D1557449

# RUSSIAN HISTORIOGRAPHY

# RUSSIAN
# HISTORIOGRAPHY
## A HISTORY

## by
## George Vernadsky

Edited by **Sergei Pushkarev**

Translated by **Nickolas Lupinin**

NORDLAND PUBLISHING COMPANY
85 Evergreen Way
Belmont, Massachusetts 02178

MAJOR WORKS by GEORGE VERNADSKY
(See the Bibliography by Nikolay Andreyev at
the end of this volume)

Library of Congress Catalogue Number 77-95207
ISBN 0-913124-25-7
© 1978 Copyright of English Translation by
**NORDLAND PUBLISHING COMPANY**
First published in Russian in *Zapiski/Transactions*
of the Association of Russian American Scholars (Vols. V–IX).

# CONTENTS

# PREFACE

George Vernadsky, professor emeritus at Yale University, died on June 18, 1973. He was truly the "elder statesman," the patriarch of Russian Historiography in the U.S.A. In 60 years of scholarly research, first in Russia and then in emigration, he worked indefatigably and fruitfully to refine the vast and rugged field of Russian history. His was a singleness of purpose. He constantly refreshed and added to his extensive historical knowledge by acquiring all new Soviet and émigré works that were of any significance. His apartment in New Haven was a huge personal library with a "reserve" consisting of old journals stored in the basement.

He retired in 1956 because of age but continued to work untiringly, literally until the last day of his life. The breadth of his interests and the depth of his erudition may be perceived from the impressive bibliography of his published works. It was compiled by Professor N.E. Andreev and can be found at the end of this book.

In his essay Professor Andreev treats George Vernadsky's biography and scholarly efforts. I wish to turn my attention to one aspect of his historical outlook. He believed that history was not made by some faceless, mechanical "laws of historical development," but by living historical personalities. Thus in his works he pays particular attention to the biographical element in the course of historical events. His own interest in the personalities and the works of the creators of Russian historical scholarship stems from this source. His knowledge of Russian historiography and bibliography was exceptional. During my long life I met many Russian historians in Khar'kov, Kiev, Prague and the U.S.A. but no one else could provide the interlocutor with so many historiographic and bibliographic references from memory without consulting reference works or personal notes (of which Professor Vernadsky had a vast quantity).

In his education George Vernadsky first completed the "Moscow school" of V.O. Kliuchevskii, then S.F. Platonov's "Petersburg school." Hence, he knew the great and the lesser Russian historians of the initial decades of the XX century personally and well. This was the period when Russian historical scholarship reached the culminating point of its development, uniting the spirit of free scholarly inquiry with respect for Russian cultural tradition. All of Professor Vernadsky's scholarly literary work was permeated with these principles. Thus it was natural that, prior to the end of his long and fruitful life, George Vernadsky wished to write a survey of Russian historiography and that his last scholarly work, presented herein, is this history. It contains much bibliographic information about Russian historians.

These "essays" which Vernadsky was able to complete himself contain data on 135 authors. This includes writers who were not professional historians but who wrote on historical subjects or played a conspicuous role in the overall cultural development of Russian society. Among these are Chaadaev, the Slavophiles and the Westernizers, Chernyshevskii, Lavrov and Mikhailovskii, Dostoevskii, Tolstoi and Mendeleev.

When he speaks of outstanding historians who were also distinguished pedagogues — those who created their own "schools" — such as A. A. Vasil'ev, N.P. Kondakov, and M.I. Rostovtsev, Professor Vernadsky also lists their disciples and successors.

In speaking of Igor Grabar', editor-in-chief of the monumental *History of Russian Art*, Vernadsky also cites the authors of the individual sections of this fundamental work.

In Vernadsky's work there is mention of those who, though not professional scholars or writers, significantly abetted historical scholarship by collecting or publishing historical materials. Among these are Count A.I. Musin-Pushkin and Chancellor Count N.P. Rumiantsev.

Of course, despite Vernadsky's encyclopedic historiographic and bibliographic knowledge, his work does not pretend to be exhaustive in terms of presentation. This would be impossible to expect from a single author within the framework of one volume written in a relatively short period of time. Severe critics might find in this, or in any other work, especially one that is so many-sided, certain deficiencies in terms of the organization of material; there might be too much biographical detail about one historian, too little about others; or there is the omission of certain writers whose works are deserving of mention. In any case, however, Vernadsky's work represents a valuable and competent description of that vast world of Russian historiography of which he was an energetic and visible participant and attentive observer for 60 years.

Out of respect for the memory of this outstanding historian and his final work, the editorial board of *Transactions of the Association of Russian-American Scholars* has decided to leave his text and organization of material basically as was. It has limited itself to correcting the considerable number of typographical errors and the very few errors in chronology and in titles of books. A small number of notes has been added and some unessential details of family biography have been shortened. An index for the book version of this work has been deemed necessary.

The editors of *Transactions of the Association of Russian-American Scholars* hope that all who are interested in Russian history — professors, students, and the reading public in general — will find many interesting and partly forgotten materials in this final work of a great historian.

George Vernadsky's sudden death interrupted this final work shortly before its completion. He had started to work on the next to last chapter, on the historiography of the Church, and managed to write only a few pages about two prominent Church historians, Metropolitan Makarii and Professor E.E. Golubinskii. At the request of the editors of *Transactions of the Association of Russian-American Scholars* the essay on the historiography of the

Church (and the Schism) was written by S. G. Pushkarev. It contains information on 30 authors and lists 175 titles.

The chapter projected by Professor Vernadsky on the historiography of Russian oriental studies, and which he was not able to write, was written by Professor A.P. Scherbatow and is titled "Oriental Studies." It contains bibliographical information about 27 authors.

S. Pushkarev

# PART ONE

## RUSSIAN SCIENCE AND SCHOLARSHIP IN THE XVIII CENTURY

### I

Ground for the growth of Russian science and scholarship had already been broken in the second half of the XVII century by the Kiev Theological Academy. This Academy provided its pupils with a solid knowledge of Latin and developed their understanding with lectures in logic, physics, and philosophy. It should not be forgotten that Latin was still the international language of European science. Many prominent Kievan scholars were invited to Moscow and opened schools there. Some of them had great influence at Court.

In 1687 Moscow founded its own academy as well — the Slavo-Greek-Latin Academy. Later, after the founding of the Petersburg Academy of Sciences, some of its students were summoned to complete their education there and became outstanding scholars.

But it was only from the time of Peter the Great that possibilities arose in Russia for the development of science in the contemporary sense of the word. In 1701 Peter established a school of mathematical and navigational studies in Moscow. The Scotsman Ferquharson was invited to be its head. In 1715 a naval academy was founded under Naryshkin's direction. His aide was the very same Ferquharson. Schools to prepare master workmen for state factories were opened in a series of cities. A medical school was founded in Moscow in 1706. In three years a similar school was established in Petersburg. All of these educational institutions were of a practical character. They were indispensable in attending to the new Russian army and navy under condition of a war with Sweden.

But Peter looked further and more deeply into the future than the majority of his collaborators. He recognized that Russia not only needed military and technical knowledge, but also required mastery of the theoretical bases of science. By his time Europe had developed a form of guiding center for scientific research — the academy of sciences. The French Academy of Sciences was founded in 1635; The Royal Society of London in 1663; The Berlin Academy of Sciences was inaugurated in 1711 on the initiative and according to the plan of the famous philosopher and mathematician, Leibniz (1646-1716). He was assigned to be its first president.

In the first years of the Swedish War [The Great Northern War] Peter was absorbed with military affairs. Only after victory at Poltava in 1708 and the resulting turning point in the war could thoughts turn to the establishment of an academy of sciences. During his trips to Germany in 1711, 1712 and 1716, Peter met repeatedly with Leibniz and discussed the dissemination of science and enlightenment in Russia with him. These discussions served as the initial impulse toward the thought of establishing an academy of sciences in Petersburg. In 1717 Peter went to Paris where he attended a session of the French Academy of Sciences and was elected a member of it. Finally, four years later, Russia's war with Sweden and its allies ended.

Peter's idea for establishing an academy of sciences now began to take on concrete forms. Peter's Chief adviser in this matter was Lavrentii Lavrentievich Blumentrost (1692-1755), a Russified German and physician-inordinary. His father, Lavrentii Alferovich [Blumentrost], also a famous doctor, left Germany for Moscow in 1668 at the invitation of Tsar Aleksei. He was well received and settled in Moscow (where he died in 1705). Peter also sought advice from the famous German philosopher, Christian Wolff. Peter invited him to Russia to found the academy of sciences. The cor-

respondence between Peter and Wolff (in which Blumentrost also participated) came to naught. Wolff refused to
come to Russia. In his opinion, prior to founding an academy
in Petersburg, it was necessary to lay the groundwork and
first establish a university. For this purpose a few professors
from Germany would be sufficient. Finally, the matter had
to be decided by Peter and Blumentrost. It was decided to
establish an academy of sciences as a scientific institution.
But, next to it, a university would be opened where academicians of professorial rank would give lectures to students.
A gymnasium would open as well where these students
would study before entering the university.

On January 28, 1724 Peter signed the charter of the
academy based on these principles. Exactly one year later he
died from a cold which he caught while helping soldiers
to push a boat from a shoal. In doing so, he saved them,
although he had to stand in water up to his waist. The
Academy of Sciences commenced its activity under Peter's
widow, Catherine I. The first organizational session took
place on November 12, 1725 and the triumphal inauguration
was held on December 27th of the same year. Blumentrost
was appointed president of the Academy. In this fashion
Peter's will was fulfilled. There can be no doubt, however,
that had Peter lived for several more years, the Academy's
activity would have unfolded immediately on a much broader
scale than it did in reality.

After the death of Catherine I, during the short reign of
Peter II, the Court moved to Moscow. Blumentrost followed
it and turned over the actual management of the Academy to
its secretary, Ivan Danilovich Schumacher (1690-1761).
Schumacher provoked great irritation among the academicians by his arbitrary rule. Nevertheless, he continued to
rule the Academy until 1757 when he was replaced by
Taubert.

In 1733, by the order of Empress Anne, Blumentrost
was dismissed from his post and sent to Moscow. His position
improved with Elizabeth's accession to the throne. In 1754
he was made curator of the University of Moscow (which

opened in 1755), but he died after one year.

The first complement of members of the Academy of Sciences was invited from abroad in accordance with Wolff's choice. Among them were such scientific luminaries as mathematicians Daniel Bernoulli and Leonard Euler (both Swiss) and the French astronomer, Joseph-Nicolas Delisle (1688-1768). Of these, Euler (1707-1783) played a particularly fruitful role in the scientific life of the Academy. Bernoulli returned to Basel in 1733 and Delisle went back to Paris in 1747.

Euler arrived in Petersburg in 1727 as a twenty year old youth. He immediately began learning Russian which he soon mastered. The period of Empress Anne's rule and particularly the brief regency of Anna Leopol'dovna (1740-1741) reflected heavily on the life of the Academy of Sciences because of the interference into its affairs by Biron and other favorites. Finally Euler could not bear it and accepted the invitation of Friedrich, King of Prussia, to move to Berlin. But he did not break his ties with Russia. He was given the title of honorary member of the Petersburg Academy of Sciences and a small yearly pension was assigned to him. Students from the Academy of Sciences were sent to Euler in Berlin to complete their education. Among them was the future astronomer, Stepan Iakovlevich Rumovskii. From Berlin Euler commenced a scientific correspondence with M. V. Lomonosov. Relations between Berlin and Petersburg almost ceased during the Russo-Prussian War of 1756-1762. After this war [the Seven Years War] ended, Euler decided to return to Russia but King Friedrich did not wish to grant him permission to do this for a long time. Euler was able to return to Petersburg only in the summer of 1766. Lomonosov had already died by this time. Despite almost total loss of sight, Euler continued his scientific work with the help of his eldest son and his students. He died from a stroke in 1783.

In accordance with the plan to fill the Academy with Russian students, recruitment of acceptable candidates began. In 1732 the Slavo-Greek-Latin Academy's twelve best students were sent for. Included was Semen Petrovich Krasheninnikov, the future geographer. In three years another group of candidates was summoned from the same source. Mikhail Vasil'evich Lomonosov was in this group. Similar recruitment continued in the future.

S. P. Krasheninnikov (1711-1755) was the son of a soldier of the Preobrazhenskii Regiment. Upon the arrival of Krasheninnikov and his partners in the Academy of Sciences, they were subjected to examinations. The best of them began to be readied for an expedition to explore Siberia. At the head of this expedition were academicians I. G. Gmelin and G. F. Müller. Krasheninnikov and his friends spent the summer of 1733 attending lectures by these professors on botany, zoology and geography.

Krasheninnikov spent ten years in Siberia (the last five on Kamchatka). In his travels he not only collected geographical and scientific information but also ethnographic and historical materials. All of his observations were unusually precise. In 1745, on the basis of Gmelin's and Lomonosov's recommendations, Krasheninnikov was made an adjunct of the Academy of Sciences. Two years later he was appointed director of the botanical garden. In 1750 Krasheninnikov was made professor of botany at the Academy's university. At the end of that year, he started writing his main scientific work: *Description of Kamchatka* [*Opisanie zemli Kamchatki*]. The book was published posthumously and was reprinted several times. The last edition was published in Moscow in 1949. Krasheninnikov's work was translated into English, German, Dutch and French.

## II

The giant figure of Mikhail Vasil'evich Lomonosov left its mark on the life of the Academy of Sciences in the 1740's and 1750's and on the subsequent growth of Russian enlightenment and the development of Russian science. It was due to his plan and initiative that the University of Moscow was established in 1755. Lomonosov was born November 8,

1711 on the White Sea coast near Kholmogory. His father, the seaman Vasilii Dorofeevich, built boats and engaged in sailing. He delivered cargo to various ports on the White Sea littoral, as far away as the docks of Norway and Sweden. Mikhail's mother — Elena Ivanovna, whose maiden name was Sivkova — was a deacon's daughter. But she died at an early age and his father remarried. His stepmother disliked her stepson and scolded him for his love of reading. Mikhail learned to read and write from his neighbor in the village and then studied with the deacon of the local parish. When Mikhail became ten years old, his father began to take him on his sea voyages. These trips, remembered throughout his life, made an indelible impression on Mikhail. At that time his inspired love of nature and his keenness of mind had already surfaced.

In 1763, describing navigational conditions on the White Sea in his work *A Short Description of Travels on the Northern Seas* [*Kratkoe opisanie puteshestvii po severnym moriam*], Lomonosov recalls: "I observed this on the shore of the Norman Sea" (during a voyage with his father).

At the age of fourteen Lomonosov learned the *Arithmetic* of Magnitskii and Smotritskii's *Slavic Grammar*. This was the apogee of wisdom then available in that remote territory. In order to study further, one had to enter the Slavo-Greek-Latin Academy in Moscow. It was there that Lomonosov headed in the winter of 1730. He went on foot in the bitter cold and with practically no money in his pocket, following wagons of fish. But he attained his goal. He was accepted into the seminary. As we have already stated, Lomonosov was summoned from Moscow in 1735 to the Academy of Sciences in Petersburg in order to enter its gymnasium. Ascertaining his knowledge and ability, the Academy's directors sent Lomonosov to Germany to complete his preparation for scientific and scholarly work. Lomonosov entered the University of Marburg where he studied philosophy, physics, and mechanics under Christian Wolff. Lomonosov also learned German and French (he had already mastered Latin and Greek at the Slavo-Greek-Latin

Academy in Moscow).

Wolff's lectures were extremely beneficial for Lomonosov. They helped him to develop his philosophical and scientific perspective, logic and clarity of thought, and also acquainted him with the scientific terminology of the time which he later adapted to the Russian language. Under Wolff's guidance, Lomonosov familiarized himself with the works of the leading philosophers, physicists and chemists of the XVII and the beginning of the XVIII centuries, among them those of the English physicist and chemist, Robert Boyle (1627-1691). Boyle accepted the existence in nature of an absolute void which contained the minutest of material particles (atoms) of specific size and form. Atoms of liquids were in constant flux; those of solids, at rest. Boyle's ideas left a great impression on Lomonosov. According to the instruction given him, upon studying with Wolff, Lomonosov was to proceed to Freiburg to learn metallurgy and mining under the guidance of Haenckel. Later, knowledge of mining helped Lomonosov considerably in research in chemistry and mineralogy. He did not stay long in Freiburg and returned to Wolff in Marburg. In 1740 he married Elizabeth Zilkh, a German. For some reason he concealed this marriage for a long time. In 1741 he returned to Petersburg. Half a year after returning to Russia, and upon presenting the preliminary report of his studies in Germany, Lomonosov was made an adjunct of the Academy.

After this, he put the notes of his research in Germany in order and began to publish works based on it. The question of making him a full-fledged member of the Academy now arose. Schumacher sent several of Lomonosov's "dissertations" to be judged by Euler in Berlin; Euler evaluated them highly. "All of these works," he wrote in his response, "are not just good, but superior. He (Lomonosov) elucidates the most necessary and difficult points of physics and chemistry which are totally unknown or are not capable of being interpreted by the most educated people. He does this on such solid ground that I am fully convinced of the accuracy of his proofs."

In 1745 Lomonosov was made a full-fledged member of the Academy of Sciences and appointed professor of Chemistry. Having consolidated his position, Lomonosov sent to Germany for his wife and his life became more orderly.

B. N. Menshutkin divides Lomonosov's subsequent scientific work into three periods. At first he concerned himself primarily with physics; then, mostly with chemistry (1749-1756). In the last decade of his life, he occupied himself with various natural sciences—geography, metereology, astronomy, mineralogy and geology.

In the physics of the first half of the XVIII century much significance was attributed to experimentation. But these experiments did not always produce clear results. Hypotheses had to be constructed to explain them. The mysterious subtle liquids—solids of heat, light, gravity, etc., figured in these hypotheses. These substances were indivisible and could not be isolated. The essence of heat was the "matter of fire" (the source of heat or the "calorific" element). "Chemistry was ruled by the phlogiston theory which lasted until the end of the XVIII century," (Menshutkin). The principle of combustion was called phlogiston. It was thought that all bodies capable of combustion or of changing from the effects of fire contained phlogiston.

Lomonosov felt that construction of a chemical laboratory was an indispensable condition for his scientific work. He sought insistently to attain this goal for several years from the academic authorities, but always received the same answer from Schumacher: there is no money. Finally Elizabeth issued a decree regarding the construction of a laboratory at her cabinet's expense. The laboratory was built in 1748 according to Lomonosov's plan and under his supervision. The building cost 1,344 rubles. This stone house was only six and one half sazhens long and five sazhens wide. There were three rooms inside. All the equipment was devised by Lomonosov. In this way Russia's first chemical laboratory was created. Later, Lomonosov also built a small laboratory in his own home.

In his chemical experiments Lomonosov was one of the

first contemporary scientists who used scales systematically. The quantitative investigation of the chemical composition of various substances was then just beginning.

With the help of this method he rejected the hypothesis of the heat source, declaring that the phenomenon which occured in the heating process was the rotating movement of body particles—of solids, liquids and gases (a "Kolovratny" method as he wrote ["circling" method − transl.] ).

Lomonosov sometimes casually employed the term "phlogiston" without paying it particular heed. But by his experiments he dealt a heavy blow to this hypothesis.

In reflecting on the processes of combustion and oxidation, Lomonosov noticed that metal increased in weight when tempered. He assumed that this derived from particles from the air flowing above it which joined to the metal. This supposition contradicted certain experiments and views of his beloved Boyle. To verify this question, Lomonosov conducted several special experiments in 1756. This time he did not agree with Boyle. He described them thusly: "the experiments were conducted in tightly closed glass vessels in order to investigate whether the weight of metals increased from pure heat. These experiments showed that the opinion of the renowned Robert Boyle was false, for without letting in outside air, the weight of annealed metal remained the same." "This proved: 1) that the increment in the weight of a metal during tempering was caused by combination with air; 2) that explaining the process of firing metal with the aid of phlogiston was impossible; if phlogiston escaped from metal, then the sealed retort containing the metal had to have a different weight after being heated" (Menshutkin). Lomonosov reported the results of his experiments to a conference of the Academy of Sciences but did not publish them.

Twenty-seven years later, the French chemist, Lavoisier, (not knowing of Lomonosov's tests) conducted the very same experiment. In so doing, he made a very important observation: only part of the air within the sealed retort combined with the metal. From this Lavoisier concluded that air consisted of two gases, one which combined with metal, one which did not (oxygen and nitrogen). Prior to this discovery by Lavoisier, air was thought to be an integral element. Advocates of the phlogiston theory commenced a desperate struggle against Lavoisier's conclusions but in the end they were forced to give up.

The basis of Lomonosov's scientific views on nature was the idea of the constancy of matter and motion. In his *Observations on the Density and Fluidity of Bodies* [*Rassuzhdenie o tverdosti i zhidkosti tel*] (1760) he wrote: "All changes which occur in nature are such that whatever is taken from one body is added onto another . . . This general natural law also extends to the laws of motion; for the body which moves another body through its own force, loses as much [force] itself as it imparts to the body being moved by it."

Lomonosov's starting point in his work on physics and chemistry was Boyle's ideas which struck him during the years of study under Wolff. Lomonosov said: "After reading Boyle, I was seized by a passionate desire to investigate the minutest particles of bodies. I reflected on them for eighteen years." On the basis of these reflections, Lomonosov thought of writing a major work regarding the significance of "particles"or "corpuscles" in understanding chemical and physical laws—"corpuscular philosophy" as he states in one of his letters to Euler. Lomonosov was not able to realize this "great undertaking" (Menshutkin's phrase). But he expounded individual parts of this plan in some of his dissertations and in his public speeches, primarily at sessions of the Academy of Sciences.

In one of his early works, *Elements of Mathematical Chemistry* [*Elementy matematicheskoi khimii*] (1741), Lomonosov already proposed his theory that matter was made up of "corpuscles" and "elements." "A corpuscle is a collection of elements which forms a single mass. . . . corpuscles are homogeneous if they consist of equal quantities of the same elements which are combined in identical fashion . . . .Corpuscles are heterogeneous when their elements are distinct and are combined in varying numbers or forms; the infinite variety of bodies depends on this." In the chemical language of the first third of the XX century, what Lomonosov called an "element" is the atom, and a "corpuscle" is the molecule. "This distinction now lies at the base of the whole harmonious structure of modern chemistry," writes Menshutkin (1937).

Lomonosov's works on geology and mineralogy have great significance. He viewed the earth's geologic life in a dynamic sense, as a long and complicated physio-chemical process. He was practically the first to evaluate the enormous role of organisms in the formation of peat, coal, and chernozem. He also intended to write "Russian Mineralogy." In 1763, through the Academy of Sciences, he appealed to factories and mines with a request to send samples of various ores and minerals to the Academy. The majority of the samples arrived at the Academy after his death. In this way the foundation of the Academy of Sciences' mineralogical collection was laid.

Among the physical problems which Lomonosov studied was the question of atmospheric electricity and aerial phenomena which, in his opinion, were related to electricity. Aurora borealis was among these. Later, he wrote: "From 1743 I rarely missed taking notes on any northern lights that I saw." His notes have not lost their significance to this day (see V.I. Vernadskii, "The Chemical Structure of the Earth's Biosphere and its Environment," p. 124 (1965)).

Continuing to concern himself with these questions, Lomonosov also observed thunderstorms, summer lightning and comet tails. Lomonosov arrived at the conclusion that all these phenomena were related to descending and ascending air currents. From 1745 Lomonosov's colleague in the Academy, the physicist Georg Wilhelm Richmann, also began to study the electricity of thunder.

In America at approximately the same time Benjamin Franklin became occupied with the properties of electricity. He posited the question of whether thunder clouds were electrified. The French physicist, Dalibar, placed a high metal pole near Paris. It was insulated by means of a wooden support. During a thunderstorm on May 10, 1752 the thunder passed over the pole. The pole was electrified and sparks emanated from it. In June of the same year, without knowing of Dalibar's experiments, Franklin sent a silk kite with a metal point attached to it into the clouds. The hempen tow line by which the kite was held was attached to the point. A key was tied to the lower end of the tow line and a thin silk rope to the key. This insulated the whole system. When the tow line was soaked by rain, sparks could be produced from the key (this description follows Menshutkin). In July 1752 Richmann built a device in his house which was called the "thunder machine." He ran a six foot long metal rod through a bottle with its bottom knocked out. To the end of the rod he fastened a metal wire and ran it through, insulated, into a room. He fastened a metal ruler to the end of it and tied a silk thread to the ruler. When there was electricity in the wire, the thread moved away and "chased the finger." Following Richmann's example, Lomonosov, too, built a similar machine in his own apartment.

Just after twelve o'clock on July 26, 1753 the Lomonosov household was preparing to sit down to dinner. At this time thunderclouds formed. "The thunder was very loud and there was not a drop of rain." Lomonosov went to his thunder machine to see what was happening. "While the table was being set," Lomonosov later wrote to I.I. Shuvalov, "I was able to see big sparks emanating from the wire. At that time my wife and the others came in . . . Suddenly, it thundered very heavily at the very moment that I was holding my hand on the metal and sparks began crackling. Everybody ran away from me . . . . My curiosity held me there for another two or three minutes until I was told that my cabbage soup was getting cold. Besides, the force of the electricity had practically ebbed by that time." Lomonosov was not able to taste his cabbage soup. Richmann's servant ran in with the report that "the professor was killed by

thunder."(Richmann, like Lomonosov, had been sitting at
his thunder machine at the same moment). Lomonosov
immediately ran to Richmann's apartment, but the latter
was already lifeless. "Thus, by a deplorable test, he (Rich-
man) proved that lightning could be averted. However, this
was to be done with a metal pole which should stand in an
open spot where lightning could strike at will. Meanwhile,
Richmann died a glorious death while fulfilling the duties
of his profession. His memory will never fade." Lomonosov
petitioned Shuvalov and obtained for Richmann's widow a
pension equal to her husband's salary.

Lomonosov was also interested in astronomy. On May
26, 1761 he observed the passing of the planet Venus over
the solar disc. He noticed a radiance "thin as a hair" which
encircled part of Venus' disc which had not yet entered onto
that of the sun. Lomonosov described this phenomenan as
"the refraction of the sun's rays in Venus' atmosphere."
At that time the existence of an atmosphere around Venus
was unknown to astronomers. Lomonosov published his
discovery in the annals of the Academy of Sciences. Thirty
years later the English astronomer Herschel rediscovered
"the atmosphere of Venus."

Navigation entered into the circle of Lomonosov's
interests. In his *Discourse on Greater Accuracy in Navigation*
[*Rassuzhdenie o bol'shei tochnosti morskogo puti*] (1759),
Lomonosov examined a series of theoretical questions
regarding navigation. He indicated better methods of deter-
mining latitude and longitude at sea and proposed a series of
practical suggestions for seafarers. In 1763 Lomonosov
wrote *A Short Description of Various Trips on the Northern
Seas and Evidence of the Possibility of Passage to East India
by Means of the Siberian Ocean* [*Kratkoe opisanie raznykh
puteshestvii po severnym moriam i pokazanie vozmozhnosti
prokhodu Sibirskim okeanom v vostochnuiu Indiiu*]. In this
work Lomonosov established the direction of the ice flow
in the North Sea and came to the conclusion that the best
way to reach the north pole lay between Spitzbergen and
Novaia Zemlia.

In 1749, among other experiments in the chemical laboratory, Lomonosov enthusiastically took on a subject new to him — mosaics. In this endeavor, art joined technique, optics and the chemistry of stained glass. Lomonosov had to make thousands of trial meltings before becoming proficient in the technique of preparing and placing pieces of glass into an artistic mosaic. Twelve of these mosaics which were made in Lomonosov's laboratory (among them "The Battle of Poltava") have been preserved. In recognition of Lomonosov's work in mosaics the Academy of Sciences of Bologna elected him an honorary member.

In the academic year 1752-1753 Lomonosov presented a course in the academy's university in physical chemistry for more advanced students. Several students signed up for the course. Of these, Lomonosov particularly approved of Stepan Rumovskii (of whom I will later speak separately). The lectures were accompanied by model demonstrations.

In the following year Lomonosov took an active part in the establishment of Moscow University. He was I. I. Shuvalov's main adviser in this matter. Shuvalov's favorite dream, which was shared by Lomonosov, was the establishment in Russia of a complete system of popular education from elementary schools to universities. The Academy's university played a major role in the training of Russian scientists but this was a closed institution for specialists with almost no link to public life. This was not a "true" university.

It was decided to establish the university in Moscow which was in the center of Russia. It would be easiest to gather a sufficient number of students there. It was resolved to open a gymnasium at the university. Lomonosov always supported the principle of teaching all social classes (a notion with which Shuvalov also sympathized). It was resolved to accept students from the gentry and the *raznochintsy* [non-gentry Russian intellectuals] into the university. But, in respect to the gymnasium, Shuvalov had to make a concession to the mores of the Moscow gentry. Two gymnasiums were opened — one for the gentry, one for the *raznochintsy*.

For serfs, access to the gymnasium and the university was blocked. Those graduating from one of the gymnasiums entered the university by taking a special entrance examination. Both Shuvalov and Lomonosov understood that, for the start, they would have to be satisfied with a university of modest scale in terms of the numbers of professors and students and in equipping the learning and teaching sectors. But both of them worked for the future with a firm faith in it. The university was organized according to the following principles: it was subject to no bureau other than to the Senate and it was not obligated to take orders from any other office.

At the head of the university were several curators. Shuvalov was the principal one. The university was divided into three departments: law, medicine and philosophy. Ten professional chairs were intended to cover all three departments. Chemistry, natural history and anatomy were taught at the medical faculty; physics — in the philosophy department.

For the start five instead of ten professors were appointed: two Russians and three foreigners. The Russians were recommended by Lomonosov: Popovskii, professor of eloquence; and Barsov, professor of mathematics. The foreigners were sent for at the direction of G. F. Müller. By 1762 the number of professors finally reached ten (one was a third Russian, the mathematician Anichkov). After this, things began to develop a bit more rapidly. In 1767 Semen Efimovich Desnitskii was appointed professor of jurisprudence. He had completed his schooling under the guidance of Hume and Blackstone in Glasgow. Desnitskii can be considered the embellishment of Moscow University in the XVIII century (he died in 1789).

Lomonosov was a universal genius. His main "pleasure," as he sometimes said, was physics and chemistry, but he had another field of creativity. He was the founder of the modern Russian language in prose and poetry. And it is precisely in this sphere that he immediately earned recognition and popularity in contemporary Russian society.

Prior to Lomonosov, from the middle of the XVII century, syllabic versification dominated Slavonic-Russian poetry. It originated because of the influence of the Polish language and was not at all natural to Russian. In his letter *On the Rules of Russian Poetry* [*O pravilakh rossiiskogo stikhotvorchestva*] (1739) Lomonosov proved convincingly that tonal versification corresponded to the Russian language. He made it the custom in Russian poetry.

Lomonosov based his teaching of literary styles on the existence in the Russian language of three categories of words: 1) those that were generally used in Church Slavonic and Russian; 2) words which were primarily scholarly, and; 3) common words, excluding "despicable foul words." From this Lomonosov inferred three styles: 1) the *high* style consisting of Slavic-Russian words, a style to be used for heroic poems, odes and prose speeches on important subjects; 2) the *middle* style — neither haughty nor base but consisting of Slavic-Russian and Russian words — for friendly poetic letters, satires, eclogues, elegies and descriptive prose; and 3) the *low* style, deriving from a combination of the middle style with common low words — for comedies, epigrams, songs, friendly prose letters and descriptions of everyday affairs.

It should be noted that Lomonosov was also the originator of contemporary Russian scientific language. He laid the proper foundations of Russian technical and scientific terminology. After the Petrine reforms, the Russian scientific and technical language was completely littered with Dutch, German and Polish words. Lomonosov elaborated the following rules: 1) foreign scientific terms must be translated into Russian; 2) words were to be left untranslated only in the event that it was impossible to find a Russian word of equal meaning or if the foreign word had already come into general use; 3) in such a case, the foreign word should be used in the form most peculiar to the Russian language. Very many scientific terms were compiled according to these rules by Lomonosov himself and became commonplace: "air pump," "laws of motion," "axis of the equator," "equilibrium of bodies," "specific gravity," etc. . . .

In 1748 Lomonosov published the first *Rhetorics*
[*Ritorika*] in the Russian language with examples taken
mostly from his own oratorical prose. His *Russian Grammar*
[*Rossiiskaia gramatika*] appeared in 1755. It was an eminent
scholarly work on the Russian language. The grammar went
through fourteen editions and was translated into German,
French and modern Greek.

Perhaps Lomonosov's best ode is "An Evening Medi-
tation on the Divine Majesty on the Occasion of the Great
Northern Lights" ["Vechernee razmyshlenie o Bozh'em
velichestve pri sluchae velikogo severnogo siianiia"] (1743).
It is tinged with a profound feeling for the cosmos.

> Day hides its face
> Dark night has covered the plains,
> A black shadow has climbed up the mountains,
> And the sun's rays have declined away from us.
> The abyss is revealed, filled with stars;
> The stars are countless, the abyss bottomless.
> Like a grain of sand in the waves of the sea,
> Like a tiny spark in perpetual ice,
> Like a speck of dust in a powerful whirlwind.
> Like a feather in a raging fire,
> So am I lost, plunged in this abyss
> And exhausted by my thoughts!
> The mouths of wise men tell us that
> There is a multitude of different worlds there.
> That countless suns burn,
> And peoples and a cycle of ages exist there:
> To the general glory of the Divinity
> The force of nature is the same there.
> But, nature, where are your laws?
> The dawn appears from the northern regions
>
> Behold, day has stepped on to the earth at night![1]

At a solemn meeting of the Academy of Sciences in

1749, Lomonosov delivered "A Poem in Praise of Empress Elizabeth Petrovna" ["Slovo pokhval'noe imperatritse Elizavete Petrovne"] in which, as in some other odes, he glorified Peter the Great, the propagator of the sciences in Russia. This "Poem" drew attention to Lomonosov at Court. At the Academy it created a number of the envious of whom Schumacher stood at the head. But the enlightened noble, Ivan Ivanovich Shuvalov (1727-1797), who was then Elizabeth's favorite, took Lomonosov under his patronage. Moreover, he took cognizance of Lomonosov's wisdom and began to consult with him on questions of popular education. In 1755, as we have already stated, he brought Lomonosov's plan for the establishment of Moscow University to fruition.

In his poem of praise to Elizabeth, Lomonosov mentioned in passing that one of the tasks of the Academy's history department was the writing of a Russian history. Elizabeth and Shuvalov assigned this task to Lomonosov. He gladly undertook this project but could not break away from his scientific work. The preparation of the Russian history moved slowly. Shuvalov hurried him along and wrote that if his other labors stood in his way, they could be set aside. At the beginning of 1755 Lomonosov replied to Shuvalov that he understood the necessity of writing a history of Russia but that "such a great matter is of a nature which demands time. . . . As to my experiments in physics and chemistry, there is no need, nor is it possible, to dispense with them. Every person demands rest from his work. Thus, in putting aside his work, he seeks to spend some time with guests or servants, playing cards, checkers or other games. Others relax by smoking. I have rejected all of these long ago in that I have found nothing but boredom in them. Thus I hope that to assuage me from the effort expended on the writing of Russian history and on the embellishment of the Russian word, I will be allowed several hours daily to devote to experiments in physics and chemistry rather than to playing billiards. These are not only a substitute for relaxation but medicinally beneficial as well. Furthermore, they can of course bring no less honor and glory to the fatherland than the first task."

Lomonosov vindicated himself and to the good fortune of science he continued his experiments in physics and chemistry. But, insofar as he was able, he fulfilled his promise regarding a Russian history. His *Short Russian Chronicle* [*Kratkii rossiiskii letopisets*] was published in 1760 and the first (and only) volume of *Ancient Russian History* [*Drevniaia Rossiiskaia istoriia*] (up to 1754) appeared posthumously in 1766. (Lomonosov died on April 4, 1765).

The *Ancient Russian History* was translated into German and from it into French. The *Short Russian Chronicle* appeared in English and German translations.

I will write below at greater length about Lomonosov the historian in connection with the works of Müller and Schlözer.

The newest edition of Lomonosov's collected works was published in ten volumes in Moscow, 1950-1957.

### III

In 1748 Stepan Iakovlevich Rumovskii (1732-1815), the son of a priest, was summoned to the Academy so as to enter the gymnasium of the Academy of Sciences. Thereafter, he was to be a student at the Academy's university. In order to complete his educational preparations, Rumovskii traveled to see Euler in Berlin. In 1752-1753, as was already noted, he took Lomonosov's course on physical chemistry. In 1760 Rumovskii was appointed instructor of mathematics to the Academy's students and several years later he became professor of astronomy. Over a period of 30 years he edited the annual publication of the astronomical calendars. In 1761 he was sent on a mission to Selenchinsk to observe the passage of Venus over the solar disc (the very same phenomenon which Lomonosov observed in Petersburg). Observations of this passage of Venus were also being conducted in France and England. Disparities appeared in some of the data. The English observer computated the sun's parallax (the angle determined by lines leading from the luminous body being observed to the center of the earth and to the observer) to be 8.5 degrees; the French — 10.5 degrees. This disparity placed the methods of observation and the mathematical apparatus for processing the data produced by the observation into doubt.

In 1769 the Petersburg Academy, at Euler's suggestion, set itself this goal: to verify and to perfect observational methods and the means of mathematical analysis. A grandiose expedition was organized. Several Russian scientists were to supply the observational materials. Rumovskii was among these. Euler took upon himself the whole management of the mathematical elaboration of the observations. Observation posts were situated in places distant from each other. Rumovskii was sent to Kola, P. B. Inokhodtsev and G. Lovits to the Gur'ev fortress at the mouth of the Ural River (at that time still called the Iaik).

According to Rumovskii's calculations, the sun's parallax was no greater than 8.62 degrees. Another computation listed it at 8.67 degrees. In this way the French calculation was repudiated.

During his travels Rumovskii determined the geographical location of many places in Russia. Later (in 1786) he published the first catalog of astronomical points in Russia. In 1800 he was appointed Vice-President of the Academy of Sciences. In addition to his work in mathematics and astronomy, he translated the *Annals* of the Roman historian Tacitus from Latin into Russian. This translation was considered a classic in its time.

When the University of Kazan was founded in 1804, Rumovskii was appointed its trustee. A mathematician and astronomer himself, Rumovskii invited leading professors of these subjects from Germany to the new university.

## IV

The year 1768 turned out to be a portentous one for the history of Russian science. The Academy of Sciences in this year organized a series of expeditions for a comprehensive investigation of Russia's nature and peoples. Their scientific work constituted an epoch in the development of geographic science. The expeditions were well planned and equipped. Outstanding scientists were placed at their heads. These expeditions lasted for six years (until 1774). To oversee the expeditions, the Academy of Sciences chose the talented German naturalist of encyclopedic knowledge, Peter-Simon Pallas (1741-1811). His principal speciality was zoology but he gradually broadened his scientific scope to include botany, geology, paleontology, mineralogy, geography, ethnography and linguistics into his course of study.

In 1767 he was chosen a member of the Academy of Sciences and moved to Petersburg from Berlin. The Academy of Sciences proposed that he first work out the plan for an expedition and draw up an instruction for the participants. For this purpose an instruction compiled by G. F. Müller for the participants of the Siberian expedition of 1733-1742 was found for him in the Academy's archives. This instruction turned out to be very useful to Pallas.

Pallas set forth the expedition's chief aims in three points: 1) to study the nationalities inhabiting Russia and their customs and rituals; 2) to investigate the country's nature; to make collections of minerals, plants and animals; 3) to study the means of working and utilizing natural resources — work in mines, ore deposits, salt mines — and to determine the condition of agriculture and forestry.

The expedition was divided into two chief sections. Pallas himself stood at the head of one. In charge of the other was an adjunct of the Academy of Sciences, Ivan Ivanovich Lepekhin (1740-1802).

The son of a soldier, Lepekhin was accepted into the Academy's gymnasium in 1751. By that time he was already literate. In 1760 he became a student at the Academy's university. At this time, Lomonosov was director of teaching at the Academy. It was under his influence that Lepekhin's scientific interests began to form. Two years later Lepekhin was sent to Strassburg where he studied mainly medicine. From Strassburg he corresponded with Lomonosov who intended the chair of botany at the Academy for him. Having received the degree of doctor of medicine in Strassburg, Lepekhin returned to Petersburg in 1767 and was appointed adjunct of the Academy.

Two Russian scientists were assigned to Pallas — V. F. Zuev and N. P. Sokolov (at that time Pallas had not yet mastered the Russian language). Three students of the Academy were assigned to aid Lepekhin — A. Lebedev, T. Mal'gin and N. Ozeretskovskii. Both sections were marvelously equipped and provided with all necessities. Each unit had artists, stuffers of animals and shooters ("to shoot birds and animals").

The routes of both sections were so planned that they periodically approached each other and diverged. Both groups started from the Transvolga and the Caspian region and then moved into the Urals. Beyond the Urals, Lepekhin only reached Tiumen. Pallas went further east across all of Siberia to Mongolia. From Tiumen Lepekhin crossed the northern Urals and came down the Severnaia Dvina to the White Sea. For more than a year he explored the White Sea and the Arkhangel'sk region. Lepekhin's group returned to Petersburg in December of 1772. In 1773, at the proposal of the Academy, Lepekhin made another trip — to Belorussia. In 1771, not yet having returned from his travels, Lepekhin was chosen a member of the Academy of Sciences.

In his travel diary Lepekhin talentedly described his observations not only of the nature of the places through which he passed, but also of the life of the populace, trade and social relations. Lepekhin gathered much valuable material on botany, the economy and ethnography. His major work is — *Daily Notes of a Journey through Various Provinces of the Russian State* [*Dnevnye zapiski puteshestviia po raznym provintsiiam Rossiiskogo gosudarstva*] in four volumes (1771-1805).

Even more significant were the materials and collections brought by Pallas — valuable information on geography, zoology, botany, geology, ethnography and archeology. In the words of L. S. Berg (1929), the reports of Pallas' expedition "still serve as a treasure-house which subsequent researchers continue to use."

In 1793 and 1794 Pallas made two trips to the Crimea and described them in detail. Pallas liked the Crimea so much that he wished to settle there. When Catherine heard this, she presented him with a house in Simferopol' and two estates. Pallas returned to Berlin in 1810 where he died one year later.

Pallas was an indefatigable writer. A bibliography of his work, compiled by his biographer F.P. Keppen, takes up more than thirty pages in small print (*Zhurnal Ministerstva Narodnogo Prosveshcheniia* [*Journal of the Ministry of Public Education*], April, 1895). Here I will cite only that Russian translation of Pallas' description of his expedition of 1768-1774, *Journey Through Various Provinces of the Russian Empire* (three volumes, 1773-1788).

## V

The state and the development of Russian natural science in the last quarter of the XVIII century have been less studied than that of the preceding period. The Academy of Sciences remained the primary focus and the breeding ground of Russian scientists. At this time natural science at the University of Moscow was weakly represented. Mathematics was taught by the talented Anichkov. He wrote and published the first Russian *Course of Pure Mathematics* [ *Kurs chistoi matematiki*].

The Medical-Surgical Academy was only founded in Petersburg at the very end of the XVIII century (1799).

There were no people of Euler's and Lomonosov's caliber among Russian scientists at the end of the XVIII century. But many of them were very capable. What is important is that the family of scientists was growing and a scientific environment was appearing in which scientific questions could be discussed. Scientific literature was growing as well. Significantly, this scientific society was not isolated. Interest in science was revealing itself in other circles of Russian society also.

The number of educated people in Russia grew steadily.

In the early 1770's the historian, Prince M. M. Shcherbatov, made a curious calculation regarding this question. He figured that in Russia there were then 50,000 of the "gentry, foreign officers, and other officials." The regular army had close to five thousand officers. The result is more or less 63,000 educated people. T.I. Rainov adds five to ten thousand people not counted by Shcherbatov — the clergy, *raznochintsy*, merchants, etc. . . . The result comes to 70,000 to 75,000 of the literate.

Rainov's figures are clearly underestimated. The number of the clergy must be added to them first of all. The clergy was the most literate class. The number of religious schools in the XVIII century grew constantly. In 1762 there were 26 of them with a total number of 6,000 students.[2] In 1783 the number of pupils studying in religious schools was already 11,000.[3]

In reference to the merchant class, the data of the fourth revision (census of taxable population) of 1783, as elaborated by academician Storkh, cites that there were 107,000 merchants in Russia.[4] By the end of Catherine II's reign the number of merchants had reached 240,000.[5]

Of them, particularly those who lived in Petersburg and Moscow, a significant number were literate. Thus, the overall number of educated people in Russia at the end of Catherine's reign must be calculated to be no less than 100,000 — 150,000.

Evidently, Shcherbatov and Rainov counted only men. However, there were also many educated women among the clergy, gentry and the *raznochintsy*. Furthermore, Shcherbatov's figures apply to the beginning of the 1770's whereas the number of educated had to rise substantially by the century's end. Of course, only a small segment was interested in the sciences but it can still be assumed that the contingent of readers of scientific books was not small for that time.

Among the aristocracy were people who occupied themselves with science or who gathered rich scientific collections — so called "cabinets of natural history."

P. G. Demidov (1738-1821) was educated at the University of Göttingen and the Freiburg Academy. He corresponded with Buffon and Linnaeus. He studied mathematics, physics, chemistry, mineralogy, botany and zoology. He compiled a large collection of natural history which he presented to Moscow University in 1802. Prince A. A. Urusov published *An Experiment in Natural History [Opyt estestvennoi istorii]* in 1780.

Prince D. A. Golitsyn (1734-1803), the diplomat, experimented with electricity and defended the vortical theory of electricity and magnetism. In 1768 he was appointed envoy to The Hague where he remained to the end of his life. He was elected chairman of the Jena Mineralogical Society. To it he willed his mineralogical cabinet. He was also a member of Petersburg's Free Economic Society, in the "Annals" of which he published several articles. Count G.K. Razumovskii was known for his work in mineralogy. The rich physics cabinet of D.P. Buturlin was purchased in 1802 by the Medical-Surgical Academy. The collections of Princess E. P. Dashkova were donated to Moscow University in 1807.

The production of Russian scientific literature (in Russian and foreign languages) in the fields of physics and mathematics increased noticeably toward the end of the XVIII century. According to Rainov's calculations, 41 books in this field were published in the decade 1771-1780. (of these, sixteen were translations). The following decade saw the publication of 121 books (of which 56 were translations); the nine years from 1791-1799 — 112 books. The number of special scientific articles in the professional journals of the Academy of Sciences grew in approximately the same proportion.

In terms of research methods, two tendencies manifested themselves in the last third of the XVIII century — one stemming from Lomonosov, the other from Euler.

Characteristic of "Eulerism" was the tendency to posit and solve certain scientific problems by means of mathematical analysis only. Euler was prepared to consider the results of an experiment which interested him in a seemingly abstract and idealized form and study it with the aid of analytical mathematical means. This method had no direct experimental value. But later, it was useful for the analysis of physical reality.

A different tradition commenced with Lomonosov — the inseparable link of theory with experimental data. He also attached great, but not exclusive, significance to mathematics.

Summarizing the results — the work of Russian and foreign scientists in XVIII Century Russia laid firm foundations for the further development of Russian Science.

## VI

From natural science let us turn to historical studies. Three outstanding scholars brought from Germany originated Russian historical scholarship in the contemporary sense of that word. These were Gottlieb-Siegfried Bayer (1694-1738), Gerhard Friedrich (Fedor Ivanovich) Müller (1705-1783), and August Ludwig Schlözer (1735-1809).

Bayer was in the first complement of foreign scholars invited to become members of Petersburg's Academy of Sciences. He graduated from the University of Königsberg. While still a student, he commenced the study of eastern languages — Chinese and the Semitic tongues. He did not know Russian or ever try to learn it. He used Russian chronicles in Latin translation. But he knew Byzantine and Scandinavian sources well. Bayer studied only the ancient period of Russian history — up to the IX century inclusive. He wrote a serious study of the Varangians and of the origins of Rus' and of the Russes' first campaign against Constantinople. With the help of V.K. Tred'iakovskii (1703-1769), he was able to determine the meaning of the Slavic names of the Dniepr rapids in the work of Constantine Porphyrogenitus *On the Administration of the Empire* [*De Administrando Imperio*]. These works by Bayer were later used by Schlözer and the Russian historian, Tatishchev.

Bayer is the founder of the Scandinavian (Norman) theory of the origin of the Russian State.

Müller, like Bayer, was brought to Petersburg in 1725, but not as a professor of the Academy's university. Rather he came as a student (he was twenty years old at the time). In contrast to Bayer, Müller began to learn Russian immediately. In the first years after his arrival, Müller taught Latin, history and geography at the Academy's gymnasium. Not later than 1730 he became interested in the history and geography of Siberia. He studied the famous work of the Dutch scholar Witsen, *Northern and Eastern Tatariia* [*Noord en Ost Tartaryen*] (1st ed. 1692; 2nd ed. 1705; Müller used both). In 1731 Müller was made a member of the Academy of Sciences and appointed professor in its university. He published his first works on Siberian history in 1732-1733.

At this time the preparation for the great Siberian expedition — the one in which Krasheninnikov participated — was in full swing. The expedition was organized jointly by the Senate and the Academy of Sciences. Besides Krasheninnikov, members appointed were two academicians — the astronomer, Delisle, and the naturalist, Gmelin.

Müller also yearned to go. Chance helped him — Gmelin fell ill. The over-secretary of the Senate, Ivan Kirillovich Kirilov, "a great zealot and admirer of the sciences," allowed Müller to go to Siberia in place of Gmelin. The latter recovered rather quickly. The Senate also allowed him to go on the expedition.

Müller was accompanied by several student helpers. Müller's main objective was to describe the archives of Siberian towns and to copy as much of the historical material in each archive as possible. But in passing, Müller also collected information on linguistics, economics, ethnography and archeology, and also compiled "a record" of Siberian towns and districts.

In so doing, Müller not only displayed his unusual capacity for work but also his firmness and insistence in obtaining the information he needed from local administrations. Müller commenced his journey from Tobl'sk, then

the capital of the Siberian province. He reached it at the end
of January of 1734. As he recalled later, he himself did not
yet know what he was to demand of the governor of Siberia
and what to ask. He did not have experience in this. It was
something which he attained with practice.

With a few exceptions, the Siberian archives were in
total disarray. The existing "registers" of activities were incomplete. Müller was forced to compile (or demand the compilation of) new inventories. He did enormous work himself.
He went over the archival books and columns chronologically
and marked for his helpers or local scribes the documents
which were to be copied. By the end of 1736, Müller reached
Iakutsk from which he returned to Irkutsk. By this time he
had overstrained himself (he fell ill with "hypochondria").
He was not able to go to Kamchatka with Krasheninnikov.
To replace him, the Academy sent Johann Eberhard Fisher
(1697-1771). Müller received notification of this in Eniseisk
in the summer of 1739 and met Fisher in Surgut (in the
province of Tobol'sk) in June of 1740. Müller gave him directions for gathering materials, promising to send a detailed
instruction from Tobol'sk. Müller sent this instruction to
Fisher on December 13, 1741, while another copy was sent
to the Senate.

This thorough and well-conceived instruction represents, in the words of A.I. Andreev, "a major scientific
work." The instruction was geared to a scientist of greater
sweep than Fisher. The latter, evidently, paid no attention to
it. Later, Pallas used it as a guide.

Müller remained in Siberia for two more years (principally in Tobol'sk) and examined archives in several towns. At
the same time he began to write his *History of Siberia* [*Istoriia Sibiri*]. As to his personal life — he was married in
Verkhotur'e in 1742. He returned to Petersburg on February
14, 1743.

From Siberia, Müller brought back a great number of
archival and other materials. These constituted the richest
of finds for the study of Russian history.

In the Academy Müller was hostilely met by Schu-

macher and some others of ill will. Among these was Fisher,
who returned to Petersburg in 1750. All kinds of squabbles
began.

In 1748 Müller became a Russian citizen and was given
the title of historiographer. His obligation was to write a
"general history of Russia."

The matter of publishing the "Siberian history" dragged. Müller wrote it in German. The translator who was
found for him was bad. Another one was found and his
translation was deemed acceptable. Schumacher sent this
translation to several people, among which was the Russian
historian V. N. Tatishchev. The latter gave it a favorable
review: "I read with great pleasure," he wrote Schumacher,
"the beginning of the Siberian history which you sent me. . .
This is the beginning of Russian regional histories and one
can say nothing about it except praise and gratitude for the
virtue displayed in it."

The first volume of Müller's *History of Siberia* was
finally published in 1750. The two succeeding volumes remained in manuscript. Finding that Müller was delaying in
writing the history of Siberia, the Academy commissioned
Fisher to write its continuation. Fisher's *Siberian History
[Sibirskaia istoriia]* (published in German in 1768 and in
Russian translation in 1774) is not a continuation of Müller
but an abridged version of Müller's work (of the published
first volume as well as of the manuscript sections).

Müller stopped writing the continuation of the history
of Siberia and began preparing to write a history of Russia.
He was one of the first Russian scholars who became interested in the later stages of Russian history. Among his works
are *Essay in Modern Russian History [Opyt noveishei istorii
Rossii]* and *Report on the Russian Gentry [Izvestie o dvor-
ianakh rossiiskikh]*.

In 1765, by a decree of Catherine II, Müller was appointed overseer of the newly established foundling hospital in
Moscow. He retained the title of historiographer. As Müller
wrote in his autobiography, he accepted this post "in the
hope that I will be able to use the Moscow archives for my

Russian history; and I was reassured of this."

In view of the move to Moscow, Müller asked permission of the Academy to take all of the archival materials which he brought from Siberia there. His request was granted. By 1766 he was removed from his post at the foundling hospital and appointed "member of the State college of foreign affairs at the Moscow archives." One year later Müller was made archival director.

Müller's goal was to create a scholarly institution from the archive. He originated a whole school of learned archivists: Stritter, Malinovskii, Bantysh-Kamenskii. Müller also placed his "portfolios" in this archive. Among them were 30 folios of acts copied from Siberian archives.

But Müller no longer had the strength to write the "Russian history." In 1767 he wrote Catherine II stating that he recommended Prince M. M. Shcherbatov for this task.

Müller was paralyzed in 1772 but he, nevertheless, continued to work indefatigably up to his very death (1783).

Müller laid a firm foundation for the study of Russian history. He collected an enormous quantity of archival material and showed the necessity of basing research in Russian history on it. Several generations of Russian historians and publishers of documents in Russian history used the treasures of Müller's portfolios.

Schlözer originated the critical study of the texts of the Russian chronicles.

Chance brought Schlözer to Russia. While still a student at the University of Göttingen, Schlözer became interested in the Biblical East. For this reason he wished to go to Palestine. But he had no money to accomplish this. He then decided to proceed to Petersburg, hoping to make money and make his way to the East from there.

In 1760 Schlözer wrote Müller regarding his intention of coming to Petersburg and asked Müller to help him obtain a position at the Academy. Müller offered him a job as tutor to his children and as aide in the publication of a series of works on Russian history (*Sammlung Russischer Geschichte*) at a salary of 100 rubles per year.

Schlözer jumped at this proposal and came to Petersburg. Immediately upon his arrival, Schlözer began to learn Church Slavonic and the Russian language.

Schlözer was not to be satisfied with his modest position in Müller's house and he did not intend to be his helper in scholarly work. He thought Müller was an ignoramus while considering himself to be an already mature scholar. Schlözer became friendly with Taubert, the Academy's secretary, who was Müller's foe. Through him he obtained adjunct status at the Academy.

Having left Müller, Schlözer began the study of Russian history. He barely touched on the documentary materials of Russian history. "If I have been correctly informed," he states, "the oldest document that has been found thus far dates to Andrei Bogoliubskii, who died in 1158." (Andrei was killed in 1174). Schlözer concentrated on studying the Russian chronicles. Taubert gave him a handwritten German translation of the *Primary Chronicle* [*Povest' Vremennykh Let*] by a monk of the Aleksandr Nevskii monastery — Adam Sellii, a Dane by birth.

Schlözer drew up a synopsis of the translation, then learned to read the *Russian Primary Chronicle* in the original. He compared renditions (among them several which are in later compilations of chronicles). Schlözer immediately noticed the dependance of the *Primary Chronicle* on Byzantine sources. Here Schlözer established his hypothesis that the different readings in the chronicle compilations resulted mainly from the mistakes of ignorant copyists. It was on this hypothesis that he based his subsequent work, critically analyzing the chronicle's text. The goal which he set for himself was the restoration of the original text of the "purified Nestor."

Not satisified with his situation in Petersburg, Schlözer, in 1764, decided to return to Göttingen. At the personal order of Catherine II, Schlözer was made ordinary academician with a salary of 860 rubles per annum. At the same time, the Empress gave him permission for a foreign passport. The contract was signed until 1770. Upon returning to Göttingen, Schlözer was given the chair of philosophy in that University. In 1769 he published an experimental compilation of the chronicle with a Latin translation and disparate renditions (*Probe Russischer Annalen*). After this, Schlözer was made honorary academician with a life long pension. Young Russian scholars were occasionally sent to him to study. His influence on Karamzin was of no little significance. When the *Society of Russian History and Antiquities* [*Obshchestvo istorii i drevnostei Rossiiskikh*] was founded in 1804, Karamzin and Schlözer were elected honorary members.

Schlözer returned to Russian chronicles only toward the end of his life when he wrote a book which he titled *Nestor*. The book was published in German in four volumes from 1802-1805 and dedicated to Alexander I. The Russian translation appeared in three volumes in 1809-1810.

Despite the fact that Schlözer pursued a false path, his book had a great positive influence on the subsequent development of Russian historical scholarship. The very fact that, be they as they were, certain critical methods were employed in the study of the chronicles' texts, was important. It was on this basis that this branch of Russian historical scholarship prospered in the future.

The fourth academician to concern himself with Russian history was Lomonosov. His aim was to write a popular history of Russia in a fluid style. It was to serve as a counterweight to Bayer and Schlözer and show that at the dawn of their history Russians had already been able to create their own government and that they were not savages. In this fashion Lomonosov's approach to historical work was literary and patriotic. Hence, it is natural that Lomonosov was against the Norman theory.

In order to understand his views, it must be recalled how Schlözer described the cultural level of Rus' in the IX—X centuries. "Of course . . . God knows since when — and whence they had come. But they were people without rule who lived like the beasts and birds which filled their forests."

In contrast to this type of the German-Normanist view,

Lomonosov, in the introduction to his *Ancient Russian History*, proclaimed: "There is much evidence that there was not the great darkness of ignorance in Russia as foreign writers represent." On this question, as subsequent research in Russian history proved, especially that of the XIX and XX centuries, Lomonosov was right.

The historian S. M. Solov'ev considers as valuable features of Lomonosov's book the author's able utilization of the information in foreign sources regarding Slavs and Rus' and also the thoughtful comparison of ancient Russian pagan beliefs with the folk customs, games, and songs that were contemporary to Lomonosov.

Lomonosov's other work, *A Short Russian Chronicle*, is a concise essay on Russian history from ancient times to Peter the Great. The essay commences with the history of the origin of the Russian nation. The main events of each reign are then given. A genealogical table of Russian rulers is appended. During the reign of Catherine II, *A Short Russian Chronicle* served as the textbook of Russian history in the schools.

## VII

Let us now turn to the works of V. N. Tatishchev, Prince M. M. Shcherbatov and I. N. Boltin. None of these men was a professional scholar. Nevertheless, the contribution of each to Russian historical scholarship was very significant.

Vasilii Nikitich Tatishchev (1686-1750), a younger contemporary of Peter the Great, was one of the talented ones who came to the fore during Peter's era. He traveled all over Russia and became intrinsically familiar with its economy, government, ethnography and the conditions of national life.

Tatishchev was the son of a merchant from Pskov. Almost nothing is known about his early years. As a youth he studied artillery and engineering in the artillery academy under the tutorship of one of Peter's most enlightened associates — Iakov Vilimovich Brius [Jacob Daniel Bruce] (1670-1735). Tatishchev participated actively in the Great Northern War. He was in Germany (1713-1714) and brought back many books. These were the foundation of his voluminous library.

In 1717 Peter sent Tatishchev to Gdansk for negotiations regarding the payment of contributions with which that city was levied.

During that same year, Tatishchev participated in the Congress of Alland which drew Russian and Swedish representatives for peace negotiations. Along with Bruce, Tatishchev was one of the two Russian plenipotentiaries. Peace could not be concluded and the Congress was dissolved.

In 1719, Peter wanted to entrust Bruce with the compilation of a geography of Russia. At the time, Bruce was up to his neck in work (he was a senator and the president of the Berg i Manufaktur Kollegiia [Department of Mines and Industry] ) and recommended to Peter that Tatishchev take his place.

Tatishchev gave Peter a report of his plan of work. Peter approved it. Already at this time Tatishchev saw that in view of the undeveloped state of Russian history, he would have to study the geography and the history of the Russian State in depth. From his library, Peter gave him *The Ancient Chronicle of Nestor* which Tatishchev soon copied.

In 1720 Bruce commissioned Tatishchev to the Urals to establish mines. It was a troublesome and responsible matter. Nevertheless, Tatishchev was able to find time for gathering historical and geographical materials. He found another copy of the *Chronicle of Nestor* and, collating it with his own copy, he discovered a significant "difference." This motivated him to continue his searches. It was at this time that he began to elaborate the plan for his *History of Russia* [*Istoriia Rossiiskaia*] .

Arriving in Petersburg at the beginning of 1722, Tatishchev showed the plan of his history to Bruce and to Archbishop Feofan Prokopovich and asked them to help with books that he needed. Some were available in Petersburg, others were brought for him from Germany.

In December of the same year Tatishchev was again sent to the Urals and the Transurals as aide to V. I. Gennin, the director-in-chief of the "Siberian factories." At the end of 1723 Tatishchev was summoned to Petersburg with Gennin's reports and remained there.

In November of 1724 Peter sent Tatishchev to Sweden "for certain secret matters." He had to familiarize himself with the state of mining, manufacture and monetary affairs in Sweden. He was to hire various masters into Russian service, "attempt to place Russians for the study of mining" and "to observe and acquaint himself with the political situation, and the open and secret intentions of this government."

Tatishchev did not fail to utilize his trip to Stockholm for his scholarly endeavors as well. He contacted Swedish historians who indicated to him the existence, important to Russian historians, of Scandinavian sagas of the pagan period. He benefited from the fact that previously, while in Siberia, he came to know several Swedish prisoners of war. Among these was Colonel Tabort who traveled across all of Siberia collecting materials for its description. Upon returning to Sweden after the war's end, he was elevated to the gentry under the name of Stralenberg. When Tatishchev met him anew in Stockholm, Stralenberg was preparing for publication (in German) his book, *The Northern and Eastern Part of Europe and Asia*. In March, 1734 Tatishchev was appointed head of the Siberian factories and those of Perm. A special point in the instruction given him noted the necessity of learning the vast countryside in which the factories were located. In all likelihood, this point was introduced at Tatishchev's suggestion. Soon after arriving in Ekaterinburg, Tatishchev drew up a questionnaire which, at his request, the Siberian governor from Tobol'sk sent to all Siberian towns. The replies came slowly and some of them were too short. Nevertheless, Tatishchev accumulated enough information to commence the compilation of *A General Geographic Des-*

*scription of Siberia* [*Obshchee geograficheskoe opisanie vseia Sibiri*]. The work progressed slowly due to the insufficiency of information sent in reply to his questionnaires.

Tatishchev was only able to write the general introduction. He sent many of his writings and materials to the Academy of Sciences. Far from all of this was preserved (probably not everything has yet been found). In their aggregate, these works by Tatishchev have major significance in the development of Russian geographical scholarship. In 1950, A. I. Andreev published *Selected Works from Tatishchev on the Geography of Russia* [*Izbrannye trudy Tatishcheva po geografii Rossii*] as a separate anthology.

While gathering geographical information and performing his administrative functions, Tatishchev continued writing his *History of Russia*. He completed it in 1746. Two years later he wrote a second edition of his work. It was this edition which was published posthumously in five volumes. The first three volumes were published by G. F. Müller (1768-1774); the fourth volume appeared in 1784; the fifth — only in 1849.

Recently the Leningrad division of the historical institute of the Academy of Sciences undertook a new edition of Tatishchev. After lengthy preparation, it was published in seven volumes (1962-1968). Such outstanding historians and archeographers as A. I. Andreev, S. N. Valk and M. N. Tikhomirov took part in editing this work. They also wrote elucidatory articles in the individual volumes of this set. The new edition takes heed of both wordings of Tatishchev's work. This is very important, especially for the second part (from the beginning of Rus' to the invasion of Batu Khan in 1238). Tatishchev "freshened up" this part somewhat. In several places he enlarged on the exposition of the ancient text of the chronicles. In the meantime it was absolutely essential for historians to familiarize themselves with the first edition which preserved Tatishchev's sources exactly as imparted. Many of these sources have been preserved. Thus, the second part of Tatishchev's *History of Russia* is like a primary source for us.

This omission has now been restored. In the new edition of Tatishchev's work, the second redaction is printed in volumes II and III, the first in volume IV. In succeeding volumes, different versions and contradictions are presented for posterity when necessary.

Tatishchev's basic sources were the chronicles. These included the later compilations, the *Khronograf*, the *Stepennaia Kniga*, and the works of A. M. Kurbskii and Avraamii Palitsyn. Besides these, he used certain juridical sources, particularly the *Russkaia Pravda* of the XI — XII centuries and the *Sudebnik of 1550*, which he had himself discovered in the 1730's. Tatishchev copied the *Russkaia Pravda* (from a compilation of the Novgorod Chronicle dating to the end of the XV century) and, providing it with a translation and notes, submitted it to the Academy of Sciences. Schlözer (basing himself on Tatishchev's manuscript) published the *Russkaia Pravda* in 1767. Tatishchev presented the manuscript of the *Sudebnik* to Empress Anne. The copy which he made from it was given to the Academy of Sciences. It was this copy which G. F. Müller used in publishing the *Sudebnik* in 1768.

In the foreword to his work Tatishchev divided Russian history into four periods: 1) the ancient (to 860) in which Scythians, Sarmatians and Slavs took part; 2) from 860 to the invasion of the Tatars in 1238; 3) from the arrival of the Tatars to their overthrow by "the first Tsar, Ivan the Great" (Ivan III); 4) from Ivan III to the election of Mikhail Fedorovich Romanov to the throne. In general, this periodic division was held to by all future Russian historians.

Tatishchev left materials on the reign of Tsar Fedor Alekseevich and the rule of Tsarevna Sofiia in a draft copy. These materials were published in volume VII of the new edition.

Tatishchev had no special training for scholarly work but he had breadth of vision and a deep sense of the past's connection to the present. He brings his life's experience to the understanding of the past. Thus, he explains the intent of Muscovite legislation by means of the juridical customs of

his time and recollections of the mores of the end of the
XVII century. The personal knowledge that he attained of
alien peoples (Kalmyks, Bashkirs, Tatars) while in government service helped him to clarify the ethnography of
ancient Russia.

Tatishchev can be labeled a utilitarian in his world view.
The basis of his views was the then fashionable theory of
natural law and natural morality. Tatishchev expounded
his ideology in the essay "Conversation Between Two Friends
Regarding The Utility of Schools and the Sciences." ["Raz-
govor dvukh priiatelei o pol'ze nauk i uchilishch"].

This "Conversation" was written bearing the influence
of Samuel Pufendorf's theory of natural law and the *Philosophical Dictionary* of Johann-Georg Walkh, the Protestant
theologian. "Natural law" does not contradict the "law of
God" because man's desire for well being stems from God. A
rational gratification of needs is virtue. Our well being demands love and the help of others. Hence, we must "show
mutual love to others."

The mind's natural powers must be developed further
by science. "The greatest science is one which allows man to
know himself." Sciences necessary to man include "bodily,"
"political," and "spiritual" self-knowledge (medicine, economics, logic, theology). Tatishchev conceived history to be
national self-knowledge.

## VIII

Prince Mikhail Mikhailovich Shcherbatov was Müller's
successor as Russian historiographer. The Shcherbatov
princes were descendants of Mikhail of Chernigovsk and were
a branch of the Obolenskii princes. Mikhail Mikhailovich was
imbued with a feeling of dignity about his aristocratic origin.

He amplified his views at sessions of Catherine's Legislative Commission (1767-1768) which gathered to draw up a
new legal code. He had been elected deputy by the Iaroslavl
gentry. Shcherbatov protested against Peter's laws by which
entry into the gentry was open through meritorious govern-

ment service. Shcherbatov tried to prove that nobility derived from ancestors who distinguished themselves by acts of valor beneficient to the fatherland. These valorous acts became hereditary traits of the noble class. This class, historically trained, must take its place at the head of the nation. Shcherbatov also protested against the assigning of peasants to the mines and demanded that only the gentry could rule over serfs.

Shcherbatov's speeches were enthusiastically greeted by the majority of the noble deputies. But they occasioned furious protests from the gentry who had achieved their noble status by service and from the deputies representing the merchants and the peasantry.

Shcherbatov's interest in the history of his family and in that of noble families in general was, by the way, expressed in the process of gathering information on the history of the nobility in Russia. This occurred before he began to write his *History of Russia* [*Istoriia Rossisskaia*]. This provided him with some knowledge of Russian history.

Shcherbatov engaged in government work in the civil service. For a time, he was the herald master, then the president of the Kamer Kollegiia [Department of State Revenues] and finally a senator.

Shcherbatov did not commence writing a history of Russia prior to 1767. Catherine granted him permission to use needed materials from the printing office of the patriarchal libraries. These were the chief repositories of the chronicles. He was also allowed to use the documents of the Moscow archives of the College of Foreign Affairs.

Despite Shcherbatov's obligations in government service, the writing of the history proceeded swiftly. Toward the middle of 1769 he had already completed the first two volumes, having reached the Tatar invasions of 1238 (they were published in 1770-1771). Later volumes followed at short intervals. The last two — volumes XIV and XV — were published posthumously. Shcherbatov was able to bring Russian history up to the deposition of Tsar Vasilii Shuiskii (1610).

Shcherbatov's *History* was the first detailed pragmatic account of Russian history in Russian historiography. Some of his contemporaries subjected Shcherbatov's work to strict criticism. In passing, they pointed out his errors. This, however, does not blight his prominence in XVIII century Russian historiography. His initial volumes, based primarily on the chronicles, are weakest. But as Shcherbatov's work draws increasingly on documentary material, its value is augmented.

Shcherbatov's fundamental view of history might be called rationalist-pragmatist. Events are explained as the result of the conscious activity of ruling personalities subjecting the will of the masses to their will.

"The duty of every sovereign is to maintain the peace and well being of his people. But, unfortunately for mankind, the history of the world frequently indicates that the common weal of the State is merely appearance. The primary reason for actions was love of glory or a personal predilection of the sovereign."

The third outstanding Russian historian of the XVIII century was Ivan Nikitich Boltin who was born in 1735 and died in 1792. He was descended from an old gentry family. He received his initial education at home and served in the army. He retired in 1768 with the rank of premier major and served in the government bureaucracy for a time. His last post was as a member of the War College with the rank of major-general.

Boltin began to write on Russian history only toward the end of his life. But he began thinking about it and collecting materials on it at an early age. No less than Tatishchev, he had an inborn feeling of the historical process, the inseparable link of the present with the past and the impossibility of understanding one without the other.

Strict in his understanding of the historian's tasks, Boltin felt that, above all, his duty was the gathering and preliminary processing of the materials needed for the writing of history.

He needed a suitable cause in order to begin using the knowledge he had attained. This cause was the appearance in

French of the *History of Russia* by the French doctor,
Nicolas LeClerc. LeClerc had come to Russia several times
under Elizabeth and Catherine. For a time, he was physician
to Count Kiril Razumovskii, president of the Academy of
Sciences and personal physician to Crown Prince Paul.
Having been in Russia, he fancied himself an expert on
Russian affairs and wrote an extensive six volume compilation of Russian history. Its first volume was published in
1783. LeClerc's *History of Russia* was written with a great
degree of self-conceit and is full of errors.

Boltin was stung to the quick and he decided to analyze
LeClerc's book. In passing, he also elected to air his views on
Russian history. Kliuchevskii feels that Boltin was moved to
this act by G. A. Potemkin, his fellow officer in the military.

Thus appeared Boltin's two volume work, *Commentary
on the Ancient and Present Russian History of M. LeClerc*
[*Primechaniia na istoriiu drevnei i nyneshnei Rossii g-na
Leklerka*] (1788). Because prior to writing his book LeClerc
had obtained a synopsis of Russian history (from Riurik to
Tsar Fedor Ivanovich) and some other materials from Shcherbatov, Boltin also criticized Shcherbatov in his book. The
latter published a rejoinder to Boltin (1789). Boltin immediately wrote a sharp retort and then began to write
*Critical Comments on Prince Shcherbatov's History* [*Kriticheskie primechaniia na istoriiu kn. Shcherbatova*]. This
two part work appeared after the death of both writers
(1793-1794).

In discussing ancient Russian history, Boltin in the main
used Tatishchev. Boltin was not so much interested in events
as in the character and the conditions of national life, laws,
institutions, cultural level, morals, and customs.

Boltin's strong side is his incisive commentary on the
texts of the ancient records of Russian law. "He explains
certain terms, institutions, and characteristics of the mode
of life of ancient Russia so thoroughly that, with minor
corrections, his explanations have validity in the present day
(for example, his interpretation of the terms in *Russkaia
Pravda*)" (Kliuchevskii).

Boltin was the first Russian historian to posit the question of serfdom. "He sees the original source of this condition in the collapse of the peasant's right to move. He (Boltin) only confuses the limitation of movement with its complete cessation which he attributes to the end of the XVI century, to Fedor's reign. According to Boltin, peasants were originally linked to the landowner by land. Then the owners attained the right to transfer peasants. Finally, they gained uncontrolled use of the peasant's person, like that of a slave" (Kliuchevskii).

## IX

Toward the end of the XVIII century, there arose a serious interest in national history. By this time, a significant number of chronicle compilations and valuable Russian legal documents had been published. A rather broad circle of students of Russian antiquity came into existence. They sought in history arguments of the defense of the distinctiveness of Russian culture. This was in contrast to the general fascination with French fashions and with French free thought.

One of these outstanding amateurs was Count Aleksei Ivanovich Musin-Pushkin (1741-1817). He was educated at the artillery school and was once an aide-de-camp to Count G. Orlov. Upon retirement, he undertook a three year trip to Europe. When he returned, he became Master of Ceremonies at Catherine's Court, the Procurator of the Holy Synod, and finally, president of the Academy of Art.

His chief passion was collecting written sources of national antiquity. In the provinces he had commissioners for the purchase of ancient manuscripts. When he was appointed Procurator of the Holy Synod (1791), he came to have knowledgeable aides from the clergy among his subordinates. At his suggestion, Catherine promulgated a decree regarding the elicitation of ancient documents from monastic archives to be at the Synod's disposal.

In this fashion, Musin-Pushkin attained an enormous

collection of valuable documents of antiquity. He only came to know them gradually himself and published his most interesting finds. Thus, in 1795, he found an anthology of ancient Russian tales compiled and recorded, by all indications, in Pskov in the XVI century. The famous *Lay of Prince Igor*[6] appeared at the end of this anthology. A copy was made for Catherine II. In 1800 Musin-Pushkin published *The Lay* according to the original with the aid of the learned archivists N. Bantysh-Kamenskii and A. Malinovskii. Not long before 1812, likely at their suggestion, Musin-Pushkin turned to Alexander I with a request to add his manuscript collection to the Moscow archives of foreign affairs.

The request was not immediately granted. In 1812 the French entered Moscow and Musin-Pushkin's home, his library and the original of *The Lay* burned to the ground.

The 1770's and 1780's were a period of unusual animation in Russia's intellectual and literary life. Many literary journals, both large and small, appeared. They polemicized against each other. At the crest of this upsurge stood Nikolai Ivanovich Novikov (1741-1818). He was also interested in Russian history and published a series of valuable historical materials (*Ancient Russian Library*) [*Drevniaia Rossiiskaia Vivliotika*]).

There appeared an interest in Russian society toward discussion of literature and social problems — in private conversation and within circles of friends. This was an era when Russian social thought was engendered.

The majority of these circles and brotherhoods were masonic lodges. During Catherine II's reign, masonry spread widely among the Russian aristocracy and among army and navy officers. The goals of XVIII century masonry were to morally ennoble its adherents and unite them in the principles of brotherhood, equality and mutual assistance. The meetings of the lodges were invested with a symbolic ritual described by Lev Tolstoi in *War and Peace*.

Prince Shcherbatov, Boltin and Novikov were masons. The future historian N. M. Karamzin joined the masons in 1785. After being in free-masonry for three years, he dropped out of the organization.

In May of 1779, M. M. Kheraskov (a mason), the curator of Moscow University, offered Novikov the rental of the university's printing press for ten years as well as the publication of the newspaper, *Moskovskie Vedomosti*. Novikov agreed and moved from Petersburg to Moscow. There, with unusual sweep, he developed his publishing and informational activity. Simultaneously, he entered Moscow's masonic organization which consisted of several lodges.

The Moscow leaders of the masonic lodges entered into relations with the Rosicrucian order which pretended to knowledge of the higher mysteries (the Rosicrucians were centered in Germany). Novikov headed the Moscow branch of the Rosicrucians and even engaged in alchemy, which was esteemed by the Rosicrucians. Novikov used his alchemical knowledge to make up medicines with which he treated his acquaintances.

Novikov's ten year contract for the rental of Moscow University's printing press and the publication of *Moskovskie Vedomosti* expired on May 1, 1789. Novikov expected renewal of the contract, but Catherine forbade the University to do so.

Even prior to this, Catherine had become suspicious of Novikov's activities. One of the reasons for her concern was her son Paul's connection with Prussia, in particular with the Berlin Rosicrucians. (She was not on good terms with Paul). Furthermore, Russia's previous alliance with Prussia was replaced by a rapprochement with Austria. Russia's relations with Prussia worsened.

The French Revolution then began. In 1792 Novikov was arrested and incarcerated in the Schlüsselburg fortress. Catherine died on November 6, 1796.

On the first day of his rule, Paul issued an order freeing Novikov. Novikov had been incarcerated in the fortress while still full of strength and energy. He emerged from there "old, bent, and decrepit." He settled in Avdot'ino, his estate in the Moscow province, and lived there practically without leaving it until his death.

Novikov's significance in the history of Russian society is very great. He awakened independent thought in his associates and infected them with the fire of his spirit. In particular, N. M. Karamzin's connection with Novikov and his circle was the turning point in his moral and literary education.

Karamzin (1766-1826) stands on the brink of two centuries. His foundations as writer and historian were laid in the XVIII century. His main work, *A History of the Russian State* [*Istoriia Gosudarstva Rossiiskogo*], opens a new era in Russian historiography.

# PART TWO

## RUSSIAN HISTORIOGRAPHY 1801-1920

### FOREWORD

My purpose in writing these "essays" was two-fold: to trace the main lines of Russian historical thought and promote the characteristics of the work of leading Russian historians. I did not attempt to offer an account of all Russian historical scholars. There were so many of them that were one to mention all, we would merely have a list of names.

I have limited myself to describing only those historians who, to my mind, had considerable influence on the development of Russian historiography. Hence, I did not touch on the work of some major scholars.

As a result of the crushing of Russian historical scholarship in 1920, a significant number of Russian historians emigrated.

I describe in detail the fate of those émigré historians who, at the moment of emigration, were fully developed scholars who continued their work abroad (Miliukov, Kizevetter) and also certain émigré historians who commenced their scholarly activity in Russia but published their main works in foreign lands.

The destinies of historians who remained in Russia are mentioned briefly. I barely touch on their works published after 1920. Their achievements belong to Russian historiography of the Soviet era.

# I

## INTRODUCTION

By the start of the XIX century Russian and Russified naturalists and historians had laid a solid foundation for the further development of Russian scholarship.

Not all of their achievements were immediately assimilated and valued by contemporaries or by posterity. Much of Lomonosov's brilliant and prescient work, for example, was either unpublished or remained in manuscript and was discovered only at the beginning of the XX century. In similar cases, scientific discoveries and hypotheses usually do not find a place in the external history of science. But, as V. I. Vernadskii points out, such discoveries and hypotheses have great meaning in understanding the inner development of mankind's scientific thought.

"The life of an individual scholar or thinker who has attained the correct view or found a proper solution of something unknown to his time does not pass in naught or without reason even though he may be removed from the main channels of human thought" (V. I. Vernadskii, *On the Significance of M. V. Lomonosov's Works in Mineralogy and Geology*, p. 2).

This idea is fully applicable to the development of historical scholarship as well. In the history of science cases where a number of scientists in different countries simultaneously, but independently of each other, take up the same problem are not infrequent. Thus, in the middle of the XVIII century, the electricity of thunderstorms was simultaneously studied by Lomonosov and Richmann in Russia, Franklin in America, and Dalibard in France. This means that in this area of knowledge the growing level of science, created by leading scientists of various countries, provided the opportunity for a problem's solution.

Let us now turn to the premises and the character of the development of historical scholarship in XIX century Russia. At the beginning of the century, several new universities were established — a German one in Derpt in 1802, a Polish one in Vilnius in 1804, that of Petersburg in 1819, and those of Kazan and Khar'kov. New Russian scholars gradually emerged from the alumni of the new universities and that of Moscow. Commencing with the 1840's, the number of Russian historians began to grow quickly.

The German idealism of Kant (1724-1804), Hegel (1770-1831) and Schelling (1775-1854) had great influence on the subsequent development of Russian historical thought.

Toward the end of the XIX century spokesmen for Marxist materialism, based philosophically on Hegelianism, begin to appear in Russia. After the Bolshevik Revolution of 1917, Marxism became obligatory and is the sole doctrine allowed.

A major push toward the development of Russian historical scholarship was provided by the emancipation of the serfs and, in general, the whole era of the reforms of Alexander II. University instruction became freer and censorship of the press more liberal. The emancipation of the serfs created a whole school of Russian historians who concentrated their attention on the history of the peasantry and the peasant problem. The works of V. I. Semevskii and several articles by V. O. Kliuchevskii were devoted to this theme; similarly, the works of N. I. Kareev (on France), I. V. Luchitskii (on Western Eurpoe) and P. G. Vinogradov (on Italy and England).

## II

### N. M. KARAMZIN

Nikolai Mikhailovich Karamzin (1766-1826) was descended from an old noble family of which there already is record in the XVI century. He was born in the province of Simbirsk on his father's estate. As a nine year old boy, he developed a passion for old novels. These cultivated his natural sensitivity. He was brought to Moscow in his fourteenth year and placed in Professor Shaden's boarding school. He attended the university as well. In 1784 he settled in Moscow and joined Novikov's masonic circle.

Karamzin remained a mason only three years before quitting but contact with Novikov's circle had a great influence on him. He matured morally and mentally and developed a taste for literature. He became interested in Russian history. In May of 1789 be undertook a long trip from which he returned in September of 1790. He traveled all over Western Europe — Germany, Switzerland, France, England. During his trip he wrote down his impressions. Upon returning to Russia, he polished them for publication and issued them in six parts, *Letters of a Russian Traveler* [*Pis'ma Russkogo puteshestvennika*], 1797-1801. This trip had colossal significance in Karamzin's development as a writer.

It resulted in the reform of the Russian literary language. Lomonosov was the creator of the literary Russian of the new period. Karamzin's goal was to eliminate the dependence of literary Russian on Church Slavonic and Latin and to substitute Lomonosov's style with the more elegant (in Karamzin's opinion) French literary style.

This reform did not bring literary Russian closer to the spoken. It "only substituted one foreign model for another. The usefulness of excluding many Church Slavonic synonyms for Russian words might be doubted: they provided color and variety. . . Karamzin increased the gap between the language of educated society and the language of the people. . . The justification for Karamzin's style is that it became the language of Pushkin."[7]

Let us now turn to the development of Karamzin's overall world view and to the initial period of his historical study. Among the European thinkers who influenced Karamzin during his journey, a place of honor is reserved by Karamzin in his *Letters* for Herder, author of the remarkable book, *Ideas on the Philosophy of Human History* (*Ideen zur Philosophie der Menschengeschichte*). Herder preached that there was no contradiction between the national and universal. In his *Letters* Karamzin expressed this thought in somewhat different fashion: "All that is *national* is nothing compared to that which is *common to humanity*. The chief thing is to be *people*, not Slavs. That which is good for people, cannot be bad for Russians. That which has been invented by Englishmen or Germans for the good and benefit of man is also mine, for I am a person."

Karamzin began to think of writing a history of Russia in 1790. His thoughts took a more definite form in 1793. In announcing to the public the cessation that year of the *Moscow Journal* which he published, Karamzin wrote: "In the place of seclusion I will begin to sort the archives of the ancient literatures. . . I will learn, and I will use the treasures of antiquity in order to later undertake a work which could eventually be a memorial to my heart and soul, if not for posterity (of which I dare not think), then at least for my few friends and acquaintances."

According to Karamzin's original conception, his life's work (*The History of Russia*) was to have a literary and patriotic character.

"Tacitus, Hume, Robertson — these are the models (wrote Karamzin in 1790 while still in Paris). People say that our history is in itself less significant than others. I do not think so. Only intellect, taste and talent is necessary. One can choose, animate, color, and the reader will be surprised how something attractive, powerful, and worthy of the attention of foreigners, not only Russians, could derive from Nestor, Nikon, and others. I agree: the genealogy of the princes, their quarrels, internecine wars, and Polovetsian attacks are not particularly interesting. But why fill whole volumes with such things? Everything which is not important should be abbreviated. But all traits which signify a characteristic of the Russian people, the character of our ancient heroes, of excellent men, of truly interesting events should be depicted vividly and strikingly. We had our Charlemagne — Vladimir, our Louis XI — Tsar Ivan, our Cromwell — Godunov, and in addition, a tsar the like of which has never been seen before — Peter the Great. Their reigns constitute the

most consequential eras in our history and even in the history
of mankind."

He studied Russian history in 1797. He was the first to
notify the European intellectual world regarding the find of
*The Lay of Prince Igor.* His report of this was published in
the Hamburg journal *Spectateur du Nord* (Oct. 1797).

During the same year, Karamzin married Elizaveta
Ivanovna Protas'eva. She died in 1802. Karamzin remarried
two years later and Ekaterina Andreevna Kolyvanovna, of the
Viazemskii family long close to him, became his wife. She
was one of the outstanding women of contemporary Petersburg society. She was well educated, was interested in literature and history, and helped her husband edit his *History*.

In 1803, through his friend Mikhail Nikitich Murav'ev,
the Minister of Public Education, Karamzin appealed to
Alexander I with a request to be appointed his historiographer. He hoped to be assigned a commensurate salary and
given the right to obtain all necessary historical sources. The
request was granted. (He was assigned a salary of 2,000 rubles
per year).

From this time on Karamzin immersed himself in the
tireless and strained effort of writing the *History of the
Russian State* [*Istoriia Gosudarstva Rossiiskogo*]. He died
while at the height of his work, having written twelve volumes and taken the account to 1610.

By the time that his work could be commenced,
Karamzin saw that his initial plan of presenting the work in
literary-patriotic terms was insufficient, that it was necessary
to provide a scholarly basis for his *History*. In other words,
primary sources had to be studied. He turned to them. As his
work progressed and he became involved in it, he displayed
an outstanding critical sense.

A dilemma now faced Karamzin — how to combine
his two plans, the literary and documentary? He got out of
the difficulty by deciding to construct his book in two tiers,
so to speak. The text of the book was written according to
literary precepts while the numerous notes follow the text
and constitute the second part of each volume, paralleling

the text. In this way the average reader could read the text without looking (or looking infrequently) at the notes. The specialist in history, or the reader seriously interested in history, could easily make use of the notes.

Karamzin's "notes" in themselves represent an individual and exceedingly valuable work. It has not lost its meaning to our day, for since then some of the sources used by Karamzin have been lost in one way or another and have not been found.

Karamzin found many materials in the synodal library. Until the destruction of the Musin-Pushkin collection in the Moscow conflagration of 1812, Karamzin obtained many valuable sources from him (he returned the *Trinity Chronicle* to Musin upon finishing with it, to be destroyed, as it turned out).

Documents in the custody of the Ministry's Moscow archive were searched out for Karamzin by Malinovskii, the archival director.

The basic idea guiding Karamzin in the writing of the *History of the Russian State* was monarchical. The unity of Russia was in the monarch supported by the nobility.

According to Karamzin, all of ancient Russian history up to Ivan III was a long preparatory process. The history of autocracy in Russia commences with Ivan III. Sequentially, Karamzin's exposition followed the *Russian History* of Prince Shcherbatov (1733-1790). But, irrespective of the fact that in terms of literature Karamzin's work is much more talented than Shcherbatov's, Karamzin used a far greater number of sources than Shcherbatov. Furthermore, he did so with a much finer sense and understanding.

The appearance of the *History of the Russian State* was an event in the intellectual life of Russian society. Of the exalted responses to Karamzin's work, let us recall those of three poets — Pushkin, Prince Viazemskii and Zhukovskii.

At this time Pushkin was bed-ridden, recovering from suppurative fever. "This was in February of 1818," noted Pushkin. "The first eight volumes of Karamzin's Russian history appeared. I read them in bed avidly and attentively. The

appearance of this book (appropriately) caused a sensation
and made a substantial impression. 3,000 copies were sold
out in one month — the sole such example in our country.
Everyone, even fashionable ladies, hurried to read the history
of their native land, a history previously unknown to them.
Ancient Russia seemed to have been discovered by Karamzin
like America was by Columbus."

Viazemskii expressed his feelings thusly: "Karamzin is
our Kutuzov of 1812. He saved Russia from the invasion of
oblivion and called it to life. He showed us that we have a
fatherland, as many found out in 1812."

Zhukovskii's response: "Karamzin's history may be
called the resurrection of our nation's prior centuries. Up to
this time they have been only lifeless mummies to us. . .
They will now be revived, arise, and assume a majestically
attractive appearance."

Pushkin valued Karamzin's work for the revival of the
Russian nation's past as well as for the author's literary style
and scholarship. Pushkin was a versatile genius. He had a
lively interest in history and a penetrating historical sense.
What is more, he not only studied history but came forward
as the author of two noteworthy historical works — *History
of the Pugachev Rebellion* [*Istoriia Pugachevskogo bunta*]
and the *History of Peter the Great* [*Istoriia Petra Velikogo*].

The *History of the Pugachev Rebellion* appeared in
1834. Chronologically speaking this is the first scholarly
book devoted to the Pugachev revolt. "It collects," writes
Pushkin in the introduction, "all that was published by the
government about Pugachev and everything which seemed reliable in foreign writers who mentioned him. I also had
occasion to use certain manuscripts, tales, and the testimony
of witnesses." Pushkin petitioned to have the Pugachev
file, which was then in the State archives, opened for him.
But Nicholas I refused. In his work, in simple and clear
fashion, Pushkin states the reasons for Pugachev's revolt,
its rapid progress, and finally its suppression by government
forces. Though basically this is a story of military operations, the background does bring out the psychology of

various strata of the population (the Iaik cossacks, serfs, mine workers, etc. . . ).

All this is far from Karamzin's literary style. Rather it is closer to the style of Tacitus. But while Pushkin was writing this book, artistic images came to him. He embodied them separately in "The Captain's Daughter" ["Kapitanskaia dochka"] (1834-1836).

From his youth, Pushkin was interested in the personality and the statesmanship of Peter. There was partly a family interest. One of Pushkin's ancestors, the Abyssinian prince, Hannibal, was Peter's associate. Pushkin gave a vivid, slightly idealized image of Peter in his tale, "The Moor of Peter the Great" ["Arap Petra Velikogo"] (1827). Having finished writing about the Pugachev rebellion, Pushkin began to collect historical materials on Peter and then to write a history of him. He did not fully complete or polish this work. Only comparatively recently was his manuscript found and published.

Pushkin's *History of Peter the Great* was written in a style different from that of the *History of the Pugachev Rebellion*. It is more unified. The author's primary attention is accorded to Peter. Peter's personality merges with his governmental activity.

The more liberal that Alexander I's policies became, the more Karamzin's views became conservative.

In 1809 Alexander entrusted M. M. Speranskii to develop a plan for government reforms. Their goal was to give the Russian monarchy the character of a legal State. Parts of the plan began to be introduced in the autumn of 1809. A State Council was created based on new foundations. It was to discuss the new laws. When disagreements arose, the Emperor was to affirm the opinion of the majority or the minority.

Speranskii was dismissed in 1812 and sent to Perm. Of course, Speranskii's plan was not a "constitution." But it led to the possibility for the introduction of a constitutional regime in the future.

Karamzin was alarmed by this possibility and wrote an

objection — *A Memoir on Ancient and Modern Russia* [*Zapiska o drevnei i novoi Rossii*]. In it he attempted to prove that Russia's sole salvation consisted of the stability of autocracy supported by the nobility. In his *Memoir* Karamzin sharply critized Alexander I's liberal policy and asserted that, instead of all the reforms, it was sufficient to find 50 good governors and guarantee the nation good spiritual fathers.

In 1811 Karamzin brought his *Memoir* to the attention of Alexander I through the mediation of Ekaterina Pavlovna, the Emperor's favorite sister. She was married to Prince Georg Ol'denburg. Their palace was in Tver.

Karamzin read his memorandum to the Emperor, but it was not approved.

## III

### GUSTAV EVERS

Another outstanding historian, Gustav Evers (1781-1830) was Karamzin's younger contemporary. The son of a Liflandian farmer, Evers studied in Germany and completed his education at the University of Göttingen. Upon graduating from the University in 1803, Evers returned to Estonia, settled near Derpt, found himself a position as tutor in the family of a local *landrat* [district administrator], and began to devote himself to Russian history. His first scholarly work, *Preliminary Critical Research for Russian History* [*Predvaritel'nye Kriticheskie issledovaniia dlia Rossiiskoi istorii*], appeared in 1808. Like his subsequent works, this book was written in German. But a Russian translation was published in 1825.

In contrast to the adherents of the Norman theory of the origin of the Russian State (which, following Schlözer, was accepted by Karamzin), Evers felt that the Rus' nation descended from the Khazars and originally inhabited southern Russia (Black Sea Rus').

During the year that this work was published, Evers

spent some time in Petersburg in conjunction with his studies. He made Karamzin's acquaintance. At this time Evers had already begun to prepare his next book — *Russian History* [*Russkaia istoriia*]. It carried through to the end of the XVII century. It was published in 1816. In 1810 Evers was appointed professor of Russian history at the University of Derpt.

Evers' major work, *Ancient Russian Law in its Historical Manifestation* [*Drevneishee Russkoe pravo v istoricheskom ego raskrytii*] appeared in 1826 (in German; later two Russian translations were issued).

The goal which Evers set for himself in this monograph was not the study of the events of Russian history but the inner development of human society.

In the introduction to his work he wrote: "Nature proceeds gradually everywhere. . . Everything is strictly interdependent." Everything in history ". . . springs from the natural course of human development. . . on the basis of Russian history, I intend to show the gradual progress of law which emerged from the so-called patriarchal condition of civil society."

Evers felt that "initially each family exists by itself. . . The kin encompasses many families; the father is master in each family . . . Tribes form from kin. The forefather becomes tribal chief. Little by little the head of the tribe becomes a powerful prince. But the original family relationship, based on nature itself still retains its strength for a long time."

Evers' theory of ancestral modes of life played a major role in the subsequent course of Russian historiography. It was later developed in somewhat altered form by Kavelin and Solov'ev.

## IV

## SOURCES FOR HISTORICAL STUDY

The first third of the XIX century was a period of

collecting and publishing historical materials. Count Nikolai Petrovich Rumiantsev (1754-1826), the diplomat, played a conspicuous role in this movement. In 1807, he was appointed Minister of Foreign Affairs and was elevated to the rank of Chancellor two years later.

Rumiantsev was interested in political and historical sciences. As already stated, the appearance of the first volume of Karamzin's *History* raised the level of interest in Russian history in Russian society. Rumiantsev understood that the time had come to solidify the documentary foundation for the future writing of Russian history and headed a whole historical archeographical movement.

A group of archeographers emerged around him — archivists of the Moscow archives of the College of Foreign Affairs: N. N. Bantysh-Kamenskii (1737-1814), A. F. Malinovskii (1762-1840), K. F. Kalaidovich (1792-1832), P. M. Stroev (1796-1876), the archeographer Ia. Ia. Berednikov (1793-1854) and also bishop (later Metropolitan of Kiev) Evgenii (Bolkhovitinov), historian and author of a historical dictionary of religious and secular writers.

Rumiantsev's chief aides were Kalaidovich and Stroev. In 1810 Rumiantsev proposed that Bantysh-Kamenskii draw up a plan for the publication of a collection of government documents and treaties. The plan was soon realized and approved by Rumiantsev. Petitioned by Rumiantsev, Alexander I established a commission at the Moscow archives to publish such a collection. Rumiantsev took all expenses upon himself.

The first volume of the *Collection of Government Documents and Treaties* [*Sobraniia Gosudarstvennykh gramot i dogovorov*] appeared in 1813; the second in 1819; the third in 1822; and the fourth in 1826 (after Rumiantsev's death).

A valuable contribution to the collection and publication of materials on Russian history was made by Aleksandr Ivanovich Turgenev (1785-1846), one of the most enlightened members of the Russian intelligentsia in the first half of the XIX century. His was a wide range of interests which included Russian history. A friend of Karamzin and Prince Viazemskii, he constantly traveled to Europe and, in a sense, served as an intermediary between the intellectual life of Russia and Europe.

Let us return to the work of the members of Rumiantsev's commission for the publication of government documents and treaties. In 1823 P. M. Stroev was elected a member of the Society of History and Antiquities at Moscow University (which was founded in 1804). In his first year upon entering, Stroev gave an inspired speech in which he proposed a grandiose plan for a series of archeographic expeditions. These were to canvass monastic and cathedral repositories of ancient written monuments of Russian history and literature.

The majority of the Society's members who were present thought Stroev's plans to be the unrealizable plans of a youthful mind. He was given the means only to review the holdings of Novgorod's Sofiia library which he did describe. Stroev's speech was not even published in the Society's proceedings. A little later, it appeared in the Petersburg journal, *The Northern Archive* [*Severnyi Arkhiv*]. Supposedly, Stroev's speech published therein drew the attention of Grand Duchess Mariia Pavlovna, sister of Alexander I. In 1804 she had married Prince Karl Friedrich, the heir of Saxony-Weimar. According to Schiller, Mariia Pavlovna possessed "great talent for art and music and a true love of reading."

Reassured by the intercession of the Grand Duchess, Stroev turned to Count S. S. Uvarov, the president of the Academy of Sciences, with a statement of his plan. The Academy accepted Stroev's plan and assigned 10,000 rubles for its implementation. Having chosen two aides, Stroev left Moscow on May 15, 1829 for the shores of the White Sea. The trip was extremely exhausting. Stroev stoically bore the poor roads, appalling hygienic conditions, illnesses, and the frequent hostility of ignorant keepers of archives and libraries. But after two months both of his helpers refused to follow him. Stroev replaced them with Ia. Ia. Berednikov who felt as passionately about the project as Stroev.

The expedition lasted for five and one half years. Stroev and Berednikov traveled all over northern and central Russia. They surveyed over 200 libraries and archives, copied up to 3,000 historical-juridical documents of the XIV-XVII centuries, and examined a great number of chronicles.

All educated Russia followed Stroev's journey. Scholars turned to him, requesting excerpts, references and advice. M. Speranskii, who was then preparing the first two volumes of the *Collected Laws of the Russian Empire* [*Polnoe Sobranie Zakonov Rosisskoi Imperii*], asked for Stroev's collaboration in assembling the materials. The expedition's progress reports were read annually on December 29, the day of the annual session of the Academy of Sciences. When the expedition ended, a permanent archeographic commission was established at the Ministry of Education for the analysis and publication of the manuscripts collected by Stroev and Berednikov. It was chaired by Prince Shirinskii-Shikhmatov, the director of the department of public education. Stroev and Berednikov were appointed members of the commission (in 1838 Berednikov was made editor-in-chief of the commission's publications).

In 1836 the Archeographic Commission published four volumes of *Documents Collected by the Archeographic Expedition* [*Akty sobrany arkheograficheskoi Ekspeditsiei*]. These were followed by *Juridical Documents* [*Akty Iuridicheskie*], *Historical Documents* [*Akty Istoricheskie*] (in five volumes) and *Supplement to Historical Documents* [*Dopolneniia k aktam istoricheskim*] (twelve volumes). Taken together, this was an enormous contribution to Russian historical study. In 1846 the commission undertook the systematic publication of the *Complete Collection of Russian Chronicles* [*Polnoe sobraniia russkikh letopisei*].

Government publications must be added to this. The second section of His Majesty's Chancellery did not limit itself to the publication of the *Collected Laws*. It also published *Diplomatic Statutes of Russian Relations with Foreign Powers* [*Pamiatniki diplomaticheskikh snoshenii Rossii s derzhavami inostrannymi*] (ten volumes), *Court Register* [*Dvortsovye rezriady*] (five volumes), and *Registers of* [*Civil and Military*] *Appointments* [*Knigi razriadnye*] (two volumes).

## V

## KARAMZIN'S SUCCESSORS

Several historians in the 1830's came to succeed Karamzin. They gave a new direction to Russian historical thought. In contrast to Karamzin, they were all *raznochintsy* in origin. The eldest of them was M. T. Kachenovskii (1775-1842). Then there were (in order of their birth dates) N. A. Polevoi (1796-1846); M. P. Pogodin (1800-1875); N. I. Nadezhdin (1804-1856); and N. G. Ustrialov (1805-1870). The jurist, K. A. Nevolin (1806-1855) can be added to them.

Mikhail Trofimovich Kachenovskii, the founder of the "sceptical school," was descended from a Russified Greek family. At the age of thirteen, he graduated from the Khar'kov Kollegium [gymnasium]. He served in the civilian and military sectors. In 1790 he obtained Boltin's works. These stimulated him to consider the critical analysis of the sources of Russian history. In 1801 Kachenovskii was appointed librarian, then head of Count Aleksei Kirillovich Razumovskii's private chancellery. From that point, Kachenovskii's career was guaranteed, the more so that Count Razumovskii was appointed trustee of Moscow University in 1807.

Kachenovskii received a master's degree in philosophy in 1811 and was appointed professor at Moscow University. He taught Russian history from 1821 to 1835. Despite the fact that outwardly Kachenovskii was a poor lecturer, he was immensely popular with his students.

The spirit of the time was changing. Youth welcomed the dethronement of former authorities. In his critical examples, Kachenovskii initially fell back on Schlözer's methods. But he later became disillusioned with him. The

German historian Niebuhr became his inspirer. Niebuhr's first volume of his *History of Rome* appeared in Berlin in 1811, and created a new era in historiography. Niebuhr rejected the whole ancient period of Roman history as being legendary.

Following in his footsteps, Kachenovskii declared the whole Kievan period to be legendary. Kachenovskii thought the sources for this period — the chronicles, the *Russkaia Pravda*, and *The Lay of Price Igor* — to be forgeries. He also criticized Karamzin sharply.

The difference between Niebuhr and Kachenovskii was that Niebuhr was a trained scholar of broad vision and systematic knowledge, while Kachenovskii, despite all of his talent, was not sufficiently schooled in systematic work.

Nevertheless, Kachenovskii and his "sceptical school" (he had several students and followers) played a positive role in the development of Russian historical scholarship. Even their opponents began to regard their research and the sources more thoughtfully and critically.

One of Kachenovskii's main opponents was Mikhail Petrovich Pogodin. Pogodin was born in Moscow. He was the son of one of the administrators (by birth a serf) of Count Stroganov. The environment of the lordly court developed in young Mikhail a certain cynicism and, simultaneously, a worldly practicality and ability to adapt to people and situations. He graduated from the first Moscow gymnasium. He bought the *History of the Russian State*, was permeated with a patriotic spirit, and continued to be an admirer of Karamzin forever. In the university, Pogodin became acquainted with the works of Schlözer, who also had great influence on him. A year after graduating from the university (in 1823), Pogodin successfully defended his master's thesis, "On the Origin of Rus'." In 1835 he attained the chair of Russian history. In 1841 Pogodin was chosen member of the Academy of Sciences in its second section (Russian language and literature). Three years later, Pogodin left the professional staff of Moscow University but continued to live in Moscow. While teaching at the university, he began to publish his *Research, Observations, and Lectures on Russian History.* [*Issledovaniia, zamechaniia i lektsii po Russkoi istorii*] — his most valuable scholarly work. In it he displayed a great critical talent.

Pogodin was an avid collector of manuscripts and various kinds of antiquities. He compiled a large and very valuable repository of antiquities. He also built up a large library. He sold his manuscript collection to the Petersburg public library in 1852.

Pogodin followed the development of European historical scholarship. He went abroad several times. In Paris, he visited Guizot. Prior to this, he had visited Prague and formed close relations with Shafarik, Haencke and Palacky. From that time on he became interested in the Slavic question and began to defend the stirrings of western and southern Slavs toward national liberation.

Politically, Pogodin was one of the eminent representatives of "official nationality." An assistant at (later minister of) the Ministry of Public Education, Count S. S. Uvarov, vividly expressed the essence of this movement in 1832 by the formula "Orthodoxy, Autocracy, Nationality." After leaving Moscow University, Pogodin worked primarily at journalism. He returned to scholarly work only toward the end of his life. He published his last book, *Ancient Russian History to the Mongol Yoke* [*Drevniaia Russkaia istoriia do Mongol'skogo iga*] in 1872. He said nothing new in it.

Pogodin was not disposed toward philosophical thought. His enthusiasm for Schelling is all the more strange. It is to be explained by an inherent sentimentality — something which also seems to be a contradiction in his personality.

In summarizing, one cannot but admit that Pogodin was an original and fairly important figure in the development of Russian historical scholarship.

Nikolai Alekseevich Polevoi is sometimes considered as one of the "sceptical school" even though he went his own special way. Polevoi was the son of a merchant of modest means from Kursk (and was born in Irkutsk). His father had a fairly large library and, while yet a boy, Polevoi hungrily threw himself into unsystematic reading. This constituted his elementary education. Later, with persistent and steady effort, he educated himself. His father was readying him for a commercial occupation and made him his overseer. From the age of fifteen, his father sent him on trade missions to, among other places, Moscow and Petersburg. In Moscow Polevoi managed to hear several of Kachenovskii's lectures. He also became acquainted with several other representatives of the contemporary Russian intelligentsia.

His work as manager left him with the commercially necessary touch of publicity and even self-advertisement.

After his father's death (1822), Polevoi moved to Moscow and no longer engaged in trade. He plunged headlong into journalism and then turned to history.

Polevoi displayed outstanding talent as a journalist. In 1825 he founded the best journal of the time — the famous *Moscow Telegraph* [*Moskovskii Telegraf*]. Polevoi wrote for it himself as well as being able to attract a whole pleiade of associates — among them, Pushkin and Prince Viazemskii. This journal had unprecedented success among readers. Four years after the journal's founding, there was almost a crisis. Polevoi, who valued Karamzin highly as a writer and recognized his significance in the creation of a new literary style, viewed him in sharply negative terms as a historian. Polevoi expressed these views in 1829, having included a review of the *History of the Russian State* in the *Moscow Telegraph*. The review incurred the resentment of Viazemskii and Pushkin who left the journal. But Polevoi's other associates remained. The journal expanded its influence ever more broadly, but a catastrophe occurred in 1834. Polevoi published an unfavorable review of Kukol'nik's patriotic play, *The Hand of the Most High Has Saved the Fatherland* [*Ruka Vsevyshniago otechestvo spasla*], which was then in its stage run. In the meantime, this play had received the approval of Nicholas I. The *Moscow Telegraph* was shut down. For Polevoi, this was a tragedy and broke him completely. Polevoi continued to write and publish in order to somehow fill his soul's emptiness. He published a *History of Peter the Great [Istoriia Petra Velikogo]*, numerous historical novels and dramas, but all of this could not compare with his previous labors. He felt this himself. Prior to his death, however, he wrote his last serious work, *A Survey of Russian History up to the Autocracy of Peter the Great [Obozrenie russkoi istorii do edinoderzhaviia Petra Velikogo]*. In it he stated a series of interesting thoughts on the essence of the historical process.

In his philosophical views, Polevoi was a follower of Schelling. Apparently the religio-mystical ideas of Herder also influenced him.

"Life is nothing other than the struggle of two principles: revival and destruction, light and darkness, the striving of parts toward distinctiveness and the striving of the whole to accommodate the originality of the parts. The end of one struggle is the beginning of another, the grave of the past existence the cradle of the new."

In contrast to Karamzin who saw the evil force of Russian history in the Asian peoples, Polevoi expressed a new view — the special place of Russia in combining and reconciling western and eastern principles. Polevoi considered Karamzin's fundamental error to be in his very approach to his task — the writing of a *History of the Russian State*. Polevoi thought that it was time to write a history of the Russian people. This he commenced to do. His chief work in history is titled precisely that way (six volumes, 1829-1833).

Polevoi proposed to take the narrative up to Peter the Great but was only able to bring it to Boris Godunov's accession to the throne (1598). In his account, Polevoi drew a parallel between historical phenomena and the social forms of Russian and European history. In studying Europe, Polevoi used the works of Michelet, Guizot and Thierry. But his main authority, like Kachenovskii's, was Niebuhr. Polevoi dedicated his work to him.

The appearance of the *History of the Russian People [Istoriia Russkogo Naroda]* was met with extreme hostility by the majority of the public. Karamzin's admirers and writers of the government camp united in this. They were joined by many journalists who were offended by Polevoi's polemical devices. They were particularly indignant at Polevoi for dedicating the work to Niebuhr.

Pushkin began his comments with an analysis of this dedication. He could not forgive Polevoi for his critical attitude toward Karamzin. As soon as the first volume of the *History of the Russian People* appeared, Pushkin decided to write a review and began to outline it. "Against one's will, we must pause at the first line of the dedication: 'To Mr. Niebuhr, the leading historian of our age'. It may be asked: how and in what way has Mr. Polevoi been authorized to determine the place of writers who have attained world wide renown?. . . 'Let my offering indicate to you that there are as many people in Russia who are able to esteem you as there are in other enlightened countries of the world'. Again! How can one pass himself off as the representative of all Russia?"

Pushkin criticized the first volume of Polevoi's *History* completely. However, he was more merciful to volume two and found certain virtues in it.

After Polevoi's death it initially seemed that his name was being boycotted and that he was forgotten. But this was only appearance. As Miliukov said, "the *History of the Russian People* was read much more than it was cited" — because it was considered improper to mention it. In reality, many of Polevoi's dictums influenced the subsequent development of Russian historical thought. Polevoi is the direct precursor of the organic view of Kavelin and Solov'ev.

Nikolai Ivanovich Nadezhdin was also a talented journalist. Nadezhdin was the son of a priest from Riazan. He studied in the Theological Seminary of Riazan, then in the Theological Academy where his main instructor was Professor Fedor Aleksandrovich Golubinskii (1797-1854), one of Russia's outstanding thinkers of the XIX century. Golubinskii studied Hegel and Schelling attentively but constructed his own religious system. Its central idea — and Golubinskii's basic intuition — was the idea of Infinite Existence. Nadezhdin became a follower of Schelling. Upon graduating from the Theological Academy, Nadezhdin took up journalism and founded a periodical, *The Telescope* [*Teleskop*], in 1831. At the same time he submitted his dissertation on romantic poetry to Moscow University and was appointed professor. He lectured on the fine arts, archeology and logic. Nadezhdin was a brilliant lecturer and his lectures made a great impression on students.

In his lectures and his disserations, Nadezhdin acquainted his audience with Schelling's ideas. Among the theses of his dissertation, Nadezhdin advanced the proposition that "where there is life, there is poetry." He asserted that creative force is nothing other than "life repeating itself."

I deem it necessary to stress (as it is frequently forgotten) that Nadezhdin was not self-taught as were Kachenovskii and Polevoi. At the Moscow Theological Academy he was trained in a fashion much more serious than that which was then provided at Moscow University.

In 1836 Nadezhdin published Chaadaev's *Philosophical Letter* [*Filosoficheskoe pis'mo*] (the first in a series of such letters) in *The Telescope*. In it the latter presented the past and present of the Russian people in gloomy tones. By order of the government, *The Telescope* was closed. Nadezhdin was exiled to Ust-Sysol'sk for a year.

Nadezhdin's spirit did not fail. While in exile, he wrote several articles for "The Reading Library" (among them, "On Historical Works in Russia' ["Ob istoricheskikh trudakh v Rossii"] ). In 1843, Nadezhdin was appointed editor of the *Journal of the Ministry of Internal Affairs* [*Zhurnal Ministerstva Vnutrennikh Del*]. He published several valuable articles therein.

Nadezhdin's remarkable article, "On the Ethnographic Study of the Russian People" ["Ob etnograficheskom izuchenii Russkogo naroda"] appeared in the *Transactions of the Russian Geographical Society* [*Zapiski Russkogo Geografichevskogo Obshchestva*] in 1847. In it Nadezhdin summarized his ethnographic research and outlined the scope and problems of ethnographic science.

In his *History of Russian Ethnography* [*Istoriia Russkoi ethnografii*], academician A. N. Pypin characterizes Nadezhdin's method as ethnographic pragmatism deriving from direct, precise facts. Pypin feels that in this Nadezhdin rendered considerable influence on the subsequent development of Russian ethnographic scholarship.

Karamzin's youngest successor, Nikolai Gerasimovich Ustrialov, a professor at the University of Petersburg, stood apart. He studied at the gymnasium in Orlov, graduated, and then entered the civil service. In 1829 he was invited to be instructor of Russian language at the University of Petersburg, but chiefly he devoted himself to Russian history.

He commenced his scholarly activity with the publication of certain important sources of Russian history of the XVI-XVII centuries — *The Epistles of Prince Kurbskii* [*Skazaniia kniazia Kurbskogo*], and *The Accounts of Contemporaries Regarding the False Dimitrii* [*Skazaniia sovremennikov o Dmitrie Samozvantse*].

Beginning in 1834 he began to lecture on Russian history. He received his doctorate for his discourse on the pragmatic system in Russian history and was then elected member of the Academy of Sciences. As a textbook for his courses, Ustrialov published his *History of Russia* [*Russkaia Istoriia*] (in five volumes). In 1842 Ustrialov was granted access to the State archives and engaged in writing the *History of the Reign of Peter the Great* [*Istoriia Tsarstvovanii Petra Velikogo*]. Five volumes (of the six planned) were issued between 1858-1864.

Ustrialov greatly benefited the growth of Russian historical scholarship by publishing a series of important sources of Russian history and also because prior to Solov'ev he provided the first systematic account of Russian history.

Konstantin Alekseevich Nevolin was a priest's son. He was educated at the Viatka Theological Seminary, then entered the Moscow Theological Academy. While not yet graduated, he — among twenty university and theological academy students — was summoned to Petersburg to prepare for the chair of jurisprudence. Beginning in the spring of

1828 all of these students commenced their studies at the Second Section of His Imperial Majesty's Private Chancellery. They were directed by Balugianskii according to a plan worked out by Speranskii.

They were examined one year later. Upon passing the test, they were sent to the University of Berlin where they studied jurisprudence under the directorship of Savigny. In addition, Nevolin attended Hegel's lectures (the last semesters of his teaching — Hegel died on November 14, 1831).

On returning from Germany, Nevolin defended his doctoral dissertation and was appointed professor at the University of Kiev. He took the chair of law and institutions of the Russian Empire. He transferred to the University of Petersburg in 1843 to take the chair of Russian civil law.

Nevolin's first work, which created his scholarly reputation, was the *Encyclopedia of Jurisprudence* [*Entsiklopediia Zakonovedeniia*] (1839-1840), the first juridical system in Russia. It provides a clear and accurate account of Hegel's philosophy of law.

Nevolin's historical works, especially his important *History of Russian Civil Law* [*Istoriia Rossiiskikh grazhdanskikh zakonov*] (1851), also are very important in scholarly terms. In the completeness and richness of material, in the care exercised in choosing facts, in the caution of his conclusion, Nevolin's work can be considered a classic.

## VI

### SCHELLINGISM. "THE LOVERS OF WISDOM." CHAADAEV.

The 1830's and 1840's were a period when Schellingism and Hegelianism flowered among the Russian intelligentsia. Schellingism had already begun to spread in Russia in the 1820's. The Slavophile, I. V. Kireevskii, recalls it as follows: "Rumors of German wisdom which spread the news of some newly discovered America everywhere and of the depth of human reason stimulated general curiosity, if not broad sympathy. The younger generation in particular avidly sought every opportunity to penetrate that mysterious world."

Schelling's (1775-1854) *Weltanschauung* might be labeled philosophical romanticism. Schelling understood the world as the product of God's artistic creativity. Any artistic work is a type of microcosm. The basic principle of Schelling's *Naturphilosophie* is unity. For man is nature's loftiest goal. The purport of the historical process is the attainment of freedom. Necessity is inherent in the unconscious aspects of the historical process, freedom in the conscious. Both paths lead toward the same goal.

The other German philosopher who put his stamp on Russian historical thought was Hegel.

"Hegel may be called a philosopher by preference, for of all the philosophers only for him was philosophy everything. In other thinkers, it is a striving to perceive the truth; in Hegel, on the contrary, truth itself attempts to become philosophy, to transform into pure thought." (Vladimir Solov'ev).

According to Hegel, the substance of knowledge, in the form of logical ideas, develops dialectically into a complete system, internally linked. Science is reason's self-creativity. The State is the highest expression of the objective spirit, the embodiment of reason in the life of mankind. The idea of history is progress in the consciousness of freedom. Only in the State is the freedom of the individual within the unity of all realizable.

"We must recognize the great merit of Hegel," says Vladimir Solov'ev, "in establishing positively in scholarship and in the general consciousness, the veritable and fruitful ideas of *process*, *development* and *history* or the sequential realization of ideal substance."

Hegel provided a "reflective analysis of the historical process" in his *Philosophy of History*. "Universal history," he states, "is the expression of the Divine and absolute process of the spirit. . . thanks to which it attains its truth. . . [and] reaches [a state of] self-consciousness."

Hegel's philosophy is dynamic and permeated with the spirit of history. He referred to the State as an organism, the builder of which was history. In Hegel's opinion, an abstract constitution could not be imposed on a nation. "Each nation has the constitution it deserves." Nevertheless, Hegel formulated the general idea of a constitutional government as a political model.

"The true State, like any expression of an absolute idea, must contain three moments within itself: 1) the moment of community which is expressed in legislative power; 2) the moment of subjecting the concrete to the general — government rule; and 3) the moment of the integral personality — kingly rule" (N. N. Alekseev).

In practice, Hegel thought the Prussian Constitution of his time to be the best expression of these principles. But he allowed the possibility that, with the passage of time, other nations could move to the forefront — in particular, the Slavs. In the *Philosophy of History*, he says: "Moreover, in eastern Europe we find the great Slavic nation whose habitat stretches from the Elbe to the Danube. . . Still, this whole mass has been excluded from our consideration because up to now it has not appeared as an independent moment in the series of shapings of reason in the world. Whether this will occur in the future is not our concern, for in history we must study of the past."

The formation of a whole series of philosophical circles for the study of Schelling and Hegel was characteristic of the 1820's, 1830's, and the 1840's. The first such circle in Russia was the "learned discussions" of the students of the Moscow Theological Academy. F. A. Golubinskii was its secretary. Evidently, he was the initiator of this circle (he entered the Moscow Theological Seminary in 1814 at the age of seventeen).

The next such circle was "The Lovers of Wisdom" ["Obshchestvo liubomudrov"], formed in Moscow in 1823. Vladimir Fedorovich Odoevskii (1803-1869) was its chairman; Dmitrii Vladimirovich Venevitinov (1805-1827) its secretary. Among its members were I. V. Kireevskii, and A. I.

Koshelev (future Slavophiles), S. P. Shevyrev and M. P. Pogodin (later professors at Moscow University), and several other people. In 1824 the society published *Mnemosyne*, an almanac and the first philosophical journal in Russia. Its editors were Odoevskii and V. K. Küchelbecker, a member of secret political groups.

Odoevskii was a man of many talents and interests — a writer, musician and musicologist, philosopher — who believed in the messianic mission of the Russian people. His main gift was musical. Inwardly music was closest and most necessary to him.

In the area of philosophy, Odoevskii, proceeding from Schelling's idea of the absolute, aspired toward a new aesthetical formulation. Odoevskii allocated the supreme position in his aesthetics to music.

Odoevskii moved away from Schellingism in the early 1830's and became absorbed in studying the mystical literature of Arndt, Eckhartshausen, San Marten, Pordedge, Baader.

In his historiosophy Odoevskii becomes disenchanted with western culture and subjects it to sharp criticism. The salvation of Europe, in his opinion, is possible only should a new nation with fresh forces come upon the historical stage. Odoevskii's conviction was that Russia was that nation. "We must save Europe's soul . . . The nineteenth century belongs to Russia."

The heart of "The Lovers of Wisdom" was D. V. Venevitinov. He was passionately carried away by philosophy and poetry and infected others with his inspiration. He undoubtedly had a great gift for philosophy and a poetic talent. In his own words, "philosophy is true poetry. . . True poets have always been profound thinkers; [they were] philosophers." In his view, philosophy's task was "epistemological." In aesthetics, Venevitinov saw a connecting link between art and philosophy. Intuition was the source of ideas ("feeling begets thought"). He died at the age of 22.

"The Lovers of Wisdom" ended its existence after the unsuccessful Decembrist Rebellion in the Senate square

(December 14, 1825). Küchelbecker, the co-editor of *Mnemosyne*, was arrested and acknowledged to be one of the major culprits of the rebellion. Odoevskii's cousin Aleksandr, was also one of the leading Decembrists. Ryleev was one of Odoevskii's friends.

Understandably "The Lovers of Wisdom" feared repression and decided to shut down the society. Odoevskii convened all the members and burned the society's charter and protocols in their presence in the fireplace.

They maintained their personal friendships and exchanged opinions for the rest of their lives. Chaadaev was friends with some of them. A particularly intimate friendship linked him to Pushkin. In essence, Petr Iakovlevich Chaadaev (1794-1856), the author of *Philosophical Letters* and the enunciator of a sceptical view of Russian culture, was a solitary thinker. He lost his parents at an early age and became the ward of his aunt, Princess A. I. Shcherbatov, who gave him a superb education. He entered Moscow University in 1809 and the military service in 1812. As an officer of the hussars, he participated in the war against Napoleon. He retired in 1821 and went abroad for six years. In 1825 Chaadaev made Schelling's acquaintance and became interested in his philosophy. In 1832 (from Russia) he wrote to Schelling (in French): "The study of your works has uncovered a whole world for me. . . It has been the source of fruitful and enchanting thoughts for me. Allow me to say, however, that though following you along your lofty paths, I have had frequent occasion to arrive at places other than yours."

Three years before, Chaadaev had written (in French) his *Philosophical Letters* but they were not yet published.

As we have stated previously, N. I. Nadezhdin published the first of these letters in *The Telescope* in 1836 (in Ketcher's clumsy Russian translation). The letter caused a furor. *The Telescope* was shut down. Nadezhdin paid with a short term exile. The whole weight of the blow fell upon Chaadaev.

He was officially declared insane. He was not committed to a hospital but continued to live in his home under house arrest (once a day, he was permitted to take a walk). A doctor and a police official visited him daily and received their recompense. The restrictions were removed after a year and a half.

Several points in Chaadaev's letter aroused indignation not only in government spheres but in fairly broad circles of Russian society as well.

Chaadaev wrote: "We never proceeded together with other nations. We never belonged to any of humanity's great families, neither to the West nor to the East. We do not possess the traditions of one or the other."

"We seem to exist outside of time and the universal education of mankind has not touched us."

"In the very beginning we had savage barbarism, then crude superstition. This was followed by a cruel degrading rule, the forces of which have not disappeared to this day. Such is the pitiful history of our early years."

"We came into the world like illegitimate children with no heritage and without ties to the people who preceded us. We did not assimilate a single instructive lesson from the past."

According to the reminiscences of contemporaries, for a month in Moscow there was hardly a house in which Chaadaev's letter was not discussed. This was a sort of accursed cry and disdain for a person who, in their opinion, dared to insult Russia. Later, everything quieted down and Chaadaev was left alone. People moved to the next sensations.

The sceptical evaluation of Russia's past expressed sharply by Chaadaev drew the principal attention of his initial readers and of subsequent generations of the Russian intelligentsia. Meanwhile, his view of Russia is not at all at the center of his historiography.

"I love my country in my own way," wrote Chaadaev in 1846. "To be one who is reputed to abhor Russia is more difficult for me than I can say." But, as "beautiful as is love for one's native land, there is one thing more beautiful still — love of truth. The road to heaven is through truth, not through one's country."

Chaadaev called himself a Christian philosopher. He does not have a theological system. But he attempts to construct a theology of culture. Chaadaev's fundamental idea is that the Kingdom of God is incarnate historically in the Church. Christianity is not only a moral system but an eternal divine power which functions in the spiritual world. He believes in the mysterious power of Providence. At the same time, however, he recognizes man's freedom as well. Hence, he also recognizes a measure of responsibility for his history.

Of the historical Christian churches, Chaadaev was negative toward Protestantism but valued Catholicism highly. Nevertheless, he remained Orthodox and did not convert to Catholicism.

## VII

### RUSSIAN HEGELIANISM OF THE 1820'S

The society of "The Lovers of Wisdom" was permeated with spiritual and philosophic idealism, but it did not have such broad social significance as did the Hegelian circles of the 1830's and 1840's, the principal one of which originated in Moscow. Many members of these groups had initially displayed interest in Schelling. Later, they fell under Hegel's influence.

The original cell of Moscow's Hegelian circles was formed in 1831. It was made up of students of Moscow University around the remarkable personality of Nikolai Vladimirovich Stankevich (1813-1840).

Stankevich was born to a rich merchant family in the Ostrogozhsk district of Voronezh province.

Among those who joined Stankevich's circle were Konstantin Aksakov and Belinskii. Mikhail Bakunin joined the group in 1834; Granovskii two years later. The circle began with reading and discussing Schelling's philosophy, then became absorbed in the study of Hegel.

Stankevich awakened the best elements of mind and feeling in his comrades. He was able to impart a lofty direction to any argument. The unworthy and petty seemed to fall away by themselves in his presence.

A significant number of students from Russia were in Berlin at the end of the 1820's to study at the University of Berlin. The majority of them were scholarship holders preparing for professorships. Many of them, including the jurists P. G. Redkin and K. A. Nevolin took Hegel's courses. I. V. Kireevskii took Hegel's courses and became personally acquainted with him.

Hegel's first student from Russia was the Estlandian [Estonian] baron, Boris Von Ikskiul'. Hegel regarded him with favor and a correspondence started between them. Ikskiul's letters have not been found to this day. Hegel's letters burned on Ikskiul's estate during the agrarian disorders, but one of them was published in 1843 (before the fire). In this letter Hegel allows for the possibility of Russia's great future more definitely than he does in the *Philosophy of History*.

Hegel writes: "You are fortunate that you have a fatherland that occupies such sizeable space in the sphere of universal history and which, undoubtedly, has even greater significance in the future. It seems that other contemporary States have, more or less, already achieved the goals of their development. It is possible that the culminating point of their development has been left behind and that their condition has become stationary. Russia, already the most powerful State among them, possibly carries within its depths great potentialities for the development of its intensive nature" (D. I. Chizhevskii's translation).

Stankevich was the creator and the soul of Moscow's first Hegelian circle. The situation changed when Mikhail Bakunin joined the group. Bakunin occupied the central spot among Russian Hegelians. In Chizhevskii's apt expression, Bakunin "was not in love with ideas as was Stankevich, but was possessed by them." Bakunin was a dictator by nature. He demanded total obedience from people. Granovskii said that there were no subjects for Bakunin, just objects.

Hegel's thoughts and utterances were debated with passion at the society's meetings.

Hegel is a difficult writer and his style is often obscure. Some of Hegel's thoughts were discussed for hours. One of the stumbling blocks was Hegel's rather famous phrase in his introduction to the *Philosophy of History*: — "All that is real is reasonable; all that is reasonable is real." This was taken to mean the justification of any governmental regime as a call to the apolitical.

Hegel himself attributed a totally different meaning to this phrase. "He viewed as 'real' all that had effect and could influence. The 'reasonable' was the basis of all things. The eternal idea of the State is reflected in each State. In this sense, it is reasonable'." (commentary by N. N. Alekseev).

Hegel felt that an idea must reach its total exposure, attain the apex of its development and then cease movement. In the religious sphere, the upper limit of the idea's development is God. In the political sphere — the perfect State.

Initially, without fully comprehending the meaning of the formula "all that is real is reasonable," Bakunin understood it to be a call to the apolitical (later he changed his explanation). Belinskii, who knew no German, followed after him.

As a man inclined toward extremes, Belinskii came forth with an *apologia* of the existing Russian social and political order. This was taken to mean that he accepted the theory of "official nationality." Very soon he saw that he had reached a dead end and turned back abruptly.

## VIII

## FOURIERISM

Many Russian Hegelians, having become professors in Russian universities, did not become "leftists" or "rightists" but remained followers of Hegel's philosophy of history in

its basics. The most famous of them were T. N. Granovskii
(1813-1857) and B. N. Chicherin (1828-1903).

Before speaking of them, I think it necessary to mention
those members of the Russian intelligentsia of the 1840's
who were carried away not so much by philosophy as by
politics. But, in contrast to Bakunin, they were enticed not
by left-Hegelian revolutionary socialism and anarchism but
by one of the forms of so-called "utopian socialism" –
Fourierism. The founder of this movement was the Frenchman, Charles Fourier (1772-1837). He was preoccupied by
his plans of transforming humanity by peaceful, not revolutionary, means. He was a man of undisciplined mind and
unbridled fantasy.

Fourier's  basic idea was the conviction that the State,
with all its instruments of coercion, was evil and that it must
be replaced by a free union of social organizations. Fourier
called such organizations, or cells, phalanges. Each cell had to
have 1,600 to 1,800 people. This way, excluding children and
the aged, each phalange would have some 810 able bodied
men and women. Each phalange would settle on its own
plot of land, approximately one square mile in size.

In relationship to each other, the phalanges are in a
state of mutual attraction – similar to the planetary system
moving according to Newton's laws.

Gradually, Fourier was able to organize a group of
followers, obtain a small sum of money, and buy a small
piece of land. Victor Considerant (1805-1893), a former
military engineer, a person of strong will and wholly devoted
to the idea of world communism, saved the situation. He became the leader of Fourierism.

According to Considerant's plan, a central world government was to be organized. It would be directed by countless
armies of industrial laborers. Great ventures would be undertaken to settle mountain ranges, transform deserts into
agricultural plantations, and build ways of communication.
A series of local administrations were to  be established
around this government. They would govern the various
parts and areas of the earth. Councils of experienced people

would meet for purposes of consultation on future plans and discussion of current affairs. There would be no more wars or dissension under such an arrangement.

Considerant dreamed that a universal social organization of this type could be introduced by peaceful means with the agreement of existing national governments because the Fourierists did not demand the forcible destruction of existing States. Hence, he .welcomed the Revolution of 1848 in France, was chosen a deputy to the National Assembly and submitted for its perusal his plan for a new social order. The plan was rejected. On December 2, 1852 Louis Napoleon was declared Emperor of France under the name of Napoleon III. After this event, Considerant lost all hope for the realization of his plan and emigrated to England. (He returned to France only after the Franco-Prussian War of 1870 and the fall of Napoleon III).

Several Fourierist groups were organized in Petersburg around 1845. At the head of the principal group was Mikhail Vasil'evich Butashevich-Petrashevskii (1819-1867). For this reason, the members of this movement were called the *Petrashevtsy*. The *Petrashevtsy* were not a strictly organized association. Weekly meetings at Petrashevskii's home were their primary manifestation of activity. Fourier's and Considerant's ideas, as well as their plans for a new order for mankind, were discussed at these meetings. Emancipation of serfs, freedom of the press, and judicial reform were also considered. Among those attending these meetings were the novelist and critic, N. D. Akhsharumov; F. M. Dostoevskii (already a famous writer); N. Ia. Danilevskii; I. I. Vedenskii (instructor of Russian literature, a talented writer, and an unsurpassed translator of Dickens' novels into Russian); the poet, Apollon Maikov; the writer M.˙ E. Saltykov-Shchedrin; and N. G. Chernyshevskii.

After a time, the Fourierist circles became known to the government. The Minister of the Interior, L. A. Perovskii, commissioned Ivan Petrovich Liprandi, an official in his department (and later to be a famous general and military writer), to "observe" these groups. On April 20, 1849

Liprandi presented the director of His Majesty's Private
Chancellery's Third Section with four lists of those involved
in the "secret society."

More than a hundred persons were interrogated. Of
them, more than fifty were arrested, but the majority were
released. Twenty-three persons were tried and twenty-one
(among them Petrashevskii and Dostoevskii) were sentenced
to death. At the last minute, when they were already on the
scaffold, the sentence was commuted to various forms of
strict punishment. Furthermore, more than 200 persons
were suspected and placed under observation.

A quarter century later, in his *Writer's Notebook*
[*Dnevnik pisatelia*] for 1873, Dostoevskii recalled the
*Petrashevtsy* affair as follows:

"We were infected by the ideas of the theoretical
socialism of the time. . . But we understood the matter in
the rosiest and moral Eden-like sense. Yes, it is true that the
embryonic socialism was compared, even by some of the ring-
leaders, to Christianity and was understood only as a correction and improvement on the past, something which con-
formed to the age and to civilization. All of us in Petersburg
loved those ideas terribly. They seemed to be saintly and
moral to the highest degree. And, above all, they seemed to
be universal, the future law of all mankind without exception."

## IX

### SLAVOPHILES AND WESTERNIZERS

Two trends of Russian social thought — Slavophile and
Westernizing — pass through the whole first half of the XIX
century, in turn approaching and spurning each other.

At their bases was a different attitude of the intellectual
circles to Russia and to Europe — a striving toward distinctiveness for some, a craving for Western culture in others.

Aleksandr Ivanovich Herzen returned to Moscow from
exile in 1840 and joined the group organized by Stankevich

(Stankevich had died prior to this in Italy from consumption). Herzen began to read Hegel and came to a conclusion completely opposite from Belinskii's. Animated debates commenced and a split occurred between the Westernizers (Herzen and Ogarev) and the Slavophiles.

They separated "with tears in their eyes." The disputants had a mutual "feeling of unlimited, all encompassing love for the Russian people, for the Russian turn of mind. The opponents, like a two-faced Janus, looked in two different directions, while their hearts beat as one" (Herzen).

Herzen, Ogarev and Bakunin moved over to the camp of the "left Hegelians" to which Karl Marx also belonged. Bakunin became the advocate of revolutionary anarchism.

The leaders of the Slavophiles belonged to a circle of rich Russian families of high lineage which preserved the basis of ancient Russian culture — Orthodoxy. Preeminent among them was their eldest, Aleksei Stepanovich Khomiakov (1804-1860), a man of brilliant talent, seething energy, and varied interests.

His father (who died in 1836) was a weak willed man, a member of the English club, and a gambler. He lost more than a million rubles and placed his fortune in a precarious state. Khomiakov's mother then barred her husband from management of their property and gradually restored, even increased, the family's wealth. They had three children — the eldest son Fedor (who died in 1828), Aleksei, and a daughter Anna.

His mother, Mariia Alekseevna, born Kireevskaiia, brought up her children in staunch devotion to the principles of the Orthodox Church and to the national foundations of life. She gave her children a fairly good, though not a systematic education. In 1812, during the Napoleonic invasion of Russia, the Khomiakov family moved to its Riazan estate. Their Moscow home was burned down. Like the majority of Russian people, the Khomiakovs felt the French invasion strongly, but then rejoiced at their expulsion. The boys, Fedor and Aleksei, dreamed of the time when they would grow up and be able to do battle.

In 1820, having completed his home study, Khomiakov passed the entrance exam for the department of mathematics at Moscow University.

In 1822 Khomiakov joined the cuirassiers' regiment, then stationed in the province of Kherson. He transferred to the cavalry regiment in Petersburg one year later. He retired in 1825 and went to Europe for a year and a half.

In 1827 a new crisis occurred in the Middle East in connection with the Greek revolt against Turkish rule. Great Britain, Russia, and France gave the sultan an ultimatum demanding recognition of Greece's independence. The sultan refused. War commenced. Khomiakov entered the service, joining the hussars' regiment. He participated in several battles and received the Order of St. Anne for bravery.

His subsequent life was not rich externally. He engaged successfully in agriculture. He spent the summer months on his estates in the Riazan and Tula provinces and usually spent winters in Moscow. He married Ekaterina Mikhailovna Iazykov, the poet's sister, in 1836. The marriage was a happy one. In 1847 Khomiakov went to Europe, visiting Germany, England, and Prague. He died from cholera in 1860.

Khomiakov spent all of these years in strenuous mental and literary activity. He wrote on the most varied themes. His fundamental goal was the elaboration of religious philosophy — teachings on the Church (Khomiakov referred only to the Orthodox Church as the Church). His historiosophic reflections are also noteworthy. The main sources of Khomiakov's theology were the works of the Holy Fathers which he read carefully and with the spirit of which he was imbued. He studied the history of the Church attentively. In all fairness, Khomiakov can be called a Christian philosopher. For all that, in his own faith, enlightened by reason, Khomiakov was exceptionally free.

In his opinion, the personality, in order to fully reveal itself, must be linked to the Church. General harmony with the Church was called *"Sobornost' "* by Khomiakov.

Khomiakov felt that because of the rationalism of

Western culture, Latinism (as he called Catholicism) and Protestantism had alienated themselves from mutual Church harmony. But he believed that the West could still return to Orthodoxy. When, in the 1840's the Anglican theologian William Palmer expressed his interest in Orthodoxy and willingness to convert to it, Khomiakov entered into correspondence with him. Nothing came of Palmer's plans and he converted to Catholicism in 1855. In his historiosophy, Khomiakov accepts the natural law of the historical process. The "matter and fate of all mankind," not of separate nations, occurs in history, though each nation "represents the same feature as does each person." Khomiakov distinguishes between two types of historical development. One represents the origin of necessity, the other — the origin of freedom. Khomiakov calls the first "Kushitic." (Kush is the ancient name for the countries south of Egypt). The other, a beneficial type, is "Iranian," as Khomiakov defines it. Despite all his passion in debates and polemics, Khomiakov respected differing opinions and was tolerant of them.

In terms of philosophy, the most gifted of the Slavophiles was Ivan Vasil'evich Kireevskii (1806-1856). Kireevskii was in constant touch with Khomiakov and it is sometimes difficult to decide who was the first to express certain views.

Kireevskii was born in a highly cultured family. His father died while Ivan was still a boy. Ivan also had a younger brother, Peter, and a sister, Anna. The children were educated by their mother, Avdot'ia Petrovna, natural cousin to Zhukovskii. She was a woman remarkable in her religiosity and strength of character. Having become a widow, she married a second time — wedding A. A. Elagin. He was a follower of Kant and Schelling and even translated Schelling into Russian. It was in such an environment, replete with intellectual and spiritual interests, that young Kireevskii grew.

In his youth Kireevskii was captivated by Schelling's philosophy. He was, in general, drawn to Western culture from which he expected a beneficial influence on Russia.

In 1832 Kireevskii commenced publication of a journal

with the characteristic title of the *European* [*Evropeets*].
Kireevskii placed his article, "The Nineteenth Century,"
which caused a sensation, in the journal. He states his ideas
on the necessity of rapprochement between and the re-
ciprocity of Russian and Western cultures in this specific
article.

This article served as cause to shut down the journal.
The government's resolution regarding this stated: "though
the author of the work declares that he speaks of literature,
not politics, he means something totally different: by the
word enlightenment he understands freedom, reason signifies
revolution, and the masterfully arrived at mean is nothing
other than a constitution."

The censor who passed this article, S. T. Aksakov
(father of Konstantin and Ivan Aksakov), was subjected to
punishment and was soon fired from his job. Kireevskii
himself avoided penalty thanks only to the intercessions of
Zhukovskii, who was at that time tutor to the heir (the
future Alexander II).

For Kireevskii, however, the closing of the journal was
a frightful blow. After this, he maintained silence for twelve
years.

During these twelve years, Kireevskii underwent a
spiritual transformation. He fell back from the Westernizers
and sided with Slavophilism. It should be noted that, in
truth, the "Slavophile" aspect did not interest him at all.
He perceived, though not immediately, the main root of the
movement to be Orthodoxy. In a letter to Khomiakov in
1844, Kireevskii states his direction as being "Orthodox-
Russian." This transformation did not occur at once but was
long and rather painful.

Kireevskii married Nataliia Petrovna Arbeneva in 1834.
She was the spiritual daughter of Saint Serafim of Sarovsk
(who died in 1833). She was deeply religious and very well
read in spiritual literature. At this time Kireevskii was still a
Schellingian and did not consider himself to be an active
member of the Orthodox Church.

In the early stage of his marriage Kireevskii and his wife

had constant arguments on religious questions. Gradually, however, his wife's fervent and concentrated faith began to win over.

Among Kireevskii's papers, an interesting note has been preserved. It is "The Story of I. V. Kireevskii's Conversion" ["Istoriia obrashcheniia I. V. Kireevskogo"] and was written by his friend, A. I. Koshelev. Evidently, it was based on information provided by Kireevskii's wife.

The note states that in the first period of clashes between Kireevskii and his wife, he promised that at least he would not blaspheme in her presence. Later they began to read Schelling together. At this point his wife surprised him by indicating that Schelling's ideas "had been known to her for a long time from patristic literature." Kireevskii began to read these works himself. He then came to have close contact with religious persons. His estate was only seven versts [verst=2/3 mile] from the Optin hermitage where the institution of the "elders" was flowering at the time. Kireevskii began to go there.

Kireevskii's conversion was total. He became completely imbued with faith and studied patristic literature thoroughly.

Kireevskii's central idea was the totality of spiritual life. The path to this consisted of inner concentration — the "gathering" of one's soul.

As to Kireevskii's historiosophy, at its foundation is the idea of a succession in historical development: in its time, each nation comes to the forefront.

## PETR VASIL'EVICH KIREEVSKII

P. V. Kireevskii (1808-1856) occupies a special place among the Slavophiles. Like his brother Ivan, he displayed ardor for only one aspect of Slavophilism. It was not so much religion as folk literature.

In terms of education and turn of mind, Petr was similar to his brother. But in character he was less sociable and more withdrawn. He remained in the background of his brilliant brother. Schelling, who knew both brothers, felt that Petr was the more intelligent of the two. Petr Vasil'evich came to the fore as a collector of folk songs.

From the end of the 1820's Petr Kireevskii became the center to which all materials collected by the members of the Moscow circle of lovers of folklore and antiquity flowed. Among the numbers of this circle were professors Pogodin, Shevyrev, Maksimovich, S. I. Aksakov and his sons, Konstantin and Ivan.

The publication of the collected materials was held up because of censorial hindrances. Uvarov's formula, "Orthodoxy, Autocracy, and Nationality" would have seemed to encourage the publication of folk literary monuments. But dignitaries and bureaucrats became worried. They perceived superstition and distortion of Orthodoxy in the spiritual poems. Religious censorship butted in as well.

For ten years, Kireevskii had to plead and appeal to patronage before he was able to obtain permission to publish an insignificant number of poems. He had to choose, strictly, that which did not arouse the suspicions of the censorship. The Society of Lovers of Russian Literature published the great numbers of *byliny* [epics] and other folkloristic works collected by P. V. Kireevskii in ten volumes in the 1860's. The work was entitled *Songs Collected by P.V. Kireevskii*. It was re-issued in the 1870's (under P. A. Bessonov's editorship).

## KONSTANTIN AKSAKOV AND IURII SAMARIN

Two younger Slavophiles, K. Aksakov and Iu. Samarin, were followers of Hegel. Hegel's influence on Aksakov was effaced fairly rapidly. Samarin retained it to the end of his life.

As Konstantin's younger brother Ivan wrote: "Hegel served them as a means to explain and sanction a newly found truth, to prove its universal historical significance. Using Hegel's principles, they made an attempt to construct a whole ideology, a whole system of a type of phenomenology of the Russian national spirit."

Konstantin Sergeevich Aksakov (1817-1860), "a pure and lofty soul" as Chicherin said of him, was a historian and philologist.

At the basis of Konstantin Aksakov's views on the essence of Russia's historical development lay the contrast of two principals — Land and State. "The power of opinion belongs to the people (the Land), the power of rule belongs to the State."

Popular life is "the path of inner (moral) truth." The substance of State activity is "organization," "order," "unlimited power — to the Tsar, complete freedom of life and spirit — to the people; freedom of action and law — to the Tsar, freedom of speech and opinion — to the people."

The cornerstone of Aksakov's social view of the world was the commune. He used this term in two meanings: the commune (capitalized) encompassing the whole Russian nation (as a counterweight to the Russian state) and the cells contained within it — local communes and village *mirs*.

Aksakov's idea was that the foundation of the Russian historical process was, in a sense, set by Providence. The duality of State and Land was expressed with particular clarity during the era of the Muscovite Tsardom (the election of Mikhail Fedorovich to the throne by the *Zemskii Sobor* [Assembly of the Land] in 1613). Subsequent events introduced change into Russian politics, but the basis was retained until the era of Peter the Great. Aksakov strove to re-establish the former equilibrium between the State and the Land.

The most illuminating historical and historico-philosophical ideas of the Slavophiles were stated in K. S. Aksakov's articles, gathered in volume one of his works (Moscow,1861). It was his conviction that "Russia is an utterly distinct country which did not at all resemble European governments and nations." Orthodoxy was the foundation of the spiritual life of the Russian people ("Holy Rus' ") whereas the West took the road of Catholicism. Western states were founded on conquest. Subsequently, their principles became those of individualism and the rule of external, formally juridical law.

The principles of Russian life were communal origins and moral truth. The Russian nation ("The Land") subjected itself voluntarily to State power (Aksakov points out the summoning of the princes and the election of the first tsar of a new dynasty by the Assembly of the Land in 1613). This authority did not interfere in the people's inner lives. In Aksakov's opinion, Peter, by his forced Westernization, violated the union of "Land" and State. He wanted to "tear Russia away from the native sources of its life and push it upon the western road, the false and dangerous road." In so doing, he provoked the split between the upper classes and the masses of the people which were loyal to age old Russian traditions.

Aksakov was guided by Hegelianism in his philological works. The most important of these is his master's thesis on Lomonosov. In it Aksakov examined the significance of Lomonosov in the history of Russian literature and on the Russian language. Aksakov equates Lomonosov's role with Peter's achievements in government reform.

Aksakov's ideas on language are most profound. For him language is a miraculous and mysterious phenomenon. Language expresses the supremacy of the spirit over all nature. Language is not only a simple instrument, not only a remedy, but a necessary concomitant to thought — in a certain sense, "the body of thought."

Iurii Fedorovich Samarin (1819-1876) was a man of different constitution than Konstantin Aksakov. S. M. Solov'ev felt that Samarin "was a remarkably smart person, but cold." According to K. D. Kavelin, Samarin had a fine mind, enormous knowledge, and great talent for writing. Furthermore, he had a character that was wholly moral and his convictions were unbending. He allowed no compromises with his conscience. At the same time, he was devoid of ambition or the craving for power and distinguished himself for his broad tolerance of other opinions.

Samarin was deeply imbued with Hegelianism. In 1842 he wrote his friend, A. N. Popov: "The task of the present day is the task of science. You know that by science I mean philosophy and that by philosophy I mean Hegel."

Samarin graduated from Moscow University and wrote his master's thesis on Feofan Prokopovich and Stefan Iavorskii — the antithesis of the Protestant and Catholic direction of Russian theological thought. In ideal Samarin contraposes Orthodoxy against both one-sided (in his opinion) Western faiths. Thus in the ideal, and in actuality, Samarin sharply criticized the synodal reform of the Russian Church introduced by Peter.

But he felt that "the Church is developing, i.e. that it constantly brings to its consciousness the eternal, unending truth which it possesses."

"The scholarly significance of Samarin's thesis is beyond all doubt. It retains its value to the present day — 95 years later. Moreover, it does so as a whole, not in some of its points as does Aksakov's work." (Chizhevskii).

Samarin's life evolved in such a way that he did not become a professional scholar. His master's thesis was his chief scholarly work. But he wrote much subsequently as well. His *Russia's Borderlands* [*Okrainy Rossii*] could not be published in Russia because of censorship (the work was published in Berlin, 1868-1876). His research on the emancipation of the serfs and on financial reforms in Prussia at the beginning of the XIX century is also valuable.

## WESTERNIZERS

The Slavophile current had a significant influence on the growth of social thought in Russia. But it was the world view of a minority. The majority of the Russian intelligentsia of the mid-XIX century was Westernizing.

This was true not only of radicals such as Herzen and Ogarev, but of moderate liberals and persons holding conservative views.

Here I deem it necessary only to mention the professors at Moscow University during the late 1830's and the 1840's, that is the very period of the origin of the Slavophile view.

The middle 1830's saw the beginning of the flowering

of Moscow University. This continued into the 1840's also. A number of talented scholars, primarily Hegelians, took chairs there. Among them were historians T. N. Granovskii, P. N. Kudriavtsev, and D. L. Kriukov, and the jurists P. G. Redkin and N. I. Krylov (the latter was not a Hegelian).

Granovskii and Kudriavtsev were professors of history in general. Kriukov taught ancient history. Russian history was taught by Pogodin until 1844; from 1845, it was taught by S. M. Solov'ev.

Like no one else, Granovskii (1813-1855) was for Russian society the symbol of scholarship, university education and humanism. He was the head of the Moscow Hegelians. But he attracted friends (who did not sympathize with Hegel's philosophy) by his personality, his sincere mildness, and the purity and honesty of his character and thought.

Granovskii learned Hegel thoroughly during his study in Berlin from 1836-1839. After this, he was appointed professor at Moscow University.

Granovskii did not become a research specialist. But he turned out to be an inspired teacher despite a quiet voice and a lisp. "This was explained by the fact that into his illuminating artistic exposition, Granovskii included those genuine and cherished convictions which fulfilled his existence. These convictions can be summarized by the proposition that the historical process consists of corrupting masses by ideas, for the masses stagnate under the weight of historical definitions from which only individuals are freed. In this way... the law of the universal historical process happens to coincide with humanity's striving toward the achievement of the loftiest moral goal. It is in this sense that Herzen said that Granovskii thought through history, felt through history, and propagandized by means of history" (Kizevetter).

Petr Nikolaevich Kudriavtsev (1816-1858), the son of a Moscow priest, was Granovskii's student, friend and successor. He studied at the Moscow Theological Seminary [Academy], then at Moscow University. In March, 1845, on Granovskii's recommendation, he was sent abroad. He studied under Schelling in Berlin and found his teachings compatible. Through Granovskii, Hegelianism had some influence on Kudriavtsev. He returned to Moscow in mid-1847 and began to lecture in the fall. Kudriavtsev is more important than his teacher as a historian.

Kudriavtsev's major work is *The Fate of Italy from the Fall of the Roman Empire to its Re-establishment by Charlemagne* [*Sud'by Italii ot padeniia zapadnoi Rimskoi imperii do vosstanovleniia ee Karlom*] (1850). In this work Kudriavtsev vividly describes the process of the conception of the Italian nationality and provides a thoughtful characterization of the Carolingian dynasty and its relations with the Papacy. Like Granovskii, Kudriavtsev was a stirring lecturer, but he was also a talented writer. His particular mastery was displayed in the subtle analysis of outstanding personalitites: "Charles V," "Catherine de Medici's Youth," and "Roman Women."

Kudriavtsev outlived Granovskii by only three years. "These two names remained inseparably linked in the memory of future generations just as they were always linked by their contemporaries" (Kizevetter).

Granovskii valued much in historical Russian culture. Kudriavtsev was a Westernizer in principle. One may say that he was in love with Italy.

The talented Stepan Vasil'evich Eshevskii (1829-1865) was a student of Granovskii, Kudriavtsev and the young S. M. Solov'ev. Eshevskii was a better historian than Granovskii or Kudriavtsev. In terms of the methodology and the utilization of sources in his works, he actually belongs to the beginning of the maturation of Russian historical scholarship. But in terms of his relationships with Granovskii and Kudriavtsev during the years of study, it is more appropriate to discuss his scholarly work in this chapter.

Eshevskii studied at the gymnasium of Kostroma, then in that of Nizhegorod. He entered Moscow University in 1846 (and graduated in 1850). In 1855 he defended his master's thesis, *Appolinaris Sidonius: An Episode from the Literary and Political Life of V Century Gaul* [*Appollinarii*

*Sidonii; epizod iz literaturnoi i politicheskoi zhizni Gallii V veka]*. In this, his first scholarly work, Eshevskii gave a brilliant picture of the condition of Gaul in that era. Eshevskii was then immediately appointed to the just vacated chair of Russian history at the University of Kazan. After Granovskii's death, Moscow University elected him to the chair of general history. But the Ministry of Public Education agreed to transfer him to Moscow only in 1858.

The first course which Eshevskii presented at Moscow University (the course was later published in his works) was *The Center of the Roman Empire and its Provinces* [*Tsentr Rimskogo mira i ego provintsii*]. Between 1859 and 1861, Eshevskii visited Germany, Italy, Switzerland and France. During this time he was readying materials for his doctoral dissertation on Brunhild, the queen of Austrasia [At that time, this was the name of eastern France (Lotharingia) including the city of Metz] at the end of the VI and the beginning of the VII centuries. She was the daughter of the Visigoth king. During the partition, Theodoric II, her youngest nephew, received Burgundy. The study of Franco-Gothic relations attracted Eshevskii to this theme.

The last complete course given by Eshevskii at Moscow University (later published) was *The Migration of Nations: The Merovingians and the Carolingians* [*Epokha pereseleniia narodov, Merovingi i Karolingi*]. Materials on Brunhild were included also. He was not able to complete his course on feudalism because of his death. All of Eshevskii's works were based on thorough study of the sources.

"As a professor and scholar, Eshevskii was distinguished by a remarkable objectivity, a liveliness of understanding and exposition. There was nothing stilted or artificial in him. He was sincere and truthful whether from the rostrum or in life." (Bestuzhev-Riumin).

## X

## S. M. SOLOV'EV (1820-1879)

Russian historical scholarship entered its mature period through the works of the generation to which S. M. Solov'ev belonged (those scholars born in the years 1817-1828). This was furthered by Solov'ev more than anyone.

Solov'ev laid the channel for the main current of Russian historical thought in the second half of the XIX century.

Sergei Mikhailovich Solov'ev was born in Moscow to an ecclesiastical family which cultivated a deep religious feeling within him. His father, archpriest Mikhail Vasil'evich, taught religion at the Moscow School of Commerce. He had a good library. While still a boy, Sergei developed a passion for reading. He was especially fascinated by historical books as well as by travel descriptions for which he maintained an interest throughout his life. He had already read Karamzin's *History* several times before he was thirteen.

Solov'ev received his primary education at the commerce school. From there, he entered grade three of Moscow's First Gymnasium. Upon graduation, he entered Moscow University.

At this time Pogodin taught Russian history at the University. Solov'ev was totally dissatisfied with his lectures. His real teacher was Granovskii. He insisted that Solov'ev learn Russian history in connection with the fate of other nations.

Solov'ev spent the first two years after graduating from the University abroad as a private tutor in Count Stroganov's family. This provided him with the opportunity of attending the lectures of German and French scholars.

In Berlin he audited the lectures of Ranke, Ritter, Raumer and Neander; in Paris — of Guizot and Michelet. Solov'ev was also in Prague where he became acquainted with the Czech scholars Haencke, Palacky, and Shafarik. This greatly increased his vision. During his trip abroad, Solov'ev thought over and prepared his master's thesis.

In 1845, after his return to Moscow and a brilliant defense of his master's thesis, Solov'ev was appointed professor of Russian history to the chair left vacant after Pogodin's departure. In the following year, he married Poliksena Sergeevna Romanova who was a descendant of a white Russian noble family. The marriage was a happy one.

From this time on, Solov'ev's life merges with his scholarly and pedagogical work — in a word, with Moscow University. Aside from his professorship, he was chosen to be dean, then rector.

His master's thesis, *Novgorod's Relations with the Grand Princes* [*Ob otnosheniiakh Novgoroda k russkim velikim kniaz'iam*] (1845) was his first scholarly work. This was followed by the *History of the Relations Between the Princes of the House of Riurik* [*Istoriia otnoshenii mezhdu kniaz'iami Riurikova doma*] (1847) — his doctoral dissertation. Both of these works definitively established him as a first class scholar.

Both dissertations were detailed investigations of historically important special problems. But as a scholar and an instructor, Solov'ev recognized the necessity of writing a learned survey of the whole panorama of Russian history. After his dissertations, Solov'ev felt himself to be sufficiently prepared for such a task and decided to execute it. He looked upon it as his social duty.

Solov'ev thought it necessary not only to set forth but also explain the past's events, to detect the law in sequential phenomenological change, to clarify the central idea, the basic origin of Russian life.

The first volume of his *History of Russia from Ancient Times* [*Istoriia Rossii s drevneishikh vremen*] appeared in 1851. From then on, punctually year after year, a volume was published. The last (the 29th) appeared posthumously in 1879. Solov'ev carried his account to 1774, but he also wrote a supplement — a survey of the diplomatic relations of the Russian Court from the Treaty [1774] of Kuchuk-Kainardzhiisk to 1780.

Solov'ev's capacity for work is truly amazing. During the years in which he was working on his monumental *History*, he also wrote a series of valuable monographs and articles, among them *The History of the Fall of Poland* [*Istoriia padeniia Pol'shii*] and *Emperor Alexander I: Politics and Diplomacy* [*Imperator Aleksandr Pervyi: Politika, Diplomatiia*]. After his death, these monographs were reprinted in his collected works (1882).

The secret of Solov'ev's capacity for work was in his feeling of responsibility to Russian historical scholarship. He set a rule for himself — never lose a minute. Every hour of his day was regulated.

The basis of Solov'ev's historiosophy was a comprehension of the course of history as an organic development. For him, the works of Gustav Evers were an affirmation of this idea (the theory of the patrimonial mode) as was Hegel's philosophy. The views of Evers aided Solov'ev in writing his doctoral dissertation (*History of the Relations Between the Princes of the House of Riurik*). Granovskii acquainted him with Hegel. Solov'ev read Hegel's *Philosophy of History* carefully. Hegel's influence was particularly apparent in Solov'ev's later article, "Observations on the Historical Lives of Nations" ["Nabliudeniia nad istoricheskoi zhizn'iu narodov"].

For Solov'ev, the historical process was not only organic but continuous as well. In the introduction to the first volume of his *History of Russia*, Solov'ev wrote: "Russian history should not be divided or split into separate parts or periods. Rather, these should be united. One should primarily look for relationships of phenomena, for the direct succession of forms. Principles should not be splintered but viewed in reciprocal terms. The attempt should be made to explain each occurrence based on intrinsic reasons before isolating it from the course of events and subjecting it to external reasons. Such is the task of the contemporary historian as the author of this work understands it."

This conception was subsequently conveyed by Solov'ev throughout all the remaining volumes. The most significant example of it is in the explanation of the Petrine reforms. According to Solov'ev, their roots must be sought in the preceding reign — that of Fedor Alekseevich (1676-1682) (*History of Russia, vol. XIII*).

His canvas is the chronological description of Russian history. Chapters on the internal state of Russian society in specific periods are placed at definite intervals. These are not mechanical insertions but elucidations of a sort of "events" from within, the real state of affairs necessary for understanding the conditions of the historical process.

The ground for the first volume was already broken by Solov'ev's two dissertations. Many of the sources necessary for the study of the Kievan period had already been published by that time. References to archival materials appear in the following three volumes. In the future, Solov'ev had to upturn new soil. Beginning with volume V, (1462-1618), archival sources constitute the foundation of his grandiose work.

Solov'ev thought the basic factors of the Russian historical process were State and people. He did not contrast them but attempted to clarify their interrelationship. He writes: "We must follow the development and growth of the State. Simultaneously, we must do the same regarding the nation — observing its development, growth, and the gradual comprehension of its consciousness of itself as a unified whole."

Solov'ev attributed considerable significance to natural conditions, the nation's ethnographic make up, and the sparseness of population. In his opinion, during the early period of its history, the Russian nation was seemingly in an unstable colonizing state, moving to the north and east away from the attacks of the steppe nomads. In this connection, Solov'ev liked to speak of the "fluid element" of Russian history.

The Moscow princes attempted to attract migrants from the south. The Mongol khans — suzerains of the Russian princes — did not impede such a policy, for their tribute corresponded to the size of the population. The Mongols en-

trusted the Moscow princes with the collection of tribute. With the end of the Mongol dominion, this tribute
now went to the exchequer of the Moscow princes.

With the growth of Muscovite autocracy, the Moscow
Grand Prince's (later Tsar's) power and guardianship over
the taxable population increased. This ended in the im-
position of serfdom.

At the universal historical level, Solov'ev deemed
Europe's centuries old struggle against Asia to be one of the
prime aspects of mankind's historical development. For him,
Russia was only a particular case of this conflict. Solov'ev
characterized the lengthy struggle of the Russian nation
against the nomadic peoples of the East who intruded into
the Russian steppes as the "conflict of the forest against the
steppe."

Solov'ev's significance in the development of Russian
historical scholarship is very great. His *History* served young
historians as a necessary introduction to their own work
while he was alive and after his death.

Despite all this, Solov'ev was of a very humble opinion
regarding the value of his work. He predicted to V. O.
Kliuchevskii, his favorite and most talented student, that his
enormous book would soon disappear from the table and be
forgotten.

In his article, "In Commemoration of Solov'ev"
["Pamiati Solov'eva"], written on the twenty-fifth anniversary of his death, Kliuchevskii refuted his teacher's ap-
prehension.

"The large compact edition of the *History* in six
weighty volumes, which was begun in 1893, soon began
to sell and when a detailed index for these books appeared
three years later, the first three volumes were already in
their second edition. The *opus* lived and continued its work
even after the author's death."

Kliuchevskii provided a penetrating characterization
of Solov'ev's personality in the same article. "This was a
scholar with a strict, well-trained mind. He did not tone
down hard truth to mollify the pathological tendencies of

the time. In opposition to the light literary tastes of the reader, he produced a lively, but serious, and sometimes stiff story in which the dry, well thought out fact was not sacrificed to the well told anecdote. This gave him the reputation of being a dry historian. His attitude toward the public for which he wrote was the same as his attitude toward the nation whose history he wrote. A Russian to the core, he never closed his eyes so as not to see the dark sides of the Russian nation's past and present. More than many patriots, he felt the great powers of his own people. He believed in their future more strongly than many others. But he did not idolize them. He was, in the highest degree, foreign to that crude disregard for the people which is frequently hidden by intemperate and unnecessary glorification of valor or a supercilious and indifferent condescension to their faults. He loved and respected Russian people too deeply to flatter them and considered them to be too mature to tell them children's tales of national knighthood under the guise of national history."

## XI

### N. I. KOSTOMAROV (1817-1885)

Kostomarov's historical conception was fundamentally opposite Solov'ev's. Solov'ev studied the fates of a united (furthermore centralized) Russian State and viewed the Russian people as a unified nation.

Kostomarov viewed the Russian State as a unification of various regions under the monarch's rule. Each of them has its own historical, cultural, and tribal peculiarities.

He considered the Malorussians (Ukrainians) to be a separate nation.

He contrasted the idea of a federation to the idea of a centralized State.

Nikolai Ivanovich Kostomarov was born in the Iurasovka settlement in the Ostrogozhsk district of the Voronezh province. His father was a noble land owner, his mother a Ukrainian peasant. She was a serf whom his father had become attached to. He sent her to a boarding school in Moscow to be educated. Later, Kostomarov's father married her but Nikolai was born prior to wedlock. His father planned to adopt him but never got around to it. He was an admirer of XVIII century French literature and was also a cruel serf owner. He was killed by his domestic serfs in 1828. They also stole all of his money.

Nikolai's mother sent him to the Voronezh boarding school but he was expelled two years later for misbehavior. He then entered the Voronezh gymnasium. Upon graduating in 1833, he entered the University of Khar'kov. The faculty of the history department was lack-lustre at that time. Kostomarov began to study classical antiquity independently. The situation changed in 1835 when the talented Mikhail Mikhailovich Lunin (1809-1844) was appointed to the chair of world history. He had graduated from the University of Derpt and received his doctorate in philosophy there. Kostomarov turned to the study of history with passion.

Kostomarov learned Ukrainian and pseudonymously wrote several collections of poetry, original and translations. Gripped by his new tendency and also influenced by Lunin's lectures, Kostomarov began to elaborate his new conception of history. The essence of his idea of the historical process consisted in juxtaposing the nation and its spiritual life with the State as an external force.

But in Khar'kov he was not only enthused over history. At this time Khar'kov was the cultural center of left-bank Malorussia. Kostomarov found himself in the romantic atmosphere of the early Slavic and Ukrainian renaissance. An almanac and literary journals were being published in Ukrainian. The popular Ukrainian poet, P. Artemovskii-Gulak, a professor at the University of Khar'kov, and the young (later famous) Slavist, Izmail Ivanovich Sreznovskii, were active participants.

During the years 1833-1838, Sreznovskii published twelve issues of ethnographic materials about the Cossacks under the title *Zaporozhskaia Starina* [*Zaporozhian An-*

*tiquity*] . These included songs and ballads.

Kostomarov passed his master's examination in 1840 and defended his master's thesis three years later. It was titled *The Historical Significance of Russian Folk Poetry* [*Ob istoricheskom znachenii russkoi narodnoi poezii*]. After this, he began to write on Bogdan Khmel'nitskii for his doctoral dissertation.

In 1846 the council of the University of Kiev chose him to be instructor of Russian history. In Kiev Kostomarov joined a circle of youth which, as he, was enthused over the ideas of nationality, folk poetry, and dreams of a Slavic federation. It was proposed that all sections of the federation have the same rights and laws, freedom of trade, and the abolition of serfdom.

Besides Kostomarov, members of this group (called the Brotherhood of Cyril and Methodius) were the writer Panteleimon Kulish; Professor N. I. Gulak; Vasilii Belozerskii, a student; Taras Shevchenko, the artist; and several other people.

The existence of the brotherhood became known to the authorities in the spring of 1847. All participants of the meetings were arrested. Kostomarov was imprisoned in the Peter-Paul fortress but released a year later and sent to Saratov. Under police surveillance, he was accepted for employment at one of the bureaus. He was forbidden to teach and to publish his works.

Kostomarov continued writing his book on Khmel'-nitskii and commenced a new work on the internal condition of the Muscovite State in the XVI and XVII centuries.

Police surveillance was removed in 1856 and the prohibition on publishing his works was lifted. Having visited abroad, Kostomarov returned to Saratov where he published his book, *The Rebellion of Stenka Razin* [*Bunt Sten'ki Razina*].

In the spring of 1859 the University of Petersburg invited Kostomarov to accept the chair of Russian history. *Bogdan Khmel'nitskii* and *Razin* were both published in 1859.

Kostomarov taught a course in ancient Russian history. Kostomarov's lectures at the university were unusually popular. They attracted a great many students and outside auditors. Kostomarov formulated his basic idea thusly: "In taking the chair, I made up my mind to present national life in its particular manifestations in the forefront of my lectures. . .The Russian State was formed out of parts which originally led an independent life and which for a long time expressed their distinctive striving in the overall system of the State. The goal of my historical studies was to find and detect these peculiarities of the national life of the various parts of the Russian State."

At this time Kostomarov was chosen to be a member of the Archeographic Commission and undertook the publication of documents on the history of Malorussia [Little or White Russia] in the XVII century. Among these, he published the nine volumes of *Documents Relating to the History of Southern and Western Russia* [*Akty otnosiashchii k istorii Iuzhnoi i Zapadnoi Rossii*].

Besides his lectures at the university, Kostomarov and several other professors organized public lectures in the municipal council's building. The contemporary press referred to these as the Free University. They were soon joined by Professor Platon Vasil'evich Pavlov (1823-1895) who had just been invited to accept the second chair of Russian history at the University of Petersburg.

At the beginning of 1862 Pavlov gave a speech at the Free University on Russia's 1,000 years (dating from Riurik). Pavlov supported the continuing development of the peasant reforms and feared the influence of the reactionary nobility on Alexander II. He finished the speech with these words: "Russia now stands at the chasm into which we will plunge if we do not turn to the last means of salvation, drawing close to the people. He who has ears to hear, hears."

The ears of the State heard. Pavlov was deprived of his position and exiled to Vetluga.

As protest against Pavlov's exile, the committee of the Free University decided to cease their lectures.

Kostomarov refused to submit to this. He felt that it was necessary, as long as it was possible, to preserve the freedom of speech and instruction. The public greeted him with hostility at his next lecture and raised such a clamor that he had to stop the lecture. Further lectures were forbidden by the administration.

On February 8, 1861, at Petersburg University's annual graduating ceremony, Kostomarov was to give a speech on Konstantin Aksakov who had died recently. But it was cancelled by order of the Ministry of Public Education.

The students, among whom revolutionary tendencies had already appeared, made a row. The University was closed indefinitely. It was decided to draw up a new university charter.

Kostomarov lost his professorship. In 1863 the University of Kiev offered him a position. In 1864 it was the University of Khar'kov, and Kiev again in 1869. But the Ministry of Public Education forbade him to accept any of these offers because his political reliability was suspect. This was mainly the result of M. N. Katkov's attacks on him in *Moskovskie Vedomosti* [*Moscow Gazette*]. A liberal in his youth, Katkov became a militant nationalist after the Polish uprising of 1863.

Kostomarov could now fully devote himself to the writing of historical books. His outstanding work, *Northern Russian Popular Rule* [*Severnorusskie narodopravstva*] (Novgorod, Pskov, Viatka) appeared in 1863. It was based on his lectures at the University of Petersburg. Another significant work appeared three years later in *Vestnik Evropy* [*European Herald*]. It was titled *The Time of Troubles in the Muscovite State* [*Smutnoe vremia Moskovskogo Gosu-darstva*]. His work *The Last Years of Poland* [*Poslednie gody Rechi Pospol'itoi*] followed thereafter.

At the same time, the indefatigable Kostomarov wrote several monographs on the history of the Ukraine. These were continuations of *Bogdan Khmel'nitskii*. He began with *The Hetmanship of Vygovskoy* [*Getmanstvo Vygovskogo*] and gradually came to *Mazepa and the Mazepians* [*Mazepa i Mazepintsy*]. These works were based on the published (partly by him) documents on the history of Southern and Western Russia.

His two volume study *Russian History in the Biographies of its Major Figures* [*Russkaia istoriia v zhizneopisanii ee vazhneishikh deiatelei*] appeared in 1874-1876. These were illuminating characterizations.

Kostomarov continued to work until his very death (his *Mazepa and the Mazepians* was published in 1882-1884). He died in 1885 after a long and agonizing illness.

Kostomarov had already expressed his ideas on Russian history in the Petersburg period of his life — *Reflections on the Federal Principle in Ancient Rus'* [*Mysli o federativnom nachale v drevnei Rusi*] and *Two Russian Nationalities* [*Dve russkikh narodnosti*] —the south-Russian (Ukrainian) and the middle-Russian (great Russian). He viewed the Novgorodians as migrants from southern Russia.

Kostomarov attributed great importance to the ethnographic foundation of the national spirit, a people's psychological cast of mind. The Ukrainian is an individualist, the great Russian — a communalist. The Great Russian people have a strong feeling of discipline and the State principle is powerful. The Ukrainian nationality is permeated with the principle of freedom. The Ukrainian nation created the *veche* [system of the town assembly] — the Great Russian, that of autocracy.

Kostomarov paid considerable attention to Poland's role in Russian and Ukrainian history. He thought that in terms of language Ukrainians were closer to the Great Russians but were closer to the Poles in national character. The difference was that the Poles were an aristocratic people; the Ukrainians — democratic.

Kostomarov was a talented writer. Only in the last years of his life, when his strength and health were strained, did his writing become the dry and merely factual exposition of events.

Many criticized Kostomarov — sometimes very sharply for being insufficiently attentive to the sources and for the resulting errors — as well as for his prejudicial attitude toward the history of the Moscow State, the negative aspects of which he frequently stressed. Here was the difference between Kostomarov's views and those of his critics. The latter were scarcely less cutting regarding Ukrainian history.

As to minor slips and errors, they are almost inescapable for every scholar. In Kostomarov they are partly to be explained by his habit of relying on his remarkable memory and partly by the diversity of his knowledge.

Nevertheless, Kostomarov's contribution to the development of Russian historiography is very substantial. He was the first to bring the abundant materials on the history of the Ukraine in the XVII century into usage within Russian historical scholarship. By his views on Russian history (regional roles) he complemented Solov'ev's scheme (they polemicized with each other).

Kostomarov's collected works were published in Petersburg from 1903 to 1905 (sixteen volumes in six books).

## XII

## A. P. SHCHAPOV (1830-1876)

In many ways Shchapov was in accord with Kostomarov in his views on Russian history. Like Kostomarov, Shchapov felt that the historian's fundamental task was the study of the history of the nation, not the history of the State. Like Kostomarov, Shchapov held to the notion of the federative origins of Russian history. But he was not interested in southern Russia. His theory might be called great Russian regionalism.

Afanasii Prokop'evich Shchapov was born in Siberia in the village of Anga, some 200 versts from Irkutsk. His father was Russian, a local reader in the church; his mother was Buriat. In 1852 he completed the course of study at the Irkutsk Theological Seminary and, as one of the best students, was sent to study to the Theological Academy of Kazan at government expense.

Shchapov studied there with great diligence and success. An important factor in the start of his scholarly labor was the fact that at this time the rich manuscript library of the Solovetskii Monastery was transferred to Kazan.

The Crimean War was in progress and the Russian government feared the incursion of the English fleet into the White Sea and bombardment of the Solovetskii Monastery. Shchapov participated in compiling the descriptions of the manuscripts and made many excerpts. His master's thesis for the Theological Academy *The Russian Schism of the Old Belief* [*Russkii raskol staroobriadchestva*] (1858) was partially based on this material (and was published in Kazan in the same year).

At this time scholarly study of the Russian Church schism was just beginning (the 200th anniversary of the start of the schism in 1667 was approaching). Metropolitan Makarii Bulgakov's work, *The History of the Russian Schism of the Old Belief* [*Istoriia russkogo raskola staroobriadchestva*], appeared in 1854. It was then considered that opposition to Patriarch Nikon and his reforms of church books and rituals was the result of the Old Believers' ignorance and indolence. Only at the very end of the XIX and the beginning of the XX centuries, through the works of such outstanding historians of the Russian Church as E. E. Golubinskii and N. F. Kapterev, was it clarified that Russian Church rituals followed those of the ancient Greek Church. Greek churchmen of the XVII century had already forgotten these. It was under their influence that Nikon instituted his reforms.[8]

Shchapov characterized the schism from the accepted view in his thesis. But he later approached the question differently, namely from the socio-political viewpoint.

In his next work, *Land and Schism* [*Zemstvo i Raskol*] (1862), Shchapov wrote that old belief was above all "a powerful, frightful communal opposition of the taxable classes, the mass of the people, against the whole governmental system — ecclesiastical and civil."

Shchapov's ideas were developed by his students and

followers — N. A. Aristov, V. Farmakovskii, V. V. Andreev, and others. Bestuzhev-Riumin also recognized the value of Shchapov's work.

From the political point of view, Shchapov's ideas concerning the Old Believers interested Herzen and Ogarev in London as well as their rather accidental friend, V. Kel'-siev, a recent émigré. It was decided to utilize the Old Believers for the struggle against autocracy. In that very year, 1862, a special journal for Old Believer readers, titled *Common Cause* [*Obshchee Delo*], began to be published in London. Herzen's circle entered into correspondence with Cossack Old Believers who had emigrated to Turkey. Nothing came of these semi-naive, semi-fantastic attempts.

Nevertheless, news of them which reached the Russian government greatly disturbed it. It was already in a state of extreme nervousness as a result of a series of peasant uprisings which had followed shortly after the announcement of peasant reforms.

In the preceding four years, while the reforms were being worked out, the peasants awaited the decision regarding their fate with unusual patience.

The Manifesto of February 19th was originally composed by N. A. Miliutin and Iurii Samarin but then it was vastly changed by Metropolitan Filaret. The Manifesto was read in all the churches and a copy of the statute of the reforms was given to each landowner and each village society. As reworked by Metropolitan Filaret, the Manifesto was written unclearly and intricately. But, according to the statute, the peasants initially remained dependent on the landowner until the reforms were put into practice.

The peasants could not understand this. They needed cogent clarifications of the state of affairs.

This task was assigned to the governors. Some of them were able to avert disturbances in their provinces. But some of them treated the matter formally and did not take the necessary measures.

The government, and Alexander II personally, relied only on military force to quell potential disturbances.

Peasant rebellions actually did take place in a series of provinces — Penza, Simbirsk, Saratov, Kazan, and Tambov.

Alexander II sent his aides-de-camp with military detachments to all the provinces. The more reasonable commanders talked the crowds of dissatisfied peasants into submitting and dispersing but in some areas the situation led to clashes.

The major tragedy occurred in the village of Bezdna in the province of Kazan. Here the peasants were particularly upset and refused to disperse. General Apraksin, who commanded the detachment, ordered to shoot into the crowd. According to official figures, 55 people were killed and close to 70 were wounded.

When news of this incident reached Kazan, Shchapov, at the head of a whole group of students, went to Bezdna in order to hold a requiem for the dead. After the requiem, Shchapov gave an emotional speech protesting sharply against the killing of the peasants. In answer, Alexander II ordered the monk who had officiated at the requiem to be exiled to the Solovetskii Monastery. Shchapov was deprived of his chair at the University of Kazan, arrested, and brought to Petersburg. Valuev, the Minister of Internal Affairs, guaranteed his bail and appointed him as an official for special assignments on schismatic affairs. But Shchapov's academic career was finished.

In Petersburg, Shchapov became acquainted with the contemporary idols of revolutionary youth — Chernyshevskii, Dobroliubov, and Pisarev. From the latter he acquired an interest in natural science and attempted to apply the scientific method to his own research.

In the meantime the political atmosphere thickened. Chernyshevskii was arrested in 1862 and incarcerated in the Peter Paul fortress. In 1864 he was sentenced to seven years at hard labor. At the same time Shchapov's relations with Herzen became known to the government and he was sent to Irkutsk.

During his stay in Petersburg, Shchapov developed his regional or landed communal-colonization theory. Then, under the influence of his passion for science, he significantly altered it.

At the root of his regional theory lay the idea that the land constituted the foundation of the whole national mode of life. "The two primary worlds — town and village — settled side by side on the same land and water. They did so themselves, without orders, in a colonial-geographic and communal-domestic tie." The district or region formed about them. "In a historically natural way, the district or regional *mirs* closed ranks with regional communes along portages and the river systems." There were two subsequently predominant forms in regional life — the distinctively regional and the united regional (federative). The latter was established after the *Time of Troubles*. Its organ was the *Zemskii Sobor* [Assembly of the Land].

Shchapov's most important article on the role of science in history was "Science and the National Economy" ["Estestvoznanie i Narodnaia Ekonomiia"]. In it he developed the notion that the task of science and medicine was the "betterment of the mental and economic state of the people."

In Irkutsk Shchapov wrote mostly on local Siberian themes. He was the inspirer of a whole series of regional Siberian public men. All of "young Siberia" was obligated to him.

Shchapov's wife, Ol'ga Ivanovna, who had dedicated herself wholly to him, died in 1874. Two years later Shchapov himself died.

## XIII

### K. N. BESTUZHEV-RIUMIN (1829-1897)

Solov'ev and his students formed the Moscow school of historians. Bestuzhev-Riumin laid the foundation of the Petersburg school.

Konstantin Nikolaevich Bestuzhev-Riumin was de-

Russian Historiography: A History                    108

scended from an old noble family of the Nizhegorod province. Konstantin was born in Kudriashki, the patrimonial
estate. His father, Nikolai Pavlovich, posessed a reverential
attitude toward Russian history and the Russian language.
His cherished dream was to see his son a professor of history.
Prior to his son's entry into the gymnasium, his father
acquainted him with the works of Tacitus and Karamzin. In
1840 Konstantin entered the first grade of the Nizhegorod
gymnasium from which he graduated in 1847.
    Of his high school teachers, Bestuzhev-Riumin was
above all obligated to P. I. Mel'nikov-Pecherskii who drew
him (and several other able students) to literary studies. Of
his high school classmates, Bestuzhev became friends with
S. V. Eshevskii. Later he married his sister.
    Upon graduating from the gymnasium, Bestuzhev
entered the law school of Moscow University. He took
Solov'ev's, Granovskii's, and Kavelin's courses. Upon
graduating from the university in 1851, Bestuzhev had to
seek a livelihood (his father had died in 1848). For the first
three years, he accepted an invitation to be private tutor in
the Chicherin family of the Tambov province. He then became editor of *Moskovskie Vedomosti*. In 1858 he inserted
a long article, "The Present State of Russian History as
a Science", ["Sovremennoe sostoianie russkoi istorii kak
nauki"], into the *Moscow Review*. This was a review of the
first eight volumes of Solov'ev's *History of Russia*.
    Bestuzhev moved to Petersburg in the fall of 1858 and
collaborated with the journal *Notes of the Fatherland*
[*Otechestvennye Zapiski*] as member of the editorial board
and permanent contributor. In 1864 he was invited to teach
native history to Grand Duke Alexander (the future Emperor
Alexander III). Prior to this, in 1863, he passed his master's
examination at the University of Petersburg and thus opened
the way to the chair of which he had long dreamed. Since he
did not yet have the doctor's degree, he was initially
appointed assistant professor. Now he could indulge in research peacefully and wrote his first outstanding work, *On
the Composition of the Russian Chronicles to the End of*

the *XIV Century* [*O sostave Russkikh letopisei do kontsa XIV veka*].Bestuzhev presented this work for his master's degree but on the basis of I. I. Sreznevskii's complimentary review (he was the dean of the historical-philological department) he was immediately awarded the doctor's degree in Russian history.

The years of Bestuzhev's professorship were the period of his scholarly and pedagogical flowering. Bestuzhev was a confirmed supporter of women's education. Beginning in 1871, aside from the university, Bestuzhev lectured on Russian history at the private (so-called Vladimir) courses for women and furthered their transformation into the first Russian women's university. (It was called the Advanced Courses for Women). He became its head in 1875. These courses came to be called the Bestuzhev courses in common parlance.

Because of Bestuzhev's strained and uninterrupted activity, he exhausted himself and went abroad in the fall of 1882. He stayed there about two years. The weakness of his health forced Bestuzhev to leave the university and the Advanced Courses for Women at the end of 1890. In March of 1890 he was elected a member of the Academy of Sciences. This was a matter of great moral satisfaction to him.

Bestuzhev was against the inclusion of abstract philosophical theories into explanations of the historical process. Of the social trends, he sympathized with Slavophilism. From 1878-1882 he was chairman of the Slavic Benevolent Committee. But he never expressed these views in his lectures or in his published works.

After Bestuzhev's dissertation on the chronicles, his major solid work was *Russian History* [*Russkaia Istoriia*] (2 vols., 1872-1885).

In his exposition of Russian history, he first provides a thorough review of the sources beginning with archeological monuments and ending with literary examples as well as those of daily life. There follows a review of the contents of scholarly works on Russian history. Bestuzhev felt that his task was to place in the reader's hands the material and varying explanations of it by different authors. He thought that the reader should grasp all of this so as to become the historian himself. For this reason, he refrained from personal evaluation of the works he noted and the opinions of their authors.

In his exposition, he separated "past" history (events, external facts) from the history of "mores and manners" or cultural history. His last student, S. F. Platonov, provided an illuminating portrayal of Bestuzhev the teacher in his memoirs. Platonov began to take Bestuzhev's courses during his first year at the university. "We were initially amazed at his external appearance." The majority of professors at the University of Petersburg wore suits when lecturing. "Bestuzhev always wore a tail-coat. He wore it as a true *barin* [lord], a temporal man. . . Upon entering the auditorium, Bestuzhev looked at us with his nearsighted, lively and kind eyes. He then sat in the arm chair and invariably began with the very same thing: he moved his left hand over his high forehead several times and pronounced the first words of the lecture quietly, so quietly that we usually did not hear them. The account heard by all began with the second phrase — and how much pleasure we derived from it. Bestuzhev was not an orator. He did not 'read', he simply discussed without worrying about the form of his speech . . . Before us was a man who moved freely in all spheres of the humanities, a man broadly learned. He knew his field brilliantly and was able to lift us to the heights of abstract speculation and lead us into the subtleties of specialized learned polemics. We seemed to live in an environment new to us, in some sort of educated brotherhood where everything breathed with mutual scholarly interest and hungered for national self-knowledge. . . At the time we did not comprehend that this was Bestuzhev's last regular course, that his health was failing, and that the sunset of his life was beginning."

## XIV

## K. D. KAVELIN (1818-1885)

In Russian historiography Kavelin could have occupied a place close to Solov'ev and Chicherin, but his life took such a turn that he had little opportunity to devote himself to Russian history.

Konstantin Dmitrievich Kavelin was descended from a noble family of the Riazan province. The family environment was a musty one — a frightful emptiness of life, the absence of intellectual interests, the mentality of serfdom, and the gentry's pretentiousness. Of the ever-changing German and Swiss tutors, the majority were worthless; some were drunkards. A bright spot for Kavelin as a boy was his friendship with his elder sister, Sofiia.

In 1827 the family moved to Moscow. Here, Konstantin's education improved. The provincial tutors were replaced by teachers — seminarians, a German and a Frenchman — who were decent this time. In 1834 it was decided to prepare Konstantin for the university. V. G. Belinskii was invited to be the mentor. His influence was decisive. Kavelin became a Westernizer for life.

In 1835 Kavelin entered Moscow University's school of law. His instructors were Redkin and Kriukov. In 1844, after the successful defense of his master's thesis on *The Basic Origin of the Russian Judicial System and Civil Legal Procedure in the Period from the Ulozhenie* [Code of Laws, 1649] *to the Establishment of the Provinces* [*Osnovnye nachala Russkogo sudoustroistva i grazhdanskogo sudoproizvodstva v period vremeni ot Ulozheniia do uchrezhdeniia o guberniiakh*]. Kavelin was appointed adjunct to the chair of the history of Russian legislation.

His course was the first experiment in Russia of the orderly philosophy of the history of Russian law and was immensely popular among students. But in 1848 Kavelin deemed it necessary to leave Moscow University because of the unworthy behavior of N. I. Krylov, professor of

Roman law. There were persistent rumors that Krylov took bribes. His colleagues demanded that he either justify himself or leave the university. Krylov did neither. Kavelin and Redkin then left the university themselves.

Kavelin moved to Petersburg and began looking for a job. In 1854 he married Antonina Fedorovna Korsh and had to support the family.

At first Kavelin joined the Ministry of Internal Affairs, then transferred to the staff of the military schools, then also accepted a position as head of a section in the chancellery of the committee of ministers (while keeping his job at military headquarters).

In 1857 Kavelin was offered the chair of civil law at the University of Petersburg. This was already the preparatory period for the emancipation of the serfs. From youth an enemy of serfdom, Kavelin participated fervently in discussing plans for the reforms. It was on this basis that he drew close to N. A. and D. A. Miliutin and Iurii Samarin and gained access to the Grand Duchess Elena Pavlovna, an ardent advocate of emancipation. Without waiting for the reforms, she decided to structure the life of her peasants on her estate, the Karlovka, in the Poltava province, on a new model. Kavelin was entrusted with drawing up the regulations. The new rules were approved on February 1, 1859.

Because of student uprisings, Kavelin and several other professors left the university in 1861. After this, A. V. Golovin, the Minister of Public Education, sent Kavelin abroad for two years to study European universities. The reports which he presented served as material for the reform of Russian universities in 1863. In the following year he again entered government service — as *juris consul* in the Finance Ministry's department of unassessed taxes. But he continued his scholarly and literary work in his spare time.

At the end of the 1870's Kavelin experienced several grave personal losses. First his son died, then his daughter, Sofiia, who was married to the artist, Briullov. Turgenev wrote an emotional reminiscence about her. Two years later, Kavelin's wife died. An opportunity to renew his teaching at the university level gave Kavelin spiritual support.

In 1878 he was given the chair of civil law at the military-juridical academy. Kavelin was 60 years old at this time but he had not lost his moral influence on youth and captured the fervent love of his new students. He dedicated his last work, *The Problems of Ethics* [*Zadachi etiki*], to youth.

Like Solov'ev and Chicherin, Kavelin is considered to be one of the founders of the so-called "Government school of Russian history." The term is not wholly accurate. The representatives of this "school" spoke not only of the State but of the people. The fundamental problem for them was the nature of the tie and the interrelationship between State and people. In his historiosophic views Kavelin, like Solov'ev and Chicherin, is guided by Evers and Hegel. Redkin, his teacher at Moscow University, acquainted him with Hegel. Granovskii did the same. Hegel's influence is apparent primarily in Kavelin's earlier works.

Kavelin already expressed his general conception of history in his first article, "A View of the Juridical Life of Ancient Rus' " ["Vzgliad na iuridicheskii byt drevnei Rus' "] (1847).

Kavelin outlines three stages in Russia's historical development. Tribal relationships predominate in the first (prior to the formation of the Kievan State). With the arrival of the princes of the House of Riurik, their clan (family) begins to rule the whole Russian land jointly. During the process of the princes' settlement in various cities, the clan was transformed into a multitude of individual independent domains. The reverse process then begins — the gathering of the lands by the Moscow members of the Riurik House. In this way an enormous patrimony, the Moscow State, was created. Only as the result of the Petrine reform was the Muscovite kingdom truly transformed into a political governmental body and became a State in the present meaning of the word.

Kavelin felt that communal land ownership and the peasants' self-government, in the form of *zemstvo* organizations and the justice of the *mir*, were the basic mainstays of Russian society. They should be freed from the gentry and the bureaucrats. Kavelin gradually came to the persuasion that for the administrative reforms to succeed, a reworking of social mores and the classification of the relationships of the individual to society was imperative. In this connection, Kavelin approached the significance of psychology and ethics. "The classification of psychological questions," he wrote at the end of the 1860's, "stands in the same theoretical, moral, and scientific relationship as do the problems of the land in the practical world. Emptiness, lack of substance, moral decay, and the corruption of the educated sector of the public is a clear indication that a new synthesis is in motion and that the old has outlived its time. . . This reflects, in particularly grievous and pernicious fashion, on the condition of the youth which needs synthesis above all. Only psychology can pave the road toward it and open the door." It was in this connection that Kavelin wrote *Problems of Psychology* [*Zadachi psikhologii*]. The reading public did not evaluate this work sufficiently. This was a great disappointment for Kavelin.

In this work, which parallels his other work, *The Problems of Ethics*, Kavelin upholds the creative source in personality. Materialism is just as unacceptable to him as spiritualism.

Psychic and material life have the same common ground — man's internal world. "The world of external realities is the continuation of the personal, individual, and subjective world." M. M. Troitskii (1835-1899), professor of philosophy at Moscow University, evaluated Kavelin's book, *Problems of Psychology* highly: "This work will forever remain one of the most interesting memorials of our philosophical literature of the 1870's."

Personally, Kavelin was an unusually humane person in whom each true misfortune, each personal sorrow, found sympathetic echo. But he was not mild to the point of indifference. He was firm and independent in his convictions.

## XV

## B. N. CHICHERIN (1828-1904) and A. D. GRADOVSKII (1841-1889)

The founder of scholarly jurisprudence in Russia was K. A. Nevolin (see Ch. V, above). To Nevolin belong the first Russian encyclopaedia of law and a series of fundamental works on the history of Russian law — both civil and public.

Chicherin studied the history of civil and public law as well as the history of political doctrines and philosophies.

Gradovskii was the author of the important work, *The Origin of Russian Public Law* [*Nachalo russkogo gosudarstvennogo prava*] and several valuable studies on the history of administrative law.

Boris Nikolaevich Chicherin was one of Russia's major historians and jurists, a man blessed with a powerful mind inclined toward systematization. Philosophically, he was a follower of Hegel — Russia's outstanding Hegelian. To test the methodological bases of his philosophy, he wrote works on the classification of animals. Chicherin's *System of Chemical Elements* [*Sistema khimicheskikh elementov*] represents an amazing example of a speculative solution of an essentially physico-chemical problem — the structure of atoms. Chicherin equated the structure of atoms with the structure of the solar system. According to his conjecture, each atom consists of a central nucleus around which particles revolve. Chicherin wrote this prior to the discovery of radioactivity and the electron.

Chicherin was descended from an old wealthy noble family from the Tambov province (he was born in Tambov). Having received a thorough preparation at home, he entered Moscow University where he studied under Granovskii, Redkin, and Kavelin. In 1861 Chicherin was appointed a professor at Moscow University, taking the chair of the history of Russian law.

Chicherin was an outstanding teacher, a master in

clearly expressing his deeply thought out ideas..He remained a professor for seven years but left the university in 1868 (along with two other professors) because of rector Barshev's unceremonious violation of the university charter.

In 1881 Chicherin was elected as Moscow's municipal head. Two years later he gave a public speech in which he pointed to the necessity of "crowning the structure" of the *zemstvo* and municipal self-government by means of popular representation. Alexander III became indignant and removed Chicherin from his post as Moscow's municipal head. After this, Chicherin lived either on his estate, participating in the activity of the Tambov *zemstvos*, or in Moscow where he became friends with the philosophers, princes S. N. and E. N. Trubetskoi.

Chicherin evaluated the significance of the State very highly. It was his notion that the State's calling was to be the sphere of the free development of the free personality. The personality, like an impenetrable "end in itself," a "spiritual monad," opposed the State. In his work, *Concerning Popular Representation* [*O narodnom predstavitel'-stve*], Chicherin writes that the State leans on the "middle classes." "In their essence the middle classes strive not so much for power as toward freedom which is necessary for the development of labor and industry. . . By their very character, the lower classes are inclined toward submission. The upper classes, in contrast, by their position of primacy, definitely strive toward power and rights." In this fashion, Chicherin's conception of "class" has the character of a certain form of socio-psychological category.

For Chicherin, Hegel remained the guide throughout his life. However, he introduced certain corrections and additions to Hegel's system. One of the major changes consisted in correction of Hegel's dialectical scheme. Chicherin replaces Hegel's tri-partite dialectical process (thesis, antithesis and synthesis) with a four part scheme: 1) original unity; the collapse of this unity into 2) the abstract aggregate and 3) the abstract particular and 4) the ultimate or final unity of both.

According to Chicherin, "the actuating cause of development is the contradiction of the principles themselves." Chicherin's outstanding works relating to the history of Russian law follow: *Regional Institutions in Russia in the XVII Century* [*Oblastnye uchrezhdeniia Rossii v XVII veke*] (1859); *Experiments in the History of Russian Law* [*Opyty po istorii Russkogo prava*] (1859); and *Concerning Popular Representation* [*O narodnom predstavitel'stve*] (1866) — which dealt with the *zemskii sobors*.

Among Chicherin's philosophical works are *The History of Political Doctrines* [*Istoriia politicheskikh uchenii*] (5 vol., 1877); *Science and Religion* [*Nauka i religiia*] (1879); *The Foundation of Logic and Metaphysics* [*Osnovaniia logiki i metafiziki*] (1894); and *The Philosophy of Law* [*Filosofiia prava*] 1901).

In Chicherin's opinion, logic was the "first and fundamental science which prescribed the law for all others." Like Hegel, Chicherin believed in the identity of laws of reason and the laws of the external world.

In his *Memoirs* [*Vospominaniia*], Prince E. N. Trubetskoi pictures Chicherin as the "completely unique personification of sincere nobleness. . . I recall such straight forwardness of heart and mind in no one else. His words could not deviate from his thoughts, even in insignificant connotations. . . This was possible thanks only to an exceptionally rare, particularly in Russia, inflexibility and firmness of spirit." But this was a quality which made many people recoil. Furthermore, in the Russian society of the last quarter of the XIX century, interest in Hegel's philosophy had almost completely disappeared. "The Hegelian at the end of the XIX century seemed to come from another planet."

Approaching death, Chicherin felt himself to be alone.

By nature Chicherin was a man with a reticent character. This quality increased still more toward his life's end.

Gradovskii, in contrast, was a man who by his very nature was convivial and who yearned for people. He was a scholar and a publicist and appeared readily at all kinds of meetings. He was a member of the *Literary Fund*.

Aleksandr Dmitrievich Gradovskii graduated from the Khar'kov gymnasium and the University of Khar'kov. He was the editor of the *Khar'kov Provincial Record* [*Khar'kovskie Gubernskie Vedomosti*], then an official on special assignments for the governor of Voronezh. In 1866, at the University of Petersburg, he defended his master's thesis, *The Central Administration in the XVIII Century and the General-Prokurors* [*Vysshaia administratsiia XVIII veka i general-prokurory*]. Thereupon he was elected permanent *docent* [assistant professor] at the faculty of law. At the same time, he was appointed to the position of extraordinary professor at the Alexandrian Lycée.

In 1868 Gradovskii defended his doctoral dissertation, *The History of Local Government in Russia* [*Istoriia mestnogo upravleniia v Rossii*] (vol. 1), after which he was elected extraordinary professor — then one year later, ordinary professor. After this he began to write his main work *The Origin of Russian Public Law* [*Nachalo russkogo gosudarstvennogo prava*] ,(3 vol.,1875-1883). For a long time this work served as the basic textbook for Russian government officials.

Gradovskii's works on foreign State laws also constitute a valuable contribution to scholarship. The most important of these are *The German Constitution* [*Germanskaia Konstitutsiia*] , (2 vol.,1875-1876) and *The National Law of Leading European Powers: Historical Section* [*Gosudarstvennoe pravo vazhneishikh evropeiskikh derzhav. Chast' istoricheskaia*] (1886).

As a professor, Gradovskii prompted his students to work hard in his subject and was strict on examinations.

As a publicist, Gradovskii wrote readily and much in newspapers and journals. He was a permanent contributor to *Golos* [*Voice*] and *Russkaia Rech* [*Russian Speech*]. A number of his articles were later reissued in the anthologies of his articles: *Politics, History and Administration* [*Politika, istoriia, administratsiia*] (1871); *The National Question in History and Literature* [*Natsional'nyi vopros v istorii i literature*] (1873); and *Difficult Years* [*Trudnye gody*]

(1880).

Politically, Gradovskii held to the moderate liberal view. In his own description, he struggled for the ideas and institutions which served to "emancipate Russia."

In his polemic with Dostoevskii, who defended the significance of the personal principle at the expense of the social, Gradovskii strove to prove that certain conditions of social and political life must prevail to achieve the full and integral development of human personality. No societal arrangements can develop or even take root if the human personality is deprived of its elementary rights.

## XVI

## N. G. CHERNYSHEVSKII (1828-1889)

Nikolai Gavrilovich Chernyshevskii was not a professional historian but he read much and wrote on historical topics. His influence on the further development of Russian historical thought was fairly significant.

Chernyshevskii, the son of a very well educated clergyman, was born in Saratov. His father destined him for an ecclesiastical career and gave him a thorough education at home. He then entered him directly into the final grade of the seminary. There, Chernyshevskii amazed his teachers and friends with his knowledge.

The Chernyshevskiis lived in the same courtyard with the family of A. N. Pypin (the future academician). Pypin was Chernyshevskii's maternal cousin (and was five years older).

Upon graduating from the seminary, Chernyshevskii, with his parents' consent, entered the University of Petersburg (in 1846). At the instruction of one of his professors, I. I. Sreznevskii, Chernyshevskii compiled an etymological dictionary for the Ipatskii chronicle which was published in the *Proceedings of the Academy of Sciences. Section II.*

During his student years, aside from scholarship, Chernyshevskii was infatuated with the ideas of utopian socialism, particularly Fourierism (he attended the meetings of the *Petrashevtsy*). In 1850, having completed courses at the master's level, Chernyshevskii left for Saratov where he obtained a position as teacher in the gymnasium. In Saratov he married Ol'ga Sokratovna Vasil'ev. Three years later, he moved to Petersburg with his wife and engaged in journalism. He headed the *Sovremennik* [*The Contemporary*].

At the same time, he decided to attain professorial rank at the university. He passed his master's examination and, in 1855, submitted for his thesis a work titled *The Aesthetic Relationship of Art to Reality* [*Esteticheskie otnosheniia iskusstva k deistvitel'nosti*]. The thesis was published immediately. His oral defense of the dissertation was successful but A. S. Norov, the Minister of Public Education, found some of Chernyshevskii's assertions "blasphemous" and voided the master's degree. It was only after three years that a new minister confirmed it. By this time Chernyshevskii was so taken up with journalism that he ceased thinking of an academic career.

Chernyshevskii wrote quite a few articles and sketches on history for *The Contemporary*. For the most part they were on topical issues — such as the history of the peasant problem (the preparation for the abolition of serfdom was then in progress). The principles and bases of the reform were being actively discussed in the contemporary press. Like Kavelin, Chernyshevskii stood for the preservation of the peasants' communal land ownership.

Their main opponents among the moderate liberals were B. N. Chicherin and the professor of political economics, Ivan Vasil'evich Vernadskii, who was the publisher of the journal *The Economic Indicator* [*Ekonomicheskii Ukazatel'*].

As already stated (see above, Ch. XII on Shchapov), peasant rebellions commenced soon after February 19, 1861. The peasants were disappointed with freedom which was "not real." There was, simultaneously, the growth of revolutionary agitation and mutinous proclamations began to appear. Arrests of persons suspected of compiling and distributing these proclamations began. Among others, Chernyshevskii was arrested in 1862. On the evidence of a spy, proclamations to the "nobility's peasantry" were attributed to him.

Chernyshevskii was turned over to the Senate to be judged. (This was on the eve of the new judicial statutes — Chernyshevskii was tried according to the old regulations).

Besides the proclamation "To the Nobility's Peasantry" (Chernyshevskii denied authorship), he was accused for the revolutionary spirit of his works (which were passed by the censor). The Senate sentenced him to fourteen years of hard labor. In its final confirmation, the term was reduced to seven years. The sentence was announced on May 13, 1864.

Chernyshevskii was sent to eastern Siberia to serve out his punishment. At the time, political "criminals" did not actually have to do hard labor. Chernyshevskii was not hindered in his dealings with other political prisoners. He was allowed to take walks. For a time he even lived in a separate house. He wrote and read much but immediately ripped up what he had written.

His wife and two young sons arrived and, for a while, he was allowed three day meetings with them. The term of his penal servitude ended in 1871 and Chernyshevskii was to be transferred to a category of settlers who were allowed to choose their place of habitat. However, Count P. A. Shuvalov, the gendarme Chief, arbitrarily sent him to distant Vil'iuisk. This was a significant worsening of his fate. It was only in 1883 that Count D. A. Tolstoi, the Minister of the Interior, allowed Chernyshevskii out of Siberia and transferred him to Astrakhan. Six years later he was allowed to return to his native Saratov, but his strength was ebbing and he died in the same year.

Chernyshevskii's philosophical views were formed through the influence of Feuerbach and Auguste Comte. His socio-economic ideas are closely linked to ethics.

This was the ethics of utilitarianism — "rational egoism." Chernyshevskii's ethical inspiration was conditioned by his fervent love for all who were repressed by life's conditions. Chernyshevskii hotly defended the individual's right to freedom.

He rejected the idealistic approach to aesthetics. In his opinion, concrete reality stood above art.

Chernyshevskii was religious from youth. While a student at the university in 1848, he noted in his diary in commenting on Feuerbach's "religion of humanity": "what if we must await a new religion? My heart is disturbed by this and my soul is uneasy. I would like to preserve the present religion. I would hate terribly to part with Jesus Christ who is so blessed, so dear in personality, so loving and reverential of mankind."

Soon thereafter, however, Chernyshevskii repudiated Orthodoxy and accepted the "religion of humanity." It was in this connection that he believed in the Russian communal system.

The cult of science ("scientism") is characteristic of Chernyshevskii. This was a true faith in science and its unlimited possibilities. Chernyshevskii fought against the conceptions of man's duality, against the antithesis of "spirit" and "nature." In defending man's unity, Chernyshevskii thought of him in biological terms.

For him man was "a being having a stomach and head, bones, tendons, muscles, and nerves".

# XVII

## SOURCES OF HISTORICAL STUDY

As previously stated (see Ch. IV, above) the work of collecting and publishing historical source materials in the 1820's and 1830's was capped by the creation of the Archeographic Commission. Its work developed uninterruptedly throughout the whole XIX and the beginning of the XX centuries.

Independently of the commission, charged by the Second Section of His Majesty's Chancellery, M. M. Speranskii labored at the compilation of the Complete Collection of the Laws of the Russian Empire beginning with 1649 (when the Ulozhenie was issued) and continuing to 1825 (1830). The first series was followed by a second (covering the years 1825-1881). From that point on, a volume was issued yearly. The last volume prior to the Bolshevik Revolution appeared in 1916.

The Kiev Archeographic Commission was established in 1843. The archives of the Kiev, Podol'sk and the Volynia provinces were transferred to it. Such outstanding scholars as N. D. Ivanishev, V. V. Antonovich, and M. F. Vladimirskii-Budanov were among its directors. The Kievan Commission published an enormous number of valuable documents relating to the history of south-western Russia. Twenty years later, the Vilensk Commission for the study of ancient documents was founded. It too was very active. The Caucasian Archeographic Commission was established practically at the same time as that of Vilensk.

Provincial learned archival commissions were institutions of a different type. They were more narrow in scope but the majority were active and useful for historical science. They were within the jurisdiction of the Ministry of the Interior. The aims of these commissions were:1) the establishment of provincial historical archives; 2) gathering information on a region's antiquities, creating of local museums, and assisting in the dissemination of archeological and historical knowledge. A. S. Lappo-Danilevskii took active part in the planning of the activities of these commissions and in the direction which their work took.

Four such commissions were established in 1884 – in Riazan, Tambov, Tver, and Orel. Others followed and gradually the network spread over all Russia. The nature of the commissions'work depended on local conditions.

The Tavridian archival commission supervised Crimean classical antiquities , the vestiges of Genoese and Venetian trading ports of the XIII-XV centuries, materials on the territory of the Crimean Tatars, and Russian historical documents. The irreplaceable chairman and soul of the Tavridian commission was Arsenii Ivanovich Markevich (1855-1942).

An important event in the development of Russian Byzantine studies was the founding of the Russian Archeological Institute in Constantinople. Academician Fedor Ivanovich Uspenskii participated in planning the project for this institution. The Russian ambassador in Constantinople, A. I. Nelidov, laid the groundwork and negotiated with the Turkish government. Uspenskii was appointed director of the Institute. The Institute published its own journal, the *Proceedings* [*Izvestiia*]. The Institute's activity was not limited to Byzantine studies. Late classical and Slavic antiquities were investigated. Systematic digs were undertaken in Bulgaria.

The Odessa Society of History and Antiquities was founded in 1839. Its journal *Transactions* [*Zapiski*] in the main published descriptions of southern Russian antiquities as well as related materials. But it also published materials on the region's history in general.

The establishment of a whole series of historical and allied learned societies had major significance for historial scholarship and for the broadening of the Russian historical horizon.

The Moscow Society of Russian History and Antiquities, founded in 1804, gradually decayed and was revived only in the 1860's. After this, the Society's *Readings* [*Chteniia*] (issued quarterly) began to publish exceedingly valuable historical materials and research.

The Russian Archeological Society was commenced in 1846 but it unfolded to its full breadth after confirmation of its new charter in 1849. The Society was divided into three branches: Russian and Slavic archeology, Eastern archeology, and Classical, Byzantine, and Western European archeology. The first volume of the *Transactions of the Russian and Slavic Archeology Section* [*Zapiski otdeleniia Russkoi i slavianskoi arkheologii*] appeared in 1851, and volume 1 of the *Transactions of the Eastern Division* [*Trudy vostochnogo otdeleniia*] five years later. Besides the special archeological materials, many purely historical monographs and sources were issued in these publications.

The Moscow Archeological Society was founded in 1864. Its first session was held in Count A. S. Uvarov's apartment and was chaired by him. Four years later, as a gift from Alexander II, the Society received its own buildings. According to its charter, the aim of the Society was the study of archeology in general, but Russian archeology in particular. Among the active members aside from the chairman, Count Uvarov, Professor Anuchin should be especially recalled. The Society organized expeditions to conduct digs and research in a whole series of provinces including the Caucasus and the Transcaucasian regions.

Archeological conferences, whose chairman was Count Uvarov, are linked closely to the activity of the Moscow Archeological Society. Members of archeological societies and other learned institutes, in addition to persons who wished to participate by paying four rubles, took part in these conferences. The conference chose an administrative committee from among its membership. In view of the varied interests of its members, the conference assigned work according to sections. The Moscow convention of 1890 had nine sections: primitive antiquities; historico-geographical and ethnographic antiquities; monuments of Slavo-Russian language and literature; classical, Slavo-Byzantine, and Western European antiquities; Eastern and pagan antiquities; archeographic monuments.

The congresses convened in turn in various cities (Moscow, Petersburg, Kiev, Kazan, Tiflis, Odessa, Iaroslavl). Some 130 people participated in the first conference; at the eighth (in Moscow) in 1890, there were 380. The fifteenth conference took place in Novgorod in 1911. The sixteenth was scheduled for Pskov in 1914 but could not be held because of the war. The proceedings of the conferences were published by the Moscow Archeological Society.

The Moscow Archeological Institute came into existence at the end of the 1880's independently of the Moscow Archeological Society. A. I. Uspenskii was its chairman. The Institute began to publish its *Transactions* [*Za-*

*piski*] in 1890. Among the valuable materials included therein, I will note as particularly important for Russian history, V. I. Klein's study of the investigations of the death of Tsarevich Dmitrii of Uglitsk [Uglich] (1591). A photocopy of the investigation itself was appended.

The Russian Geographic Society was founded in 1845 in Petersburg. Its work also had great significance for history as well.

Such prominent scholars as K. M. Ber, P. I. Keppen, V. I. Dal', P. P. Semenov-Tian'shanskii, Iu. M. Shokolai, and I. V. Mushketov participated actively in its founding. The Society was made up of four sections: mathematical geography; physical geography; ethnography; statistics. Branches of the Society uniting local regional specialists were opened in Tiflis, Irkutsk, Orenburg, Omsk, Khabarovsk, and Tashkent. The studies and publications of the ethnographic and statistical divisions are particularly valuable for historians.

The Russian Historical Society of Petersburg was founded later than others (1866). According to its charter, the aims of the Society were to gather and process the materials and documents of Russian history. This not only applied to items in government and private archives and libraries but also those in the hand of individuals, in Russia and abroad.

Commencing in 1867, the Society began to publish its *Sbornik*[9] [lit. "collection"] which featured materials on Russia's internal history and on foreign policy.

The *Russian Biographical Dictionary* [*Russkii Biograficheskii Slovar'*] published by the Society is another indispensable source for historians. Twenty five volumes were published up to 1916. The Society was closed after the October Revolution of 1917. Publication of the *Sbornik* and the *Biographical Dictionary* ceased.

It should be noted in this connection that no less a valuable collection of Russian historical documents is the *Russkaia Istoricheskaia Biblioteka* [*Russian Historical Library*] published by the Archeographic Commission (one volume annually).

In 1873 the Historical Society of Nestor the Chronicler was founded in Kiev. The Society published its *Readings* [*Chteniia*]. These contained valuable studies and materials on history and the history of law. Professor Ikonnikov, Vladimirskii-Budanov, and Dovnar-Zapol'skii were active members of the society.

Historical societies were also established at many universities. They were of lesser scope but aided the scholarly intercourse of historians. Primarily at Kareev's initiative, a historical society was founded at the University of Petersburg in 1889. The Society published a journal called the *Historical Review* [*Istoricheskoe Obozrenie*]. A society was founded at the University of Moscow four years later as well as a society of archeology, history, and ethnography at the University of Kazan.

An indication of the constantly growing interest in history among broad circles of Russian society was the appearance of several popular historical journals which were semi-literary in character. However, they also published competent historical studies. In 1856 M. N. Katkov began to publish the *Russian Herald* [*Russkii Vestnik*]. Seven years later, also in Moscow, P. I. Bartenev founded the *Russian Archive* [*Russkii Arkhiv*]. In Petersburg, M. I. Semevskii founded *Russian Antiquity* [*Russkaia Starina*] (1870). The *Historical Herald* [*Istoricheskii Vestnik*], edited by S. N. Shubinskii, came into existence ten years later.

Museums of antiquities were established in conjunction with each archeological society.

At the beginning of the 1870's, a decision was made to found a museum of nationwide Russian significance. Between 1875-1883, the architect Sherwood built special buildings for it in a style which was rather widespread at the time — the imitation of XVI century Russian architecture. The museum exists to this day and is one of Moscow's notable sights. Antiquities dating to the bronze and stone ages have been collected there as well as antiquities from the Crimea and the Caucasus. There is also a collection of manuscripts.

The main collection of antiquities from southern Russia is in the Hermitage museum in Petersburg with its famous hall of Scythian treasures. But the Hermitage collected, and continues to collect, monuments of Russian culture of the X-XVIII centuries. The Hermitage publishes its yearly illustrated *Reports* [*Soobshcheniia*]. The last one known to me, volume XXIX, was issued in 1968.

The Russian museum of Alexander III was established in Petersburg in 1898. Originally it was meant for Russian art. But later archeological and ethnographic sections were opened and historical manuscripts and antiquities began to be deposited therein.[10]

## XVIII

## V. O. KLIUCHEVSKII (1841-1911)

In the period of the 1840's a whole pleiade of prominent Russian historians and historians of law was born — Kliuchevskii, Ikonnikov, Gradovskii (all three in 1841), Vladimirskii-Budanov (1838), Semevskii (1848), Kareev (1850), Maksim Kovalevskii (1851) and Shmurlo (1853).

The most famous of these in Russian society at the turn of the century was Vasilii Osipovich Kliuchevskii, "a great scholar and brilliant professor" (Kizevetter).

Like Solov'ev, Kliuchevskii came from a clerical family. But Solov'ev's father was a teacher of religion at Moscow's School of Commerce and belonged to the upper circle of Moscow's educated and prosperous clergy.

Kliuchevskii, born in the village of Voskresenskoe in the Penza district, came from the poorest strata of the rural clergy. His great-great-grandfather was a priest, his great-grandfather a reader, his grandfather a deacon, his father a priest.

Kliuchevskii lost his fathèr when he was eight. His mother took the children (Vasilii was the eldest) and moved to Penza.Vasilii was placed in a religious school. In 1856 he was accepted into the Penza seminary. However, Kliuchevskii did not wish to devote himself to an ecclesiastical career. He was attracted to the university and to secular learning.

It was with some difficulty that he moved to Moscow and entered the historico-philological department of Moscow University.

Study captivated him immediately but, at the beginning, he had financial problems until he found means of earning money.

Kliuchevskii wrote his first work while still a student. It dealt with Muscovite Russia and was his candidate's paper. Titled *Foreign Accounts of the State of Muscovy* [*Skazaniia inostrantsev o Moskovskom gosudarstve*], it was published immediately.

Kliuchevskii studied under Solov'ev but was also much taken by the lectures of two other of his professors – F. I. Buslaev in Russian literature and S. V. Eshevskii in world history. Shchapov's ideas influenced him greatly. The latter's works were just beginning to appear in print.

Kliuchevskii entered the university during the year of the emancipation of the serfs, in the atmosphere of incipient reforms. He perceived this period to be a turning point in Russian history and was deeply gripped by the new trends. In this connection he developed a desire to re-think anew the whole previous course of Russian history. It is from this that he derived his lively interest in the social and economic history of ancient Rus', the history of classes, and the history of serfdom.

In 1867 Solov'ev, who was lecturing on Russian and world "political history" at the Alexandrian Military School, recommended Kliuchevskii as tutor for his course. When Solov'ev stopped teaching there, Kliuchevskii was appointed lecturer in history in his place.

In 1871 he was appointed instructor in Russian history at the Moscow Theological Academy and in 1872 at the Advanced Courses for Women. During this very year he defended his master's thesis, "Ancient Russian Hagiographies as Historical Sources" ["Drevnerusskie zhitiia sviatykh,

kak istoricheskii istochnik"]. Soon thereafter, he began to
write his principal monograph *Ancient Russia's Boiar Duma*
[*Boiarskaia Duma drevnei Rusi*] (1882). This was his doctoral dissertation.

In 1879 Kliuchevskii had already been elected a docent
at Moscow University where he soon took the place of
Solov'ev who had died. Upon receiving the doctor's degree,
he was appointed professor.

In 1889 Kliuchevskii was chosen a member of the
Academy of Sciences, in the historico-political division.
In 1900 he was made ordinary academician, over and above
staff, in Russian history and antiquity.

Kliuchevskii commenced teaching his course in Russian
history in 1879. He immediately captivated his listeners and
practically became the most popular professor in Moscow
University. S. F. Platonov later recalled how as a student at
the University of Petersburg he found out from his Moscow
friends about Kliuchevskii's initial steps in Moscow.

Higher circles in Petersburg, including the royal family,
gradually noticed Kliuchevskii. In 1893 he was invited to
present a course on political history to Grand Duke George,
then the heir to the throne. Due to illness, he was then living
in Abastuman.

When Alexander III died (1894), Kliuchevskii gave
a memorial lecture wherein he praised him as a Tsar-peace-
maker for his foreign policy. Kliuchevskii did not touch on
his domestic policy. Nevertheless, a group of radical students
hissed at Kliuchevskii at his next lecture.

Kliuchevskii had no sympathy for Alexander III's
domestic policy. It was expected in Russian society that the
new Tsar, Nicholas II, would be inclined to relax the State's
guardianship. Some *zemstva* drew up statements wherein
they carefully expressed the hope that they would be given
the right to state their desires to the Tsar. These hopes were
not justified. In replying to greetings at the solemn reception
of the representatives of the nobility, *zemstva*, municipalities,
and peasant communes, Nicholas referred to the hopes of
the *zemstva* addresses as "senseless dreams." In this way, the

split between the government and society was underscored. This laid the groundwork for the "liberation movement" which led to the fall of autocracy.

After the Tsar's comment regarding "senseless dreams," Kizevetter went to see Kliuchevskii. The latter said: "Mark my words — Nicholas is the last Tsar of the Romanov dynasty. If he has a son, he will not rule."

In July of 1905 Kliuchevskii was invited to Peterhof for consultation on the project for the creation of a State Duma. The sessions were personally chaired by Nicholas II. At these sessions Kliuchevskii repeatedly stated the necessity of broad participation of peasants in the elections. "Let God preserve us from the danger that the grim specter of a class Tsar will arise in the people's imagination."

The project was made public in August. It was nicknamed "Bulygin's Duma" (after Bulygin, the Minister of the Interior). The Duma was to be consultative and did not satisfy the radicals.

The revolutionary movement continued and on October 17, 1905 the Manifesto for a legislative Duma was issued. Simultaneously with the creation of a Duma, the State council was reorganized. Half of the positions at its sessions were given to elected members. Elections were held according to *curiae*. One of them consisted of the Academy of Sciences and the universities. Kliuchevskii took part in the meetings of electors but refused to be a candidate himself.

Of the parties which arose, Kliuchevskii joined the National Freedom Party (the Cadet Party).

Physically Kliuchevskii was unusually strong and hardy though this was not the impression at first sight. But his powerful organism gradually weakened. He died on May 12, 1911.

In his historical views Kliuchevskii followed Solov'ev, his teacher. But he took much from Chicherin, Buslaev, and Shchapov. Following Solov'ev, Kliuchevskii considered colonization to be one of the basic factors of Russian history. In his speech in honor of Solov'ev, Kliuchevskii defined Solov'ev's view of the Russian historian's task to be "the development of political forms and social relations." This formula can be applied to Kliuchevskii. The difference is that for Solov'ev the stress is on its first part; for Kliuchevskii on its second.

Solov'ev created an integrated and harmonious course of Russian history. It was based on the solid foundation of primary sources (the majority of which were then yet unpublished). This greatly aided Kliuchevskii in elaborating his own historical world view. Kliuchevskii recognized this himself. Every beginning Russian historian, he said in his memorial speech on Solov'ev, "must start from the point were Solov'ev left off."

Besides Solov'ev, Chicherin had much influence on Kliuchevskii. Kliuchevskii attended Chicherin's lectures after he had already graduated and when he was an assistant at the university. These lectures, like Chicherin's works in general, furthered the development of Kliuchevskii's taste for legal problems. They directed his thought to the history of society's institutions, primarily from the juridical point of view.

"Kliuchevskii's works on the history of *kholopstvo* [status of servitude] can be viewed as the direct continuation of Chicherin's articles on unfree classes. Does not a theme like *Ancient Russia's Boiar Duma* derive from the same cluster of problems to which the famous *Regional Institutions in Russia in the XVIII Century*, the title of one of Chicherin's books, belongs?" (M. M. Bogoslovskii). Kliuchevskii dedicated his work, *The Composition of the Representatives to the Zemskii Sobors of Ancient Russia* [*Sostav predstavitel'stva na Zemskikh Soborakh drevnei Rusi*] (1890-1892), to Chicherin as the author of *Concerning Popular Representation* [*O narodnom predstavitel'stve*], (1866).

Kliuchevskii also valued the language of Chicherin's writings. It was crystal clear, compressed and precise, and unusually adapted to expressing juridical concepts and relationships. Following Buslaev and Shchapov, Kliuchevskii thought deeply of the role of popular psychology in history. For Kliuchevskii, the people are a living personality.

To all of this we must add that Kliuchevskii contributed a thorough study of Russia's economic and agricultural development to the science of Russian history. In Kliuchevskii's articles on special historical problems, his style is concise and matter of fact (Chicherin's style). In contrast, in his monographs dealing with general topics, the style becomes artistic. Kliuchevskii attains the heights of this artistry in *The Course of Russian History* [*Kurs russkoi istorii*]. Aside from its scholarly significance, this course represents one of the remarkable memorials of Russia's refined literature at the end of the XIX and the start of the XX centuries.

At the same time, the *Course*, like all of Kliuchevskii's works, is based on a thorough study of historical sources. Erika Chumachenko showed this convincingly in the book, *V. O. Kliuchevskii — Student of Sources* [*V. O. Kliuchevskii — istochnikoved* (1970).

Kliuchevskii worked out the basic content and form of his *Course* during his first ten years of teaching. But he then constantly continued to include partial changes and to make additions. In this fashion, the *Course* lived together with its lecturer. Kliuchevskii knew the *Course* by heart. Nevertheless, on the rostrum he always had the manuscript of the lectures before him. He constantly turned the pages (without looking at them).

"When Kliuchevskii lectured with masterful artistry, signifying every connotation of his thought with corresponding intonations, all distinctly felt the clarity with which the lecturer pictured those phenomena of history's past upon which he constructed his general conclusions. I have no doubt that, while speaking, Kliuchevskii saw that of which he spoke." (Kizevetter).

Initially, Kliuchevskii allowed his students to write down and lithograph his lectures. But in 1885 students were forbidden to do this. Nevertheless, they continued to do this without Kliuchevskii's permission.

In September of 1893 Kliuchevskii received a letter from the Minister of Education, I. D. Delianov, in which

Delianov asked him to send a copy of the lithographic edition. Kliuchevskii replied that he had only one copy, issued prior to 1885, but that it was "studded with my corrections and additions." "Should I succeed in finding a neat copy of the course, I will consider it my duty to supply Your Eminence with it." In conclusion, Kliuchevskii wrote that he hoped to publish his course. He was able to do this only in the 1900's.

The first volume was published in 1904. The last (fifth) volume was published posthumously in 1921 according to the notes of Ia. L. Barskov, Kliuchevskii's student.

Kliuchevskii's *Course of Russian History* is the sole course of its type which represents, in execution and design, a monolithic and complete work. At the very beginning of his course, Kliuchevskii raises the questions of the scholarly goal of local history (i.e. in this case, Russian history). He approaches this problem from a sociological point of view.

"In studying local history," says Kliuchevskii, "we became acquainted with the composition of the human community and the nature of its component elements. From the science of the structure of the human community, there might, with time, develop — and this would be a triumph of historical scholarship — its general sociological feature — the science of the general laws of the structure of human communities irrespective of transitory, local conditions." Placing colonization at the basis of the periodization of Russian history, Kliuchevskii establishes the following four periods in Russian history: 1) the Dnepr; 2) the upper Volga; 3) the great Russian; and 4) the all Russian.

Kliuchevskii understands the fourth period to be from the beginning of the XVII century to the commencement of Alexander II's reign (1613-1855). "This period is of special interest to us. This is not merely a historical period but a whole chain of epochs through which a series of important facts proceeds. They constitute the deep foundation of the contemporary cast of our life. True, this foundation is decaying but it has not yet been replaced. This, I repeat, is not one of the periods of our history: it is all of our modern history."

Having established the chronological periods, Kliuchevskii subsequently pays little attention to chronology. In his whole course, Kliuchevskii always thinks of all Russian history as a single whole.

"In the concepts and relations forming during these two and a half centuries, we notice the early germs of ideas which touch upon our consciousness. We observe the springing up of customs which were the first social impressions of people our age."

Throughout his whole course, Kliuchevskii traces the fate of these "early germs" of the historical process, their subsequent manifestation in new forms or the unsuccessful attempts to ignore them.

Let us cite a characteristic example. In the first lecture of his course, Kliuchevskii states: "In 1699 Peter the Great directed Russian merchants to trade as trade is conducted in other countries. This was to be done by companies and the pooling of capital. Due to the want of habit and lack of trust, things went poorly. Ancient Russia had developed a form of commercial association in which persons, not capital, united on the basis of kinship and indivisibility of property. . .This was the commercial house and consisted of the merchant-owner with his 'brothers in trade', 'sons in trade', etc. . .This form of co-operation graphically shows how the need of collective activity, in the absence of mutual trust within society, sought means of fulfillment in the shelter of the home by grasping at the remains of the blood tie."

This organically bred form was precisely what Peter wished to replace by the Western model — the trade (or commercial-industrial) company. He was able to achieve the establishment of these companies thanks only to his persistence and the pressure of government power (vol. IV, lecture LXIV).

The exposition of the *Course* is thus constructed in rings or circles which are partly parallel (for various aspects of socio-economic life) and which partly intertwine.

The majority of the chapters of the *Course* are devoted to the description of the history of administrative institutions and of estates, particularly the enserfment of classes. According to the *Ulozhenie* of 1649, "the peasant lost his freedom of movement and became enserfed to the owner under conditions of land tenure. . . For this reason, subsequent legislation did not devise limits and conditions to serfdom as a law, but merely means of exploiting serf labor. It was a two-sided exploitation; fiscal from the treasury's view; agricultural from the perspective of the landlord."

In carrying out the military-tax reforms, Peter the Great introduced universal military conscription and established the soul tax for serfs and *kholops* [slaves] alike. This erased the distinction between serfs and *kholops*. Serfdom, in actuality, was transformed into slavery. "Peter thought of his treasury, not of people's freedom. He sought laborers, not citizens."

As a result, as Kliuchevskii notes, "previously unknown obligatory service for all classes was being introduced into government." Serfs (who in 1724 numbered more than 4,000,000 "registered males") and the lower class of towns-people (169,000 "registered males") were subject to it.[11]

From the nobility Peter demanded permanent obligatory service, military or civil. The nobleman was allowed to go to his estate to live out his life only in case of mutilation in war or the infirmities of old age. It was only Peter III who, on February 18, 1762, "bestowed liberty and freedom on the whole Russian nobility."

"By the demands of historical logic or social justice," says Kliuchevskii, "the following day, February 19, should have witnessed the abolition of serfdom. It did follow on the following day but 99 years later."

Kliuchevskii attaches particular significance to exhaustive wars in the development of what may be called the statutes of serfdom within the Russian socio-governmental system of the XVII and XVIII centuries. During the reign of Tsars Aleksei and Peter, Russia was almost constantly at war; furthermore, with several adversaries at once.

In his characterization of the Russian governmental system, Kliuchevskii makes broad use of sharp irony and sarcasm. In the treatment of pre-Petrine Russia, the irony is often scoffingly indifferent. In treating Peter and his successors and their government managers (Kliuchevskii prefers the term "manager" to the term "statesman"), the sarcasm becomes merciless.

But Kliuchevskii also presents positive types among XVII century Russian statesmen — Tsar Aleksei, F. M. Rtishchev, A. L. Ordin-Nashchokin.

Rtishchev was constantly at Tsar Aleksei's side. "This was one of those rare and somewhat strange people who was totally devoid of vanity. . . He used his influence as the Tsar's favorite to be the conciliator at Court, to eliminate enmity and hostility, and to restrain arrogant or uncompromising people such as the *boiar* Morozov, archpriest Avvakum, and Nikon himself."

Kliuchevskii thought that A. L. Ordin-Nashchokin was the most remarkable of Muscovite statesmen in the XVII century.

"This statesman is doubly interesting for us in that he introduced a dual groundwork for the reforms of Peter the Great. First of all, no Muscovite statesmen of the XVII century expressed so many reforming ideas and plans which Peter later realized as he did. Secondly, by birth he did not belong to the society within which he had to function. . . Ordin-Nashchokin was perhaps the first provincial noble to pave his way into the circle of the conceited aristocracy."

Of the XVIII century statesmen, Kliuchevskii particularly singles out Anisim Maslov, *ober-prokuror* of the Senate. In his reports to Empress Anne and to Biron, he "constantly reiterated the poor state of the peasantry." In 1734, "Maslov carried out the Empress's strict instructions to the cabinet ministers to draw up a gentry institution, wherein it could maintain its villages and which could provide any needed help. . . This raised the burning question of serfdom's legislative norm."

Kliuchevskii did not acknowledge the significance of abstract philosophy. But he thought much about the role of nature in history and the correlation between natural and historical science. In his diary entries for 1903, he noted the impression upon him of the ideas of Helmholtz, the German physicist and physiologist. These concerned logical induction in the study of nature and its foundation – the universality of phenomena, its unvaried repetition. Kliuchevskii contrasts "historical induction" to it. Its method is "popular psychological feeling."

During his student years, Kliuchevskii lived through a complex religious crisis. Born in a religious family and a pupil of the Penza religious school, Kliuchevskii naturally absorbed the atmosphere of religion and did not subject it to doubt. At the university the lectures in theology by Fr. Nikolai Sergievskii made a great impression on him. Kliuchevskii wrote: "His lectures acquaint us not only with contemporary theology but with philosophy as well. . . He boldly opposed Feuerbach, the inveterate contemporary materialist. . . who rejects God."

Kliuchevskii, however, did not stop here. He decided to examine the opinions of Christianity's opponents.

He read Chernyshevskii's article on religion in *The Contemporary*, after which he attentively read Feuerbach's book, *Lectures on the Essence of Religion*.

"Christianity, it seems, is subjected to the very severest criticism," wrote Kliuchevskii in November, 1861, to his friend, Porfirii Petrovich Gvozdev, teacher of Latin at Kazan's second gymnasium.

"Feuerbach has definitively rejected all of the existing religions. He has labeled them the creations of human fantasy. In view of these circumstances, one feels the need to better acquaint oneself with the history of Christianity. Today, like in all transitional periods, there is no salvation without history. . . One must examine the whole historical path of Christianity, to verify it impartially. And it matters not to what this examination may lead, even though it be to the rejection of Christianity."

In the end, Kliuchevskii remained a Christian in the traditional sense, though in essence he became an agnostic.

In his course, Kliuchevskii was generally very critical of the XIX century Russian tsars (including Alexander II) and of the results of the Russian government's action.

In this activity he found an insufficient understanding of the course of Russian history and the true needs of the Russian people.

In his diaries, where he expressed himself with complete frankness, Kliuchevskii arrives at pessimistic conclusions: "History teaches even those who do not learn from it: it teaches them a lesson." (note from 1893). . . "During the whole XIX century, beginning in 1801 with the accession of Alexander I to the throne, the Russian government's policy was purely provocational. It gave society just enough of the freedom it needed to bring out its initial manifestations. It then covered careless simpletons."

Foreign policy — war — played a fatal role.

"After the Crimean War, the Russian government understood that it was worth nothing. After the Bulgarian War (1877-1878), the Russian intelligentsia also understood that its government was worth nothing. Now, during the Japanese war, the Russian people begin to understand that its government and its intelligentsia are both worth nothing."

Kliuchevskii recognized that war was not just a Russian but a universal phenomenon. He had a prophetic presentiment that wars would bring the old world to catastrophe. Still in 1893 he wrote to V. I. Ger'e: "I am thinking of going somewhere, but do not know where. Most of all, I would like to go to the West, to Europe, in order to see Europe before the war, perhaps the last European war. For after this war, I fear that there will be no one to fight anybody."

## XIX

### P. N. MILIUKOV (1859-1943)

Pavel Nikolaevich Miliukov occupies a prominent place in Russian historiography and in Russian political life.

Miliukov was born in Moscow.[12] His father, Nikolai Pavlovich, was the city architect, then an appraiser in one of Moscow's banks. His mother, whose maiden name was Sultanova, then Baranova upon marriage to her first husband, was a passionate and imperious woman. Hers was the primary role in the family. His father seemed to retire into the background before her but occasionally he objected. Stormy scenes resulted. Miliukov did not feel close to his parents at all. But he was friends with his younger brother, Aleksei.

His father had a large library, principally on architecture and the history of art. But there were volumes of *Russkii Arkhiv* [*Russian Archives*] for the first four years of its existence and Homer's *Illiad* in Gnedich's translation.

The parents sent both sons to Moscow's first gymnasium. According to Miliukov's memoirs, most of the teachers were dull. Latin was taught by a Czech who spoke poor Russian. But the Greek teacher, Petr Aleksandrovich Kalenov, loved the culture of the ancient world. He was able to transmit this love to his pupils, including Miliukov. "Kalenov caught fire when commenting on classical works," recalls Miliukov. "In his interpretation, the Greek texts came to life before us and became close to us."

Miliukov formed good relations with his comrades at the gymnasium. Somehow by itself a circle of friends formed. It was united by common aspirations. Meetings were held quite frequently in one of the members' homes. Usually one participant prepared an opening lecture. Aside from Miliukov, the princes Nikolai Dmitrievich Dolgorukov (the group's actual chairman), Konstantin Starinkevich, and Konstantin Ikov were active in the circle. Miliukov gave two lectures in the circle; one of them was on the theme of "Exclusiveness and Imitation." "Exclusiveness" was understood to mean intolerant ideological nationalism. Before it, Miliukov defended the right of imitation as an inevitable and progressive phenomenon. Some of the characteristics of Miliukov's future sociological and political views were already visible in the very choice of theme.

In 1876, in response to one of the protest demonstrations held by Moscow students, the butchers from Moscow's Okhotskii district beat up the students. The gymnasium circle could not comprehend this event. The students were considered to be "intercessors for the people." Why did "the people" beat them up?

The group's members avidly followed each issue of Dostoevskii's *Diary of a Writer*. They decided to turn to Dostoevskii for precept and counsel. The group entrusted Miliukov to write a letter to Dostoevskii and ask: "Wherein are we wrong in what has happened?"

Dostoevskii replied — you are not wrong. The society to which you belong is wrong. In breaking with the falsehood of this society, you turn to Europe, not to the Russian people in whom is all our salvation.

The revolts of the Balkan Slavs, which began in 1875, and their cruel suppression by the Turks, disturbed Moscow's gymnasium students as it did Russian society in general. Russian action became a moral necessity. The declaration of war on Turkey in April 1877 was supported by Russian public opinion.

Upon graduating from the gymnasium, Miliukov, in the summer of 1877, served in a medical unit in the Transcaucasian theater of military operations. In his free time he read Danilevskii's *Russia and Europe* [*Rossiia i Evropa*]. Miliukov did not then comprehend its political tendency, but he became interested in the theory of cultural types and its natural-historical foundation. Subsequently, Miliukov repeatedly returned to Danilevskii's ideas.

Miliukov returned from the Caucasus when studies at the university had already begun. He registered for courses in comparative linguistics (taught by F. F. Fortunatov), Sanskrit (taught by Vsevolod Müller who also included commentaries on folklore and the myths of popular literature), and Troitskii's course on the history of Greek philosophy. Miliukov did not immediately become interested in history.

Miliukov thought that V. I. Ger'e's lectures in world history were dry and insipid. S. M. Solov'ev was completing his professorial career. He taught advanced courses in Russian history. Miliukov went to one of his lectures once. Solov'ev spoke in an exhausted voice about the "fluid element" in Russian history. He died in the following year.

Miliukov finally found his true teachers in the persons of Kliuchevskii in Russian history and Vinogradov in world history.

Miliukov and his classmates were Kliuchevskii's first students after he became an instructor at Moscow University. The students in this course had the opportunity of coming closer to Kliuchevskii than later graduates. Kliuchevskii conducted his seminar at his home. Miliukov's class attained the privilege of unconstrained personal discussion after each session of the seminar. "Anna Mikhailovna (Kliuchevskii's wife) gave us tea," recalls Miliukov. "We raised political questions (there were so many of them at the time) and beleaguered Vasilii Osipovich, wishing to know his opinion. He escaped by joking, bandied paradoxes about, and so our evening would end."

*Russkaia Pravda* and other ancient monuments were analyzed at the seminars. Kliuchevskii conducted his wonderful digs among these esteemed ruins of antiquity — and returned with valuable finds. . . One could not learn one's own personal scholarly work at these seminars. All that was left to do was to write down the professor's personal commentaries.

Miliukov was deeply moved by Kliuchevskii's lectures. "He overwhelmed us with his talent and scholarly perspicacity. His perspicacity was amazing. Kliuchevskii detected the idea of Russian history with an inner eye, so to speak. He re-lived the psychology of the past as a member of the clergy, the class which above others preserved the link to the old historical tradition. . . Another trait adjoined this one: the charm produced by the artistic side of Kliuchevskii's lectures. . . We saw that Russian history too could be the subject of scholarly study."

Miliukov valued Vinogradov in a different way, though perhaps even more deeply. "He returned (from foreign assignment) with a completed work on the Lombards of Italy. It was based on the archives right on location. It truly showed what could be expected of him. . . But his seminar was even more important than his lectures. It was only from Vinogradov that we understood what true scholarly work meant. . . he could assign work to us based on primary sources without fearing (as Ger'e did) to fall behind us. On the contrary, he welcomed all new conclusions."

Miliukov also took part in the student movement. He was elected chairman of the illegal student mutual aid fund. After the assassination of Alexander II on March 1, 1881, student gatherings were forbidden. But at the insistence of the students' left wing, it was decided to organize one more meeting. Miliukov went there in order to convince the gathering to disperse. Discussion commenced and there were passionate speeches. At their peak, the police and the gendarmes arrived unexpectedly. All the participants of the gathering were taken to the Butyrsky jail overnight. On the basis of the police list, all of the students were turned over to be judged by the professors. Tikhonravov, the rector, summoned all of the guilty students and freed from punishment those who agreed to say that they had come to the gathering accidentally. Miliukov refused to do this and was expelled from the university. He was given permission to re-apply for the same course of study in the fall.

Miliukov decided to go to Italy for the summer to acquaint himself with monuments of art. To do this, he borrowed money from a friend. He returned to Moscow when lectures at the university had already resumed. His former classmates had already graduated from the university and gone on to their life's endeavors.

In this, his last year at the university, Miliukov again took Vinogradov's seminar.

After the final exam, Vinogradov and Ger'e offered Miliukov to stay on and prepare for a professorship in world history. Both professors knew that Miliukov intended to devote himself to Russian history. Through Vinogradov's allusions, Miliukov concluded that Kliuchevskii did not wish to keep him at the department of Russian history. But Kliuchevskii kept him.

His main task was, of course, preparing for the master's examinations. The usual time allotted for this was three years and Miliukov could prepare himself in this period (1883-1885). The points of departure for this preparation were programs of questions compiled by agreement with the examiners. The program in his major subject — with Kliuchevskii — consisted of twelve questions. In addition, he was to be examined in his minors — world history and political economy.

In world history Vinogradov gave Miliukov a theme that he was working on himself — colonization in the Roman Empire. For A. I. Chuprov in political economy, Miliukov chose the theme himself — theories of rent. This provided Miliukov with opportunity to acquaint himself with Ricardo's book, Ziber's on Ricardo, and Tiunen's book on "isolated government."

Of the themes in Russian history, Miliukov became particularly interested in two — *The Peasant Question from Catherine to Nicholas I* [*Krest'ianskii vopros ot Ekateriny do Nikolaia I*] and the emancipation of the serfs under Alexander II.

After successfully passing the master's examinations, Miliukov, as was the custom, gave two trial lectures and was given the rank *privat-docent*. As themes for his trial lectures Miliukov chose "The Juridical School in Russian Historiography" and "The Origin and Authenticity of the Earliest '*Razriadnaia Kniga*' " [Book of Civilian Military Appointments] — a paramount source for the history of the Russian military class and the organization of the military system in the Muscovite State. Both lectures were soon published (1886-1887).

As a *privat-docent*, Miliukov announced two courses — the history of Russian colonization and Russian historiography.

Both courses were not required for students and only a few registered. But those that did register were truly interested in the subject and wished to work seriously. Some of Miliukov's younger friends from the university also attended the lectures.

One of them, A. A. Kizevetter, vividly described his impression in his memoirs. "Miliukov's lectures made a powerful impression on those students who were already preparing to devote themselves to the study of Russian history precisely because before us was a lecturer who introduced us to the current work of his laboratory and the exuberance of this research infected and animated attentive listeners."

At this time, there was a substantive change in Miliukov's personal life. In 1888, he married Anna Sergeevna Smirnova, Kliuchevskii's student at the Advanced Courses for Women.

In 1886, Miliukov began to write his dissertation. The theme chosen was "The State Economy in Russia and Peter the Great's Reform." He decided to base his work primarily on archival materials. Miliukov's basic idea was the thesis that the Europeanization of Russia was not the product of borrowing but the inevitable result of an inner evolution. This was the same in Russia because of historical circumstances. In this scheme, Peter's personality was cast into the background. Miliukov recognized that shaping and writing his dissertation would take several years. But he did not fear this.

He recalls: "I not only had to work on the materials of Peter's time but also on the materials of the preceding period (beginning with the XVI century) to be found in Moscow's archives. In order to personally master Petrine materials, I had to broaden my studies to include work in Petersburg. There the richest of sources awaited me in the thickest volumes of Peter's cabinet. I spent two consecutive summers at this work. The feeling of constant effort and delight at almost daily important discoveries never left me. The latter seemed to fit by themselves in the overall, truly grandiose canvas."

In stating the idea that the Europeanization of Russia was the inevitable result of an internal evolution, Miliukov followed in Solov'ev's footsteps.

In 1898 Miliukov summarized his views of Peter and his reforms in the encyclopedic dictionary of Brockhaus-Effron (half-volume 46). There, in passing, he writes: "The question of the degree of Peter's personal participation in the reforms of the last period is still debatable."

This is a masked retreat from the views which Miliukov expressed in his dissertation. He could not but respond to the new materials contained in N. P. Pavlov-Sil'vanskii's just published book, *Reform Projects in the Memoranda of the Contemporaries of Peter the Great*. [*Proekty Reform v zapiskakh sovremennikov Petra Velikogo*].

These memoranda were presented either voluntarily or by commission to Peter by many Russians and foreigners. Measures to better the government's state of affairs were proposed in their projects. Peter read many of these memoranda himself, particularly those on raising State revenues and developing Russia's natural resources as well as the reports on trade policy and administrative reform. Therefore, Peter's personal role in the preparation of reforms and, in many cases, his initiative are not subject to doubt.

Kliuchevskii was not in agreement with the fact that Miliukov chose to write a dissertation that demanded so much time.

Kliuchevskii himself had been assigned a master's thesis topic by Solov'ev — ancient Russian hagiographies. It was laborious work but did not demand much time. It was only for the doctoral dissertation that Kliuchevskii chose a broad topic (*Ancient Russia's Boiar Duma* [*Boiarskaia Duma Drevnei Rusi*]).

For this reason Kliuchevskii advised Miliukov to postpone the theme of the Petrine reforms until his doctoral dissertation and analyze the documents of one of the northern monasteries for his master's thesis. Miliukov categorically rejected this advice. "I could not tear myself away from my work" he writes in his memoirs. "Master, doctor — it matters not when I receive those degrees. So I continued to work without heeding Kliuchevskii's opinion." Thus occurred the first disagreement between teacher and student.

When Miliukov completed his thesis, S. F. Platonov did him a big favor by arranging for its publication, by individual chapters, in the *Journal of the Ministry of Public Education* [*Zhurnal Ministerstva Narodnogo Prosveshcheniia*].

The individual reprints of these chapters were bound as a book and the thesis was thus presented by Miliukov to the historico-philological faculty of Moscow University.

At Platonov's recommendation, the Academy of Sciences commissioned Miliukov to write a review of A. S. Lappo-Danilevskii's book, *The Organization of Direct Taxation in the Muscovite State from the Time of Troubles to the Reform Era* (1890) [*Organizatsiia Priamogo Oblozheniia v Moskovskom Gosudarstve so Vremeni Smuty do Epokhi Preobrazovanii*]. Instead of a review, Miliukov wrote a whole study, *Controversial Problems in the Financial History of the Muscovite State* [*Spornye Voprosy Finansovoi Istorii Moskovskogo Gosudarstva*].

In discussing Miliukov's thesis in the department, Vinogradov and Ger'e proposed to grant Miliukov the doctor's degree at once (by-passing the master's) but — as Vinogradov related to Miliukov — Kliuchevskii did not agree to this.

The thesis defense took place on May 17, 1892. The department gave Miliukov the master's degree.

"I immediately made a promise," writes Miliukov in his memoirs, "which I kept — never to write and defend a doctoral dissertation." When Platonov found out the outcome of the Moscow dispute, he proposed that Miliukov present his *Controversial Problems in the Financial History*

*of the Muscovite State* to the Petersburg historico-philological faculty as a doctoral dissertation. Miliukov refused.
In 1893 Miliukov received the S. M. Solov'ev prize for
his thesis. It was a sum large enough to enable him and his
wife to go abroad. The Miliukov's spent the summer on the
Brittany shore not far from Brest. Before departing in the
fall, Miliukov had a lengthy conversation one morning in
the hotel with a Frenchman who turned out to be a mason
and who proposed that Miliukov join a masonic lodge.
Miliukov rejected the offer. "Thereafter, I was repeatedly
given offers to join the masons," he recalls. "I think that this
insistence was one of the reasons for my stubborn refusal.
Such power of the collective seemed to be incompatible
with the preservation of individual freedom."

In Paris, Miliukov first visited P. L. Lavrov. Lavrov
spoke of scholarship, not politics, with Miliukov — evidently
in connection with the major work which he was preparing.
Miliukov also met in Paris Ivan Mikhailovich Grevs from
Petersburg. He was writing his dissertation on the history of
Roman landownership. Grevs introduced Miliukov to M. P.
Dragomanov whom Miliukov came to like exceedingly. It
turned out that they had many similar views. In particular,
both viewed Slavophilism negatively.

Prior to his departure abroad, Miliukov had already been
approached by organizers of pedagogical courses in Moscow
with an offer to present a series of lectures on the history
of Russian culture. Miliukov agreed. Upon returning from
abroad, Miliukov decided to write a book on this theme
which would be based on these lectures. Thus arose his
famous *Outlines of Russian Culture* [*Ocherki po Istorii
Russkoi Kul'tury*]

Simultaneously, Miliukov participated actively in
educational activity modeled on the English university ex-
tension program. The publication of a "home reading
library" and the organization of public lectures in Moscow
and the provinces were included here. Nizhnii Novgorod was
chosen to be the first province for the test. I. I. Ivanov gave
a series of lectures there on Russian literature. Miliukov was

the next lecturer. He announced a six lecture course on "social movements in Russia."

The lectures were held in the large hall of the gentry. The lieutenant-governor (the governor was away) and the bishop attended. In his lectures Miliukov attempted to show how the weak shoots of the social movement in the era of Catherine II proceeded to grow and strengthen gradually. The conclusion suggested itself: the time had come for the fulfillment of general expectations. The last lecture contained obvious hints at this. The public listened to the whole course with strained attention. At the end, it gave the lecturer a stormy ovation.

Miliukov did not escape without penalty. The Ministry of Public Education fired him from the university and forbade him to teach anywhere. The Ministry of the Interior began an investigation concerning the "nature of Miliukov's crime" in Nizhnii Novgorod and ordered his expulsion.

Miliukov went to Riazan alone. His wife Anna and the children (a second son, Sergei, was born) temporarily remained in Moscow. In Riazan Miliukov met people who sympathized with him. They found Miliukov a roomy house with a large garden on the church square. Miliukov moved his now substantial library there. In addition, the city had a rather good library at the archival commission. Miliukov began to work on his *Outlines of Russian Culture*. They were published in the Petersburg journal, *The Lord's World* [*Mir Bozhii*] before they appeared as a separate book.

During the second year of Miliukov's Riazan exile, he received an offer from the University of Sofiia (in Bulgaria) to accept the chair of world history which was vacant because of Dragomanov's death. His wife went to Petersburg to clarify matters. Mikiukov was given a choice: a one year jail sentence in Ufa or a two year exile abroad (this was a masked permission to accept the Bulgarian offer). Miliukov chose exile. This occurred in the spring of 1897. The lectures in Sofiia were to begin in the fall.

Miliukov left for Paris to prepare for his world history lectures. For the topic of his first course he chose that which he knew best from studying under Vinogradov — the transition from the fall of the Roman Empire to the Middle Ages. As an addition, he announced a course on Slavic archeology. According to his contract with the University of Sofiia, Miliukov was given the same salary as Dragomanov (18,000 *levs* per annum). This sum would be forfeited should the contract be breached. These were terms which exceeded the usual salaries of Bulgarian professors.

Miliukov immediately became friends with Professor Ivan Shishmanov, who was married to Dragomanov's daughter, Lidiia. Among other Bulgarian scholars and politicians with whom Miliukov became acquainted were the Russophile, Karavelov, with his wife, who united love of Russia with an ardent Bulgarian patriotism, and with the young V. N. Zlatorskii who taught Bulgarian history.

Miliukov's relationship with the Russian embassy in Sofiia turned out badly. Miliukov, like many of the radical intelligentsia of the day who were enthused over their struggle with the Russian government, had no feeling of responsibility to his government even as a representative of the Russian nation. Even when they were abroad, they did not hide their alienation from Russia's official representatives. December 6, the namesday of Nicholas II, came. On this day a thanksgiving service was held at the cathedral. Miliukov went to church with his Bulgarian colleagues.

After the thanksgiving service, everyone went to the reception held by Iu. P. Bakhmetev, Russia's ambassador in Sofiia. Miliukov did not go. His absence was noted and, with the assistance of Bulgarian Russophiles, it was interpreted as a demonstration against Russia.

Bakhmetev then, in a formal note, demanded Miliukov's removal from the university. The ambassador's demand was granted. But, in accordance with the contract, Miliukov forfeited a year's salary.

Miliukov's exile was far from over and he decided to utilize this time to become acquainted with Macedonia.

Miliukov's stay in Bulgaria gave him a feeling of deep respect for the Bulgarian people. He felt that Russia's protective policy toward Serbia, the government of which at this time was Austrophile, was in error. Preparing for his trip, Miliukov began to study Turkish and modern Greek.

Miliukov first went to Constantinople where he had never been. He was not so much attracted by the city as by the Russian Archeological Institute headed by the famous Byzantine scholar, F. I. Uspenskii. The institute possessed a good library.

From Constantinople, Miliukov went by rail to Saloniki (Solun' in Slavic). There he was especially interested in the colony of Macedonian Bulgars — an important base of revolutionary agitation. He also visited Skoplje, the center of Serbian propaganda.

Besides his specific aims, Miliukov took part in Uspenskii's expedition and the digs in Bulgaria and Macedonia.

In the meantime, his two year term ended. He returned to Russia and decided to base himself in Petersburg. Suddenly he received a proposal from academician N. P. Kondakov to participate in his expedition to Macedonia. Miliukov happily accepted. Pokryshkin, an architect, also took part. Kondakov charged Miliukov and Pokryshkin to inspect ancient Serbia. They surveyed Prizren, D'iakovo, and Pech. The Turkish authorities provided them with a military escort for this.

In Petersburg Miliukov immersed himself in the tense political atmosphere. "There was no time for scholarship." Miliukov joined the Literary Fund wherein Petersburg's finest social forces were concentrated: K. K. Arsen'ev, N. K. Mikhailovskii, N. F. Annenskii and their comrades. In a sense, this was the headquarters of the radical movement of that time.

In the spring of 1900, a meeting in memory of the sociologist P. L. Lavrov (who had died in Paris in February, 1900) was scheduled in the Mining Institute, a haven for secret student meetings. Miliukov was asked to take part and say a memorial word about Lavrov. He agreed. Fairly soon after this meeting Miliukov was arrested and placed in the house of preliminary detention. There he spent close to six months. During this time he wrote the next section of the third volume of *The Outlines of Russian Culture*. Necessary books were brought to him from the public library. Gradually they filled the whole corner of his cell.

After a series of questions which uncovered nothing, Miliukov was told that he was free but that he was forbidden to live in Petersburg. The Miliukov's settled in Finland near the Russian border and the Udel'naia station.

Not long thereafter, two Americans arrived in Petersburg — Samuel Harper, President of the University of Chicago, and the enlightened millionaire, Charles Crane, who was interested in the Slavs and in Russia. Crane provided money in order to fund a series of lectures at the University of Chicago on Slavic studies. The first lecturer to be invited was Professor Masaryk (the future President of Czechoslovakia). The second projected lecturer was Miliukov.

Miliukov happily agreed but asked for time to perfect his English. This was taken into account and his course was slated for the summer of 1903 when a conference of teachers was planned at the University of Chicago.

In the meantime, the revolutionary movement continued to flare. In 1902 liberal and moderate-socialist circles began to publish the journal *Liberation* [*Osvobozhdenie*] in Germany. In 1902 *Revolutionary Russia* [*Revoliutsionnaia Rossiia*], the organ of the socialist revolutionaries, began to be published abroad. Earlier, in Switzerland, Plekhanov, by agreement with Lenin and Martov, founded the social-democratic (later bolshevik) *Spark* [*Iskra*].

The time left prior to his trip to America was utilized by Miliukov for the preparation of his Chicago course. He decided to construct his course as the history of political thought in Russia and divided it into three sections: conservatism, liberalism, and socialism. The history of the revolutionary years 1902-1903 demanded special elaboration. Miliukov decided to undertake this at the Lowell Institute at Harvard University in Cambridge. It was also through Crane that he was given an offer there.

The verdict in the "Lavrov affair" came out in the

meantime. This time Miliukov was placed in the so called "*Kresty*" ["*Crosses*"]. His wife Anna visited him, brought him news, and sent food. Miliukov was provided with books from the public library as well as from his personal one. He continued to work on the third volume of his *Outlines of Russian Culture*.

In this fashion Miliukov spent half of his term when suddenly he was summoned by the Minister of the Interior, Pleve, in December, 1902. Pleve informed him that Kliuchevskii had written him and requested that the investigation be speeded up. Kliuchevskii had also written the Sovereign with a like request. (Kliuchevskii wrote to S. D. Sheremet'ev for transmittal to the Sovereign). Miliukov was deeply impressed by Kliuchevskii's concern. It was unexpected in view of the long break in their relations.

Pleve asked Miliukov what he would say were he offered the post of Minister of Public Education. Miliukov replied that he would express his gratitude but would refuse. Why? "Because there would be nothing to do for me in this post. However, if Your Excellency proposed that I take your position, I would then give it some thought."

The interview ended with this. One week later, Pleve again summoned Miliukov and announced his verdict. "I have concluded from our discussion that we cannot be reconciled. But at least do not enter into open battle with us. Otherwise, we will sweep you away. . . I have given the Sovereign a favorable report regarding you. You are free."

Returning to freedom, Miliukov wrote a heart-felt letter of gratitude to Kliuchevskii. The latter also replied warmly. Their former friendly relationship was fully re-established.

The teacher's conference in Chicago was held during a period of terribly humid summer heat. The lecturer had to wear a black robe and hat. Formal wear was required at dinner. This, of course, was exhausting to Miliukov and to the Americans. But such were the rules of the time.

In addition to Miliukov's course on Russia, there was a Japanese lecturer for a course on Japan. The Japanese lecturer attended Miliukov's lectures and Miliukov replied in kind. The former knew American psychology well and constantly maintained the listeners' interest with jokes. Apart from the jokes, he propagandized very capably on Japan's behalf. His lectures were very popular with the auditors.

A significantly smaller number of people signed up for Miliukov's course. But they listened very attentively and kept careful notes. By their questions after the lectures, Miliukov saw that they were mastering what they had heard.

There was a good amount of time left between the completion of the Chicago lectures and the commencement of the fall course at the Lowell Institute. Miliukov decided to use the time to polish his course for the Institute. For this reason, he went to Cambridge early. Lawrence Lowell, President of Harvard University, invited Miliukov to stay at his home and provided him with a comfortable room. He introduced him to the director of the University library. There Miliukov found much that was useful.

Lowell personally introduced Miliukov to the audience prior to the first lecture of his course. The auditors were not students primarily but adults wishing to supplement their life's experience and reading. After the lectures, they asked Miliukov many questions.

Miliukov united the two series of lectures into a book and titled it *Russia and Its Crisis* [*Rossiia i ee Krizis*]. This book was also translated into French.

Meanwhile, the indefatigable Crane gave Miliukov another task — to give a course on the Balkan Slavs at the University of Chicago. Crane knew of Miliukov's stay in Bulgaria and his trips to Macedonia. Miliukov agreed but said that he needed to enlarge his knowledge of the western section of the Balkan peninsula. It was agreed that Miliukov would visit these countries in the summer of 1904 and give the course in Chicago in the semester covering 1904-1905.

Miliukov decided to spend the time that was left before the Balkan trip in London. He suffered from the cold houses in winter, became sick, and spent some time in bed under a doctor's care. At the British Museum Miliukov decided to continue the third volume of *Outlines of Russian Culture*. He discovered many materials that he needed. Aside from his scholarly study, Miliukov made the acquaintance of a number of well known Russian émigrés then living in England — Kropotkin, Breshko-Breshkovskaia, N. V. Chaikovskii, and I. V. Shkalovskii.

Miliukov was visiting Kropotkin on February 10, 1904 when the first telegrams arrived in England of Japan's sudden attack on Port Arthur without a declaration of war. Kropotkin was very indignant at the Japanese treachery. Instinct and Russian national feeling arose in the anarchist and opponent of war and Russian policy. Miliukov expected anything, but not this.

But the most powerful impression made on Miliukov was not so much by the Russian emigration as by English political life. This he followed very closely.

Miliukov became especially interested in the moderate socialist group — the Fabians (gradualists). Sidney Webb, Bernard Shaw, and Ramsey McDonald, younger than the rest and the future Labor Party leader, belonged to it. Miliukov made closer acquaintance with the latter.

The main aim of Miliukov's western Balkan trip was to get to know the underground national movement which was then flaring up in the popular masses. The western Balkan Slavs were politically divided between Austria and Hungary. The Croations were included in Hungary, the Slovenes in Austria. In Bosnia and Herzegovina, occupied by Austria, the Serbs were of three faiths — Orthodox, Catholic, and Moslem.

The idea of a united Yugoslavia was already gaining strength among these splintered groups of Slavs. Open political activity was possible only in Croatia, the most cultured of the western Balkan regions.

Generally, Miliukov was able to collect abundant and valuable materials in the western Balkans — notes on his secret personal discussions, statistical data, and newspapers and journals.

In November Miliukov left for America. He arrived in Chicago in the depth of winter. In contrast to his first American trip, he now had to present at the University of Chicago a course for students, not for teachers. It was a special course on the Slavs. He had given five lectures when telegrams about "Bloody Sunday" in Petersburg (which occurred on January 9, 1905 — old style—) appeared in the newspapers.

Miliukov immediately felt that the turning point in laying the groundwork for the Russian revolution had come and that his duty as one of the leaders of Russian liberalism was to be where the events were. Miliukov announced to Crane that he could not complete the course but that he would remain in America for a time in order to prepare a book on the southern Slavic national movement (the theme of the course) for publication. This he did.

Miliukov's subsequent political activity, right up to the February revolution of 1917, blends in with Russian political life in general and this is not the place to mention it.

After the October revolution of 1917 and the civil war in Russia, Miliukov based himself in Paris. He became the editor of the newspaper, *The Latest News* [*Poslednie Novosti*]. This newspaper was a unifying center for the radical wing of the Russian emigration.

Its conservative counterweight was *Renascence* [*Vozrozhdenie*] whose editor was P. B. Struve.

After a while Miliukov was again drawn to scholarly work. In Paris in the years 1932-1933 a three volume *History of Russia* [*Istoriia Rossii*] was published in French at his initiative. It was an authoritative collective work in which Miliukov participated (Miliukov, Seignobos, Eisenmann. *Histoire de Russie*).

Simultaneously, his friends and admirers proposed that he rework and add to his *Outlines of Russian Culture*. Sufficient means were gathered for this. Miliukov aimed not only to use the new scholarly literature which had appeared from the beginning of the XX century and new publications of sources, but also to bring the exposition of the text to the current moment.

To a considerable degree he was able to accomplish this for volume two — *Faith, Creativity, and Education* [*Vera, Tvorchestvo, Obrazovanie*]. The volume turned out to be so big that it had to be split into two sections (1931).

Volume three (1930) — *Nationalism and Europeanism* [*Natsionalizm i Evropeizm*] was brought to the end of Catherine II's reign and her repressive measures against masonry, Novikov, and Radishchev.

The most difficult task was the re-working of volume one. In its first edition (1896), it represented a concise outline of Russia's geographic base, and the history of its government, economic system, military, and finances.

For the new edition Miliukov endeavored to develop this schematic essay into a major study. He began with the territory and the history of its colonization — the fates of the Eastern Slavs after they left their homeland. Miliukov places the original homeland of the Indo-Europeans, including the Slavs, in central Europe. According to his hypothesis, the Slavs moved from West to East along Russia's northern (forest) line. Miliukov researched an enormous quantity of linguistic and historical data for this study.

Mikhail Ivanovich Rostovtsev, who also worked on the question of the origin of the Russian State, highly valued Miliukov's work, though he arrived at different conclusions.

Miliukov was able to publish only the first part of the reworked first volume (Paris, 1937). Part two, *From Pre-History to History* was preserved in manuscript by B. I. El'kin, Miliukov's friend and executor.

El'kin entrusted its editing to N. E. Andreev. Andreev treated his task with great diligence and supplemented the bibliography with new data (*Outlines*, volume one, part 2, The Hague, 1964).

The book contains five chapters: "Southern Russia and the Nomads of the Steppe"; "The Forest Zone and the Settlement of the Eastern Slavs"; "The First Zone of Russian Expansion" (Volga and Ural areas); "The conquest of Siberia"; and "The Problem of a Russian Anthropological

Type."

In essence, the theme of the book might be called the study of the Russian nation's spatial development. The term *"spatial* development" ["Mestorazvitie"] was borrowed by Miliukov from the founder of the Eurasian trend in Russian historiography, P. N. Savitskii. He did give it a somewhat different formulation.

In his introduction Andreev attached significant importance to Miliukov's new conception for the subsequent development of Russian historical thought.

In the introduction to volume one, Miliukov labels his fundamental approach to history "sociological." Following N. Ia. Danilevskii, Miliukov rejects the idea of world history. He replaces it with the comparison of the histories of individual human societies. In Danilevskii's and Miliukov's opinion, traits can be found in the evolution of each national organism which are comparable to those in the evolution of another organism. It is here that Miliukov sees historical law.

Miliukov's life was split between politics and scholarship. In his subversive struggle against autocracy, Miliukov proved to be a brilliant and successful tactician. But he was unable to make use of his success. He was not able to stop in time so as to solidify positions already won.

Miliukov's chief accomplishments were scholarly. His early work on the Petrine reforms and the *Controversial Problems in the Financial History of the Muscovite State* [*Spornye Voprosy Finansovoi Istorii Moskovskogo Gosudarstva*] have not lost their importance to this day. His *Outlines of Russian Culture* still are a valuable introduction to the history of Russian thought and society for broad circles of readers.

# XX

## HISTORIANS OF THE SOUTHWESTERN REGION

In this chapter I write of a group of prominent Russian historians whose main contribution to Russian historical scholarship consisted of the study of southwestern Russia (the Ukraine and white Russia in today's terminology). The majority of them also produced major works in Russian history in general. Here I will discuss the work of the seven most important of these historians. Leontovich and Antonovich were the eldest among them. They were followed by Vladimirskii-Budanov, Liubavskii, Dovnar-Zapol'skii, and Lappo, (for Kostomarov, see Ch. XI above).

## LEONTOVICH (1833-1911)

Fedor Ivanovich Leontovich graduated from the juridical faculty of the University of Kiev. He received the master's degree for *A Historical Investigation into the Rights of Lithuanian-Russian Jews* (Kiev, 1863) [*Istoricheskoe Issledovanie o Pravakh Litovsko-Russkikh Evreev*], and the doctor's degree for his dissertation titled *Ancient Croatian-Dalmation Legislation* (Odessa, 1869) [*Drevnee Khorvato-Dalmatskoe Zakonodatel'stvo*]. He was professor of the history of Russian law at Odessa University. In 1891 he was given a chair at the University of Warsaw.

Leontovich was a thoughtful scholar of broad perspective. He wrote *The Peasants of South-Western Russia According to Lithuanian-Russian Law in the XV and XVI Centuries* (Kiev, 1863) [*Krest'iane-Iugo-Zapadnoi Rossii po Litovsko-Russkomu Pravu XV i XVI Vekov*] as well as *The Council of the Grand Lithuanian Princes* [*Rada Velikikh Kniazei Litovskikh*] (*Journal of the Ministry of Public Education*, 1907). His interests included eastern law. The following works pertain to this field: *The Ancient Oirotian Charter of Punishments* (Odessa, 1879) [*Drevnii Oiratskii Ustav Vzyskanii*], *Kalmyk Law* (Odessa, 1880) [*Kalmytskoe Pravo*], and *Customs of the Caucasian Mountaineers* (Odessa, 1880) [*Adaty Kavkazkikh Gortsev*].

Leontovich's most important contribution to Russian historical scholarship was his work, *The Family-Communal - Societal Character of the Political Customs of Ancient Russia* [*Zadruzhno-Obshchinnyi Kharakter Politicheskogo*

*Byta Drevnei Rusi*] (*Journal of the Ministry of Public Education*, 1867, IV, and 1874, VI and VII). In this work, Leontovich incidentally expressed the idea that the "*Ver'v*" of the *Russkaia Pravda* should be interpreted as a patriarchal community. This explanation of the term "*Ver'v*" was accepted by K. N. Bestuzhev-Riumin and M. M. Kovalevskii.

## ANTONOVICH (1834-1908)

Vladimir Bonifat'evich Antonovich, like Leontovich, was one of the pioneers in the field of the history of southwestern Rus'. But, in contrast to Leontovich, he was a Ukrainian nationalist, thought Ukrainians to be a separate nation, and idealized the Cossacks.

From 1863 to 1880 Antonovich was the editor-in-chief of the Temporary Commission for the Analysis of Ancient Documents in Kiev. From 1878, he was professor of Russian history at the University of Kiev. In 1862 he was a contributor to *Osnova* [*The Foundation*], a Petersburg journal edited by Kostomarov. This was the organ of moderate Ukrainian populism. Nevertheless, it was soon shut down by the government.

At the beginning of the 1870's in Kiev, the southwestern division of the Russian Geographical Society was founded. M. P. Dragomanov played an important role in it. For a time, it became the center of Ukrainian thought and scholarship. Together with Dragomanov, Antonovich published two volumes of *The Historical Songs of the South Russian Nation* [*Istoricheskie Pesni Iuzhno-Russkago Naroda*] (1874-1875).

The south-western branch of the Russian Geographical Society was closed by the government in 1876. Simultaneously, a decree was issued forbidding the publication of books in the Ukrainian language (except for *belles-letters*, ethnographic materials, and historical deeds).

Dragomanov was fired from the professorial staff of the University of Kiev and emigrated to Switzerland (see Ch. XXI below).

Antonovich's noteworthy works are: *An Essay on the Grand Duchy of Lithuania* [*Ocherk Istorii Velikogo Kniazhestva Litovskogo*] (Kiev, 1882) and *On the Origin of the Shliakheta Families in Western Russia* [*O Proiskhozhdenii Shliakhetskikh Rodov v Zapadnoi Rossii*] (*South-Western Russian Archives*, volume IV, Kiev, 1867).

## VLADIMIRSKII-BUDANOV (1838-1916)

Mikhail Flegontovich Vladimirskii-Budanov was the son of a village priest. He studied in the theological seminary in Tula, then in the Kiev Theological Academy, and later in the department of history and philology at the University of Kiev. He graduated from the university in 1864. This was a period of intellectual uplift in Russia — the period of Alexander II's reforms. The superintendent of the school district was the famous surgeon and pedagogue, N. I. Pirogov. The rector of the university was N. Kh. Bunge, who had been a professor of political economy and who was later to be the Minister of Finance.

In 1869 Vladimirskii-Budanov defended his master's thesis on the theme *German Law in Poland and Lithuania* [*Nemetskoe Pravo v Pol'she i Litve*]. This work was based on unpublished documents in the central Kiev archives.

After this, Vladimirskii-Budanov received a year's commission abroad. Thereupon, he was appointed professor of the history of Russian law at the Iaroslavl juridical lycée. There he wrote his doctoral dissertation on the government's relation to public education from the time of Peter the Great (1874). One year later, he transferred to Kiev, taking the chair of the history of Russian law.

In 1882 he was appointed editor-in-chief of Kiev's Temporary Commission for the Analysis of Ancient Documents. Five years later, he was elected chairman of the Historical Society of Nestor the Chronicler.

Vladimirskii-Budanov possessed a keen analytical mind, a critical sense in the study of sources, and an ability to express his thoughts clearly. Among his works were detailed investigations of individual problems as well as general studies. He was also an outstanding teacher. His works and lectures were always based on the sources, often on the archives.

Vladimirskii-Budanov developed his doctoral dissertation into a major study, *The Government and Public Education in Russia from the XVII Century to the Establishment of the Ministries.* [*Gosudarstvo i Narodnoe Obrazovanie v Rossii c XVII Veka do Uchrezhdeniia Ministerstv*] (1874). Of his specialized works I will note *The Pomest'ia of the Lithuanian State* [*Pomest'ia Litovskogo Gosudarstva*] (Kiev, 1889), and *The Legal Code of 1589. Its Significance and Sources* [*Sudebnik 1589 Goda. Ego Znachenie i Istochniki*] (Kiev, 1902).

His chief contribution to Russian Historiography is his *Survey of the History of Russian Law* [*Obzor Istorii Russkogo Prava*] (7th ed., Kiev, 1915). In the introduction to this work Vladimirskii-Budanov states that his book was conceived as a "handbook," not as a "textbook". A handbook must only aid in study. A textbook "includes the contents of a science which is necessary for the student. It has no place in institutions of higher learning." The book is divided into the following three parts: 1) the history of Russian public law; 2) the history of Russian criminal law; 3) the history of Russian civil law. An extensive bibliography is contained at the end. This work became a classic immediately and has not lost its significance to this day.

An indispensable supplement to it is the *Reader in the History of Russian Law* [*Khristomatiia po Istorii Russkogo Prava*] in three parts. It was compiled by Vladimirskii-Budanov and was issued several times. The first part contains such important legal monuments as *The Russian Law* [*Russkaia Pravda*] (XI-XII Centuries), *The Legal Charter of Pskov* [*Pskovskaia Sudnaia Gramota*] (1397-1467), and *The Legal Charter of Novgorod* [*Novgorodskaia Sudnaia Gramota*] (1471).

The second part contains the charter of privilege [these

are the *"Zemskie Ustavnye Gramoty"* which confirmed old customs, rights, and privileges — N. L.] of the Lithuanian-Russian State (1457-1509); *The Administrative and Criminal Charters of Belozersk* [*Ustavnaia i Gubnaia Belozerskie Gramoty*] (1488-1639) and *The Legal Code of Ivan the Terrible* [*Sudebnik Ivana Groznogo*] (1550).

The third part contained documents from the second half of the XVI and from the XVII centuries: *The Collection of Financial Decisions* [*Ukaznaia Kniga Vedomstva Kaznacheev*], *The Decisions of the Supreme Court for Criminal Affairs* [*Ustavnaia Kniga Razboinogo Prikaza*], and *The Collection of the Decisions of the Moscow Judicial and the Pomestnyi Prikazy* [*Ukaznye Knigi Zemskogo i Pomestnogo Prikazov*].

In the introduction to part one of the *Reader*, Vladimirskii-Budanov explains that this collection of documents is intended for educational use as a source for students having independent (so called practical) assignments in the history of Russian law. The aim of the commentaries on the text was to aid each student in making independent decisions. For a long time, this *Reader* was also an irreplaceable source for professors in conducting seminars on the history of Russian law. It is still useful today.

## LIUBAVSKII (1860-1936)

Matvei Kuz'mich Liubavskii studied in the Riazan seminary, then in the historico-philological department of Moscow University. He was Kliuchevskii's student. Upon graduating from the university, he was kept in Russian history to prepare for a professorship. Having passed the master's examinations, he was given the rank of *privat-docent*. In 1893 he defended his master's thesis on the theme *Regional Division and Local Administration in the Lithuanian-Russian State* [*Oblastnoe Delenie i Mestnoe Upravlenie Litovsko-Russkogo Gosudarstva*]. In 1901 he received his doctor's degree for his work, *The Lithuanian-Russian Seim* [*Litovsko-Russko Seim*], but was made professor only ten years later.

Under the re-organization of the Academy of Sciences by the Soviet government in 1928, it was decided to expand significantly the number of active members of the Academy of Sciences. An attendant decision meant to add Marxist scholars as members of the Academy of Sciences. The right to nominate new members was extended to "social organizations and institutions." The choices were the result of compromise between active members of the Academy and "social organizations." Liubavskii was one of the candidates chosen. But in 1931 he was arrested, expelled from the Academy, and exiled to Ufa where he died.

Liubavskii was totally engrossed in his scholarly work and in teaching at the university and the Advanced Courses for Women. Furthermore, he was an active member of the Moscow Society of Russian History and Antiquities where his main scholarly works were published. He participated energetically in this society's meetings, gave lectures, and shared in the disputations.

Liubavskii avoided non-academic social activity. He did not at all participate in the nation's political life.

Liubavskii's first major scholarly work was *Regional Division and Local Administration in the Lithuanian-Russian State to the Period of the First Lithuanian Statute* [*Oblastnoe Delenie i Mestnoe Upravlenie Litovsko-Russkogo Gosudarstva ko Vremeni Pervogo Litovskogo Statuta*] (1892-1893). To write this work, Liubavskii spent several years in the Moscow archives of the Ministry of Justice. There he studied the materials found in the volumes of the state archives of the Grand Duchy of Lithuania [*"Metrika Litovskaia"*]. He published some of these materials as an introduction. This work was epochal in the study of Western Russia and laid the groundwork for future studies of Liubavskii himself and other scholars as well.

There then followed another fundamental work — *The Lithuanian-Russian Seim* [*Litovsko-Russkii Seim*] (1911). On the firm foundation of his research, Liubavskii also wrote two valuable works of a more popular character —

*An Essay on the History of the Lithuanian-Russian State Through the Union of Liublin* [*Ocherk Istorii Litovsko-Russkogo Gosudarstva do Liublinskoi Unii Vkliuchitel'no*] (Moscow, 1910), and a parallel work, *Lectures on Ancient Russian History to the End of the XVI Century* [*Lektsii po Drevnei Russkoi Istorii do Kontsa XVI Veka*] (3rd ed., Moscow, 1918). This work is a collection of essays on the history of Kievan and north-eastern, i.e. Muscovite-Suzdal Rus'.

Liubavskii views Lithuanian Rus' as the direct successor of Kievan Rus' and Muscovite-Suzdal [Rus'] as the contrasting tendency, but one which flowed from the same channel.

Liubavskii considered the socio-political system of Lithuanian Rus' to be feudal, similar to western feudalism. He also found characteristics of feudalism in the north-eastern Rus' of the XIII-XV centuries.

"We find here the same institutions, the same relationships and attitudes as those in the feudal West. Sometimes they are fully developed. At other times they are in less definite forms. . . In its development, Russian feudalism did not go beyond initial embryonic forms which were not able to harden and solidify."

Liubavskii's last major work was published in 1929. Its title is: *The Formation of the Basic Territory of the Great Russian Nation: The Settlement and Unification of the Center* [*Obrazovanie Osnovnoi Gosudarstvennoi Territorii Velikorusskoi Narodnosti: Zaselenie i Obedinenie Tsentra*].

Most of the time, Liubavskii was very careful in his conclusions. He was sceptical of the various theories of different scholars on a number of issues. That is his attitude toward the theories of familial modes (Evers, Solov'ev, Kavelin), communal modes (Konstantiń Aksakov), and family-communal social modes (Leontovich). Liubavskii feels that all of these theories are one-sided.

"In my opinion," he writes, "each of the cited theories has a portion of truth. We must only isolate these parts and combine them into a coherent and integral view."

Liubavskii was a man of reserved character but he participated actively in academic life. He was Bogoslovskii's first opponent at the latter's master's debate (the second was Kizevetter). According to Kizevetter's memoirs, the debate was very interesting and was, in tone, that of scholarly comrades. The same thing happened at Bogoslovskii's doctoral defense with the very same opponents.

In his relations with students, Liubavskii was strict but fair and knew how to reconcile conflicts. The episode which occurred during the finals at Moscow University in 1904 is characteristic. During the world history examination, a sharp clash took place between the Professor, V. I. Ger'e, and his student and future historian of the Old Believers, S. P. Mel'gunov. Mel'gunov was late for the start of the examination. Ger'e told him he would now be examined last since he had missed his turn. Mel'gunov turned to Sokolov, chairman of the examining commission, with a demand that he be examined immediately. Sokolov became flustered. Liubavskii then interceded and was able to bring Mel'gunov to reason. The latter agreed to wait his turn.[13]

Liubavskii admired Solov'ev and his teacher Kliuchevskii but frequently disagreed with their theories.

On the question of Ivan the Terrible's *oprichnina*, Liubavskii combined the opinions of Kliuchevskii and Platonov and even sharpened Platonov's conclusions.

Kliuchevskii recognized and valued Liubavskii as an outstanding scholar. In his letter to Liubavskii written at the beginning of December 1909, Kliuchevskii calls him "my close friend." Evidently, however, Kliuchevskii and Liubavskii were never really close friends.

## DOVNAR-ZAPOL'SKII (1867-1934)

Mitrofan Viktorovich Dovnar-Zapol'skii graduated from the University of Kiev in 1894. In 1901 he defended his master's thesis titled *The State Economy of the Grand Duchy of Lithuania under the Jagellons* [*Gosudarstvennoe Khoziaistvo Velikogo Kniazhestva Litovskogo pri Iagellonakh*] and was made a professor at the University of Kiev. Four years later he received his doctor's degree for his study, *Essays on the Organization of Western-Russian Peasantry in the XVI Century* [*Ocherki po Organizatsii Zapadno-Russkogo Krest'ianstva v XVI Veke*]. Both of these works were based on archival materials.

Dovnar-Zapol'skii was a talented researcher and teacher of history. He wrote on Western-Russian and general Russian themes.

His work *The Polish-Lithuanian Union at Seims Prior to 1569* [*Pol'sko-Litovskaia Uniia na Semakh do 1569 Goda*] (Antiquities of the Moscow Archeological Society, Transactions of the Slavic Commission, 2) appeared in 1897. The first volume of his work, *The History of the Russian National Economy* [*Istoriia Russkogo Narodnogo Khoziaistva*] was published in 1911. This work was subjected to sharp criticism by the Marxist historian, M. N. Pokrovskii. Dovnar-Zapol'skii replied with a letter to the editor of the Moscow journal *Voice of the Past* [*Golos Minuvshego*] in 1913.

Dovnar-Zapol'skii was also interested in the history of Russian social and political ideology. In his anthology of articles, *From the History of Social Movements in Russia* [*Iz Istorii Obshchestvennykh Techenii V Rossii*] (2nd. ed., Kiev, 1910) there is, among others, his article on Granovskii. During the years 1906-1907, he published three volumes of materials on the Decembrists — *The Secret Society of the Decembrists* [*Tainoe Obshchestvo Dekabristov*], *Memoirs of the Decembrists* [*Memuary Dekabristov*], and *The Ideals of the Decembrists* [*Idealy Dekabristov*].

After this, he undertook a collective work of which he was the editor and one of the contributors: *Russian History in Essays and Articles* [*Russkaia Istoriia v Ocherkakh i Stat'iakh*] (3 vol. Moscow, 1909-1912). The majority of these articles are very valuable.

Dovnar-Zapol'skii participated actively at archeological conferences. It was in this connection that he closely followed the work of provincial learned archival commissions.

In conclusion, I will note that N. D. Polonskaia compiled the *Historical Cultural Atlas of Russian History* [*Istoriko-Kul'turnyi Atlas po Russkoi Istorii*] (Kiev, 1913) under his editorship.

## I. I. LAPPO (1869-1944)

Ivan Ivanovich Lappo was born in White Russia [Belorussia]. In 1892 he entered the historico-philologic department of the University of Petersburg. His teachers were S. F. Platonov, V. G. Vasil'evskii, and V. I. Lamanskii. His main tutor was Platonov at whose recommendation Lappo was left at the university to prepare for professorship. Under Platonov's supervision, Lappo wrote his first scholarly work, *The District of Tver in the XVI Century: Its Population and Domain* [*Tverskii Uezd v XVI Veke. Ego Naselenie i Vidy Zemel'nogo Vladenie*] (Moscow, 1894). This thorough investigation was based on the statistical processing of the census books [*"pistsovye knigi"*].

After this, Lappo occupied himself with the history of the Grand Duchy of Lithuania from the Union of Liublin to the death of Stefan Batorii (1569-1588) (2 vol., Petersburg, 1902). This was his maters's thesis.

In 1905 Lappo was invited to take the chair of history at Iur'evsk University. There he continued to study the history of Western Russia. The task that he set this time was to clarify the role of the local shliakhta [szlachta] organizations which sent deputies to the lower house of the Seim (*"posol'-skaia izba"*).

Thus arose his second fundamental work, *The Grand Duchy of Lithuania in the Second Half of the XVI Century. The Lithuanian-Russian Povet [district] and Its District Assembly* [*Velikoe Kniazhestvo Litovskoe vo Vtoroi Polovine XVI Veka. Litovsko-Russkii Povet (Uezd) i Ego Seimik*] (Iur'ev, 1911 — his doctoral dissertation).

Lappo took a very active part in the life of Iur'evsk University. He established close relations with his colleagues — both professors and students.

After peaceful life and work, a difficult time came —
the devastation of the civil war (1918-1920).

In 1919 Lappo moved to Prague where the so-called
"Russian action" was already commencing. With the support
of President Masaryk and the Czech government, a powerful
center of Russian culture in exile was created.

In Prague, Lappo was chosen to be a member of the
Russian Education Board (a professorial council). During his
years in Prague, Lappo wrote many valuable works in Czech.
His extensive article, "An Essay on the Development of Rus-
sian Historical Science" ["Ocherk Razvitiia Russkoi Istori-
cheskoi Nauki"] was published in 1922 in *Cesky Casopis
Historichký*, vol. XXVIII, a Czech historical journal. Another
Czech periodical, *Sbornik ved pravnich a statnich* [*An-
thology of Juridical and Government Sciences*] published
Lappo's articles "The Lithuanian Statute: Its Sanctioning in
1588" ["Litovskii Statut i Ego Sanktsionirovanie v 1588
Godu"] (1922) and "The Fundamental Laws of the Grand
Duchy of Lithuania and of Poland" ["Osnovnye Zakony
Velikogo Kniazhestva Litovskogo i Pol'shi"] (1923).

In 1924 Lappo published a small book in Russian in
Prague. It was significant in content and profoundly thought
out. This book, *Western Russia and Its Unification with
Poland in their Historical Past* [*Zapadnaia Rossiia i ee Soedinenie s Pol'shei v ikh Istoricheskom Proshlom*], in a
sense provides the key to understanding the complicated
problems of Western Russian history.

In 1928 Lappo participated in the fourth congress of
Russian Academic Organizations in Belgrade (Oct. 16-23).
Lappo was a member of this conference's ruling board. At
one of the sessions he lectured on "The Lithuanian-Russian
State and Poland in the XVII Century" ["Litovsko-Russkoe
Gosudarstvo i Pol'sha v XVII Stoletii"].

This lecture was published with the title of "The Equalization of Rights of the Grand Duchy of Lithuania with those
of the Polish Crown in 1697" (*Transactions of the Russian
Educational Institute in Belgrade*, I., 1930). Lappo begins
his article with an analysis of the Union of Liublin in 1569

and interprets it in a new way. It was usually thought (not only in Polish historiography) that the incorporation of Lithuania into Poland resulted from a decision of the Liublin Seim. In reality, as Lappo proved, something else happened. The plan to incorporate Lithuania into Poland, presented by the Poles, was decisively rebuffed by the Lithuanian delegation.

Lappo writes: "In such a state of affairs, the Union of Liublin naturally represented a compromise between Polish and Lithuanian demands which was full of contradictions. It did not co-ordinate them organically. Having declared the merging of two governments and nations . . . the act of union simultaneously recognized the Grand Duchy of Lithuania as possessing national, not provincial, rights. Among these were the ancient State title and seal, ancient State posts including those of previously existing ministries, a separate army and military command, a State Treasury and fiscal administration."

Twenty one years later, the significance of the Grand Duchy of Lithuania's national independence was consolidated by the Third Lithuanian Statute. This Statute never mentioned the Union of Liublin and recognized Poles to be "foreigners."

Throughout the XVII century, the Polish-Lithuanian Seim acted not as the parliament of one State but as a congress of the representatives of two nations. The Lithuanian members ("*posly*") of the Seim protested every Polish attempt to impose their decisions on them.

Finally, on March 9, 1652, Sitsinskii, a Lithuanian member, protested that the Seim was invalid and left Warsaw.

Lappo explains: "The Seim was frustrated by the vote of one delegate of The Grand Duchy of Lithuania. The *liberum veto* commenced its destructive effect on the Commonwealth of Poland and Lithuania."

The culmination of the Grand Duchy of Lithuania's independent national life was the already cited Lithuanian demand: "The Equalization of Rights of the Grand Duchy of Lithuania with those of the Polish Crown." It was presented in 1697 to Augustus II, the newly elected king.

This document agreed on the extent of the obligations of Lithuania and Poland for the mutual needs of the federated Commonwealth. Poland offically recognized the Lithuanian Statute of 1588 to be the fundamental law of the Grand Duchy.

In 1928, Russian activity in Prague began to diminish gradually. Some of the Russian professors found positions in Czech universities and schools. The majority moved to other countries.

In 1933 Lappo was invited to the University of Kovno in the capacity of *privat-docent* and moved to Kovno [Kaunas].

There Lappo occupied himself fully with research into and preparation for publication of the Lithuanian Statute of 1588 (the so-called Third Lithuanian Statute). This was the culmination of his scholarly life.

The stimulus for the study of this statute was the proposal given him in 1912 by M. A. D'iakonov — to prepare a critical edition of the text of this document. The intention was to publish it at the Academy of Sciences.

Lappo agreed and began by studying the Statute's origin in connection with its text. He then proceeded to work on the text.

As stated above, Lappo's work in Iur'ev was disrupted by the civil war of 1918-1920 and his move to Prague. In Prague he could only work on the Statute sporadically. He devoted himself fully to it in Kovno.

Lappo divided his work into two volumes: 1) research into the Third Lithuanian Statute and 2) a critical edition of its text.

The research itself is a monumental work of more than 1,000 pages, split into two parts. In the introduction to part one, Lappo states: "In view of the fact that the author had to solve the lengthy series of questions linked to the Third Lithuanian Statute in a manner totally at variance with the existing literature about them, he felt it necessary to make it as easy as possible for the reader to verify the propositions expressed in his work. Hence, he attempted not to limit himself to simple footnotes with appropriate page references of cited works and published sources or to simple references to manuscript sources. In the majority of cases he has cited the corresponding passages."

In part one of volume one Lappo first investigates the history of the preparation and the composition of the Second Lithuanian Statute (1566). He then proceeds to the Union of Liublin of 1569 and only then does he discuss the development of the Third Statute's final draft.

In part two Lappo analyzes the content and the idea of the fundamental laws of the Third Statute and the order of its confirmation.

Then there follows a chapter on the Vilensk press of the Mamoniches (at which the Statute was printed) and a chapter on the typographical technology of the Statute's first edition. In the same chapter Lappo characterizes the Russian language in which the Statute is written.

"This was the language used by the Russian population of the Grand Duchy of Lithuania. Over the course of several centuries it was accepted as the State language." (p. 337).

The last chapter is devoted to the history of scholarship dealing with the Third Statute from the beginning of the XIX century to the 1930's.

Lappo's work was published in Kovno during the years 1934-1936. The critical edition of the text of the Statute followed in 1938.

During the Second World War, Lappo moved from Kovno to Dresden.

## A. Ia. EFIMENKO (1848-1918)

The family-communal theory of Leontovich has an adherent in Aleksandra Iakovlevna Efimenko.

A. Ia. Stavrovskaia (Efimenko by marriage) was born in the family of an official of the Arkhangel'sk province. She studied at the Arkhangel'sk gymnasium. She was a teacher in Kholmogory where she married Petr Savvich Efimenko, the exiled ethnographer.

Her main interest was the study of folk customs, beliefs, and legal concepts in the extreme Russian north.[14]

She was fascinated by "the great Russian tribe's exceptional tendency toward collectivism [and] its ability to create social forms." From the study of artels in the north, she moved to the study of the problem of the origin of the village landed commune. She plunged into the archives for two years. The result was her famous work, *Peasant Landownership in the Far North* [*Krest'ianskoi Zemlevladenie na Krainem Severe*] (in the journal *Russkaia Mysl'*, 1882).

She valued this work above all of her other works on common law.

In the meantime her husband's exile ended and they moved to Little Russia. Efimenko now turned to the study of southern Russia and the Ukrainian people. Her studies in this field were gathered in her books *Southern Russia* [*Iuzhnaia Rus'*] (2 vol., 1905) and the *History of the Ukrainian Nation* [*Istoriia Ukrainskogo Naroda*] (two issues, 1906).

In the introduction to the latter book, Efimenko found it necessary to note that "the author of this work devoted to southern Russian history must not be suspected of southern-Russian national subjectivism. This should be so because of her great Russian background as well as by the sympathies discovered in the study of northern Russian juridical folklore."

At the archeological congress of 1893 in Vil'nius, Efimenko lectured on peasant courts in the left-bank Ukraine. This presentation led to an impressive ovation.

At the proposal of V. G. Vasil'evskii, the session's chairman, the congress welcomed her as an outstanding Russian woman who had already made herself a celebrated name in scholarship.

Around 1907, Efimenko moved to Petersburg. Her husband died in 1908. She joined the staff of the Advanced Courses for Women.

In 1910, on the occasion of her forty years of teaching, the University of Khar'kov presented her with a doctor's degree. Efimenko primarily taught the history of southern Russia and held a seminar on juridically related themes. During the revolution and the civil war Efimenko moved to Khar'kov. There she was killed at the end of 1918. At this time, Khar'kov was already under bolshevik control.[15]

## XXI

## M. P. DRAGOMANOV (1841-1895)

Mikhail Petrovich Dragomanov occupies a special place in the history of Russian social thought and in Russian historiography. His image is double sided. He felt himself to be both Russian and Ukrainian.

Dragomanov was a writer and scholar of broad vision and diverse interests. He was historian, geographer, publicist, literary critic, and expert in national poetry and folklore.

Dragomanov was born in Gadiach in the province of Poltava to a family descended from Cossack elders. In XIX century terminology, this was a noble family.

He studied at the Poltava gymnasium and at the University of Kiev. Upon graduation, he was appointed instructor in geography in the Kiev gymnasium, then made a *docent* at the University of Kiev in world history. He wrote several articles in defense of the usage of the Malo-Russian (Ukrainian in present day terminology) tongue in public schools. He felt that this necessity derived not from the view-point of Ukrainian nationalism but from the pedagogical aspect. (This was similar to the approach taken by such prominent Russian teachers as Ushinskii and Vodovozov).

In 1870 Dragomanov defended his master's thesis on the theme "The Question of the Historical Significance of the Roman Empire and Tacitus" ["Vopros ob Istoricheskom Znachenii Rimskoi Imperii i Tatsit"]. For its time, this is a marvelous scholarly investigation which has not been sufficiently valued.[16]

After the defense of the thesis, Dragomanov received

an education assignment abroad.

Returning to Kiev, Dragomanov participated actively in the just opened division of the Russian Geographical Society. Governmental circles in Petersburg were suspicious of the section's activity, for they perceived Ukrainophilism in it. This branch of the Society was closed in 1876. Dragomanov was removed from the professorial staff of the University of Kiev.

He then decided to emigrate and went to L'vov where he became friends with Ivan Franko, the young Ukrainian poet. They both took active part in Galician political life, attempting to create an Ukrainian people's socialist party.[17]

Dragomanov did not stay long in Galicia. The political situation there was tense. He could not occupy himself with literature and scholarship. Furthermore, he was always under the threat of arrest.

In 1877, Dragomanov moved to Geneva. There he established a Russian-Ukrainian press.

As he personally declared in his autobiography, he accepted the following principle for the division of his writings into Russian and into Ukrainian:

1) To write in Ukrainian all that related directly to the Ukraine and to the spread of socialistic ideas within it.

2) To write in Russian on topics of a liberal-political bent, observing all events which agitated the Russian reader.

Dragomanov wrote his autobiography in Russian but it was published in Ukrainian translation.[18]

In 1889, the Bulgarian government invited Dragomanov to take the chair of world history at the University of Sofiia. In all likelihood the initiator of the request was the Bulgarian professor, Ivan Shishmanov, who was married to Dragomanov's daughter Lidiia. At Sofiia Dragomanov taught in Russian for four years with much success.

In 1894 there was a triumphal celebration of his thirtieth anniversary in scholarly and literary work. One year later he died from a heart attack.

Like Kostomarov, Dragomanov attached great historical significance to Western Russia — the triangle of interrelations among Poland, the Ukraine and Belorussia, and Russia.

His major historico-sociological work, *"Historical Poland and Great Russian Democracy"* [*"Istoricheskaia Pol'sha i Veliko-russkaia Demokratiia"*] (Geneva, 1882; reissued in Paris, 1905) is devoted to this theme.

In the introduction Dragomanov discusses the relations of the Poles to the Russian revolutionary movement of 1860-1863. There then follows an analysis of the geographic conditions of Eastern Europe and a historical survey of the vacillation of the Ukrainian-Belorussian population between Poland and Moscow from the XV through the XVII centuries.

Later Dragomanov stresses the concomitance of views of the Polish aristocracy and great Russian bureaucracy and society on the so-called Western region and on the independent origin of the renascence of the plebeian nations of this region in the XIX century.[19]

The next two chapters of Dragomanov's book are devoted to A. I. Herzen and his relationship to the Polish revolution of 1863.

"It is apparent in everything," writes Dragomanov, "that Herzen possessed specious information on the history and ethnography of the 'Western Russian provinces'. It is likely that he did not, for example, even read the works of Kostomarov. His reserve of factual knowledge on this subject did not exceed that possessed by the average Russian metropolitan literateur, i.e. it was quite meager."

But in Dragomanov's opinion, Herzen had an inborn feeling for the understanding of political phenomena and a great reserve of observations on the political life of the contemporary era. "Taken together, this, in a peaceful time, provided him with the possibility of properly surmising the basic characteristics of the Polish question in Russia — the truth and falsehoods of the strivings of Polish patriots of all shades "whom he had occasion to meet."

At the same time he recognized that only Poles had the right to decisive say on the question of Poland's fate. Dragomanov writes: "The whole problem is that Herzen's understanding of what truly constituted Poland was quite vague. Despite all his respect for nationalities above that for government he was still capable of forgetting that the words "Poland" and "Russia" represent governments, not peoples. When the Polish revolution started, Herzen (partly influenced by Bakunin) came to the conclusion that Polish victory would lead to the commencement of revolution in Russia. Both Herzen and Bakunin were pleased with the indefinite declaration of the Warsaw committee regarding the "guarantee of the broadest development of their nationality and language to the fraternal peoples of Lithuania and Russia, united with Poland."

Herzen published the declaration of the Polish revolutionary committee in *The Bell* [*Kolokol*]. In his own name he published an appeal for Russian officers to transfer to Polish service. There were several officers who did so. Naturally, all of them lost their lives.

In view of such a policy, Herzen undermined his popularity even in radical Russian circles. The circulation of *The Bell* dropped immediately and Herzen ceased to publish it for a time.

Two years after his book, *Historical Poland and Great Russian Democracy*, Dragomanov published *An Experiment in an Ukrainian Politico-Social Program* [*Opyt Ukrainskoi Politiko-Sotsial'noi Programmy*] in Geneva. This work was appended to the 1905 edition of *Historical Poland and Great Russian Democracy*.

The title of "Ukrainian" given by Dragomanov does not encompass the whole breadth of the program. Evidently, Dragomanov initially approached his task from the Ukrainian viewpoint, but later applied the same principles to the composition of the All-Russian regional federation.

Dragomanov even compiled a model list of such regions. It is:
1) the Northern (the Arkhangel'sk and Vologda provinces).
2) the Lake (the provinces of Olonetsk, Petersburg, Pskov, Novgorod, and Tver).
3) the Baltic (Estland, Lifland, and Kurland).

4)  the Lithuanian (the provinces of Kovno, Suval'sk, and the north-western half of the Vilensk province).

5)  the Polish (the provinces of the Polish kingdom).

6)  the Belorussian (the provinces of Vitebsk and Mogilev and a large part of the provinces of Grodnensk and Smolensk).

7)  the Forest (parts of the Sedletsk, Minsk, Liublin, and Volynsk provinces).

8)  the Kiev (the south-western part of the Volynsk province, the Kiev and Chernigov provinces, and a large part of the province of Poltava).

9)  the Odessa (the provinces of Podol'sk, Bessarabia, and Kherson, the western part of the Ekaterinoslavsk province, and a large part of the Taura province).

10) the Khar'kov (part of the Taura, Ekaterinoslavsk, Poltava, Kursk, and Voronezh provinces and the whole province of Khar'kov).

11) the Moscow (the provinces of Moscow, Riazan, Orlov, Kaluga, and Smolensk − exluding the Belorussian provinces).

12) the Nizhegorod (the provinces of Nizhegorod, Iaroslavl, Kostroma, and Vladimirsk).

13) the Kazan (the provinces of Viatka, Kazan, Simbirsk, and Samara).

14) the pre-Urals (the provinces of Perm, Ufa, and Orenburg).

15) the Saratov (the provinces of Saratov, Tambov, Penza, and Astrakhan).

16) the Caucasus (the province of Stavropol and the Transcaucasus).

17) Western Siberia.

18) Eastern Siberia.

19) the Cossack lands (the Don, Kuban, Terek, and Ural).

20) The Central Asian. These regions, writes Dragomanov, "are too diverse in their populations and have just recently been annexed. They must be governed according to their special statutes. Where possible, measures of autonomy must be applied."

I have given this list of regions *in toto* since it has great importance in understanding Dragomanov's ideas on the nature and essence of the federal principle.

Dragomanov's "regions" do not coincide with ethnic boundaries (or coincide just partly). The majority of them are not territorially large. This, in his opinion, was to impart a more solid and binding character to the All-Russian Federation.

According to Dragomanov's plan, this federation was to be founded on the democratic principles of political freedom and equality.

The words *political freedom*, says Dragomanov, must be understood to mean:
A)   The rights of man and of the citizen — the inviolability of the body for shameful punishments and the death penalty; the inviolability of the personality and of one's home to the police without a court order.
B)   The inviolability of private letters and telegrams.
C)   The freedom to choose one's residence and occupation.
D)   The inviolability of nationality (language) in private and public life.
E)   The freedom of conscience (faith and disbelief) and of every public worship and ritual not offensive to social custom.
F)   Freedom of speech, press, theater, and education.
G)   The freedom to gather without thereby violating order and security.
H)   The freedom of association and membership in societies.

According to Dragomanov, the federation's governmental system was to be established along the lines of self-government beginning from the village and municipal commune right up to the State Duma.

To carry out this program in practice, Dragomanov thought it necessary to organize the public opinion of the moderate circles of Russian society as a counterweight to revolutionary terrorism. His ideas were one of the sources for the liberal movement in Russia which led to the Revolution of 1905 and to the establishment of the State Duma.

## XXII

## A. S. LAPPO-DANILEVSKII (1863-1919)

Aleksandr Sergeevich Lappo-Danilevskii was a descendant of nobles from the Ekaterinoslavsk province. He was born on the Udachnoe estate near the village of Malo-Sofievka in the Verkhnedneprovsk district. His father was the marshal of the nobility, for several three year terms. His mother, Natal'ia Fedorovna (Chuikevich by her maiden name) was also of the province's nobility and lived in Udachnoe with her family. It was there that he received a domestic education. After the family's one and a half year stay in Switzerland, Lappo-Danilevskii entered the Simferopol gymnasium from which he graduated with a gold medal in 1882.

While in the upper classes of the gymnasium, aside from the required assignments, he read much and, as he writes in his autobiography,[20] "was becoming somewhat acquainted with philosophy through Lewis' book, with the systems of Kant and Mill, and by means of the influence of Taylor, Spencer, and Grote discovered a proclivity toward the study of primitive culture and the ancient world."

Upon graduating from the gymnasium, Lappo-Danilevskii entered the historico-philologic department of the University of Petersburg. He graduated in 1886 and was kept at the department for professorial training.

While still a student, in connection with his interest in primitive culture, he compiled "A Review of Scythian Antiquities" ["Obozrenie Skifskikh Drevnostei"] (Petersburg, 1887). Six years later he published a study of the antiquities of the Karagodeuashakh burial mound in the pre-Kuban district (IV - III c. B. C. ). This work appeared in the *Materials on the Archeology of Russia* [*Materialy po Arkheologii Rossii*] published by the Archeological Commission (No. 13, 1893).

For his master's thesis Lappo-Danilevskii decided to take a theme from the Moscow period. Thus arose his fundamental work *The Organization of Direct Taxation in the Muscovite State from the Time of Troubles to the Reform Era* [*Organizatsiia Priamogo Oblozheniia v Moskovskom Gosudarstve so Vremeni Smuty i do Epokhi Preobrazovanii*] (Petersburg, 1890).

At that time, the financial history of the Muscovite State had been little worked on. At the basis of his thesis were extensive archival materials. Lappo-Danilevskii subjected a whole series of debatable points to study. This work was the foundation for subsequent researchers of the Muscovite State system and finances.

Upon defense of his master's thesis, Lappo-Danilevskii began, as a *privat-docent*, to lecture on Russian history at the University of Petersburg. He also did this at the Historico-Philological Institute where he was elected professor in 1891.

In 1899, Lappo-Danilevskii was chosen adjunct at the Academy of Sciences. Three years later he was made extraordinary academician, and ordinary academician in 1905. Having become a member of the Academy of Sciences, he left the Historico-Philological Institute but continued to lecture at the university.

Lappo-Danilevskii's subsequent activity went in two directions: his personal scholarly creativity and the organization of the work of other scholars and learned societies and institutions.

Let us first look at Lappo-Danilevskii's major scholarly works.

He did not cease studying the Muscovite period. But, besides that, he studied the historical problems of the XVIII century. To the Moscow period belong his article, "Research Into the History of Attaching Peasants to the Land" (1901) and the long and very valuable "Essay on the History of the Education of the Major Categories of the Peasant Population in Russia" (1905). This included the characterization of these categories as they formed in the XVIII century.

Of Lappo-Danilevskii's works pertaining to the XVIII

century, it is necessary to mention his "Russian Industrial and Trade Companies in the First Half of the XVIII Century" ["Russkie Promyshlennye i Torgovye Kompanii v Pervoi Polovine XVIII Veka"] (1899) and "The Collection and the Code of Laws of the Russian Empire Compiled in the Years 1775-1783" ["Sobranie i Svod Zakonov Rossiiskoi Imperii, Sostavlennye v 1775-1783 Godakh"] (*Journal of the Ministry of Public Education*, 1897). This attempt at codification of Russian laws during the reign of Catherine II was a continuation of the work of the famous Legal Commission of 1767-1768 which did not complete its task.

From the mid 1890's, Lappo-Danilevskii began to give a course at the university on the theory of social and historical sciences. In this connection, he studied the problems of sociological and historical method in his seminar. He particularly stressed cause and effect, chance, and evolution. Several published works by his students derived from this seminar.

In this field, he wrote a study of the fundamental philosophical principles of A. Comte (published in the anthology titled *Problems of Idealism* [*Problemy Idealizma*], 1902).

Beginning in 1906, he began to teach a course on historical methodology. Two volumes were published (1910 and 1913).

The first deals with the theory of historical knowledge in its two principal directions, the pneumatetic and the idiographic, and also with the doctrine of the object of historical knowledge. The second volume contains an analysis of the main problems of historical study.

In addition, he held a seminar on archeography (on the diplomacy of private documents). Several young scholars came out of this seminar. Among them was S. N. Valk.

We turn to Lappo-Danilevskii's organizational activity. As an academician and a member of the Archeographic Commission he played a prominent role in planning the tasks of Russian historical scholarship and the publication of historical materials.

He headed two new scholarly enterprises — the *Documentary Collection of the former College of Economics* [*Sbornik Gramot Byvshei Kollegii Ekonomii*] and *Documents of Russian Legislation* [*Pamiatniki Russkogo Zakonodatel'stva*]. Moreoever, he supervised the publication of *Letters and Papers of Peter the Great* [*Pis'ma i Bumagi Petra Velikogo*] and the anthology *Russia and Italy* [*Rossiia i Italiia*].

In 1900, he presented the Academy of Sciences with a plan to publish Russian archival documents of the XV-XVIII centuries. Initially he projected the publication of the materials of the former College of Economics.[21]

His reports on the preparatory work for the publication of these materials are to be found in the *Proceedings* [*Izvestiia*] of the Academy of Sciences.

Up to his death (1919) Lappo-Danilevskii was able to complete for publication the first volume of the *Documentary Collection of the former College of Economics*. It was published in 1922.

Lappo-Danilevskii also participated in archeological conferences. He was the chairman of one of the sections of the Novgorod congress of 1911. He attentively followed the development of the learned activity of the provincial archival commissions. He took part in their creation (see above, Ch. XVII).

Lappo-Danilevskii's organizational activity was not limited to Russia. He was a member of the International Sociological Institute. In 1913 he took part in the International Historical Congress in London and gave a lecture on the "Development of the Idea of the State in Russia from the Time of Troubles to the reforms of the XVIII century."[22]

Petersburg was scheduled to be the conference site of the 1918 International Historical Congress. Lappo-Danilevskii was appointed chairman of the executive committee for the arrangement of this congress. The congress could not convene because of World War I.

For Europe and America, Lappo-Danilevskii was a living connection with Russian historical scholarship. When any

foreign scholars came to Russia for archival or library research, he first contacted Lappo-Danilevskii at the Academy
of Sciences. He introduced the scholar to Russian colleagues,
and education institutions.
   He invited many of these scholars to evening receptions
at his home. During the years 1915-1916, I attended these
learned discussions which, as I recall, were held on Mondays.
The meetings were not crowded and were very beneficial to
the participants.
   Aleksandr Sergeevich first talked with each guest
individually. The others, in the meantime, talked among
themselves.
   The individual discussions were extremely valuable for
the participants. Each one had the opportunity to speak of
his study's progress and get Aleksandr Sergeevich's advice
on literature and the nature of the required sources.
   There followed a general discussion in which Lappo-
Danilevskii participated enthusiastically. Scholarly tidings,
new directions in historical science, and historical methodology were talked about.
   I tried never to skip any of these evenings, but this
was not always possible. Among the steady visitors were M.
A. D'iakonov, historian of Russian law and the archeographer, S. N. Valk. (The latter was in Lappo-Danilevskii's
seminar on the diplomacy of private documents).
   Foreign scholars were frequently in attendance. Among
them were two Americans — Frank Golder (who was studying Siberian history) and R. G. Lord (who was researching
the history of Poland). These discussions were an echo of
Lappo-Danilevskii's broad organizational activity, be it
Russian or international.

## XXIII

## THE PHILOSOPHY OF HISTORY

   From the middle of the 1820's to the 1860's inclusive,
the main thrust of Russian historico-philosophic thought

was reflective of Hegelianism's influence.

The sociological positivist trend was represented far more weakly. In contrast, the positivist trend in Russian social thought comes to the forefront in the 1870's and 1880's. One of the acute questions is the relationship between society and the individual.

The most prominent representatives of the sociological trend in Russian philosophy were N. I. Kareev, P. L. Lavrov, and N. K. Mikhailovskii.

Great significance to the philosophy of history was also attached by Mikhail Matveevich Stasiulevich (1826-1911), historian of the Middle Ages and ancient Greece.

His major work in this field was *An Experiment in the Historical Observation of the Main Systems of the Philosophy of History* [*Opyt Istoricheskogo Obzora Glavnykh Sistem Filosofii Istorii*] (1866). It went from Augustine to Buckle. In this book, he limited himself to fundamental systems which, in his opinion, "had the broadest and most widespread influence on historical thought. . . and which, simultaneously, represented a certain link transferring its task from one generation to another."

In the presence of so many different theories, Stasiulevich still found it possible to reduce them to two categories: the theory of constant historical immutability and the theory of constant historical progress.

Nikolai Ivanovich Kareev (1850-1931) was born in Moscow. His youth was spent in the Smolensk province. He studied at the fifth Moscow gymnasium. In 1869 he entered Moscow University where his principal instructor was V. I. Ger'e. Kareev was an active participant in his seminar. It was then that he developed an interest in the era of the French Revolution of 1789.

Kareev wrote his candidate's thesis on the topic of the state of the French peasantry prior to the Revolution. Upon graduating from the university, Kareev stayed at the history department to prepare for professorship. He passed his master's examination in 1876 and received an assignment to go to France in order to write his master's thesis. This work,

*Peasants and the Peasant Problem in France in the Last Quarter of the XVIII Century* [*Krest'iane i Krest'ianskii Vopros vo Frantsii v Posledniiu Chetvert' XVIII Veka*] (1879) was based on archival materials previously unused. French historians recognized Kareev's work to be groundbreaking for the subsequent study of the peasant question in France.

After defense of his master's thesis, Kareev received a chair at the University of Warsaw where he taught until 1881. He then moved to Petersburg. He was first given a chair at the Alexandrian Lycée, then at the University of Petersburg and at Bestuzhev's courses for women.

By order of the Minister of Public Education, Kareev was removed from the university in 1899. It was only in 1906 that he returned to a university post. In 1910 the Academy of Sciences elected him associate member.

Kareev turned to his ideas on the philosophy of history in the writing of his doctoral dissertation. The work was published as *Fundamental Problems of the Philosophy of History* [*Osnovnye Voprosy Filosofii Istorii*] (2 vol., 1883).

The first part chiefly contains the history and criticism of "historiosophic ideas" and an analysis of the methods of the philosophy of history. The second part contained a criticism of contemporary teachings in biology, anthropology, psychology, and sociology and the general views of progress which were based on them. In this work, Kareev produced a critical review of an enormous amount of literature on the subject.

Moreover, he anticipated the ideas of the German philosophers Windelband and Rickert. Some ten years before Windelband, Kareev established the distinction between two categories of knowledge — between (in his terminology) the pneumatological and the phenomenological (history belonged to the latter).

Windelband's corresponding terms are pneumatetic and diographic. Another work by Kareev was the continuation of his *Fundamental Problems of the Philosophy of History*. It was titled *The Essence of Historical Progress and the Role of the Personality in History* [*Sushchnost' Istoricheskogo Progressa i Rol' Lichnosti v Istorii*] (1890). In this book Kareev strove to clarify "how one personality acts upon another and why isolated examples of such activity represent extreme inequality." Kareev recognized the relative independence and originality of the personality without rejecting the action of general causes and influences upon it. The "hero" acts on the crowd, the crowd on the "hero." Kareev defines the essence of historical process as being the interaction of individuals and the environment.

Kareev's first book (*Fundamental Problems of the Philosophy of History*) made a great impression and led to fervent debates.

The second, (*The Essence of Historical Progress. . .*), to which he attached primary importance, passed almost unnoticed. This was a great disappointment to him.

Kareev was an indefatigable teacher and a prolific writer. His series called *Typological Courses* [*Tipologicheskie Kursy*] is interesting. In it he examined the various forms of government. Included in this series were: "The City-State of the Ancient World" ["Gosudarstvo-Gorod Antichnogo Mira"] (1903), "The Monarchies of the Ancient East and the Greco-Roman World" ["Monarkhii Drevnego Vostoka i Greko-Rimskogo Mira"] (1904), "The Patrimonial State and Class Monarchy in the Middle Ages" ["Pomest'e Gosudarstvo i Soslovnaia Monarkhiia Srednikh Vekov"] (1906), and "Western European Absolute Monarchy in the XVI-XVIII Centuries" ["Zapadno-Evropeiskaia Absoliutnaia Monarkhiia XVI-XVIII Vekov"].

His multiple work, *The History of Western Europe in Modern Times* [*Istoriia Zapadnoi Evropy v Novoe Vremia*], was of major importance. It dealt with cultural and social relations and appeared in seven weighty volumes (1892-1917).

## PETR LAVROVICH LAVROV (1823-1900)

Lavrov was the son of a general, a rich Russian landowner. As a youth, Petr Lavrovich entered the artillery school from which he graduated at age nineteen. He stood out through his exceptional erudition. Aside from mathematics and natural science, he also studied the history of scientific thought.

In 1844 Lavrov was appointed teacher of mathematics at the artillery school. Later, he was given the rank of professor. Lavrov was famous for his radical political views. In 1861 he was arrested and exiled to the Vologda province. There he wrote his *Historical Letters* which, pseudonymously under the name of "Mirtov," were published in Petersburg in 1870. These *Letters* had great influence on Russian radical youth.

Lavrov himself strove only toward scholarly work. Aware that under the conditions of the Vologda exile he could not engage in scholarship, he escaped abroad and settled in Paris. He truly did occupy himself with sociology. But, in 1872, he bowed to the request of a delegation of his adherents and founded a revolutionary journal, *Forward* [*Vpered*]. Despite this diversion, he continued his scholarly study. He continued to be published in Russia, but under a pseudonym.

Lavrov's basic conviction was determined by his faith in science and the rejection of metaphysics. One of the chief sources of his doctrine was ethical inspiration.

In his words, "philosophy is the comprehension of all that is real as a unity and the embodiment of this idea in artistic images and in moral actions."

Lavrov felt that the question of free will was unsolvable in its metaphysical formulation. He states: "In man one can not eliminate the phenomenon of self-obligation, of self-judgment. . . I proceed from the fact of the consciousness of freedom, the fact of creating ideals. And, on the basis of these facts, I structure a coherent system of moral processes."

Lavrov's philosophy of history flows from his ethics. The idea of the intelligentsia's guilt before the "people" and the demand that the intelligentsia "pay its debt" to the people derives from this.

"Mankind has paid dearly so that a few thinkers in their studies could speak of its progress. If it were calculated how many lost lives pertained to each presently living individual, our contemporaries would be horrified at the thought of what capital in blood and labor had been spent on their development."

## NIKOLAI KONSTANTINOVICH MIKHAILOVSKII (1842-1904)

Mikhailovskii was born to a poor gentry family of the Meshchovsk district of the Kaluga province. He studied at the mining school but did not graduate. Instead, he took up publicism.

In contrast to Lavrov, who wrote in a laborious style, Mikhailovskii was a brilliant literary talent. Basically, in his views, Mikhailovskii followed in Lavrov's footsteps. But his popularity among readers was far greater than Lavrov's. Furthermore, he lived in Russia, not abroad.

From 1869, Mikhailovskii became a permanent contributor to *Notes of the Fatherland* [*Otechestvennye Zapiski*], a journal published by Nekrasov. After Nekrasov's death (1877), he became one of the journal's three editors (the other two were Saltykov and Eliseev). The journal was closed down in 1885.

From the beginning of the 1890's Mikhailovskii headed *Russian Resplendence* [*Russkoe Bogatstvo*]. He remained its editor until his death.

At the center of Mikhailovskii's world view and ethics was his concept of the individual. "The personality must never be sacrificed — it is sacred and inviolable." The notion of integrity in men and integrity within spiritual activity in and of itself is linked to this.

It is from here that the concept of "dual truth" stems — truth-verity (which is theoretical and objective) and truth-justice (which is social).

"Truth in this vast sense of the word," wrote Mikhailovskii, "always constituted the goal of my strivings. . . Everything engaged me exclusively from the viewpoint of dual truth."

Lavrov was the first to express the idea of the "payment of debt" by the intelligentsia to the people. Mikhailovskii popularized the phrase "repentant noble."

Mikhailovskii perceived the idea of social life in the personality and its harmonious development.

"Human personality, its fate, and its interests — that is what must be placed at the head of our theoretical thought in the area of social problems and our practical activity." In so doing, he establishes differences in types and degrees of development.

If in society there is an increase in the division of labor and individuals specialize, like workers in a factory, their type is reduced (relative to the peasant in the village who does everything himself). But the degree of their development can be very high.

From this point of view, according to Mikhailovskii, the highest form of social development is the Russian peasant commune.

Mikhailovskii felt that one must struggle to achieve the social ideal. The sociologist should not look upon progress as on an indifferent evolution. This constituted his "subjective method."

Prior to the revolutionary crisis of 1879-1881 which culminated in the murder of Alexander II, Mikhailovskii attached little significance to forms of government.

In 1879 the leaders of the *zemstvo's* liberal movement raised the question regarding the necessity of agitating for a constitution. I. I. Petrunkevich, the liberal leader, wished to attract Mikhailovskii to this program. Mikhailovskii asked him: could he (Petrunkevich) take upon himself an obligation wherein all of the land would be transferred to the peasants?

Petrunkevich observed that this would depend on the Constitutional Congress which, alone, could decide this question.

"In that case," declared Mikhailovskii, "the people

spit on your landowners' constitution. When the people take power into their own hands, they will write their own constitution."[23]

At that time, Petrunkevich did not know that Mikhailovskii, who had until then shunned revolutionary activity, had participated in the committee of the "People's Will" ["Narodnaia Volia"] party.

After the assassination of Alexander II, the executive committee of the "People's Will" addressed the new Tsar, Alexander III, with a letter which promised to cease revolutionary activity on two conditions: if the government announced a general amnesty for all political crimes and if it would convene the "representatives of all the Russian people to review the existing government and social forms and to revise them in accordance with national desires." (Vl. Burtsev, in the anthology, *During a Hundred Years* [*Za Stolet*], London, 1897, The Hague, 1965; p. 178).

## NIKOLAI NIKOLAEVICH STRAKHOV (1828-1896)

Strakhov was born in Belgorod. His father was a master of the Kiev Theological Academy and archpriest and instructor of philology at the Belgorod seminary. After his death, the boy Nikolai was taken for upbringing by his mother's brother, the rector of the Kamenets-Podol'skaia, and later of the Kostroma, seminary. Strakhov finished the course in Kostroma.

In 1845 he entered the mathematics department of the University of Petersburg, then transferred to the mathematics-natural science division of the General Pedagogical Institute. He graduated in 1851. He taught physics and mathematics in Odessa, then natural history in Petersburg's second gymnasium.

Strakhov defended his master's thesis in zoology at the University of Petersburg in 1857 and received an offer of the chair of zoology at the University of Kazan. He did not go there, wishing not to part with Petersburg.

During the 1860's, he became friends with Dostoevskii

and collaborated with him in his journals, *Time* [*Vremia*] and *Epoch* [*Epokha*]. In 1873 he was made librarian of the public library's juridical division. In the 1890's he became an associate member of the Academy of Sciences.

Strakhov was a confirmed Hegelian. He valued Hegel's "logic" and dialectical method highly. "This," he wrote, "is an eternal monument of human genius. . . one of the greatest examples of man's philosophical ability."

Hegelianism, for Strakhov, is a pre-requisite of the philosophy of history striving to understand the individuality of nations. Specifically, Hegelianism lies at the foundation of Slavophilism, understood in the broad sense of the word. Strakhov felt that the concept of historical development as a sequential change in a series of spiritual images serving the spirit of nations was an incontestable legacy of the philosophy of history for which we are indebted to Hegel. Strakhov wrote: "National spirit — that is what we shall call the mysterious force upon which the manifestation of human souls at their deepest source depends."

In connection with this notion, Strakhov became an ardent follower of N. I. Danilevskii's ideas on the difference in cultural-historical types and in the development of mankind. The first edition of the latter's book, *Russia and Europe* [*Rossiia i Evropa*] appeared in 1871.

Strakhov considered himself to be a religious man. But this opinion of himself demands qualification. E. L. Radlov, professor of philosophy at the Alexandrian lycée, expressed the profound opinion that Strakhov understood religion more with his mind than with his heart. And in truth, in one of his letters to L. N. Tolstoi, Strakhov admitted that it was only from Schopenhauer that he learned to understand religion.

Strakhov had great philosophical abilities.

"All the qualities necessary to write a major philosophical work were united in him: a broad and diverse education, critical capacity, thoughtfulness, and methodical reflection. He lacked only true creativity through which the new is created." (Radlov).

Strakhov was a close friend and fervent follower of L. N. Tolstoi. They continuously maintained a lively correspondence. Strakhov attempted to draw Tolstoi into Hegelianism but, for Tolstoi, it was completely unacceptable. For a time, in contrast, Strakhov fell under the influence of Tolstoi's mystical ideas.

In one of his letters to him, Strakhov wrote: "that eternal spiritual source which contains the root of all being is recognizable in our consciousness. Everything proceeds from God, leads to God, and is crowned in God. . . I now reject that the mind governs history, that it is the development of ideas."

## FEDOR MIKHAILOVICH DOSTOEVSKII (1821-1881)

Dostoevskii inspires philosophic thought to this day.

He provides a religious basis to the metaphysics of history. He thought that at God's design, human freedom was a prerequisite of historical dialectics. The problem of good ("salvation") is sharply contrasted with the problem of evil.

Rationalism leads to the crushing of human freedom ("Legend of the Grand Inquisitor" in *The Brothers Karamazov*). The way out for Dostoevskii is a free movement toward the Churchification of culture. In addition to Christian ethics, Dostoevskii believed in the purifying power of beauty. "Beauty will save the world." "The Holy Spirit is a direct comprehension of beauty, a prophetic consciousness of harmony and hence a steadfast striving toward it."

## LEV NIKOLAEVICH TOLSTOI (1828-1910)

At the conclusion of his novel *War and Peace*, — that grandiose historical panorama — Tolstoi wrote a long discussion on the philosophy of history. The majority of readers did not, and do not, read this discussion. Almost all of Tolstoi's contemporaries viewed it with bewilderment and mockery. Turgenev, in a letter to his friend Botkin, characterized Tolstoi's discourse as the charlatanism of a self-taught person. It must be said that Turgenev also did not initially like *War and Peace* in artistic-literary terms. It was only later that he conceded Tolstoi's genius as a writer.

One of the few who took Tolstoi's philosophy of history seriously was Kareev. Kareev carefully analyzed Tolstoi's views in his article "The Historical Philosophy of Count L. N. Tolstoi" ["Istoricheskaia Filosofiia Grafa L. N. Tolstogo"] (*European Herald*, 1887), but did not accept his conclusions.

Twenty years ago, a new evaluation of Tolstoi's historiosophy was given by Isaiah Berlin in his paper, *Leo Tolstoy's Historical Scepticism.*[24]

"Tolstoi," writes Berlin, "felt reality in its multiformity as the totality of individual essences. He looked into their depth with rare perception. But he personally believed only in the all-encompassing and unified whole."

Berlin stresses the fact that Tolstoi was interested in history from an early age. In Tolstoi's view, history is the sum of concrete events in space and time. Tolstoi approaches the study of history in the spirit of the anti-theological and the anti-metaphysical thinkers of the XVIII century.

"The subject of history," writes Tolstoi, "is the life of nations and of humanity. To catch at first hand and describe the life not only of humanity but of one nation is impossible."

Tolstoi then examined the methods used by historians in order to "capture the seemingly elusive life of a people."

"For the ancients, these problems were solved by the deity's direct intervention in human affairs."

"The new history rejected the beliefs of the ancients. It did not replace them with new attitudes. The logic of the situation forces the historians, who allegedly rejected the divine rule of kings and the Fate of the ancients, to arrive at the same conclusion by different means: to come to the recognition that 1) nations are ruled by individuals, and 2) there is a well-known goal toward which mankind is moving."

"It would seem that, having rejected the beliefs of the ancients regarding man's subjection to God and the definite goal toward which nations were moving, the new history should study the causes forming it, not the phenomena. But the new history failed to do this. Having, theoretically, rejected the ancients, it follows them in practice."

With merciless sarcasm, Tolstoi summed up the view and methods of historians in his satirical parody of their reasoning.

"You wish to know what this movement (of peoples) means, why it occurred, and what force produced these events? Listen. Louis XIV was a very proud and presumptuous person. He had such and such mistresses, such and such ministers, and ruled France poorly. Louis's heirs were weak people and also ruled poorly over France. They also had various mistresses and favorites. Furthermore, some people wrote books at this time. At the end of the XVIII century in Paris, some twenty people met. They began to say that all men are free and equal. In France, because of this, people began to kill and drown each other. These people killed the king and many others as well. At this very time in France, there was a genius — Napoleon. He always won everywhere; that is he killed many people, because he was a genius. For some reason he went to kill Africans. And he killed them so well, and was so smart and so sly, that arriving in France, he ordered all to obey. And all obeyed him. Having become emperor, he again went to kill people in Italy, Austria, and Prussia. And he killed many. In Russia there was Emperor Alexander who decided to restore order in Europe. Hence, he warred with Napoleon. But in 1807 he suddenly became friendly with him. In 1811 he again quarreled and they began to kill many people anew. Napoleon brought 600,000 men to Russia and conquered Moscow. He then suddenly ran from Moscow and Emperor Alexander, with the help of advice from Stein and others, unified Europe in defense against the violator of their peace. All of Napoleon's allies suddenly became his enemies. And this militia took to the field against Napoleon's newly gathered forces. The allies

defeated Napoleon. They entered Paris. They forced Napoleon to renounce the throne and forced him to go to the
island of Elba. They did not strip him of his imperial rank
and showed every respect despite the fact that five years
prior, and a year later, they all thought him to be an un-
lawful robber. Louis XVII, at whom Frenchmen and allies
had only laughed up to that point, now came to rule. Napoleon, shedding tears before the old guard, renounced the
throne and left for exile. Then, statesmen and diplomats
(particularly Talleyrand who was able to be the first to
sit in the well-known seat and thereby increased France's
boundaries) talked in Vienna and these talks made nations
happy or unhappy. Suddenly the diplomats and monarchs
almost quarreled. They were already prepared to order their
armies to kill each other when Napoleon arrived in France
with a battalion. And Frenchmen who hated him immediately submitted to him. But the allied monarchs became
angry because of this and again proceeded to fight the
French. The brilliant Napoleon was defeated and taken to
the island of St. Helena. He was suddenly recognized to be a
thief. There the exile, who was separated from the beloved
France and those dear to his heart, was dying a slow death
on the cliff and left his great deeds to posterity. There was
reaction in Europe and all States again began to abuse their
people."

"The oddity and comedy of these answers," observes
Tolstoi, "derive from the fact that the new history is like
a deaf mute who answers questions which no one puts to
him. If the goal of history is the depiction of the progress of
humanity and nations, then the first question without the
answer to which all else is incomprehensible is the following:
what force moves nations?"

The only concept known to the new history of such a
force is power.

For the new historiography, "power is the aggregate of
the will of the masses which, whether through expressed or
silent agreement, is transferred to rulers chosen by the
masses."

This theory is merely a paraphrase, an expression of the question by means of other words.

"What is the cause of historical events? — Power. What is power? Power is the aggregate of wills transferred to an individual. Under certain conditions it is the expression of the people's will by one person. That is, power is power. Which means that power is a word whose meaning is incomprehensible to us."

Tolstoi defines power as "a relationship of a famous person to other people in which the person participates all the less in an operation the more that he expresses the opinions, assumptions, and justifications of an aggregate action which is being performed."

"Movement in nations is not produced by power, by intellectual activity, or even by a combination of both as historians thought. It is produced by the action of all the people who participate in an event and who always unite in a way such that those who participate the most in an event take the least responsibility upon themselves, and vice versa."

Tolstoi feels that the causal concept is not applicable to history.

"In speaking of the interaction of heat and electricity, and of atoms, we cannot say why this occurs. We say, this must be so, it is a law. The same thing applies to historical phenomena. We do not know why war or revolution occur. We only know that to accomplish one action or another, people unite in various combinations. Everyone participates in this. And we say that such is the way things are, for this is the law and it is inconceivable that things be different."

"If history concerned itself with external phenomena, the ascertainment of this simple and obvious law would be sufficient. We would end our discourse. But historical law refers to man. A particle of matter cannot tell us that it does not at all feel the need of attraction and repulsion, and that this is false. A person who is the object of history says bluntly: I am free and therefore am not subject to laws. The presence of the question of free will, though it may not be openly stated, is felt at history's every step."

"If reason views the concept of freedom as a senseless contradiction, this only proves that consciousness is not dependent on reason."

For Tolstoi, this constitutes the main riddle of history.

"If each person possessed free will, that is if each person could do just as he wished, then all history would be a series of disconnected accidents. . . If there is even one law which governs human action, there cannot be free will for the will of people would have to be subjected to this law."

In real life every action of man is represented as nothing other than a certain unification of freedom and necessity.

"In every action analyzed we see a certain measure of necessity. And always, the more freedom there is apparent in any action, the less necessity there is. The more apparent the necessity, the less the freedom."

"Man is the creature of the almighty, all-blessed, and omniscient God."

The notion of sin ("the problem of theology") derives from the consciousness of human freedom. For Tolstoi, in this fashion, God's manifestation is a historical law.

## DMITRII IVANOVICH MENDELEEV (1834-1907)

Mendeleev was not only a scholar with a powerful mind but a person of diverse erudition and interests. Fundamentally, he was a naturalist (chemist, physicist, and mathematician). At the same time, he also profoundly thought out a series of problems in the social sciences.

In addition to his works in natural science, he wrote penetrating articles on economic problems. He advocated the necessity of developing national industry.

"Science and industry — those are my hopes." But he attached no less significance to upgrading agriculture.

Mendeleev made wide use of statistical material in his economic research. An analysis of the data of the first Russian census of 1897 is at the basis of his last work, *Toward a Knowledge of Russia* [*K Poznaniiu Rossii*].

Historiosophic thoughts and observations are scattered about in many of Mendeleev's works. They are summarized in his remarkable book *Cherished Thoughts* [*Zavetnye Mysli*], published in 1904. Here Mendeleev states the basis of his philosophy of history. We shall now turn to the characteristics of this philosophy of history.[25]

In chapter one of *Cherished Thoughts*, Mendeleev writes: "In ordinary conversation, people have become used to distinguishing only between idealism and materialism. The latter is sometimes referred to as realism. Words, of course are conditional in meaning. But in accordance with their origin, the three cited words represent completely different meanings. Realism should be placed in the middle."

V. Kirichenko, the communist editor of the anthology, and a candidate in economics, found it necessary to make this addition to Mendeleev's introduction:

"D. I. Mendeleev's assertion regarding the presence of a special ideological trend, which he calls "realism" and which is to be distinguished from materialism and idealism, is wrong. The founders of Marxism proved that only two philosophic camps exist: those of materialism and idealism. Being a materialist, Mendeleev as a rule included materialist content in the idea of 'realism'."

According to Mendeleev's own definition, realism "strove to express reality in the highest degree of human objectivity. Common sense should be employed without any tinge of the preconceived judgments of which both idealism and materialsim are full. Such a realism lies at the basis of all natural science and from it, in the aggregate, the development of contemporary thought. . . True idealism and true materialism are products of ancient times. Realism is a new matter when compared to the length of historical ages. Thus, for example, the yearning for wars of aggression is peculiar to both idealism and materialism. . . realism is always opposed to all aggressive wars and strives to eliminate all contradictions. It proceeds from real circumstances, from government affairs and from history. Idealism of the Greek or Chinese type considers all those who do not hold to their ideal to be barbarians. Modern materialism, most clearly expressed among the Anglo-Saxons, holds that people of other colors — Indians, Negroes, Chinese (red, black, and yellow) — are barbarians in essence and also because of the poverty that is generally prevalent among them. For realism, all people are the same. They are simply in different periods of their evolutionary development."

"Realism is primarily inherent in certain nations like idealism and materialism are in others. And I dare say that our Russian nation, which occupies the center of the ancient continent, represents the best example of a realistic nation with real ideas. This is observable in the attitude of our people toward all others, their ability to get along with them and absorb them. Above all, it is apparent in the fact that our whole history is an example of the unity of Asiatic concepts with the western European."

Touching upon domestic State policy, Mendeleev attached primary significance to the necessity of universal public education. "Realism clearly suggests that universal public education is unthinkable without the accumulation of a certain degree of national riches. . . The matter of development and the growth of universal public education are incomprehensible without the broad development of science in general. But it demands great resources."

In this way, we see that the theory of realism which Mendeleev placed at the source of his philosophy of history was also, for him, an actual factor in the transformation of Russian national life.

## XXIV

## THE DEVELOPMENT OF WORLD HISTORY AT THE END OF THE XIX AND THE BEGINNING OF THE XX CENTURIES

In 1893 Vinogradov, one of the most prominent representatives of world history in Russia, wrote: "It would not be paradoxical to say that it is precisely world history which must become a Russian science. Russians have even less right to seclude themselves in their isolated national culture than do Englishmen, Frenchmen, or Germans. . . . On the other hand, if Russians need, and are kindred to man's universal civic mindedness, they have no reason to bind themselves with the study of just one branch of learning or science."

## V. I. GER'E (1837-1919)

The founder of the Russian school of world history was Vladimir Ivanovich Ger'e.[26]

Ger'e was born in Moscow and studied at Moscow University. He had occasion to study under Granovskii and Kudriavtsev. He held them in reverence all his life. He was closely linked to the Stankeviches. Ger'e later married N.V. Stankevich's niece, Evdokiia Ivanovna Tokarev.

Upon graduating from the university, Ger'e was kept on to prepare for professorship. At the same time he became instructor of literature and history at the first cadet school.

The theme chosen by Ger'e for his master's thesis was "The Struggle for the Polish Throne in 1733" ["Bor'ba za Pol'skii Prestol v 1773 Godu"]. This was a topic suggested by Solov'ev. Among Ger'e's works this occupies a special place. Ger'e is primarily a historian of culture and ideas.

Evidently Solov'ev felt that Ger'e also had to take cognizance of foreign diplomatic history.

Ger'e's book came out in 1862 — right at the time when the Polish question had become the burning issue of the day. The Polish revolution began in 1863.

After teaching his first university course, Ger'e was sent abroad. He spent nearly three years in Germany, Italy, and France. There he collected materials for his doctoral dissertation, "Leibniz and his Age" ["Leibnits i Ego Vek"] (1868).

Ger'e's goal was to describe Leibniz's life and works in relation to his age and contemporary society. Ger'e strove to clarify Leibniz's philosophic, religious, and political ideas, his work in searching for archival materials, and his recognition of the importance of gathering and publishing the records of cultural history.

When Ger'e was completing his dissertation, he found out that there was important material on Russia and Peter in Hanover. He decided to devote a separate work to this topic. Thus arose his book *Leibniz's Relations with Russia and Peter the Great* [*Otnosheniia Leibnitsa k Rossii i Petru Velikomu*] (1873). Ger'e then published *An Anthology of Leibniz's Letters and Materials Relating to Russia and Peter the Great* [*Sbornik Pisem i Materialov Leibnitsa Otnosiashchikhsia k Rossi i Petru Velikomu*] (1873).

Ger'e felt an attraction for the philosophy of history. The introduction to his first university course served as an essay on the development of historical science. It was published immediately.

In essence, this was an attempt at historical philosophy. Half a century later Ger'e reworked this essay and published it with the title of *The Philosophy of History from Augustine to Hegel* [*Filosofiia Istorii ot Avgustina do Gegelia*]. In the work, Ger'e spoke out against the application of scientific methods to history. He wrote: "History will always permit subjective creativity and will approach art. . . The principal role in the lives of nations is not played by climate, food, or physical conditions but by forces about which no scientist can give an account. For example, what enormous influence ideas have on the fates of nations and on the course of civilization."

In 1885 Ger'e commenced lecturing at the *privat-docent* rank. Later, upon attaining professorship, he first lectured on Medieval history, then on Roman and modern.

One of his students of 1899, M. O. Gershenzon, later recalled: "Each of Ger'e's lectures was a holiday. I think I would not tire of listening to him for five hours" (this was written after Ger'e's death).

Besides his dissertations, Ger'e wrote a whole series of useful books and articles on various aspects of world history.

In Roman history, I will note his compilation of three

articles, *Augustus and the Establishment of the Roman Empire* [*Avgust i Ustanovlenie Rimskoi Imperii*] (1877). Twenty years later he wrote an article titled "Scholarly Trends in Ancient Roman History" ["Nauchnoe Dvizhenie v Oblasti Drevneishei Rimskoi Istorii"].

Over a period of years Ger'e wrote a series of articles on the history of the Middle Ages. They dealt primarily with the medieval world view. He then united these articles under the overall title, *Architects and Devotees of the Heavenly Kingdom* [*Zodchie i Podvizhniki Bozh'ego Tsarstva*] (3 parts, 1910-1916). The first part treats St. Augustine. The second and third parts discuss the papacy and monasticism. His essay, *St. Francis: Apostle of Poverty and Love* [*Frantsisk, Apostol Nishchety i Liubvi*] (1908) also belongs to this series.

Ger'e's basic viewpoint contrasts the papacy with St. Francis.

"The more that the Western Church succeeded in its aspiration of subjecting and ruling the world, the more it managed to become the "heavenly kingdom" on earth, the more it became an *earthly* kingdom."

This historical and psychological paradox, says Ger'e, "constitutes the essence of medieval history and ensures an eternal interest inherent to it."

Ger'e's speciality in modern history was the XVIII century — the *ancien régime*, the Enlightenment, and the French Revolution. His 1873 article, "A Republic or a Monarchy Will be Established in France" ["Respublika ili Monarkhiia Ustanovitsia vo Frantsii"] applies here. It was written in connection with his university course of that year. France was then experiencing a difficult crisis after defeat by the Prussians and the Paris commune of 1870. Its political future was unclear.

*The Origin of France's Present System*, the work of H. Taine, a French historian, began to appear in 1876.

As the separate parts of this work were issued, Ger'e acquainted the Russian public with it in the pages of the *European Herald*. Then, having reworked them, he compiled a book, *The French Revolution According to H. Taine* [*Frantsuzkaia Revoliutsiia v Osveshchenii I. Tena*] (1911).

In 1884 Ger'e published a book called *The Concepts of Power and Nation in the Instructions of 1789* [*Poniatiia o Vlasti i Narode v Nakazakh 1789 goda*].

Ger'e idealized the French Revolution. At the end of the 1870's he wrote that "the year 1789 will always be considered one of the remarkable movements on humanity's road to civic progress . . . . For the historian, the French Revolution is of considerable importance in four essential aspects. First, it was the narrow result of XVIII century European culture; then, the Revolution was a catastrophe of the feudal order; at the same time, it was the culmination of the centralization and unification of France, and finally, its declaration of rights became the great charter of European democracy."

During his many years of teaching at Moscow University, several generations of future Russian historians attended his lectures and studied in his seminars. In this sense he had many students, and academic grandsons and great-grandsons. More specifically, his most distinguished students were V. O. Kliuchevskii, N. I. Kareev, P. G. Vinogradov, and A. A. Kizevetter.

Ger'e was a confirmed supporter of higher education for women. In 1871 he petitioned the Minister of Public Education regarding the establishment of advanced courses for women under his directorship at Moscow University. The rector of the university, the historian S. M. Solov'ev, supported this solicitation. Only the humanities were taught in these courses. Among the professors whom Ger'e enlisted to teach were two young historians — Kareev and Vinogradov. Both of them were his students.27

In 1888 the Ministry of Public Education issued a decree closing all women's courses in Russia. Ger'e's courses were also shut down. The only ones to remain were Bestuzhev's Advanced Courses for Women in Petersburg.

Ger'e could not reconcile himself to the destruction of his offspring and gradually continued to lay the groundwork for the re-establishment of the Advance Courses for Women in Moscow.

These courses were opened on new and solid foundations in September of 1900. They were placed under the jurisdiction of the superintendent of the Moscow school district. Ger'e was made director.

The courses were split into two departments — the historico-philological and the physico-mathematical. The majority of the instructors were professors of Moscow University. The course was based on a four year program.

Ger'e could not reconcile himself to the October Revolution of 1917. He was already 82 and felt himself to be derailed. He had no more strength to live and died in 1919.

## ANCIENT HISTORY

## M. S. KUTORGA (1809-1886)

Ger'e studied ancient, medieval, and modern history.

The first independent student of ancient Greek history was Mikhail Semenovich Kutorga. Having spent one year at the University of Petersburg, he entered the professorial institute at the University of Derpt in 1827. He was then sent abroad and attended lectures in Paris, Heidelberg, Munich and Berlin.

Having been superbly trained, he was given a chair at the University of Petersburg in 1835.

Kutorga was mostly interested in the history of the Athenian republic. He devoted the first of his main works to this history (from the murder of Hipparchus to the death of Miltiades).

Kutorga paid much attention to chronology. His second major work, *The Persian Wars: A Critical Investigation of the Events of this Period of Greek History* [*Persidskie Voiny, Kriticheskie Issledovaniia Sobytii Etoi Epokhi Drevnei Grecheskoi Istorii*] (1858), was based on his research in this field.

He attached great significance to Greek history for

Russians, for "it serves toward a more accurate comprehension of our nation." "The ancient world did not die and was not destroyed by Teutons or Slavs. It existed and functioned in an altered form and over a greater area. Byzantine-Slavic history is a direct and uninterrupted continuation of Hellenic history with principles transformed by Christianity. . . in studying the history of the ancient Greeks, we study the history of our ancient forefathers."

In more recent times, the most prominent historian of the ancient world was M. I. Rostovtsev. We will speak of him in a different connection (Ch. XXX, "Archeology and the History of Art").

## THE MIDDLE AGES

### V. G. VASIL'EVSKII (1838-1899)

The oldest of the prominent Russian medievalists (and we include Byzantine history in the medieval period) was Vasilii Grigor'evich Vasil'evskii (1838-1899).[28]

Vasil'evskii was the son of a village priest in the Iaroslavl province. In 1852 he entered the middle division of the Iaroslavl Seminary. He moved to Petersburg in 1856 and was granted a scholarship to the General Pedagogical Institute. Three years later he switched to the historico-philological department of the University of Petersburg. Upon graduation, he was sent abroad to prepare for professorship. He attended Mommsen's and Droysen's lectures in Berlin and those of Adolf Schmidt in Jena.

Upon returning from abroad, he lacked funds and accepted a position as teacher of Russian literature at the Novgorod gymnasium. During that very year, he was transferred to the Vil'nius gymnasium to teach history and geography.

In Vilnius, besides teaching at the gymnasium, Vasil'evskii began to work on his dissertation. Furthermore, he began to collect and study sources on the history of Vil'nius. His work based on this was issued in two volumes in 1872 and titled *Essay on the History of the City of Vil'nius* [*Ocherk Istorii Goroda Vil'no*].

He wrote his master's thesis on "Political Reform and the Social Movement in Ancient Greece During the Period of its Decline" ["Politicheskaia Reforma i Sotsial'noe Dvizhenie v Drevnei Gretsii v Period ee Upadka"]. He defended it at the end of 1869.

In March of 1870, Vasil'evskii was confirmed as *privat-docent* at the University of Petersburg. In 1879 he was promoted to professor extraordinary, to ordinary professor in 1884, and was made professor emeritus in 1895.

In 1879 Moscow University honored him with the doctor's degree in history *honoris causa*.

In 1876 Vasil'evskii became an associate member of the Academy of Sciences. He became an active or full member of the Adacemy in 1890. Such is the outline of his life.

Vasil'evskii's scholarly legacy is extremely valuable and diverse in theme and approaches to historical problems.

During a period of close to thirty years, he taught a survey course in medieval history, choosing Byzantium as the subject of his particular studies.

Vasil'evskii's first important work in Byzantine studies was his study "Byzantium and the Pechenegs" ["Vizantiia i Pechenegi"] (1872). This article made a great impression in the scholarly world. It commences the steady growth of Russian Byzantinology up to 1920.

Of Vasil'evskii's other solid works, I will note his "Materials for the Internal Domestic History of the Byzantine State" ["Materialy dlia Vnutrennei Istorii Vizantiiskogo Gosudarstva"] (1879) and "Russo-Byzantine Studies" ["Russko-Vizantiiskie Issledovaniia"] (1893). The latter essay contains the lives of St. George of Amistridia and Stefan of Surozhsk (the Slavic-Russian text).

After Vasil'evskii's death, the Academy of Sciences resolved to publish his selected works. Four volumes were published (1908-1930).

## F. I. USPENSKII (1845-1928)

Fedor Ivanovich Uspenskii was born on February 7, 1845 to a priest's family in the settlement of Gorki, the Galich district, province of Kostroma.[29] Uspenskii received his first education in his father's home. He entered the Galich religious school in 1854. From there, he entered Kostroma's seminary from which he graduated in 1866. After one year, he went to Petersburg and entered the university's historical-philological department. He was given a scholarship.

He described his student years in his memoirs of his sojourn at the university (the journal *Dela i Dni*, 1920, I).

At the university Uspenskii studied Greek language and literature under professor K. Ia. Liugebil. His main teachers were V. I. Lamanskii and Bestuzhev-Riumin. Among his close student friends were Vladimir and Viacheslav, the two sons of I. I. Sreznevskii, dean of faculty.

Through them, Uspenskii and some other students were received by the dean's family and were occasionally invited for evening tea. This created friendly relations between professors and students.

Upon graduating from the university, Uspenskii was kept at the chair of Russian history.

His first published work, *The First Slavic Monarchies in the North-West* [*Pervye Slavianskie Monarkhii na Severe-Zapade*] appeared in 1872.

Uspenskii wrote his master's thesis on "A Byzantine Writer, Nicetas Acominatus of Chonae" ["Vizantiiskii Pisatel' Nikita Akominat iz Khon"]. Two years later, Uspenskii was appointed *docent* at the chair of world history at the University of Odessa.

His later life can be clearly divided into two periods — the Odessa period (1874-1894) and the Constantinople period (1894-1914). The latter was as director of the Russian Archeological Institute.

Uspenskii wrote his doctoral dissertation on the theme, "The Formation of the Second Bulgarian Kingdom" ["Obrazovanie Vtorogo Bolgarskogo Tsarstva"] (1879).

In 1893 he was elected associate member of the Academy of Sciences; in 1900, ordinary academician. Uspenskii was both an outstanding historian and archeologist. He participated actively in archeological congresses as well as personally conducting digs for antiquities (particularly in the Constantinople period of his life).

Uspenskii's role in producing the *Byzantine Annals* [*Vizantiiskii Vremennik*], which commenced publication in 1894, was very important. This was the first international journal of Byzantine studies. Uspenskii was its irreplaceable editor. He was surrounded by a multitude of contributors — Byzantinists and specialists in kindred studies (Slavists, archeologists, orientalists).

Uspenskii's scholarly works are numerous and diverse.

I will mention only the most important (his two dissertations, the master's and the doctor's, have been cited above).

Of great interest is his *Essays on the History of Byzantine Civilization* [*Ocherki po Istorii Vizantiiskoi Obrazovannosti*] (1891). In breadth and organization, this is one of Uspenskii's best works.

"Before us is the philosophic and theologic movement, the intellectual life of XI-XIV c. Byzantine society, political motifs and their interrelationships; and, the European East, the West, and Russia" (Buzeskul).

His *History of the Crusades* [*Istoriia Krestovykh Pokhodov*] (1900) was a more general work. It was rather of the popular-scholarly type.

Uspenskii's hope after this was to write a general history of Byzantium. The first volume of his work, *A History of the Byzantine Empire* [*Istoriia Vizantiiskoi Imperii*] appeared in 1913 in the superb edition of the Brockhaus-Efron company. The first half of volume two appeared after a long interval.

Volume three, (from 1081 to the end of the Byzantine Empire), remained in manuscript.

On October 16, 1914, Turkey joined the Central Powers

and broke relations with Russia.

Uspenskii was forced to leave Constantinople in a hurry, leaving the Russian Archeological Institute and almost all of his personal property to the mercy of fate. He returned to Petersburg. In the summer of 1916, and again in the summer of 1917, Uspenskii was sent on a scholarly mission to Trabezond. The fruit of his research there was his last significant work, *Essays on the History of the Trabezondian Empire* [*Ocherki po Istorii Trapezundskoi Imperii*] (published posthumously in 1929). From 1922-1927 Uspenskii lectured on Byzantine history at the University of Petersburg. He died on September 10, 1928.

## M. M. KOVALEVSKII (1851-1916)

Maksim Maksimovich Kovalevskii was born in Khar'kov in a rich noble family. His father was a participant of the War of 1812, subsequent battles, and the capture of Paris. When the war ended, he was elected district, then provincial marshal of the nobility. His mother was an intelligent woman with aesthetic inclinations. She selflessly loved her only son.[30]

His mother reared Maksim carefully. As a child and youth he mastered French, German, and English (later, as an adult, he learned Italian and Spanish). His mother aroused Maksim's interest in history. Under her influence, he read much.

While not yet seventeen, he entered the University of Khar'kov. An inept professor taught history in the historico-philological department. For this reason, Kovalevskii entered the department of law. There his teacher and inspirer was the talented professor of international and government law, D. I. Kachenovskii. (The latter came from the same family which previously gave us a representative of the sceptical school of Russian history, M. T. Kachenovskii).

In his autobiography, Kovalevskii writes' "He (Kachenovskii) taught international law so well that many years later I was able to prepare for the master's examination in this subject merely with the aid of his lectures alone."

He often said: "Were there no Kachenovskii, there would not have been Kovalevskii."

Kachenovskii died the year that Kovalevskii was graduated from the university (1872).

Kovalevskii went abroad, first to Berlin where he utilized the counsel of Gneist and Brunner, then to Paris. Guided by French scholars, Kovalevskii learned the methods of studying sources at the charter school.

From Paris Kovalevskii went to London to study at the British Museum.

In England he made the acquaintance of several outstanding English scholars — Maine, Spencer, Bryce, and Karl Marx.

On the basis of the materials he collected, published and unpublished, Kovalevskii wrote his master's thesis on "The History of Police Administration and the Criminal Court in the English Shires from Ancient Times to the Death of Edward III" ["Istoriia Politseiskoi Administratsii i Politseiskogo Suda v Angliiskikh Grafstvakh s Drevneishikh Vremen do Smerti Eduarda III"]. In the form of a separate appendix, he issued a collection of previously unpublished acts and documents which characterized English police administration in the XII, XIII, and XIV centuries.

While in England, Kovalevskii also began to collect materials for his doctoral dissertation, "The English Social System at the End of the Middle Ages." Kovalevskii was a pioneer in this field. At the time there were no serious works available on this problem.

Upon defending his dissertation, Kovalevskii received a professorship at Moscow University's department of law. His chair was in government law.

Kovalevskii felt no inclination for jurisprudence or the theory of law. He studied State and society in their historical aspect. Additionally, he was keenly interested in ethnography and common law.

Soon after receiving the professorship, Kovalevskii went abroad for two years on a scholarly assignment. He first traveled to Italy and Spain where he surveyed the major libraries and archives, then to America. Upon returning to Moscow, Kovalevskii, along with Vsevolod Miller, made several trips to the Caucasus in order to study the daily life of the native peoples. The result was the following valuable works by Kovalevskii: *Contemporary Custom and Ancient Law* [*Sovremennyi Obychai i Drevnii Zakon*], *Ossetian Common Law* [*Obychnoe Pravo Osetin*] (1886), and *Law and Custom in the Caucasus* [*Zakon i Obychai na Kavkaze*] (1890).

Government circles in Petersburg thought Kovalevskii was "unreliable" and feared his "pernicious influence" on youth. In 1887, Del'ianov, the Minister of Public Education, fired Kovalevskii "according to point three." This deprived him of the right to teach in Russian universities in general.

Kovalevskii moved abroad, lived partly in France, partly in Italy, and sometime visited England and America. Occasionally he went to Russia. In Paris, he founded the Russian Higher School of Social Sciences. At the same time he lectured in a series of European universities and in America.

In Chicago he had a course on Russian political institutions; in London, on Iranian culture in the Caucasus; in Stockholm, on the origin of the family and property.

In 1905 Kovalevskii returned to Russia and lectured at the University of Petersburg. In 1906 he was elected to the State Duma, and then he was elected a member of the State Council (division of the Academy of Sciences and universities). He was elected member of the Academy of Sciences in 1914.

He died in 1916.

Kovalevskii's most important works, (aside from those of the Moscow period of his life) are: *The Origin of Contemporary Democracy* [*Proiskhozhdenie Sovremennoi Demokratii*] (4 vol., 1895-1897); *Europe's Economic Growth to the Emergence of Capitalist Economy* [*Ekonomicheskii Rost Evropy do Vozniknoveniia Kapitalisticheskogo Khozia-*

*istva*] (3 vol., 1878-1903); and *From Direct Rule by the People to Representative Government and From Patriarchal Monarchy to Parliamentarianism* [*Ot Priamogo Narodo-pravstva k Predstavitel'nomu i ot Patriarkhal'noi Monarkhii k Parlamentarizmu*] (3 vol., 1906).

In terms of his scholarship Kovalevskii was not a jurist but a historian and sociologist. In his eyes the critical-historical method is not only a means toward constructing the new science of the natural growth of human societies (descriptive sociology), but also the mandated method for the study of the history of law of one nation or another.

Considering the diversity and volume of his works, it is understandable that there are a number of blunders, inaccurracies, and errors. But they are overshadowed by their virtues.

## P. G. VINOGRADOV (1854-1925)

Pavel Gavrilovich Vinogradov was born in Kostroma. His father, the son of a Suzdal priest, was a history teacher and later the director of the Kostroma men's gymnasium. He subsequently transferred to Moscow as director of the first men's gymnasium, then became head of all women's gymnasiums which were under the jurisdiction of the Empress Mariia.

His mother, Elena Pavlovna Kobeleva, was the daughter of Lt. General P. D. Kobelev, participant in the War of 1812.[31]

Until age twelve, Pavel was educated by his mother. While still a youth, he obtained good knowledge of foreign languages.

He then studied at Moscow's first gymnasium. During his gymnasium years, Vinogradov was interested in Western European literature and philosophy and particularly in European history.

In 1872 he entered Moscow University with the firm intention of studying world history. Ger'e was his adviser in university study. Vinogradov was already in his class in his freshman year and studied in his seminar. He read much in European history. He was impressed by the works of Ranke and de Tocqueville. He also acquainted himself with the major works in law and political economy. His student graduation (medal) essay was written on "Merovingian Landownership" ["Zemlevladenie u Merovingov"].

Upon graduating from the university, Vinogradov went to Germany for two years. In Berlin he studied enthusiastically in Mommsen's seminar. Later, he called these studies his primary scholarly inspiration in life.

In 1878 he went to Italy to gather materials for his master's thesis. As a topic, he chose the origins of feudal relations in Lombard Italy. In this work he discovered roots of feudal relations in the III and IV century Roman Empire.

The book's first chapter deals with the colony's civilization; the second, with the Lombard conquests; the third, with the Lombard kingdom's political system; the fourth with the social system. He defended this thesis in 1880.

For his doctoral dissertation, Vinogradov decided to choose English social history in the Middle Ages as his topic. The starting point of his research was the XIII century, for medieval English society of this period lends itself to a more precise investigation. He drew on an enormous quantity of archival materials to accomplish this goal.

Vinogradov came to the conclusion that the feudal system was not so much to be explained by the development of bonded relationships as by the degeneration of the social organization of the free village.

Upon returning to Russia, Vinogradov published his dissertation in the *Journal of the Ministry of Public Education*. This was later issued as a separate book (*An Examination of Medieval English Social History* [*Issledovanie po Sotsial'-noi Istorii Anglii v Srednie Veka*]). He defended his doctoral dissertation in 1887.

By that time Vinogradov was already extraordinary professor at Moscow University. Two years later he achieved the ordinary rank. He lectured on the history of Greece and on the Middle Ages and held corresponding seminars.

According to all of the reviews and recollections, the seminars were particularly valuable.

In 1891 Vinogradov again went to England. There, at the invitation of Oxford University, he presented a course on Slavophilism and its influence on Russian culture.

His book, *Villainage in England*, was published in Oxford in 1892. It was his doctoral dissertation, expanded and reworked. Its Russian recension was published in Petersburg in 1910.

In 1895 Vinogradov was elected associate-member of the Academy of Sciences; in 1914 — active member.

At the end of 1901 there were student disorders at Moscow University. Vinogradov was chosen chairman of the university commission on student affairs. He wrote a memorandum on this affair which was signed by many professors. Vinogradov's plan was rejected by Vanovskii, the Minister of Public Education. Vinogradov then withdrew from the university's professorial staff and went abroad.

In 1903 Oxford University invited him to accept the chair of comparative jurisprudence.

In the fall of 1908 and in the spring of 1910 Vinogradov came to Moscow and, in the capacity of a supernumerary professor, lectured on the history of jurisprudence and the social history of medieval England.

But in 1911, L. A. Kasso, the Minister of Public Education, illegally fired the rector, associate rector, and the assistant rector of the University. Vinogradov, along with many other professors, handed in his resignation and came to Russia no more.

It pleased fate, after the bolshevik overthrow and the civil war, to have Russia — in the person of a number of scholars and statesmen — come to Vinogradov in London. He could not refuse to participate in Russian affairs.

Of those newly arrived, the closest to Vinogradov was Mikhail Ivanovich Rostovtsev. Rostovtsev was one of the founders of the Russian Committee of Liberation. One of the activities of this committee was the publication of anti-communist brochures. Vinogradov joined this movement.

Vinogradov then participated in the major international project of the Carnegie Foundation in America — the *Economic and Social History of the World War* (World War I). Vinogradov agreed to be the editor of the volumes devoted to Russia. He invited M. T. Florinskii to be his aide. They discussed the Russian series, projected the authors of the individual volumes, and entered into correspondence with them.

Vinogradov died before publication commenced. Florinskii completed the project.

## Iu. A. KULAKOVSKII (1855-1920)

Iulian Andreevich Kulakovskii was the son of a priest in the town of Ponevezh in the province of Kovno.

He received his secondary education at the Vil'nius gymnasium, then enrolled in the Katkov lycée in Moscow. Thereupon he entered Moscow University.

He was sent on an education assignment to Berlin where he worked under Mommsen. Among other things, he analyzed epigraphic texts.

Mommsen had a powerful influence on Kulakovskii's scholarship.[32] After Mommsen's death, he dedicated an article to him (*Journal of the Ministry of Public Education*, 1904). It was written with great feeling.

Kulakovskii's first works dealt with allotment of land to veterans and military settlements in the Roman Empire.

He wrote his master's thesis on public organizations which played an important role in Roman social, economic, political, and religious life — "Kollegiums in Ancient Rome" ["Kollegii v Drevnem Rime"] (Kiev, 1882).

From the beginning of the 1880's, Kulakovskii began to teach Roman history at the University of Kiev, first with the rank of *privat-docent*, then as professor.

Kulakovskii's doctoral dissertation was titled "Regarding the Question of Rome's Origin" ["K Voprosu o Nachale Rima"] (Kiev, 1888).

Despite his firm reverence for Mommsen, Kulakovskii

differed on the question of Etruscan dominion. Mommsen rejected Etruscan influence; Kulakovskii attached great significance to it. His major work is *History of Byzantium* [*Istoriia Vizantii*] (3 vol., Kiev, 1910-1915). Kulakovskii begins his exposition with 395 and takes it to 717. This is one of the best surveys of Byzantine history in Russian scholarship. His essay, "The Alans According to Classical and Byzantine Writers" ["Alany po Svedeniiam Klassicheskikh i Vizantii-skikh Pisatelei"] (Kiev, 1899), is also very valuable.

In addition, Kulakovskii wrote a marvelous book, *The Past of the Tauris* [*Proshloe Tavridy*] (2nd ed., Kiev, 1914).

In the introduction to the *History of Byzantium* Kulakovskii defines the goal of his work as follows: "My goal was to present a sequential, chronologically accurate, and where possible a complete picture of the life of the empire. This was to be based on a first hand study of the sources at the level of their present refinement. These appear in monographs concerned with this period as well as in the many studies on separate problems which appear in the various periodicals devoted to Byzantine studies. Since the empire lived under the powerful influence of the ancient principle of symphony of Church and State, I have, in my account, tried to allot equal attention to Byzantium's religious and political life."

Kulakovskii was also an admirer of the Roman State religion. His attitude toward historical Christianity was negative, for he felt that Christians impaired the foundations of the Byzantine State. He gave a public lecture on this theme which was published in the *Transactions of the University of Kiev*. This lecture provoked furious attacks on him by certain professors of the Kiev Theological Academy. He was nicknamed "Julian the Apostate," parodying the nickname of Julian, the Roman Emperor (361-363). Christians nicknamed Julian "the Apostate" since he strove to inspire the pagans and to create a new philosophical religion on the foundation of paganism. For this reason, he persecuted

Christians.

## I. M. GREVS (1860-1941)

Ivan Mikhailovich Grevs was born on his father's estate near the village of Lutovinov, Biriuchinsk district, Voronezh province.[33]

Both of his parents were from the vicinity of Khar'kov. His father, Mikhail Mikhailovich Grevs, was a descendant of an Englishman who had entered Russian service under Peter the Great. He was in the military as a youth. During the Crimean War he was wounded at Sevastopol and retired with the rank of lieutenant.

His mother, Anna Ivanovna (Bekariukova) gave her all to bring up her children (Ivan had a brother and sister).

Until the age of twelve, Ivan studied at home. Student teachers were not talented and had little influence on their pupil. Still, it was likely at their suggestions that Ivan read S. T. Aksakov's *Chronicle of a Russian Family* [*Detskie Gody Bagrova-Vnuka*] and Goncharov's *The Frigate Pallas* [*Fregata Pallada*]. Later on, Grevs continued to enjoy reading about trips and liked traveling.

In 1872 his mother moved to Petersburg with her children. One year later Ivan entered grade III of the Karin classical gymnasium. During those years, the majority of secondary schools in Russia were very poor. Formalism ruled and pupils met with rudeness and indifference from their teachers. The exception in this bleak panorama was Viktor Petrovich Ostrogradskii, teacher of Russian. His lessons were captivating and wakened young minds.

Upon graduating from the gymnasium in the autumn of 1879, Grevs enrolled in the University of Petersburg. This was an uneasy period. The revolutionaries were attempting to assassinate Alexander II and captured offenders were being executed.

Grevs sympathized with the revolutionaries. By this time he had recognized his predilection for history, but during the first year was not able to choose an adviser.

At the start of the second year the choice was made. Grevs turned to V. G. Vasil'evskii and became his faithful student and eventually a friend.

It was under Vasil'evskii's influence that Grevs became a medievalist. Vasil'evskii was not a brilliant lecturer. One had to get used to his difficult and sometimes awkward phrasing. But everything was expiated by the content of his lectures. Students "learned scholarship" from Vasil'evskii.

In order to achieve the rank of "candidate" in the first rank, a student had to write a competitive essay in medal competition. Topics were announced a year or two in advance of submission of the essay. Grevs chose the topic of "The Roman-Byzantine State According to the Legal Codes of the V-VI Centuries." He received a medal at the university's graduating ceremony on February 8, 1884.

Grevs was kept at the chair of world history in order to train for professorship.

Besides preparing for the master's examinations, he began to teach history in the upper classes of the men's and women's gymnasiums and the cadet school.

Grevs taught there with enthusiasm and continued to do so later when he had become a professor at the university.

At the end of his student years, and those immediately following, Grevs found a circle of people consonant with his views. He participated in the students' Scientific-Literary Society and joined the comradely association which formed the so-called "Priutino Brotherhood."[34] Several students from the University of Petersburg belonged to it — historians, philologists, jurists, and natural scientists. The brothers F. F. and S. F. Ol'denburg, A. A. Kornilov, V. I. Vernadskii, D. I. Shakhovskoi and several other persons belonged to this group.

In 1885 Grevs married Mariia Sergeevna Zarudnaia, daughter of the famous statesman involved in the judicial reforms of the 1860's.

"The brotherhood," wrote Grevs in his memoirs, "was a fact in the life of a tightly knit group of people which developed along moral lines. But a strong public element was present within it as well. Our brotherhood strove to unite firmly into a single, integral union. But there was never an element of monastic seclusion in it. We strove not toward self-containment but, so to speak, toward a social synthesis . . . (we tried) to serve our nation's progress by means of the constructive labor of peaceful cultural forces."

As a result, Grevs, in his own words, was delivered from the "pressure of contemporary revolutionary groups which were foreign to me in spirit."

Upon passing his master's examinations and receiving the rank of *privat-docent*, Grevs took his first trip abroad in the summer of 1889. Europe made a very powerful impression on him. His Parisian stay decisively persuaded him to study the Roman middle ages.

Fustel de Coulanges had just died but in French academic circles his name was still on everyone's lips. Subsequently, Grevs said that he considered Coulanges to be one of his teachers.

Upon returning to Russia, Grevs commenced to lecture as a *privat-docent*. His first course dealt with the history of the State and society during the period of the Roman Empire's decline. Two years later (1892) he presented his introductory lecture at the Advanced Courses for Women.

When Vasil'evskii became ill, the university entrusted Grevs to teach the survey of the Middle Ages.

Stormy student riots took place at the University of Petersburg in 1899. The police began to arrest and exile the "insurgents." Professors who sympathized with the students were also subjected to repressions. Grevs was among those who were fired from the university. He regained his rights in 1902.

At this time Grevs had already begun to write his master's thesis. In its final form it appeared as the first volume of *Essays on the History of Roman Landownership* [*Ocherki iz Istorii Rimskogo Zemlevladeniia*].

The book is based on the genetic principle. The socio-economic history of the Roman world, particularly its latter phase, is viewed as the ground on which the medieval system

*Russian Historiography: A History*

grew. The construction is thereby oriented toward the future (the Middle Ages) though it begins from afar.

The central figures in the *Essays* were the poet Horace (b. 65 B.C.) and the writer Pomponius Atticus (b.109 B.C.). Grevs defended his thesis in 1900. His official opponents were N. I. Kareev and F. F. Sokolov.

By this time, volume II of his *Essays*, which he had begun to write for his doctoral dissertation, was almost complete. In this volume Grevs intended to clarify the problem of the causes for the fall of the Roman Empire. But it turned out that at this time the German scholar Otto Hirschfeld published statistics on Roman landownership in the imperial period in a German journal. It was material that was rich, newly gathered, and never used by anyone prior to him.

Grevs' work not only included statistical data; it also depicted a broad historical canvas. Nevertheless, Grevs did not then begin to write volume two. He returned to this work only toward the twilight of his life.

After the first Russian revolution, Grevs gave much of his time to public activity. He participated in the congresses of the All-Russian union of professors and in the elaboration of a new university statute and university autonomy.

In the re-organized universities, Grevs sided with the thematic system of instruction. Five "seminars" were created at the University; one of them was in history. Each seminar was in a sense a study with a good sized library and reading room. Grevs labored much to organize the history seminar.

After the October Revolution, the universities had a difficult time. M. N. Pokrovskii's school with its slogan, "history is the politics of the past," came to prevail. The teaching of history in universities died out.

The history departments were re-established only in 1934 and scholarly instruction of history commenced anew. Grevs was able to continue his favorite activity. With the introduction of degress, he was given the degree of doctor of historical sciences.

Grevs turned his main attention to the "aspirants"

[graduate students]. (This was a new term which replaced the old phrase of "kept at the chair"). He did not refuse anyone advice and guidance.

Grevs died on May 16, 1941, failing by one day to attain his 81st birthday. His wife and his daughter Catherine died in Leningrad during the German blockade.

After defending his master's thesis, Grevs took up the study of feudal France, the spiritual culture of the early Renaissance, and Dante's creative work. He published a series of valuable articles on these topics.

Grevs' long articles on feudalism in France (in *The Brockhaus-Efron Encyclopedic Dictionary*, half-volume 70, 1902) and in Italy (*ibid.*) are thorough and profound.

In half-volume 72 of the *Encyclopedic Dictionary*, Grevs published an article on the famous French historian, Fustel de Coulanges whom he listed as one of his teachers (as noted above).

From his youth Grevs liked Turgenev. They had much in common.

Grevs wrote two books about Turgenev — his biography and a thoughtful, one may say poetic, étude *Turgenev and Italy* [*Turgenev i Italiia*].

During the last years of his life, Grevs returned to the theme of his master's thesis. He reworked and added to the *Essays on the History of Roman Landownership*. The result was a magisterial two volume work. Grevs wrote with his youthful enthusiasm and was able to complete it. I have no information as to whether this work was published.

Grevs's last book was *Tacitus* (published posthumously in 1946). Grevs felt that Tacitus was the best Roman historian.

Grevs had many students — at the university and at the Advanced Courses for Women. Far from many chose the scholarly career.

Of those who took the scholarly path, those closest to him were L. P. Karsavin, O. A. Dobiash-Rozhdestvenskaia, and A. I. Petrunkevich.

# D. M. PETRUSHEVSKII (1863-1942)

Dmitrii Moiseevich Petrushevskii graduated from the historico-philological department of the University of Kiev. He was the student of I. V. Luchitskii. Somewhat later, he took part in Vinogradov's seminar in Moscow. Thus, he can also be considered Vinogradov's student.

In 1892 he wrote a long article on Vinogradov's book, *Villainage in England*. His main work, *The Revolt of Wat Tyler*, [*Vosstanie Uota Tailera*] appeared in two parts, 1897-1901. The individual parts were submitted respectively as the master's thesis, then the doctoral dissertation.

He was then granted a professorship at Moscow University.

Petrushevskii was a thoughtful guide in the seminar on medieval history.

He spoke rather quickly. Frequently, he covered his mouth with his hand and turned half-way around. But the students accustomed themselves quickly. In their content his lectures were very pithy (I write through personal recollection about this).

In 1911, along with many of his colleagues, Petrushevskii left Moscow University in protest against the illegal actions of Kasso, the Minister of Public Education. He received a chair at the Petersburg Polytechnic Institute and moved to Petersburg. He was elected active member of the Academy of Sciences in 1929.

Of Petrushevskii's many works, aside from *The Revolt of Wat Tyler*, I will note his excellent *Essays on the History of English State and Society in the Middle Ages* [*Ocherki is Istorii Angliiskogo Gosudarstva i Obshchestva v Srednie Veka*] (1903; 4th ed., 1937), and *The Great Charter of Freedoms and the Constitutional Struggle in English Society in the Second Half of the XIII Century* [*Velikaia Kharta Vol'nostei i Konstitutsionnaia Bor'ba v Angliiskom Obshchestve vo Vtoroi Polovine XIII Veka*] (1915).

Petrushevskii's approach to medieval England's social

and economic system was historical.

"All social sciences," he writes in the introduction to his *Essays on the History of English State and Society*, "orient themselves toward history. More properly speaking, they are the component parts of history — history of the science of both the general and the individual alike."

"With the success of comparative historical studies, it became even more clear that the feudal order was not the product of local European medieval development. Feudal aspects are observable in ancient Greece and Rome, in ancient Eastern societies, among the Slavic peoples and Arabs, and in China and Japan. Feudalism was ceasing to be a purely historical category and was becoming an obviously sociological category."

"The history of the Roman Empire casts a bright light on the processes of political and social development occurring in Muscovite Russia. At the same time, it may be said that the science of Russian history totally ignores the edifying lessons which the empire of Diocletian and Constantine generously offers. It is enough to compare the Roman colonies with Moscow's serfdom to be struck by the amazing parallel between these institutions themselves and the reasons which brought them into existence."

"Thus, feudalism does not signify a decay of State unity fully compatible with broad governmental organization but even represents one of its varieties."

## A. A. VASIL'EV (1867-1953)

Aleksandr Aleksandrovich Vasil'ev was born in Petersburg. His father was a lieutenant-colonel in the army and headed the military detachment of the Peter-Paul fortress where Aleksandr spent the first years of his childhood.[35] His mother, Ol'ga, came from the Chelpanov family of merchants.

In 1880 Aleksandr entered the second grade of Petersburg's first classical gymnasium. He graduated with a gold medal in 1887.

Among his comrades at the gymnasium, Vasil'ev retained for life the friendship of V. N. Zlatarskii, a Bulgarian.

Upon graduating from the gymnasium, he enrolled in the historico-philological department of the University of Petersburg where his adviser was V. G. Vasil'evskii. In addition, he studied Arabic at the Near Eastern department under the guidance of Baron V. R. Rozen.

Vasil'ev graduated from the university with a gold medal in 1892. Upon graduation he received a post as Latin teacher in the very same gymnasium that he had attended.

One of his classmates in his student years was M. I. Rostovtsev who practically became his closest friend.

Three years later, Vasil'ev realized that his job at the gymnasium hindered the continuation of his scholarly studies. He quit teaching at the gymnasium and received a foreign assignment from the university. With interruptions, he spent three and a half years abroad (1897-1900).

Vasil'ev spent the first year in London, then studied in Paris. Toward the end, after a short stay in Vienna, he went to Prague to attend the commemoration of the 100th anniversary of Polacky's birth. The celebration was a triumphal one.

Vasil'ev spent the second year of his assignment in the Near East. At this time his headquarters was the Russian Archeological Institute in Constantinople. There he met F. I. Uspenskii. But they did not become fiends.

In Europe Vasil'ev wrote his master's thesis, "Byzantium and the Arabs" ["Vizantiia i Araby"]. The first volume served as his master's thesis (which he defended in 1901), the second — as his doctoral dissertation (which he defended in 1902).

In 1904 Vasil'ev was elected to the chair of world history at Iurevsk University at the rank of ordinary professor. Simultaneously, he was made instructor in medieval history at the Women's Pedagogical Institute in Petersburg. In order to combine these two duties, Vasil'ev traveled twice monthly from Iur'ev to Petersburg.

As a representative of the University of Petersburg, Iur'ev University, and the Women's Pedagogical Institute, he went to Australia in 1906 to attend the 50th anniversary of the University of Melbourne.

In 1917 Vasil'ev was made professor at the University of Petersburg, and in 1919, chosen as associate member of the Academy of Sciences.

The Academy for the History of Material Culture was established in Petersburg in 1918. Vasil'ev was elected member and was its chairman for a time.

In 1925, because of the difficulties of scholarly work in Petersburg (by that time Leningrad), particularly for historians, Vasil'ev accepted an invitation from the University of Wisconsin to teach a course in Ancient History. After his first year of teaching there, Vasil'ev received a professorship.

In 1936 Vasil'ev was elected a member (fellow) of the American Medieval Academy in Cambridge, Massachusetts.

Upon reaching his retirement age at the University of Wisconsin (in 1937), Vasil'ev was invited to be a Fellow at Dumbarton Oaks, Harvard University's Byzantine Institute in Washington.

Vasil'ev moved to Washington and continued his scholarly work. Conditions for this were exceedingly favorable – there was a large library and collection of antiquities. Besides Vasil'ev, a whole consortium of major scholars who studied Byzantine history and related disciplines gathered there.

Vasil'ev established friendly relations with his colleagues.

At the end of 1952, Vasil'ev was invited to the Byzantine Congress in Saloniki (1953). He was chosen to be the Congress's honorary president and presented a lecture. It may be said that this Congress took place under the symbol of honoring Vasil'ev.

Bearing this impression, Vasil'ev flew to Washington. Upon arrival, he died in his sleep.

Vasil'ev had many students, male and female, in Russia and in America. Among those who specialized in Byzantine history we can cite: M. A. Andreeva (a member of the

Seminarium Kondakovianum in Prague), A. F. Vishniakova, E. Ch. Skrzhinskaia, A. P. Smirnov, P. A. Iakovenko, F. von Steinmann. In America — John S. Schneider, Miss Hazel Ramsay, and Peter Charanis.

We will now review Vasil'ev's major scholarly works. The first of these appeared in two volumes in 1901-1902. These were: *The Political Relations of Byzantium and the Arabs During the Period of the Amorian Dynasty* [*Politicheskie Otnosheniia Vizantii i Arabov za Vremia Amoriiskoi Dinastii*] and *The Political Relations of Byzantium and the Arabs During the Period of the Macedonian Dynasty* [*Politicheskie Otnosheniia Vizantii i Arabov za Vremia Makedonskoi Dinastii*].

Thirty years later, Vasil'ev revised and amplified this work for the French edition. It also appeared in two volumes and was titled *Byzance et les Arabs* (Brussels, 1935-1950).

Thereafter, Vasil'ev's work took two directions. On the one hand, he prepared an overall course of Byzantine history; on the other, he wrote specialized monographs.

In 1917 Vasil'ev published volume one of his *Lectures in Byzantine History* [*Lektsii po Istorii Vizantii*] in Petersburg. It covered up to the period of the Crusades. In America, Vasil'ev reworked and significantly expanded his lectures.

His monumental English history of the Byzantine Empire — *History of the Byzantine Empire, 324-1453* was created in this fashion. The first English edition appeared in two volumes in 1928-1929.

Four years later, Vasil'ev reworked and expanded the text for the French edition which was published in Paris in 1932.

Vasil'ev revised this French edition anew for the second English edition which was published in Madison in 1952.

I cite this detailed bibliographic data because it is valuable in characterizing Vasil'ev as a scholar. He never stood still but moved constantly forward, inquisitively and indefatigably.

The principal monographs written by Vasil'ev in English in America are three: *The Goths in the Crimea* (1936), *The*

*First Russian Attack on Constantinople in 860-861* (1946), and *Justin the First: An Introduction to the Epoch of Justinian the Great* (1950). All three works are very valuable. In his works Vasil'ev turns his primary attention to the political, social, and economic aspects of Byzantium's historical development. But (particularly in his *History of the Byzantine Empire*) he also provides a superb survey of cultural history. Each chapter of the *History of the Byzantine Empire* contains a section on literature, learning, and art.

Music had a considerable place in Vasil'ev's life. Throughout his life, he preserved a passion for it which he had from childhood.

While a pupil in the gymnasium, Vasil'ev attended the première of *Eugene Onegin* and saw P. I. Chaikovskii [Tchaikovsky]. He already played the piano well. Subsequently he became an excellent pianist and expert on musical literature. In America he constantly attended piano recitals and symphonic concerts.

In his own words, he loved music more than scholarship.

## O. A. DOBIASH-ROZHDESTVENSKAIA
## (1875-1939)

Ol'ga Antonovna Dobiash-Rozhdestvenskaia (the name Rozhdestvenskaia derives from her husband) graduated from the Advanced Courses for Women in Petersburg. She was a student of Grevs, an outstanding medievalist and paleographer, and associate member of the Academy of Sciences.

Upon graduating from the Advanced Courses for Women, she studied in Paris under Ch. V. Langlois, a professor of paleography. Influenced by Langlois, she wrote her dissertation on the life of French ecclesiastical parishes in the XIII century. She received the doctor's degree.

Three years later, she published an expanded version of this work in Russian. It was titled *French Ecclesiastical Society in the XIII Century: Part I, the Parish* [*Tserkovnoe*

*Obshchevtvo Frantsii v XIII Veke, chast' I, Prikhod*].
She received the master's degree in world history —
the first such award to a woman in Russia.
Her next major work was devoted to the cult of Arch-
angel Michael in the Middle Ages (1918).
A summary in the form of a small book appeared in
Paris in French in 1922.

## A. M. PETRUNKEVICH (1876-1965)

Aleksandra Mikhailovna Petrunkevich was the daughter
of the chief doctor of the Tver provincial hospital.
His brother, Ivan Il'ich, was a public figure and member
of the first State Duma.
Aleksandra Mikhailovna graduated from the Advanced
Courses for Women in Petersburg. She was a student of
Grevs. Afterwards, she was elected professor of world history
there. Of her scholarly works of this period, the most sig-
nificant are: *Cola di Rienzi* [*Kola Di Rienzi*] (an episode
from the history of XIV century Rome), and *Catherine of
Aragon* [*Ekaterina Arragonskaia*] (dealing with XVI century
Anglo-Spanish relations).
In 1920 she emigrated to France and settled in Paris.
She joined the Association of Russian Scholars in Paris. Her
old friends, the French historian F. Lot and his Russian wife,
the daughter of Professor I. Borodin, were among the organ-
izers of this group.
Like her teacher Grevs, Petrunkevich was a follower of
Fustel de Coulanges and wrote a penetrating article about
him which was published in the *Transactions of the Russian
Education Institute* in Belgrade (No. 5, 1931, pp. 291-334).
After a long illness, she died in a nursing home outside
Paris in June of 1965.

## L. P. KARSAVIN (1882-1952)

Lev Platonovich Karsavin was born in Petersburg in an
artistic family. His father was a ballet master, his sister

Tamara, a famous ballerina.

Karsavin graduated from the historico-philological department of the University of Petersburg. He was a student of Grevs.

His master's thesis was "Essays on Religious Life in Italy in the XII-XIII Centuries" ["Ocherki Religioznoi Zhizni v Italii XII-XIII Veka"] (1912). His doctoral dissertation was "The Origins of Medieval Religiosity in the XII-XIII Centuries, Principally in Italy" ["Osnovy Srednevekovoi Religioznosti v XII-XIII Vekakh, Preimushchestvenno v Italii"] (1915). Both of these fundamental works were similar in theme and historical method. Karsavin strove to depict the "religiosity of the masses." He sets Catholicism's dogma aside. At the center of his attention is the problem of "the nature of religious life, of religions and religio-moral feelings." In so doing, Karsavin brought together the orthodox and heretical trends.

In 1922, by Trotsky's order, he was exiled abroad and settled in Paris.

He participated in the Eurasian movement. (The Eurasian movement was founded by Prince N. S. Trubetskoi and P. N. Savitskii in 1920).[36]

In 1928 Karsavin was invited to be professor of world history at the University of Kovno. At the time, Kovno (Kaunas) was the capital of the Lithuanian republic.

Karsavin was a man of unusual abilities. Among them was a talent for languages. He learned Lithuanian to perfection and lectured in Lithuanian.

According to the 1939 agreement between Hitler and Stalin, Lithuania was occupied by Soviet forces. Karsavin was arrested and sent to a concentration camp in Siberia. He died there in July of 1952.[37]

Of Karsavin's works written abroad, the most important is *Philosophy of History* [*Filosofiia Istorii*] (Berlin, 1923). The book's basic idea is the unity of the world created by God. Man also shares in this unity. Therefore he is capable of mentally encompassing all eras and regions.

## MODERN HISTORIANS

## I. V. LUCHITSKII (1845-1918)

Ivan Vasil'evich Luchitskii was born in Kamenets-Podol'skii where his father taught in the seminary. He studied at this seminary. Luchitskii transferred from the seminary to the gymnasium. (He graduated from the gymnasium in Kiev). While still a gymnasium pupil, Luchitskii read Guizot's *General History of European Civilization* [*Istoriia Tsivilizatsii v Evrope*] and Schlösser's *A History of the XVIII and XIX Centuries* [*Istoriia XVIII i XIX Stoletii*]. Upon graduating from the gymnasium, he enrolled in the historico-philological department of the University of Kiev. At the time, this department was in great decline. World history was taught by an untalented professor. Luchitskii did not have a real adviser. Left to himself, he read books rather indiscriminately. He read Gervinus, Bücher, and Feuerbach. Auguste Comte's positivism made a great impression on him.

His first published work was a critical analysis of Dobriakov's book, *Russian Women in the Appanage-Vech Period* [*Russkaia Zhenshchina v Udel'no-Vechevoi Period*] (in the newspaper *Kievlianin*, 1863).

Luchitskii graduated from the university in 1866. The senior thesis necessary to receive the rank of *privat-docent* was written on the bourgeoisie and the Huguenot aristocracy in southern France after the Massacre at St. Bartholomew's in 1572.

His master's thesis is titled "Feudal Aristocracy and Calvinists in France" ["Feodal'naia Aristokratiia i Kalvinsity vo Frantsii"] (1871).

Luchitskii approached his topic from the socio-political, not the religious, angle. He proved that the first phase of the struggle was basically that of the aristocracy against royal power. This struggle was not democratic as formerly thought.

Luchitskii establishes the connection between the Huguenot movement, the extreme Catholic party, and feudal reaction.

Primarily he used published materials for this study but also drew on the unpublished. He found correspondence of contemporaries of this era in the Petersburg public library. For a long time, the Calvinist era in France was the focus of Luchitskii's attention.

Luchitskii's work drew notice not only in Russia but in France as well. A. Morie wrote an article on Luchitskii's book in *Journal des Savants*.

Luchitskii defended his master's thesis in Kazan. The department awarded him the *privat-docent* rank but he was blackballed by the university council. Nevertheless, the university gave him a foreign assignment.

Luchitskii went to Paris. He worked in the national library and the national archives. He became friendly with Gabriel Monod, editor of the journal *Revue Historique*. At Monod's request, Luchitskii began to contribute surveys of Russian historical literature to this journal.

Luchitskii also made the acquaintance of the representatives of positivism — the Frenchman Littre and the Russian G. N. Vyrubov. He also became acquainted with figures of the French Revolution of 1848, among them Louis Blanc.

In the search for unpublished materials on Calvinism, Luchitskii went to the south of France — Grenoble, Nimes, Montpelier, and Toulouse. In those archives he truly did find a great number of valuable materials unknown to French historians. He also researched archives in Germany — those in Heidelberg and Leipzig.

In 1874 the University of Kiev chose Luchitskii as a *docent* and he returned to Kiev. His doctoral dissertation appeared in 1877: "The Catholic League and Calvinists in France During the Second Half of the XVII Century" ["Katolicheskaia Liga i Kal'vinisty vo Frantsii vo Vtoroi Polovine XVII Veka"]. He defended it in Petersburg after which he attained professorship at the University of Kiev.

Subsequently, Luchitskii turned to the history of economic relations in Europe, chiefly to the history of the peasantry in France before and after the French Revolution of 1789. But he also studied the history of the peasant commune in Spain, wrote on peasant reform in Denmark and Lifland, and on the population of German cities in the XV and XVI centuries.

Luchitskii's main works at the end of the XIX and the beginning of the XX centuries dealt with the problem of peasant landownership in France prior to and during the French Revolution of 1789.

There was disagreement in the historical literature on this subject. In his book on the peasants in France in the last quarter of the XVIII century (1789), Kareev held to the opinion that peasant landownership on the eve of the Revolution was insignificant.

Maksim Kovalevskii felt that the transference of land during the Revolution principally benefited the middle and upper bourgeoisie.

Luchitskii decided to base himself primarily on statistical data. Beginning in 1894, he annually, until the commencement of World War I, (and with breaks only in 1906 and 1908), conducted research in more than twenty provincial archives. He worked from early morning to late evening.

The main sources for his study were the tax rolls, cadastres, and the sales records of national properties.

Luchitskii came to the conclusion that peasant landownership in France was already widespread prior to the Revolution. In his opinion, the composition of the peasant population was heterogeneous but there was no peasant group which did not possess at least a piece of land. The Revolution did not hinder the transfer of private property and in some degree abetted it.

However, the idea of agrarian reform was foreign to the majority of legislators. In the sale of national properties, financial aims were in the forefront.

As a university professor, Luchitskii had great influence on youth. He did not like to give survey courses but preferred to present courses on special topics and to hold seminars.

Several prominent scholars came out of his seminars —
N. N. Liubovich, D. N. Molchanovskii, V. P. Kliachin, V. K.
Piskorskii, and E. V. Tarle.

During his lifetime, Luchitskii built an enormous library in many languages encompassing the history of many
centuries.

He wrote: "For the historian, there should be no
breakdown between interesting and uninteresting nations.
The historian may not be interesting but history is alway
interesting." He willed his library to the Kiev public library.

Luchitskii was active in public work. He was a member
of the Kiev municipal council and of the *zemstvo*.

In Paris, along with M. M. Kovalevskii, he took part in
founding the Russian advanced school of social studies.

In 1908 Luchitskii was elected to the Third State Duma
and moved to Petersburg for a time. However, he paid little
attention to it. He lectured at the Advanced Courses for
Women and at the University of Petersburg as a *privat-
docent*.

He died on his estate in the Poltava province in 1918.

## UNIVERSAL HISTORY OF THE MODERN
## PERIOD [38]

### R. Iu. VIPPER (1858-1954)

Robert Iur'evich Vipper graduated from the historico-
philological department of Moscow University.

His teacher was V. I. Ger'e, but he later broke with him.

For a long time, Vipper taught in the secondary school
system in Moscow.

The first topic of Vipper's specialized study was the
XVI century — the study of the religious and political
theories of Calvinism in Geneva.

Vipper based his work on a broad range of published
and archival material. Vipper carefully traces the relations

between Church and State in Geneva. Vipper brought the detailed exposition down to the mid 1580's; but in the final chapter, he gave a general survey to 1602.

For this outstanding work, the historico-philological department of Moscow University granted him the doctor's degree immediately, skipping over the master's. The sole chair of world history at Moscow University was held by M. S. Kavelin. Vipper lectured at the *privat-docent* rank. Only after Kavelin's death (1899) did Vipper get a professorship.

Vipper's lectures were enormously popular with students. Mostly he taught modern history. He used his lecture material for his interesting articles: "Social Teachings and Historical Theories of the XVIII and XIX Centuries in Connection with the Social Movement in the West" ["Obshchestvennye Ucheniia i Istoricheskie Teorii XVIII i XIX Vekov v Sviazi s Obshchestvennym Dvizheniem na Zapade"] (1900), "Essays on the Theory of Historical Knowledge" ["Ocherki Teorii Istoricheskogo Poznaniia"] (1914); and "The Crisis of Historical Scholarship" ["Krizis Istoricheskoi Nauku"] (Kazan, 1921).

In 1922, on Trotsky's order, Vipper was exiled from Russia. He was given a professorship at the University of Riga.

His book, *Ivan the Terrible* [*Ivan Groznyi*] appeared in the same year. In this work Vipper turned his major attention to Ivan's foreign policy on the background of European history. He arrived at the conclusion that Ivan the Terrible played a more prominent international role than it was generally supposed.

Stalin's "cult of personality" began ten years after this book's appearance. Ivan the Terrible was pronounced a brilliant statesman. The terror of the *oprichnina* period was justified by government necessity.

Vipper's book on Ivan the Terrible was caught up in this wave. It was re-issued in Moscow in 1944. Its English translation also appeared in Moscow (1947).

## A. N. SAVIN (1873- 1923)

Aleksandr Nikolaevich Savin was born, and spent his early childhood, in a village in the Kaluga province. His father was a doctor's assistant. Savin graduated from the historico-philological department of Moscow University. His principal instructor was P. G. Vinogradov.

Vinogradov, as stated in the chapter about him, studied the social history of XIII century England; Petrushevskii worked on the XIVth and Savin on the XVth and XVIth. Together, they can be called the Russian school for the study of medieval England.

In 1900 Savin received an educational assignment for England. There, in the British Museum and in the government archives (the Public Record Office), he collected an enormous amount of material for his master's thesis titled "The English Village in the Tudor Era" ["Angliiskaia Derevnia v Epokhu Tiudorov"] (Moscow, 1903). His extensive work consists of three chapters: 1) the end of villeinage; 2) the juridical history of common hold; and 3) the decline of the manorial economy.

His doctor's dissertation, "English Secularization" ["Angliiskaia Sekuliarizatsiia"] (Moscow 1906) is a continuation of this work.

Savin arrived at the conclusion that during the partition of confiscated monastic lands, the greater share was obtained by military servitors and, primarily, the managers of the central State mechanism.

"The government factor influences the redistribution of landed property, the growth of the middle and rich landowners of the gentlemen serving class, and the subsequent successes of the landed gentry."

Although Savin's main interest focused on England, he was also engaged in broad European problems, including Russia.

His article, "Nicholas I and Friedrich-Wilhelm IV (1840-1848)" ["Nikolai I i Fridrikh-Vil'gelm IV (1840-

1848)"] appeared in the anthology *Russia and the West* [*Zapad i Rossiia*] in 1923. His death did not enable him to complete it. After his death, one of his students, P. F. Preobrazhenskii, finished it.[39]

After the defense of his master's thesis, Savin was chosen extraordinary professor at Moscow University; upon the defense of his doctoral dissertation, he was given one of the chairs of world history.

At the university, Savin lectured on European history, primarily of the XVI-XVII centuries. His lectures were serious and pithy.

He also ran the seminar very well. Savin was a man of poor health. He had rheumatism (or arthritis) in his legs. He came to the university to lecture and to hold the seminar. But the members of the seminar, in order to speak on the topic of their work, had to visit him at his home.

He lived in the house of the Glesin music school (he was married to one of the Glesin sisters).

At the end of 1922, Savin left on his regular trip to England. There in January of 1923 he died from the Spanish flu.

Savin was a historian-analyst. He was very careful in his conclusions and avoided synthesis and broad generalizations.

According to Petrushevskii's testimonial, Savin was "a man of extraordinary intellectual power, extensive education, and profound scholarship."

## E. V. TARLE (1875-1955)

Evgenii Viktorovich Tarle graduated from the historico-philological department of the University of Kiev. He was the student of I. V. Luchitskii.

Upon graduating from the university, he moved to Petersburg and joined the staff of the *privat-docents* at the University of Petersburg.

In 1901 he published two books on Italy: *The History of Italy in the Middle Ages* [*Istoriia Italii v Srednie Veka*] and *The History of Italy in Modern Times* [*Istoriia Italii v*

*Novoe Vremia*]. Both were in the series titled *The History of Europe by Eras and Nations* [*Istoriia Evropy po Epokham i Stranam*].

His book, *The Social Views of Thomas More as Related to the Economic State of Contemporary England* [*Obshchestvennye Vozzreniia Tomasa Mora v Sviazi s Ekonomicheskim Sostoianiem Anglii ego Vremeni*] also appeared in that year. Some critics attacked the book sharply.

Tarle's fundamental work appeared in 1909-1911 in two parts. It is called *The Working Class in France in the Era of the Revolution* [*Rabochii Klass vo Frantsii v Epokhu Revoliutsii*]. The first part deals with the National Assembly of 1789-1791; the second with the 1792-1799 period.

In the first part, Tarle focuses principally on the Parisian workers; in the second — on the provincial workers. The first part primarily discusses the social aspect of the problem; the second also treats the economic.

Tarle discusses the state of the workers in connection with the fate of French industry. He notes its technical backwardness.

This work was followed by another major two-volume work, *The Continental Blockade: I — A Study of the History of the Industry and Foreign Relations of France in the Napoleonic Era* (Moscow, 1913); *II — The Economic Life of the Italian Kingdom in the Reign of Napoléon I* (Iur'ev, 1916) [*Kontinental'naia Blokada. I. Issledovanie po Istorii Promyshlennosti i Vneshnei Torgovli Frantsii v Epokhu Napoleona. II Ekonomicheskaia Zhizn' Korolevtsva Italii v Tsarstvovanie Napoleona I*].

In this work Tarle studies the governing principles of Napoleon's economic policy and the extent of French foreign trade in the Napoleonic era.

Tarle's next significant work was *Europe in the Age of Imperialism* [*Evropa v Epokhu Imperializma*] (1928). Tarle places the major share of the blame for the start of World War I on Germany.

The end of the 1920's was a period wherein M. N. Pokrovskii's dictatorship over Russian historical scholarship was established. He routed the "bourgeois" historians. Tarle, among others, also suffered. He was exiled to Tashkent. Only in 1934 was he given permission to return from exile.

His book *Napoleon* was published in 1937. In describing the French invasion of Russia, Tarle asserted that, in contrast to Spain, there was no mass uprising against the French in Russia. On the contrary, there were cases when peasants informed on their landowners to the French.[40]

But in one year Tarle's new book appeared: *Napoleon's Invasion of Russia* [*Nashestvie Napoleona na Rossiiu*]. In it he glorifies the unity of the Russian nation (including peasant serfs) in the struggle against the French.

What happened during the year which forced Tarle to change his opinion?

It became clear to the Soviet government that Hitler was preparing for a war with Russia. Thus, psychological preparation for this war and an appeal to patriotism was begun. Tarle took stock of this.

Tarle's last major works were two brilliantly written books — *The Northern War and the Swedish Invasion of Russia* [*Severnaia Voina i Shvedskoe Nashestvie na Rossiiu*] (Moscow 1958) and *The Crimean War: 1853-1856* [*Krymskaia Voina 1853-1865 Godov* ] (Moscow 1960). Both of these books were published posthumously. In summary, it might be said that Tarle was an unusually talented man and an outstanding historian. But, whenever he found it necessary, he did not hesitate to change his views to please the Soviet government or the reading public.

## XXV

### PLATONOV (1860-1933), D'IAKONOV (1855-1919), IKONNIKOV (1841-1923)

Platonov's and D'iakonov's creative work ran parallel in many ways.

Both were outstanding scholars. Platonov was a historian. D'iakonov was a jurist and legal historian and also occupies a prominent place in the development of Russian historical scholarship. To a certain extent, their main works belong to the same group of Russian historical problems and to the same period — the Muscovy period (XVI-XVII centuries).

Sergei Fedorovich Platonov was born in Chernigov where his father held a government post as a typographical technician. His parents were both from Moscow by birth and they longed to return. Under their influence the boy Sergei became a Russian patriot. In 1869 the family moved to the north from Chernigov. They visited Moscow but settled in Petersburg. The elder Platonov received a rather good salary there. His dream was to give his son a good education and see him graduate from the university. The son was placed in a gymnasium to prepare for the university.

While in the gymnasium, Platonov already displayed an interest in literature and history and decided to enroll in the philological-historical department at the University of Petersburg. In the spring of 1877, when Platonov was to go from grade seven to grade eight in the gymnasium, he became seriously ill with typhus. During his illness, the Russo-Turkish War of 1877-1878 began. It made a deep impression upon him.

For rest and recuperation his mother took him to Moscow in the summer of 1877. There he made close acquaintance with the family of Evgeniia Antonovna Selivanova. She was a widow and lived in her summer cottage with her two daughters — also widows — and two granddaughters.

"The spirit of the old Moscow intelligentsia, of a somewhat Slavophile hue, permeated this family," Platonov later wrote in his memoirs.

Platonov became friendly with the eldest granddaughter, Evgeniia Nikolaevna Kolaidovich. She was six years older than he and greatly influenced his intellectual development. She awakened in him a lively interest in literature and history.

"Returning to my gymnasium in the fall," says Platonov, "I was already different from what I had been prior to my illness. I recall this last winter at the gymnasium with pleasure. Above and beyond class assignments, I read and wrote much."

Evgeniia Nikolaevna Kolaidovich married V. N. Berkut, a philology student at Moscow University. From him, Platonov received news of the upgrading of historical study at Moscow University. There were courses by professors Ger'e, Solov'ev, and Vinogradov, and Platonov was almost sorry that he decided to enroll in the University of Petersburg, not Moscow University.

Platonov was disappointed with his first year of study at the University of Petersburg. The course schedule offered little room for the specialty which Platonov had chosen — literature. Greek was taught by an old wreck of a professor, Liugebil who was lame, deaf, and voiceless. O. A. Shebor, the Latin professor, was a Czech by origin. He taught with great enthusiasm but soon lost popularity because he introduced *extemporalia* into his teaching. Students were already tired of this in the gymnasium.

F. F. Sokolov was the professor of ancient history and was a good scholar. An enthusiast of ancient Greece, he previously had many students. He began each lecture with the words "the Greeks were an amazing people." His course was laden with facts but short on historiography, guiding ideas, and enlightened generalizations.

The famous Sreznevskii taught the "Encyclopedia of Slavic Philology." Students listened to his lectures with great attention and benefit for themselves. This was Sreznevskii's last course — he died in 1880.

Very popular with students was Orest Fedorovich Miller, professor of Russian literature. He was a confirmed Slavophile and expounded his views with unusual fervor.

Konstantin Nikolaevich Bestuzhev-Riumin turned Platonov's attention from literature to history. Platonov became his student.[41]

Platonov was disappointed because, with the exception of Sreznevksii and Bestuzhev, students were not given introductory or general courses in world literature, history, linguistics, philosophy.

He sought a guiding synthesis among the jurists. For Platonov, Gradovskii's and Sergeevich's lectures were a certain corrective.

Platonov writes: "Gradovskii taught government law and was a keen and refined lecturer. He knew how to clothe risky contemporary political topics in proper form and to thoroughly illuminate problems of governmental structure without encouraging the censorship of the time. . . My conceptions of State and society, government aims, the relationship of the State to the individual, and the welfare of personal freedom and 'independence', were initally formed from Gradovskii's lectures."

"I am, by the way, also obligated to Gradovskii for the stubbornness with which I always opposed all partisanship or clanishness. I jealously guarded the right of every individual to use his own powers in the direction which his own inner motive dictated. Gradovskii's powerful influence upon me forces me to recognize him as one of my teachers in the best sense of that word."

Sergeevich's lectures were of a different character. Students — Platonov among them — were enraptured by them. "He spoke splendidly. His serious and smooth phrasing always contained a precise and clear thought. Sergeevich's oral speech was like his literary style which one could admire."

However, Sergeevich did not influence Platonov's thought.

"I now feel," wrote Platonov in his memoirs, "that Sergeevich little knew and understood Russian life because he was not familiar with the national mode of life. . . A powerful logic, straightforward conclusions, the disregard of historical perspective for the sake of schematic clarity and juridical constructions — such were the general characteristics of Sergeevich's exposition.[42]

Platonov's second year at the university (1879-1880) was a cheerless one. These were troubled times. Terroristic attempts on the life of Alexander II began. There were murders of governors and top police officials.

With the exception of Bestuzhev, the second year courses were of no interest to Platonov. Two lectures had not yet finished when his father fell dangerously ill.

In his memoirs, Platonov writes: "It was necessary to maintain constant watch by the sickbed. For this task we were able to get only one person in addition to my mother and myself. My share of the duty was eight hours per day on top of various cares and necessary absences. University studies were pushed into the background. For a time I made an effort and sat up at night over psychology notes. But then I fell behind here as well and attended the university only when I had a minute. I tried not to miss Bestuzhev's lectures. Matters dragged on like this until spring."

Platonov passed a part of his exams in the spring and received permission to take the others in a year. He was conditionally passed on to his junior year.

The junior year was a bright period in Platonov's student life. The main event was the appearance of a new professor of world history — Vasilii Grigor'evich Vasil'evskii. He presented a general course in medieval history and a special course for history majors. It had no particular title and was not specifically listed. It may best be called "Russo-Byzantine topics."

"Vasil'evskii acquainted us with the results of his particular research, the texts which he was working on, and with the research methods which he had become accustomed to. At the same time, he inclined those so desiring to write essays and attentively checked such labors."

Vasil'evskii proposed that Platonov take the theme of the inhabitat of the southern Goths. Platonov agreed. Vasil'-evskii placed these Goths "somewhat above Anapa, closer to the Straights of Kerch." Platonov placed them directly on the Taman peninsula. In the main, he based his account on the *History of the Wars* by Procopius of Caesarea (VI c.).

Vasil'evskii read Platonov's essay attentively and spoke with him for an hour about it.

"Many years later," writes Platonov, "I heard from one of my friends that Vasil'evksii did not forget my eager essay and had formed a good opinion of me because of it. . . This was my first acquaintance with Vasil'evskii and it served as the start of long and close relations with an unforgettable teacher."

During the junior year, according to established custom, Platonov was to receive a theme from Bestuzhev for his graduating examination in Russian history. Platonov contemplated the problem of the *zemskii sobors* [national assemblies]. Here was the influence of the historical moment. This was the short period of Loris-Melikov's reforms.

Bestuzhev approved the topic but, in accordance with his pedagogical principles — to let students work independently — he did not give Platonov any bibliographic references.

Platonov then turned to *privat-docent* E. E. Zamyslovskii. The latter gave Platonov useful instructions regarding the relevant literature and sources. This helped Platonov a great deal in the first phase of his work.

Platonov presented his work to Bestuzhev in January of 1882. The latter read it at length and then told Platonov that the work fully satisfied the requirements of a candidate's thesis. According to the supposed rules of the colloquium, Bestuzhev suggested that he write another work on the topic of the collected divisions of the *Pomestnyi Prikaz*.[43]

Platonov was surprised and offended at Bestuzhev's new demands.

But it so occurred that in the spring of 1882 Bestuzhev fell seriously ill and left for abroad. His students were given to E. E. Zamyslovskii.

Zamyslovskii passed Platonov's essay on the *zemskii sobors* for his candidate's paper and left Platonov at the chair of Russian history to prepare for the professorial calling.

Platonov's father died in November of 1881. Platonov had loved and respected him deeply. Difficult property cares now fell upon him. He was able to find earnings immediately — he gave history lessons in A. K. Neigard's private women's school.

In May, 1881 Platonov's classmate, Count A. F. Geiden, who was then close to Vladimir Solov'ev, proposed that Platonov join a new venture — "The Student Scientific-Literary Society." Professor Orest Fedorovich Miller became the organizer and head of this society. According to the charter, professors and university instructors, not just students, could join this society. Among those who joined the society were Platonov and D'iakonov.[44]

Upon graduating from the university, Platonov was invited to lecture on modern Russian history at the Alexandrian Lycée in Petersburg. In addition, he taught Russian history at the historico-philological institute. This was a difficult time for him as he had to prepare for the master's examinations (after which he received the rank of *privat-docent*), and then write the master's thesis. The topic that he chose was "Old Russian Legends and Tales About the Time of Troubles of the XVII Century as a Historical Source" ["Drevnerusskie Skazaniia i Povesti o Smutnom Vremeni XVII Veka kak Istoricheskii Istochnik"]. He defended this thesis successfully in 1888.

Professor Zamyslovskii became hopelessly ill in 1889 and thus the chair of Russian history at the University of Petersburg became vacant.

Having discussed the question of a replacement for the post, the historico-philological department decided to invite Platonov. Since the latter had only the master's, not the doctor's, degree he was chosen as one carrying out professorial duties. He was to be a full-fledged faculty member with all rights and duties.

In the process of working on his master's thesis, Platonov thoroughly mastered the whole body of literary sources on the Time of Troubles. The goal which he set for himself for his doctoral dissertation was to study the whole period of the Time of Troubles comprehensively — its causes, development, and consequences. Thus arose the famous *Essays on the History of the Time of Troubles in the State of Muscovy in the XVI-XVII Centuries [Ocherki po Istorii*

*Smuty v Moskovskom Gosudarstve XVI-XVII Vekov]* (1890; 2nd. ed., 1901). Platonov felt this work to be the main achievement of his scholarly life.

Platonov defended his dissertation in Kiev. At that time there were three doctors of Russian history at the University of Kiev: V. S. Ikonnikov, P. V. Golubovskii, and B. V. Antonovich. All three were solid scholars.

Until 1896 Platonov was an assistant editor of the *Journal of the Ministry of Public Education.* He was also a member of the academic committee of the Ministry of Public Education and the administrative section of Slavic and Russian archeology of the Russian Archeological Society.

At the very beginning of 1917 Platonov was elected member of the Academy of Sciences.

Platonov's pedagogical activity at the University of Petersburg spread broadly in the 1890's. He lectured and presented a seminar. Such major future historians like S. V. Rozhdestvenskii, A. E. Presniakov, I. I. Lappo, P. G. Vasenko and many others received their training in his seminar.

Simultaneously, Platonov gave a survey course in Russian history. It was very popular. In 1899 two of Platonov's regular auditors issued Platonov's course by lithographic means. Platonov checked the text and authorized the book.

After this, the lectures were published. The sixth edition (revised and expanded) appeared in 1909. The eighth edition came out in 1913.

Platonov's *Lectures* and Kliuchevskii's *Course* are the two pillars of Russian historiography at the end of the XIX and the beginning of the XX centuries. Tens of thousands of students heard them in the university. Tens of thousands of educated Russians read them. Russian society was brought up by them.

Russian public opinion at the end of the XIX and the beginning of the XX centuries was built on them.

As we have seen (see Ch. XVIII above), Kliuchevskii's *Course* was not a factual exposition of the course of the external events of Russian history. It was the elucidation of the inner content of the historical process from the social point of view. The *Course* is tendered in an inimitable artistic style that is peculiar to Kliuchevskii alone.

Platonov's *Lectures* are of a different character. They are a systematic survey of Russian history from ancient times through the reign of Nicholas I. The presentation of events is linked to the history of institutions, classes, and society. Compressed but expressive characteristics are given of prominent people — Ivan the Terrible, Boris Godunov, Kuz'ma Minin, Tsar Aleksei, Patriarch Nikon, Peter the Great, Catherine II.

In an introduction to the *Lectures*, Platonov gave an excellent concise essay on Russian historiography and a survey of the sources of Russian history.

Platonov was against the appropriation by historical science of another (more general) discipline — sociology. In his opinion, sociology's goal was to discover the general laws of the development of the life of society without applying them to a specific place, period, or nation.

In Platonov's definition, "History is a science which studies concrete facts precisely in terms of time and place. Its main goal is recognized to be the systematic depiction of the development and changes of distinct historical societies and all mankind."

"In order to give a scholarly-precise and artistically-whole picture of any era or the complete history of a nation, it is necessary 1) to collect historical materials; 2) determine their trustworthiness; 3) precisely establish individual historical facts; 4) indicate a causal relationship between them; and 5) bring them together to form a general scholarly survey or an artistic portrayal."

The critical methods of researchers "are perfected with the development of historical science. But until now, neither these methods nor the science of history itself have attained their full development."

After the simple analysis of historical phenomena, a broader problem presents itself to the historian — "historical synthesis, the goal of which is to recreate the course of universal history in its totality." Into the foundation of this synthesis, Russian history can put in its stone as well — observation as to how the basic phenomena of Russian historical life developed.

Despite the fact that in the introduction to his *Lectures* Platonov dissociates sociological goals from those of history, the background of his *Lectures* must be recognized as sociological. It is within this background that Platonov unfurls the sequence of "events."

Platonov's *Lectures* are divided into three parts. The first part proceeds from ancient times to Tsar Ivan the Terrible; the second — from Ivan the Terrible to Tsar Fedor inclusive; the third — from Fedor's death (1682) to the death of Nicholas I.

Platonov commences his account of Russian history with a brief characterization of the geographical bases of Russian history. There follows a review of the original territorial structure of the future Russian State.

Platonov's principle attention is given to the problem of the internal organization of the Slavs. Analyzing the discussion of this problem in Russian historiography, Platonov begins with Evers' theory of familial modes (upheld by Solov'ev and Kavelin). Konstantin Aksakov contrasted this theory with his own view that the basic organization of the Slavs was not that of kin, but of the commune.

In Platonov's opinion, Leontovich's theory of the familial-communal social mode of the ancient Slavs, based on territorial and regional associations, was more successful.

"The existence of distinctive communes of archaic type among Russian people in historical times is indicated in the works of the modern ethnographers" writes Platonov (particularly true in the works of Aleksandra Ia. Efimenko).

Regarding the formation of the Kievan State, Platonov gives primacy to the Varangians (Normans) — to that branch which inhabited the Scandinavian peninsula.

The chronicle contains an account of the summoning of the Varangians to Novgorod by the Slavs around the middle of the IX century. From Novgorod they then went to

Kiev down the Dniepr. Some of the chronicle rolls link the name Rus' with the Varangians.

Trying to comprehend this intricate problem, Platonov, following in Vasil'evskii's footsteps, notes the presence of the Rus' people on Black Sea at the beginning of the IX century, hence prior to "the summoning of the Varangians." "It would be natural to conclude·therefrom that the name Rus' belonged to the Slavs, not to the Varangians, and that it always meant what it did in the XII century, i.e. the Kiev district with its population." But, Platonov thinks that there is insufficient cause to consider Rus' as a Slavic tribal name.[45]

Platonov considers Christianity, which had already penetrated into Kiev in the X century, to have been a powerful force in the unification of Rus'.

In the first part of the *Lectures*, Platonov gave a concise survey of the development of Russian socio-political and cultural history to the middle of the XIII century. The second part, from the second half of the XVI century, contains the basis of his course.

In his evaluation of Ivan the Terrible, Platonov distinguishes between the Tsar's personality and his policies. In the characterization of Ivan the Terrible's personality, Platonov agrees with Kliuchevskii. But in his *Essays on the History of the Time of Troubles in the State of Muscovy in the XVI-XVII Centuries*, Platonov feels that the *oprichnina* established by Ivan the Terrible was not only a senseless example of panic and the Tsar's sadistic cruelty, but also an attempt, by means of the bloody extermination of the boyar aristocracy, to create a new social foundation for Muscovy. This was to move the middle classes of Russian society — the gentry and the townspeople — to the forefront.

This concept held sway in Russian historiography for a long time. After Platonov's death, this problem was revised anew by S. B. Veselovskii in his articles on the *oprichnina* in the 1940's and 1950's.[46]

Veselovskii subjected Platonov's conclusions to severe

criticism. Having paid his due to the eminent scholarly value of Platonov's work on the literary monuments and the events of the Time of Troubles, Veselovskii says that "the introductory chapters of his *Essays on the Time of Troubles*, and in particular the chapter on the *oprichnina*, are not independent investigations based on the study of old and new sources, but are an attempt to generalize the historiographic achievements contemporary to him. . . Platonov's concept definitely needs criticism because it has had great success and, as is usually the case, it has, in simplified form, found its way into survey courses and textbooks."

In objecting to Platonov, Veselovskii, in a series of essays based on concrete, partly archival, material analyzed in detail Ivan the Terrible's establishment of the *oprichnina*. He examined the initial territory and administration of the *oprichnina*, the expansion of this administration, the expulsion of the *zemshchina* people from the districts confiscated by the *oprichnina*, the service records of the *oprichniks*, and the register of persons who were in Tsar Ivan's disfavor.

Veselovskii writes, "Much in the establishment of the *oprichnina* seemed incomprehensible to historians precisely because they felt it to be directed against the service princes and the boyars, i.e. the upper class of the sovereign's court."

"In reality, Ivan the Terrible was not able to remove all those who were objectionable to him in the old court. Therefore, he established a new and special (*oprichnyi* [separate] ) court in which he expected to be total ruler."

Veselovskii comes to the conclusion that princely and untitled boyar families predominated at both the old and new royal court.

During the period of the *oprichnina*, Tsar Ivan executed boyars of the *zemshchina* and the *oprichnina* who were disagreeable to him. But *oprichnina* terror was not merely directed against the boyars. It was also directed against the nobility and the lower classes of the population.

In 1581, during a family squabble, the Tsar hit his son, Tsarevich Ivan, with his staff with such force that he died

several days later. The Tsar had no intention of killing him.
This was a deep emotional experience for him. The Tsar
began to visit monasteries, made large financial contributions
to them, and ordered that requiems for Tsarevich Ivan be
held daily.

This gave the Tsar the idea of compiling memorial
*sinodiks* of all those martyred by him.

For prayers on their behalf, the Tsar again gave large
sums of money to various monasteries.

The more complete *sinodiks* list some 3,300 people.
Of them, more than 2,000 are shown nameless. There is no
doubt that all of these belonged to the lower classes of the
population. In this fashion, Veselovskii convincingly dem-
onstrated the groundlessness of the opinion that Tsar Ivan's
terror was directed exclusively at the boyars.

Early in 1920 Platonov wrote a short, but very intriguing article titled "Rusa." Rusa is what Platonov called
the former administrative city of the Novgorod province. The
city was located to the south of Lake Il'men. Prior to the
1917 revolution, it appeared on maps and in dictionaries as
"Old Rusa" ["Staraia Rusa"].

In this article Platonov relies on A. A. Shakhmatov's
work, "The Ancient Fate of the Russian Tribe" ["Drevneishie Sud'by Russkogo Plemeni"] (*Russian Historical Journal*, 1919 — [*Russkii Istoricheskii Zhurnal*]). Shakhmatov
felt that in the IX-X centuries, Rusa was the political center
of the Varangians from which they ruled over neighboring
Slavic and Finnish tribes. Shakhmatov attributes the evidence
regarding "a Russian island" in the eastern historian, Ibn-
Rusta, to this center. The region of Old Rusa is full of rivers
and lakes and could be called an island. But there is no
agreement among researchers on this score. Some scholars
feel that Ibn-Rusta's evidence must be attributed to the
Tmutarakan region (beyond the Straights of Kerch between
the Kuban river and the Sea of Azov). Other opinions have
also been stated.

Platonov's articles are therefore just one of the hypotheses without which we cannot delve into the history of

the "Rus' " tribe.

It may be said that Platonov wrote "Rusa" in passing. At this time he was absorbed in writing one of his most important works — the book *Boris Godunov* (1921). This book is not a history of Boris's reign but a penetrating study of Boris's personality and psychology and elucidation of the reasons for his fatal destiny.

Boris's personality and historical role had long interested Platonov in connection with the tales and legends about the Time of Troubles. These Platonov had studied thoroughly for his master's thesis.

Platonov had already come to the conclusion at that time that "Boris Godunov's personality and public activity could be newly interpreted if it were possible to show the bias of certain narrators, his enemies. . . "

When Boris became the actual ruler under the weak-minded Tsar Fedor, his enemies — personal and political — began a bitter slandering campaign of rumor and accusation against him. The major accusation was that of the murder, through an agent, of Tsarevich Dmitrii of Uglich in 1591. In his *Lectures on Russian History*, Platonov wrote that the evaluation of Boris's personality depended on this accusation. "If Boris is the murderer, then he is the villain that Karamzin depicts him as being; if not, he is one of the most attractive of Muscovite tsars."

In his book on Boris, Platonov returned to the essence of this question. The book has three chapters: "Boris's Career," "Boris's Policies," and "The Tragedy of Boris." The third chapter commences with an investigation of Tsarevich Dmitrii's death.

In contrast to Solov'ev and Kliuchevskii who unreservedly accepted the version of the Tsarevich's death at the hands of Boris's agent, Platonov gives an unbiased and detailed analysis of the event. He based it on the inquest (published in a photo-type edition by V. Klein in 1913).

During the noon hours on May 15, 1591, when all life came to a standstill, Tsarevich Dmitrii was in an isolated inner yard of the court grounds. With him were his wet-nurse, his governess, who was in charge of the women who looked after him, his nanny, and his chambermaid. Also, there were four boys with whom he was playing a knife throwing game. According to the testimony of the women and the boys, the Tsarevich, in an epileptic fit, fell on the knife throat first and stabbed himself.

The Tsarevich's mother and his uncle, Mikhail Nagoi, ran over from the palace. His mother accused the nurse and began beating her screaming, in the meantime, that her son and the son of the d'iak [secretary] Bitiagovskii had stabbed the Tsarevich.

Mikhail Nagoi ran out into the street and began to incite the crowd against Bitiagovskii. A pogrom started in the town. The crowd killed Bitiagovskii and his son, and looted his house and office.

As soon as news of the events in Uglich reached Moscow, an investigative commission was sent there to ascertain the circumstances of the Tsarevich's death and the uprising in the town. The government appointed Vasilii Ivanovich Shuiskii to head the commission. Metropolitan Gelasii was sent by the Patriarch as his representative.

The commission was ordered to interrogate all witnesses and record all of the testimony, even though it be contradictory.

Returning to Moscow, the commission first presented its perquisition (inquiry) to the partriarchal sobor [council]. The council offered its conclusions that "death came to Tsarevich Dmitrii by the will of God, and that the Nagois' " were at fault for inciting the revolt. It turned the matter over to the Tsar and boyars for a decision. Tsarina Mariia (the Tsarevich's mother) was tonsured as a nun and took the name of Marfa. Mikhail Nagoi was exiled but was accepted into the service in 1600 and made a voevoda [military commander] in Tsarev-Sanchursk (in the Viatka district).

In May, 1606, after the death of the pretender (the false Dmitrii), Prince Vasilii Ivanovich Shuiskii was proclaimed Tsar. To solidify his position and prevent the appearance of new pretenders, Tsar Vasilii decided to canonize

Tsarevich Dmitrii. (New pretenders appeared later anyway). A *vita* was written wherein it was maintained that he was killed at the order of Boris Godunov.

Patriarch Ignatii, a Greek and bishop of Riazan who had been appointed in place of Iov by the False Dmitrii, readily agreed to the canonization.

Fundamentally, the canonization was a political, not a religious, act. Tsarevich Dmitrii was buried in Uglich immediately after the departure of the investigative commission. But the location of his grave was soon forgotten. When ecclesiastical figures came from Moscow in 1606 to transfer the Tsarevich's remains, no one in Uglich could indicate the burial site. Nevertheless, the Moscow emissaries declared that they found the Tsarevich's "relics" in one of the abandoned graves of Uglich, and transported them to Moscow.

Platonov asserts that Dmitrii's death "evidently passed without noticeable clamor or action in daily Muscovite life. It should be remembered that as one begotten from a sixth or seventh wife (Tsar Ivan's) Dmitrii could not be viewed as fully legitimate" (the Church at the time did not even crown a third marriage).

It should also be remembered that in May, 1592, a daughter was born to Tsarina Irina (wife of Tsar Fedor, sister of Boris). The daughter could be considered heir to the throne. Though she died soon thereafter, others could be expected.

The situation changed with the death of Tsar Fedor (January 7, 1598). Fedor willed the rule to Irina but she refused to accept it and was tonsured as a nun with the name Aleksandra. A period of interregnum ensued. A new Tsar had to be chosen.

Among the possible candidates were Boris Godunov, Prince F. I. Mstislavskii, F. N. Romanov, and B. Ia Bel'skii. A national assembly was convened. Boris was chosen.

The majority of late researchers felt that the assembly was fixed and that Boris's election was a comedy.

However, in his article "The Composition of the Representatives to the *Zemskii Sobors* of Ancient Russia,"[47] Kliuchevskii, on the basis of detailed lists of the assembly's members (there were 512 of them) showed that the composition was completely normal and corresponded to the XVI century conception regarding the order of representation.

Boris's position as Tsar became much more difficult than his role as ruler under Tsar Fedor. In the struggle for election, Boris lost almost all of his friends from the ruling boyar class. The Godunovs were left almost isolated.

In his government policy, Boris sought the support of the middle classes – the gentry and the merchants.

The titled boyars (the princes) were, as a whole, loyal aides to Boris. But the untitled high born boyars, headed by the Romanovs, attempted to lead a struggle against Boris using all possible means, including the cultivation of a pretender ( a false Dmitrii).

Natural calamity was added on top of this – the catastrophic harvest and famine of 1602.

Platonov thinks that Boris's tragedy was the tragedy of fate. In the conclusion to his book, Platonov writes: "During death Boris was not wearied by a battle with his own conscience upon which (by the measure of the time) there were no particular sins or crimes, but rather by the exceedingly trying conditions of his government work. . . The complexity and versatility of his work uncovered his ruling talent in its full glory; also, his good qualities – gentleness and kindness. But these very qualities not only made him an object of astonishment, enthusiasm, and praise, but of envy, hate, and slander."

After the appearance of "Boris," Platonov, in a sense, summarized the results of his study of the Time of Troubles in the popular book *The Time of Troubles* [*Smutnoe Vremia*] (1923). This monograph was meant for the broad reading public. A supplement titled *The Social Crisis of the Time of Troubles* [*Sotsial'nyi Krizis Smutnogo Vremeni*] appeared a year later. This is a well selected anthology of documents and excerpts from the memoirs of that era. It began with V. I. Shuiskii's oath upon accepting the reign in 1606 and went up to the election of Mikhail Romanov to the throne (1613).

Platonov's remarkable study, *Moscow and the West in the XVI-XVII Centuries* [*Moskva i Zapad v XVI-XVII Vekakh*], (1925) appeared thereafter. This book is of a different order than *Boris Godunov*. In *Boris Godunov* Platonov gave a psychological characterization of a prominent personality and his fate.

*Moscow and the West* represents a brilliant essay on the fundamental landmarks of Muscovite society's cultural development — the process of its Europeanization in various aspects.

Platonov feels that Moscow's relations with the West began earlier and were stronger than it was commonly thought in his day. It was to these earlier periods that he turned his principle attention.

It was erroneous to think, he said, that Moscow's isolation was the result of its unwillingness to have intercourse with the West. On the contrary, in the middle of the XVI century the West tried to isolate Moscow. The cities of the Hanseatic League and Poland feared the "Muscovite danger." They felt that Western trade with Moscow and Moscow's engagement of needed technicians would increase the military power of Muscovy.

A historical accident — the English discovery of the northern route to the White Sea in 1553 — renewed Moscow's direct trade relations with the West. The Dutch and the French followed the English. Gradually the Dutch gained superiority over the English. The whole XVII century was a period of uninterrupted Dutch successes in the Moscow State.

Aside from the voluntary arrival of foreigners to Russia, there was also involuntary colonization. After the conquest of Livonia in 1558, Moscow's forces took a large number of captives to Russia. The upper crust was composed of Livonian nobility. The majority were Estonian and Latvian common folk. These made up the work force.

The Muscovite government took the Livonian nobility (Germans) into its service. From them, they formed garrisons for cities in the eastern reaches of the country.

Some of these captives made brilliant careers for themselves at the Tsar's Court, e.g. Johann Taube and Elert Kruze (both subsequently fled from Russia to Poland).

Ivan the Terrible liked to talk with foreigners not only on political and economic topics. He was also very interested in religion.

His famous disputation on the faith with Jan Rokyt, a prominent figure of the commune of Czech Brothers (of the Hussite tradition) took place on May 10, 1570. Each remained true to his persuasion.[48]

Like Ivan the Terrible, Boris Godunov also kept in close contact with foreigners arriving in Moscow. A new element in his discussions with them was his creative idea to found a school of higher education in Moscow — something akin to a university. In this connection, it was decided to send gifted Russian youths to the West to "learn different languages and other studies." Initially, eighteen persons were sent — six each to England, France, and Germany. None of them returned. By the time their courses of study were over, Boris had died and disturbances had begun. Understandably, they had no desire to return.

The people of Muscovy came out of the Time of Troubles materially ruined. The country returned to a normal state but slowly. With the first signs of calm, foreigners again made their way to Arkhangel'sk. Trade between Muscovy and European countries was reborn and a spontaneous influx of foreigners to Moscow began. An important role among them was played by merchants and technicians of all kinds, as well as by officers and soldiers (*Landsknechte*). The government of Moscow decided to form regiments based on the foreign model from Russians.

Mostly Protestants, and to a lesser degree Catholics, were invited to Russia. Fearing their religious influence on Russian people, the government of Moscow, at Patriarch Nikon's insistence, evicted all foreigners from Moscow (except those who had converted to Orthodoxy). Land beyond the city was given them for settlement (1652). Thus arose the *Nemetskaia Sloboda*, a prosperous corner of Europe in Muscovy. Lutherans and Calvinists were permitted to build churches there but this was denied to Catholics.

In Moscow, not only the *"Nemtsy"* (a general term for all Europeans) but also those from the western Russian districts of the Polish and Lithuanian Commonwealth were looked upon with suspicion. Their number began to increase greatly after 1620.

"After the Time of Troubles," writes Platonov, "it was difficult for the people of Muscovy to tell who was from Lithuania and Poland, who was Orthodox, Uniate, or Catholic."

In Moscow itself there were people who were perplexed by the new cultural and religious beliefs. Such a person was Ivan Andreevich Khvorostinin, "the first swallow of the cultural spring," as Platonov calls him.

He felt bored in Moscow: "all the people are stupid; there is no one to live with." He began to ponder theological problems, to reject the resurrection of the dead, and the necessity of prayer and fasting. For this he was sent to the Kirillov monastery in 1623 to do penance. He soon repented, took an oath, and promised that he would adhere strictly to Orthodoxy. Thereupon he was returned to Moscow. The Tsar and Patriarch forgave him fully. He died in 1625.

Platonov takes his account to the beginning of Peter's reign. He draws a convincing picture of cultural uplift in mid-XVII century Moscow. He stresses the importance of the learned Kievan monks who were invited to Moscow. His characterizations of the prominent figures of this time are illuminating.

Platonov's last book is devoted to Peter: *Peter the Great. Personality and Activity* [*Petr Velikii. Lichnost i Deiatel'nost*] (Leningrad, 1926).

The cause for writing it was the appearance of romanticized biographies of Peter in Russian *belles lettres*. In Platonov's view, these represented a crude libelous caricature.

These were Aleksei Tolstoi's "Peter's Day" ["Den' Petra"] (a preliminary essay to the book on Peter which followed later) and B. Pil'niak's *His Majesty Kneb Piter Komondor* [*Ego Velichestvo Kneb Piter Komondor*].

"In both," says Platonov, "Peter appears as a dirty and sick drunkard who is devoid of common sense and all elemental decency."

Platonov thought it necessary to restore the true image of Peter as a sovereign and as a man, and as a counterweight to such debunkings of Peter which were widespread in Russian society.

Platonov first looks at the publicistic and philosophic evaluations of Peter in the XVIII century and the first half of the XIX century.

He then turns to the scholarly evaluations of Peter in modern times (Solov'ev, and Kavelin, Kliuchevskii, Miliukov).

Solov'ev and Kavelin, brought up on methods of the German historical school, looked upon the historical process as the organic development of national life.

From their point of view, Peter not only received his notions for the necessity of reforms from the old order, but he acted along previously marked paths.

Solov'ev's students introduced a somewhat different understanding of Peter's historical role. "They began to think that under Peter Russia lived through a shock which, nevertheless, was not a revolution." Platonov highly values Kliuchevskii's views on Peter and the Petrine reforms.

"In the person of Kliuchevskii, our scholarship first raised itself to the height of a fully realistic idea of Peter, his personality, and his historical role."

As to Kliuchevskii's student, Miliukov, Platonov recognizes the great value of his basic work, *The State Economy in Russia and Peter the Great's Reform*. But he feels that in the final analysis, in his books, and particularly in his *Outlines of Russian Culture*, Miliukov distorted Peter's image. He pictured him as passively accepting the projects for reforms which were submitted to him by foreign and Russian advisers. Furthermore, according to Miliukov, these projects were not co-ordinated.

In subsequent chapters, Platonov first speaks of Peter's

childhood and youth and of his first trip abroad (1699). There follows a chapter on Peter's military talent. The most vividly written chapter is the last one, "Peter the Great in the Last Period of His Life." In conclusion, Platonov writes: "Peter's working life and his close knowledge of governing developed in him one most valuable quality — he liked truth and hated falsehood, deception, and extortion. He viewed governing as a sacred duty and carried out his duties with extreme conscientiousness. . . He gave himself to government service and demanded the same of his subjects. In his government there were no privileged people and no privileged groups. They were all equal in their lack of rights before the State."

Platonov, Kliuchevskii, and Lappo-Danilevskii occupy a prominent place in the development of Russian historical thought at the end of the XIX and the beginning of the XX century and the dissemination of historical knowledge in contemporary Russian society.

Kliuchevskii and Platonov both produced a whole pleiade of talented scholars (the "Moscow" and "Petersburg" schools of historians).

Lappo-Danilevskii had less immediate students as such. But the influence of his organizational ideas spread to many of the young scholars who, formally, were not his students.

In the aggregate, all of them charted the subsequent development of Russian historical scholarship.

## MIKHAIL ALEKSANDROVICH D'IAKONOV

Mikhail Aleksandrovich D'iakonov was born on December 31, 1855 to the family of a bureaucrat in Ekaterinburg in the province of Perm. During the peasant reforms, his father was a mediator of the peace [*Mirovoi posrednik*].

Mikhail received his initial education at home and entered grade two of the Ekaterinburg gymnasium. He studied there until grade seven. He then transferred to the Perm gymnasium where he received his diploma in 1873. During the same year, he enrolled in the Medical-Surgical

Academy but left in his third year and enrolled in the juridical department at the University of Petersburg. He was graduated in 1880.

At V. I. Sergeevich's proposal, D'iakonov was retained at the university. At the end of 1883, he presented his master's thesis on the topic of "The Power of the Moscow Sovereigns" ["Vlast' Moskovskikh Gosudarei"]. Thereafter, he was appointed professor at Iur'ev (Derpt) University.

For his doctoral dissertation, D'iakonov presented his "Essays from the History of the Rural Population in the State of Muscovy" ["Ocherki iz Istorii Sel'skogo Naseleniia v Moskovkom Gosudarstve"]. He defended this dissertation in 1900.

In 1905 D'iakonov was chosen adjunct of the Academy of Sciences; four years later, he was chosen extraordinary academician, and ordinary academician in 1912. Thereafter, he moved from Iur'ev to Petersburg.

While in Iur'ev, D'iakonov prepared for publication a course of lectures which he taught there — *Essays on the Social and Governmental System of Ancient Russia* [*Ocherki Obshchestvennogo i Gosudarstvennogo Stroiia Drevnei Rusi*] (1906). The book had great success. The second edition appeared two years later after which two more editions were issued. This historical survey became an indispensable source for both sudents and instructors and for all those seriously interested in the history of Russian government and society.

The primary attention of D'iakonov as a researcher dealt with the history of the peasantry and their gradual enserfment. Diakonov's youth was spent in the atmosphere of their emancipation. He set as his goal the study of the conditions and circumstances of the peasants' foregoing history — the gradual growth of serfdom.

Simultaneously, he also attentively studied the history of government in the State of Muscovy — the relation between the new means of local government and the reconstruction of the central institutions. He also studied Muscovy's financial history.[49]

For D'iakonov, the basic problem in the history of peasant enserfment became the question of "precedent" and of peasants who were "long term tenants." He was particularly interested in clarifying the relationship of "precedent" to the "precedent of *tiaglo*" [sum total of peasant obligations] on the one hand, i.e. the attaching of peasants to the *tiaglo*, and on the other hand — to the liabilities of peasants who received loans and advances from the landowner. D'iakonov feels that the common institution of long term tenancy was the foundation stone of enserfment.

D'iakonov was a careful historian. In his work, striving and doubt predominated over absolute assertions and conclusions. For the latter, D'iakonov felt that historical science did not yet possess enough finished materials or data.

"D'iakonov's works, above all, teach us critical alertness. They bring to the forefront the need for a broad and systematic work on disused archives" (Presniakov).

D'iakonov died in 1919.

## V. S. IKONNIKOV (1841-1923)

Vladimir Stepanovich Ikonnikov was descended from a gentry family in the Kiev province.[50] He studied at the cadet school in Kiev, then enrolled in the historico-philological department of the University of Kiev. He graduated from the university with a gold medal. He was then retained as a fellowship holder to prepare for the professorship.

He wrote his master's thesis on *Maksim the Greek* [*Maksim Grek*]. He defended it in 1867 at the University of Odessa. His doctoral topic was *An Experiment in Research on the Cultural Significance of Byzantium in Russian History* [*Opyt Issledovaniia o Kul'turnom Znachenii Vizantii v Russkoi Istorii*]. He defended it likewise at the University of Odessa, in 1870. After this he was elected extraordinary professor at the University of Kiev. In 1871 he was made ordinary professor.

From 1874-1877 and from 1893-1895 he was the

chairman of the Historical Society of Nestor the Chronicler
in Kiev.

In 1914 Ikonnikov was elected a fellow of the Academy
of Sciences. Of his monographs, in addition to the two books
cited above, I will note his important work, *Count N. S.
Mordvinov* [*Graf N. S. Mordvinov*] (Petersburg, 1873).
Ikonnikov paid considerable attention to questions of
Russian Historiography. His articles on Bodianskii, Count
Rumiantsev, Boltin, Schlözer, and Karamzin are in this
category.

All of this was groundwork for his monumental *Russian
Historiography* [*Opyt Russkoi Istoriografii*] (vol. I, in 2
books, Kiev, 1891; vol. II, also in 2 books, Kiev, 1908).

# XXVI

## KLIUCHEVSKII'S STUDENTS
## A. A. KIZEVETTER (1866-1939)

Kliuchevskii's favorite student was Aleksandr Aleksandrovich Kizevetter.

Kizevetter was an outstanding historian and public
figure. From 1903-1906 he was very active in politics.

He was frank and direct with friend and foe. He occupies
a prominent place in the Moscow intelligentsia of the time.

Kizevetter was born in Orenburg.[51] He was graduated
from the Orenburg gymnasium in 1884. The closest university to Orenburg was that of Kazan. But Kizevetter was
irrepressibly drawn to Moscow. While in the middle grades of
the gymnasium, he had already decided to devote himself to
the study of Russian history. The name of Kliuchevskii
also drew him to Moscow. It had just thundered across the
scholarly world thanks to the doctoral disputation at which
he had defended his dissertation, "Ancient Russia's Boiar
Duma."

Arriving in Moscow in mid-summer of 1884, Kizevetter
first applied to the historico-philological department. Some
two months remained prior to the commencement of cour-

ses. Unhindered, Kizevetter could devote himself to learning the noisy and multicolored Moscow which immediately enchanted him for life.

Among Kizevetter's university instructors, Kliuchevskii of course took first place. It so happened that Kizevetter entered the university in a year when Kliuchevskii was beginning his course with ancient Russia (the course took two academic years). Kizevetter was immediately fascinated by the lecturer (Kizevetter's impression of the course was already cited in the chapter on Kliuchevskii).

At this time, the patriarch of the historico-philological department was Vladimir Ivanovich Ger'e, professor of world history and one of Kliuchevskii's teachers. Kizevetter took his courses on Roman history and on European history of the XVIII century (enlightened absolutism). Despite a certain old fashionedness in these courses, Kizevetter found both of them useful.

The second instructor in world history was P. G. Vinogradov. Like Miliukov,[52] he rated him exceedingly highly as a teacher, particularly within his seminar. Kizevetter also recalls the lively discussions of Moscow's historians in Vinogradov's apartment. "At these meetings we heard lectures by Miliukov, Fortunatov, A. Guchkov, Kavelin, Petrushevskii, and others." He studied the history of Russian literature under N. S. Tikhonravov and linguistics under F. E. Korsh and F. F. Fortunatov.

Also valued very highly by Kizevetter was S. F. Fortunatov, "an enthusiast of the cult of political freedom." He taught a course on the history of England, the United States of America, and the French Revolution.

During these years, the student body was divided into three parts — "the politicians, the future average man, and the future scholars."

Kizevetter joined the latter group primarily because he felt an inconquerable passion for scholarship and also he saw little sense in the contemporary student movements.

From time to time, studies were diversified "through visits to the gallery of the Little Theater where at that time, for 30 kopeks, one could experience minutes of the greatest esthetic pleasure from the performances of Ermolova, Fedotova, Medvedeva, Nikulina, the Sadovskiis, Lenskaia, and Iuzhina."

Passion for the theater did not interfere with Kizevetter's studies. In his junior year, under Kliuchevskii, he chose his senior thesis — the history of State servitor landownership in XVI and XVII century Muscovy.

"Toward the end of my university studies, I already felt myself to be well grounded, so to speak, in Russian history. I could visit Kliuchevskii without fearing to be the yellow beaked nestling who needlessly took his teacher's time. Kliuchevskii greeted me most heartily and our discussions belong to my most pleasant memories of those distant years."

Kizevetter graduated from Moscow University in the spring of 1888. In the fall of that year Kliuchevskii kept him at the chair of Russian history to prepare for the professorship.

After passing the master's examinations, Kizevetter received the rank of *privat docent* and commenced to lecture at the university. After the Advanced Courses for Women were opened by Ger'e in 1902, he also began to teach Russian history there.

For his master's thesis, Kizevetter chose to study the Petrine innovations, based on foreign models, in the organization of Russian towns. Scholarly literature could give no answer to this question while archival material relating to the correspondence of XVIII century municipal administrations remained untouched. This was the goal which Kizevetter set for himself.

He had other stimulating considerations. Though he had not yet entered politics, his political convictions had already formed. He was already a confirmed constitutionalist. A question now arose before him as a historian: what prerequisites for the possibility of transforming the Russian political system could be found in our historical past? In both Muscovite Russia and the Empire of the XVIII-XIX centuries, local self-government did exist — at the municipal and rural levels. Kizevetter chose to work on the municipal aspect — "to plow the great and previously untouched field." Kliuchevskii approved the theme. The materials which Kizevetter needed were in the archives of the Ministry of Justice on *Devich'e Pole*. He delved into them. He worked there enthusiastically every day. "There are special charms in archival documents." Soon after Kizevetter began to work in the archives of the Ministry of Justice, two younger colleagues began work there as well — M. M. Bogoslovskii and N. A. Rozhkov. Having worked on archival documents for several hours running, the three would go out for a stroll to refresh themselves. They had lively friendly discussions. In the future the three turned out to be political foes: the Cadet (Kizevetter), the Octobrist (Bogoslovskii), and the Bolshevik (Rozhkov).

The fundamental conclusion of Kizevetter's dissertation was the assertion that throughout the XVIII century, right up to Catherine II's municipal reform, the typical urban *mir* of Muscovite Russia continued to exist under the cover of Peter's reforms. The thesis published in 1903 was titled *The Urban Commune in XVIII Century Russia [Posadskaia Obshchina v Rossii XVIII Stoletiia]*.

The disputation occurred in December of 1903. Kliuchevskii and Liubavskii were the official opponents. Kliuchevskii led the dispute in a vein totally alien to him. There was no "cat and mouse game" combined with an easy examination for the defender. Kliuchevskii let it be clearly known to all present that he recognized his student to be his brother in scholarship. Liubavskii was most correct.

Kizevetter's doctoral dissertation dealt with Catherine II's charter of the cities in 1785. It was also based on previously untouched archival materials. The defense took place in 1909. Kliuchevskii could not take part this time since he was out of Moscow because of illness. The opponents were Liubavskii and Got'e. The disputation had the character of unforced scholarly discussion.

In 1893 Kizevetter became engaged to Ekaterina Aleksandrovna Kudriavtseva. She was the widow of his friend Aleksandr Alekseevich Kudriavtsev (who was Vinogradov's student). She already had children from her first marriage — a son, Vsevolod (who was a mathematician) and a daughter, Nataliia. The marriage took place in the summer of 1894. A daughter, Ekaterina, was born to them.

Aside from his scholarly work and university teaching, Kizevetter took an active part in the Moscow Committee on Literacy. In this connection he also participated in the broad-based educational movement, the so-called "Commission on Reading in the Home" and the lecture bureau for organizing lectures in the provinces by professors.

The Moscow Committee on Literacy had been founded in 1845 for "the nationwide dissemination of literacy based on religio-moral foundations." The activity of the Committee, at first stagnant, was temporarily revitalized in the 1870's when the Committee entered into relations with the *zemstvos* on matters of public education. Then, it quieted down anew.

In 1892 a large number of new members joined the Committee simultaneously. There were professors, municipal figures, and members of the *zemstvos* and they verified the Committee's activity. This drew the government's suspicion as to the unreliability of this institution.

Pobedonostsev gave an accusatory speech in the committee of ministers. No investigation of the Committee's activities was undertaken. But, on November 17, 1895 the Moscow Committee on Literacy (as well as that in Petersburg) was shut down.

"Societies of literacy" were established in place of these committees. The change was not only in the name. According to the new charter, the chairman of such a society was to be appointed by the Ministry of Public Education. In fact, public sessions were abrogated. The society's activity was constrained by various strict restrictions.

The closing of the committees of literacy led to strong annoyance in social circles. The members of the Petersburg committee, seeing no possibility of continuing new and fruitful work under the new charter, unanimously decided not to join the Society of Literacy.

Opinion was split in Moscow. Some of the members (Kizevetter among them) favored withdrawal. Others, headed by such popular figures as Chuprov and Gol'tsev, thought it imperative to work in the Society of Literacy irrespective of the charter which fettered its activity.

The matter was stormily and passionately discussed. In the end, the vast majority of members dropped out of the society.

A small group remained. The activity of the society faded. The pessimists turned out to be correct.

The "Commission on the Organization of Reading in the Home" arose due to the initiative of E.N. Orlova, a public figure, Miliukov, and Vinogradov.

The organizational session for the Commission was held in the large hall of the Polytechnic Museum. Many professors and *privat-docents* from Moscow University (Kizevetter among them), as well as secondary school teachers, were in attendance. It was decided to form "a university outside university walls," i.e. to elaborate a program of correspondence teaching within the framework of university instruction in all university departments except the medical. It was decided to publish textbooks on all aspects of the programs. These would be appropriate works by competent authors. The Sytin publishing firm, Moscow's largest, readily took the publication of these texts upon itself. This series was called "Library for Self-Education" ["Biblioteka dlia Samoobrazovaniia"].

A lecture bureau, for lecturing in provincial towns, was organized within the Commission. Kizevetter took an active part in it. His first trip was to Nizhnii Novgorod. The permission of the local governor was necessary to organize the lectures. It was to be granted by a preliminary finding of the superintendent of the school district. The superintendent declared that he could not give a positive reply until he was given the written text of the lectures. (Kizevetter intended to present a whole course on the state of Russian society at the end of the XVIII century). Kizevetter submitted the text. In speaking of the relations between noble landowners and serfs, Kizevetter used the expression "slave-owning." The superintendent said that he could not allow such expressions because this would cause dissatisfaction among the gentry. Kizevetter said: "If deniable, I can replace the term 'slave-owning' with the term 'ownership of souls'."

The superintendent thought a bit and said: this is permissible.

Kizevetter's lectures were very popular. After Nizhnii-Novgorod, he traveled to a number of other towns. He arrived in Tver right during the *zemstvo* meeting.

Tver was always famous for the high cultural level of its *zemstvo* officers. Kizevetter recalls: "The two days that I spent among these people (these were the Petrunkevich brothers, Bakunin, Kuz'min-Karavaev and others) left a most gratifying impression upon me."

In 1903, at the invitation of Gol'tsev, Kizevetter joined the editorial staff of the journal *Russian Thought* [*Russkaia Mysl'*]. In this journal, and a series of others, Kizevetter wrote many clearly written articles on various problems of Russian domestic history.

An anthology of these articles appeared in 1912 with the title *Historical Essays* [*Istoricheskie Ocherki*]. His long study on the relations between Alexander I and Arakcheev is included. The second volume of *Historical Essays* appeared in 1915.

After the Constitutional Manifesto of October 17, 1905 was issued, Kizevetter wrote a leaflet in order to clarify the true meaning of the Manifesto to people of little knowledge in a forthright manner. He wished to translate its juridical formulations into a language intelligible to common folk. I. D. Sytin published this leaflet and it had great success.

Thanks to this leaflet, Kizevetter began to be invited to clarify the Manifesto to popular audiences. In his *Memoirs*, by the way, Kizevetter tells of one such invitation. This time he was invited by some of his students at the Advanced Courses for Women who worked at a school. The other teachers at the school were Social Democrats. The Social Democrats stood for boycotting the elections. Having finished his talk, Kizevetter invited questions from the floor. One worker said: "It is said (by the Social Democrats) that there should be no elections to the Duma, there will be fraud." Kizevetter replied: "What will happen if the workers do not vote? Others will vote in their own representatives. Who will then represent your interest in the Duma?"

This dialogue later led to stormy arguments and quarrels among the school-teachers. The Social Democrats screamed that the bourgeoisie should not be allowed to talk to the people. So great was their fear of the free exchange of opinions.

Before the very issuance of the Manifesto of October 17, a constitutional convention of the Constitutional Democratic (Cadet) party (the People's Freedom Party) took place in Petersburg.

Because of the railroad strike, there were very few participants. Kizevetter also could not come.

In actuality, the party was organized at its second convention, January 5-11, 1906.

Kizevetter was elected a member of the party's central committee.

In February and March, he participated energetically in the pre-electoral debates among the Cadets, the Octobrists, and the Social-Democrats.

After the dissolution of the first Duma and the ill-starred Vyborg Manifesto, all those who had signed it were brought to trial. This led to only a three month jail term but it deprived them of the right to stand for election.

Almost all of the Cadet members in the First Duma — the flower of the party — were thereby removed from political life.

At the beginning of December, 1906, it was announced that the Second Duma would convene on February 20. The pre-election period thereby opened officially.

Countless meetings again took place. Kizevetter was

projected as one of the candidates to the Second Duma from the party of national freedom. He had to speak almost daily. The discussions were more varied than those prior to the First Duma. The leftist parties had already rejected political boycott and joined into a bloc. Parties to the right of the Cadets also participated actively in the pre-election campaign.

The Cadets attained complete victory in Moscow and in Petersburg. Moscow elected Kizevetter, Prince Pavel Dolgorukii, Maklakov, and Teslenko to the Duma.

The political cast of the Second Duma differed significantly from that of the first.

Instead of the Cadets, the laborites held the center. The number of deputies from the People's Freedom Party declined significantly. However, F. A. Golovin, a Cadet, was elected chairman of the Duma.

The labor faction consisted primarily of peasant deputies at the head of which were a few members of the intelligentsia — moderate socialists. But the peasants only occasionally followed their lead. They conducted their own policy of which the main goal was to achieve a new land law which would transfer the greatest amount of land possible to the peasants.

The watchword of the peasantry and the majority of the members of the Second Duma was to avoid conflicts with the ministry and to "preserve the Duma" for active legislative work. But this could not be done in view of the lack of an absolute majority of any one group and the presence of a series of minor groups with implacable interests.

To the right of the Cadets was a small layer of Octobrists and then an extreme right wing of Black Hundreds deputies (the Russian national union). The Duma's left wing consisted of the moderate Popular Socialists, the Socialist Revolutionaries, and the Social Democrats (Mensheviks and Bolsheviks). The Polish group held to itself.

Kizevetter gave several speeches in the Duma and participated in commissions.

Stolypin's ministry was totally dissatisfied with the

Duma and sought only an excuse to dissolve it. On June 1, Stolypin demanded that the Duma expel from its membership the whole Social Democrat group of 55 deputies. It was accused of a criminal military conspiracy. The Duma formed a commission composed of deputies-jurists in order to determine the validity of the ministry's demand. Kizevetter was chosen chairman of this commission. The commission was in session until 1:00 a.m. on the night of June 3 in order to renew and finish the work on the next day.

But during the night, Stolypin was able to secure a decree from Nicholas II which not only dissolved the Duma but provided for the issuance of a new electoral law which gave a majority to the parties of the right. This was done in defiance of the fundamental laws.

"After the dissolution of the Second Duma," writes Kizevetter in his memoirs, "everything indicated that the moment of political crisis had passed and that many humdrum days lay ahead . . . The whirlwind has subsided. The ship of State entered quiet waters. Now political labor could be offered to those who had an inner taste and a direct inclination for it. . . I categorically refused to put forth my candidacy for the State Duma."

In 1911 Kizevetter, along with the majority of university professors and instructors left Moscow University in protest against the illegal actions of Kasso, the Minister of Public Education. Kasso fired Manuilov from his post as rector as well as relieving the associate and assistant rectors.

The majority of the professors and instructors who withdrew from the university including Kizevetter, were immediately invited to teach in the just created free People's University (named after Shaniavskii).

In 1922 Kizevetter, along with a large group of Russian scholars and philosophers, was exiled abroad at Trotsky's orders. His wife, daughter, and stepdaughter left with him. They settled in Prague.

It was during these years that Prague had become a

Russian cultural center. The so-called "Russian action" had begun. The Czechoslovak government allocated significant sums for the arrival of Russian professors and students in Prague. For several years, Prague became the "Russian Athens."

Under these conditions Kizevetter was able to successfully continue his scholarly and pedagogical activity. He joined the Russian Education Collegium and was made a professor at the Russian Department of Law (he received the chair in Russian history). In addition, he became a member of the Russian Historical Society in Prague and gave several lectures there.

Kizevetter also took an active part in Russian public life in Prague, participating, for example, in the annual meetings called anniversary days of Russian culture. These might be called a sort of tribute and reminder of the cultural significance of the Russian diaspora abroad.

During his years in Prague, Kizevetter wrote and published his memoirs and many scholarly works. Let us cite the most important of these: *Ivan Peresvetov* (a collection of articles in honor of P. B. Struve; Prague, 1925); *The First Five Years in the Reign of Catherine II* [*Pervoe Piatiletie Pravleniia Ekateriny II*] (a collection of articles in honor of P. N. Miliukov; Prague, 1929); historical essays on the history of XV-XVI century Muscovy, the history of Russia in the XVII century, and the history of the reign of Alexander I (published in French in the collective edition — Milioukov, Seignobos, Eisenmann, *Histoire de Russie*; Paris, 1932-1933).

In the last year of his life Kizevetter was extremely ill and despondent over the death of his wife, his faithful companion.

## M. M. BOGOSLOVSKII (1867-1929)

Mikhail Mikhailovich Bogoslovskii, upon graduating from the gymnasium, enrolled in the historico-philological department of Moscow University (he was one year behind

Kizevetter). He wrote his senior thesis on the *pistsovye knigi* [books containing detailed description of all taxable objects]. Kliuchevskii praised it highly and left Bogoslovskii at the chair of Russian history to prepare for the professorship. For his master's thesis Bogoslovskii chose Peter the Great's provincial reform of 1719. The thesis was principally based on archival documents. A gifted and pithy book resulted (1902).

At the defense Bogoslovskii's official opponents were Liubavskii and Kizevetter. "The disputation was most interesting. We talked like gentlemen — as colleagues in scholarship" (Kizevetter).

Several years later Bogoslovskii completed his doctoral dissertation, *Landed Self-Government in the Russian North in the XVII Century* [*Zemskoe Samoupravlenie na Russkom Severe v XVII Stoletii*] (2 vol.).

This book was an even greater contribution to scholarship than the first. At its base lay a great quantity of archival materials drawn from the correspondence of the administrative department of the Ustiug district.

Bogoslovskii's talent for research expressed itself in full force in this work. From the enormous block of archival documents he was able to carve out a harmonious image of the northern Russian littoral. He illuminated many aspects of its life which previously had appeared to historians in vague outlines.

The doctoral defense took place in 1910. Kizevetter and Liubavskii were again the opponents.

"We argued animatedly, not without biting jests from both sides. The public applauded each of us gayly several times" (Kizevetter).

In 1911 (after Kliuchevskii's death), Bogoslovskii was elected to the second chair of Russian history (the first was held by Liubavskii). Ten years later he was elected member of the Academy of Sciences.

Bogoslovskii was also interested in local lore, particularly that of northern Russia. His article, "Russian Regional History: Its Scholarly Peculiarities and Contemporary Aims"

["Oblastnaia Istoriia Rossii, ee Nauchnye Osobennosti i Sovremennye Zadachi"] was published in the anthology, *Problems of Local Lore* [*Voprosy Kraevedeniia*] (Nizhnii Novgorod, 1928).

Kizevetter provided a vivid characterization of Bogoslovskii in his memoirs.

"Bogoslovskii spoke with a bass voice and had the look of a staid and positive person. He tread solidly and his body movements were slow, but weighty. At first appearance he could be taken for a person who was grave in all aspects. But is was enough to meet him and become acquainted with his work to pleasantly discover a person of graceful and keen mind and of a vividly expressed talent. He treated liberal ideas with considerable scepticism and was persistent in the defense of his opinions."

As was already stated, Bogoslovskii chose a topic from the Petrine era for his master's thesis. Thus, he became well versed in the methods and the character of Peter's reforming work. Though his doctoral dissertation dealt with a different topic and an earlier age, the subject of Peter became firmly entrenched in his thought.

During the difficult period of the First World War, Bogoslovskii planned, and began to prepare, a multi-volume biography of Peter.

Bogoslovksii placed an excerpt, titled "Peter the Great in Vienna in 1698," from volume II in the journal *Dela i Dni* [*Days and Works*] (1921). By this time the first volume was already completed.

It may be surmised that Bogoslovskii commenced his gigantic work under the influence of the impression of catastrophic (for Russia) war time events. He felt the approaching end of the Empire created by Peter and turned to a thorough analysis of Peter's life and work in order to engrave on the consciousness of Russian society a panorama of a heroic era in Russian history.

Bogoslovskii's work is constructed in very original fashion. Peter's personality stands at the center. But around it, within the author's narrative, enter all those with whom

Peter came into contact according to the measure of their appearance and importance. Commencing with his childhood, the whole setting of Peter's life is depicted. Reading this book, one seems to see Peter and live with him in the surrounding reality. Bogoslovskii worked on Peter's biography until his very death. Five volumes remained in manuscript after his death. The last volume published by him covers Peter's activities in 1698 and 1699 — prior to the conclusion of peace with Turkey. The last page carries the date upon which he completed this volume — April 6, 1929. The account of the Northern War was to follow, but Bogoslovskii died on April 20 and his work remained unfinished. But even the part which he was able to write is a major contribution to historical scholarship. The work was published in 1941-1948.

## N. A. ROZHKOV (1868-1927)

Rozhkov came to Moscow from Perm in the mid-1890's. In Perm he was a history teacher at the gymnasium. The gymnasium's library contained a rich collection of books on Russian history. It was there that Rozhkov prepared for his master's examination. Upon passing the exam, he was kept at the chair by Kliuchevskii.

At that time Rozhkov held most definitely to populist views. But he gradually became a Marxist.

He wrote his master's thesis very rapidly, passing both Kizevetter and Bogoslovskii. The topic of his thesis was "The Agricultural Economy in Russia in the XVI Century" ["Sel'skoe Khoziaistvo v Rossii v XVI Veke"]. He based it on the study of the *pistsovye knigi*. He gathered a mountain of material. Methodologically, the work was very weak.

At the defense Kliuchevskii dissected the inadequacies of the thesis mercilessly. Kizevetter was the second opponent. He attempted to smooth the impression left by Kliuchevskii's remarks, but still pointed to a series of errors.

Nevertheless, Kliuchevskii and Kizevetter both recommended that the department grant the master's degree to Rozhkov. Rozhkov did not begin the doctoral dissertation. He joined the editorial staff of the bolshevik *Bor'ba* [*Struggle*], was arrested, spent a long time in jail, and was exiled to Irkutsk.

After the October Revolution of 1917, Rozhkov returned from Siberia but immediately split with his former party friends. He remained true to the Marxist dogma which he had accepted but saw that the Bolsheviks had altered it in their actions. He could not compromise on this score. The private press was still in existence in this transitional period and he wrote a letter in which he sharply criticized the party's ongoing policy. For this he was arrested and imprisoned. Finally he gave up and wrote a letter of repentance. Thereafter, he was made the head of one of the educational institutions and died at this post.

Rozhkov was a prolific writer. The majority of his works was written from a sociological point of view. *City and Village in Russian History* [*Gorod i Derevnia v Russkoi Istorii*] (3rd ed., Petersburg, 1913) is worthy of attention.

His main work is *Russian History in the Comparative Historical Perspective* [*Russkaia Istoriia v Sravnitel'no-Istoricheskom Osveshchenii*] (12 vol., 1918-1926). It is practically the first effort at a generalizing survey of Russian history from the sociological point of view. Rozhkov placed the evolution of economic forms, the replacement of a natural economy by a money economy, at the basis of the periodization of the Russian historical process.

Rozhkov counts nine periods in Russian history: primitive society, savage society, pre-feudal society (events in Russian history begin with this period), the feudal revolution, feudalism, the noble revolution, the accendancy of the nqbles, the bourgeois revolution, capitalism.

## Iu. V. GOT'E (1873-1943)

Iurii Vladimirovich Got'e was a talented historian and archeologist. He graduated from the historico-philological department of Moscow University in 1895 and was kept at the chair by Kliuchevskii. His two other teachers were Ger'e and Vinogradov.

From 1903-1915 Got'e was a *privat-docent*, then a professor at Moscow University.

From 1898 Got'e was the secretary of the Rumiantsev Library, then its assistant director. He remained at this post until 1930. (After the establishment of Soviet rule, the library was renamed the Lenin Library).

In 1939 Got'e was elected a member of the Academy of Sciences.

Got'e was a scholar of broad vision and diversity of theme.

His first substantial work was *The Trans-Moscow Region in the First Half of the XVII Century* [*Zamoskovnyi Krai v Pervoi Polovine XVII Veka*] (1906; re-issued in 1927). This was his master's thesis.

This work was based on a thorough analysis of the data in the *pistsovye knigi* and presents a picture of the gradual overcoming of the catastrophic ravages of the Time of Troubles.

The anthology of documents published by Got'e and titled *A Memoir of the Defense of Smolensk, 1608-1611* [*Pamiatnik Oborony Smolenska 1608-1611*] (1913) also treats the Time of Troubles.

After the XVII century Got'e turned to the XVIII. The first volume of his extensive *History of Regional Administration in Russia from Peter to Catherine II* [*Istoriia Oblastnogo Upravleniia v Rossii ot Petra do Ekateriny II*] (his doctoral dissertation) was published in 1913.

Got'e begins where Peter the Great left off — the the abolition of the costly provincial institutions in 1727.

All functions of government and justice were placed upon the governors and the *voevodas* [military commanders] and their offices. The order to the *voevodas* repeated in significant measure the instructions they had received in the XVII century.

Subsequently, matters moved in the direction of the expansion of the rights of local gentry in local life. This process was described by Got'e in volume II of his book which appeared in 1944 (this volume is unavailable to me; I know of it from the Soviet encyclopedia's article on Got'e). The new era was heralded by Peter III's "Manifesto on the Freedom of the Nobility." [53]

In 1915 Got'e published his *Essay on the History of Landownership in Russia* [*Ocherk Istorii Zemlevladeniia v Rossii*].

From 1900 Got'e began to study archeology, which had already interested him previously. He upheld the necessity of drawing upon historical and archeological data in the study of ancient Russian history. He conducted many digs in central and southern Russian districts.

His two works, *Essays on the History of Eastern Europe's Material Culture* [*Ocherki po Istorii Material'noi Kul'tury Vostochnoi Evropy*] (1925) and *The Iron Age in Eastern Europe* [*Zheleznyi Vek v Vostochnoi Evropy*] (1930) were based on the results of these excavations.

These books contain the first scholarly survey of Russian pre-history in Russian historiography. They have retained their significance to this day.

## S. V. BAKHRUSHIN (1882-1950)

Sergei Vladimirovich Bakhrushin was born in Moscow. In 1904, upon graduating from Moscow University, he was also retained at the chair by Kliuchevskii.

His first work was on the history of the princely economy (1909). There followed a study of the Moscow revolt of 1648 (1917). His article, "Native Legends in S. Remizov's 'Siberian History' " ["Tuzemnye Legendy v 'Sibirskoi Istorii S. Remizova' "] appeared in 1916.

Bakhrushin's main works were written after the October

Revolution of 1917.

Bakhrushin worked primarily on two problems: the history of Siberia in the XVI and XVII centuries and the enterprises of Russian merchants in the same period and, in this connection, studied the pre-requisites of the Russian marketplace in the XVI century. Bakhrushin's *Scholarly Works* [*Nauchnye Trudy*] were published in four volumes (Moscow, 1952-1959).

## A. I. IAKOVLEV (1873-1951)

Aleksei Ivanovich Iakovlev studied at Moscow University. Student unrest started when he was in his third year and a stormy strike occurred in February of 1899. More than 150 students were expelled by the university's administration. Iakovlev was expelled for his "escapades."

On February 20th Kliuchevskii wrote a letter to the university's rector petitioning for Iakovlev's re-admission. "He wrote a marvelous essay on Russian history in medal competition while he was still in his first year — a rare case in the history of Russian universities. . . The more that I came to know him, the more I became convinced of my opinion of him. I laid the highest hopes upon him. I believe that his act was the result of an extremely agitated state and that it was not induced by irremediable motives. . . I am perfectly willing to guarantee his trustworthy behavior upon his return to Moscow University."

Iakovlev was finally re-admitted to the university. Kliuchevskii retained him at the chair.

Upon passing the master's examination, Iakovlev became a *privat-docent*.

His work, *The Defense Line in the XVIII Century* [*Zasechnaia Cherta v XVIII Veke*] appeared in 1916. In it Iakovlev described the system of Russian defense fortifications against Tatar raids. This work is valuable to this day for the history of military affairs in Russia and for Russian historical geography.

Iakovlev's work, *The Department of Military Affairs*

[*Prikaz Ratnykh Del*] came out in the following year. After this, Iakovlev was given a professorship.

Iakovlev continued his scholarly work after the October Revolution of 1917. His work *Slaves and the Status of Servitude in the State of Muscovy* [*Kholopy i Kholopstvo v Moskovskom Gosudarstve*] was published in 1943. A large collection of documents, *Novgorodian Service Contract Books* [*Novgorodskie Zapisnye Kabal'nye Knigi*] was published under his editorship a few years earlier (in 1938).

## Ia. L. BARSKOV (1863-1937)

Iakov Lazarevich Barskov was the oldest of Kliuchevskii's students and was utterly devoted to his teacher.

Upon graduating from the university, Kliuchevskii did not keep Barskov at the chair. I do not know whether Barskov wished to pursue an academic career. Evidently, he did not feel the calling. In any case, he and Kliuchevskii remained friends for life.

Upon graduating from the university, Barskov became a history teacher in Moscow's secondary schools. He taught history in the upper grades of Moscow's fifth gymnasium when I was a pupil there (I graduated from this gymnasium in the spring of 1905). In his lessons Barskov strove not only to have his pupils know the subject but to reflect upon it and learn to think about the historical process in an independent fashion. Barskov instilled the interest in and love of history in me. When I was graduating from the gymnasium, I had already decided to enroll in the historico-philological department of Moscow University.

From time to time Barskov traveled to Petersburg. There he met with scholars and men of letters. Sometimes he carried out an errand for Kliuchevskii and informed him of news of Petersburg.

In 1902 V. K. Pleve, chief secretary of Finland, asked Kliuchevskii to gather materials on the history of Finland. Kliuchevskii used illness as an excuse to dissuade him and suggested Barskov in his stead. The assignment was a ticklish one: the preparation to limit Finland's autonomy was begun in 1899 (when Pleve was placed in charge of Finnish affairs). It was in this connection that Pleve needed historical data. Pleve did not summon Barskov. Evidently, he entrusted this task to one of the officials of his chancellery.

In 1909 students, friends, and admirers of Kliuchevskii dedicated a collection of articles to him on the anniversary of his thirtieth year as a professor at Moscow University. Barskov compiled a bibliography of Kliuchevskii's works for the *Festschrift*.

Barskov labored much to put Kliuchevskii's *Course of Russian History* in order. While yet a student, he had written down Kliuchevskii's lectures of 1883-1884. The course was lithographed according to his notes. Twenty years later Barskov helped Kliuchevskii to prepare the first four parts of the course for publication. The fifth part was published by Barskov in 1921.

After Kliuchevskii's death Barskov moved to Petersburg. There he received a post as an official in the State archives. This work was exactly what he needed in terms of his inclinations and abilities. He quickly mastered his new duties.

In addition, he became acquainted with the materials in other Petersburg archives and in the public library.

Barskov understood the needs of both Russian and foreign scholars who studied in the archives and was always ready to help them with advice and direction.

Among those he helped much was I when, in 1913, I moved from Moscow to Petersburg and was preparing for my master's examination and thesis under S. F. Platonov.

Despite all of this, Barskov was able to indulge in his own scholarly work. In 1915 he wrote a biography of the mason, I. V. Lopukhin, for the *Russian Biographical Dictionary*. In that same year he gave a lecture at the Military Historical Society on the correspondence between Counts N. I. and P. I. Panin and Grand Duke Paul [the heir to the throne]. In 1915 Barskov published the interesting correspondence of Russian masons in the years 1780-1792.

Barskov was an Old Believer and an expert in Old
Believer literature. Aware of this, V. G. Druzhinin, a member
of the Archeological Commission, asked him to compile an
anthology of documents for the initial years of Russian old
belief. Barskov worked for several years on the study of this
valuable material. The anthology was edited by Barskov and
published in 1912 in volume XXIV of the *Annals of the
Archeological Commission* [*Letopisi Zaniatii Arkheologiche-
skoi Kommissii*].

In 1922 Barskov published an extensive review of
Platonov's book, *Boris Godunov*, in book 8 of the *Russian
Historical Journal*. Barskov notes that Platonov's interest in
Boris's personality and fate had already manifested itself in
his work on his master's thesis, "Old Russian Legends and
Tales About the Time of Troubles. . . " [1888]. It was later
revealed in his *Lectures on Russian History* and in his *Essays
on the History of the Time of Troubles in the State of
Muscovy in the XVI-XVII Centuries* (1890).

"Years and decades passed," writes Barskov, "and the
author continued to have not only an unfailing scholarly
interest in but also a deep sympathy for Boris. He persis-
tently built arguments to justify him." Barskov continues:
"Platonov's new work has the basic aim of justifying Boris."

Barskov highly evaluates Platonov's literary talent.

"Anyone can talk much and say little. But only a great
master of his craft can enclose vast material within closely
prescribed boundaries. In the symmetry and the harmony of
the whole, in the arrangement and proportionality of the
parts, in the elegance and ease of language, Platonov's book is
comparable only to the works of the best French historians —
G. Bossier, Sorel, and Taine."

"The book contains nothing new in comparison with
Platonov's other works. But in its style and construction,
in its treatment of the basic theme, this is a major and pre-
cious novelty in Russian historiography."

Barskov's last work is his article on Radishchev. It
is titled "A. N. Radishchev — Torzhok." It is a sort of commentary to the chapter so titled in Radishchev's sensational

book, *Journey from Petersburg to Moscow* [*Puteshestvie iz Peterburga v Moskvu*] (1790).[54]

The article contains an analysis of Radishchev's opinions on freedom of the press and censorship. It was published after Barskov's death.

Barskov's contribution to Russian historical scholarship was not limited to his own research and publications. One must take cognizance of his aid to Kliuchevskii and his assistance to a whole series of other Russian historians and historians of Russian literature who turned to him for help in their work.

## XXVII

## PLATONOV'S STUDENTS

## S. V. ROZHDESTVENSKII (1868-1934)

In terms of age Sergei Vasilevich Rozhdestvenskii was Platonov's oldest student.[55]

Rozhdestvenskii graduated from the historical-philological department of the University of Petersburg. On the advice of Platonov, he took for his master's thesis a theme from Muscovite Russia's socio-economic history — "Servitor Landownership in XVI Century Muscovy" ["Sluzhiloe Zemlevladenie v Moskovskom Gosudarstve XVI Veka"]. In the introduction to his work he expresses his sincere gratitude to Platonov for his "unfailing attention and varied assistance."

The work was completed in 1896 and the book published in 1897.

The defense was successful and Rozhdestvenskii received his master's degree. He began to lecture at the University of Petersburg.

In 1920 Rozhdestvenskii published his keenly felt article "In Memory of S. M. Solov'ev" (on the 100th anniversary of his birth) ["Pamiati S. M. Solov'eva"] in the journal *Dela i Dni*, book one.

This is a thoughtful and broad evaluation and is one of

the best articles about him. Rozhdestvenskii concluded his essay with the following words:

"Let the memory of how Solov'ev lived and worked give more inspiration and strength to our own younger generation that is entering the historical field."

Prior to the appearance of Rozhdestvenskii's study, the history of servitor landownership primarily drew the attention of legal historians. The works of Nevolin and several others exhausted the material contained in Moscow's legal documents and ancient acts and provided a more or less detailed construction of hereditary and political rights in the XVI and XVII centuries.

"This artificial scheme of legal relationships," writes Rozhdestvenskii, "frequently hides the living historical perspective, the odd sequence of the various processes of which the history of the phenomenon studied is composed."

Chronologically, Rozhdestvenskii limits his research to the XVI century. He writes: "In this era all the essential and original traits of the topic studied are particularly vivid and salient. It is precisely in the XVI century that the fundamental principle of servitor landownership — land must not be taken out of service — is stated firmly and in full realization by the Muscovite government. It is implemented in practice in an especially strong manner."

In this aspect the study of the history of servitor landownership touches on the problems of Muscovy's financial history as it was depicted in the works of Lappo-Danilevskii and Miliukov. Rozhdestvenskii relies on these works.

In the various series of chapters of his study, Rozhdestvenskii examines the questions of mobilizing the patrimonial landowners, the economic crisis, the hereditary properties of princes, the servitor significance of monastic patrimonies, the Moscow landed aristocracy of the XVI century, the foundation of the *pomest'e* organization of the XVI century, and the types of *pomest'e landownership*. True to his principle — to grasp the actual everyday conditions in which the government tried to implement legislation concerning patrimonies and *pomest'e* — Rozhdestvenskii comes to the conclusion that the legal consciousness of the servitor class and its opposition to government measures undermined the government's attempts.

Upon writing his master's thesis, Rozhdestvenskii set the Muscovite period aside and studied the history of public education in the XVIII and XIX centuries.

His substantial work, *A Historical Survey of the Operation of the Ministry of Public Education* [*Istoricheskii Obzor Deiatel'nosti Ministerstva Narodnogo Prosveshcheniia*] appeared in 1902.

In 1910, in a supplement to it, Rozhdestvenskii published *Materials for the History of Educational Reform in Russia in the XVIII — XIX Centuries* [*Materialy dlia Istorii Uchebnykh Reform v Rossii v XVIII — XIX Vekakh*]. In 1920 he published *The University of Petersburg in the First Century of Its Activity: Materials for Its History* [*Sanktpeterburgskii Universitet v Pervoe Stoletie ego Deiatel'nosti, Materialy po Istorii*], Vol. I, 1819-1836.

Rozhdestvenskii's second fundamental work appeared in 1912. It was titled *Essays on the History of the Systems of Public Education in Russia in the XVIII — XIX Centuries* [*Ocherki po Istorii Sistem Narodnogo Prosveshcheniia v Rossii v XVIII — XIX Vekakh*], Vol. I, the XVIII century.

The book consists of three essays: "Questions of Public Education in the XVIII Century During the Reign of Catherine II"; 2) "Projects for Educational Reform in the Reign of Catherine II Prior to the Establishment of the Commission on Public Schools"; and 3) "The Commission for Establishing Public Schools." The appendix contains materials drawn from the archives.

The content of this work is significantly broader than might be judged from the title. Rozhdestvenskii not only examines "systems" of public education but also the main currents of Russian educational thought in the XVIII c.

Questions of public education were not only legislative items but were avidly discussed in the press.

The striving for a professional gentry education predominated in the second third of the XVIII century.

A gentry land corps was instituted in 1731 under the Empress Anne. But the idea of the necessity for universal education was already being expressed.

This idea was realized with the foundation of Moscow University. Its principal advocate was I. I. Shuvalov. Later, in the reign of Catherine II, a structured system of educational institutions was created. It was headed by Moscow University. A new and broad reform of the public education system and the creation of a net of universities was begun under Alexander I. The beginning point was where Catherine's reforms had left off.

Rozhdestvenskii intended to write of educational reforms in the Alexandrian era in a second volume but had no time.

He died in exile in 1934, one of the many Russian historians who perished at this time.

## A. E. PRESNIAKOV (1870-1929)

Aleksandr Evgen'evich Presniakov graduated from the historico-philological department of the University of Petersburg. Platonov retained him at the chair.

Presniakov deeply felt his teacher's friendly attitude toward him.

In the introduction to his master's thesis, "Princely Law in Ancient Russia" ["Kniazhoe Pravo v Drevnei Rusi"] (1909) Presniakov writes: "It is particularly difficult for me to evaluate in words the many things for which I am obligated to my lengthy personal and scholarly association with my dear teacher Platonov. Without his friendly insistence, this book would not have been written."

In 1913 Presniakov published his valuable study of the so-called *Tsarstvennaia Kniga* — treating its contents and origin.

The *Tsarstvennaia Kniga* covers the period from September of 1533 to 1555. It was published by Prince M. M. Shcherbatov in 1769 according to the only manuscript of it which he knew. It was preserved in the Moscow Synodal (previously Patriarchal) Library. This edition is completely unsatisfactory. Shcherbatov presented the manuscript itself to Empress Catherine II.

The *Tsarstvennaia Kniga* is one of the chief sources for the study of events at the beginning of Ivan the Terrible's rule and is the sole reliable description of the boyar disturbance of 1553.

In view of the historical value of the *Tsarstvennaia Kniga*, Presniakov raised the question of its publication. Platonov took this upon himself. Under his editorship the *Tsarstvennaia Kniga* was published in the second half of volume XIII of the *Complete Collection of Russian Chronicles* [*Polnoe Sobranie Russkikh Letopisei*].

Five years later two of Presniakov's books appeared in print — *The Moscow State* [*Moskovskoe Tsarstvo*] and *The Formation of the Great Russian State* [*Obrazovanie Velikorusskogo Gosudarstva*] (his doctoral dissertation).

In 1922 Presniakov published two articles from the period of XVI century Muscovy — "The Testament of Grand Prince Vasilii III" ["Zaveshchanie Velikogo Kniazia Vasiliia III"] (in an anthology of articles dedicated to S. F. Platonov) and "The Era of Ivan the Terrible in the Overall Historical Perspective" ["Epokha Groznogo v Obshchem Istoricheskom Osveshchenii"] (*Annals* [*Annaly*], No. 2).

After this, Presniakov turned his attention to XIX century Russian history. He wrote a book about Alexander I (1924) and an essay on the Decembrist revolt (1926). His *Lectures on Russian History: I. Kievan Rus'.* [*Lektsii po Russkoi Istorii: I. Kievksaia Rus'*] and II (issue I) *Western Russia and the Lithuanian State* [*Zapadnaia Rus' i Litovsko-Russkoe Gosudarstvo*] were published posthumously. These lectures were given by him at the University of Petersburg in 1908-1909 and 1909-1910.

A major contribution to Russian historical scholarship by Presniakov is his master's thesis, "Princely Law in Ancient Rus' " (1909). As Presniakov explains in the introduction to this work, the book consists of two essays. The first is dedicated to inter-princely relations in pre-mongol times. The

second essay is devoted to an attempt to illuminate the
social position of the prince: the particular circle of relations which served as the basis of the prince's independent
position in the ancient Russian principality.
Presniakov discusses the characteristics of ancient
Slavic law in the opening chapter. He recognizes the value of
the concept of the ancient communal association or the
family commune which was advanced by F. I. Leontovich.
But he does not accept this theory *in toto*.[56]

In the conclusion to his work, Presniakov analyzes the
question of the origin of Church ownership of land and finds
that grants of land by princes played an important role in this
process.

Presniakov's next major work was *The Moscow State*.
The book consists of an introduction and eleven chapters.
In them Presniakov treats the following topics: the great
Russian concept; the popular life of the great Russian north;
the formation of the great Russian State; hereditary autocracy; the great Russian boyars; Church and State in Muscovite Rus'; the fate of hereditary landownership; servitors of
the sovereign; the sovereign's obligated poor; the governmental system of the Muscovite tsardom; the Muscovite
tsardom and the Russian Empire.

M. A. D'iakonov, who was strict with others and with
himself, wrote a critical review of this work. He found much
that was unclear in the author's (Presniakov's) judgments. In
conclusion, however, he recognized that many features of the
social system "will be extremely intriguing and the book
will be read with much interest and benefit by anyone who is
capable of handling it."

The third, and perhaps Presniakov's outstanding, work is
*The Formation of the Great Russian State*. In the author's
words, the fundamental aim of this study "is to reinstate,
insofar as it is possible, the rights of source and fact in the
presentation of one of Russian history's most important
phenomena — the formation of the great Russian State. The
early history of north eastern Rus' has, in our historiography,
fallen victim to the theoretical approach to material. This has

transformed the data of primary sources into a series of illustrations for a scheme which did not derive from them.

"Therefore, on the one hand, there is quite a bit of this material which has not fit the accepted scheme and has remained outside of historians' attention and generalization, and on the other hand, the broad generalizations disregarded the chronological sequence of the basic phenomena of the evolution under study and severed their true interrelation." In Presniakov's opinion "the historiographic tradition founded by Solov'ev has, in Kliuchevskii's works, become an axiom of sorts in our field." It is therefore all the more sharply, in Presniakov's view, that the fundamental sin of this axiom — sociological dogmatism — becomes apparent.

The formation of the great Russian State, not the elevation of Moscow, writes Presniakov, must be the basic concept which should be adhered to in the new structuring of the history of north-eastern Rus' in the XII—XV centuries. The complex and variable interlacing of external interests and the relations of the great Russian nation which led to cohesion around one of the centers of the struggle for national interests must be stressed, not the organic process of the growth of the princely patrimony into the State; and, the unification of great Russia by the grand princes, by the Moscow methods of gathering power — and not lands — must be viewed.

In book five of the *Russian Historical Journal* (1918), S. V. Rozhdestvenskii wrote a thoughtful review of what he referred to as Presniakov's "fundamental" work.

"Presniakov's book," writes Rozhdestvenskii, "is a major gain for our historiography. If he was not able to shake the foundations of the dominant view of the history of north-eastern Rus' in the XIII—XV centuries, then substantial results were attained in the criticism of the certain one-sidedness of this interpretation by means of a model verification of the factual material. The new points of view advanced by the author regarding the nature of the development of great power rule and the nature of the *udel* proprietorship must enliven the attention of historians to these basic problems of our antiquity."

## M. A. POLIEVKTOV (1872-1942)

Mikhail Aleksandrovich Polievktov was graduated from the historico-philological department of the University of Petersburg in 1894. Platonov retained him at the chair to prepare for a professorship.

In 1907 Polievktov defended his master's thesis on the theme of "The Baltic Question in Russian Policy After the Treaty of Nystadt (1721-1725)" ["Baltiiskii Vopros v Russkoi Politike Posle Nishtadskogo Mira 1721-1725"].

In 1917, he published a bibliographical article, "Literature on XVIII—XIX Century Russian External History During the Years 1910-1915" ["Literatura po Vneshnei Russkoi Istorii XVIII—XIX vv. za 1910-1915 g."] (in *Historical News* [*Istoricheskie Izvestiia*]). Another bibliographical article followed, "Historical Literature on the Era of Nicholas I During the Years 1900-1916" ["Istoricheskaia Literatura po Epokhe Nikolaia I za 1900-1916 gg."] (*Russian Historical Journal*).

After the defense of his thesis, Polievktov was chosen professor at the Advanced Courses for Women. In addition, he lectured as a *privat-docent* at the University of Petersburg.

At the Advanced Courses for Women Polievktov gave a course surveying the era of Nicholas I. Simultaneously, he wrote a biography of Nicholas I for the *Russian Biographical Dictionary*. The publication of the *Dictionary* ceased in 1917. Polievktov was given an offer by the Sabashnikov publishers in Moscow to publish this work as a book. It came out in 1918, titled *Nicholas I: Biography and Survey of His Reign* [*Nikolai I. Biografiia i Obzor Tsarstvovaniia*].

Polievktov's "Baltic Question" (1907) is a work of paramount importance for Russian foreign affairs in the first quarter of the XVIII century.

In his introduction, Polievktov characterizes the five year period from 1721 to 1725 as a "time of systematic

diplomatic struggle which was a direct and logical continuation of the just-ended armed conflict for the Baltic coast-
line."

In order to comprehend the historical aspects of this
struggle from behind the scenes, Polievktov prefaces his
study with an essay on the Baltic question during the second
half of the Northern War (1709-1721).

As the basis for his work, Polievktov used a broad array
of materials drawn from both Russian and foreign archives.
These materials had not been used until that time.

In the concluding section of his introduction, Polievktov
expresses his gratitude to two of his university professors —
S. F. Platonov and G. V. Forsten. Platonov, writes Polievktov, taught him to "respect accuracy and methodicalness in
scholarly research and prudence in his conclusions. In addition, he gave him real support in his scholarly studies."

"But above all, and most of all, he (Polievktov) felt
obligated to his mother who was able to instill in him a respect for the scholarly endeavor. Later, by her indefatigable
efforts, she created the most favorable conditions for his
study. In truth, this work must be dedicated to her."

In 1930 Polievktov was made professor of Russian
history at the University of Tiflis and moved to the Caucasus.

Let us turn to a discussion of his book on Nicholas I.

"The reign of Nicholas I," writes Polievktov in his
introduction to this work, "is a definite era in Russian history, an era, above all, in the history of absolute monarchy in
Russia. This political form became a militant slogan in this
period. It trumpeted its victory and was transformed from a
simple historical fact into a sanctioned political principle. . .
The life of Nicholas Pavlovich, the sovereign, explains much
in the governmental activity of Emperor Nicholas."

The opening chapter, "Childhood and the Years of
Study of Grand Duke Nicholas," follows the introduction.
Three years after his birth, his grandmother, Catherine II,
died and care for Nicholas was shifted to his parents, Emperor Paul and his wife (by a second marriage) Maria Fedorovna. After Paul's death, Maria Fedorovna remained in charge

of Nicholas's upbringing.

Later, when Nicholas turned fifteen, academician Heinrich Storch was invited to give him a course on political economy. Afterwards, Nicholas thought these lectures were too abstract, but some of Storch's ideas did have an influence on him. Nicholas studied engineering with enthusiasm. He was developing into a knowledgeable engineer.

From childhood, the combination of sincerity and directness with cruelty and rudeness was observed in Nicholas's character. Subsequently, these contradictions were expressed in his function of sovereign.

In 1814 and 1815 the Grand Duke Nicholas and his younger brother Michael traveled to the theater of military operations against France. Their instructor was P. P. Konovnitsyn, an experienced combat general.

Parting with the grand dukes at the beginning of 1816, Konovnitsyn wrote them a letter in which he warned them against becoming enthused over the callous front line soldiery.

As Nicholas matured, his mother, Empress Maria Fedorovna, began to look for a suitable bride for him. Her choice fell on Charlotte, the Prussian princess. In June she arrived in Petersburg with her retinue, converted to Orthodoxy and was named Aleksandra Fedorovna. The marriage took place in the Winter Palace on June 1, 1817.

In the familial sense, the marriage was a happy one. A son — Alexander, the future Emperor Alexander II — was born on April 17, 1818.

This marriage had significant political consequences — Nicholas's close ties with the Prussian royal house.

At the end of 1826, Nicholas ordered that a compilation of the Decembrists' testimony on the nation's internal state be made for him. This collection was presented to him in February of 1827. From that time on, it was always in the sovereign's cabinet. In this way Nicholas had before him a picture of the chaotic state of the Russian administration, police, tax system, and the difficult condition of peasant serfs.

The liberal ideas of the Decembrists ("prattle") were, of course, unacceptable to Nicholas. But he decided to carry out the reforms within the framework of bureaucratic government and under his personal supervision. The focus of his supervision over the conduct of the reforms became His Majesty's Private Imperial Chancery. The First Section carried out the functions of the Emperor's personal private chancery.

The Second Section was entrusted with bringing the laws into order. Under Speranskii's direction, the *First Complete Collection of Laws* was compiled (1649-1825) and, on its basis, the *Code of Laws* (first ed., 1832). After this, there was an annual compilation of statutes that had come into effect during the year.

The Third Section was in charge of the government police and the gendarmes corps. General and Count A. Kh. Benkendorf was placed at its head. His main task was the struggle with undesirable political ideas. In this connection a series of measures in the area of loyal politics, censorship, and public education were undertaken.

The Fourth Section was "The Department of Empress Maria" (women's gymnasiums, institutes, hospitals, homes for the blind, etc. . . ).

Nicholas paid considerable attention to the state of the peasantry. The sovereign's aide in this matter was General P. D. Kiselev whom the Tsar jokingly called his chief of staff on the peasant question and who, as Minister of State Properties, did much to regulate the administration and raise the economic and cultural question as a whole. It was discussed in a series of secret committees and a number of partial measures were accepted for the benefit of the peasantry.

No matter how timid these attempts were, Polievktov feels that Kiselev's attraction to the solution of the peasant problem constitutes an epoch in this respect. And, truthfully, what was significant was that the peasant question had been placed in the order of business. Furthermore, the materials collected by Kiselev turned out to be extremely useful in the work of the commissions on peasant freedom in 1861.

In the first half of his reign Nicholas was able to attract a whole series of talented aides to his side — Kiselev, Speranskii, Admiral Mordvinov, Kankrin, Count (from 1831 on Prince) V. P. Kochubei.

In military affairs the chief authority for Nicholas from 1821 was General Ivan Feodorovich Paskevich ("father commander," as Nicholas called him).

As a strategist, Paskevich thoroughly thought through and planned each of his campaigns. Only then did he strike at the enemy. But during the Crimean War of 1854-1855, his carefulness, which turned into indecision, undermined his military authority.

During the second half of his reign, Nicholas began to surround himself with advisers who were of little use — such as Admiral Prince A. S. Menshikov and General Aleksandr Ivanovich Chernyshev.

A fateful circumstance was that under the influence of protracted successes in his reign, Nicholas became convinced that he was all-powerful in international affairs and could allow himself anything. His new advisers only supported him in this conviction. All this led to catastrophe.

In Tiflis Polievktov predominantly worked on Caucasian topics.

His study, *Russian Academic Study of the Caucasus in the XVIII Century* [*Russkoe Akademicheskoe Kavkazovedenie XVIII Veka*] was published in the *Izvestiia* of the Academy of Sciences (social science division) in 1935.

During that same year, Polievktov compiled a bibliography of European travelers in the Caucasus in the XIII-XVIII centuries. Two years later he published *Materials on the History of Russo-Georgian Relations 1615-1640* [*Materialy po Istorii Gruzino-Russkikh Otnoshenii 1615-1640*].

## P. G. VASENKO (1874-1934)

Of all of Platonov's students, Vasenko was closest to him. Vasenko himself revered him deeply.

In the introduction to his main work *Kniga Stepennaia Tsarkogo Rodosloviia*, Vasenko writes: "The author is deeply grateful to his dear teacher, S. F. Platonov, discussions with whom helped to conceive the ideas for the proposed study and who, during the course of the work itself, supported it with his valuable suggestions and sincere participation."

In 1908 Vasenko published an article dealing with a topic from the Time of Troubles titled "D'iak Ivan Timofeev, Author of 'Vremennik' " ["D'iak Ivan Timofeev, Avtor Vremennika"] (*Journal of the Ministry of Public Education*, No. 3, 1908). D'iak Timofeev was one of the most brilliant of the publicists of the Time of Troubles. Vasenko returned to this period in 1923 and wrote of another outstanding writer — Avraamii Palitsyn. The work was *Social Disruption During the Time of Troubles as Depicted by Avraamii Palitsyn* [*Obshchestvennoe Razlozhenie v Smutnoe Vremia v Izobrazhenii Avraamiia Palitsyna*] and appeared in *Russkoe Proshloe* [*The Russian Past*], book 5, 1923.

In book I of *Dela i Dni* in 1920, Vasenko published a short study, "Notes on the History of the Servitor Class in the State of Muscovy. Servitor and *Pomest'e* Hetmans" ["Zametki k Istorii Sluzhilogo Klassa v Moskovskom Gosudarstve. Atamany Sluzhilye-Pomestnye"]. In his *Essays on the History of the Time of Troubles* Platonov defined the *pomest'e hetmans* as a special rank. Vasenko clarified that these hetmans came to Moscow from the Don, strove to merge with the Muscovite rank of *deti boiarskie* [lesser gentry], and petitioned the Moscow government to that effect. The latter readily satisfied these requests.

The center of Vasenko's historical research was the *Stepennaia Kniga*.

This book had already been known to V. N. Tatishchev in the XVIII century. It was published by G. F. Müller in 1775.

This book is a type of religio-philosophical history of the Russian Tsars. It is arranged in sequence of generations commencing with Riurik. Information is given on the Russian metropolitans.

In this fashion the *Stepennaia Kniga* was conceived as a collection of articles primarily of a hagio-biographical content and arranged according to a genealogical scheme. In its goals the *Stepennaia Kniga* is a "triumphal book" which glorifies the "Lord's confirmed holders of the sceptre, hallowed in their piety" and in general "the holy seed of St. Vladimir" with whom the most famous and most holy of the Moscow metropolitans have been also glorified.

During the course of his work, Vasenko not only studied Müller's published edition but all other texts which he was able to find. He noted all the various readings and the heterogeneity of the contents of all these sources.

In the first chapter of his book, Vasenko provides a survey of the discussions of the *Stepennaia Kniga* which had previously appeared in Russian historical literature.

In chapter two he analyzes Müller's published edition and various texts of the *Stepennaia Kniga*.

The question of who was the compiler of the *Stepennaia Kniga* is discussed in chapter four.

Some historians believe that the compiler was Metropolitan Kiprian (1370-1406). Vasenko proved the groundlessness of this view.

Vasenko personally came to the conclusion that the idea for compiling the *Stepennaia Kniga* belongs to Metropolitan Makarii (d. December, 1563) and that Makarii gave his blessings for this task to elder Afanasii (who was elected metropolitan after Makarii's death).

Vasenko surmises that the book was compiled between 1560 and 1563 and that its final re-working dates to March-December, 1563. This conclusion, to me, seems to be firmly established.

To all this we may add that the *Stepennaia Kniga* played a significant role not only in the history of Muscovy's religio-political ideas but also in the history of Muscovy's foreign policy.

According to the *Stepennaia Kniga*, the Moscow Tsars are the successors of Vladimir Sviatoslavich and Vladimir

Monomakh and do not need to be confirmed in their rule by either the Roman Pope or the German Emperor. They are self-ruling.

On this basis Ivan the Terrible commenced an international campaign for the acceptance of his title of Tsar. But England recognized the title as Ivan's without any ado. After the English opened the northern sea route to Rus' via the White Sea in 1553, they received trading privileges in Russia. The growth of Anglo-Russian trade was exceedingly beneficial to England and to Moscow.[57]

Vasenko published his study of the *Stepennaia Kniga* in 1904. When he began, he already foresaw that this work would have to be completed with a new critical edition of the *Stepennaia Kniga*.

This edition was published by him in two parts (in 1908 and 1913) in volume 21 of the *Complete Collection of Russian Chronicles*.

No works by Vasenko appeared in print after 1923. In all probability he was tortured to death in prison and exiled by the Bolsheviks at the same time as Rozhdestvenskii. Their teacher Platonov died in exile in 1933.

## A. I. ZAOZERSKII (1874-ca. 1933)

Aleksandr Ivanovich Zaozerskii graduated from the historico-philological department of the University of Petersburg in 1910. He was retained at the chair of Russian history by Platonov and, upon passing the master's examinations, received the rank of *privat-docent*.

In 1912 he published his article on the assemblies of the land in the anthology *Three Centuries* [*Tri Veka*] (Moscow 1912, vol. I).

Zaozerskii worked mostly at home.

I do not believe that his means were extensive (I think he taught at women's gymnasiums). But he bought very many books and manuscripts from second hand book dealers and stores.

There were two desks and shelves with books in the big

room of his apartment. In addition, along one of the walls, the volumes of the Complete Collection of Laws for the second half of the XVIII century lay in heaps (I write from personal recollection).

Zaozerskii wrote his master's thesis on "Tsar Aleksei Mikhailovich in his Economy" ["Tsar Aleksei Mikhailovich v Svoem Khoziaistve"] (1917). The second edition appeared in 1937 under the title of *The Royal Patrimony in the XVII Century [Tsarskaia Votchina XVII Veka]*.

Within the circles of scholars and Platonov's friends there were rumors that Platonov intended to give Zaozerskii the doctoral degree immediately (by-passing the master's). But Platonov granted him the master's.

Evidently, Zaozerskii later intended to continue his study chronologically and to broaden the theme. In 1922, in book eight of the *Russian Historical Journal*, he published a lengthy article "The Boiar Household. A Page from the History of One Boiar Household" ["Boiarskii Dvor. Stranitsa iz Istorii Odnogo Boiarskogo Dvora"] (end of the XVII century).

Let us turn to the contents of Zaozerskii's work on the royal patrimony.

To manage this patrimony, a special *"Prikaz"* was established (this was the name of central administrative organs in Muscovy). This institution was called the *Prikaz Tainykh Del* or *Tainyi Prikaz* [Bureau of Secret Affairs]. It was founded *circa* 1658.

The bureau was under Tsar Aleksei's personal direction and was in a sense his private chancery.

The Tsar created this office partly in order to hasten the pace of affairs in the old bureaus (which continued to function) and partly in order not to be dependent on the Boyar Duma and the Assembly of the Land.

Among the Tsar's advisers in the Bureau of Secret Affairs were his most trusted boyars — Princes N. I. Odoevskii and A. N. Trubetskoi and a few others.

Concentrated in the Bureau, without any plan, were questions of the utmost variety — partimonial and those relating to the State. The Bureau conducted investigations into the most important governmental matters, for example, the affair of Patriarch Nikon and the issuance of counterfeit coins. Factories and explosives were under the Bureau's jurisdiction. Simultaneously, the Bureau was in charge of the Tsar's favorite amusement — falconry. The economic base of the Bureau was the royal patrimony. It is only this aspect of the Bureau — the royal economy — which Zaozerskii examines in his work. His main source was the archive of the Bureau of Secret Affairs.

In the first chapter Zaozerskii describes the history of the formation of the Bureau of Secret Affairs.

In chapter two Zaozerskii discusses the history and methods of the growth and development of the royal patrimony's land fund. The possessions of the Bureau were not in an unbroken block but were scattered about in twenty districts of the central region around the Moscow district.

In choosing land to be taken under the Bureau's jurisdiction, the heads of the Bureau considered the benefits of the economic exploitation of the land, the familial relations of the Tsar, and sometimes political aspects.

All lands controlled by the Bureau of Secret Affairs were called the sovereign's. Some of them had previously belonged to the sovereign. Others were taken away from individuals.

In a quantitative sense, of former individual possessions, the first place belongs to the patrimonies of his first cousin, once removed, and uncle, N. I. Romanov (he died childless in 1682). Tsar Aleksei had right to these patrimonies by escheat. He took them into his patrimony and Bureau of Secret Affairs.

In 1665 the Tsar ordered the local military commander to transfer the patrimonies of boyar N. A. Ziuzin of the Nizhegorod province. The patrimonies were confiscated without indemnification and were placed under control of the Bureau of Secret Affairs. This was an act of revenge by Tsar Aleksei for Ziuzin's unsuccessful attempt to reconcile the Tsar with Patriarch Nikon and to convince the Tsar to return Nikon to the patriarchy. This occurred in December of 1664.

In the third chapter Zaozerskii describes the forms and the degree of the Tsar's participation in the Bureau's economic activity. The Tsar had a special table with special writing implements at the Bureau. The Tsar heard the matters and issued his orders regarding them.

Aleksei was constantly and well informed regarding the state of affairs in his economy and took notice that his orders be realized.

In the fourth chapter Zaozerskii surveys industrial undertakings on the royal patrimony — the production of potash, salt, glass, the establishment of factories for bricks and the production of Morocco leather, and also the organization of the land plowed in obligation to the sovereign. There followed stock raising (horses, cattle, swine, sheep), raising of poultry (geese, ducks, chickens), and the raising of fruits and vegetables.

The fifth chapter speaks of the condition of patrimonial peasants and other categories of workers.

Insofar as peasants are concerned, the Bureau of Secret Affairs generally followed the Code of Laws of 1649 (the *Ulozhenie*). Nevertheless, in contradiction to the principles of the *Ulozhenie*, Aleksei did not hesitate to forcibly resettle peasants from one region to another when this seemed economically advantageous.

The sixth chapter discusses distillation and the pay scale for advisers to and employees of the Bureau as well as trade with Persia.

In the seventh (and final) chapter, Zaozerskii treats the correlation and synchronization of the activities of the Bureau of Secret Affairs with the work of other *prikazy*.

In addition, in the same chapter Zaozerskii sketches Tsar Aleksei's political ideology. Aleksei received his political training under the guidance of boyar B. I. Morozov and Patriarch Nikon.

For him, the paradigm of the autocratic sovereign was

Ivan the Terrible.

One of the Swedish agents who was in Moscow at the beginning of the 1650's wrote: "The Tsar is so taken up with reading works on the history of Ivan the Terrible and his wars that he probably wishes to follow in his footsteps. . . By nature the Tsar is proud and cruel like a barbarian. Consequently, he is capable of anything. He must find pleasure in stories of Ivan Vasil'evich and his tyranny."

Of course, Tsar Aleksei does not approach Ivan the Terrible's cruelties but he did have a cruel streak in his character (side by side with external mildness).

After 1922, no works by Zaozerskii appeared in print.

The second edition of his master's thesis (with the changed title of *The Royal Patrimony in the XVII Century*) was issued by the Government socio-economic publishing house and edited by N. L. Rubinshtein. The author, evidently, took no part in it whatsoever.

It may be thought that Zaozerskii spent the last years of his life in prison and exile — like Vasenko and Rozhdestven-skii.

### P. G. LIUBOMIROV (1885-1935)

Pavel Grigor'evich Liubomirov graduated from the historical-philological department of the University of Petersburg. In Platonov's seminar he wrote a work on the topic, "Essay on the History of the Nizhegorodian Militia" ["Ocherk Istorii Nizhegorodskogo Opolcheniia"]. (It was published in the *Journal of the Ministry of Public Education* in 1913 and 1914).

For his master's thesis on the same topic, Liubomirov reworked and expanded his essay. It was published in 1917.

The defense of the thesis (Platonov was the chief opponent) was successful.

In 1918, in book five of the *Russian Historical Journal*, Platonov wrote a detailed review of Liubomirov's book. "Only lengthy and intent labor," says Platonov, "could have led the author to such a fortunate and rich result in his research."

"A third of a century ago," Platonov continues, "when I was writing my master's thesis on ancient Russian stories and legends regarding the Time of Troubles, I intended to study this very topic but was halted because of insufficient materials."

The state of the sources changed for the better at the beginning of the XX century.

"Liubomirov's task was to collect in one place the factual data available in print and to supplement it, insofar as it was possible, with archival references. He was to review and check the results of the scholarly investigations of preceding researchers and, finally, to include within his exposition themes uniting the scholarly synthesis or the integration of the scholarly-artistic depiction."

"The first and second parts of Mr. Liubomirov's task are executed very well. Our author seems to feel that part three is superfluous."

In conclusion, Platonov states, "P. G. Liubomirov has written a large and valuable work. . . . All subsequent works will be based on it."

Liubomirov followed some of Platonov's suggestions and, on their basis, re-worked his study for a new edition. It appeared posthumously in 1939.

In 1922 Liubomirov was appointed professor at the University of Saratov. There he wrote a valuable study, *Trade Relations of Ancient Rus' with the East in the VIII-XI Centuries* [*Torgovye Sviazi Drevnei Rusi s Vostokom v VIII-XI Vekakh*] (*Transactions of the University of Saratov*, I, issue III, 1923) and an essay on the history of old belief titled "The Vyg Commune" ["Vygovskoe Obshchezhitel'stvo"] (1924).

Liubomirov's next basic work was his *Essays on the History of Metallurgical and Metal Working Industry in Russia (in the XVII, XVIII, and XIX Centuries): The Geographical Distribution of the Metal Industry* [*Ocherki po Istorii Metallurgicheskoi i Metalloubrabatyvaiushchei Promyshlennosti v Rossii (XVII, XVIII, i XIX Vekov): Geo-*

*graficheskoe Razmeshchenie Metallo-Promyshlennosti*] .
Liubomirov finished the work in 1934 but the book
came out only in 1937 after the author had died.
In his introductory note for the publication of this book
the communist editor found it necessary to note that "P. G.
Liubomirov does not utilize the most valuable indications of
Lenin and Stalin on the question of pre-Petrine and Petrine
industry. The essay published is not, as a whole, a Marxist
investigation into the history of industry."

Liubomirov states in his introduction that at the basis
of his work "there is the gathering of rich published materials
on metallurgy. Various data from archival and manuscript
collections have also been drawn on. As to metal working,
one had to gather materials of the most varied sorts from
various sources. . . To provide a finished all-sided characterization of industrial regions and points in this work would be
premature."

Liubomirov's study is full of factual material. It is
extremely valuable for Russian social and economic history
in general and for the history of metallurgy in Russia in particular. But it is not easy to read. It must be intently studied.

## A. I. ANDREEV (1887-1959)

Aleksandr Ignat'evich Andreev was born in Petersburg
where his father, a peasant from the Pskov district, worked as
a guard at the commercial board. His father arranged his stay
at one of the shelters of the merchant society. Upon finishing
education at this shelter, Aleksandr received a scholarship to
the Petrine commerical school in Petersburg. Upon graduating from this school, Aleksandr Ignat'evich enrolled in the
economics department of Petersburg's Polytechnic Institute.

In 1909 he passed the gymnasium course in Greek and
Latin and transferred to the historico-philological department
of the University of Petersburg. At the university Andreev
studied under Lappo-Danilevskii, Presniakov, and Platonov.

In 1913 Andreev participated in the compilation of the
catalogue of the particular acts of the Muscovite State. It

was being produced by students of Lappo-Danilevskii. The "Terminological Dictionary of the Particular Acts of the Muscovite State" ["Terminologicheskii Slovar' Chastnykh Aktov Moskovskogo Gosudarstva"] was published in 1922 under his editorship and carried his introduction. From 1918 to 1925 Andreev was the director of the archives of the Ministry of Ways and Means and did much to bring it into order.

Andreev spent the period from the fall of 1931 to the spring of 1935 in Eniseisk. He worked in the regional museum and in the city library where there was a fairly large collection of books on Siberian geography, ethnography, and history.

Siberia captivated Andreev and broadened his vision.

Returning to Leningrad, Andreev broadly unfurled his work on the study of Siberia's historical ethnography and history.

The work began with the preparation and publication of the works of G. F. Müller. The first volume of Müller's *History of Siberia* appeared in 1937, the second in 1941, under the editorship of Andreev and S. V. Bakhrushin. The third and fourth volumes remain in manuscript. In the appendix to the first volume, Andreev wrote an introductory article, "G. F. Müller's Manuscripts on the History, Geography, Ethnography, and Languages of Siberian Peoples."

In 1940 Andreev defended his doctoral dissertation, "Essays on the Source Study of Siberia in the XVII-XVIII centuries" ["Ocherki po Istochnikovedeniiu Sibiri XVII-XVIII Vekov"] (three issues, 1940-1965). His opponents were S. V. Bakhrushin, Iu. V. Got'e, and B. D. Grekov. All of them evaluated Andreev's work highly.

During the Second World War, in June of 1942, Andreev was evacuated to Tashkent. At the end of the year he moved to Moscow. In 1949 he returned to Leningrad. In Moscow he was mostly interested in the history of Russian geographical discoveries.

He published two collections — *Russian Discoveries in the Pacific Ocean and in North America in the XVIII Century*

[*Russkie Otkrytiia v Tikhom Okeane i Severnoi Amerike v. XVIII v*] and *The Russian Fleet and Geographical Discoveries* [*Russkii Flot i Geograficheskie Otkrytiia*].
During the last ten years of his life, Andreev worked primarily on the history of the Academy of Sciences in the XVIII century. His primary attention was given to M. V. Lomonosov. He participated actively in the preparation of Lomonosov's collected works. He was the editor of volumes V, VI, and IX of this publication.

In addition, in 1950, he issued *Selected Works on Russian Geography* [*Izbrannye Trudy po Geografii Rossii*] by V. N. Tatishchev.

Andreev also studied Peter the Great. The Academy of Sciences entrusted him with editing the second issue of volume XIII of *The Letters and Papers of Peter the Great* [*Pis'ma i Bumagi Petra Velikogo*] (which were published in 1946 and 1948). From 1943 Andreev was in charge of the group studying Peter at the Historical Institute. The result was the publication of an anthology titled *Peter the Great* which was edited by Andreev. Two of Andreev's own articles were published in this anthology — "The Foundation of the Academy of Sciences in Petersburg" ["Osnovanie Akademii Nauk v Peterburge"] and "Peter the Great and England in 1698" ["Petr Velikii i Angliia v 1698 g."].

Andreev was also one of the editors in the preparation of the new edition of Tatischev's *History of Russia*. This extremely valuable publication appeared in seven volumes from 1962-1968 (after Andreev's death). Andreev died on June 12, 1959.

Scholarly work was the basic and beloved work of his life. He was wholly dedicated to it.

But he did not close himself in. Individuals and educational institutions constantly turned to him for advice and direction. He was always ready to help them without lamenting the loss of his time.

## S. N. VALK (1889-ca. 1964)

Sigizmund Natanovich Valk enrolled in the historico-philological department of the University of Petersburg in 1907. He graduated in 1913. At the university, for the most part, he studied under Lappo-Danilevskii, Presniakov, and Platonov, but also under N. I. Kareev and I. M. Grevs. Valk's major subject — one may say his passion at the university and throughout his life — was Russian archeography. But he also familiarized himself well with the achievements of Russian and universal historical scholarship.

Together with Andreev, Valk was an active participant in Lappo-Danilevskii's seminar on research into and compilation of the *Terminological Dictionary of the Particular Acts of the Muscovite State*. (It was published in 1922 and contained Andreev's notes. The latter also was its editor).

Valk published an article in *A Collection of Articles on Russian History Dedicated to S. F. Platonov* [*Sbornik Statei po Russkoi Istorii, Posviashchennyi S. F. Platonovu*] on the "*Gramota Polnaia*,"[58] one of the forms of these acts (1922).

In 1949 Valk published *Documents of Novgorod the Great and Pskov* [*Gramoty Velikogo Novgoroda i Pskova*] a very valuable historical source. Together with Andreev, Valk was one of the chief editors in the preparation of the monumental new edition of V. N. Tatishchev's *History of Russia* (seven volumes, 1962-1968). Neither Valk nor Andreev lived to see this publication.

Valk's main work is his *Soviet Archeography* [*Sovetskaia Arkheografiia*] (Moscow, Leningrad, 1948). In the introduction he writes: "Up to this time even a general survey of the abundant result of the works of our historians in the matter of publishing documents has not been available in our literature. One need not mention how such a state of affairs impedes the use of the fruits of this work in historical scholarship. This was what led to the idea for compiling a survey of published documents which have appeared in Soviet print . . . In the main, our survey includes documents published in book form."

In the first chapter Valk gives a survey of the organization of archeographic work in the Soviet Union.

Created first, according to a resolution of the Soviet of People's Commissars of the RSFSR (September 25, 1920), was a commission for the study of the history of the Russian Communist Party and the October Revolution (*"Istpart"*).[59] It commenced wide ranging work in the capital and in the provinces where local *"istparty"* were organized. There were almost 100 of them in 1927.

Prior to the October Revolution, the central institution for the publication of historical documents and chronicles was the famous Archeographic Commission (founded in 1834). In 1922 it was transferred to the institutional groupings of the Academy of Sciences. Its main organ was the *Letopis' Zaniatii* [*Annals of Study*].

The Central Archive of the RSFSR was created in 1922. It published several series of documents, among them *Materials on the History of the Peasant Movement in Russia* [*Materialy po Istorii Krest'ianskogo Dvizheniia v Rossii*].

The same year saw the commencement of the publication of *Krasnyi Arkhiv* [*Red Archive*] which appeared right up to the beginning of World War II. Initially, and in the main, it published documents on Russia's foreign policy (among them were Russia's secret agreements with its allies during World War I).

Later, materials on the history of the revolutionary movement in Russia (beginning with the Decembrists) and on domestic policy came to be included.

The *Trudy Arkhiva Akademii Nauk i Instituta Literatury* [*Transactions of the Archives of the Academy of Sciences and the Institute of Literature*] (the "Pushkin houses") have great value for the history of Russian scholarship and literature.

In 1948 the Academy of Sciences of the USSR published S.N. Valk's book, *Soviet Archeography*. The author treats the literature of Soviet archeography and questions relating to Soviet archeographic practice. He then provides a survey of the publication of documents on Russian history prior to the XIX century, then on the history of the XIX and XX centuries, and finally, on the history of the USSR.

## A. A. VVEDENSKII (b. 1889)

In his scholarly work Andrei Aleksandrovich Vvedenskii devoted himself to one theme which he studied throughout his life. This theme was the origin of the "famed Stroganovs" and the creation by them, in the XVI and XVII centuries, of a powerful commercial-industrial economic base.

The Stroganovs played a major role in the conquest of Siberia at the end of the XVI century and helped the government of Muscovy to recover from the devastation of the Time of Troubles. Evidently, Vvedenskii became interested in the Stroganovs while he was a student in the historico-philological department at the University of Petersburg (1907-1911).

Upon graduating from the university, he prepared to study the genealogy and the economy of the Stroganovs.

In the summer of 1920 Vvedenskii received a scholarly assignment to Perm for gathering archival material on the economic history and the organization of peasant economy on the Stroganov patrimonies in the XVI and XVII centuries.

Vvedenskii familiarized himself with the archives of the city of Perm as well as with the factory and industrial archives of the Ural and Kama areas of the Perm province. He found that the Perm archives were in a chaotic state but that these archives, particularly those of the Stroganovs, had great scholarly value.

It should be kept in mind that this was the civil war period. Not long before Admiral Kolchak's forces, basing themselves in Siberia, took Perm but were not able to hold it. They were soon forced to retreat.

In his future work, Vvedenskii's basis was mainly the archives of the Stroganovs' Sol'vychegodsk patrimony.

In 1922, in the *Collection of Articles on Russian His-*

*tory Dedicated to S. F. Platonov*, he published his article "Anika Stroganov in His Sol'vychegodsk Business" ["Anika Stroganov v svoem Sol'vychegodskom Khoziaistve"].

In addition, in this and the following year he published several other articles and notices on the Stroganovs' activities in several publications.

His valuable collection of materials, titled *The Trading House of the XVI-XVII Centuries. Documents* [ *Torgovyi Dom XVI-XVII v.v. Dokumenty*], appeared in 1924. There then ensues a long interruption in his publications. It may be thought that this was an enforced break.

In 1938 Vvedenskii was appointed professor at the University of Tiflis. His article, "Peasants — Stroganovs in the XVI-XIX Centuries" ["Krest'iane — Stroganovy v XVI-XIX-m Vekakh"] (1939), appeared in volume ten of the *Transactions* of this university.

From Tiflis, Vvedenskii was transferred to Kiev and received a professorship at the University of Kiev. There he lectured on documentary source study (diplomacy). These lectures were published in 1963.

His article, "The Stroganovs in Kazan in the XVI-XVII Centuries," ["Stroganovy v Kazani v XVI-XVII Vekakh"], was published in volume three of the *Transactions of the History Department of the University of Kiev* in 1939.

In 1955, in *Voprosy Istorii* [*Problems of History*], Vvedenskii wrote an article called "The Class Struggle and 'Isolation' on the White Sea Littoral in the XVI-XVII Centuries" ["Klassovaia Bor'ba i 'Odinochestvo' v Pomor'e v XVI-XVII Vekakh"].

Finally, in 1962, the main work of his life was published, *The Stroganov House in the XVI-XVII Centuries* [*Dom Stroganovykh v XVI-XVII Vekakh*].

In the introduction Vvedenskii provides a survey of the historical literature on the Stroganovs in Siberia beginning with the remarkable work by the Dutch scholar Witsen, *On the Nations of Northern and Eastern Asia and Europe* [*O Stranakh Severnoi i Vostochnoi Azii i Evropy*] (Amsterdam, 1692; 2nd ed., 1705; 3rd ed., and the most valuable, 1785).

Vvedenskii then notes the significance of G. F. Müller's works on Siberia (*Description of the Siberian Kingdom* [*Opisanie Sibirskogo Tsarstva*], 1750). "It was G. F. Müller who first brought a significant quantity of documentary materials into scholarly use."

Vvedenskii states: "The problems connected with the Stroganov conquest and annexation of Siberia, the Stroganov school of iconography, and the political activity of the Stroganovs as agents of the government of the Russian State have been studied relatively well and completely in historical literature." Regarding these problems already discussed in scholarship, Vvedenskii, in his new work, reports new materials and substantiates new conclusions.

"The varied life of the Stroganov house," writes Vvedenskii in the conclusion to his introduction, "represents significant scholarly interest. It need be stressed that their diverse economic and political activity goes far beyond the confines of the Stroganov house. In the XVI-XVII centuries, they influenced the whole nation's economic life. Therefore, the disclosure of the history of the Stroganov's commercial-industrial house can aid in the study of problems in the development of the all-Russian market and the origin of the process of the so-called initial accumulation of capital."

In the eight chapters of his book, filled with factual data gathered from the Stroganov archives, Vvedenskii studies the business of the Sol'vychegodsk and partly the Perm Stroganovs.

In chapter one Vvedenskii analyzes the formation of the commercial-industrial house of the Stroganovs in the XVI century.

. In the second chapter he speaks of Tsar Ivan the Terrible's commission to the Stroganovs regarding the defense of Muscovy's eastern frontiers and of the sending of Ermak by the Stroganovs to conquer Siberia. The theme of the third chapter is the Stroganovs' role in the history of the Time of Troubles and the beginning of the XVII century.

After these historical chapters, the fundamental part of Vvedenskii's work follows: the Stroganov organization of agriculture (chapter four); the organization of manufacture and industry on the Stroganov patrimonies (chapter five); Stroganov trade in Sol'vychegodsk (chapter six); Stroganov trade in Vologda (chapter seven); and finally, Stroganov trade in Kazan and other cities (chapter VIII). In the conclusion of his book Vvedenskii states that "in the activities of the Stroganovs we see a typical example of the transformation of usurious and commercial capital into industrial capital. This is accomplished by organizing large enterprises together with specialized handicrafts, and applies to the free technical intelligentsia as well as to peasant serfs and to laborers."

"The contribution of the Stroganov masters to the development of Russian culture in the XVI-XVII centuries is significant. The work of their icon chambers laid the foundation for a new direction in Russian painting. It created the decorative-festive 'Stroganov' school of iconography. The Stroganovs spread polyphony in church choirs throughout the nation through their servitor, composer and choirmaster, Diletskii. They distributed hand written calligraphically designed books, which were written in their workshops, into the book market."

## B. A. ROMANOV (1889-1957)

Boris Aleksandrovich Romanov was graduated from the historico-philological department of the University of Petersburg in 1912. Platonov retained him at the chair of Russian history. Of Platonov's older students, Romanov became especially friendly with Presniakov who also helped him in the preparation for a scholarly career.

Romanov provided a bibliography of Platonov's works in the *Anthology in Honor of Platonov* [*Sbornik v Chest' Platonova*] (1911).

While a student and member of Presniakov's seminar, Romanov gave a report there titled "The Smerd Horse and the Smerd in the Chronicle and in the *Russkaia Pravda*"

["Smerdii Kon' i Smerd v Letopisi i *Russkoi Pravde*"] . Presniakov found that Romanov was giving a new notion about the *smerdy* (state peasants in Kievan Rus'). Romanov's report was published in the *Proceedings of the Russian Language and Literature Division of the Academy of Sciences* (Vol. XIII, 1908). Upon passing his master's examinations, Romanov received the *privat-docent* rank. He taught at the University of Petersburg (Leningrad) from 1917 to 1927 and from 1944 to 1951.

From 1923-1926, he wrote a series of articles on the basic features of Russian policy in the Far East. From this, Romanov developed a plan for the monographic study of the Russian autocracy's foreign policy during the imperialistic era. The fruit of his study in this field was his outstanding work, *Russia in Manchuria 1892-1906* [*Rossiia v Man'-zhurii 1892-1906*] (1928).

There then follows a long break in his publications, evidently "owing to the circumstances" of Soviet life. In 1941 Romanov received the doctor's degree in history.

Romanov's essay "Land and People in Ancient Rus'" ["Zemlia i Liudi Drevnei Rusi"] appeared in 1947. The same year saw his second fundamental work, *Essays on the Diplomatic History of the Russo-Japanese War* [*Ocherki Diplomaticheskoi Istorii Russko-Iaponskoi Voiny*]. (A second revised and expanded edition came out in 1955).

Again in 1947, in volume two of the Academy of Sciences publication of *Pravda Russkaia* as edited by V. D. Grekov, Romanov was one of the collaborators of the Leningrad division of the Academy of Sciences' Institute of History which was entrusted with the preparation of commentaries to the text.

In 1952 Romanov was a member of the editorial group for the Academy's publication of *Legal Codes in the XV-XVI Centuries* [*Sudebniki XV-XVI Vekov*]. He wrote the commentary for the Legal Code of 1550 [the *Sudebnik* of 1550].

Appearing in the same year was Romanov's article,

"On the Fully Bondaged Slave and the Village Priest in Ivan the Terrible's Legal Code" ["O Polnom Kholope i Sel'skom Pope v Sudebnike Ivana Groznogo"]. (It appeared in the *Festschrift, To Academician B.D. Grekov on the Occasion of His Seventieth Birthday* [*Akademiku B.D. Grekovu ko Dniu Semidesiatiletiia*)].

Romanov was a talented scholar of broad vision and diverse interests. He studied problems of both ancient and modern history, wrote important works and detailed analyses of individual problems of the social and economic life of Russia's past. His works were based on a thorough study of archival and published sources and of the literature on the subject. S.N. Valk compiled a bibliography of Romanov's works (*Historical Transactions* [*Istoricheskie Zapiski*], vol. 62, 1958).

## XXVIII

### V.I. SEMEVSKII (1848-1916)

Vasilii Ivanovich Semevskii graduated from the first Petersburg gymnasium after which he enrolled in the Medical Surgical Academy for two years. He then transferred to the historico-philological department of the University of Petersburg.

While still a student, Semevskii decided to devote himself to the history of the peasantry. In *Russian Antiquity* [*Russkaia Starina*] in 1876, he published an article titled "Peasant Serfs Under Catherine II" ["Krepostnye Krest'iane pri Ekaterine II"]. This was the start of his work on a broad investigation of this theme. His monumental work was published in 1881 in the *Transactions* of the historico-philological department of the University of Petersburg.

Semevskii presented the book as a master's thesis to the historico-philological department of Moscow University and defended it successfully.

In December of 1882 Semevskii began to lecture on Russian history at the University of Petersburg as a *privat-*

*docent.* His lectures were popular with students but, by orders of the administration, were terminated in 1886.

In 1889 Semevskii presented his book, *The Peasant Question in the XVIII and the First Half of the XIX Century* [*Krest'ianskii Vopros v XVIII-m i Pervoi Polovine XIX-go Veka*], to Moscow University for the doctorate. The department, based on Kliuchevskii's review, allowed Semevskii to defend the dissertation and awarded him the doctor's degree.

In 1891, a Siberian owner of gold mines, I. M. Sibiriakov, who provided financial support for the publication of scholarly works on Siberia, proposed that Semevskii take up the study of the history and the present state of workers in the gold fields. Semevskii went to Siberia and gathered a mass of materials. His study, *Workers in the Siberian Gold Fields* [*Rabochie na Sibirskikh Zolotykh Priiskakh*] came out in 1898.

Besides these learned works, Semevskii wrote popular publicistic pieces in the journals *Russkaia Mysl, Russkaia Starina* and *Vestnik Evropy* [*Russian Thought, Russian Antiquity, European Herald*]. I will here mention his articles on Princess E. R. Dashkova, V. I. Vodovozov (one of the founders of the new Russian pedagogy), and N.I. Kostomarov.

Besides the history of the peasants and the peasant movement, Semevskii was also interested in the history and ideology of social movements. But because of censorship nothing of this could be published before 1905.

In 1905 Semevskii, V.I. Bogucharskii, and P.E. Shcheglov published a book titled *Social Movements in Russia in the First Half of the XIX Century* [*Obshchestvennye Dvizheniia v Rossii v Pervuiu Polovinu XIX Veka*] (Vol. I, Decembrists M.A. Fonvizin, Prince E.P. Obolenskii, and Baron V. I. Shteingal'). Semevskii's *Political and Social Ideas of the Decembrists* [*Politicheskie i Obshchestvennye Idei Dekabristov*] saw the light of day in 1909.

## KORNILOV (1862-1925) and STRUVE (1870-1944)

Kornilov and Struve were persons of a different caliber and different emotional and intellectual temperament. Both occupy a prominent portion in the history of Russian society and Russian liberalism. Both opposed the autocracy and, for a time, belonged to the same political party (the "Cadet" — the People's Freedom Party).

### A.A. KORNILOV

Aleksandr Aleksandrovich Kornilov was born in Warsaw where his father was the director of Warsaw's governor-general's chancellery. His mother was a sincere person of broad mind and rare kindness. Her stamp lay on the whole family of many children (from the memoirs of I.M. Grevs).

Kornilov graduated from Warsaw's Russian gymnasium and then enrolled in the department of law at the University of Petersburg. His father died soon after.

During his student years, Kornilov joined the circle of friends which later received the name "Priutino Brotherhood."

The brotherhood's goal was moral perfection and mutual aid. The majority of the brotherhood's members were under the influence of Tolstoiism and the "religion of humanity" preached by William Fry. But, in contrast to Tolstoi, the brothers recognized the value of education and mental labor. A whole series of outstanding educators came out of the brotherhood.

The principal members of the brotherhood besides Kornilov were D.I. Shakhovskoi (the future social and political figure), V.I. Vernadskii (the future geologist and founder of bio-geo-chemistry), the Ol'denburg brothers, Sergei (the future orientalist) and Fedor (later a teacher), and I.M. Grevs (subsequently medieval historian).

Upon graduating from the University of Petersburg's law school, Kornilov served as Commissar for peasant affairs in the Polish Kingdom. He then received a position as head of peasant and migrant affairs at the Irkutsk governor-general's office.

Service in Warsaw and Irkutsk gave Kornilov an excellent knowledge of peasant affairs and served as a firm foundation for his subsequent learned and social activity. Kornilov took the winter of 1892-1893 off in order, at the request of friends, to take charge of aid to starving peasants in the Morshanskii district of Tambov province. Money for this purpose was collected by his Moscow and Petersburg friends. Many of them came to help him for several months at various intervals.

Kornilov gave a detailed account of his strenuous labor in the book *Seven Months Among Starving Peasants* [*Sem' Mesiatsev Sredi Golodaiushchikh Krest'ian*] (1893).

In the conclusion of the book he writes: "All of us (he and his friends) felt that between them and the population they helped, in their hearts there had developed a certain spiritual tie . . . During these months spent in direct contact with the people, in their very midst, their whole life became immeasurably clearer and more understandable to us (many of whom were city dwellers) than it could have been through the study of books even though the latter were studied over a longer period of time."

The famine of 1892-1893 was, in a sense, a turning point in Russian social life. The government was unable to handle this calamity through bureaucratic means. It was forced to permit social initiative by the *zemstvos* and private organizations.

This was a moment when collaboration between the bureaucracy and the *zemstvos* could be thought of. But these hopes were soon smashed.

On December 17, 1895, at a reception in the Winter Palace for deputies of various classes, Nicholas II called the *zemstvos'* striving for the participation of their representatives in government affairs "senseless dreams."

From this time on, the Priutins and other *zemstvo*-constitutionalists opposed the autocracy directly. The

"Union of Liberation" was formed in Germany in 1903. The Constitutional Democratic Party (the "Cadet" or "People's Freedom Party") was formed at conferences of the *zemstvo*-constitutionalists in Moscow, October 1905, and Petersburg, January, 1906. Kornilov was elected a member and secretary of its cultural committee. The main brunt of organizational problems and relations with the central committee for the Duma faction as well as local party units lay upon him. Members of the party constantly came to him for all kinds of information and for the solution of various misunderstandings.

Despite all that, Kornilov found time for scholarly activity. His book, *The Social Movement Under Alexander II* [*Obshchestvennoe Dvizhenie pri Aleksandre II*] came out in 1909. He published *The Bakunin Family* [*Semeistvo Bakuninykh*] in 1914. It was based on the documents of the Priamukhin archive of the Bakunin family ("The Youthful Years of Mikhail Bakunin" — ["Molodye Gody Mikhaila Bakunina"] ).

In 1909 Kornilov was chosen to be lecturer at the Petersburg Polytechnic Institute. He was to present a course on XIX century Russian history. This course was published in three volumes in 1912. Up to this time, such a course was not in the curriculum of Russian institutions of higher learning.

Kornilov's works as secretary of the Central Committee of the People's Freedom Party became constantly more tense in connection with the conflict between Nicholas II and the State Duma and social organizations (1915-1916). A particularly strained atmosphere resulted after the February Revolution of 1917.

At a conference of the Cadet Party's central committee in July of 1917, Kornilov had a stroke. He was taken to his home half-paralyzed. When he became a bit better, I took him to a sanatorium in Kislovodsk. There, he gradually improved and later, having returned to Petersburg, could again indulge in learned study. Its fruit was his last book, *Mikhail Bakunin's Years of Wandering* [*Gody Stranstvii Mikhaila*

*Bakunina*]. It was published posthumously.
The main themes of Kornilov's historical works were:
1) The Freeing of the Peasants and the Peasant Question.

Pertinent here is his book, *The Peasant Reform* [*Krest'i-anskaia Reforma*] (Petersburg, 1905, in the series "The Great Reforms" ["Velikie Reformy"]); the article "Basic Trends of Government and Social Thought During the Elaboration of the Peasant Reform" ["Osnovnye Techeniia Pravitel'stvennoi i Obshchestvennoi Mysli vo Vremia Razrabotki Krest'ianskoi Reformy"] (in the anthology *Freeing of the Serfs* [*Osvobozhdenie Krest'ian*] 1911); and, *Essays on the History of the Social Movement and Peasant Affair in Russia* [*Ocherki po Istorii Obshchestvennogo Dvizheniia i Krest'ianskogo Dela v Rossii*] (1905).
2) The Land Reform and the *Zemstvo*.
Of significance here is his detailed review of B.B. Veselovskii's book, *History of Zemstvo Over Forty Years* [*Istoriia Zemstva za Sorok Let*] (*Proceedings of the Petersburg Polytechnic Institute*, economic and judicial section, no. 14, 1910.).
3) *The Social Movement Under Alexander II* (Paris, 1905. Second, and expanded, edition. Moscow, 1909).
All of these works also served as basis for his course "The History of Russia in the XIX Century" ["Istoriia Rossii v XIX Veke"].

## P.B. STRUVE (1870-1944)

Petr Berngardovich Struve was the grandson of Wilhelm Struve, professor of mathematics and astronomy at the University of Derpt from 1819. He had emigrated from Germany. Wilhelm's eldest son, Bernhard, who was Petr's father, was born in Derpt (1827).[60]
Bernhard Struve's mother was German. Bernhard graduated from the lycée at Tsarskoe Selo in 1847 and entered the service in one of the Petersburg chancelleries. He was then assigned to the Governor of Eastern Siberia.

He served under his direction for five years. He traveled the length and breadth of Siberia. In 1853 Bernhard married Anna Fedorovna Rosen, a Baltic German.

Upon returning from Siberia, Bernhard was appointed lieutenant governor of Astrakhan and, in 1865, governor of Perm. It was there that his youngest son, Petr, was born on March 5, 1870 (he had seven children in all — all boys). Petr and his parents were not close.

Petr was placed in Petersburg's third classical gymnasium. He graduated in the spring of 1889.

His father had died in February of the same year. After the funeral Struve moved in with his gymnasium friend, Andrei Dmitrievich Kalmykov.

In his memoirs, Kalmykov writes that Struve was the leader in their circle of friends for self-education.[61]

Andrei Kalmykov's mother, Aleksandra Mikhailovna Kalmykova (1850-1920), was an outstanding figure in public education. In collaboration with Kh. D. Alchevskaia, she published a book called *What People Should Read* [*Chto Chitat' Narodu*]. In Petersburg she taught in Sunday and in public schools and was an active member in the commission of literacy of the Free Economic Society.

Upon graduating from the university, Andrei joined the Ministry of Foreign Affairs and soon received an assignment in Persia. Struve stayed at Kalmykova's home.

He married Nina Aleksandrovna Gerd in the spring of 1897. She was the daughter of a famous Petersburg teacher. The newlyweds found a small apartment.

The 1890's in Russia were a period of bitter polemics between the populists and the Marxists.

Struve's sensational book, *Critical Observations on the Question of the Economic Development of Russia* [*Kriticheskie Zametki k Voprosu ob Ekonomicheskom Razvitii Rossii*] appeared in 1894.

In this book Struve analyzes the problem of capitalism on an international scale and insists on the necessity of the development of capitalism in Russia for the growth of its productive force. The book concludes with an appeal: "We recognize our lack of culture and will go to capitalism to be trained."

Struve also viewed the Russian bourgeoisie in its contemporary state to be uncultured. In the manifesto of the first Russian social-democratic congress in Minsk in 1898, Struve wrote that the further east from Europe one went, the bourgeoisie became weaker, more cowardly and baser. Struve sent the text of the manifesto to the bureau of the congress but was not present personally. His authorship was known only to a few of the initiated. Therefore, though the participants of the congress were arrested, Struve did not suffer.

Though Struve was the author of the revolutionary manifesto of the first congress of the Social-Democratic Party, he was, at this time, opposed to revolutionary methods. In his book, *Critical Observations . . .*, he said: "It is not people's conciousness which determines their existence, but, on the contrary, existence which determines their conciousness."

"At a certain level of social development, productive forces enter into conflict with the existing means of production. Only then does the era of social revolution ensue. . . History is an unswerving process."

With such views it is understandable why Struve, like the historian of the Russian factory, M.I. Tugan-Baranovskii, received the nickname of "legal Marxists."

Struve attentively followed the polemic among the German Marxists. He came to sympathize with the moderate trend of German Bernsteinism.

During his student years, Struve was friendly with Lenin. But now Lenin attacked him furiously in a series of articles.

After 1898 Struve departed from socialism and sided with the constitutional democratic movement. He became friends with the *zemstvo*-constitutionalist circles. It was precisely at this time that these groups began to prepare for active opposition to the autocracy. Necessary preliminary steps regarding this began to be discussed in Moscow in the years 1900-1902.

The creation of a free press and the organization of a secret society for the propagation of constitutional ideas were outlined.

On March 4, 1901 there was a rather inspiring demonstration on the square near the Cathedral of Our Lady of Kazan on the Nevskii Prospekt in Petersburg. Struve went to the demonstration. It was dispersed by the mounted police. The majority of the participants, including Struve, were arrested.

Thereupon, Struve was exiled from Petersburg. He was offered a choice of several cities. He chose Tver so as to be in contact with the Petrunkevich group and other *zemstvo*-constitutionalists.

Struve decided to emigrate to Germany. He was entrusted with the editing of the constitutionalists' printed organ, *Liberation* [*Osvobozhdenie*]. The first copy appeared in Stuttgart in June of 1902.

Struve's anthology of articles (for the years 1893-1901) came out in Petersburg in that same year. It was titled *On Various Themes* [*Na Raznye Temy*].

After the publication of the constitutional manifesto of October 17, 1905, and the declaration of amnesty, Struve returned to Petersburg. From 1907 to 1918 he was the editor of the journal *Russkaia Mysl'* (which was published in Moscow).

He also wrote much (on various themes). He published his articles for the years 1905-1910 in his second anthology, *Patriotica — Politics, Culture, Religion, Socialism* [*Patriotika — Politika, Kul'tura, Religiia, Sotsializm*] (Petersburg, 1911).

In January of 1907 Struve was chosen a delegate to the Second State Duma by the Cadet Party. Struve and the Cadet Party entered the Duma with the intention of working seriously on legislation. But with the presence in the Duma of a significant number of leftist delegates (Social-Democrats, Socialist-Revolutionaries, and *"Trudoviki"* ["laborites"]) the harmonious work of the Duma and the government could not take place. On June 3, 1907 the Duma was dissolved.

At the last minute, just before the dissolution of the Duma, four Cadet members made an attempt to dissuade the government from dissolving the Duma. But Stolypin had already made his decision and did not intend to change it. In 1913 Struve was chosen professor in the economics division of the Petersburg Polytechnic Institute. Among his courses was the *Historical Introduction to Political Economy* [*Istoricheskoe Vvedenie v Politicheskuiu Ekonomiiu*] which was published in 1916. During his professorship at the Polytechnic, he wrote one of his most remarkable works, *Price and Economy* [*Khoziaistvo i Tsena*] (2 volumes, 1913-1916).

In 1916 he received an honorary doctor's degree from Cambridge University in England. In the following year he was elected Fellow of the Russian Academy of Sciences.

After the Bolshevik coup and the dispersal of the Constituent Assembly, civil war started in Russia. The volunteer army based in southern Russia began an attack on Moscow. But, after a successful beginning, it was thrown back by the Red Army. Only the Crimea held on.

General P.N. Wrangel' was elected ruler of South Russia and the commander of its armed forces.

In the spring of 1920 Wrangel appointed P.B. Struve to be in charge of foreign affairs (i.e. Minister of Foreign Affairs). He commissioned him to go to Paris in order to conduct negotiations for French recognition of his (Wrangel's) government.

The negotiations were successful and played an enormous role in the fate of very many Russians evacuated from the Crimea.[62]

Struve stayed in Paris until the beginning of 1922. He then moved to Prague where he received a professorial scholarship from the Czechoslovak government and joined the Russian educational collegium.

At this time Prague was a major cultural center of the Russian emigration. Struve found many friends there. Among them were P.I. Novgorodtsev, and Struve's student from the Polytechnic Institute, K.I. Zaitsev.

Among the Czechs, Struve associated with the Russo-phile K.P. Kramarzh and the historian of comparative Slavic law, K. Kadlets. In Prague Struve participated in the Russian Historical Society. In 1923 he read a lecture titled "Foreign Published Works as a Source for Russian History and Russian Studies" ["Inostrannye Pechatnye Proizvedeniia, kak Istochnik Russkoi Istorii i Russkovedeniia"].

His article, "Certain Fundamental Concepts of Economic Science" ["Nekotorye Osnovnye Poniatiia Ekonomicheskoi Nauki"] appeared in the following year in the *Transactions of the Russian Educational Collegium in Prague.*

In 1925 Struve received an offer from A.O. Gukasov, the oil industrialist, to become the editor of a conservative newspaper that he had planned (it was to be a counterweight to the radical-democratic *Latest News* of Miliukov). Gukasov promised Struve complete independence in editorial policy. Struve agreed and moved to Paris. The newspaper was called *Vozrozhdenie* [Rebirth].

Struve edited *Vozrozhdenie* talentedly and enthusiastically. He himself published articles and reviews in the newspaper on current events. He invited several prominent émigré writers − I.A. Bunin, I.S. Shmelev, I.S. Surguchev, and A.V. Amfitiatrov − to contribute to the newspaper.

After a time, however, friction developed between Struve and Gukasov. Gukasov absolutely did not value literature and art and was unhappy with many of Struve's articles on these and other topics. He found them to be too profound and insufficiently militant. Gukasov wished *Vozrozhdenie* to have a purely political and nationalistic character.

In August of 1927 Gukasov removed Struve as editor. Iu. F. Semenov was appointed as the new editor. He was a physics teacher. He was an old friend of Struve, but now their relations were severed.

Struve started his own newspaper, *Rossiia*. (It was a weekly and was later renamed *Rossiia i Slavianstvo* [*Russia and Slavism*] ).

In the fall of 1938 Struve moved to Belgrade where he was promised a lectureship in Russian history. Extreme rightists held sway among Russian émigrés there. They were hostile to Struve as a former Marxist and liberal. Struve was in a difficult position. Nevertheless, he began to lecture in Subotica (where there was a branch of the University of Belgrade).

In 1941 German forces invaded Yugoslavia. Struve was arrested and was initially held in the Gestapo building in Belgrade, then in a prison in Graz. In 1942 Struve and his wife were allowed to move to Paris where their two sons lived. Nina Aleksandrovna died in May of 1942, Petr Berngardovich in February of 1944.

Struve's scholarly-literary heritage is abundant and multiform. His primary scholarly works are *Price and Economy* [*Khoziaistvo i tsena*] (1913-1916) and *The Social and Economic History of Russia* [*Sotsial'naia i Ekonomicheskaia Istoriia Rossii*]. (The latter was published posthumously in Paris in 1952). In the appendix to this last work, several brilliant articles on Solov'ev, Chicherin, Kliuchevskii, Platonov, and Kizevetter were reprinted. These were written by Struve in the 1930's. There is much valuable material in these articles for the comprehension of Struve's own ideas.

We shall now proceed to the characterization of the main tendencies of Struve's thought and scholarly creativity. Insofar as it is possible, I shall try to confine myself to Struve's own words and figures of speech. At the basis of Struve's world view was the feeling and consciousness of the historical process — the history of culture as a whole, of personality and society.

"Society as a sociological concept," writes Struve in the first chapter of his *Social and Economic History of Russia*, "signifies interpersonal relations of all types and forms. Society is not some sort of "being." Society is a system of relationships or a certain environment. The primary and national "beings" in this system of relationships are human personalities, live people — and only they. Society is formed by the interaction or contiguity between these living people — be it physical, spiritual, or emotional. Therefore, it would be more correct to speak of interaction, not of society."

Boris Sergeevich Izhboldin sees the basis of the economic theory created by Struve in this type of thought. Izhboldin calls it "automistic-nominalistic."[63]

"All interpersonal relations," Struve continues, "are the essence of contiguity, are social relations. But in the narrow sense of the word, we shall label social the relationships of power and supremacy. The relationships of submission and dependence stand in correlation to them. . . . The system of the interpersonal relations of supremacy and submission which form according to the above stated cultural substances of human life is what we call the social structure or system."

Another aspect of human society is the economic system.

"Economics is an activity directed at receiving or obtaining the means necessary for the satisfaction of human needs. It is not consumption. Economics is always directed toward obtaining the means and is thus continued."

"In terms of economics, human society can be built or organized in three ways. It can either represent: 1) the aggregate of economies existing side by side; 2) a system of interacting economies; or 3) a unified society-economy."

For his work Struve studies interpersonal social relationships as an aspect of the historical process.

"The historical is differentiated from the non-historical in that the 'new' always arises within the first. We attempt to trace it causally to the former. Within the non-historical, everything repeats itself and nothing comes into being."

Struve provides a periodization of Russian social and economic history in chapter two. He outlines seven periods:

1) the early medieval period (850-1240)
2) the middle medieval period (1240-1500)
3) the later middle ages (1500-1648)

4) the Muscovite period (1648-1700)
5) the Petersburg period (1700-1800)
6) the all-Russian period (1800-1917)
7) the Bolshevik period

"The Bolshevik overthrow and the Bolshevik supremecy," reflects Struve, "is a social and political reaction of the
egalitarian lower classes against the centuries old social and
economic Europeanization of Russia. An almost total economic, social, political, and cultural isolation. of the Russian
expanse and its population advances within the framework
of the communist party dictatorship and in the image of the
socialist "fatherland." In its internal structure Russia is cut
off from European-American culture at a time when the
ruling communist atheist leaders attempt, in all possible
ways, to forcibly import European-American Technology
into the country. They implant it by party and government
fiat. Since ideologically the Soviet system is egalitarian
socialism, and emotionally and historically the Bolshevik
Revolution was an egalitarian reaction of the uncultured
and blinded lower classes against more differentiated forms
of social and political being, the bearers of which were
supreme power and the society's cultural elite, the Russian
social and political crisis unfolds into a universal crisis of
socialism."

## XXIX

### RUSSIAN HISTORICAL SCHOLARSHIP AT
### THE END OF THE XIX AND THE FIRST
### HALF OF THE XX CENTURIES

The beginning of the XX century is a portentous moment in the development of Russian historical thought. This
is a period of its creative fermentation and the re-appraisal of
the bases of the historical world view.

New trends appear in the theory of historical scholarship and in the exploitation of its materials. On the one hand,

there appears the inclination to study the problems of man's intellectual development. On the other — an intensification of the methods of developing the history of economics and material culture in general. A new historico-philosophical factor comes onto the stage — Marxism. Young and middle aged scholars take part in this displacement. From the middle of the XIX century, ties between Russian historians and their Western European colleagues became ever closer. At the beginning of the XX century an international organization of historical study, in which A.S. Lappo-Danilevskii played a prominent role, is formed. The broadening of the horizon of Russian historians was the result of displacements and the revolutionary movement in Russia. On the other hand, there were world wide shocks — the ill-fated Russo-Japanese War of 1904-1905, the German war of 1914-1918, and the civil war which followed.

## HISTORIANS AT THE END OF THE XIX AND THE BEGINNING OF THE XX CENTURIES
### (given in order of their birth dates)

Shmurlo, Bagalei, Shakhmatov, Pavlov-Sil'vanskii, Veselovskii, Priselkov, Grekov, A.V. Florovskii, Vernadsky, Pushkarev, Karpovich; MARXIST HISTORIANS: Plekhanov, Pokrovskii

### E.F. SHMURLO (1853-1934)

The eldest of the historians discussed in this group was Evgenii Frantsovich Shmurlo. He was the son of an exiled Pole or Polonized Lithuanian and was born in the Altai.

Shmurlo was graduated from the historico-philological department of the University of Petersburg. He was Bestuzhev-Riumin's student. After the latter's death (1897),

Shmurlo dedicated a special book to him, *The Life and Work of K.N. Bestuzhev-Riumin* [*Ocherk Zhizni i Deiatel'nosti K.N. Bestuzheva-Riumina*] (1899). Upon passing the master's examinations, Shmurlo received the rank of *privat-docent* and commenced to lecture at the University of Petersburg. In 1889 he defended his master's thesis on the theme, "Regarding the Memorandum of Sil'vestr Medvedev." ["O Zapiskakh Sil'vestra Medvedeva"].

Sil'vestr Medvedev was a learned monk and a student of Simeon Polotskii. He participated actively in the debates between the Latinizing pupils of the Kiev Theological Academy and Orthodox Muscovites and Greeks living in Moscow (second half of the 1680's during the reign of Sofiia). One of the points of debate was the exact moment of transubstantiation at the end of the liturgy. Passions flowed. Medvedev (accused of the "Latin heresy") was executed.

After the defense of the thesis, Shmurlo received the chair of Russian history at the University of Derpt (Iur'ev).

At the XI archeological congress in Kiev in 1899, Shmurlo presented a paper on the necessity of establishing in Rome a permanent historical commission to search for materials on Russian history in Italian archives and libraries. Shmurlo's idea was a fruitful one. In 1903, in the historico-philologic division of the Academy of Sciences, the position in Rome of a "learned correspondent" was established. Naturally, Shmurlo was assigned to this duty. His reports of his activity there were published in the book, *Russia and Italy: A Collection of Historical Materials and Studies on Russia's Dealings with Italy* [*Rossiia i Italiia, Sbornik Istoricheskikh Materialov i Issledovanii, Kasaiushchikhsia Snoshenii Rossii s Italiei*].

Shmurlo then resigned from the professional staff of the University of Derpt. Over a period of several years, from 1887 to 1900, Shmurlo made trips of an ethnographical-geographical nature beyond the Urals in order to study the spread of Russian colonization to the East. He went to the Turgai steppe, the Semipalatinsk and the Ak-

molinsk districts, and to the southern Altai. He published vivid descriptions of his trips in the *Transactions* of the Western Siberia Division of the Russian Geographical Society.
Shmurlo, generally speaking, responded keenly to life around him, in particular to the Russian famine of the 1890's. His dispatches were published in the *St. Petersburg Gazette*, then were issued separately as a book titled *Years of Famine* [*Golodnyi God*].
A short while after the Bolshevik overthrow the Soviet government sent a new "learned correspondent" to Rome.
Shmurlo moved to Prague. He was elected member of the Russian Educational Collegium and continued his scholarly and social work. He spent the last fifteen years of his life in Prague.
Shmurlo was one of the initiators of the founding of the Russian Historical Society in Prague and was its first chairman. The Society organized lectures which were open to all those who were interested and published its *Transactions*. Two volumes were issued (1927-1929) but funds for more ran out. The contents of the *Transactions* were at a high scholarly level.
In the first volume of these *Transactions*, Shmurlo wrote a thoughtful article titled "When and Where was St. Vladimir Baptized?" ["Kogda i Gde Krestilsia Vladimir Sviatoi?"] This étude is one of the best studies on the circumstances of Vladimir's christening.
Shmurlo played a conspicuous role in the intellectual life of Prague's Russian colony. He was one of the popular orators at the yearly celebration of Russian culture days which were held on June 8 (Pushkin's birthday according to the new style calendar).
Shmurlo's scholarly-literary production is very voluminous. His literary comments, those written in Russia and in Prague, are vivid and of a keen style.
His scholarly works are based on precise data drawn from the sources and from previous historical literature. Thematically they can be divided into several groups.

Shmurlo was principally interested in intellectual movements and religious questions — the correlation of Catholicism, Orthodoxy, and Lutheranism. Pertinent here are his works, *The Roman Curia in the Orthodox East 1609-1654* [*Rimskaia Kuriia na Pravoslavnom Vostoke v 1609-1654 Godakh*] (Prague, 1918); *Iurii Krizhanich* (in Italian, Rome, 1926); and his address in September, 1928, to the IV congress of Russian Academic Organizations in Belgrade (it was published in the *Transactions* of this Congress, part I, pp. 65-111). Shmurlo titled this work "Russian Relations with the Papal Throne During the Reign of Peter the Great" ["Snosheniia Rossii s Papskim Prestolom v Tsarstvovanie Petra Velikogo"] (1697-1707).

Shmurlo studied Russia's relations with the papacy within the framework of the Great Northern War (between Russia and Sweden). He treated the gradual replacement of the old methods of the Office of Foreign Affairs by the more flexible methods of the time which were more adaptable to the contemporary conditions and circumstances of international life. The "grand embassy" to Europe (1697-1700) was not officially headed by Peter (he went "incognito" under the name of Petr Alekseevich Mikhailov, a sergeant in the Preobrazhenskii Regiment). The Tsar's arrival made a great impression on European diplomats. Specifically, favorable reports on Peter which reached the Roman curia gave it the most optimistic expectations for the generation of Catholic propaganda into Russia. His main goal at this time was the creation of an international coalition against Turkey. The Roman curia would have to play a key role in such a coalition.

Further along in his article, Shmurlo traces the tortuous path of the negotiations which continued even after the conclusion of peace with Turkey.

In the conclusion of his article, Shmurlo states: "If, in moments of greatest difficulty, the Russian Tsar was able to refrain from formal obligations to the Roman curia, then now, having become the master of the situation in Eastern Europe, he would be all the more free and independent in regard to relations with the papacy, and all the less would he consider its demands and desires."

Generally, Shmurlo wrote much about Peter the Great. His first work on this subject was *Peter the Great in Russian Literature. An Experiment in the Historico-Bibliographic Survey* [*Petr Velikii v Russkoi Literatury. Opyt Istorika-Bibliograficheskogo Obzora*] (1889). During his many trips to Europe in the 1890's, Shmurlo gathered many valuable materials from its archives. He published part of them in *Collection of Documents Relating to the Reign of Peter the Great* [*Sbornik Dokumentov, Otnosiashchikhsia k Tsarstvovaniiu Petra Velikogo*] vol. I, 1693-1700, (1903).

In Prague he published the book, *Peter the Great and His Heritage* [*Petr Velekii i ego Nasledie*] (1925). His biography of Peter came out (in German) in 1931 in the series *Menschen die Geschichte Machten.*

In connection with his interest in Peter, Shmurlo treated a broader problem — *The East and West in Russian History* [*Vostok i Zapad v Russkoi Istorii*] (1926); and, *Russia in Asia and Europe* [*Rossiia v Azii i Evrope*] (in Czech, Prague, 1926).

Shmurlo was the author of two valuable surveys of Russian history: *History of Russia 862-1917* [*Istoriia Rossii: 862-1917*] (München, 1922), and *A Course in Russian History* [*Kurs Russkoi Istorii*] (in a hectographic edition of only 100 copies, Prague, 1931-1934). The latter was in two volumes, each in two issues. This course could appear thanks to the assistance of the Slavic Institute in Prague which covered part of the publishing expenses.

His goal in the München book was to provide Russian émigré youths with a reliable textbook of Russian history.

"But a textbook," writes Shmurlo in the preface, "will never replace the living words of the instructor . . . it is necessary to bring the student to reflection, to aid him in making an appropriate conclusion which still escapes him . . . To provide such an interpretation in the field of Russian history is the goal of the present book . . . The book is meant least of all for reading, but more for reflection and analysis."

Every section of the book ends with a special rubric — "Monuments of Russian Culture." Noted here, in addition to literary works, are items of material antiquity: churches, icons, frescoes, artistic needlework, and other art objects. The Prague *Course in Russian History* is a different book. It is geared to a reader better prepared.

During the process of writing the *Course*, Shmurlo constantly reviewed, revised, and supplemented it. He took personal charge of the publication to the last minutes of his life. His closest assistant in the publication of the *Course* was V.V. Sakhanev. The Slavic Institute placed the responsibility for the subsequent realization of the edition on him.

Let us glance at volume two of the *Course*. In the initial issue there is first a chronological account of Russian history, intellectual and social trends in Muscovy (1462-1613), then a survey of history and culture in Russia, Poland, and Lithuania (1613-1654).

The second issue is an appendix, "Controversial and Unresolved Problems of Russian History" ["Spornye i Nevyiasnennye Voprosy Russkoi Istorii"]. Many of Shmurlo's commentaries are thorough studies in themselves. Such, for example, are "the origin of the Stoglov," "the *oprichnina*, its goals and achievements," "how did the notion of Moscow as the Third Rome originate?," "how did Tsarevich Dmitrii die?," "when was the Assembly of the Land summoned in the reign of Ivan the Terrible?," "how did the election of M.F. Romanov to the throne take place?"

During his life, Shmurlo built up an extremely valuable archive and large library. After the end of World War II, both were moved to Moscow.

## D.I. BAGALEI (1857-1932)

Dmitrii Ivanovich Bagalei received his higher education at the Universities of Kiev and Khar'kov.

Upon passing his master's examinations, he became a

*privat-docent* at the University of Khar'kov. In 1887 he defended his thesis on the topic, "Essays on the History of the Colonization of the Orthodox Steppe Districts of the Muscovite State" ["Ocherki po Istorii Kolonizatsii Stepnoi Okrainy Moskovskogo Gosudarstva"] and received a professorship.

Bagalei lived in Khar'kov until 1918. He participated actively in the city's intellectual and public life. He responded as well to all overall Russian interests and events. The question regarding the establishment of the Ukrainian Academy of Sciences in Kiev arose in 1918. V.I. Vernadskii and N. P. Vasilenko were the initiators of this plan. Both knew Bagalei personally and knew of his scholarly works.

Therefore, when in their preliminary meetings on the organization and make up of the Ukrainian Academy conversation turned as to whom to invite as members of the Academy, the decision was made to summon Bagalei to Kiev. Bagalei came immediately. The principles of the organization and the charter of the Ukrainian Academy were worked out in a special commission in October, 1918.[64] Then, new members of the Academy were proposed.

The first session of the Academy took place on October 27, 1918. In a secret ballot, V.I. Vernadskii (a member of the Russian Academy of Sciences) was unanimously elected president of the Academy, and Bagalei vice-president.

We turn to Bagalei's works. Until 1918, he published his works in Russian; after that, in Ukrainian.

His first major work was the above-cited master's thesis (1887). A supplement to this is his publication of documents, *Materials for the History of the Colonization and the Life of the Khar'kov and Partly the Voronezh Provinces* [*Materialy dlia Istorii Kolonizatsii i Byta Khar'kovskoi i Otchasti Voronezhskoi Gubernii*] (1886-1890).

His *Essays* provide a broad picture not only of Russia's impulsive colonization southward, but also the sociology of this elemental Russian flow. He described its significance for the settlers themselves and for Russia's general economic development and for historical geography and demography.

The *Essays* have not lost their value to this day.

Bagalei then wrote *A History of the University of Khar'kov* [*Opyt Istorii Khar'kovskogo Universiteta*] (Khar'-kov, 1893-1894). There then followed an article on the XVIII century Ukrainian philosopher, Grigorii Skovorada ("Kievskaia Starine" ["Kievan Antiquity"], 1895, I-II). Volume I of *Russian History* [*Russkaia Istoriia*], a major work by Bagalei, was published in Moscow in 1914. This work is interestingly conceived and constructed. At its beginning, Bagalei, partly under M.I. Rostovtsev's influence, devotes considerable time to archeology. Bagalei also relied on Rostovtsev on the question of the role of Hellenism and Iranianism in the early history — rather the pre-history — of Kievan Rus'.

Bagalei's chief works during the Kievan phase of his life are *Ukrainian Historiography* [*Naris Ukrainskoi Istoriografii*], volume I (in two editions, Kiev, 1923-1926). Works which followed were: *Decembrists in the Ukraine* [*Dekabristy na Ukraine*] (Khar'kov, 1926), and *A Socio-Economic History of the Ukraine* [*Naris Istorii Ukrainy na Sotsial'no-Ekonomicheskom Grunti*] (Khar'kov, 1928).

## A.A. SHAKHMATOV (1864-1920)

Aleksei Aleksandrovich Shakhmatov was one of the outstanding philologists of his time.

Simultaneously, his whole creative thought was imbued with a living sense of the history of the development of the Russian language and Russian literary depiction.

Shakhmatov was born in Narva.[65] He spent his early childhood in Odessa where his father served in the judicial administration. His mother passed away in Odessa in 1870. His father died in January, 1871. His father's brother took Aleksei with his two sisters for upbringing. Aunt and uncle replaced his parents. The family lived in a village near Saratov until 1876.

It was here that learning started. A.F. Petrunkevich's *Whence the Russian Land* [*Otkuda Poshla Russkaia Zemlia*], then Karamzin's *History of the Russian State* elicited an interest in history in Aleksei. In addition, he learned some Sanskrit words from A.S. Khomiakov's book on the relationship of Slavic languages to Sanskrit. In 1879 Shakhmatov entered grade four of the gymnasium. At this time he was already greatly carried away by philology. He collected Sanskrit, old German, Gothic, Persian, Arabic, and Celtic words for a comparative study of their roots. He made the acquaintance of philology professors Vsevolod Müller, F.E. Korsh, and F.F. Fortunatov. In 1881 Fortunatov gave Shakhmatov permission to attend his linguistics seminar.

Shakhmatov graduated from the gymnasium in the spring of 1883 and enrolled in the historico-philological department of Moscow University.

In the following year, the historico-philological department provided for assignment during the summer vacation for a trip to the Olonetskaia province to study local dialects and folklore.

Shakhmatov prepared his *Research on the Language of Novgorodian Documents of the XIII and XIV Centuries* [*Issledovanie o Iazyke Novgorodskikh Gramot XIII i XIV Veka*] for publication in December of 1884.

At the proposal of Academician I. B. Iachich, with whom Shakhmatov became acquainted in 1881, this work was published in an anthology of the Academy of Sciences' division of Russian language and literature.

Shakhmatov was graduated from the university with the candidate's degree in 1887.

Upon passing the master's examinations in 1890, he received the rank of *privat-docent* and was to commence lecturing. However, "in connection with certain heartfelt matters" (as he writes in his autobiography) he decided to leave Moscow. He accepted a part as *"zemskii nachal'nik"* [superintendent of the peasantry] in the Saratov province (the post was open in the summer of 1891).

The year 1891 was a frightful one for Russia — first famine, then cholera which lasted until the new harvest of

1892. Shakhmatov took an active part in helping the population.

Shakhmatov wrote his master's thesis from 1892-1893. It was titled "Studies in Russian Phonetics" ["Issledovaniia v Oblasti Russkoi Fonetiki"]. He defended it on March 12, 1894. The department gave him the doctor's degree in Russian language and literature (by-passing the master's).

In the following year Shakhmatov was elected adjunct of the Academy of Sciences and moved to Petersburg. Three years later he was chosen extraordinary academician, and made ordinary academician in 1898.

As to his private life, he married Nataliia Aleksandrovna Gradovskaia (daughter of Professor Gradovskii) in 1896.

Shakhmatov participated actively in the life of the Academy of Sciences. He worked in many of the Academy's commissions. Among them were the commission for the removal of restrictions on publishing books and journals in the Malorussian (Ukrainian) language (1911), and in the commission on the question of simplifying Russian orthography (1917).

In 1910, Shakhmatov was chosen to be supernumerary ordinary professor at the University of Petersburg. Despite all of this, he steadily continued his own learned work. He wrote large works and detailed studies on specialized problems.

Shakhmatov's scholarly heritage is rich and varied. Here I can cite only his most important works briefly.

They can be separated into two headings — linguistic works (historical phonetics) and studies on the composition of ancient Russian chronicles and the history of the writing of these annals.

His interest in historical ethnography is linked to this. He was the first to teach a course on the historical ethnography of eastern Europe and the history of Russian geography (settlement and tribal movement of Russian Slavs, colonization, dialectology).

Shakhmatov summarized his research in a small, but very profound work, *The Ancient Fate of the Russian*

*Tribe* [*Drevneishie Sud'by Russkogo Plemeni*] (1919). "In the general perspective of his scholarly work, Shakhmatov can be called a historian of the Russian nationality. An outstanding linguist, he placed the history of the Russian language at the center of his linguistic studies" (Presniakov). In this respect, Shakhmatov's fundamental work is his thesis, "Studies in Russian Phonetics." In addition, he wrote several other outstanding linguistic studies.

The valuable article on the "Russian Language" ["Russkii Iazyk"] in the Brockhaus-Effron encyclopedic dictionary (volume XXVIII, pp. 564-581, 1899) belongs to him.

Shakhmatov's basic work in the study of chronicles is *Findings Regarding the Ancient Russian Chronicle Compilations* [*Razyskaniia o Drevneishikh Russkikh Letopisnykh Svodakh*] (1908).

"Prior to Shakhmatov," wrote Presniakov, "our compilations of chronicles were viewed almost exclusively as historical sources, as collections of heterogeneous historical materials . . . In Shakhmatov's works, the chronicle compilations were revivified as a whole, essential division of ancient Russian written language, as monuments of ancient literary creativity and the steadfast labor of the social concepts of the ruling circles on the the basic trends of contemporary political reality."

Presniakov continues: "Shakhmatov truly had a calling for scholarship. He was precisely a 'servant' in the sense that ecclesiastics are 'servants of the altar' . . . Recognizing more deeply than anyone the many sided complexity of scholarly tasks and the inexhaustibility of study, Shakhmatov measured his achievements according to the distant ideal of a complete solution to the more complicated problems of cultural history. He was frequently very brave in his constructions but judged them more strictly than anyone else. He constantly checked, corrected, and reconstructed them like an indefatigable seeker."

## N. P. PAVLOV-SIL'VANSKII (1869-1908)

Nikolai Pavlovich Pavlov-Sil'vanskii was graduated from the historico-philological department of the University of Petersburg. He was a member of Platonov's seminar. Upon graduating from the university, he entered the service of the Ministry of Foreign Affairs. He died from cholera.

His scholarly work took two directions. Initially he worked primarily on the Petrine era. Later, he became absorbed in the field of the political and social history of ancient Rus'. He devoted his attention to the question of feudalism in Russia in a comparative historical light.

His fundamental work, *Reform Projects in the Memoranda of the Contemporaries of Peter the Great*, dates to this early period of Pavlov-Sil'vanskii's activity. In this work he showed that during the second half of his reign (after the victory at Poltava in 1709), Peter proceeded toward the realization of his plan for reform in Russia whereas previously his full attention was taken up by the ongoing developments of the Northern War and prevention of catastrophe. This disproved the views of Miliukov. In his book, *The State Economy in Russia and Peter the Great's Reform in the First Quarter of the XVIII Century* (1892), Miliukov came to the conclusion that the reform, during the whole period of Peter's reign, was erratic and that the desires of his advisers were similarly chaotic and inconsistent. The fact was that the material of the proposals of Peter's advisers got into two different archival collections, only one of which Miliukov knew about. The second was discovered by Pavlov-Sil'vanskii. In his biography of Peter in the *Encyclopedic Dictionary of Brockhaus-Effron* (half volume 46 (1898), pp. 487-495), Miliukov recognized the significance of Pavlol-Sil'vanskii's studies.

Let us turn to the second period of Pavlov-Sil'vanskii's scholarly development — his works on feudalism in Russia.[66]

His main works in this field are two: *Feudalism in*

*Ancient Rus'* [*Feodalizm v Drevnei Rusi*] (1907), and *Feudalism in Appanage Rus'*, [*Feodalizm v Udel'noi Rusi*] (1910). In Pavlov-Sil'vanskii's view, feudalism in Russia derived from the blending of State and private principles. Pledging, immunity, patronage, and benefices existed in ancient Rus'. In appanage Rus' we meet the same institutions, attitudes, and relationships as those in the West. Sometimes they are, however, in less definite forms. In the Russian documents of the time, there are phrases which appear as if they are literal translations from corresponding Latin texts.[67]

Pavlov-Sil'vanskii's premature death cut off the further development of his studies.

## S. B. VESELOVSKII (1876-1952)

Stepan Borisovich Veselovskii was born in Moscow to the family of an agronomist.[68]

At first he studied in Moscow, then at the Tambov gymnasium. He was graduated from it in 1896, then enrolled in Moscow University's school of law. In 1903, upon graduating from the university, Veselovskii began systematic work in the Moscow archives. Principally he studied the history of the national economy and the finances of the State of Muscovy in the XVI-XVII centuries.

In May of 1917 Veselovskii was elected extraordinary professor at Moscow University to the chair of the history of law; in the following year he was chosen ordinary professor. In 1929 he was elected associate member of the Academy of Sciences and academician in 1946. Veselovskii taught at Moscow University until the liquidation of the social science department in 1925.

From 1928-1930 he directed the doctoral candidates in the scientific-research Institute of the Peoples of the Soviet East. From 1938 to 1941 he was a professor at the Moscow State historico-archival institute.

I turn now to a survey of Veselovskii's scholarly works.

After ten years of preparatory work, his monumental work, *Compilation of Census Books. A Study in the History of Cadastres and Sokha Taxation in the State of Muscovy* [*Soshnoe Pis'mo. Issledovanie po Istorii Kadastrov i Pososhnogo Oblozheniia Moskovskogo Gosudarstva*] appeared in two volumes in 1913-1915.

This work was based on an enormous amount of, and profoundly studied, material which was introduced into scholarship for the first time.

The Academy of Sciences awarded Veselovskii the Uvarov prize for this work and Moscow University granted him the doctorate in the history of Russian law.

In addition, between the years 1911 and 1917, Veselovskii published a series of studies on the history of the central Muscovite institutions in the XVII century.

During those years he wrote several works in the field of ecclesiastic, monastic, and lay land ownership. Among these were: *Village and Settlement in North-Eastern Rus' in the XIV-XVI Centuries* [*Selo i Derevnia v Severo-Vostochnoi Rusi XIV-XVI Vekov*]; *Feudal Landownership in Muscovite Rus'* [*Feodal'noe Zemlevladenie v Moskovskoi Rusi*]; *Monastic Landownership in Muscovite Rus'* [*Monastyrskoe Zemlevladenie v Moskovskoi Rusi*]; and *On the Question of the Origin of Patrimonial Rule* [*K Voprosu o Proiskhozhdenii Votchinnogo Rezhima*].

After 1940, Veselovskii turned his attention to the study of Ivan the Terrible's *oprichnina*. He wrote a series of articles on topics of the general notion of the *oprichnina* and its separate institutions. He collected them so as to publish a special anthology. This anthology was ready in 1945 but could not be published at that time.

This was still the period of Stalin's "cult of personality" and the glorification of Tsar Ivan and the *oprichnina*.[69] Veselovskii's work *Studies on the History of the Oprichnina* [*Issledovaniia po Istorii Oprichniny*] appeared only in 1963. Veselovskii rejected the approach of understanding the *oprichnina* by preceding historians who saw in the *oprichnina* a policy of expediency by Ivan the Terrible, the nobility, and the townsmen — to crush the boyars and elevate the middle classes.

According to this view, Ivan the Terrible was charitable to the lower classes (peasants and farm laborers). The last to express this opinion was Platonov. His rejoinder is chiefly to him.

Veselovskii established that the same type of noble princely and boyar families predominated in Tsar Ivan's princely court as in the *zemshchina* and that the outbreaks of terror were directed equally by the Tsar against both. There was no "elevation" of the middle classes and townsmen. The more complete lists of Ivan the Terrible's *sinodik* cite 3,300 people who were executed; 1,240 people are listed by name in the *sinodik*. Of them, 400 belong to the servitor class of privileged landowners. The majority of the 2,060 people who are nameless and just listed numerically belonged to the lower classes of the population. All of these figures refer to people executed by Ivan's orders. The number of those killed during the *oprichniks'* sacks of Novgorod and other cities was much greater.

Veselovskii's work in the publication of valuable documentary materials is of great importance. I will here note his *Acts of Suburban Moscow's Militias and the Zemskii Sobor of the Years 1611-1613* [*Akty Podmoskovnykh Opolchenii i Zemskogo Sobora 1611-1613 Godov*] (1911); *Census Acts: Materials for the History of the Cadastre and Direct Taxation in the State of Muscovy* [*Akty Pistsovogo Dela, Materialy Dlia Istorii Kadastra i Priamogo Oblozheniia v Moskovskom Gosudarstve*] (2 vol., 1913-1917); *Documents on Muscovy's Socio-Economic History in the XIV-XVII Centuries* [*Pamiatniki Sotsial'no-Ekonomicheskoi Istorii Moskovskogo Gosudarstva XIV-XVII Vekov*] (1929); *Acts of the Socio-Economic History of the North-Eastern Rus' from the End of the XIV to the Beginning of the XVI Century* [*Akty Sotsial'no-Ekonomicheskoi Istorii Severo-Vostochnoi Rusi Kontsa XIV-go Nachala XVI v.*] (1952).

## M. D. PRISELKOV (1881-1941)

Mikhail Dmitrievich Priselkov was Shakhmatov's student and successfully continued the work of his teacher on the study of Russian chronicles.

Priselkov was born in Petersburg. His father (who died in 1909) was a man of means. Mikhail graduated from the historico-philological department of the University of Petersburg.

Upon passing his master's examinations, Priselkov received the rank of *privat-docent* and began to lecture at the university.

He wrote his master's thesis on the theme, "Essays on the Ecclesiastical-Political History of Kievan Rus'" ["Ocherki po Tserkovno-Politicheskoi Istorii Kievskoi Rusi"] (1913). His principal opponent at the defense was his teacher, Shakhmatov. Their dialogue was that of a lively scholarly discussion.

His first published work was an article, "The Writing of Chronicles in the XIV Century" ["Letopisanie XIV Veka"] (in an anthology on Russian history dedicated to Platonov, 1911). His first major work was his master's thesis. This is an inspiring and fascinating book.

Its principal idea is the struggle of the young Russian Church for independence from Byzantium, the more so that Byzantine emperors felt that when "barbarian" peoples converted to Christianity, this not only led to the recognition of the supremecy of the "ecumenical" (Byzantine) Church over them but that of the Byzantine empire as well.

The sole exception to this custom was the temporary recognition of Bulgarian autocephaly (of the archbishopric then in Ochrid).

In counterbalance to Byzantine claims, the Kievan princes strove to get an autocephalous metropolitan from Byzantium. The history of this struggle constitutes the canvas of this book.

Priselkov's principal sources were Russian chronicles (Shakhmatov's and his own interpretations), the Serbian historian B. Prokich, and Iakh'ia, the Arab chronicler (born at the end of the X century, died 1066).

Proceeding from there, Priselkov weaves an elegant lacework of his suppositions and hypotheses. The reader involuntarily falls under the spell of Priselkov's conjectures. But if one is to think more deeply, some doubts arise.

The point is that Priselkov provides neither a complete picture of political and ecclesiastical events nor diverse motives in international affairs. He reduces everything exclusively to the struggle of the Russian princes and ecclesiasts with the Byzantine demands. Not infrequently, a simplification of reality results.

But, at the end of his thesis, Priselkov leads the reader to his main conjecture — the identity of the famous Metropolitan Illarion (author of "Of Law and Grace" ["Slovo o Zakonakh i Blagodati"]) with the founder of the Monastery of the Caves in Kiev, Nikon the Great. This, of course, is also a hypothesis and is not formally proven. But it is convincing internally and psychologically. This is the end of Priselkov's book.

Priselkov's article, "The Lay of Prince Igor as a Historical Source" ["Slovo o Polku Igoreve kak Istoricheskii Istochnik"] (in the *Marxist Historian* [*Istorik-Marksist*], no. 6) appeared in 1938.

Priselkov's very thorough study of the Laurentian chronicle came out in the following year. It was called "The Laurentian Chronicle: History of the Text" ["Lavren't-evskaia Letopis', Istorii Teksta"] (*Transactions of the University of Leningrad*, issue 2). In this work Priselkov parted with many aspects of Shakhmatov's conclusions.

Priselkov also studied the writing of chronicles in the Western Ukraine and White Russia (*Transactions of the University of Leningrad*, no. 7, historical science series, issue 7, 1941).

The apogee of Priselkov's amazing penetration into the letter and spirit of Russian writing of chronicles is his reconstruction of the Trinity Chronicle.

The Trinity Chronicle burned up in the Moscow conflagration of 1812. But Karamzin had used it prior to this and made many extracts in his notes to the *History of the Russian State*. In addition, several of the XV century chronicles retained excerpts from the Trinity Chronicle. Priselkov was able to complete his painstaking work. It was published posthumously as a separate volume.

## B. D. GREKOV (1882-1953)

Boris Dmitrievich Grekov was born in Mirgorod in the Poltava province.[70] He was graduated from the gymnasium in 1901 and enrolled in the historico-philological department of the University of Warsaw. He transferred to Moscow University in 1905. D. M. Petrushevskii was his principle teacher. In 1914 Grekov defended his master's thesis, "The House of St. Sofiia in Novgorod. An Experiment in the Study of the Organization and the Internal Relations of a Large Patrimony" ["Novgorodskii Dom sv. Sofii. Opyt Izucheniia Organizatsii i Vnutrennikh Otnoshenii Krupnoi Votchiny"], part I.

During the 1917-1918 academic year, Grekov was professor at the University of Perm. He taught a course in ancient Russian history and held a seminar.

From Perm he made his way south to Simferopol and was invited to take the chair of ancient Russian history in the just opened University of Taura.

After the Red Army's takeover of the Crimea (autumn, 1920), Grekov returned to the north. He taught at the University of Leningrad. From 1937 to the end of his life he headed the Institute of History at the Academy of Sciences.

He was chosen associate member of the Academy of Sciences in 1934 and fellow in 1935.

At the same time he was active in public life. He was successfully elected to Leningrad's municipal council, as deputy of the Supreme Soviet of the U.S.S.R.

Grekov was an outstanding and prolific historian-researcher and publisher of documents.

He was the editor of the monumental edition of the *Russian Law [Pravda Russkaia]*. It was published by the Academy of Sciences: volume I (1940), the texts; volume III (1963), facsimile reproduction of the texts. The last volume came out after Grekov's death.

The second fundamental work edited by Grekov was *Legal Codes of the XVI-XVII Centuries [Sudebniki XVI-XVII Vekov]* which was similarly published by the Academy of Sciences.

The first *sudebnik* [legal code] to be compiled was that of 1497 (elaborated under Ivan III). Prior to its appearance, the norms of the *Russkaia Pravda* and local decrees [promulgated by local administrators] held sway in Rus'. The government of Ivan III recognized the necessity of codifying former laws. The *sudebnik* responds to this need.

The Legal Code of 1550 was compiled under Ivan IV (after he took the title of Tsar in 1547). Hence it is called the *Royal Sudebnik [Sudebnik Tsarskii]*. It is more significant in content than the preceding one. It was affirmed by the assembly of church and land [the so-called *Stoglav*].[71] The Academy of Sciences published them in 1952.

Grekov touched on feudalism and feudal relations in ancient Rus' in a series of his works, particularly in connection with the history of the Russian peasantry and the feudal patrimony. Grekov approached the problem of feudalism from the socio-economic, not the juridical point of view. In his opinion, the formation of feudal relations in ancient Rus' corresponds to the process of enserfment.

Muscovy in the XVII century and Imperial Russia prior to the emancipation of the serfs are essentially phases in the development of the feudal system.

Grekov's fundamental work in the history of the Russian peasantry is *Peasants in Rus' from Ancient Times to the Middle of the XVII Century [Krest'iane na Rusi s Drevneishikh Vremen do Serediny XVII Veka]* (1946; second expanded edition, 1954).

Grekov's works on the history of southern and western Slavs constitute a separate group. Pertinent here are the

Croatian Vinodol Statute (1288), the Politskii Statute (1662), and the Polish law, *Kniga Pravda*, of the XIII century (*Selected Works*, volume I).

Grekov wrote several valuable works on the history of Kievan Rus'. I will note the two following: "Kievan Rus'" [*Kievskaia Rus'*] (4th ed., 1944), and *The Culture of Kievan Rus'* [*Kul'tura Kievskoi Rusi*] (1944).

His work (together with the orientalist A.I. Iakubovskii) *The Golden Horde and Its Collapse* [*Zolotaia Orda i ee Padenie*] (1950) treats the history of Russo-Tatar relations. Grekov was also interested in Russian historiography. Of importance here are his essays: "Lenin and Historical Science" ["Lenin i Istoricheskaia Nauka"]; "Lomonosov-Historian" ["Lomonosov-Istorik"]; and "Pushkin's Historical Views" ["Istoricheskie Vozzreniia Pushkina"] (all three were published in Grekov's *Selected Works*, volume III).

"Pushkin," wrote Grekov, "lived within broadly outlined time limits; he conceived of the distant past, the present, and the future as something that was unified, unbroken, and interconnected."

"Pushkin did not imagine an enlightened person who did not know history. In one of his notes he equates the knowledge of history with enlightenment. In another, he ridicules those who are not interested in history."

Pushkin studied the French historian Guizot very attentively and made excerpts for himself. One such characteristic excerpt is: "Society, its composition, its form of life, the relations among various classes and persons — in a word, the civic life of people — is undoubtedly the first question which draws the attention of the historian who writes to know how nations lived and the journalist who writes to know how they were governed."

Pushkin's views were reflected in his *History of the Pugachev Rebellion* as well as several of his literary works like *Boris Godunov* and "The Captain's Daughter."

"Lomonosov was not a professional historian in the narrow sense of the word," writes Grekov. He did not dedicate his life to this field of knowledge and could not do so because life made too strenuous demands on him for him to concentrate on just one thing."

"His main motivating reason," continues Grekov, "was an energetic love of his native country. Lomonosov strove to know Russia in order to exalt it, to defend it from all sorts of attacks on it whether real or even imagined." Lomonosov's reports on the progress of his preparatory work for the writing of Russian history display how serious was his attitude toward his task.

In his notes for 1751 it states: "Read books for collecting materials for writing a history of Russia: Nestor, Iaroslav's laws, the first volume of Tatishchev" (etc. . .).

In notes for 1752 there is: "For obtaining materials on Russian history, I read Krantz, Praetorius, Muratori, Jordanes, Procopius" (etc.).

In a report for 1753 he wrote: "1) I organized the notes from previously mentioned authors into chronological columns; 2) I read the Academy's Russian chronicles without notes in order to have a broad understanding of Russian deeds." In 1756, "the Russian history was ready. The Academy printed 2,000 copies of it. It appeared after Lomonosov's death."

## A. V. FLOROVSKII (1884-1968)

Antonii Vasil'evich Florovskii was graduated from the historico-philological department of the University of Odessa.[72] While still a student, he wrote his first learned work — on the compositions of Catherine II's legislative commission. This essay served as the foundation of his master's thesis, "The Composition of the Legislative Commission 1767-74" ["Sostav Zakonodatel'noi Kommissii 1767-74"] (1915). He was made professor after its defense.

At the end of the Civil War in 1920 Florovskii moved to Bulgaria and a year later to Prague. In Prague he was elected to the Russian Educational Collegium and made a professor at the Russian juridical faculty.

Florovskii was one of the founders of, and friend of the chairman of, the Russian Historical Society in Prague (the chairman was E. F. Shmurlo).

After the establishment in Prague of the Seminarium Kondakovianum, devoted to archeology and Byzantine studies, Florovskii became a member. Subsequently, he was appointed professor at the University of Prague.

In the summer of 1967 the Belorussian Academy of Sciences invited Florovskii to participate in the 450th anniversary of the publication of the first Belorussian book. It was published by Frantsisk Skorina, a native of Polotsk. Skorina was a Russian (as he considered himself) scholar of the early XVI century. He was a typographer in Prague, then in Vilnius. The celebration took place in Minsk and Polotsk.

From there Florovskii went to Leningrad to visit scholars in that city. He derived great satisfaction from the recognition of the value and significance of his scholarly works by his colleagues there.

At the beginning of 1968 asthma was detected in Florovskii. In the intervals between attacks, he displayed good spirits and continued to be passionately interested in problems of Russian history. A fateful attack of uncommon strength and pain ended his life (March 27).

A talented man of broad vision, Florovskii devoted his whole life to indefatigable scholarly creativity. He avoided broad generalizations in his works. He based his work on a thorough analysis of historical materials and a critical study of them.

The range of his works is extraordinarily varied — the history of Russian and Slavic culture and inter-Slavic ties, Biblical and Byzantine influences, information from the East on ancient Rus', the history of trade, Jesuits in Russia at the end of the XVII and the start of the XVIII century, Peter the Great and Ethiopia, new information on Pushkin — Florovskii studied all this from primary sources.

Each of his works, no matter its size, is at the same level as his major works.

Florovskii's major fundamental work is *Czechs and the Eastern Slavs. Essays on the History of Czech-Russian Relations in the X-XIII Centuries* [*Chekhi i Vostochnye Slaviane. Ocherki po Istorii Cheshsko-Russkikh Otnoshenii X-XVIII vv.*].
The first volume of this work appeared in Prague in 1935. Volume two was ready for publication in 1941 but, in view of the war and the German occupation, it could not be published at that time. It came out only in 1947.

In its construction the book consists of a series of individual essays, each of which contains a completed exposition of concrete problems from the past of Russo-Czech relations. "In their internal link," writes Florovskii in the introduction to volume one, "these essays constitute three groups . . . In terms of their basic content, the first four essays touch on the Kievan period of the history of Rus' from the IX-XII centuries." The fifth chapter treats the relations between Czechoslovakia and the principality of Galicia in the XII, and partly in the XIV centuries.

"The second part of our work," continues Florovskii, "consists of essays which essentially treat the relations of Czechoslovakia and Czechs with the Rus' and the Russians encompassed by the boundries of the Polish, and especially the Lithuanian states. The chronological limits of these essays are the XIV and XVII centuries. The last third of the book contains a survey of information on mutual relations between Czechs and Russians during the era of Peter the Great and his closest successors."

Florovskii's second major work was dedicated to the theme of Czech Jesuits in Russia at the end of the XVII and in the XVIII centuries. It was written and published in Czech and published in Czechoslovakia.[73]

The book consists of two parts. The first speaks of the organization of Jesuit schools in Czechoslovakia in the XVII and XVIII centuries and of scholarships granted for study to Eastern Slavic youths.

The second part speaks of the trips of Czech Jesuits to Muscovy commencing with the time of Tsarevna Sofiia, then under Peter the Great. The Jesuits did not conduct open Catholic propaganda. Rather they offered their services for the dissemination of enlightenment in Russia.

Nevertheless, Patriarch Ioakim and the Greek brothers Likhud who resided in Moscow protested against their activity and they were banished from Moscow. But, little by little, some of them were able to penetrate into Moscow incognito. They were again banished in 1719.

The book is richly illustrated. Most of the illustrations were taken from Prague archives and libraries. Among these illustrations there are portraits of Jesuits, Tsarevna Sofiia, Prince V. V. Golitsyn, the young Peter, views of the Kremlin, the German settlement in Moscow, and sketches of Kalmyks. This work by Florovskii (like all his others) is built on a firm foundation of archival sources and literature on the subject.

There is no complete bibliography of Florovskii's works. His two major works and a large number of reprints of his smaller works are in my personal library (they were sent to me by the author). Besides that, see Antoine Florovsky, "La Litterature historique russe. Emigration, Compte-rendu, 1921-1926," *Bulletin d'Information des Sciences Historiques en Europe Orientale*, Vol. I (Warsaw, 1927); *Materials for the Bibliography of Russian Scholarly Works Abroad* [*Materialy dlia Bibliografii Russkikh Nauchnykh Trudov za Rubezhom*] (1920-1930) issue I, (Belgrade, 1931), pp. 340-343; issue II (1941), pp. 372-374.

## G. V. VERNADSKY (1887-1973)[74]

Georgii Vladimirovich Vernadsky was born in Petersburg. He was the son of Vladimir Ivanovich and Natalia Egorovna Vernadsky.

He was graduated from Moscow's fifth classical gymnasium with a gold medal in the spring of 1906. He became a student of the historico-philological department at Moscow University.

He attended Kliuchevskii's lectures (though Kliuchevskii

no longer conducted his seminar). Vernadsky's teachers were:
M. M. Bogoslovskii (Russian History), D. M. Petrushevskii
(Middle Ages), and A. N. Savin (Modern History).
Vernadsky married Nina Vladimirovna Il'inskaia in
1907, a faithful life's companion (she died in 1971).
Upon graduating from the university in 1910, he com-
menced independent scholarly work and began the study of
Siberian history. He studied the sources in the archive of
Moscow's Ministry of Justice which had had little elabora-
tion. The fruit of this work was three articles, one of which
was already a serious scholarly piece. This was "The Sovereign's Servitors and Tradesmen in Eastern Siberia in the
XVII Century" ["Gosudarevy Sluzhilye i Promyshlennye
Liudi v Vostochnoi Sibiri XVII Veka" (*Journal of the Ministry of Public Education*, new series, IV, 1915).
   Ascertaining his ability for scholarly creativity, thanks
to archival research, Vernadsky turned to S.F. Platonov in
1911 with a request that he oversee his preparation for the
master's examinations and then the writing of the master's
thesis. Platonov agreed.
   In 1913 Vernadsky moved to Petersburg (where his
parents lived). He received the rank of *privat-docent* in
1914 and began to lecture at the University of Petersburg.
   In 1915 Vernadsky wrote an article, "The Hungarian
Campaign of 1849" ["Vengerskii Pokhod 1849 Goda"]
(*Russkaia Mysl'*, 1915, no. 2).
   In America, in 1971, Vernadsky returned to the theme
of this work. He revised, reworked, and significantly expan-
ded it for *Ferdinandy Festschrift*, a collection of articles in
honor of the Hungarian historian Michael Ferdinandy, who
was professor of European history at the University of
Puerto Rico. The *Festschrift* was in honor of his 60th birth-
day.[75]
   Vernadsky chose the theme of "Russian Freemasonry
During the Reign of Catherine II" ["Russkoe Masonstvo v
Tsarstvovanie EkaterinyII"].[76]
   Vernadsky was never a mason. The topic of freemasonry drew his attention in that it provided the possibility of

studying one of the important intellectual currents of that era against a background of European intellectual growth (both rationalistic and mystical).

In addition to Platonov, Vernadsky consulted with A. S. Lappo-Danilevskii on his choice of theme and his work on it. Ia. L. Barskov also gave Vernadsky invaluable help. At this time Barskov was the senior scholarly official in the State Archives. He also knew thoroughly what other Petersburg archives and libraries contained materials on the topic of freemasonry.

The manuscript of the thesis was ready by the beginning of 1917. Platonov approved it and set the disputation for October 22. The defense of the thesis was successful and the department unanimously granted Vernadsky the master's degree in Russian history.

At the same time, at the proposal of Vera Aleksandrova Pypina-Liatskaia, A. N. Pypin's daughter, he reworked, corrected, and expanded Pypin's collection of articles on Russian freemasonry in the XVIII and the first quarter of the XIX century (they were written during the years 1870-1873).[77]

Later, on the suggestion of the editors of the next issue of the *Russian Biographical Dictionary*, Vernadsky wrote a long essay on N. I. Novikov. Vernadsky treated Novikov extensively in his dissertation on Russian freemasonry, but there was much material on Novikov which he had not utilized.

The publication of the *Russian Biographical Dictionary* was stopped after the October Revolution. Vernadsky's book on Novikov was published as a separate volume in 1918.

Vernadsky was invited to be professor of modern Russian history at the University of Perm for the 1918-1919 academic year.(B. D. Grekov held the chair of ancient Russian history).

Vernadsky was one of the founders and a Fellow of the "Society of Historical, Philosophical, and Social Sciences" at the University of Perm. He wrote an article titled

"Empress Catherine II and the Legislative Commission of 1767-1768" ["Imperatritsa Ekaterina II i Zakonodatel'naia Komissiia 1767-1768 Godov"] for the first collection published by the Society.

Perm in the autumn of 1918 was virtually autonomous and not subject to the central Soviet government. The situation changed by the spring of 1919. The Bolsheviks gained the majority in the Perm soviet of worker's deputies. Agents of the Cheka were sent from Moscow. Arrests began. Well wishers advised Vernadsky to leave for the summer, assuming that the situation would change by fall.

Vernadsky and his wife went south to Simferopol. There Vernadsky was invited to accept the professorship in modern Russian history in the just opened University of Taura.

As in Perm, the craving of youth for a higher education amazed one. Student composition in Simferopol was heterogeneous. There were older students as well as very youthful ones who had just graduated from gymnasiums, many of them in Simferopol.

Besides lecturing and conducting a seminar at the university, Vernadsky was an active member of the Tauridian Learned Archival Commission. At its head was Arsenii Ivanovich Markevich, an outstanding scholar and a profound expert on Crimean antiquity. Despite the age difference (Markevich was much older than Vernadsky), they formed a close friendship.

In the Crimea many valuable family archives were in private hands. Because of the unsettled conditions resulting from the 'Civil War, many of the possessors, prior to the founding of the University of Taura, handed them over to the Archival Commission.

From Markevich Vernadsky learned that the substantial and exceedingly valuable archive of V.S. Popov, the head of Potemkin's chancellery, was at the Tavel' estate. The owners willingly agreed to transfer this archive to the library of the University of Taura. N. L. Ernst, the university's librarian, took the duty of supervising the transfer upon himself.

Thus, the archive was saved and Vernadsky gradually began to sort it out.

Toward the end of the Civil War in the autumn of 1920, Vernadsky and his wife evacuated to Constantinople. From there, in March of 1921, they moved to Athens where they spent eleven months. In Athens, Vernadsky received a position as inspector of the Russian gymnasium.

During his stay in Greece, Vernadsky became familiar with classical antiquities and also became interested in monuments of Byzantine antiquity. This served as the origin of his subsequent works in Byzantine studies.

At the beginning of February, 1922, Vernadsky received news that he had been elected a member of the Russian Educational Collegium in Prague.

At the end of February the Vernadskys moved to Prague. Many Russian professors and students had already gathered there and continued to arrive. For a few years at this time, Prague seemed to become a piece of Russia — a major center of Russian culture.

Vernadsky was chosen professor of the history of Russian law in the just founded Russian Juridical Faculty He presented a course on Russian State law in the imperial period.

On the basis of these lectures he wrote *An Essay on the History of Law in the Russian State in the XVIII-XIX Centuries* [*Ocherk Istorii Prava Russkogo Gosudarstva XVIII-XIX Vekov*] (Prague, 1924).

In addition, Vernadsky was elected member of the Slavic Institute (a Czech scholarly organization) and became friends with prominent Czech scholars — Karl Kadlets (historian of Slavic law) and Liubor Niderle (Archeologist).

In the autumn of 1922 academician N. P. Kondakov, the famous archeologist, historian of art, and Byzantinist, came to Prague from Bulgaria. He began to lecture (in Russian) at the Czech university. Russians and Czechs who knew Russian were among the auditors. Vernadsky also attended these lectures. A circle of Kondakov's admirers was formed among the Russian auditors which met once weekly at his home. Vernadsky also attended. Kondakov's 80th birthday was in November, 1924. Vernadsky gave a speech regarding the significance of his scholarly work at the III congress of Russian historians in exile which took place in Prague on September 25. Kondakov died on February 17, 1925.

The circle of students, friends, and admirers of Kondakov decided not to disband but to establish in his memory an association along comradely-scholarly lines. This was the "Kondakov Seminar" (Seminarium Kondakovianum). For the start, it was decided to publish a collection of international articles dedicated to Kondakov's memory (*Recueil Kondakov*, Prague, 1926).

Russian and foreign scholars participated in this collection. Vernadsky wrote an introductory essay on Kondakov's life and work (which was published in French).

In addition, Vernadsky also included an article in this anthology. It was titled "Byzantine Doctrines Regarding the Power of Tsar and Patriarch" ["Vizantiiskie Ucheniia o Vlasti Tsaria i Patriarcha"].

Among the members of the Kondakov seminar were archeologist N. P. Toll; art historian N. M. Beliaev, artist Princess N. G. Iashvil' and others. The leaders of the seminar were Vernadsky and the archeologist A. P. Kalitinskii.

The first volume of the Seminarium Kondakovianum appeared in 1927. A volume was issued yearly thereafter.

For volume one Vernadsky wrote an article called "The Golden Horde, Egypt, and Byzantium in their Relations During the Reign of Michael Paleologus" ["Zolotaia Orda, Egipet, i Vizantiia v ikh Vzaimotnosheniiakh v Tsarstvovanie Mikhaila Paleologa"]. A series of articles and notes by Vernadsky appeared in subsequent volumes. Of these we will note "M. I. Rostovtsev: On His Sixtieth Birthday" ["M.I. Rostovtsev. K Shestidesiatiletiiu Ego"] (Seminarium Kondakovianum, IV, 1931); "A. A. Vasil'ev: On His Seventieth Birthday" ["A. A. Vasil'ev: K Semidesiatiletiiu Ego"] (Annales de l'Institut Kondakov, X, 1938). (This is a continuation of the Seminarium Kondakovianum).

In 1925 Vernadsky published a study on "The Government Statutory Charter of the Russian Empire of 1820" ["Gosudarstvennaia Ustavnaia Gramota Rossiiskoi Imperii 1820 Goda"]. This is a project for restructuring Russia on the principles of moderate constitutionalism. This project was drawn up by N. N. Novosil'tsev. It was commissioned by Alexander I. Alexander kept this project for a long time but never did affirm it.

At the beginning of the 1930's Vernadsky expanded and completely revised this work. The book was published in a French translation done by S.S. Ol'denburg (Paris, 1933).

In May, 1926, Vernadsky participated in the International Byzantine Congress in Belgrade.

A turning point in his life occurred a year later. He received an offer from Yale University in the U.S.A. in August, 1927, to be a research associate. He was made professor in 1946 and retired in 1956 due to age.

### FURTHER BIBLIOGRAPHICAL LISTINGS OF VERNADSKY'S WORKS

*Materialy dlia Bibliografii Russkikh Nauchnykh Trudov za Rubezhom*, 1920-1930. Vyspusk I (Belgrade, 1931, pp. 65-67); Vyspusk II (1941), pp. 83-85.

A.D. Ferguson and Alfred Levin, editors. "Essays in Russian History." A Collection Dedicated to George Vernadsky (Hamden, Conn., 1964, pp. XIII-XXV).

*Who's Who in America*, 37th edition, 1972-1973, vol. 2, page 3262.

Also see below (in this volume).

### S. G. PUSHKAREV (b. 1888)

### Autobiography[78]

Sergei Germanovich Pushkarev was born in the Starooskol'sk district of the Kursk province.

His parents were German Iosifovich (a notary and land-owner) and Aleksandra Ivanovna (maiden name Shatilova).

Pushkarev was graduated from the Kursk gymnasium with a gold medal and enrolled in the historico-philological department at the University of Khar'kov. He studied there from 1907 to 1910. From 1911 to 1914 he was a student at the universities of Heidelberg and Leipzig.

He returned to Khar'kov in 1915 and in 1917 was kept at the chair of Russian history at the proposal of Professor M. V. Klochkov to prepare for the professorship. From 1917 to 1919 he prepared for the master's examinations.

In June, 1919 Pushkarev joined the Volunteer Army, infantry. He was seriously wounded, then served on armoured trains. In November, 1920 he was evacuated to Turkey with General Wrangel's army.

From there, at the end of 1921, he moved to Prague where he received a scholarship for study from the Russian Educational Collegium. He prepared for the master's examinations under the guidance of Professor I.I. Lappo. He passed them in 1924 and received the rank of *privat-docent*.

He was elected member of the Russian Educational Collegium. He taught at the Russian Free University as a *docent*.

He was a member of the learned council of the Russian Foreign Historical Archives in Prague which was administrated by the Czechoslovakian Ministry of Foreign Affairs.

Pushkarev also was an associate of the Scholarly Research Union which published its *Transactions*.

In addition, he participated in the Russian Historical Society in Prague. He read two papers at sessions of this society — "Principles of Peter the Great's Trade and Industrial Policy" ["Printsipy Torgovoi i Promyshlennoi Politiki Petra Velikogo"] and "Pososhkov and His Importance in the History of Russian Culture" ["Pososhkov i ego Znachenie v Istorii Russkoi Kul'tury"].

During these and the following years, Pushkarev published a whole series of scholarly works.[79]

Pushkarev married Iuliia Tikhonovna Popova on September 2, 1927 (she died in America on August 19, 1961). Their son, Boris, was born in 1929.

Prague was occupied by the German army in the spring of 1939. The Czech university was closed. The Russian Free University came under German control.

But the turning point in the war came. In the spring of 1945 the Soviet army approached Prague from the east, the American army from the west. Pushkarev and his family were able to go to the American zone.

During the time spent in camps of "displaced persons," Pushkarev was the director of and teacher in a secondary school for Russian children.

In 1949 the UNRRA began to transfer refugees to America from the German camps. The Pushkarevs arrived in New Haven on July 21, 1949. In 1950 Pushkarev was appointed Russian language instructor at Yale University.

His son, Boris, enrolled in the school of architecture in 1950 and was graduated therefrom in 1954. From 1954-1956 he proceeded to study "city planning."

### A SURVEY OF S. G. PUSHKAREV'S SCHOLARLY WORKS (compiled by G.V. Vernadsky)

All of Pushkarev's works are based on thorough preparation and on a profound knowledge of sources and the literature on the subject.

Thematically the range of his work is very broad. Here are the main themes he elaborated on during the course of his indefatigable and fruitful work:

1). History of the Russian peasantry; the origin of the commune; peasant self-government.

2). The city-state in northern Russia (Pskov).

3). The popular origin of the Muscovite tsardom.

4). Don Cossacks and their relations with Moscow.

5). The significance of the Church in Russian history.

6). Peter the Great.

7). Lenin.

8). Russia and the West.

Pushkarev's brochures, "An Essay on the History of Peasant Self-Government in Russia" ["Ocherk Istorii Krest'-ianskogo Samoupravleniia v Rossii"] (Prague 1924) and the large and very valuable study, "The Peasants' Repartitional Land-Commune in Russia" ["Proiskhozhdenie Krest'-ianskoi Pozemel'no-Peredel'noi Obshchiny"] (2 parts, Prague, 1939-1941) relate to the first group.

Pushkarev's articles should also be cited. "The Political Movement and Political Organization of the Russian Peasantry in the 20th Century" (in the anthology: *A Systematic Source Book in Rural Sociology,* P. A. Sorokin, ed., vol. II Minneapolis, Minnesota, 1931), and "The Russian Peasants' Reaction to the Emancipation of 1861" (Russian Review, vol. 27, no. 2, April, 1968).

To group two (on the city-state) belongs his marvelous study, "The Internal Structure and External Situation of the State of Pskov in the XIV-XV cc." ["Vnutrennee Ustroistvo i Vneshnee Polozhenie Pskovskogo Gosudarstva v XIV-XV Vekakh,"] (in Czech; Prague, 1925, *Sbornik ved Pravnich a Statnich*).

Pushkarev devotes his article "The Russian Land Without Sovereignty 1606-1613" ["Russkaia Zemlia v Bezgosudarnoe Vremia 1606-1613"][80] to the turning point in the history of the Muscovite tsardom — the Time of Troubles and the national election of a new Tsar.

Pushkarev vividly describes the destruction of the Time of Troubles, the Polish intervention, the uniting of Russian cities for the purpose of re-establishing order, and the election of Mikhail Fedorovich Romanov as Tsar.

Also in the topic of Muscovy's internal structure are the articles, "Sworn Men in the Court and Administration of Muscovite Russia" ["Tseloval'niki v Sude i Upravlenii Moskovskoi Rusi"] and "Sworn Men in the State Economy of Muscovite Russia" ["Tseloval'niki v Gosudarstvennom Khoziaistve Moskovskoi Rusi"] (*Transactions of the Russian*

*Educational Institute in Belgrade*, issue 9, 1933; issue 13, 1936).

Pushkarev's work, "The Don Cossacks and the Muscovite State in the XVII Century" ["Donskoe Kazachestvo i Moskovskoe Gosudarstvo v XVII Veke"] treats the theme of Don Cossacks.[81]

Pushkarev begins his article with the origin of the Cossacks and the formation of a unique military-democratic republic (the "Great Don Host"). He notes the role of the Cossacks in the Time of Troubles. The military union of Moscow and the Don continued, with brief interruptions, throughout the whole XVII century.

On the significance of the Church in Russian history, Pushkarev wrote two short books. These were: *The Holy Trinity Monastery* [*Sviato-Troitskaia Sergieva Lavra*] (Prague, 1928), and *The Role of the Orthodox Church in the History of Russian Culture and Statehood* [*Rol' Pravoslavnoi Tserkvi v Istorii Russkoi Kul'tury i Gosudarstvennostii*] (Ladomirovo, Czechoslovakia, 1938).

He also speaks considerably about the Church in his article on the Time of Troubles.

In 1926, Pushkarev wrote an article on the principles of Peter the Great's trade and industrial policy, (in Czech) in the series *Sbornik ved Pravnich a Statnich*, XXI.

At the beginning of the 1970's, Pushkarev returned to Peter and wrote two articles for the *Transactions of the Association of Russian American Scholars in the USA* (vol. VII, 1973). They were: "The Personality and Works of Peter the Great" ["Lichnost' i Deiatel'nost' Petra Velikogo"] and "A Survey of His Reign" ["Obzor Tsarstvovaniia"] (both were united under the general title of "Peter the Great."

We will now observe Pushkarev's articles on Lenin.

Pushkarev's article "The October Revolution of 1917 Legend Free" ["Oktiabr'skii Perevorot 1917 Goda Bez Legend"] appeared in book 89 of the *Novyi Zhurnal* [*New Review*] (1967).

In book 100 of the same journal (1970) Pushkarev wrote an essay on "Lenin and the USA" ["Lenin i S.Sh.A."].

In volume IV of the *Transactions of the Association of Russian-American Scholars in the USA*, Pushkarev wrote an article titled "Lenin's Foreign Policy 1914-1922" ["Vnesh-naia Politika Lenina 1914-1922"] (1970). These works were founded primarily on Soviet sources and materials.

According to Pushkarev, the most thorough and correct description of the October Revolution is to be found in S.P. Mel'gunov's Book, *How the Bolshevicks Seized Power* [*Kak Bol'sheviki Zakhvatili Vlast'*] (Paris, 1953).[82]

In his article "The October Revolution of 1917 Legend Free," Pushkarev describes the chaotic situation which prevailed in Petrograd toward the end of the existence of the Provisional Government, the loss of initiative by the latter, the neutrality of the enormous mass of soldiers, the confusion of the "mandatory democracy" — of the SR's and the Mensheviks.

But the Bolsheviks also did not have enough reliable forces.

On October 25, [1917], the Bolsheviks met no serious resistance in Petrograd. The Winter Palace was taken at night without "storm" after its few defenders either dissipated or ceased to resist.

In his article, "Lenin's Foreign Policy 1914-1923," Pushkarev stresses the significance of Lenin's fundamental slogan regarding the "transformation of an imperialistic war into a civil war." In fact, Lenin's defeatist propaganda in Russia occasioned direct aid to Germany from whom the Leninists received subsidies in the millions.

After Germany's defeat and the Peace of Versailles of 1919, Lenin's policy was a dual one. On the one hand, he organized the Third (communist) International and headed communist movements throughout the world. On the other hand, he strove to sow discord among the Western nations and attract European capitalists to financial aid for Russia via loans and "concessions."

In his article, "Lenin and the U.S.A.," Pushkarev analyzes Lenin's attempts to achieve recognition by the United

States and the re-establishment of diplomatic relations between the Soviet Union and the U.S.A. These attempts ended
in failure.

We will now survey Pushkarev's works on the theme of
Russia and the West.

Much material on the many sided relations and ties of
pre-revolutionary Russia and the Western world, particularly
in the sphere of spiritual culture, is cited in the article "Russia and the West: Ideological and Personal Contact before
1917" (*Russian Review*, vol. 24, no. 2, 1965).

A historical essay on Russo-American relations is given
by Pushkarev in his article "Russia and the U.S.A." ["Rus-
siia i SShA"] (*Novyi Zhurnal*, no. 88, 1967).

Pushkarev begins with Catherine's era. Catherine did not
recognize the American colonies as a belligerent. In fact, she
provided real help to them by her refusal to send a Russian
corps to America to help England and by her declaration of
armed neutrality which aimed to paralyze the English blockade of the North American states.

The era of Alexander II was the apogee of Russo-American friendship.

This friendship began to ebb in the 1880's. America
cooled toward Russia primarily because of the Russian government's discrimination against Jews and its aggressive policy in the Far East.

In the 1950's, Pushkarev wrote two volumes on Russian
history for the general reader: *A Survey of Russian History*
[*Obzor Russkoi Istorii*] (New York, 1953), and *Russia in the
XIX Century* [*Rossiia v XIX Veke*] (New York, 1953).

Pushkarev provides many citations from the sources in
his account so that the reader "would see our antiquity with
his own eyes and hear its voice."

Each of these works is an essay on the political and
social history of the Russian nation. Pushkarev just briefly
touches on the history of Russian spiritual culture. He treats
the history of the Russian Church only insofar as the Church,
particularly in pre-Petrine Russia, was closely linked to the
overall social and political life of the Russian nation.

A lengthy bibliography of the works used by the author appears at the end of each volume.

The latter book was translated into English by Professor Robert McNeal and published with the title of *The Emergence of Modern Russia, 1801-1917.*[83]

In the 1950's Russian-American historians in the U.S.A. conceived the idea of the need of publishing a solid "source book" on Russian history. Such an anthology was necessary for students and, in general, for all those who were interested in Russian history but did not know the Russian language. But an anthology of this sort can also be useful for people who know Russian in that the sources from which translations have been made are limited.

An editorial committee was formed to realize this plan. It consisted of: G. V. Vernadsky, editor-in-chief, Ralph Fisher, managing editor, Alan Ferguson and Andrew Lossky, committee members, and S.G. Pushkarev, compiler.

The anthology was titled *A Source Book for Russian History from Early Times to 1917* (1972). It was published in three volumes: I. *Early Times to the Late Seventeenth Century*; II. *Peter the Great to Nicholas I*; III. *Alexander II to the February Revolution.*

Pushkarev took the task of preparing the excerpts from the sources. The majority of these were excerpts from Russian sources, though a part were from English. Excerpts from the Russian sources were translated into English by competent aides.

As the work proceeded, Pushkarev compiled a dictionary of historical terms that were found in the sources.[84] This dictionary is necessary for readers of the anthology, but is exceedingly valuable in and of itself.

A source book as detailed as this has yet to be published in the Soviet Union.

### M. M. KARPOVICH (1888-1959)

Mikhail Mikhailovich Karpovich was born in Tiflis. His father was a railroad engineer, a Pole by origin; his mother —

a Russian, sister of the historian Professor A. E. Presniakov. Karpovich studied at the second classical gymnasium in Tiflis where instruction was at a high level.[85]

During his last year of study at the gymnasium, Karpovich was seized by the rising revolutionary tide in Russia and joined the Socialist Revolutionary party. He was arrested twice but graduated from the gymnasium.

As Professor Mosely fairly notes, the liberal democratic program of the Cadet Party was closer to Karpovich's temperament than was revolutionary terrorism.

He enrolled in the historico-philological department of Moscow University in the fall of 1906 but left for Paris in 1907 where he attended the lectures of Diehl and Luchaire.

Karpovich returned to Moscow in 1908. His instructors at Moscow University were M. M. Bogoslovskii (in Russian history) and D. M. Petrushevskii (in the Middle Ages).

Karpovich spent the winter of 1913-1914 in Petersburg where he wrote a work on Alexander I and the Holy Alliance. He passed the government examinations in the spring of 1914 and began to prepare for the master's examinations under the guidance of Bogoslovskii. He received a post as an assistant to the science secretary of the Moscow science museum. This, in essence, was a *sinecure* and Karpovich had much free time to continue his scholarly preparation.

Peaceful studies were interrupted by World War I. Karpovich was assigned to the War Ministry. The February Revolution of 1917 freed him from this service.

A chance meeting with B. A. Bakhmetev on the Nevskii Prospekt turned Karpovich's whole life around. Bakhmetev had just been appointed ambassador to the United States and was looking for a personal secretary whom he could fully trust. Bakhmetev had previously lived in the Caucasus and knew Karpovich's father well. He offered the job to Karpovich. The decision had to be made immediately and Karpovich agreed. Bakhmetev and his retinue left for America in the middle of May.

After the October Revolution, the government of the United States did not recognize Bolshevik rule and considered Bakhmetev to be the legal Russian representative. However, the activity of the Russian embassy was greatly curtailed. The embassy's personnel was decreased compared to before.

During the five years from mid 1917 to mid 1922, Karpovich was not only Bakhmetev's personal secretary but was, *de facto*, the embassy's first secretary. At this time, Karpovich made the acquaintance of Harvard University Professor Archibald C. Coolidge whose idea it was to introduce Russian history into the Harvard University course of study.

In December of 1918 Bakhmetev went to Paris in order to take part in the Russian committee formed to represent Russia's interests at the Paris peace conference. However, the representatives of the Russian committee were not allowed at the conference.

After the conclusion of the peace (at which Russia as such was not represented), the Russian embassy in Washington was closed down. Bakhmetev and Karpovich moved to New York. Karpovich helped Bakhmetev to liquidate embassy affairs.

It was decided to utilize the remaining unspent money to establish a special fund whose goal would be to support scholarly endeavors (Humanities Fund of New York City).

In January, 1927, at the proposal of Professor Archibald Coolidge, Karpovich was invited to be lecturer of Russian history at Harvard University. Teaching had to commence immediately in the spring semester. In his course on Russian history, Karpovich spoke not only of Russia's political history but also of the history of Russian society and Russian culture. Subsequently, following the traditions of Moscow University, he began to conduct a seminar in Russian history.

This seminar produced a pleiade of talented students later to become professors of Russian history in America.

The first to come under Karpovich's instructorship was Philip Mosely.

In 1949, while remaining a member of the history department, Karpovich was made chairman of the department of Slavic languages and literature.

During his years at Harvard, Karpovich published many articles and his first book, *Imperial Russia* [*Imperatorskaia Rossiia*] (New York, 1932). (We will discuss his scholarly works after the biography).

In addition to his basic scholarly work as an American professor of Russian history, Karpovich had another sphere of cultural work in America — the Russian immigration. He gave it much attention and time. He was frequently invited to New York by Russian organizations there for lectures, discussions, and consultations of all kinds. He never refused these invitations.

Karpovich deserves much merit for his leadership in Russian public opinion in America in his role as editor of *Novyi Zhurnal*.

*Novyi Zhurnal* was founded by Karpovich's friends, M. Aldanov and M. Tsetlin in 1942. In 1946 Karpovich became its irreplaceable editor — a position he held until his very death.

Karpovich himself also wrote for the *Novyi Zhurnal* on various themes: "Miliukov as a Historian" ["Miliukov kak Istorik"], "America, Russia, and Europe" ["Amerika, Rossiia i Evropa"] (on the Truman doctrine and the Marshall plan), and "M. I. Rostovtsev and A. A. Vasil'ev." He reviewed contemporary problems and events in his thoughtful "Commentaries."

Karpovich's bride, Tat'iana Nikolaevna Popova, arrived from Moscow in 1923 and they were wed.

I now proceed to a survey of Karpovich's scholarly works.

The book on Imperial Russia (already cited) provides the reader with a brilliant and concise essay on the basic lines of Russian development from Peter the Great to Nicholas II.

Karpovich treated Russia's economic development in this period in two chapters of the collaborative work, Borodin, Karpovich, Usher, *Economic History of Europe* (1937).

Karpovich wrote a thoughtful article on "Vladimir Solov'ev on Nationalism" ["Vladimir Solov'ev o Natsionalizme"] for the *Review of Politics* in 1946. In this article Karpovich pointed out the uncompromising conflict between a nationalism narrowly conceived and Christian ethics.

On the occasion of the 100th year anniversary of Pushkin's death, Karpovich gave a speech in New Haven at the meeting of the Connecticut Academy of Arts and Sciences. It was published in the *Transactions* of this Academy in 1937. In that same year Karpovich wrote an article, "Pushkin as Historian" (*Centennial Essays for Pushkin* edited by S. H. Cross and E. J. Simmons, 1937).

A valuable article by Karpovich appeared in 1943. It was devoted to recurrent problems of Russian historiography.[86]

Karpovich feels that in the XIX and the beginning of the XX century there were three attempts in Russian historical study at a general historical synthesis. Karamzin's and Solov'ev's attempts were soon forgotten but Kliuchevskii's was protracted.

In Karpovich's opinion, Kliuchevskii's synthesis approximated Russian populism. In essence, it rejected the State as an external superstructure.

Karpovich welcomed new tendencies in Russian historiography. In these new trends he included the views of M. I. Rostovtsev (on the necessity of archeology for the study of the ancient period of Russian history) and Grushevskii's [Hrushevskii's] protest against the traditional schematization of Russian history.

Karpovich felt that one of the weaknesses of Kliuchevskii's synthesis was its absence of intellectual and cultural currents.

At the end of the 1930's, Vernadsky and Karpovich conceived the plan of writing (in English) a history of Russia in ten volumes. Vernadsky took upon himself the survey of ancient Russian history (to the end of the XVII century). Karpovich was to do the modern period.

Yale University Press took on the task of publishing this series of volumes on condition that the Humanities Fund would subsidize each volume. Vernadsky carried out his promise. His first volume of the series (*Ancient Russia*) appeared in 1941, the last and fifth volume (*The Tsardom of Moscow 1547-1682*) in 1969. Because of his duties at Harvard University, his editing the *Novyi Zhurnal*, and his involvement in Russian affairs in New York in general, Karpovich was constantly forced to postpone the writing of his volumes. He commenced this only in the last winter of his life but could not realize his dream because of the fateful illness which led him to the grave.

## MARXIST HISTORIANS

### G. V. PLEKHANOV (1857-1918)
### M. N. POKROVSKII (1868-1932)
### N. A. ROZHKOV (1868-1927)[87]

The basic trait of Marxism is its historical character, its bent for historicism.[88]

Marx borrowed the scheme of universal history from Hegel. Only for the absolute Spirit as the prime mover of history, Marx substituted the development of productive forces and economic relations.

At the same time, Hegel's idea that human history was a movement in the direction of freedom was close to Marx. But he arrived at a notion of totalitarian society in which all private forces would blend with the social and man would become a totally patrimonial being (Alekseev, p. 29).

### G. V. PLEKHANOV (1857-1918)

Georgii Valentinovich Plekhanov, the founder of Russian social-democracy, was a populist in youth. He participated in the organizations "Land and Freedom" ["Zemlia i Volia"] and "Black Partitions" ["Chernyi Peredel"].[89] Plekhanov emigrated to Europe in 1881. There he became acquainted with the doctrine of Marx and Engels, accepted it, and together with Leo Deutsch and Vera Zasulich formed the first Russian social-democratic group. It was called "Liberation of Labor" ["Osvobozhdenie Truda"]. The group's goal was to propagandize Marxist ideas in Russia.

During the following decade, Plekhanov wrote a series of works to clarify and defend Marxism: *Socialism and Political Struggle* [*Sotsializm i Politicheskaia Bor'ba*] (1883), *Our Differences* [*Nashi Raznoglasiia*] (1885), *Toward the Development of the Monistic Conception of History* [*K Voprosu o Razvitii Monisticheskogo Vzgliada na Istoriiu*] (1895), and *Essays on the History of Materialism* [*Ocherki po Istorii Materializma*] (1896).

Plekhanov felt that Russia, because of the insufficient development of its industry and the comparatively small labor class, was not ready for a socialist revolution.

The initial goal, in his opinion, should be political revolution in order to attain free political institutions. Therefore, he deemed it necessary to establish contact with the liberal movement.

There was complete agreement between Lenin and Plekhanov until about 1900.

Lenin came to Switzerland in the spring of 1895 in order to make Plekhanov's acquaintance. Plekhanov made a deep impression upon him. In his reminiscences of this meeting Lenin wrote: "Never in my life did I feel such a sincere reverence for someone."

Five years later, in August, 1900, Lenin again came to Switzerland to discuss with the "Liberation of Labor" the creation of a social-democratic journal or newspaper. Plekhanov considered himself to be the true leader of the Russian social-democracy. Lenin wished to run the party press organ. There was a sharp conflict between Plekhanov and Lenin. A decision was postponed. Lenin's reverence for Plekhanov disappeared at once and forever.

The second congress of the RSDLP [Russian Socialist Democratic Labor Party] took place in London in the Summer of 1903.

A resolution was passed regarding the necessity of overturning the tsarist autocracy and substituting a democratic republic in its place.

Between 1905 and the First World War, Plekhanov devoted most of his attention to scholarly work.

He studied the history of Russian social thought. He carried his account to the end of the XVIII century. This is an outstanding work.[90]

When the war started, Plekhanov moved to Petersburg.

Lenin advanced the slogan "turn the imperialist war into a civil war" and directed defeatest propaganda in the army. Actually, this was aid to Germany.

Plekhanov took the opposite position. Viewing Germany as the aggressor, the French socialists and Plekhanov supported resistance to the Germans. Regarding Russia, Plekhanov also upheld defense.

He organized a moderate socialist group, "Unity" ["Edinstvo"]. Kropotkin, N. A. Morozov, and Potresov belonged to it. The group was small. Nevertheless, it possessed much moral authority.

Plekhanov died in 1918 when the Bolsheviks were already in power.

Plekhanov contributed nothing essentially new to the theory of orthodox Marxism.

As to Plekhanov the historian, his fundamental work, *History of Russian Social Thought* [*Istoriia Russkoi Obshchestvennoi Mysli*], was greeted unfavorably by Soviet scholars.

I. I. Smirnov writes: "At the root of Plekhanov's idea is the theory of the non-class character of Russian absolutism which stood above the classes and which oppressed all the classes."[91]

## M. N. POKROVSKII (1868-1932)

Mikhail Nikolaevich Pokrovskii was graduated from the historico-philological department of Moscow University. Upon graduating from the university course, Pokrovskii passed the basic master's examinations (under Kliuchevskii) and received the *privat-docent* rank. But he did not utilize it and did not join the staff of the *privat-docents*.

He lectured at the pedagogical courses, taught history at the women's institute, wrote eight articles for an anthology of medieval history edited by Vinogradov, and worked on a committee for organizing home reading. But, he kept his distance from the university.

Kizevetter provides a vivid description of Pokrovskii in his memoirs.

"He was of short height and had a squeaky voice. He was conspicuous by his erudition, the glibness of his literary speech, and the ability to infuse it with sarcastic digs against his opponents. Quiet and humble in appearance, he concealed an overly sensitive pride."

"Later, in 1905, Pokrovskii participated in the conferences dedicated to the establishment of the Constitutional Democratic Party. In discussions regarding the party's program, he held the more rightist position — literally to the very eve that he became a Bolshevik."

In the fall of 1902 the superintendent of the Moscow school district forbade Pokrovskii to teach in the schools. He could devote his whole time to writing.

Between 1907 and 1910 Pokrovskii wrote 30 chapters in the collective *History of Russia* by Granat publishing house. Then, he personally wrote a four volume *History of Russia From Ancient Times* [*Istoriia Rossii s Drevneishikh Vremen*] (1910-1914).

There then followed the *Essay on the History of Russian Culture* [*Ocherk Istorii Russkoi Kul'tury*] in two parts (5th ed., Petrograd, 1923). This was a rebuff of sorts to Miliukov's *Outlines*.

In his works on XIX century Russia Pokrovskii devoted

much attention to Russian foreign policy. He felt that Russian foreign policy was a reflection of domestic policy and that it was dictated by the interests of the ruling classes of Russian society. In Pokrovskii's opinion, the class struggle was at the root of scientific history. History is the most political of all the sciences. Pokrovskii states: "History is the past of politics without the knowledge of which contemporary politics cannot be conducted."

After the October Revolution, Pokrovskii published a book, *Russian History in Its Most Concise Outline* [*Russkaia Istoriia v Samom Szhatom Ocherke*] (1920). The book was approved by Lenin.

Pokrovskii played a visible role in Lenin's government.

He was appointed assistant to the commissar of public education and made the chairman of the State soviet of public education. In the post the central archives were placed under his control. The reform of the universities was entrusted to him. The teaching of history was abolished. It was replaced by Marxist sociology.

Pokrovskii, in addition, was made a member of the commission on the history of the October Revolution and the Communist Party (abbreviated, this commission was known as the "ISTPART").

He was also the chairman of the presidium of the Communist Academy. The publication of *Red Archives* [*Krasnyi Arkhiv*] and the journal, *Marxist Historian* [*Istorik-Marksist*] was also entrusted to him.

In this fashion Pokrovskii seized the command heights of surveillance over the direction of Russian historical scholarship.

But one sphere did not subordinate itself to him. The majority of Russian historians, including the most important ones, continued their scholarly work without heeding Pokrovskii's dictates.

Pokrovskii could not bear this. Only one course of struggle remained open to him: the physical extermination of opponents.

By his orders, a series of outstanding Russian historians were tortured to death in prison and exile (Platonov, Liubavskii, Rozhdestvenskii, Vasenko, Zaozerskii). Pokrovskii's star began to fade around 1930. Many were annoyed at his dictatorial habits. Others criticized his university reform, in particular the exclusion of history from the university (and from the overall school) curriculum. Theoreticians of communism accused him of perverting communist doctrine. Pokrovskii defended himself energetically until his death (he died in 1932). The teaching of history was re-introduced in 1933.

## XXX

## THE HISTORY OF THE CHURCH[92]

This chapter will speak of the historians of the Russian Orthodox Church and the Old Believers.

I will speak of the history of Russian sects only in passing, when and if this will be necessary in connection with the opinions of one historian of the Church or another. Russian sectarianism is a special field.

I will touch on special theological questions only when this is necessary for the characterization of historical thought within the framework of Church history.[93]

### METROPOLITAN MAKARII BULGAKOV (1816-1882)

The first major historian of the Russian Church who laid the foundation for subsequent studies was Metropolitan Makarii Bulgakov.[94]

Mikhail Petrovich Bulgakov (the future Metropolitan Makarii) was born in the village of Surkovo, district of Novyi Oskol in the Kursk province. His father was the priest of Surkovo village. He died while still young, leaving a widow and six orphans without any means.

Mikhail studied at the parish school in the town of Korocha, then in the district ecclesiastical school in Belgorod and at the Belgorod seminary. At the seminary he mastered language well, particularly French. While in the seminary, he read Karamzin's *History* and became enthused over Zhukovskii's poetry which he imitated not without some success.

In 1837 Bulgakov enrolled in the Kiev Theological Academy. He received the master's degree for his work, *The History of the Kiev Theological Academy* [*Istoriia Kievskoi Dukhovnoi Akademii*]. It was published in 1843.

During his years at the Academy, he felt a calling to monasticism. He was consecrated a monk in February of 1841 and received the name Makarii. Upon graduating from the Academy, Makarii (because of his baccalaureate) was retained at the chair of Russian and Church history.

He was transferred to the Petersburg Theological Academy in the following year. In 1843 he was appointed extraordinary professor and made ordinary professor one year later. In addition, he was a member of several committees and commissions on ecclesiastical administration.

In 1847 he published his lectures on basic theology. They were titled *Introduction to Orthodox Theology* [*Vvedenie v Pravoslavnoe Bogoslovie*]. He received the doctor of theology degree for this work.

This was followed by his *Dogmatic Theology* [*Dogmaticheskoe Bogoslovie*] (1851-1853). This was an attempt at a scientific classification of accumulated dogmatic material. Makarii subjected it to the strictest unification. He accepted the suitable and rejected the outmoded. In this fashion, a summing up of the whole preceding development of dogmatic theology in Russia was made.

Makarii was elected ordinary member of the Academy of Sciences in 1854.

Three years later, he was appointed eparchial [diocesan] bishop in Tambov. He was transferred to the Khar'kov seat in 1859, to the Lithuanian in 1868, and made Metropolitan of Moscow in 1879.

His *History of the Russian Schism of the Old Belief* [*Istoriia Russkogo Raskola Staroobriadstva*] appeared in

1854. This was the fruit of his work as preceptor of the missionary anti-schismatic class at the Petersburg Theological Academy. This is a purely polemical and accusatory work. In their criticism of the reforms of Church ritual introduced by Patriarch Nikon in the XVII century, the Old Believers relied on the decisions of the *Stoglav Sobor* of 1551 and the collection of Church decrees known under the heading of "*Stoglav.*" Makarii passes strict judgement on this monument of Russian Church antiquity.

But Makarii was a writer of unusual scholarly fairness. When he subsequently studied the matter more profoundly, he did not hesitate to change his opinion. In volume VI of his *History of the Russian Church* [*Istoriia Russkoi Tserkvi*] he gave a completely different evaluation of the "*Stoglav.*"

"Its authenticity [the *Stoglav's* book] as a synodical book which contains actual decisions (canons) of the *Stoglav Sobor*, or the "council's statutes," cannot be presently doubted."

Already in the 1840's Makarii conceived of writing a history of the Russian Church. But teaching and other responsibilities at the Petersburg Theological Academy, then the responsibilities of eparchial hierarch in various cities seriously impeded his work.

Makarii placed a single principle at the basis of the structure of his history — the Russian Church is not an independent whole. It is a part of the one ecumenical apostolic Church. That is why the history of the Russian Church consists of its relations with the ecumenical Church.

Makarii divided his history into three periods: (1) The Russian Church in Dependence on the Patriarch of Constantinople (992-1448), (2) The Russian Church (1448-1588), (3) The Period of the Patriarchy. This was to have been followed by the period of synodal administration. Makarii was not able to complete his monumental work. In the twelfth and in the unfinished thirteenth volume he commenced the history from Nikon to the Synod.

For the first six volumes, and partly later as well, Makarii had to be both the researcher and the seeker of manuscript materials. The appendices to these volumes, where the documents discovered by Makarii are published, were a series of sensational discoveries which attract the attention of historians to this day.

## E. E. GOLUBINSKII (1834-1912)

Evgenii Evstigneevich Golubinskii was born in the Kostroma province to a priest's family.[95]
He was educated at the Soligalich ecclesiastical school, then at the Kostroma seminary, and later at the Moscow Theological Academy (from which he graduated in 1858). There he received the master's degree and was made baccalaureate of Russian Church history and the German language.

In 1870 he was advanced to the rank of extraordinary professor. In 1880, after the defense of his dissertation, "History of the Russian Church" ["Istoriia Russkoi Tserkvi"], volume I, the first half (the pre-Mongol period), he received the doctor of theology degree and was elected as associate member of the Academy of Sciences. He was made ordinary academician in 1903.

Golubinskii's major scholarly work is the *History of the Russian Church*; volume I, two parts (1880); volume II, in two parts, the first of which appeared in 1900. Its second part came out under the editorship of S.A. Belokurov. The account is inclusive of Metropolitan Makarii (1542-1562).

Another basic work by Golubinskii is the *History of the Canonization of Saints in the Russian Church* [*Istoriia Kanonizatsii Sviatykh v Russkoi Tserkvi*] (1903).

In addition, Golubinskii wrote *A Short Outline of the History of the Orthodox Church of Bulgaria, Serbia, and Rumania* [*Kratkii Ocherk Istorii Pravoslavnoi Tserkvi Bolgarskoi, Serbskoi, i Rumynskoi*] (1871).

In 1905 he wrote an article for *Readings of the Society of History and Antiquities* [*Chtenie v Obshchestve Istorii i Drevnostei Rossiiskikh pri Moskovskom Universitete*][96] titled "On Our Polemic With the Old Believers" ["K Nashei Polemike so Staroobriadtsami"] (which was also published

separately). In this article he expressed the opinion that the
Council of 1667, which anathematized the Old Believers
(with the participation of the Eastern patriarchs) simply
was ill informed, that the differences between the Russian
and the new Greek regulations of the mid XVII century
occurred not because of Russian errors but because of
changes made in the statutes by the Greeks themselves.
Golubinskii, in acerbic expressions, insisted that history should be written unadorned and without any ideali-
zation of the past.
"History is of three types. There is the obtuse type
which accepts everything which the past has left us with the
label of historical material at face value and therefore tells
us old wives tales. There is the prevaricating type which
does not fool itself but cheats others, which because of
various practical considerations depicts white as black and
black as white, and reviles what is praiseworthy and praises
the reproachable. There is the real type which strives insofar
as it is possible, to correctly and thoroughly know the
past and thereupon just as accurately and thoroughly to
recreate it." (Citation from N. N. Glubokovskii's "Russian
Theological Scholarship in its Historical Development").

## THE HISTORIOGRAPHY OF THE RUSSIAN
## ORTHODOX CHURCH

### by SERGEI G. PUSHKAREV

### Foreword

Professor George V. Vernadsky, who died in June of
1973, was truly a patriarch in the field of the contemporary
study of Russian history. He worked indefatigably in culti-
vating the broad and rugged field of Russian history for over
60 years, literally to the last day of his life. A sudden death
did not permit him to complete the last great work of his
life — the essays on the development of Russian historical
scholarship. Among the last unwritten chapters was a chap-

ter on the historiography of the Russian Church.

Among Professor Vernadsky's papers, we found only the text he had written on the two most outstanding historians of the Russian Church — Metropolitan Makarii and Professor E.E. Golubinskii. These were the last of the countless pages written by George Vernadsky. The editors of the *Transactions of the Association of Russian American Scholars*, out of respect for the memory of the deceased historian, decided to print these last pages in the form in which they appeared. I was entrusted with writing the general essay on the historiography of the Russian Church.

Among Professor Vernadsky's papers, in addition to the above cited text, I found (in the folder entitled "History of the Church") only scattered notations of the names of certain authors about whom he wished to write and the titles of a few of their works. Thus, I had to write the essay on the historiography of the Russian Church on my own, according to my own plan and understanding. To accomplish this, I used my previously "collected" excerpts from the literature. These were supplemented by the material available in the great riches of the Yale University library.

My present essay states a limited goal. I set forth the historiography of the Russian Orthodox Church and, briefly, the historiography of the Old Belief (the "schism" in older terminology). I do not touch on the boundless quantity of publications of primary sources of Russian Church history, on theological tracts, the broad sphere of ecclesiastical art (architecture, painting, and singing), and the history of Russian sectarianism (Old Believers are not included in the sectarians).

\* \* \*

## METROPOLITAN PLATON

The pioneer in the elaboration of the history of the Russian Orthodox Church was the famous Metropolitan

Platon of Moscow (1737-1812), Petr Georgievich Levshin prior to tonsure. He was born in the village of Charushnik-ovo, some 40 versts from Moscow, to a family of a church servitor (later to be a priest). He studied at the Kolomna seminary, then at the Slavo-Greco-Latin Academy in Moscow. Upon graduating from the academy (1759), he was consecrated a hieromonk [priest monk] and appointed prefect and instructor in Philosophy at the seminary of the Holy Trinity Monastery. In 1766 he was elevated to the rank of archimandrite and was made archbishop of Tver in 1770. In 1775 he became archbishop of Moscow and Metropolitan of Moscow in 1787. During his student years, he was distinguished by his inquisitiveness and diligence. He learned Latin, Greek, and French thoroughly. As a prefect and instructor of the Trinity seminary, he became famous for the eloquence of his sermons which left a deep impression on listeners, among them Empress Catherine II who visited Moscow and appointed him to be Court preacher and religious teacher of Paul, heir to the throne. But his heart remained closer to his native Moscow than to St. Petersburg and the Imperial Court. Having become the archbishop, then the Metropolitan, of Moscow, Platon work-ed for the regulation of church life in the Moscow eparchy and for the raising of the clergy's educational, material, and social level. Regarding this, subsequently he wrote: "I found the clergy in bark shoes and dressed them in boots. From outer rooms led them to the reception rooms of gentlemen."

Platon was against the severe persecutions of the "schismatics" (these were eased during the reign of Catherine II). He strove to find ways of compromise between the ruling Church and the Old Believers. This goal was to be served by *"edinoverie"* — the permission granted to Old Believers to hold their services according to the old (pre-Nikonian) books on the condition that those believing in *"edinoverie"* recognize the Orthodox hierarchy. Platon compiled a set of rules for them. These were confirmed by the Synod in 1801. The first *"edinoverie"* church opened in Moscow in that same year.

From youth, Platon displayed a lively interest in history in general and in the history of the Russian Church in particular. In his notes he wrote of himself that he "attained a knowledge of history by the constant reading of history books, something which he continued throughout his life. . ." During the 1760's and 1770's, Platon wished to introduce Church and civil history into the curriculum of the Trinity seminary. The new subject of instruction took hold slowly and Platon had to issue reminders more than once: "The authorities of the seminary are reminded to be assiduous in seeing to it that the students learn the history of the Church and civil history. For these above all make a person enlightened" (A. P. Lebedev, *Historiography of the Church* [*Tserkovnaia Istoriografiia*], p. 492).

Utilizing his broad erudition, Metropolitan Platon compiled a survey of the history of the Russian Church (to 1700). It was titled *A Short History of the Russian Church* [*Kratkaia Tserkovnaia Rossiiskaia Istoriia*] (in 2 parts). It was published in 1805; a second edition appeared in 1821, a third in 1834. Regarding his work, Platon humbly wrote that he did not consider it to be perfect. Perhaps it was even erroneous in some parts. But at least in the absence of any history of the Russian Church, it would be of some use in the ecclesiastical schools. On this point, archbishop Filaret (Gumilevskii) notes (in his *Survey of Russian Spiritual Literature* [*Obzor Russkoi Dukhovnoi Literatury*]) that "Platon's history was not only useful to the schools but to the whole Russian public as well." Historians observe Platon's literary talent and his striving to write truthfully and impartially without closing his eyes to the dark events in the life of the State and society. Also, his was a critical attitude toward historical sources and ancient legends, particularly regarding the legend of Apostle Andrew's journey to Scythia and his preaching of Christianity on the "Kievan hills" (A. Kartashev, *Essays*, vol. I, pp. 15-16). In addition to his *History*, Metropolitan Platon compiled the *Rolls of the Muscovite and Kievan Metropolitans* [*Spiski Moskovskikh i Kievskikh Mitropolitov*] (to 1804); the *Vita of St. Sergius* [*Zhitie Prepodobnogo Sergiia*]; autobiographical *Notes*; and a *Catechism for the Schools* [*Katekhizis dlia Shkol'nogo Obucheniia*]. In a word, Metropolitan Platon was an outstanding Church administrator, pedagogue, historian, theologian and preacher.[97]

At the beginning of the XIX century, two future hierarchs, Amvrosii, bishop of Penza and Saratov, and Evgenii, Metropolitan of Kiev, worked diligently and fruitfully on the study of the sources of Russian Church history.

## BISHOP AMVROSII

Amvrosii, (d. 1827), who was Andrei Antonovich Ornatskii prior to tonsure, was the son of a deacon in the church of the settlement of Chudi in the Cherepovetskii district of the province of Novgorod. He received his education at the Aleksandr Nevskii Seminary in Petersburg. He became a monk in 1805, was elevated to the rank of archimandrite in 1808 and made abbot of the Antoniev Monastery of Novgorod as well as rector of the Novgorod seminary. In 1816 he was made bishop of Starorussk and, in 1819, bishop of Penza and Saratov. He resigned from the post of bishop in 1825 and withdrew to the Kirillobelozerskii Monastery. There he led the severe life of an anchorite and ascetic and worked on the preparation of the second edition of his fundamental work, *History of the Russian Hierarchy* [*Istoriia Rossiiskoi Ierarkhii*], published in six parts in Moscow, 1807-1815. Amvrosii worked on this enormous study principally while he was rector of the Novgorod seminary, in collaboration with bishop Evgenii of Starorussk (later to be Metropolitan of Kiev). At the basis of this work was the unpublished Latin book on the Russian hierarchy written by the monk Nikodim Sellii (a Dutchman by descent). The latter was Latin teacher at the Aleksandr Nevskii Seminary. Of course, enormous labor was demanded from the Russian compilers regarding the translation of and additions to Sellii's *History*. The *History of the Russian Hierarchy* contains much information not only on the hierarchy in the precise meaning of that word but also on councils, Russian saints, monasteries, and ecclesiastical schools (A. Kartashev, *Essays*, vol. I, pp. 13, 18). In the appraisal of archbishop Filaret of Chernigov, an outstanding Church historian (see below), the multi-volume work of Amvrosii and Evgenii "does not lose its classical significance to this day. In its time, this work was of great importance, dear to the holy Church." (*Survey of Russian Spiritual Literature*, vol. II, 3rd ed., 1884).

## METROPOLITAN EVGENII

Metropolitan Evgenii of Kiev (Evfimii Alekseevich Bolkhovitinov prior to tonsure, 1767-1837) was the son of a priest in the Voronezh province. He was educated at the Voronezh seminary, then at the Moscow Theological Academy. At the same time, he attended lectures at Moscow University. Upon graduating, he returned to Voronezh where he was an instructor at the seminary. He moved to Petersburg in 1800, entered monkhood, and became an instructor at and prefect of the St. Petersburg Spiritual Academy. In 1804 he was made bishop of Starorussk (vicar of the archbishop of Novgorod). From 1808-1822 he held the bishoprics of Vologda, Kaluga, and Pskov respectively. From 1822 to the end of his life in 1837, he was Metropolitan of Kiev.

The monk and hierarch Evgenii displayed a lively and constant interest in Church history and archeology and in the biographies of figures of the Russian Church and of Russian culture in general. He transformed his monastic cell into a scholarly library of books and manuscripts and into the study of a scholar. In studying history and archeology, Evgenii collected and worked on historical and archeological materials in the monasteries and churches of the Novgorod, Pskov, and Kiev eparchies that were so rich in ancient documents. He concerned himself with the preservation of ancient manuscripts and books in monasteries, the organization of monastic archives and libraries, and the preservation of valuable objects of Church archeology. He wrote a multitude of works on Church history, archeology, and bibliography. He was a member of the Academy of Sciences and many learned societies. Let us cite some of his works:

*Historical Dictionary of Writers-Ecclesiastics in Russia* [*Slovar' Istoricheskii o Byvshikh v Rossii Pisateliakh Dukhovnogo Chinu*] (St. Petersburg, 1818); reissued in 1827, 1836, and 1862.

After Metropolitan Evgenii's death, M. P. Pogodin published his *Dictionary of Russian Secular Writers, Compatriots, and Foreigners Writing on Russia* [*Slovar' Russkikh Svetskikh Pisatelei, Sootechestvennikov i Chuzhestrantsev Pisavshikh o Rossii*] (2 vols., Moscow, 1845). The alphabetical index contains the names of 470 authors. And this is not simply a listing. Fairly long articles are devoted to the most important of them: M. V. Lomonosov — 22 pp.; G. R. Derzhavin — 11pp.; V. N. Tatishchev — 13pp.; F. G. Volkov, founder of the Russian theater — 14 pp.

*Discourse or Historical Investigation Into Russian Church Councils* [*Rassuzhdenie ili Istoricheskoe Issledovanie o Soborakh Rossiiskoi Tserkvi*] (SPT, 1808); *History of the Principality of Pskov* [*Istoriia Kniazhestva Pskovskogo*] (Kiev, 1831); *Discussions on the Antiquities of Novgorod the Great* [*Razgovory o Drevnostiakh Velikogo Novgoroda*] (1818); *Description of the St. Sofiia Cathedral in Kiev and the History of the Kievan Hierarchy* [*Opisanie Kievo-Sofiiskogo Sobora i Istoriia Kievskoi Ierarkhii*] (Kiev, 1825); *Description of the Kiev Monastery of the Caves* [*Opisanie Kievo-Pecherskoi Lavry*] (Kiev, 1826).[98]

## METROPOLITAN MAKARII

Two outstanding historians-hierarchs in the field of Russian Church history appear in the middle of the XIX century: Makarii (Bulgakov), Metropolitan of Moscow, and Filaret (Gumilevskii), archbishop of Chernigov. Metropolitan Makarii's twelve volume *History of the Russian Church* (see Professor Vernadsky's description above) was a work as fundamental and unsurpassed in size in the scholarship on Russian Church history as was S.M. Solov'ev's enormous 29 volume *History of Russia From Ancient Times* in the field of secular Russian history. But the scholarly merits and achievements of Archbishop Filaret, Metropolitan Makarii's contemporary, were also great. Makarii's *History* takes the account only through the Moscow Councils of the 1660's. Basically it is a collection of historical materials whereas archbishop Filaret's *History* includes for the first time a survey of the synodal period (to 1826). According to Professor A. V. Kartashev, "we have a true scholarly history of the Russian Church only from the appearance of archbishop Filaret's *History of the Russian Church* [*Istoriia Russkoi Tserkvi*] (*Essays*, I, p. 23).

## ARCHBISHOP FILARET (GUMILEVSKII)

Archbishop Filaret (1805-1866), who prior to tonsure was Dimitrii Grigor'evich Gumilevskii, was the son of a village priest in the Shatskii district of Tambov province. He received his education at the Shatskii ecclesiastical school, the Tambov seminary, and the Moscow Theological Academy. He accepted monkhood in 1830 and, upon completion of the academy's course, remained there as an instructor of Church history and Holy Scriptures. He was appointed academy inspector in 1832 and became rector in 1835. He was made bishop of Riga in 1841, of Khar'kov in 1848, and archbishop of Chernigov in 1859. For his many and important scholarly works, Filaret was elected fellow or honorary member of many ecclesiastical and secular learned societies and organizations; as a specific example, he was an honorary member of the Imperial Academy of Sciences.

Of his works, the most important in terms of Russian historiography was the *History of the Russian Church* [*Istoriia Russkoi Tserkvi*]. Initially, it was published in five separate issues in Riga and Moscow in 1847-1848. It was re-issued frequently later. The 6th edition appeared in one large volume in St. Petersburg in 1895.

Filaret divided Russian Church history into five periods:
1) from the origins of Christianity in Russia to the invasion of the Mongols (988-1237);
2) from the invasion of the Mongols to the division in the Russian metropolitanate (1237-1410);
3) from the division in the metropolitanate to the establishment of the Patriarchy (1410-1588);
4) the patriarchal period (1589-1720);
5) synodal administration (1721-1826).

The end of each issue contained an alphabetical index of persons and subjects — a very useful innovation which, unfortunately, was not generally accepted in Russian scholarly works until the very end of the XIX century.

The account, within the framework of each period, encompasses the spread of Christianity, Church doctrine and service, ecclesiastical administration, and the life of Christian society (including the monastic and the Church Schism). Professor Kartashev notes that in Filaret's *History* there is a "mass of information and minute detail, partly from manuscript sources" (*Essays*, vol. I, p. 24).

An extremely important reference work for Russian Church history is archbishop Filaret's two volume work *Survey of Russian Spiritual Literature* [*Obzor Russkoi Dukhovnoi Literatury*]. It was first published in the *Transactions* of the Academy of Sciences in 1856, then separately in Khar'kov in 1859. The third edition, with the author's corrections and additions, appeared posthumously in St. Petersburg in 1884. Volume I includes spiritual authors from 862-1720; volume II — from 1720 to 1863. Filaret's *Survey* includes a far greater number of authors than does Evgenii's *Dictionary*. By my count, the index to volume I contains 405 names; that for volume II — about 425. The author observes that he not only had to make significant additions to Evgenii's *Dictionary*, but also to make many corrections and classifications. At the same time, he had to shorten the unnecessary details of personal biographies. Besides the purely spiritual authors, archbishop Filaret includes in his *Survey* those secular authors who wrote on religio-ecclesiastical themes like Prince Kurbskii, Speranskii, Nadezhdin, Khomiakov. In the preface to the second edition of book two (1863), Filaret speaks of the contiguity of spiritual and secular literature and observes: "Christianity in itself does not shun anything worldly; it is a sinful world which shuns Christianity."

We will cite several other historical works by archbishop Filaret: *Russian Saints Revered by the Church as a Whole or Locally. An Exercise in the Description of their Lives* [*Russkie Sviatye, Chtimye Vseiu Tserkoviiu ili Mestno. Opyt Opisaniia ikh Zhizni*], in four parts, Chernigov, 1861-1865; 3rd. ed., SPB, 1881; *Lives of the Saints Revered by the Orthodox Church* [*Zhitiia Sviatykh, Chtimykh Pravoslavnoi Tserkvo'iu*] in twelve books, Chernigov, 1861; 3rd ed., SPB, 1900; *A Historico-Statistical Description of the Khar'kov Eparchy* [*Istoriko-Statisticheskoe Opisanie Khar'kovskoi Eparkhii*], in five parts, Moscow and Khar'kov, 1849-1859; *Description of the Chernigov Eparchy* [*Opisanie Chernigovskoi Eparkhii*] in seven parts. In addition, Filaret wrote many articles on Church history in religious and secular journals.[99]

## METROPOLITAN FILARET (DROZDOV)

An outstanding figure in the field of Church administration, religious enlightenment, and Russian spiritual culture in general was Metropolitan Filaret of Moscow (1782-1867). His name prior to entry into monkhood in 1808 was Vasilii Mikhailovich Drozdov. He was the son of a cathedral archpriest of the city of Kolomna in the Moscow province. Upon graduating from the Holy Trinity Seminary, he was appointed instructor of Greek and Hebrew languages there. In 1809 he was transferred to St. Petersburg and appointed rector of the Aleksandr Nevskii Seminary. In 1810 he was transferred to the St. Petersburg Theological Academy to teach theology and Church history. In 1812, (with the rank of archimandrite), he was appointed rector of the academy and worked hard to improve instruction there.

During the second decade of the XIX century, Filaret stood at the head of a complicated and difficult task — the translation of the Holy Scriptures into the Russian language (only the books of the New Testament were completed). His closest collaborator in this work was the learned philologist, archpriest G.P. Pavskii (1783-1863), professor of Hebrew at the academy.

In 1819 Filaret was appointed archbishop of Tver; in 1820 — of Iaroslavl'; in 1821 — of Moscow whose Metropolitan he became in 1826. At this point he showed himself to be an able and energetic administrator and was famed for his eloquence and broadly based charity. His many scholarly works in the field of Theology and Church history gained him honorary membership in theological academies, Moscow University, and a series of learned societies. The *Catechism of the Orthodox Faith* [*Katekhizis Pravoslavnoi Very*] (1st ed., SPB, 1823) and the *Short Catechism* [*Kratkii Katekhizis*] (1824) were re-issued many times and translated into foreign languages. He was the author of the Manifesto of February 19, 1861 regarding the freeing of the peasantry. From 1885-1888, archbishop Savva (Tikhomirov) of Tver published in five volumes the *Collection of the Opinions and Comments of Metropolitan Filaret on Educational and Church-State Problems* [*Sobranie Mnenii i Otzyvov Mitropolita Filareta po Uchebnym i Tserkovno-Gosudarstvennym Voprosam*].[100]

## RESEARCH IN THEOLOGY AND CHURCH HISTORY

During the second half of the XIX and the beginning of the XX century, the literature of theology and Church history in Russia attained a broad development. The principal centers of these studies were four theological academies: those of Moscow, Kiev, St, Petersburg, and (from 1842) Kazan. The academies published their *Transactions*, translations of the Church fathers and the supplements to their work, and substantive articles of a theological and religio-historical character.

Many religious journals appear during this period. They

brought up and discussed problems of Church life and Church history. The two previously existing journals, *Church Herald* [*Tserkovnyi Vestnik*] and *Christian Readings* [*Khristianskoe Chtenie*] are joined by new ones: *Sunday Readings* [*Voskresnoe Chtenie*] (Kiev, 1837-1862); *Orthodox Interlocutor* [*Pravoslavnyi Sobesednik*] (Kazan, 1855-1917); *Orthodox Review* [*Pravoslavnoe Obozrenie*] (Moscow, 1860-1891); *Virtuous Readings* [*Dushepoleznoe Chtenie*] (Moscow, 1860-1916); *Wanderer* [*Strannik*] (SPB, 1860-1916); *Readings in the Moscow Society of Lovers of Spiritual Enlightenment* [*Chteniia v Moskovskom Obshchestve Liubitelei Dukhovnogo Prosveshcheniia*] (Moscow, from 1863); *Orthodox Palestinian Collection* [*Pravoslavnyi Palestinskii Sbornik*] (SPB, 1881-1914); *Faith and Reason* [*Vera i Razum*] (Khar'kov, 1884-1917); *Church Record* [*Tserkovnye Vedomosti*] (SPB, 1888-1917); *Theological Herald* [*Bogoslovskii Vestnik*] (Sergiev Posad, 1892-1917); *Faith and Church* [*Vera i Tserkov*] (Moscow, from 1899). Special missionary journals were: *Fraternal Word* [*Bratskoe Slovo*] (Moscow, 1875-1899); *Orthodox Harbinger* [*Pravoslavnyi Blagovestnik*] (Moscow, from 1893); *Missionary Review* [*Missionerskoe Obozrenie*] (SPB, from 1896). Each eparchy published local "eparchial news" which frequently contained historical articles.

Because of the close connection of the Orthodox Church and its institutions to the political, socio-economic, and cultural life of Russia, many documents relating to the Church were (in the XIX and the beginning of the XX century) published in the major general historical collections of historical information and various documents. Among them were: *Complete Collection of Russian Chronicles, Collection of Government Documents and Treaties, Documents Collected by the Archeographic Expedition of the Academy of Sciences, Historical Acts and Supplements to Historical Acts, Complete Collection of the Laws of the Russian Empire* and other official publications of the "synodal period," *Russian Historical Library, Documents of Ancient Writing, Readings of the Imperial Society of Russian History and*

*Antiquities at Moscow University* and many other publications of the Academy of Sciences and all the universities. In view of that same historical link between Church and State in Russia, many secular historians and journalists began to show interest in Church history in the XIX century. They published many monographs and articles. Some were exceedingly valuable, scholarly, and objective. Others were publicistic and "accusatory." (I do not here speak of the Soviet period which crushed any possibility of scholarly Church history in the USSR).

In studying Russian Church history as a whole, the attention of historians naturally turned particularly to three focal points: the beginning of Christianity in Russia, the Church reform of Patriarch Nikon and the Church Schism in the second half of the XVII century, and the introduction by Peter the Great of the synodal-ministerial type of Church administration.

Existing information in the chronicles regarding the acceptance of Christianity by St. Vladimir appears — after analysis of their texts by scholars at the end of the XIX and the beginning of the XX century — to be unclear, incomplete, and contradictory. This analysis discovered that the text known as the *Primary Kievan Chronicle* (*Tale of By-Gone Years*) is the result of a significant editorial treatment or reworking of the initial chronicles of the XI century. Particularly subject to doubt is the traditional view of Russian Church history that the first Metropolitan of Kiev was Mikhail, a Greek, who was sent from Byzantium at the very time of Russia's Christianization.

At the beginning of the XX century the Petersburg professor M.D. Priselkov in his book, *Essays on the Ecclesiastical-Political History of Kievan Rus' X-XII cc.* (SPB, 1913), after the analysis of "obscure and fragmentary evidence" regarding the christening of Vladimir and Rus' and comparison of the Russian evidence with the Byzantine and Eastern, came to the conclusion that the Orthodox faith and the Church hierarchy came to Rus' not from Byzantium but from Bulgaria. He felt that the first head of the (autonomous) Russian Church was not the Greek Patriarch of Constantinople but the Bulgarian Patriarch of Ochrid. This lasted until 1037 when the chronicles indicate the establishment in Kiev of a Greek metropolitanate with Feopempt [Theopemptus] (p. 42). "The Russian Church was part of the Ochridian patriarchate and the conquest of it by the Greeks (i.e. the conquest of Bulgaria by Byzantium) led us into the fold of the empire of the New Rome" (p. 44). Actually, the author himself refers to his theory as a "supposition" ("if our supposition is correct...," p. 42) or a "conjecture" ("but this conjecture is valid" p. 34).

Priselkov's "Bulgarian theory" naturally led to many differences and disagreements in ecclesiastical-historical literature.

The most recent historian of the Russian Church, Professor A.V. Kartashev (in his *Essays on the History of the Russian Church*) accepts Priselkov's theory approvingly (though he does call it a "nimble *hypothesis*"). He writes: "The honor of the scholarly unraveling of the obscure knot of contradictions of the evidence and the omissions of the official chronicle regarding the initial hierarchical organization of the Russian Church belongs to M.D. Priselkov." His "nimble hypothesis, after the lengthy opposition by some Russian scholars, has gained its citizenship" (*Essays*, I, 160). The establishment of a Greek metropolitanate in Kiev in 1037 was a "whole canonical upheaval" which led to the inclusion of the Russian Church under the jurisdiction of the Patriarch of Constantinople and to the subsequent reworking of the chronicles and literature on the origins of the Russian Church (*Essays*, I, 165-167).

The patriarch of Russian historiography in the U.S.A., the late Professor G.V. Vernadsky, after some hesitation, came to different conclusions concerning Priselkov's theory. I cite from his book *Kievan Russia* (p. 67):

In 1913 the late M.D. Priselkov suggested that Vladimir, unable to come to terms with Byzantine authorities, addressed himself to Bulgaria and placed the Russian church under the authority of the archbishop of Ochrida. The theory seems at first glance very ingenious, and for a number of years I was prepared to accept this view. However, after giving more attention to the problem, I have been obliged to reject it. Priselkov was not, in fact, able to produce any direct evidence for his Bulgarian theory. There is no mention of the dependence of the Russian church on the archbishop of Ochrida in any of the sources, either Russian or Bulgarian.

Evidently, some questions on the history of the birth of the Russian Church will have to remain questions in view of the incompleteness, the vagueness, and the contradictions of the primary sources.

## NIKOLAI FEDOROVICH KAPTEREV

A distinguished Church historian at the turn of the century was Nikolai Fedorovich Kapterev (1847-1917), doctor of Church history and honored professor at the Moscow Theological Academy. Kapterev was the son of a village priest in the Podol'sk district of Moscow province. Upon graduating from the ecclesiastical school and the seminary, he enrolled in the Moscow Theological Academy in 1868. Upon graduating from it in 1872, he was retained at the Academy with the rank of *privat-docent* at the chair of civil history. He received his master's in divinity in 1874 and the degree of doctor of Church history in 1891. He was made extraordinary professor in 1883, ordinary in 1896, and received the title of honored ordinary professor in 1898.

Let us first look at his lengthy monograph, *The Nature of Russian Relations with the Orthodox East in the XVI and XVII Centuries* [*Kharakter Otnoshenii Rossii k Pravoslavnomu Vostoku v XVI i XVII Stoletiiakh*] (first published in 1884; 2nd ed. 1914; re-issued by Mouton Publishers in 1968). This book was written on the basis of a lengthy study of a multitude of unpublished primary sources — manuscripts from the Turkish and Greek affairs of the former *"Posol'skii Prikaz"* [bureau of foreign affairs]. These were preserved in the Moscow archives of the Ministry of Foreign Affairs. Professor Kapterev's book clearly and in detail describes that religious self-conciousness and attitude of Moscow's ecclesiastical society in the XVI-XVII centuries which served as the subsoil for the subsequent Church schism. Already in the XV century the authority of the Greek Church and Greeks in general fell considerably in the eyes of Muscovite society. This was influenced by two historical events: the Florentine Union (1439) with "Latinism" (after the Greeks had for centuries incited Russians against the impious Latin "heretics"), and the conquest of Constantinople by the Turks (1453) in which devout Muscovites saw God's punishment for the Greeks' defection from Orthodoxy. As the XV century turned into the XVI, a proud theory arose in Moscow: Moscow, the "Third Rome," becomes the sole keeper of the Orthodox faith ("the New Israel," "Holy Russia"), and the Muscovite sovereign, as the sole Orthodox ruler in the world, becomes the defender and protector of ecumenical Orthodoxy.

Muscovy's relations with the Orthodox East continue in the XVI-XVII centuries but the nature of these relations and the roles of both sides alter significantly. Many Greek ecclesiastical figures — hierarchs and monks — came to Moscow. But they arrive not as teachers or instructors in the spiritual life but as suppliants for the "sovereign's charity." The Muscovite government endowed them generously with sable fur (because of the lack of metal money in the State treasury). Now Muscovite people saw themselves, not the Greeks, as the preservers of true piety. They were convinced that it was preserved in the Church services and rituals which they inherited from their fathers and grandfathers.

In this period the religious relations between Russians and Greeks contained another very important element. The Greek hierarchs and monks who came from the East brought, as presents for Muscovy's sovereign, many various holy relics. These ranged from the relics, or parts of the relics, of saints venerated by the Eastern Church to a multitude of various items of religious veneration (including "three buttons from the chasuble of Mary," p. 99). They presented these sacred objects to the Tsar. The Tsar, in each case, gave them as many sable "as were dictated to the sovereign by God," i.e. as many as he wished (and, of course, according to the evaluation and advice of experts). Formally these were exchanges of gifts. But, in essence, this constituted sale by the Greeks of religious sacred objects which were dear to every Orthodox. This meant that the Orthodox East was being denuded of religious objects venerated from time immemorial whereas the State of Muscovy, more precisely its churches, were being filled with them. In the eyes of Muscovites, this elevated the concept of "Holy Russia" still more and dropped still further the authority of the Greeks, who for the "fur of a sable" were willing to remove their sacred objects to a foreign country.

Correspondingly, among the Greeks who did arrive, there were sometimes various adventurers, imposters and fakes; for example, former hierarchs stripped of their rank, or merchants, under the guise of monks, who came for commercial operations.

At a time when Russian Church society was convinced of its superiority over the Greeks, the "Grecophile" Nikon ascended the patriarchal throne in 1652 and began to "change ancient Russian religious practice to the contemporary Greek mold." He "corrected" the Church service books according to the Greek models and altered some Church customs and external aspects of Church observances (p. 444). Naturally, "Nikon's Church reform was slated to bring a deathly blow to the historically formed Russian view of their religious superiority over all other peoples, particularly the Greeks" (p. 445). It "led to a strong protest by the adherents of and believers in the ancient Russian Church traditions" (p. 446).

Kapterev's book, *Patriarch Nikon and His Opponents in the Matter of Reforming Church Rituals. Issue I. The Peri-*

od of Iosif's Patriarchy (to 1652) [*Patriarkh Nikon i ego Pro-
tivniki v Dele Ispravleniia Tserkovnykh Obriadov. Vyp. I.
Vremia Patriarshestva Iosifa*] appeared in 1887. In this work
the author describes the function of the "correctors" of
Church service books in the pre-Nikon period. But at this
point I would like to mention one fact which played such a
tragic role in Russian history, namely the question of the
two-fingered or the three-fingered method of making the sign
of the cross. The Church Council of 1666-1667, which condemned the "schismatics," decided that the Stoglav Council
(1551), which was headed by Metropolitan Makarii, and
which approved the two-fingered method and the double
halleluja, did so "through its simplicity and ignorance." In
reality, the ancient Russian Church took these customs from
the Greek Church which switched to the three-fingered
method only in the XV century (p. 24). In the thousand year
history of the Christian Church the method of making the
sign of the cross changed more than once: ". . . in the Christian Church the means of making the sign of the cross was
very different at different times; the sign of the cross was
made with one, two, and three fingers" (p. 87). Professor
Kapterev feels that no form of making the sign of the cross
can be viewed as the only Orthodox form and be attributed
a dogmatic significance (pp. 89-90).

In this respect, both sides, in bowing to ritual, sinned
against the spirit of Christianity. The two-fingered method
could not be considered sacred dogma for adherence to
which one was to undergo torture and death. Similarly,
those who crossed themselves in this fashion could not be
termed evil heretics and subjected to cruel repression.

Kapterev's lengthiest monograph was his two volume
study, *Patriarch Nikon and Tsar Aleksei Mikhailovich* [*Patriarkh Nikon i Tsar' Aleksei Mikhailovich*] (Sergiev Posad,
vol. I-II, 1909-1912). This work is not only a personal history of the famous patriarch but also a general survey of
Church-State relations in Muscovite Russia (which appears
in volume II). In both the pre-Muscovite and the Muscovite
periods there was a close union of Church and State. But the

decisive word in both ecclesiastical and secular affairs belonged to the sovereign, particularly after the Moscow metropolitans began (from the middle of the XV century) to be appointed independently of the patriarch of Constantinople. The power of the Muscovite sovereign over the Church in no way diminished when, after 1589, there was a patriarch rather than a metropolitan at the head of the Church. The patriarchs, like the metropolitans, were "appointees and protégés of the sovereign and gave no thought to independence from secular rule" (p. 61). Only Patriarch Filaret, as the father of a weak Tsar, occupied a special place. Sovereigns interfered in purely ecclesiastical affairs, chose bishops, and summoned Church councils. "Our Muscovite Church councils of the XVI and XVII centuries were merely simple advisory panels before the sovereign's person. They were only organs of the Tsar's rules regarding Church matters. For us, the sole source of any law, be it ecclesiastical or civil, was the Tsar" (p. 104). "Our sovereigns always fully held Church rule completely at their disposal" (p. 120).

Nikon, who ascended to the patriarchy in 1652 at the wish of Tsar Aleksei, and who was simultaneously the Tsar's friend, had completely different ideas regarding the relationships of spiritual and lay rule. Theoretically, he accepted the medieval idea of "two luminaries," i.e. the conviction that the hierarch's rule superseded kingly rule as much as the sun's light exceeded that of the moon. For the hierarch's rule derived directly from God whereas the Tsar accepted anointment and coronation from the hierarch as the moon "takes light from the sun." The hierarchal role is that of rule "over souls whereas kingly rule is rule over the things of this earth" (p. 129).

In practical politics, of course, Nikon could not proclaim the primacy of his rule over the Tsar's. But he strove to establish the co-operation of the "wise dyad" — the two supreme rulers appointed by God — "great sovereign Tsar" and "great sovereign Patriarch." It is precisely this that Kapterev views as Nikon's primary goal, not reform of ritual. "The goal was to free the Church, in the person of the Patriarch, from its overwhelming and total subjection to the State, to make the Patriarch, as the spiritual head of the Church, not only independent of the sovereign but place him equal to the Tsar as another great sovereign, and to place under his control, as the defender and protector of the eternal and immovable divine laws, not only the life of the Church, but of the State and society as well" (Introduction, p. v).

In addition to the above-cited monographs, Kapterev wrote: *Lay Hierarchical Officials in Ancient Russia [Svetskie Arkhiereiskie Chinovniki v Drevnei Rusi]* (Moscow, 1874); *Relations of Dosifei, Patriarch of Jerusalem, With the Russian State 1669-1707 [Snosheniia Ierusalimskogo Patriarkha Dosifeia s Russkim Pravitel'stvom v 1669-1707 gg.]* (Moscow, 1891); and two other studies of the relations of the Jerusalem patriarchs with Russia in the XVI-XIX centuries. These appeared in the *Journal of the Imperial Palestinian Society*, vol. XV, SPB, 1895. Besides these monographs, Kapterev wrote many historical articles in various periodicals (see listing thereof in the *Orthodox Theological Encyclopedia*, vol. VIII, pp. 558-559).

## M. V. ZYZYKIN

After the War and the Revolution, the personality, work, and ideas of Patriarch Nikon attracted the sympathetic attention of Warsaw professor M. V. Zyzykin (1880-1960). He wrote a three volume work titled *Patriarch Nikon. His Governmental and Canonical Ideas [Patriarkh Nikon. Ego Gosudarstvennye i Kanonicheskie Idei]* (Warsaw, Synodal Typography, vol. I-II, 1931, vol. III, 1938). At the beginning the author provides a survey of the previous historical literature on Nikon. Then he presents his own understanding and evaluation of his ideas and aims. Instead of a re-telling, we provide some citations from volume I. "Nikon drew the reminder that the local Church cannot be an independent Church, that it was merely a part of the one Ecumenical Church, that the parts of this Church were to be in contact and in agreement" (p. 9). "He was creating an enlightened Orthodox culture and was learning it from the Greeks as the sons of the Mother Church" (p.18). In terms of Church and State, Nikon "was preserving the Church from its impending absorption by the State"; "in defending the rights of the Church, he was not striving to give it political power" (p. 10). He defended the idea of symphony or union of Church and State with the complete and independent power of each in its own sphere. "At the same time he set the religio-moral duty of political power to be penetrated by religious principles." (p. 12).

Nikon "provided a theory of the Orthodox tsardom" and rejected the doctrine of unlimited royal rule." His Tsar is not dressed in a military uniform, but rather in the dress of a Muscovite Tsar with a cross on his chest" (p. 13). "The Tsar cannot be father of the Church but (must be) its son" (p. 280). "The theory of symphony, in recognizing the primacy of the Church over the State, indicates the State's goal in which, in serving completely voluntarily, the State finds its meaning and purpose" (p. 283). "The State itself subordinates its activity to the higher religious interest and authority of the Church. The Church does not interfere in State affairs based on its right. Here the subordination is of a purely moral character" (p. 297). Both sides must mutually respect each other. There is no striving for secular primacy in the Orthodox Church. In an Orthodox State the Church is called upon to influence and regenerate the State, not to run the State" (p. 306).

In accordance with his views on Church-State relations, Professor Zyzykin treats Peter the Great's Church reform in a sharply negative manner. "Tsar Peter de-churchifies the State. Both literally and figuratively, he removes the ecclesiastical vestments from the Tsar" (p. 21). His goal is the glory of the fatherland "in a purely pagan sense." The imperial period, in terms of Church-State relations, is the "rebirth of paganism" when the "all-powerful autocrat," the Emperor, occupies a position of *Pontifex maximus* in relation to the State" (p. 24). "Peter destroyed the concept of the Church as a special organism which has its own laws, administration, and justice" and "undermined the vital activity of the Church" (p. 21). "The enthralment of the Church was led to its apogee by Peter I. The Revolution was the atonement for two centuries of this enslavement and self-willed power" (p. 26).

## P. V. VERKHOVSKOI

P.V. Verkhovskoi devoted a broad and richly documented study to Peter the Great's Church reform. He was a Warsaw professor and the study was titled *The Establishment of the Ecclesiastical College and the Spiritual Reglament. On the Question of the Relationship of Church and State in Russia* [*Uchrezhdenie Dukhovnoi Kollegii i Dukhovnoi Reglament. K Voprosu ob Otnoshenii Tserkvi i Gosudarstva v Rossii*] (vol. I, Investigation, vol. II, Materials; Rostov on the Don, 1916).

In the preface to volume I there is a thorough survey of the sources and literature on the problem. Here, as well, the author provides a general evaluation of Peter's Church reform. Having effected the complete secularization of the Russian State, Peter subordinated the Orthodox Church to the State. The "Ecclesiastical College is a State establishment which totally changed the position of the Church in the Russian State," for "in the relations of the Moscow Tsars to the State, one cannot perceive their juridical ascendancy over it."[101]

In his conclusion, the author states: "Peter deprived the Russian Church of its distinctive and independent existence as a definite juridical insitution." "There was not, and could never be . . . " the juridical subordination of the Church to the State prior to him; ". . . factually, there was only a collaboration in the attainment of mutual goals" (p. 684). On page 685 the author formulates the summation of his study in this way: ". . . 6) The decisive event of Peter's Church reform was the establishment of the Ecclesiastical

College; 7) The Ecclesiastical College, as it was conceived by Peter and Feofan, is nothing other than a General Church Consistory of the Germano-Swedish type. The Spiritual Reglament is a free copy of Protestant Church charters (*Kirchenordnungen*). The Ecclesiastical College is a State institution, the creation of which completely changed the juridical position of the Church in the Russian State"; 9) Doubtlessly, Peter's Church reform significantly aided in regulating the heavily neglected Church affairs and the introduction of cultural bases into the rather rough forms of Church life of the Muscovite era. But at the same time, the reform made the Church a *servant of the State* and thereby reflected very disastrously on its external structure and its internal being. First, the Russian Church ceased to exist as a juridically independent institution. It was replaced by an "Administration of the Orthodox Faith" at the head of which was a *State college* [kollegium] called the Holy Synod. It was controlled by the Chief Procurator [*Ober Prokuror*] who, from the beginning of the XIX century, gradually became the minister of the "Administration of the Orthodox Faith." (p. 685).

The position of the clergy in the State also changed. The title of chapter XIII, which formulates its contents, reads: "The Affixation of the Clergy to Government Service and the Adaptation of Church Doctrine to the Life and Demands of State Problems" (p. 606).

The clergy "was, when possible, drawn into State service and, within it, constituted a semi-privileged service class" (p. 621).

Besides his monumental monograph on the establishment of the Ecclesiastical College, Professor Verkhovskoi published a book titled *Essays on the History of the Russian Church in the XVIII and XIX cc. [Ocherki po Istorii Russkoi Tserkvi XVIII i XIX st.]*, issue I (Warsaw, 1912). In its evaluation of the Petrine reform and the subsequent state of the Russian Church this book expresses the very same pessimism that appeared in the monograph following it. During the synodal period "external regulation of Church affairs" was achieved. But it was accompanied by a "decline in faith and piety and the clergy's loss of authority" (p. 2). Crushed by the weight of the "police State," "the Synod was deprived of creative canonical activity in the stabilization of Church life" (p. 117). It could not support the religious animation of Church people, a significant segment of which turned to the Old Belief and sectarianism for the gratification of its religious needs.

Actually, Professor Verkhovskoi recognizes that "the Russian Church, though paralyzed from the outside, is alive in its inner spiritual life." But for its renascence "religious consciousness, at present, insistently demands the re-establishment of its juridical freedom" in order to eliminate the consequences of "the disaster which occurred 200 years ago" (p. 87).[102]

## P. N. MILIUKOV

P. N. Miliukov's three volume *Outlines of Russian Culture* came out in its first edition in 1896 and was re-issued many times thereafter. Part two is titled *Church and School* (Faith, Creativity, Education) [*Tserkov' i Shkola* (Vera, Tvorchestvo, Obrazovanie)]. As a left liberal politically and a positivist in his world view, Miliukov, naturally, could not be sympathetic to the Russian "official" Church. But his book contains much factual material and statistical data on the state of the Church, the clergy, and the ecclesiastical schools. The social state of the Church and its role in the State is defined by Miliukov by the fact that (after the Schism) "the Russian Church gave itself fully into the hands of the State power" (p. 155 in the 3rd ed. 1902). The clergy was forming a closed State class and the religious strivings of the faithful found satisfaction in the Old Belief and sectarianism. Miliukov devotes four chapters of volume two of the *Outlines* to the history of these.

In the conclusion to volume two, Miliukov observes that "Russian religion" did not motivate thoughts toward activity (as did "British religion") and did not persecute it by means of inquisitional tribunals (as did "French religion"). That is why the attitude of the Russian intellectual toward religion was what history had made it to be — one of indifference (p.402).[103a]

## P. N. ZNAMENSKII

Turning to the works of the "official" historians of the Russian Church, i.e. to the surveys and "manuals" compiled by professors of Church history at the theological academies which were geared for purposes of teaching this history in the schools, I must note to begin with that I have neither the inclination nor the possibility within the framework of this essay to provide any type of complete survey of this historico-pedagogical literature. I will speak only of the works of its two most prominent representatives at the turn of this century, professors P. N. Znamenskii and A. P. Dobroklonskii.

It should be observed at the start that during this period the works of "official" Church historians were completely devoid of that spirit of servility to the government (eulogizing or vilifying in compliance with its directives) which became mandatory for all historians in the totalitarian states of the XX century.

Petr Vasil'evich Znamenskii (1836-1917) was an honored ordinary professor of the Kazan Theological Academy, an associate member of the Academy of Sciences, doctor of Russian history at Moscow University, and an honorary member of the Kazan and St. Petersburg theological academies. He was born in Nizhnii Novgorod to the family of a deacon. He received his education at the Nizhegorod seminary, then at the Kazan Theological Academy. Upon graduating from the latter, he became (from 1862 on) the instructor in Russian Church history there. He remained in this position for more than 30 years.

His *Guide to Russian Church History* [*Rukovodstvo k Russkoi Tserkovnoi Istorii*] appeared in Kazan in 1871. It was re-issued in 1876, 1880, 1886, and 1888. Later it was reworked into the *Educational Guide to the History of the*

*Russian Church* [*Uchebnoe Rukovodstvo po Istorii Russkoi Tserkvi*]. The second corrected and expanded edition appeared in St. Petersburg in 1904. Znamenskii's book was broadly disseminated. According to the article in the *Orthodox Theological Encyclopedia*, "Znamenskii is the spiritual teacher of all Russia's youth."

In the introduction to his *Guide* (the 1904 ed.), Znamenskii defines the content of the field of Russian Church history. It must describe: 1) how the Church grew among Russians and foreigners; 2) the internal hierarchical structure of the Church and its relationship to the State and to the people; 3) what and how did the Church teach the people; 4) features of service and rituals; 5) success, i.e. the degree of success of Christian moral life among the people (pp. 7-8).

The account of each period of Church history is organized according to these five rubrics. In the history of the original religious education of the Russian nation, the author stresses the dominant role of Bulgaria from which "came to us the first Christian teachers, books, and Slavonic writing itself" (p. 39). The author observes the close link of the Church hierarchy with secular rule both in the ancient and in the Muscovite periods. Supporting E. E. Golubinskii's pessimistic view of ancient Russian Orthodoxy, Znamenskii observes the preponderance in ancient piety of the "ritualistic trend" and "a weak knowledge of Orthodoxy's spirit" (p. 54). "Ritualistic piety could not aid much in the development of moral life. The general impression derived from studying the customs of the period described (XIII-XVcc.) is a very sad one" (p. 108). As to Muscovite Russia in the XVI-XVII cc. : "an Asiatic crudity of manners was to be found in society beneath external piety"as well as a weak development of "sincere religious feeling" (p. 154). The only bright spots were individual religious ascetics of whom the author speaks.

Regarding Church-State relations, the author ascertains that the Russian hierarchy, having become independent of foreign Church rule (i.e. of the patriarch of Constantinople), "had to find itself in greater subordination to local governmental rule" (p. 132).

In speaking of the Church Schism of the XVII century, the author — teacher of future Orthodox priests — was, naturally, negative in viewing the "schismatics" (pp. 294-295). But at the same time he recognizes that Patriarch Nikon handled the matter of Church reforms "too abruptly" and "aroused much personal animosity against himself" (p. 292).

In the history of the synodal period the author speaks of the broad development in the XIX century of missionary activity, theological studies, and spiritual enlightenment. But he views negatively the mystical movement popular in the first quarter of the XIX century. It "was engraved with the stamp of sanctimony and hypocrisy" (p. 431).

The last pages of the book are devoted to a survey of the history of monasteries wherein tens of thousands of lay people found "spiritual healing for their sorrows and illnesses" (p. 482).

Professor Kartashev, in his survey of previous historiography, highly evaluates Professor Znamenskii's work (in his *Essays*, vol. I, pp. 30-31). "Professor Znamenskii's 'Guide' must doubtlessly be considered among the independent Church history systems. This is true for its plan, the selection of facts, and the artistry of structure. True, the author presents the history dogmatically, without citations and scholarly criticism. But throughout his account one uncovers a solid knowledge of primary sources from which many valuable facts are extracted independently, facts which are furnished with very significant and accurate characteristics and which shed light on the nature of whole eras . . . His *Guide* is the best 'book for reading' on this subject that we have. Among the distinguished virtues of the *Guide's* contents is also the fact that it devotes less space even than it was formely the custom to a description of external affairs. With great detail and attention it depicts the internal life of the Church and the religio-moral attitude of Russian society."

In addition to the *Guide*, Professor Znamenskii wrote

many works on the history of various aspects of the life of the Russian Orthodox Church. Among these are: *Parish Clergy in Russia from the Period of the Petrine Reforms* [*Prikhodskoe Dukhovenstvo v Rossii so Vremeni Reform Petra*] (Kazan, 1873; 850 pp.). The book draws a dismal picture of the material, legal, and social condition of the parish clergy, "far from spoiled by concern or solicitude for its welfare," as the author notes at the end of his book: *History of the Kazan Theological Academy in the First (pre-reform) Period of Its Existence (1842-1870)* [*Istoriia Kazanskoi Dukhovnoi Akademii za Pervoi (doreformennyi) Period ee Sushchestvovaniia (1842-1870)*] (Kazan, vol. I-III, 1891-1892); *Ecclesiastical Schools in Russia Prior to the Reform of 1808* [*Dukhovnye Shkoly v Rossii do Reformy 1808*] (Kazan, 1881). To Professor Znamenskii's pen also belong many articles on the History of the Orthodox Church. They were published in the *Orthodox Interlocutor* and other ecclesiastical and secular journals. (A list is available in the *Orthodox Theological Encyclopedia*, vol. V, pp. 722-724).

## A. P. DOBROKLONSKII

The other outstanding expert on the history of the Russian (and ancient Christian) Church, and teacher of Russia's clerical youth, was Professor Aleksandr Pavlovich Dobroklonskii (1856-1937). He was the son of an archpriest in the Pavlovsk settlement in the Moscow province. He was graduated from Moscow Theological Academy in 1880. From 1881-1899 he was instructor of Russian civil and Church history at the Riazan, then the Moscow seminary. From 1899 he was extraordinary professor at Novorossiisk University, holding the chair of Church history. In emigration he continued his scholarly and pedagogical work as a professor at the University of Belgrade.

His significant scholarly-pedagogical service was his *Guide to the History of the Russian Church* [*Rukovodstvo po Istorii Russkoi Tserkvi*] in 4 volumes which appeared in Riazan and Moscow between 1884-1893. I did not find this volume in the Yale University library catalogue. Hence, I must limit myself to the comments of Professor A.V. Kartashev, an expert on Russian ecclesiastical-historical literature, who values Professor Dobroklonskii's *Guide* highly. It is "truly the most useful" guide for students and teachers, for theologians and lay readers, "not only because of the orderly system by means of which the materials of the discipline are presented at the subject's contemporary level, but also as the single source book of its type which serves as an introduction to the literature on the subject. The enrichment of the subject with new data in the *Guide*'s narrative increases with time. The final (4th) volume of the *Guide* is an even more original creation which contains an abundance of citations from primary sources... To this day, this volume remains the most complete summary that we have of historical information on the synodal period as a whole. After Professor Dobroklonskii, no one has yet been inspired to write a new general history of the Russian Church" (*Essays*, vol. I, p. 36). In this respect, there has been a 70 year hiatus. (Currently, this gap has been filled by Kartashev's *Essays*, see below).

## SCHOLARSHIP IN EMIGRATION

Over a short period of time after the Bolshevik Revolution, theological and ecclesiastical-historical scholarship was destroyed in the Soviet Union. But it was preserved, and continued its creative life in the "true diaspora" of émigré Russia. Some of the former professors of the theological academies became university professors in Orthodox countries (N. N. Glubokovskii in Sofiia, A. P. Dobroklonskii in Belgrade). Other religious and religio-philosophical writers and scholars, both clerical and lay, formed groups and worked in several newly organized centers of Russian spiritual culture abroad. Such centers were "Russian" Harbin in the Far East, and, in Europe, Belgrade, Sofiia, Prague, Berlin, and Paris. In Czechoslovakia, aside from Russian scholars and educational organizations in Prague, a spiritual enlighten-

407     *Russian Historiography: A History*

ment center was established in Ladomirov (or Vladimirov). In Slovakia, archbishop Vitalii (the former head of Orthodox ecclesiastical publishing at the Pochaevskaia Lavra) established a typography and created a publishing house for spiritual-educational literature.

Paris became the major center of Russian theological and Church historical scholarship and Orthodox enlightenment in Europe. Here the St. Sergius "household" was established and in it the Russian Theological Institute (transferred from Berlin in 1925). It was also called the Spiritual Academy. The center of the Russian Students Christian Movement was here; it published its periodical *Vestnik R.S.Kh. D.* [*Herald of the Russian Students' Christian Movement*]. Russian organizations worked in close contact with the "Union of Christian Youth" and the publishers of this Union (transliterated *IMKA* (or YMCA) in Russian) published many Russian books of spiritual and secular content.

Two centers of Russian spiritual (Orthodox) culture were established in the U.S.A. — in New York and in Jordanville. In New York there is the Russian Orthodox Theological Fund and a school for advanced theological education. This is the St. Vladimir's Seminary which publishes its own *Quarterly* and which has attracted into its ranks of instructors a number of prominent lay and ecclesiastical scholars.

The Holy Trinity Monastery in Jordanville (New York) has become another center of Russian Orthodox culture in the U.S.A. It is the spiritual center of the "synodal" or the Russian Church "in exile." It has its own seminary and its publishing house which not only publishes new works but also reprints pre-revolutionary works of spiritual content.

Prior to commencing a survey of works in Church history by émigré authors, I must express a deep gratitude to Professor N.M. Zernov for his new work, *Russian Émigré Writers* [*Russkie Pisateli Emigratsii*].103 This work helped me significantly in organizing this section of my historico-bibliographic survey. Professor Zernov's book contains biographical and bibliographical data about clerical and lay authors not only in the field of Orthodox Church culture but also in other areas of Russian spiritual culture. By my count, the alphabetical index of authors contains 304 names. It is difficult to imagine how much effort and time was needed in order to gather 50 years worth of biographical and bibliographical data on some 300 Russian émigré authors, living and dead, scattered all over the globe. I have taken the majority of my biographic information on émigré authors from Zernov's book.

In my essay on émigré literature on Church history, I limit the survey to the history of the Russian Church prior to 1917. I do not touch on the Church Council of 1917-1918, the history of the Church in the Soviet Union, and the Russian Church abroad.

## A. V. KARTASHEV

For our theme — the historiography of the Russian Church — the most important work was Professor Kartashev's *Essays on the History of the Russian Church*, vol. I-II ("IMKA", Paris, 1959). Anton Vladimirovich Kartashev (1875-1960) was originally from the Urals. He was graduated from the Perm seminary, then from the St. Petersburg Theological Academy (in 1899). Initially he taught Church history at the academy, then at the Advanced Courses for Women. He was the chairman of the Religio-Philosophical Society in St. Petersburg. After the February Revolution, he was (the last) Ober-Procurator of the Holy Synod, then — Minister of Faiths in the Provisional Government. He left Russia in 1919 and was professor at the Theological Institute in Paris from 1925 to the end of his life.

The first volume of Kartashev's *Essays* encompasses the period from the beginnings of Christianity in Rus' to the establishment of the Patriarchate in 1589. Volume two includes the history of the patriarchal and synodal periods (to 1801). In the introduction (pp. 1-39) the author presents the reader with a historiographic survey of the literature on the history of the Russian Church.

In the chapter "The Pre-Governmental Era," the author ascertains that "a deep darkness hides from us the origins of the historical life of the Russian nation and with it the origin of its introduction to the Christian religion" (p. 52). He supposes that the "first baptism of Kievan Russes [Russians] occurred back in the period of the Byzantine patriarch Photius about 860. Regarding the baptism of the Kievans under St. Vladimir, he accepts M. D. Priselkov's hypothesis that the initial Church hierarchy and the origins of Christian enlightenment came to Rus' not from Byzantium but from Bulgaria (see above).

Speaking of the Muscovite period, the author indicates the complete dependence of the upper Church hierarchy on government power. Furthermore, the patriarchal title for the head of the Russian Church (from 1589) "added not a drop of power to the head of the Russian Church and did not diminish by a drop its complete dependence on the State" (p. 380).

The last section of volume one, "The South-West Metropolitanate, from the Division of the Russian Church (in the mid XV century) to the Union of Brest in 1569" (pp. 531-681), describes in detail the cheerless situation of the Orthodox Church in the Polish-Lithuanian State. Depicted is the ugly and burdensome "right of patronage" of Catholic sovereigns and lords over Orthodox churches and monasteries and the preparation and execution by the Western Russian episcopate of Brest's church union contrary to all protests by Orthodox laymen and clergy.

Kartashev's second volume of *Essays* describes the history of the patriarchal and synodal periods (the account is taken to 1801).

In describing the history of the patriarchy's establishment in Russia (pp. 10-46), the author indicates that the initiative for the realization of this major reform of the Russian Church's central administration (in 1589) was the work of the secular government which strove to elevate the prestige of the State of Muscovy both in the eyes of Muscovites and in foreign relations, particularly among the

Orthodox nations of the Near East. The hierarchs of the Russian Church did not, of course, object to a reform whose goal was to elevate its prestige. But they played no active role in this process. The official document cited by the author proclaims: "and the holy council, in speaking of and discussing this whole matter, willed it that the pious sovereign and Tsar and the Grand Duke Fedor Ivanovich of all Russia do as he desires" (p. 27). The real head of government at this time, under the weak Tsar Fedor Ivanovich, was the Tsar's all powerful brother-in-law, the boyar Boris Fedorovich Godunov. He conducted the negotiations regarding the establishment of the patriarchate in Moscow with Patriarch Jeremiah of Constantinople who had come to Moscow. He also "installed" his close friend, Metropolitan Iov [Job] of Moscow, on the patriarchal throne. Kartashev notes: "The Russian patriarchy is the child of royal will" (p. 33); and, during the "ordination" of a new patriarch, the Tsar invested him with the pastor's staff (the crozier).

Patriarch Nikon, with his ideas of the supremacy of the "priesthood" over "kingdom," attempted to realize the Church's independence from the State and, in the person of the patriarch, to create a second "great sovereign." But his attempt suffered defeat.

Kartashev's history of the patriarchal period, like all courses in Russian Church history, includes the sad story of the beginning of the Church Schism, of the persecution of the "schismatics," and of their self-immolation.

I would like to view in some detail Kartashev's description and evaluation of the history of the synodal period on the principle *audiatur et altera pars*. For Kartashev's positive judgement of the Petrine Church reform and the whole synodal period diverges from the opinion of the majority of the "non-official" historians of the Russian Church. Professor P. V. Verkhovskoi directly labels the Petrine reform as a "misfortune which overtook the Russian Church." The author of this essay also is not an "adherent" of it.[104]

In the section, "Basic Character and Evaluation of the Synodal Period" (pp. 313-320), the author first of all observes that Peter's Church and cultural reforms were totally "within the spirit of the time." In the European nations there was occurring "a breaking away from the decayed form of medieval theocracy" and an all around *secularization* of government and spiritual culture. Ideas of "natural law," intertwining with Protestant notions, did not allow for the existence of the Church as a special organization independent of the State. Religion and the Church had to subordinate themselves to government rule which took upon itself the overall concern for the material and spiritual well being of its citizens (or for the "national good" in the words of Peter's decrees).

Peter's striving to secularize Russian life and culture could not, of course, meet with sympathy from the Muscovite (great Russian) priesthood headed by the conservative patriarchs Ioakim [Joachim] (1673-1690), and Adrian (1690-1700). In their eyes, the mere shaving of beards constituted a powerful sin against the Orthodox Church and Muscovite tradition. On the other hand, writes Kartashev, the bloody *streltsy* rebellion of 1682 left a lifetime mark on Peter which was a "deep spiritual revulsion to the savage image of the wild, obscure, ignorant and in no way Christian, ancient Muscovite fanaticism" (p. 323). Under such conditions, "it was impossible to harmonize the views of Peter and Patriarch Adrian theoretically or practically . . . Accord (i.e. agreement) was mathematically excluded. The new idea of (an all-powerful) State did not tolerate dualism. . . Religion and Church could only be subordinate to it" (p. 327).

Kartashev recognizes that Peter's Church reform was of a "radical" and revolutionary character. But, in contrast to the majority of historians and publicists, he asserts that it did not paralyze but "stimulated" the Church's creative powers. "Peter the Great's revolutionary reform, which was sharp to the point of pain, was beneficial suffering for the Russian Church and stimulated its creative strengths" (p. 318).

The author indicates various spheres of the manifestation of the Church's creative powers in the imperial period which, in terms of both State and Church, represented "an ascending life in the biological evolution of the indivisible Russian organism" (p. 317).

First of all, Kartashev points to the enormous, almost ten-fold quantitative growth of the Church in the imperial period. And, "this quantitative growth is not just the automatic result of population growth; it is also the result of active and systematic external and internal missionary work on an unprecedented scale" (p. 317).

There was broad development of an orderly system of spiritual education. At the turn of the XX century there were in Russia four theological academies, 55 seminaries, 100 ecclesiastical schools and 100 parochial schools (for girls). The overall number was 75,000 students.

The broad development in the synodal period of scholarly theological knowledge made the Russian Church "the most elevated, the most powerful, and, one may say, the predominant one in all of Eastern Orthodoxy" (p. 318).

"The educational-theological growth of the powers of the Russian Church during this period increased yet in connection with another original cultural phenomenon – the appearance of secular theologians and religious philosophers – Khomiakov, the Aksakov brothers, Vladimir Solov'ev, the Trubetskoi brothers" (N.O. Losskii). "We must place on a parallel plane the religio-Orthodox force in Russian literature, which became universal" (p. 319). The creative powers of the Orthodox Church also manifested themselves in iconography, Church music, and architecture.

"To avoid undue doubt and vacillation in evaluating the development of the Russian Church let us apply an undeniable measure for all churches and all times. We mean the measure of holiness." Just as in preceeding periods, new saints did appear in the synodal era and canonization of former ascetics took place.

The last section of volume two speaks of the development of spiritual education in Russia.

In the overall evaluation of Kartashev's book, it should be said that it displays the author's broad and multilateral erudition and contains rich factual material in the description of all aspects of the life of the Russian Church: the administrative structure of the Church and the relationship of Church to State; the hierarchy, monasteries, and parish clergy; Church councils; ideological differences in the Church, heresies and schisms; the degree of Christianization of Church goers and the nature of ancient piety. Finally, the author provides a substantial bibliography for each period of Church history.

After Kartashev's "monumental" work, two more large and valuable surveys of the history of the Orthodox Church were published — by N.D. Tal'berg and I.K. Smolitsch.

## NIKOLAI DMITRIEVICH TAL'BERG

Nikolai Dmitrievich Tal'berg (1886-1969) graduated from the imperial school of jurisprudence in 1907. He worked in the government, left Russia in 1922, lived in Germany and Yugoslavia, and in the U.S.A. from 1950 where he was an instructor at the seminary of the Holy Trinity Monastery in Jordanville.

His large (925 p.) book, *History of the Russian Church* [*Istoriia Russkoi Tserkvi*] appeared in 1959. In the preface the author states that his book is the course given by him at the Holy Trinity seminary and does not pretend "to have a scholarly significance." He utilizes the pre-revolutionary studies of Russian Church history of Metropolitan Makarii, archbishop Filaret, E.E. Golubinskii, P.V. Znamenskii, and others. From all of these works, as well as from S.M. Solov'ev's *History of Russia from Ancient Times*, the author provides many substantial quotes. Two points, which touch on important events in Russian Church history and in which Tal'berg's account agrees with that of Kartashev, should be noted. The establishment of the patriarchate occurred on the initiative of the Tsar who "arrived at this idea" (presumably on the advice of Boris Godunov) "in order to give our country a patriarch" (p. 302). The author discusses the establishment of the Synod without praise or reproach. However, he notes that Peter, who left the patriarchal throne vacant for many years, became ever more convinced that, in the overwhelming majority, the Russian hierarchy was not sympathetic to his reorganizations. He "did not see a future primate on whom he could depend" (p. 547). "Peter sought a way out" (p. 548) and finally arrived at the Protestant system of Church administration. However, upon establishing the Synod, he turned to the four Eastern patriarchs with a request to recognize the legality of the reform which he had carried out. It should also be noted that the sixth section of Tal'berg's book is titled "The Flowering of Church Life." The book's last five pages (pp. 920-924) are devoted to Father Ioann [John] of Kronstadt, "a great luminary of Orthodoxy shining at the beginning of our age."

## IGOR KORNILIEVICH SMOLITSCH

Igor Kornilievich Smolitsch (1898-1970), a "Russian scholar working within the body of German scholarship" (in Kartashev's expression) left Russia in 1920 and settled in Berlin. He graduated from the University of Berlin and (in terms of language) became a German scholar. As a youth he was a member of the Russian Students Christian Movement. His superb book, *History of the Russian Church 1700-1917* [*Istoriia Russkoi Tserkvi 1700-1917*] came out in Leiden in 1964. Unfortunately, only the first volume (734 pp.) covering the period from 1700 to 1869 was published. At the beginning of the book there is an extensive list of sources and literature (42 pages of small print). On the basis of a thorough study of extensive materials, the author presents the history of the Russian Church in detail. It is done thoughtfully and objectively. The book is divided into five major chapters. The first two speak of Church-State relations, of the introduction by Peter the Great of "State religiosity," i.e. the establishment of the Holy Synod, the Spiritual Reglament, and the power of the *Ober Procurator*. Chapter three discusses eparchial administration; the fourth — the parish clergy; and the fifth — the ecclesiastical schools. On pages 691-713 are tables which clearly show the various sides of Church life in the XVIII-XIX centuries (ending in 1914). Indexes follow: one treats subject; the other names; the latter also provides the dates of birth and death. Another substantial (556 page) book belongs to Smolitch's pen. It is a valuable study of the history of Russian monasticism: *Russian Monasticism: Its Origin, Development, and Essence* [*Russkoe Monashestvo. Ego Vozniknovenie, Razvitie, i Sushchnost'*] (Würzburg, 1953). Smolitsch also devoted special attention to the subject of monastic "elders" in the book *Lives and Teachings of the Elders* [*Zhizn' i Uchenie Startsev*] (Vienna, 1936, Köln, 1952). The original German titles of Smolitsch's books may be found below in the bibliography.

Before speaking of the scholarly-monographic literature of the Russian emigration in the field of Church history, I would like to say a few words on two pre-revolutionary and three post-revolutionary autobiographies of outstanding Church figures of the XIX-XX centuries. These contain a wealth of information for acquainting one with the socio-ecclesiastical life of the era.

## ARCHPRIEST SAVVA OF TVER

For the second half of the XIX century, there is much material in the enormous autobiography of archbishop Savva of Tver (Tikhomirov, 1819-1896). Titled *Chronicle of My Life* [*Khronika moei Zhizni*], it was published posthumously in nine volumes, from 1897-1917. He was a priest but, having become a widower, he was consecrated a monk and took the course of study at the Moscow Theological Academy. In 1850 he was appointed sacristan of the synodal sacristy in Moscow, and became absorbed in the study of Church antiquities. Subsequently, he was the rector of the Moscow Theological Academy, then, in successive order, bishop of Mozhaisk, Polotsk, Khar'kov and archbishop of Tver. His work, *Paleographic Depictions from Greek and*

*Slavonic Manuscripts of the VI-XVII cc.* in the Moscow
Synodal Library [*Paleograficheskie Snimki Grecheskikh i
Slavianskikh Rukopisei Moskovskoi Sinodal'noi Biblioteki
VI-XVII vv.*] appeared in Moscow in 1863. His *Guide to
the Survey of the Moscow Patriarchal Sacristy* [*Ukazatel'
dlia Obozreniia Moskovskoi Patriarshei Riznitsy*] had been
published previously (4th ed., Moscow, 1864). It contained
tables of various Church antiquities. Later, he compiled
for publication the five volume *Collection of the Opinions
and Comments of Metropolitan Filaret in Educational
and Church-State Problems* (Moscow, 1884-1888).

## ARCHPRIEST IOANN OF KRONSTADT

At the turn of the century, the most popular Church
figure among the Orthodox people, and one known all over
Russia, was archpriest Ioann of Kronstadt (1829-1908). Ivan
Il'ich Sergiev, the son of a psalm reader, was born in the
village of Suro, district of Pinega, province of Arkhangel'sk.
He graduated from the Arkhangel'sk seminary, then from the
St. Petersburg Theological Academy. In 1855 he was or-
dained priest and placed in charge of the St. Andrew Cathedral in Kronstadt. This is where his half-century of pastoral
service took place, one which transformed him from a parish
priest into an "all Russian pastor." In his work, *My Life in
Christ, or Minutes of Spiritual Sobriety and Contemplation,
Pious Feeling, Reform of the Soul, and Tranquility in God.
Excerpts from the Diary* [*Moia Zhizn' vo Khriste, ili Minuty
Dukhovnogo Trezveniia i Sozertsaniia, Blagogoveinogo Chuv-
stva, Dushevnogo Ispravleniia i Pokoia v Boge. Izvlechenie
iz Dnevnika*], and many other works and sermons (published during his lifetime or posthumously), he sets forth his
thoughts and precepts on all the fundamental problems of
Christian philosophy and ethics. (It was published in Moscow
and the work was re-issued many times in Russia, Ladomirov,
and Jordanville). Father Ioann's penetrating sermons had
great success. His ascetical life gave him, according to the belief of the faithful, the gift of insight and miracle working.

[The Synod of the Russian Church in Exile canonized
Father Ioann of Kronstadt on November 1, 1964.] Unhappy
with the spiritual enlightenment of the Orthodox people,
Father Ioann developed charity at a wide level in Kronstadt.
With the aid of the "Church trusteeship" which he created
and with contributions received from all corners of Russia,
he founded the "House of Industry" in Kronstadt. It soon
developed into a little town which contained many institutions of economic, medical, and educational assistance to
the poor of Kronstadt.

The left and left-liberal intelligentsia did not like, and
reviled, Father Ioann for his political conservatism. In the
autocratic Tsar he saw the anointed of God who was to
concern himself for his people's welfare. In the atheistic
intelligentsia and the revolutionary movement he saw a
destructive force which threatened Russia with destruction. ("The Russian Tsardom is wavering, reeling, close to
collapse . . .").[105]

## METROPOLITAN ANTONII

Bishop Nikon (N. P. Rklitskii) of the Russian Church in
exile, archbishop of Washington and Florida has compiled a
ten volume work, *Biography of the Most Blessed Antonii,
Metropolitan of Kiev and Galich* [*Zhizneopisanie Blazhennei-
shego Antoniia, Mitropolita Kievskogo i Galitskogo*] (New
York, 1956-1963; volume one was re-issued in 1971). True,
this is a biography, not an autobiography. But N.P. Rklitskii,
presently archbishop Nikon, was Metropolitan Antonii's
closest friend and colleague in the emigration. If the latter
had the time or desire to write ten volumes of his biography,
he would have likely written much the same thing.

Metropolitan Antonii (Aleksei Pavlovich Khrapovitskii
1863-1936) was graduated from the St. Petersburg Theological Academy in 1885 and became a monk. Initially he was
the rector of the Moscow, then the Kazan, Theological
Academy. From 1900-1902 he was bishop of Ufa; from
1902-1914, bishop of Volynia. From 1907 he was a member

of the government Duma where he was a member of the
"rightist" faction. By his speeches he elicited the enmity of
the "liberal" press. From 1914-1917, he was the archbishop
of Kharkov; from 1918-1920, Metropolitan of Kiev and
Galich. He participated in the all Russian Church Council
of 1917-1918 and was one of the three candidates to the
patriarchal throne. In the emigration he headed the Russian
Church in Exile (the "Synodal" Church). Metropolitan
Antonii was an outstanding spiritual writer. His many works
on theological-dogmatic, politico-ecclesiastical, and literary
problems made up seven volumes. These were prepared for
publication by his biographer and friend, archbishop Nikon
(and were published in New York from 1963-1969). The
first four volumes of his biography deal with the pre-1920
period; the last set with the emigration era.

## METROPOLITAN EVLOGII

Another outstanding Russian and émigré hierarch was
Metropolitan Evlogii (Vasilii Semenovich Georgievskii 1868-
1946). He was born to a priest's family in the Tula province.
He graduated from the Moscow Theological Academy in
1892 and was tonsured in 1895. From 1897-1902, he was the
rector of the Kholm seminary. In 1903 he became the vicar
bishop of the Warsaw eparchy. He was a member of the second and third Duma (1907-1912) and aided Prime Minister
P.A. Stolypin in passing a law on the formation of a special
province and eparchy of Kholm. The goal was to counteract
Polonism, Catholicism, and Uniatism in the Kholm region. He
was archbishop of Kholm from 1912-1914 and archbishop of
Volynia from 1914-1919. He left Russia in 1920. He lived in
Paris as an émigré and was the Metropolitan of the Western
European Russian churches.

Metropolitan Evlogii's memoirs have the title *My Life's
Path. The Memoirs of Metropolitan Evlogii, Based on His
Own Accounts by T. Manukhina [Put' Moei Zhizni. Vospominaniia Mitropolita Evlogiia, Izlozhennye po ego Ras-
skazam T. Manukhinoi]* ("YMCA," Paris, 1947). The first

half of this large (676 p.) book contains the interesting story of Russian life at the turn of the XX century. Naturally, Church life is treated in the main, but it is tightly interwoven with overall public life. The second half of the book presents in detail the history of the Russian émigré Church in Europe with all its difficulties and conflicts.

## ARCHPRIEST SHAVEL'SKII

The fifth autobiography that I wish to mention is the memoirs of archpresbyter Shavel'skii, *Memoirs of the Last Arch-Presbyter of the Russian Army and Navy* [*Vospominaniia Poslednego Protopresvitera Russkoi Armii i Flota*] (Chekhov Publishing House, New York, 1954). Georgii Ivanovich Shavel'skii (1871-1951) was born near Vitebsk to the family of a deacon. He graduated from the Vitebsk seminary and was ordained a priest in 1895. He then graduated from the St. Petersburg Theological Academy (1902). In 1911 he was appointed chief priest (arch-presbyter) of the army and navy. From 1915-1917 he was a member of the Holy Synod. In emigration he was a professor at the University of Sofiia. During the war he was assigned to the staff of the Supreme Commander in Chief (first Grand Duke Nikolai Nikolaevich, then Emperor Nicholas). His proximity to the "highest spheres" left him a broad field for interesting observations. It should be noted only that his memoirs are clearly expressive of the fashionable "accusatory" tendency regarding "Tsarist" times.

In surveying the field of monographs on the history of the Russian Church which came out in the emigration (besides the above-cited ones of A.V. Kartashev, N.D. Tal'berg, and I.K. Smolitsch), I will treat five authors: N.S. Arsen'ev, S.N. Bulgakov, N.M. Zernov, G.P. Fedotov, and G.V. Florovskii. I do not know in what scholarly-hierarchical order to take them, thus I do so alphabetically [i.e. according to the Russian alphabet].[106]

## NIKOLAI SERGEEVICH ARSEN'EV
## (1888-1977)

Nikolai Sergeevich Arsen'ev (b. 1888) graduated from the historico-philological department of Moscow University (see his recollections of Moscow University in volume one of the *Transactions of the Association of Russian-American Scholars*). He passed his master's examinations in 1912 and became a *privat docent* at the chair of Western European literatures. In 1918 he was appointed professor at the University of Saratov. He left Russia in 1920. He was lecturer, then professor, at the University of Königsberg (where he received the doctor of philosophy degree in 1924). Simultaneously, he was a professor in the department of Orthodox theology at the University of Warsaw. From 1948 he was professor at St. Vladimir's Seminary in New York.

Professor Arsen'ev has written many books on topics of Russian spiritual culture in Russian, English, German, and French (for a bibliogarphy, see Professor Zernov's book on Russian émigré writers, pp. 10-11).

Professor Arsen'ev possesses a broad and deep erudition in the field of Russian spiritual culture, particularly in the history of the Orthodox Church and Russian literature. Beginning with his short, *The Eastern Church* which appeared (in German) in Berlin in 1926, he has published many valuable monographs on the history of Russian spiritual culture. He includes the history of the Russian Church in his works, for it was his conviction that throughout Russian history the Orthodox Church was the major moving force for the cultural development of the Russian nation. "The Eastern Church was the great educator of the Russian nation. From it, it received its 'vertebrae', the spiritual content and meaning of life. The highest achievements of Russian culture and spiritual life and of Russian artistic creativity are — directly or indirectly — linked with this spiritual foundation" (*On the Spiritual Fate of the Russian People*, in German, p. 85). In the just cited book, chapter four discusses the basic character of the Eastern Church. It particularly singles out the sacrament of the Eucharist and the feast of Christ's Resurrection. The fifth chapter speaks of the Church's influence on the spiritual life of the nation. Many examples of piety, heroism, and self-sacrifice are given from life and from literature. In this, and in other books by Arsen'ev, many literary citations are given. The author is a great expert on and connoisseur of Russian literature, particularly poetry.

Characteristics of the Orthodox Church and Russian piety are contained in the book *Russian Piety* (in French). The role of Church rituals and customs in the life of the Russian people is described and many examples given.

In the book *Holy Moscow* (in English), the author paints a picture of Russia's spiritual life in the XIX century. He describes how closely Russian cultural life was connected to the religious foundation of Russian culture, how fully Russian habit was filled with religious rituals and customs. He speaks of Church and monastic devotees and of secular religious philosophers.

It must be said that Arsen'ev is not a one-sided "worshiper" of pre-revolutionary Russia and does not view Orthodox Russia as an isolated cultural island. In his book, *From Russian Cultural Creative Tradition* [*Iz Russkoi Kul'-turnoi Tvorcheskoi Traditsii*] ("Posev" publ., 1959) he states: "Of course, it will not do to idealize in a one-sided fashion. There was much, very much that was grievous and negative in the fabric of Russian life, many faults and sins. Frequently, the fates of the Russian people, particularly the peasantry, were burdensome and dark . . ." (p. 10). He views the basic trait of XIX century Russian culture to be the creative synthesis of a national-religious Russian culture with the secular culture of the West: "The great cultural synthesis of the XIX century occurred as a result of the meeting of two spiritual principles, two cultures: the national Russian source, to a significant degree, fed and fertilized by the traditions of the Orthodox Eastern Church, and the Western source. . ." (p. 11). "Especially significant for XIX Century Russian culture was the creative interaction of

West and East, the creative synthesis of the native and the Western European inheritance" (p. 152).

## SERGEI NIKOLAEVICH BULGAKOV

Sergei Nikolaevich Bulgakov (1871-1944) was the son of a priest. He studied at a seminary but lost his faith in early youth (ages 14-15), left the seminary, and in the expression of his autobiographical works, became a "prodigal son" of Orthodox Russia, "the victim of dismal revolutionary nihilism" in its Marxist variety. He graduated from a Moscow gymnasium and from Moscow University. He was professor of political economy, first at the Kiev Polytechnic Institute, then in the Moscow Institute of Commerce, then at Moscow University. He published several substantial works in political economy, initially in the Marxist vein. But a transformation within him occurs at the beginning of the XX century. It is "from Marxism to idealism" (the title of an anthology of articles published in 1903). He accepted the priesthood in 1918. He left Russia in 1923 and from 1925 to the end of his life, he was professor of dogmatics and dean of the Orthodox Theological Institute in Paris.

Fr. Bulgakov wrote many theological works in emigration. Within Church circles they elicited both high praise and objections right up to accusations of heresy.

Fr. Bulgakov's vividly written *Autobiographical Notes* [*Avtobiograficheskie Zapiski*], published posthumously (1946) with an introduction and notes by his close colleague, L. A. Zander, are of doubtless interest for the history of the Russian Church and the general state of the Russian cultured class at the turn of the XX century. Bulgakov's disillusionment with Marxism was soon joined by his disillusionment with the Russian leftist intelligentsia as a whole. In 1907 he was a member of the Second Duma. And this leftist Duma made a depressing impression upon him. "It was unfit for any task and was drowning in endless chatter" (p. 80).

Bulgakov's book *Icons and the Veneration of Icons* [*Ikona i Ikonopochitanie*] was published in Paris in 1931.

His book *Orthodoxy* [*Pravoslavie*] appeared in French in
1932. It sets forth the dogmas of the Orthodox Church,
the hierarchical structure, sacraments, rituals, veneration of
icons, mysticism, the foundations of Christian ethics, the
attitude of Church to society and the State.
Fr. Bulgakov's book, *Orthodoxy. Essays on the Doctrines of the Orthodox Church* [*Pravoslavie. Ocherki Ucheniia Pravoslavnoi Tserkvi*] appeared, in Paris, in 1965
("YMCA" Press). The text is preceded by L.A. Zander's
"Brief essay of the life and creative exploits of our unforgettable priest and teacher."

## NIKOLAI MIKHAILOVICH ZERNOV

Nikolai Mikhailovich Zernov was born in 1898 in Moscow to a doctor's family. He left Russia in 1921 and graduated from the department of theology at the University of
Belgrade in 1925. In Paris (from 1925-1932) he was the
secretary of the "Russian Students' Christian Movement"
and editor of *Vestnik R.S.Kh.D.* He moved to England
where he was a lecturer on Eastern Orthodox Culture at
Oxford University. He is a doctor of philosophy and doctor of theology of Oxford University. He is the author of
many surveys and monographs in the history of the Russian
Orthodox Church (a listing of these is provided on p. 54 of
Zernov's very useful book, *Russian Émigré Writers*, see
above).
In Professor Zernov's exposition the history of the
Russian Church is interwoven with the history of the Russian
State and the people, and with the history of Russian spiritual culture — just as they were "intertwined" in reality.
Most of Zernov's books were published in English. I
will give the titles of some of his books and their contents
(see the bibliographical listing at the end of this chapter).
Zernov's book, *The Russians and Their Church* [*Russkie i ikh Tserkov'*], came out in London in 1945. The first
chapter describes the initial changes introduced into the
life of Kievan society and government by the acceptance of

Christianity. Chapter two describes the creation of Russian nationality and Russian culture under the influence of the new religion. In the 250 years from Russia's baptism to the Tatar invasion the Christian Church created a nation with its own language and culture out of a series of separate tribes. "For the Russian person, the Christian Church was his university and the church building was his theater, his concert hall, his art gallery" (p. 17). In the XIV century, crushed by the Tatar yoke, Rus' began to recover. This was accomplished by the administration of the Muscovite princes and collaboration by Metropolitans Petr and Aleksei and, especially, St. Sergii of Radonezh (to whom the author devotes all of chapter five). "St. Sergei created a miracle with the Russian people: he transformed a defeated (oppressed) people into the creators (builders) of a great State" (p. 42). The following chapters speak of the origin of the proud idea, "Moscow the Third (and last) Rome"; of the Church's life in the XVI century; of the Church's important national-State role (especially of Patriarch Germogen and the Holy Trinity Monastery) during the Time of Troubles; of Church life in the XVII century and the tragedy of the Church Schism for which the author's opinion holds Patriarch Nikon to be responsible more than others (see below); of the Petrine Church reform which he views as the "misfortune" and the "imprisonment" of the Russian Church (see below); of the life of the Church in the XVIII-XIX centuries when the Church, crushed by bureaucratic wardship of the "police State" nevertheless "survived this misfortune" and preserved its "vitality." Chapter fifteen is titled "Saints, Missionaries, and Prophets" and describes the spiritual-cultural achievements of the Russian Church in the XVIII-XIX centuries. It includes the recrudescence of monasticism (after the wounds inflicted upon it by Peter I and Catherine II), the appearance of elders (Optin Hermitage), the flowering of theological literature, and the broad spreading of missionary activity (both within and outside the Empire). The author observes the "strange contradiction" in the life of the Russian Church at this time: weighed down

from the outside by the wardship of the Imperial bureaucracy, the "Church was inwardly free and experienced the
breath ('effusion') of the Holy Spirit more than at any
time in its history" (p. 139).

Zernov's book, *The Ecumenical Church and Russian
Orthodoxy* [*Vselenskaia Tser'kov i Russkoe Pravoslavie*]
was published in Paris in 1952 ("YMCA" Press). Two large
chapters (ch. 3 and 4, pp. 98-240) are devoted to the history of the Russian Church. We will observe two key points
here. The author accuses Patriarch Nikon for the origin of the
Schism. His methods in the correction of the books and
reform of ritual were "despotic." He "acted not as a pastor,
but as an oppressor" and alienated "the best Church people"
(p. 160). "The fundamental reason for the Schism (I would
say "primary cause," as the author himself states on the
same page – S.P.) was the opposition of the best part of the
Russian clergy and flock to the violation of the Church committed by the Patriarch" (p. 160). Insofar as his talents were
concerned, "Nikon could have done much good for the
Church and the people. But his conceit and pride made him
not a creator but a destroyer – one of the perpetrators of
the Schism in the Orthodox Church" (p. 163). Zernov is
severely critical of Peter's Church reform. The Spiritual
Reglament, in his opinion, is "closer to captious and mali-
cious satire then to an act of supreme legislation." "Peter
the Great deprived the Church of its independence. It became one of the parts of the government mechanism" (p.
177). "Beginning with Peter the Great, the Russian Church
was the Empire's captive. . . The Spiritual Reglament was an
act of State oppression over the Church which bore it until
the Revolution of 1917" (pp. 181-182).

Zernov's *Eastern Christendom. A Study of the Origin
and Development of the Eastern Orthodox Church* was
published in London in 1961. It provides an account of the
Church's history from the life of Christ to the XX century.
The history of the Russian Church is included in the survey. The last chapters set forth the dogmas of the Church,
the services, sacraments, rituals, and Church art.

Besides general surveys, Professor Zernov has published a number of monographs on Russian Church and general cultural history: *Moscow the Third Rome* (London, 1937); *St. Sergius Builder of Russia* (London, 1939); *Three Russian Prophets* (*Khomiakov, Dostoevsky, Soloviev*) (London 1944; re-issued, 1973); *The Russian Religious Renaissance of the XX Century* [*Russkoe Religioznoe Vozrozhdenie XX Veka*] (in Russian and English; Paris and London, 1973).

## GEORGII PETROVICH FEDOTOV

Georgii Petrovich Fedotov (1886-1951) was a Marxist and member of the Social Democratic party during his student years. He emigrated in 1906 and studied history in Germany. Upon returning to Russia (in 1908), he was graduated from the historico-philological department of the University of St. Petersburg and was an instructor of history in St. Petersburg, then in his native Saratov. He left Russia in 1925. He was instructor at the Theological Institute in Paris and editor of the *Novyi Grad* anthologies (1931-1940). He moved to the U.S.A. in 1943 and taught at St. Vladimir's Seminary in New York.

Fedotov's book, *Saints of Ancient Russia, X-XVII cc.* [*Sviatye Drevnei Rusi, X-XVII st.*] was published in Paris in 1931 (by "YMCA" Press; re-issued in 1960). In it the author, utilizing his extensive knowledge of hagiographical literature, depicts the lives and the characteristics of the outstanding saints of the Russian Church — from the holy martyrs, princes Boris and Gleb to Serafim of Sarovsk. He also expresses general judgements on the nature of Russian holiness and we cite some of his conclusions. The primary impression derived from the study of Russian holiness is "its radiant regularity, the absence of radicalism and extreme and sharp departures from the Christian ideal bequeathed by antiquity. In monasticism, we almost fail to see cruel asceticism or the practice of self-torture. The dominant asceticism of Russian saints is fasting and labor" (p. 248). The socio-agricultural life of the monastery "derives its religious justification only in its social service to the world. With uncommon force, all Russian holy monks insist on giving alms and providing charity as conditions for the spiritual blossoming of their cloisters" (*ibid.*).

In Fedotov's opinion, vital holiness left Russia in the last quarter of the XVII century: "Peter destroyed only the decayed shell of Holy Russia" (p. 204). However, even during the Imperial period, "spiritual life glimmered in the monasteries, hermitages, and in the world" (p. 253). Serafim of Sarovsk ("the greatest of the saints of ancient or modern Russia") "broke the synodal seal placed on Russian holiness" and the elder, Paisii Velichkovskii, resurrected the mystical tradition of the elders. "The Optin Hermitage and Sarov became the two centers of Russian spiritual life; two fires by which a frozen Russia warmed itself" (pp. 253-254).

In 1946 Harvard University Press published Fedotov's *The Russian Religious Mind. Kievan Christianity: the 10th to the 13th Centuries* (It was re-issued in 1960 and 1966 — and has now been published as volume III (paper) in Nordland's *The Collected Works of George P. Fedotov*). It contains a detailed and comprehensive description of the religious life and creativity of the first centuries of Russian Christianity (the author commences with a characterization of Byzantine Christianity). He also discusses Christain doctrine, ethics, monasticism, ancient Russian saints, asceticism, ritualism, preaching, the Russian chronicles in relation to religion. One chapter is devoted to "The Lay of Prince Igor" ["Tale of Igor's Campaign"], the only work of secular literature of this period that has come down to us. The continuation of this work: *The Russian Religious Mind: The Middle Ages — The Thirteenth to the Fifteenth Centuries* (1946; 1966) [Volume IV (paper) in Nordland's *The Collected Works of George P. Fedotov*] contains the history of Russian Christianity in this period.

Fedotov's *A Treasury of Russian Spirituality* appeared in 1948 (in English; New York and London) [Volume II (paper) in Nordland's *The Collected Works of George P. Fedotov*]. In it the author provides a description of the lives and spiritual work of the outstanding spiritual pillars of Orthodox Russia: Feodosii of Pechersk, Sergii of Radonezh, Nil Sorskii, Archpriest Avvakum, Tikhon of Zadonsk, Serafim of Sarovsk, Innokentii Borisov, Archbishop of Kherson ("the most famous Russian preacher of the XIX century"), Father Ioann of Kronstadt, Father Aleksandr Elchaninov. In addition to the above-cited works, Fedotov's book, *St. Filipp: Metropolitan of Moscow* [*Sviatoi Filipp, Mitropolit Moskovskii*] was published in Paris (1928; "YMCA" Press) [It is volume I (cloth) in Nordland's *The Collected Works of George P. Fedotov*, translated by R. Haugh and N. Lupinin].

## GEORGII VASIL'EVICH FLOROVSKII

Professor and archpriest Georgii Vasil'evich Florovskii was born in Odessa in 1893 and graduated from Novorussia University in 1916. In the emigration in the 1920's he engaged in scholarly and pedagogical work in Prague, then was professor of patristics at the Theological Institute in Paris (1926-1939). In the U.S.A. he was professor and dean of St. Vladimir's Seminary in New York (1939-1955), professor at Harvard, then at Princeton.

Fr. Florovskii is the author of two monographs on the Eastern and Byzantine Church fathers (IV-VIII cc.) published in Paris in 1931 and 1933. In 1972-1973, Nordland Publishing Company (Belmont, Mass.) commenced the publication of *The Collected Works of Georges Florovsky* [vol. I — *Bible, Church, Tradition: An Eastern Orthodox View*; vol. II — *Christianity and Culture*; vol. III — *Creation and Redemption*; vol. IV — *Aspects of Church History*. Volumes V and VI, under the editorship of Richard Haugh, Visiting Professor of Church History at Rice University, are *Ways of Russian Theology* with extensive footnoting and bibliographic material. Other volumes, including the two on the Church Fathers, are forthcoming.

His fundamental work, *Ways of Russian Theology* [*Puti Russkogo Bogosloviia*] (published in Paris in 1937 and re-issued by the University of Michigan in 1964) is very important for the history of the Russian Church. I do not take it upon myself to judge Fr. Florovskii's book in terms of the history of Russian theology (due to my incompetence in theological sciences). But, as an historian, I must note the extraordinary breadth and depth of the author's erudition in the fields of Russian Church history and general Russian cultural development. His extensive bibliography takes up 54 pages of small print (pp. 521-574) and includes many works on the history of Russian culture aside from works that are purely theological or ecclesiastico-historical.

I will provide the contents of Florovskii's book in brief insofar as it "intertwines" with Russian Church history.

Chapter 1: "Crisis of Russian Byzantinism"; Chapter 2: "Meeting with the West" (XVII c.); Chapter 3: "Contradictions of the XVII Century" (History of the Schism).

Chapter 4: "The Petersburg Revolt." Peter's Church reform "was an imperious and radical experiment in State secularization" (p. 82). "The clergy was transformed into a special serving class" (p. 84). "Peter wanted to organize Church administration in Russia according to the way it was organized in Protestant countries" (p. 85). The Petrine reform "commences the Babylonian captivity of the Russian Church" (p. 89). The Petrine reform, as a whole, was "not successful," and the Spiritual Reglament "is only a program" (p. 88).

Chapter 5: "The Struggle for Theology" contains the history of the Church and spiritual enlightenment in the first half of the XIX century; the opening of four theological academies; the Biblical Society and translation of the New Testament into Russian; the work of the theological academies and seminaries. Accusors of the seminary told "too much that was bad and dreary" about the ecclesiastical schools of the first half of the XIX century. "And it must be recognized that it had many defects: crudity of manners, material poverty, formalism in instruction" (p. 230). "However, in the final analysis, all of these unquestionable shortcomings did not enfeeble the creative bursts of those generations. The historical-cultural significance of these pre-reform ecclesiastical schools must be recognized as positive and evaluated highly. For it was precisely the Church-school network which turned out to be the true social basis for the whole development and growth of Russian culture and education in the XIX century . . . It was precisely the "seminarian" who over a period of decades remained the producer of Russian culture in the most varied fields. . . The 'raznochinets' was, after all, most frequently a seminarian. . . The history of Russian scholarship and learning in general is linked to the ecclesiastical school and the clerical class" (p. 231).

In Chapter 6 ("Philosophical Awakening") the author asserts that "the whole history of the Russian intelligentsia proceeds in the preceding century under the sign of religious crisis" (p. 292).

Chapter 7 ("The Historical School") discusses the activities of the Church school, religious periodicals, and the development of Church history study in the XIX century. Furthermore, the author provides characteristics of the works of all the major Church historians. He gives a high opinion of the historical works and method of archbishop Filaret Gumilevskii (pp. 365-366) whereas Metropolitan Makarii "remains in history merely as a collector of information and texts" (p. 366). The author is not too sympathetic to the "denunciatory" critical-skeptical method of the most prominent historian of the "Moscow school," E.E. Golubinskii. "Golubinskii transformed common distrust and suspicion into historical method"; "this was a historian-publicist" (p. 372).

Chapter 8: "On the Eve." Here the history of the Church and religion at the end of the XIX and the beginning of the XX century is set forth. He treats the striving toward Church reform (to the re-establishment of the patriarchy and the conciliar system) and work on the "pre-Council conferences"; the development of the scholarly activity of the theological academies; the awakening of religio-philoso-

phical interests in intellectual society which was expressed
by religio-philosophical meetings in St. Petersburg from
1901-1903. This was followed by the establishment of a
religio-philosophical society named after Vladimir Solov'ev
(1907) and by the publication of a number of works on
religio-philosophical themes. However, the author, as an
Orthodox priest, notes the "ambiguity and unsteadiness"
of the intelligentsia's religio-philosophical movement (p.
493).

The final and 9th chapter — "Breaks and Links" — explains the author's religio-philosophic views.

My essay, of course, is far from exhaustive of the rich
contents of Russian literature on Church history. Two bibliographic lists are added as supplements to it. The first contains
books in Russian not mentioned in the text; the second lists
books by Russian and foreign authors in foreign languages.
It includes the works whose title was given in Russian translation in the text. See the appendices at the end of the
book.

## HISTORIOGRAPHY OF THE SCHISM OF THE
## OLD BELIEF

Before presenting the reader with a brief essay on the
historiography of the "Schism," we should recall those
religio-ritualistic differences which "split" the Russian
Church in the middle of the XVII century and of that religio-
national psychology of the Russian society of that time
which made this split possible (or inevitable).

Let us enumerate those liturgical-ritualistic particulars
which distinguished the "old belief" from the texts and
rituals accepted by the Orthodox Church after the correction
of Church service books (according to Greek models) by
Patriarch Nikon.

The sign of the cross was made with two, not three,
fingers. A dual, not triple, "alleluja" was sung. Isus, not
Iisus, was Christ's name. Seven (not five) communion breads
were to be used during the liturgy. In the second article of

the Creed, "Jesus Christ, Son of God, begotten but not created," the conjunction 'but' is omitted. In the seventh article of the Creed about the Son of God: "His Kingdom has no end [*nest' kontsa*]," the corrected version reads "there will be no end." In the eighth article of the Creed: "In the Holy Spirit, True God and Life-Giver," the word "True" is omitted. In the Paschal prayer: "death is stepped upon by death" is changed to "death is trampled upon by death." In the prayer of the Blessing of the Water: "sanctify this water by Thy Holy Spirit and fire," the words "and fire" are omitted. The liturgy was to be conducted only according to the old (pre-Nikonian) books, the processions around the church were to be according to the sun, i.e. from east to west, not the opposite way.

There were some other differences in the number of bows during the liturgy, church vestments, and iconography. In daily life the "old ritualists" rejected and reproached imitation of Western customs and dress, shaving of beards, smoking tobacco, etc. . . . In the area of religio-social life, the Old Believers thought it a vice of the dominant Church that parish clergy were appointed by eparchial rule in abrogation of choosing candidates for the priesthood by the parishoners.

This may appear strange to the contemporary reader: how could such insignificant differences in the texts and rituals beget an irreconcilable and age old internecine enmity and struggle in the Russian Church and State? Here we must above all indicate two peculiarities of the national-religious psychology of Muscovite society in the XVI-XVII centuries.

Russian piety of this time, as acknowledged by both ecclesiastical and secular historians, had more of an external-ritualistic rather than a religio-moral character. According to N.I. Kostomarov, a popular historian of the mid XIX century, "Orthodoxy affected the Russian person not as a doctrine but as a custom." And it was carefully preserved as a custom inherited from ancestors and unchangeable ("from ages unto ages"). Or, according to E. E. Golubinskii, a prominent historian of the Russian Church, "the schism of the old belief arose because our forefathers equated Church customs and rituals with dogmas of the faith." Historians constantly cite this "belief in ritual" as a characteristic trait of ancient-Russian religiosity.[107]

In addition to "belief in ritual," an extremely important trait of the religio-national psychology of Muscovite ecclesiastical society in the XVI and the first half of the XVII century was a conviction in the greatness and holiness of the Russian land. From the middle of the XV century, the Russian Church which, formally, up to that time, was one of the metropolitanates under the jurisdiction of the patriarch of Constantinople, became independent of the Greek Church. In the meantime, the State of Muscovy experienced a period of enormous foreign policy successes: the overthrow of the Tatar yoke, the unification of all great Russian territories under the Muscovite sovereign, the conquest of the enormous territory of the three Tatar kingdoms — Kazan, Astrakhan, and Siberia. The authority of the Greek Church fell considerably in Moscow's eyes after it subscribed to the Union of Florence (1439). The conquest of Constantinople by the Turks (1453) was seen in Moscow as a punishment of Byzantium which had fallen into the "Latin heresy." Now, all Orthodox kingdoms in the Balkans became provinces of the Turkish Empire and the Eastern patriarchs became "slaves" of the Turkish sultan. A proud theory then arises in Russia: after the fall of Byzantium, the "Second Rome," Moscow became the Third and Eternal Rome ("a fourth is not to be"). It becomes the head and patron of all Orthodoxy. Rus' is recognized and characterized as "Holy Russia," as the "New Israel" chosen by God, and as the sole keeper of true Orthodoxy in all of its immaculate purity (the aggregate of these ideas is vividly expressed in the writings of the founder and apostle of old belief, archpriest Avvakum).

Moscow's link with the Orthodox East does not cease but it attains a totally different character. Greek hierarchs and other ecclesiastics frequently came to Moscow — but not as mentors and teachers, rather as recipients and petitioners of the "sovereign's alms." Moreover, it is suspected in Moscow that Greek Orthodoxy, and Church service in particular, has been "tainted" by the influence of the "Latin heresy" and Turkish enslavement. It was natural, writes N.F. Kapterev, that Nikon's Church reform (i.e. the correction of texts and rituals according to Greek models) "had to deal a deathly blow to the historically formed notions of the Russians regarding their religious superiority over all nations, particularly the Greeks" and "elicited a powerful protest among the adherents and admirers of the Russian Church's past."

The protest movement, in the expression of S.M. Solov'ev, was headed by the "hero archpriest" Avvakum. The fact that the conflict between the "reformers" and their opponents was of such a sharp and acerbic nature from the very beginning is also to be explained, in addition to the above-cited reasons, by the personal characters of the leaders of the two parties. Nikon and Avvakum were both men of strong character. They possessed indomitable energy, unwavering confidence in their own rectitude, and had no inclination or ability for concession or compromise.

Patriarch Nikon was filled with the consciousness of the grandeur of his hierarchical power. He imagined that it exceeded any secular power, including that of the Tsar. The patriarch viewed any resistance or even insubordination to upper Church authority as a crime and was ready to crush it by any means. According to N.I. Kostomarov, "Nikon treated the question of reform as a military commander treated a military matter. It was to be done. Disobedience was to be met with harsh punishment."

Meanwhile, Nikon's major opponent, archpriest Avvakum Petrovich (from the town of Iurevets) was unshakeably convinced of the rectitude of his ancient cherished religious views and had not the slightest desire to carry out the "profane" orders of the religious reformers. Avvakum considered and called Nikon a "borzoi hound, an apostate and heretic," and "what peace could there be with a heretic? Fight him, and do not obey his perverse mind until death."

With such attitudes on both sides no peace or agreement between them was possible. The Church Council of 1666-1667 (after Nikon's fall) condemned the Old Believers as "heretics" and excommunicated them. Secular authority aided the ecclesiastical in uprooting the "heresy." This deplorable internecine strife clouded the history of the Russian Church and the Russian nation over the course of the next two centuries.

A very important source for the history of the rise of the Schism and for Russian Church history in general is the autobiography of archpriest Avvakum; *Life of Archpriest Avvakum, Written by Himself* [*Zhitie Protopopa Avvakuma, im Samim Napisannoe*]. This is not only an important document of Church history but also a marvelous literary work written in a vivid and expressive folk tongue.[108] Avvakum's *Life* has been preserved in many manuscripts and was issued and re-issued repeatedly in the XIX and XX centuries. In view of the significance of the *Life* for the history of the Church and of literature, I will provide a number of its editions: N. Tikhonravov, *Annals of Russian Literature* [*Letopisi Russkoi Literatury*], vol. III, sect. II, pp. 117-173, Moscow, 1861; N. Subbotin, ed., *Materials for the History of the Schism During the First Period of Its Existence* [*Materialy dlia Istorii Raskola za Pervoe Vremia ego Sushchestvovaniia*], vol. V, pp. 1-113, Moscow, 1879; A. K. Borozdin, *Archpriest Avvakum* [*Protopop Avvakum*], 2nd. ed., SPB, 1900, appendix no. 25, pp. 71-116; Ia.L. Barskov, ed. *Documents of the First Years of Russian Old Belief* [*Pamiatniki Pervykh Let Russkogo Staroobriadchestva*] SPB; 1912, pp. 163-228; *Life of Archpriest Avvakum Written by Himself* [*Zhitie Protopopa Avvakum, im Samim Napisannoe*] published by the Imperial Archeographic Commission, ed. V.G. Druzhinin, Petrograd, 1916; *Russian Historical Library* [*Russkaia Istoricheskaia Biblioteka*], vol. 39; published by the Historico-Archeographic Commission of the Academy of Sciences of the USSR, Leningrad 1927; *Documents on the History of the Old Belief in the XVII c.* [*Pamiatniki Istorii Staroobriadchestva XVII v.*], book 1, issue 1;

*Life of Archpriest Avvakum* in three editions, introduction by Ia. L. Barskov, columns 1-240; *Archpriest Avvakum, Life. Correspondence with Boiarinia Morozova* [*Protopop Avvakum. Zhitie. Perepiska s Boiarinei Morozovoi*], Paris, 1951; *Archpriest Avvakum's Life and Other Works by Him* [*Zhitie Protopopa Avvakuma i Drugie ego Sochineniia*], ed. by N. K. Gudzii, Moscow, 1960.[109]

During the second half of the XIX century and in the XX century, many documents and materials on the history of old belief and sectarianism were published. These were edited by Ia.L. Barskov, E.V. Barsov, V.D. Bonch-Bruevich, V. G. Druzhinin, N. Popov, N. I. Subbotin.[110]

With the existence of a strict censorship, i.e. to the end of Emperor Nicholas I's rule (1855), old believer authors (or those sympathetic to the "Schism") could not legally publish their theological or historical books. The history of the "Schism" was interpreted only in historical or polemical works of Orthodox authors of the "ecclesiastical class."

The origin of this type of literature is be found in the work of the Metropolitan of Rostov, Dimitrii (Tuptalo, 1651-1709). It was titled: *An Inquiry Into the Pernicious Faith of the Old Belief: Its Doctrine and Works, in Which It Is Shown How Their Faith is Untrue, Their Doctrine Injurious and Their Works Displeasing to God* [*Rozysk o Raskol'nicheskoi Brynskoi Vere, o Uchenii i o Delakh ikh, v Kotorom Pokazano, Iako Vera ikh Neprava, Uchenie ikh Dushevredno i Dela ikh ne Bogougodny*]. Metropolitan Dimitrii completed his work not long before his death (1709). It was first published in 1745. In its new edition this book appeared in 1803 (published by the Moscow Synodal Typography). The title of Metropolitan Dimitrii's book speaks clearly enough of its contents and aims.

During the first half of the XIX century, several works published by ecclesiastical authors were directed at "condemning" the Schism. At the end of this period (1855), the *History of the Russian Schism, of the Old Belief* [*Istoriia Russkogo. Raskola, Izvestnogo pod Imenem Staroobriadstva*] was published. It was written by Makarii, bishop of Vinitsk and rector of the St. Petersburg Theological Academy (later Metropolitan of Moscow and author of the monumental *History of the Russian Church*). In the first part of the book, the author discusses the "seeds and germs" of the Schism, i.e. religious differences since the beginning of the XV century. He then sets forth the history of the Schism in detail commencing with 1667. The book is full of factual material, devoid of a sharply polemical tone, and ends in a prayerful hope for the re-unification of the "schismatics" with the Orthodox Church.

The books of the ecclesiastical authors "interpreted" the Schism only from the viewpoint of religious differences between the Orthodox and the "schismatics." A totally new approach to the history of the Schism is to be found in the book by the Kazan professor, A.P. Shchapov; *The Russian Schism of the Old Belief. Viewed in Connection With the Internal State of the Russian Church and the Civic Body in the XVII Century and the First Half of the XVIII Century. An Experiment in the Historical Investigation of the Causes of the Origin and Dissemination of the Schism* [*Russkii Raskol Staroobriadstva, Rassmatrivaemyi v Sviazi s Vnutrennim Sostoianiem Russkoi Tserkvi i Grazhdanstvennosti v XVII Veke i v Pervoi Polovine XVIII v. − Opyt Istoricheskogo Issledovaniia o Prichinakh Proiskhozhdeniia i Rasprostraneniia Raskola*], Kazan, 1859. I will give several quotations from the introduction to Schapov's book, for it was the take off point for the new "interpretation" of the Schism in Russian historical and publicistic literature. The author acknowledges that the "main initial source of the Schism" was the "superstitious attachment (of Muscovite society) to just external ritualism without the spirit of faith." But he also indicates other reasons for the successful spread of the Schism: "The religio-civic democratism of the Schism under the cloak of mystical-apocalyptical symbolism, the rejection of Peter the Great's reform, the revolt against foreign sources in Russian life, protest against the Empire and the State, the courageous protest against the censuses, taxes, and 'many tributes', against recruitment, serfdom, regional authority, and the like — this is the very significant expression of the nation's view of the social and governmental system of Russia, the manifestation of dissatisfaction by the lower classes, the fruit of a painful, suffering, and irritated state of the nation's spirit" (introduction, p. II). Nevertheless, the Schism itself does not instill Shchapov with special sympathy. It is "a dark side of our people's moral and social development, the fruit and expression of the extreme inadequacy of the clergy's moral influence on the nation, and the absence of a national education and upbringing." The strength of the Schism, in Shchapov's opinion, is not in its external nature, rather in its role as a religio-ritual sect. The strength of the Russian Schism is chiefly in the religio-civic democratism "when it moved from the purely ecclesiastical to the sphere of civic public life" (p. 55). Under Peter the Great, the "Schism became even more powerful and complex and clearly took on the character that was religious, national, and democratic" (p. 103). "It took on the character of a popular-democratic opposition against the transformation of Russia into an European Empire, against the new European order and the direction of Russia's inner life" (p. 131). "As a splinter of ancient and obsolete Russia, the Schism fell away from the new Russia organized by Peter the Great." And, in the introduction to his work, Shchapov writes: "A petrified splinter of ancient Russia was, so to speak, preserved in the Schism."

In several chapters of his work Shchapov describes the historically formed weaknesses and inadequacies of Russia's Church, social, and government life which were conducive to the rise and dissemination of the Schism.

However, as seen from the above-cited quotations, Shchapov, at this time, did not view the Schism to be a positive and progressive phenomenon. In the argument between Avvakum and Nikon, he clearly stands on the side of the latter: "The ecumenical patriarchs unanimously approved and confirmed Nikon's great task and viewed him as a great defender of the Orthodox Church" (p. 53). Nikon was "our great pastor, a truly remarkable genius of his age" (p.

56), a "strict zealot of truth" (p. 339), and the organizer of grandeur and devotion in Church services" (pp. 320, 331 and throughout).

If in 1855-1858 Shchapov characterized the Schism as "a pertified splinter of an obsolete Russia," then over a few years immediately following, his convictions moved substantially to the side of democratic populism. In the brochure *Zemstvo and Schism* [*Zemstvo i Raskol*] (SPB, 1862), Shchapov understands "*zemstvo*" in the populist-slavophile vein, as the whole national mass contraposed against the government and the upper classes (in the official language of the XVIII-XIX c.c., this was was called "the burdened classes," in contrast to the upper classes which did not pay a "head tax"). In XVII-XVIII centuries, "the burdened people of the land," writes Shchapov, "felt sorrow and difficulty from the obligations due to the State treasury, the abuses of government bureaucrats, and coercion by boyars" (p. 3). The Schism is a "mighty and terrible communal opposition of the taxable *zemstvo*, the popular mass against the whole governmental structure — ecclesiastical or civil" (p. 28). Teachers and adherents of the Schism "appeared in all strata of the popular mass," including rich merchants who by means of their capital supported, organized, and strengthened old believer communes (p. 35).

Here the Schism is represented not as "a petrified splinter of ancient Russia" (as in the introduction to the 1859 book) but as a mighty opposition movement of the popular mass against political, social, and religious oppression.[111]

## PAVEL IVANOVICH MEL'NIKOV

An expert on the religious life and everyday customs of the "schismatics" was the famous writer and ethnographer Pavel Ivanovich Mel'nikov ("Andrei Pecherskii" 1819-1883). An official on special assignments for the governor of Novgorod (during the reign of Nicholas I), he took a direct part in government surveillance of the "schismatics."

He learned their life and character intimately both through documentary materials and personal observation. An oppressor of the Schism in his work, Mel'nikov, after the end of Nicholas I's gloomy reign, spoke out (in an official memorandum on the state of the Schism) for a policy of complete toleration for the Schism and the "schismatics." In an 1868 article he wrote that with civic equality and the development of public education the Schism would gradually "fade away" — but on the "indispensable condition that the system of repressions, which in practice only contributed to an increase in the number of schismatics and a strengthening of the Schism's fanaticism, would never be re-instituted in any form" (*Complete Collected Works*, 2nd. ed., 1909, vol. VII, p. 409).

Mel'nikov's *Historical Essays on the Priestists* [*Istoricheskie Ocherki Popovshchiny*] (which was included in volume seven of his collected works, 1909 ed.) came out in 1864. Written in a popular-literary style it, however, is abundantly documented by many notes with extensive quotations from both official sources and "schismatic" works. In particular detail, the author sets forth the "search for a hierarchy" by the priestists-Old Believers as well as the history of the Old Believer Rogozhsk community in Moscow. The latter was, during the first half of the XIX century, the spiritual and economic focus of the "priestists." At their head was a group of rich Moscow merchants who owned factories, plants, and commercial enterprises and who gave the "old faith" a significant socio-economic weight and influence in the surrounding environment. Thrifty, prudent, careful, and opponents of luxury and extravagance, they increased their fortunes and "their children did not turn into squandering nobility because they were merchants handling millions" (p. 207).

In the 1870's Mel'nikov published a broad series of essays titled *In the Forests* [*V lesakh*] and *On the Mountains* [*Na Gorakh*]. These, in belletristic form, contained a detailed description of the religious beliefs, the everyday customs, and the *mores* of the Old Believers and the sectarians of the

Volga region (*In the Forests*) and of the pre-Urals (*On the Mountains*). In the *Complete Collected Works* (1909), *In the Forests* constitutes volumes two and three and *On the Mountains* volumes four and five. These volumes were published anew in 1963 in the Moscow (incomplete) collection of Mel'nikov's works.

The unreasonable, immoral and unjust persecution to which the "schismatics" were subjected by the governing and ecclesiastical powers also elicited interest in and sympathy for the "schismatics" by those circles of the positivist, liberal, and revolutionary intelligentsia for whom the firm religious nucleus of old belief was totally alien.

In 1870 V.V. Andreev's book, *The Schism and Its Importance in Popular Russian History* [*Raskol i ego Znachenie v Narodnoi Russkoi Istorii*] was published in St. Petersburg. The author begins his introduction with the words: "The adherents of the Schism are unquestionably also the representatives of our *zemstvo*, our popular mass. The representatives of the Schism are the most sober, hard working, enterprising, and literate segment of our peasantry. The representatives of the Schism are doubtlessly both the spokesmen of sense and civic mindedness among the Russian common people." (p. III).

The religious element, in the author's opinion, played an utterly secondary role in the Schism's rise: "Is it really possible that because some crossed themselves with two fingers, honored the old books . . . and sang the dual alleluja, and the law of the others prescribed the three fingered sign of the cross and a triple alleluja . . . can it really be that because of this ten million people fell away from the remaining mass of the Russian populace . . . Common sense refuses to believe that the Schism was the result of deviation in the secondary details of religious dogmatism and church ritualism. − No, these were not the deviations that split the Russian people into two halves" (p. 1).

In actuality, in the author's opinion, the Schism was a movement of popular protest against political and social oppression − the "*zemstvo* rights" and the introduction of

serfdom. "The abolition of the *zemstvo* rights, crowned by
the final enserfment of the peasants — that is where the
source of the Schism must be seen" (p. 10). "Serfdom was
the main cause of the Schism's origin as popular protest"
(p. VII)[112] and in response to the reforms undertaken in the
reign of Alexander II, "the Schism loses its former fiercely
oppositional character" (p. 366).

The famous historian, N.I. Kostomarov, expressed an
original view of the nature of the "Schism" and the schismatics in an article, "History of the Schism and the Schismatics." It appeared in *European Herald* [*Vestnik Evropy*] (no.
4, 1871) and was later reprinted in volume XII of his monographs. Kostomarov decisively rejects the standard view that
sees in the Schism only a blind love for antiquity, a senseless
adherence to the letter, intellectual inflexibility, and an
ignorant hostility to enlightenment. In contrast, in Kostomarov's opinion, the Russian nation, in the Schism, expressed
an "original energy in the area of thought and conviction.
The Schism was a major phenomenon in intellectual progress" (p. 469). In contrast to the Old Believers, it was
precisely the "common person of Orthodox faith who, like
his fathers and forefathers before him, was very frequently
distinguished by a coolness toward religion, ignorance,
and apathy in the area of spiritual growth" (p. 498). "We
will not agree with the opinion long spread and which is, so
to speak, a truism: that the Schism is allegedly ancient Russia. No, the Schism is a new phenomenon, foreign to ancient
Russia. The old believer does not resemble the ancient
Russian person; the Orthodox commoner resembles him
much more. The old believer chased after antiquity and tried
to maintain it accurately — but he deluded himself. The
Schism was a phenomenon of the new, not the ancient life.
In ancient Russia people thought little about religion, and
were little interested in it. The old believer thought only of
religion. The whole interest of his spiritual life was concentrated upon it. In ancient Russia ritual was a dead form and was
poorly executed. The old believer sought meaning in it and
tried to carry it out as accurately and religiously as possible.

Literacy was rare in ancient Russia. The old believer read and tried to educate himself. In ancient Russia the absence of thought reigned and there was an imperturbable submission to the ruling authorities. The old believer liked to think and debate; he did not lull himself by thinking that if he was ordered from above to believe in a certain way and to pray in a specific manner, that this had to be. The old believer wished to make his own conscience the judge of the order given. The old believer attempted to check and investigate everything himself" (pp. 498-499). "But another notion which also predominates is also completely fair — that the Schism is supported, as it was formerly upheld, by the absence of public education and that knowledge is the sole means for its eradication" (p. 499). Despite all of its delusions, the Schism represents an "original, though imperfect and erroneous organ of public self-education" (p. 500).

## A. K. BOROZDIN

At the turn of the XX century a competent researcher in the field of the history of the Schism and sectarianism was Professor A. K. Borozdin. In his monograph *Archpriest Avvakum. An Essay from the History of the Intellectual Life of Russian Society in the XVII c.* (1st. ed., 1898; 2nd ed.; revised and supplemented, SPB, 1900), the author not only describes the life and works of the leading schismatic, but provides a general characterization of the Schism which he acknowledges basically to be a religious movement not a socio-political one. The book contains many appendices, including Avvakum's *Life*.

When the government commenced the cruel persecution of the schismatics, a question arose within their midst: was it permissible to pray for the Tsar, the persecutor of the true faith? "It is from this moment that the Schism attains the coloration of social protest though the basis of the protest always remains strictly religious. Secular government was viewed as impious, one that rejected the true faith. As a result, it lost its authority to some. Preaching about opposition to secular authority and all that emanated from it began (it was, of necessity, a passive opposition but one which, in the presence of favorable conditions, could become active). This exhortation grew in force to the degree that the influx of Western innovations increased and paralleled the intensification of government repression. However, it should not be forgotten (and here was the root error of Shchapov's theory) that social protest was directed not at government *per se* but exclusively against the government that was recognized as impious. In precisely the same way the national element, in playing the prominent role in the rise and development of the Schism, nevertheless, in the eyes of the schismatic teachers, was subordinate to purely religious motives of defending the ancient, true faith which, according to former traditions was recognized to be only the Russian faith, one which preserved the doctrine and rituals of the Ecumenical Church in their inviolability" (p. 144).

Summarizing his study, Professor Borozdin formulates thirteen points in his conclusion. The first of these states: "The movement expressed in the activities of Avvakum was of a purely religious character. The national and social elements play a subordinate role but their significance cannot be denied . . . The protest against the Tsar's government, though not in itself a religious phenomenon, proceeded from religious motives since the State broke away from Orthodoxy" (p. 319).

## A. S. PRUGAVIN

A prolific writer on subjects of the Schism and sectarianism and an assiduous collector of materials was A. S. Prugavin. We will give a few citations from his book *The Schism and Sectarianism in Russian National Life* [*Raskol i Sektanstvo v Russkoi Narodnoi Zhizni*] (Moscow, 1905) in order to show with what tender sympathy our leftist publicists treated the Schism and sectarianism without bothering to differentiate between these two very dissimiliar and unidentical movements.

"The Schism is a whole religio-domestic cult generated and created by the historical process of Russian national life. In a most amazing fashion it mixes purely religious ideas and strivings with questions of a purely internal and social cast and character" (p. 9). "The Schism reveals the striving of the awakened popular mass toward light, freedom, and space" (pp. 13-14). Under Peter, "the nation rejected innovations which forced authority in it because it gave it nothing besides fearful oppression, backbreaking obligations . . . conscription, recruitment, passports, etc. . . " (p. 16).

"During the first period of the Schism, the notion was to end it by means of cruel persecution and repression. This failed to work. The Schism not only did not weaken but, on the contrary, it grew and took root everywhere. It encompassed the greater part of Russia, penetrated the capitals, consolidated itself in the border regions, and wove a nest in Russia's very heart. The persecutions did the job of the bellows; they blew the sparks into a fire, the fire into a terrible flame, and this flame enveloped half of Russia" (p. 89).

"The 'Schism' developed enormous cultural-education activity. The old believers have their schools, teachers, and their own literature. Being totally deprived of the right to openly publish and print their books, they form secret typographies and organize matters such that, despite strict surveillance by the police and civil and State authorities, these presses exist for decades and publish thousands of volumes" (p. 91).

Sectarianism not only grows, it progresses. "The teachings of the Schism, which flowed directly from the popular spirit, do not represent something that is constant and immovable. . . No! Splitting and modifying, the various doctrines of the Schism constantly absorb new influences and devour new ideas and trends. These do not allow them to harden, stiffen, or decay and introduce new forces, new energy, and vitality" (p. 93).

"In all movements which are religio-ethical in character, we see the fervent sincere striving of the people to arrive at the truth" (p. 94).

In his understanding of "the Schism," Prugavin evidently includes not only the schismatics — Old Believers — but also all mystical and rationalistic sects, the life and doctrines of which he knew not only from written and published sources but also from personal observations and impressions gleaned from his associations with sectarian acquaintances and friends. His exalted admiration of sectarian apostles of "truth" are much more relative to the "new ideas" of these sects than to the firm ritualistic piety of the followers of archpriest Avvakum.

## S. P. MEL'GUNOV

The historian and journalist S.P. Mel'gunov (one of the leaders of the "People's socialist" party) in his book, *Religio-Social Movements in the XVII-XVIII cc.* [*Religiozno-Obshchestvennye Dvizheniia XVII-XVIII vv.*] (Zadruga, Moscow, 1922), stresses the connection of the Schism to the sociopolitical protest movements of the time. The author asserts that in the XVII century the Schism had "encompassed great popular masses" (p. 70) and "was a major phenomenon of the nation's popular life . . . The feeling of conscious religiosity awakens in the Schism for the first (*sic!*) time" (p. 76). The Schism intertwines with popular movements against a "regimented and serf-like system" and the "old belief" is the political banner of this ferment (p. 129). "The Schism and the rebellions are inseparably linked" (p. 69).

## LITERATURE OF THE OLD BELIEVERS

In the last decade of the XIX and at the beginning of the XX century, many books and articles (in ecclesiastical and secular journals) devoted to the Schism and sectarianism appeared in Russia. The works of ecclesiastical authors or professors of the theological academies were, naturally, critical of the movements of the Schism and sectarianism. Secular writers who were in opposition to the government treated these movements sympathetically as opposition movements subjected to State persecution.

During the Monarchy and Duma period (1906-1916) when all persecutions of the Old Believers ceased[113] and complete freedom to publish was established in Russia, a third category of authors appeared. These were Old Believers who wrote and published books in defense of the "old faith" and its traditions.

In the present essay we do not, of course, have the possibility of providing a survey of this extensive "third side" literature and only append a list of books on the "Schism" in the appendix. It supplements those books of which we speak or note above.

## S. A. ZENKOVSKII

The last word (at least chronologically) of Russian historical scholarship in regard to the study of the Schism was the book of the contemporary Russian-American historian, Professor S.A. Zenkovskii, *Russia's Old Believers: Spiritual Movements of the Seventeenth Century* [*Russkoe Staroobriadchestvo: Dukhovnye Dvizheniia Semnadtsatogo Veka*] (München, 1970). At the beginning of the book, the author presents a short historiographic survey then, sequentially, sets forth the religio-social psychology of the era. Among these are: the pre-Nikonian attempts to eliminate disorders in the Church and in the church services undertaken by a group of archpriest-devotees or "Zealots of Piety" (including Avvakum); the struggle between the Byzantine and Western influences in Moscow, after which he sets forth Patriarch Nikon's Church reform in detail and toward which he is sharply negative. For example: "Nikon's attempt to transform Russian ritual according to the Greek model was totally unwarranted and senseless" and offended the "loyalty of the zealots of Russian liturgical tradition" (p. 210). The changes introduced into the new *Sluzhebnik* [service book] were, "in the majority of cases, unnecessary and extremely questionable as they were based on more recent Greek texts than those upon which the Russian printed editions were based" (p. 225). A long chapter of the book (the 5th; pp. 258-374) describes the rise of the Church Schism and the work of Avvakum. Chapter six describes the growth of old belief and the split into groups (pp. 375-486).

In the book's conclusion the author writes: "Now, of course, it is difficult to judge. But one must assume that were it not for the violent Nikon's absurd ventures (*sic!*) Russian Church problems would not have taken the tragic turn they did take as the result of the introduction of the new ritual." — "The standard of the defense of the Russian faith was created as much by Patriarch Nikon's imprudence as by the support of his innovations by the Tsar and the ruling class" (p. 496).

It should only be mentioned that the term "violent" is also fully applicable to Nikon's arch enemy, archpriest Avvakum, who in his writings writes colorfully about how he would deal with the "Nikonian dogs" were he to take the upper hand . . .

## CHAPTER XXXI

## ARCHEOLOGY AND THE HISTORY OF ART

### Introduction

I will begin with the work of three luminaries of Russian scholarship — M.I. Rostovtsev, N.P. Kondakov, and his student, Ia. I. Smirnov. S.A. Zhebelev was also a prominent archeologist.

I then discuss the author of the monumental *History of Russian Art* [*Istoriia Russkogo Iskusstva*], I.E. Grabar', then A.N. Grabar', historian of Byzantine art. I then proceed to V.V. Stasov, to researchers of primitive archeology (A.A. Spitsyn, V. A. Gorodtsov),[114] classical antiquities (B. V. Farmakovskii) and the history of Byzantine art (D.V. Ainalov, V.N. Lazarev).

The herculean figure of V.V. Stasov stands apart — a

man of seething energy, insatiable curiosity, and a broad range of interests. He did much work in both archeology and the history of art.

## LIST OF SCHOLARS MENTIONED IN THIS CHAPTER ACCORDING TO BIRTHDATE

V. V. Stasov   1824-1906
Count A. S. Uvarov   1824-1884
N. P. Kondakov   1844-1925
A. A. Spitsyn   1858-1931
V. A. Gorodtsov   1860-1945
A. V. Ainalov   1862-1939
S. A. Zhebelev   1867-1941
Ia. I. Smirnov   1869-1918
M. I. Rostovtsev   1870-1952
B. V. Farmakoskii 1870-1928
I. E. Grabar'   1871-1960
A. N. Grabar'   b. 1896
V. N. Lazarev   b. 1897

On Eastern archeology, see the following chapter (XXXII. Oriental Studies).

A general survey of the fate of Russian archeological scholarship is given by M. A. Miller, *Archeology in the U.S.S.R. [Arkheologiia v SSSR]* (München, 1954).

## M. I. ROSTOVTSEV (1870-1952)

Mikhail Ivanovich Rostovtsev occupies a prominent place among the leading historians of the ancient world. In this capacity he should have been discussed in chapter XXIV on the development of universal history in Russia. But he was also an outstanding archeologist and historian of art.

In order not to split his sketch into two halves, I will view Rostovtsev's scholarly work as a unified whole. We will begin with his biography.

Rostovtsev was born in Zhitomir on October 28, 1870.

His father was the director of the gymnasium. His mother, Monakhova by birth, was from a military family.[115]

Rostovtsev graduated from the Kiev gymnasium in 1888 and enrolled in the historico-philological department of the University of Kiev. There he studied for two years. He took Russian history under Antonovich and classical philology under Kulakovskii.

Thereupon Rostovtsev moved to Petersburg and transferred to the University of Petersburg. There he completed the third and fourth years.

At this time his main subject of study was classical philology. At the university he became friends with S. A. Zhebelev and Ia. I. Smirnov.

Rostovtsev graduated from the university in 1892 with a decision to devote himself wholly to scholarly study. He received a study assignment abroad in 1895 and spent three years in Constantinople, Athens, Italy, Vienna, and Spain.

He defended his master's thesis in 1898 on the topic "History of State Farming in the Roman Empire" ["Istoriia Gosudarstvennogo Otkupa v Rimskoi Imperii"], and the doctoral dissertation in 1903 on "Roman Lead Tesserae" ["Rimskie Svintsovye Tessery"]. After this, he received a chair at the University of Petersburg and at the Advanced Courses for Women.

Many of his students developed into scholars, among them Count I. I. Tolstoi, Vol'demar Borovka (director of the Hermitage), S. I. Protasov, M. I. Maksimova, El'za Maler.

Rostovtsev married one of his students, Sofiia Mikhailovna Kul'chitskaia, in 1901. She was well-informed in her husband's scholarly work and was his constant companion on his scholarly trips abroad. In Petersburg, Rostovtsev's apartment became one of the centers of the scholarly and literary world. Scholars, artists, and writers attended their home on "Tuesdays."

After the October Revolution of 1917, the Rostovtsevs moved to Oxford in England. There Rostovtsev continued his scholarly work and also participated actively in Russian affairs. He was one of the founders of the Russian "Committee of Liberation." He wrote many articles and brochures against the Bolshevik seizure of power.

Rostovtsev's absorbingly written book on one of his favorite themes, *Iranians and Greeks in South Russia*, was published at Oxford in 1922.

In 1920 Rostovtsev had received an invitation to accept the chair of ancient history at the University of Wisconsin in the U.S.A. The Rostovtsevs stayed there until 1925 when he was offered a professorship at Yale University. It was in New Haven that Rostovtsev died. His wife died three years after him.

Rostovtsev continued his scholarly work in New Haven. At Yale, he lectured on ancient history (giving the survey as well as more specialized courses for advanced students). He was given a large office at the university. There he kept part of his library and held seminars and discussions for his students. Rostovtsev had many students at Yale. Bradford Welles succeeded him in his chair. Clark Hopkins was the field director of the Dura excavations until 1936. Frank Brown was the director of the Dura excavations from 1934-1936. He is a director of the American Academy (Archeological Institute) in Rome. Howard Porter is the chairman of the department of classics at Columbia University. Frank Gilliam is a member of the Institute for Advanced Studies in Princeton. He is preparing a book on the epigraphy of Dura. Lawrence Richardson is a professor at Duke University. Henry Immerwahr is a professor at the University of North Carolina. Elizabeth Holworth Gilliam is at Princeton. Christopher Dawson was a professor at Yale University. The youngest of Rostovtsev's students, Larry Richardson, is a professor at the University of North Carolina.[116]

Rostovtsev was also elected as president of the American Association (the president of this association is chosen for one year terms). He was a member of the American Academy of Arts and Sciences (Boston), the American Archeological Institute, the Connecticut Academy of Arts and Sciences (New Haven), and many European academies.

I will now survey Rostovtsev's learned works, after

which I will speak of his work as an archeologist.[117]

Rostovtsev's scholarly legacy is rich and varied. He wrote major works as well as articles and reviews on specialized problems. If all of his articles were collected and published, the result would be several very valuable volumes. Everything was collected and unified in Rostovtsev's mind. His fundamental works on ancient history are *Social and Economic History of the Roman Empire* [*Sotsial'naia i Ekonomicheskaia Istoriia Rimskoi Imperii*] (2 vol., 1926) and *Social and Economic History of the Hellenistic World* [*Sotsial'naia i Ekonomicheskaia Istoriia Ellinisticheskogo Mira*] (3 vol., 1941).

In addition, he wrote a marvelous concise history of the ancient world in two volumes (I — the Near East and Greece, 1926; II, Rome, 1927). All of these books have been published in English.

Rostovtsev was particularly attracted to the history and archeology of south Russia in connection with the question of the influence of Iranian culture on the Hellenic-Roman. He sought parallels for this in India and China. Art objects served as the chief documentation.

In 1914 Rostovtsev published a large album, *Ancient Decorative Art in South Russia* [*Antichnaia Dekorativnaia Zhivopis' na Iuge Rossii*], volume I, plus an atlas with 112 tables. (It was published by the Archeological Commission). The edition stopped at volume one because of World War I.

Fifteen years later, in America, Rostovtsev wrote a book small in bulk but one that was very important and of broad scope. This was *Central Asia, Russia, China, and the Savage Style* [*Sredniaia Aziia, Rossiia, Kitai i Zverinyi Stil'*]. It was published by the *Seminarium Kondakovianum* in Prague in 1929. This is an artistic edition with illustrations.

Rostovtsev spoke of his methodological approach in his approach to almost every topic that he treated in the introduction to his book, *Iranians and Greeks in South Russia*.[118]

"In my brief account, I attempted to give the history of the south Russian lands in the pre-historic, the proto-historic, and the classical periods prior to the migration of nations.

By 'history' I do not mean the repetition of the meager facts derived from classical writers as illustrated by archeological materials but rather the attempt to establish the role of south Russia in world history and determine the contribution of south Russia to human culture."

"In order to do this, I had to draw on all sorts of materials, especially the rich evidence of excavations in south Russia. But despite the predominance of archeological material, this book is not a guide to south Russian archeology . . . I have attempted to write the history (of south Russia) using archeological material in the same measure that I used written documents and literary sources."

Rostovtsev's main achievement as an archeologist was his direction of excavations in Syria.

These excavations were begun by the French *Academie des Inscriptions* in 1925. But the French lacked funds to proceed with them. An agreement between the French and Yale University was reached in 1927 regarding mutual work on the excavations which were to be funded by Yale. Rostovtsev took the major supervision of these excavations upon himself.

As chief aide he took N. P. Toll, a disciple of Kondakov and head of the Kondakov Institute in Prague.

The projection of the center of the excavations was the location of the ancient city of Dura on the Euphrates River. It was covered by the sands of the neighboring desert.

This city was at the confluence of several caravan routes where peoples and goods of various nations flowed together. Meetings and, in part, mixings of various cultures took place — the Iranian, Hellenic, Roman, Judaic. At different periods, the city had Roman and Parthian garrisons.

The results of the excavations were rich and varied. The most sensational find was a Jewish synagogue with frescos on the walls. This is practically the only known case of finding wall murals in a synagogue. The frescos of Dura were done in 250 B.C. There is a marvelous edition of them by Professor Kraeling. All the frescos were removed from the walls by Henry Pearson in 1936.

Herbert Gute, professor of art at Yale University, copied the frescos precisely. The copies were displayed at Yale University's Art Gallery. Preliminary reports of the progress of work at Dura were published yearly by the Yale University Press. The detailed research and description of items found by Rostovtsev, Toll, and other scholars were published as study of them was completed. Among these, Rostovtsev's work, *Dura and the Problems of Parthian Art*, has great significance. This is a vital contribution to the scholarly literature on the Parthians and their art.

In 1922, in the introduction to his book, *Iranians and Greeks in South Russia*, Rostovtsev lamented that we were poorly informed about the Iranian world. Since then, the situation has changed thanks to the works of Rostovtsev and other scholars. The excavations at Dura were an enormous step forward in the study and understanding of Iranian culture.

## N. P. KONDAKOV (1844-1925)

Nikodim Pavlovich Kondakov was born in the Novo-skol'sk district of Kursk province.[119]

His father was the steward of the estates of the Trubetskoi princes.

Kondakov studied in an ecclesiastical school in Moscow, then in Moscow's second-classical gymnasium. Upon graduating from it in 1861, he enrolled in the historico-philological department of Moscow University. His teachers were K.K. Gerts (history of art) and F. I. Buslaev (Russian Literature and archeology).

Upon graduating from the university, Kondakov was a teacher of Russian literature at the Alexandrian military school and of Russian history and archeology at the School of Art, Sculpture, and Architecture. He became a member of the just organized Society for Lovers of Ancient Russian Art.

In 1867 Kondakov studied classical archeology and Italian art at the museums of Berlin, München, and Dresden. In 1870 he was chosen *docent* of the history of art at the University of Odessa. Three years later, he defended his master's thesis on the theme "Monument to the Harpies of Xanthus in Lycia" ["Pamiatnik Garpii iz Ksanfa v Likii"]. He defended his doctoral dissertation in 1876. It was titled "History of Byzantine Art and Iconography According to the Miniatures of Greek Manuscripts" ["Istoriia Vizantii-skogo Iskusstva i Ikonografii po Miniatiuram Grecheskikh Rukopisei"].

Between 1879 and 1889 Kondakov undertook a series of trips in the Middle East to survey Christian antiquities. He visited Constantinople, Greece, Egypt, the Sinai peninsula, Mt. Athos, and Jerusalem.

In 1889 he traveled to the monasteries and ancient churches of Georgia to describe the most important antiquities, among them Georgian icons decorated with Byzantine enamel partitions.

In 1888 Kondakov was appointed professor of the arts at the University of Petersburg and assigned as the keeper in charge of the Hermitage's medieval division.

Two years later, in addition, he was made director of the committee for the trusteeship of Russian iconography. He organized iconographic schools with workshops in the iconographic settlements of the Vladimir province.

In 1892 Kondakov was elected an associate member of the Academy of Sciences, and ordinary academician in the following year.

After the October Revolution of 1917, Kondakov left for Odessa, then, at the beginning of 1920, for Bulgaria. In the fall of 1921, the Czechoslovakian Charles University invited Kondakov to give a two year course on the history of Eastern European art.

Kondakov agreed. At the end of March, 1922, he left Sofia for Prague and commenced his course in May.

This was after the start of the so-called "Russian shares" when, on the means of sums allotted by the Czech government, many Russian professors and students came to Prague. A Russian educational collegium was established.

Kondakov gave his course in a large auditorium of Charles University. He gave it in Russian but a fairly large number of Czechs who knew Russian also took it. Kondakov also conducted a seminar at the university. In addition, something like a special seminar — *'privatissima'* — was organized in Kondakov's home.

After Kondakov's death, the participants of this tightly knit scholarly circle felt it their obligation not to separate and cease not their learned and friendly fellowship. This was Kondakov's last group of students. I list them in alphabetical order [according to the Russian alphabet]: M.A. Andreeva, N.M. Beliaev, G.V. Vernadsky, A.P. Kalitinskii, K.M. Katkov, L.D. Kondaratskaia, V.N. Losskii, T.N. Rodzianko, D.A. Rasovskii, N.P. Toll, Princess N.G. Iashvil'. Kondakov's principal student and successor in his work was N. P. Toll.

Let us turn to a survey of Kondakov's scholarly works.

## I. BIBLIOGRAPHY

1.) *Dictionary of Members of the Academy of Sciences*, I (1915). Kondakov's autobiography is on pp. 340-342.
2.) *Recueil Kondakov*, pp. XXXIV-XL.
3.) Supplement — *Seminarium Kondakovianum*, I; p. 315.
4.) the Belgrade *Materials*, issue I (1931), pp. 158-159.
5.) The Prague *Fetschrift* of 1924, pp. 75-85.

## II. POSTHUMOUS EDITIONS OF KONDAKOV'S WORKS
   (not included in the above-cited bibliographies)
1.) *Reflections and Recollections* [*Vospominaniia i Dumy*] (Prague, 1929).
2.) *Essays and Notes on the History of Medieval Art and Culture* [*Ocherki i Zametki po Istorii Srednevekovogo Iskusstva i Kul'tury*] (Prague, 1929).
3.) *The Russian Icon* [*Russkaia Ikona*].
   I. Album of 65 Colored Plates (*Seminarium Kondakovianum*, 1928).

II. Album of 136 plates (*Seminarium Kondakovianum*, 1929).

III. Text, part one (*Seminarium Kondakovianum*, 1931).

IV. Text, part two (*Kondakov Institute*, 1931).

4.) A shortened English translation of the *Russian Icon*; *The Russian Ikon* by N.P. Kondakov. Translated by E.E. Minns. (Oxford, 1927).

Kondakov's scholarly works may be divided into four parts: 1) Archeology; 2) Byzantine art; 3) Study of nomads; 4) Icons and Iconostasis.

Between 1889 and 1899 the set *Russian Antiquities in Monuments of Art Published by Count I.I. Tolstoi and N.P. Kondakov* [*Russkie Drevnosti v Pamiatnikakh Iskusstva, Izdavaemye Grafom I.I. Tolstym i N.P. Kondakovym*] appeared in six volumes.

In 1896, outside of this series, Kondakov published his *Russian Treasures of the Period of the Grand Princes* [*Russkie Klady Velikokniazheskogo Perioda*] containing 20 tables of drawings and 122 reproductions.

These publications of Kondakov introduced a new approach to ancient Russian history based on archeology in scholarly consciousness.

Kondakov's first major work on Byzantine studies was his doctoral dissertation, "History of Byzantine Art and Iconography According to the Miniatures of Greek Manuscripts" (Odessa, 1876).

Kondakov contrasts the miniature to monumental Byzantine art and mosaics. "These are two poles."

Miniature art developed primarily in the monasteries. Biblical and New Testament subjects were illustrated. Kondakov finds more spirituality and vitality in the Byzantine miniature than in mosaics.

Kondakov also turned his attention to Byzantine enamels. In 1892 he published an album with text, *Byzantine Enamels. The Collection of A.V. Zvenigorodskii. History and Examples of Byzantine Enamels* [*Vizantiiskie Emali. Sobra-*

*niia A.V. Zvenigorodskogo. Istoriia i Pamiatniki Vizantiiskoi Emali*] (this work was simultaneously published in French as well).

In 1880 Kondakov examined the mosaics of the Kariye Djami mosque in Constantinople (the former Christian monastery of Chora). Like everything he did, he studied them thoughtfully. At the time it was felt that these mosaics were an imitation of Italian *trecento* art and were the works of an Italian master. Kondakov decisively opposed this view.

"The mosaics of the Kariye Djami mosque," he asserts, "in their style and technical execution as well as in their internal content are the work of real Byzantine art. There is no participation of any sort by Western artists and they belong to the second flowering of Byzantine art in the XI and XIII centuries" (Kondakov, *Mosaics of the Kariye Djami Mosque* [*Mozaiki Mecheti Kakhrie Dzhami*] Odessa, 1881).

In 1888 he published an article on "The Frescos of the Staircases in the St. Sofiia Cathedral in Kiev" ["O Freskakh Lestnits Kievo-Sofiiskogo Sobora"] in the *Transactions of the Archeological Society.*

In 1906 the Academy of Sciences published Kondakov's work, *The Depiction of the Russian Princely Family in Byzantine Miniatures of the XI Century* [*Izobrazhenie Russkoi Kniazheskoi Sem'i v Vizantiiskikh Miniatiurakh XI Veka*].

Let us now turn to Kondakov's works on the icon and iconography. These works occupy the largest spot in his scholarly legacy and represent the main part of his study. There is the *Iconography of Our Lord God and Savior, Jesus Christ. A Historical and Iconographical Essay* [*Ikonografiia Gospoda Boga i Spasa Nashego Iisusa Khrista. Istoricheskii i Ikonograficheskii Ocherk*]; text and atlas of tables.

His *Iconography of the Mother of God: The Relation of Greek and Russian Icon Painting to Italian Art of the Early Renaissance* [*Ikonografiia Bogomateri: Sviazi Grecheskoi i Russkoi Ikonopisi s Ital'ianskoi Zhivopis'iu Rannego Vozrozhdeniia*] appeared in 1911.

His *Iconography of the Mother of God* [*Ikonografiia Bogomateri*] came out in two volumes, 1914-1915.

On the basis of the profound study of Russian icon painting and its history, Kondakov began to write a book on the Russian icon in the early 1900's. He brought a completed manuscript to Prague and continued to revise and add to it until the day of submitting it to press.

The text of *The Russian Icon* takes up two volumes, some 382 pages in a large format.

The first volume contains an introduction and eight chapters.

The first chapter is an introductory one: "The Veneration of Icons in Russia. The Icon in Religious Custom and Ritual."

The contents of the other chapters follow:

Ch. II: "The Contemporary State of Icon Veneration, Iconography, and the Study of Icons"

Ch. III: "Transference and Painting in Russian Iconography"

Ch. IV: "Paints"

Ch. V: "Monuments of Byzantine Iconography"

Ch. VI: "The Most Ancient Iconography of Kievan Rus' and the Suzdal Region"

Ch. VII: "The Most Ancient Iconography of Novgorod"

Ch. VIII: "Characteristics of Greco-Italian, Italo-Cretan, and Russian Korsun Styles of Iconography"

Volume two has six chapters:

Ch. IX: "The Fourteenth and Fifteenth Centuries. Andrei Rublev"

Ch. X: "Novgorodian Iconography of the XI Century"

Ch. XI: "Mystical-Didactic Icons"

Ch. XII: "Novgorodian Iconography of the XVI Century"

Ch. XIII: "The Iconography of Moscow in the Early Period"

Ch. XIV: "The Iconography of Moscow in the XVI Century"

In the introduction Kondakov provides a brief, though clear, characterization of ancient Russian iconography and its study.

"The Russian icon was the most artistic phenomenon of Russian antiquity, an age-old and primary implement, and a gift of its religious life. In its historical origin and formation the icon was an experience of the most elevated spiritual tradition. In its development it represented a marvelous phenomenon of artistic mastery."

"In its decorative virtues and unusual compositional traits, the austerity of types, the idealism and spiritual profundity of the religious ideas, the icon stands on a par with the early medieval art of Western Europe."

His *Essays and Notes on the History of Medieval Art and Culture* is different in character and concept. This was Kondakov's last major work. He was not able to polish and complete it, but even in such form, this book is of great scholarly significance. The *Essays* consist of notes of one of Kondakov's students, N. M. Beliaev, who took the course and took upon himself the correction and editing of the manuscript. The book is richly illustrated and has six chapters:

I. Antiquities of the Eastern Nomads in South Russia
II. The Art of Medieval Barbarians in Europe.
III. Bulgarian Antiquities
IV. Of the Savage Style in Medieval Art
V. Byzantine Clothing
VI. Byzantine and Eastern Medieval Fabrics

In the introduction to chapter one, Kondakov expresses his views on the scholarly approach to the history of art.

"In contemporary literature the history of art is usually defined as the history of the art form. The latter is taken in the broad sense of the historical development of the forms of architecture, sculpture and art in all applied arts. . . The historian of art is thus obliged to briefly denote the content of a given moment but does not have the obligation or need to enter into a historical analysis of this content."

For Kondakov such a division between form and content is not only senseless but clearly deleterious to the subject itself.

"The medieval antiquities of Eastern Europe," says Kondakov, "are closely linked with Scythian-Sarmatian antiquities . . . The literature of Scythian-Sarmatian archeology represents such a high level in the study of its materials that it provides a sufficient basis in order to structure the investigation of the medieval art of Europe's eastern territories upon it."

"The nomads of Central Asia, the Altai, and Western Siberia had long lived next to highly cultured nations: Sogdiana, Bactria, Parthia, Persia, India, and China. They were in constant contact, or in a state of war, with them. The nomads developed horse-breeding to a colossal degree . . . culture came to the nomads before it came to the sedentary settler."

"Within its forms, the antiquities of the eastern nomads in south Russia combined the whole strength of the ancient tenor of life and the stability of an age-old world view. This was not affected, rather just strengthened by cultural yet related influences. In the midst of these antiquities the image of a deer lying peacefully at pasture represents a totem of primitive nomadism and a real condition of life and a magic formula accompanying the spirit of the dead into the next world."

In nomadic art much is linked to horse breeding and the horse's gear. "The beautiful *nashchechnik* of the Krasnokutsk burial mound has two horse-heads whose neck coils in knots and forms a separated palinette which reminds us of a later branch of this ornamentation in the folk crafts of the Scandinavian and Russian north."

The nomads also evolved clothing geared to riding horseback. This is the so-called "skaramanchii" — the riding caftan. This form was reflected in Byzantine clothing and then spread through almost all of Europe.

In these observations Kondakov fully develops the

thoughts which he expressed in his *Russian Antiquities*, particularly in the third volume (*Antiquities of the Period of the Migration of Nations* [*Drevnosti Vremeni Pereseleniia Narodov 1890*).

Unfortunately, Kondakov was not able to write chapter IV, "On the Severe Style in Medieval Art." His manuscript contained only preliminary notes.[120]

Kondakov crowned his many years of study of iconography with *The Russian Icons*.

In *Essays and Notes on the History of Medieval Art and Culture* he summarized his research on the nomads and the archeology of south Russia.

## Ia. I. SMIRNOV (1869-1918)

Iakov Ivanovich Smirnov was born in Irkutsk where his father was director of the gymnasium.[121]

His mother, Anna, was the niece of D.I. Mendeleev.

Having qualified for a pension, his father moved to Petersburg. Iakov entered the second grade of the gymnasium at the Historico-Philological Institute. Upon graduating from the gymnasium, he enrolled in the historico-philological department of the University of Petersburg.

His principal instructor was N.P. Kondakov. Smirnov also took seminars from V.G. Vasil'evskii and F.F. Sokolov (one in Greek inscriptions, from the latter). In this way he received an excellent education and a superb knowledge of ancient languages.

Soon after graduating from the university, Smirnov took part in Kondakov's archeological expedition to Syria and Palestine.

In 1894 Smirnov left for a scholarly assignment abroad. He spent many months in Athens and explored a large part of Greece. He mastered modern Greek perfectly.

In the autumn of 1895 he made a substantial archeological trip through Asia Minor. He spent two weeks in Cyprus.

When Kondakov left Smirnov at the chair to prepare for a professorship, he and the whole department looked upon

Smirnov as Kondakov's successor.

However, it so happened that soon after Smirnov's departure on a foreign assignment, Kondakov was forced to leave Petersburg for a long time due to illness. In 1897 Kondakov completed his thirtieth year and the chair at the University of Petersburg became vacant. It was taken by A.V. Prakhov.

In 1899 Smirnov was appointed keeper of the Medieval and Renaissance divisions of the Hermitage and keeper-in-chief ten years later. In 1917 he was elected member of the Academy of Sciences in the field of Russian language and literature.

By this time his health had become shaky. He died on October 10, 1918 from the Spanish flu that was raging.

I turn to Smirnov's works. They are not so much in number but are all valuable in terms of quality.[122]

Smirnov's monumental work is *Eastern Silver [Vostochnoe Serebro]*. This is "an atlas of ancient silver and gold china of Eastern origin found principally within the boundaries of the Russian Empire" (published by the Archeological Commission, St. Petersburg, 1909 and containing 130 plates). Smirnov supplies an eight page explanatory introduction.

Smirnov spent many years gathering and studying materials. His preliminary *études* might be considered his articles "Sassanid Plates" ["O Sassanidskikh Bliudakh"] (*Findings of the Society of History, Archeology, and Ethnography at the University of Kazan [Izyskaniia Obshchestva Istorii, Arkheologii, i Etnografii pri Kazanskom Universitete]*, XII, 1894), and "A Syrian Silver Plate found in the Perm Region" ["Serebrianoe Siriiskoe Bliudo Naidennoe v Permskom Krae"] (*Materials on Russian Archeology [Materialy po Arkheologii Rossii]*, no. 22, 1899).

Smirnov's work, *A Bronze Water Carrier of Western European Make and Other Similiar Finds Within Russia [O Bronzovom Vodolee Zapadno-Evropeiskoi Raboty, i o Drugikh Podobnykh Nakhodkakh v Predelakh Rossii]* was published in Khar'kov in 1902. The name water carrier was given to figured wash basins used in lay and religious life. Lapkovskaia's article has several references to Smirnov's work.[123]

In concluding the bibliographical survey of Smirnov's works, I will note his review of F.I. Schmidt's study, *Kariye Djami* (*Protocols of the General Sessions of the Russian Archeological Society 1899-1908* [*Protokoly Obshchikh Sobranii Russkogo Arkheologicheskogo Obshchestva za 1898-1908 Gody*]. Petersburg, 1915).

As Zhebelev states, Smirnov "was distinguished by a complete absence of what may be called learned egoism. As soon as a scholarly problem was touched, even if it did not relate to his more immediate scholarly interests, Smirnov seemed to forget that it was not he who was interested in the question but someone else. Iakov Ivanovich would forget about his own work and fervently surrender to the work of the person who had turned to him for assistance of reference. Iakov Ivanovich did not limit himself to just giving the reference. He layed out before his interlocutor all that he knew on the given question. Furthermore, he was inclined to broaden and deepen it."

## S. A. ZHEBELEV (1867-1941)

Sergei Aleksandrovich Zhebelev was born in Petersburg in 1867.

His father, a native of the town of Vereia (in the Moscow province), was a merchant of the second guild. He died in 1876. Sergei entered the preparatory class of Petersburg's second classical gymnasium. He graduated therefrom with a silver medal in 1886.[124]

He enrolled in the historico-philological department of the University of Petersburg where he attended both the historical and the classical divisions. Upon graduating from the university, he was kept at the chair of classical philology to prepare for a professorship.

During his student years, Zhebelev became friends with M.I. Rostovtsev and Ia. I. Smirnov. He made the acquaintance of N. P. Kondakov. In 1898 Zhebelev passed his master's examinations and defended his master's thesis. In 1904 he defended the doctoral dissertation. Thereupon he was made extraordinary professor of the University of Petersburg. He was made ordinary professor in 1913.

Zhebelev was elected member of the Archeological Society in 1894 and of the Archeological Commission in 1901.

In 1914 he was elected associate member of the Academy of Sciences and a fellow in 1927.

Zhebelev was an indefatigable researcher of complex historical problems and a prolific writer.[125]

The philologist-classicist, the epigraphist, the archeologist and historian were combined in him. Of Zhebelev's early work we should note his *Religious Healing in Ancient Greece* [*Religioznoe Vrachevanie v Drevnei Gretsii*) (1893).

His master's thesis entitled "From Athenian History, 229 B.C. − 31 B.C." ["Iz Istorii Afin, 229−31 do R.Kh."], is devoted to a period that had not yet been studied. In this work, Zhebelev wrote a thoroughly based essay on the history of "Athens' fall" (1898).

Zhebelev's doctoral dissertation, "Achaica" (1903) represents a series of *études* on the area of the ancient Greek province of Achaica.

Zhebelev's *Introduction to Archeology* [*Vvedenie v Arkheologiiu*] in two parts is very valuable: part I − "History of Archeological Knowledge" ["Istoriia Arkheologicheskogo Znaniia"]; part II, "The Theory and Practice of Archeological Knowledge" ["Teoriia i Praktika Archeologicheskogo Znaniia"] (1923-1924).

This is the best of the archeological surveys which retained its significance over many years.

Methodologically, Zhebelev is a follower of Kondakov. Kondakov felt that, methodologically, the most perfect area of archeological knowledge was classical archeology. This was precisely Zhebelev's specialty.

In 1926, in a *Festschrift* in memory of Kondakov (*Recueil Kondakov*), a long article appeared by Zhebelev: "Iconographic Schemes of Christ's Ascension and the Sources of their Origin" ["Ikonograficheskie Skhemy Vozneseniia

Khrista i Istochniki ikh Vozniknoveniia"]. Zhebelev distinguishes two such themes. One of them "may, in all fairness, be called the Eastern scheme. A second scheme is the Western."

In the first volume of the *Kondakov Seminar* (Prague, 1927), Zhebelev wrote an article titled "Oranta (On the Question of the Origin of a Type)" ["Oranta (K Voprosu o Vozniknovenii Tipa)"]. Zhebelev provides a historical survey of the image of the Mother of God — Oranta ("the praying one") in ancient Christian art.

Kondakov felt that the Oranta type of the Mother of God originated from the apocryphal representation of the Virgin Mary as a servant of the Jerusalem temple. Zhebelev agreed with this opinion.

At the beginning of the 1920's, Zhebelev was partly translating and partly editing the works of Plato with E.L. Radlov. His book on Socrates (Berlin, 1923) is connected to this work.

At this time, two beautiful books appeared in the scholarly-popular series, *Introduction to Scholarship* [*Vvedenie v Nauku*]: *Hellenicism* [*Ellinstvo*] (1920) and *Hellenism* [*Ellinizm*] (1922).

The Archeological Commission was closed down in 1919 and the Russian Academy for the History of Material Culture (RAIMK) was established in its stead. In 1924 it was renamed the State Academy of Material Culture (GAIMK). The Philologist N. Marr was assigned as its first director. Zhebelev became a member of GAIMK. At the end of the 1930's, he was made head of the Institute of Ancient Archeology.

Zhebelev died in Leningrad during the German siege in 1941.

## I. E. GRABAR (1871-1960)

Igor' Emmanuilovich Grabar was a talented artist and art historian, an archeologist (restorator of ancient icons), portraitist, and a person whose creative mind had a broad sweep.

The major monument which he erected for himself was the monumental history of Russian art.

Grabar developed the principal plan for the publication, wrote several chapters and parts of chapters, and enlisted a number of other outstanding Russian art critics to work on the other segments. Among them were Aleksandr Benois, N.N. Vrangel, and N.K. Roerich.

In the introduction Grabar states that the historian of Western European art has at his disposal an enormous quantity of material which provides him with firm ground for confident constructions and precise conclusions (he has documents, letters, memoirs, millions of photographs and drawings made from all movements of significance). In part, this material has already been excellently worked. This material, gigantic in scope, significantly simplifies the historian's work.

The historian of Russian art is in an incomparably poorer position. Many valuable documents were also published in Russia. Many artistic movements have been found. But this material does not exhaust all the branches and eras of art. Moreover, research methods for artistic movements have only begun to be applied recently.

Under such conditions the historian of Russian art must think not so much of conclusions to be derived from material previously obtained as of obtaining material.

Published between 1905-1909 were: volumes I, II, and III on architecture — (written by Grabar himself), V — on sculpture (written by Baron N.N. Vrangel'), and VI — on painting (the general essay to the mid XVII century was written by P.P. Muratov; the additional essays on the art and frescos of the second half on the XVII century were written by Grabar).

At the beginning of the 1950's, Grabar decided that the time had come for a second, thoroughly revised and significantly expanded edition of the *History of Russian Art*. Publication was undertaken by the Academy of Sciences. The edition was published under the general editorship of Grabar.

Also participating were V.S. Kemenov, fellow of the Academy of Art and V.N. Lazarev, associate member of the Academy of Sciences.

The first volume (the ancient era) appeared in 1953. Among the authors of the individual chapters were Grabar, his editorial associates, and other Russian historians and art critics. Many of them were from younger generations.

As an example, let us open volume III of the new edition (1955). It has three chapters:

I. The Art of the Central Russian Principalities of the XIII-XV Centuries. The authors are N.N. Voronin and V.N. Lazarev.

II. The Art of the Grand Principality of Moscow. The compilers of this chapter were N.N. Voronin, P.N. Maksimov, V.N. Lazarev, and B.P. Rybakov.

III. The Art of the Russian Centralized State. Authors were N.E. Mneva, P.N. Maksimov, V.V. Kostochkin, V.N. Lazarev.

This volume, like the others, has many illustrations, but they are not in color. There is an extensive bibliography at the end of the volume.

The fourth volume is devoted to the culture of the XVII century.

The book begins with a general survey of this era authored by Iu.N. Dmitriev and I.E. Danilova.

Seven chapters follow on the theme of "Architecture and Decorative Ornament in the XVII Century." The authors are M.A. Il'in and P.N. Maksimov.

Chapter eight is "Carving and Sculpture in the XVII Century." The authors are N.E. Mneva, N.N. Pomerantsev, M. M. Postnikova-Loseva.

The following three chapters discuss painting, miniatures, and engraving in the XVII century. Authors were: I.E. Danilova, N.E. Mneva, M.M. Postnikova-Loseva, and A.A. Sidorov.

The theme of chapter twelve (authored by M.M. Postnikova-Loseva) is applied art in the XVI-XVII centuries.

In the final concluding chapter N.N. Voronin discusses the "results of the development of ancient Russian art." Voronin writes: "In the strict sense of the word, we label the art of medieval Rus' to be ancient Russian art. Its origin is linked to the era of early feudal Kievan government in the X-XI centuries and the formation within the bosom of that State of the ancient Russian nation. Its end is in the XVII century when a new period of Russian history begins. It is marked by the formation of the great Russian nation. Pertaining conditions were the development of trades, the growth of commercial ties, and the establishment of a Russian wide market."

Extensive and competent bibliographies appear at the end of volumes three and four.

According to the established Soviet model a general bibliography is prefaced with a bibliography of the founders of Marxism-Leninism — Marx and Engels, Lenin and Stalin. Among the Lenin works cited, by the way, are his articles "What Are the 'Friends of the People' and How They Fought Against the Social Democrats" and "To the Village Poor."

Among the Stalin works cited are: "Marxism and the National Question" ["Marksizm i Natsional'nyi Vopros"] and the "Economic Problems of Socialism in the USSR" ["Ekonomicheskie Problemy Sotsializma v SSSR"].

The unbiased reader may rightfully experience doubt as to whether these works by the heads of Russian Bolshevism will aid him in understanding aspects of art history.

In conclusion it is necessary to say something, even though briefly, regarding Grabar's work on the cleaning of icons.[126]

In the first volume of "Problems of Restoration," there is a short preface by Grabar on "eight years of restoration work" and a major study titled "Andrei Rublev." It is an essay on the artist's work based on restoration work from 1918-1925 (pp. 7-112).

The second volume contains Grabar's report on his trip to the Urals, to Niznii Tagil, to verify the sensational news that an original Raphael had been found there (pp. 5-101).

From Grabar's preface to volume one of the "Problems of Restoration," it is apparent the Commision of Restoration, which arose from the depths of the division of museum affairs and the preservation of monuments of art and antiquity, commenced its activity on June 10, 1918.

This was a severe time. The chaos of civil war had started. It was necessary to concentrate all thoughts on the preservation of artistic monuments that were in danger. A significant chunk of this work fell on the Commission of Restoration.

The basic task of this organ was care for the preservation of artistic monuments. In 1924 it received the name "Central Government Restoration Workshops."

The work proceeded along two lines: along the line of registering and investigating artistic monuments with the goal of clarifying the presence of valuable art in Russia, and along the line of conservation, i.e. repair, restoration, and protection of art monuments from destruction and damage. This work of eight years was a fine school for elaborating work methods.

During these eight years an enormous amount of material was accumulated, something that could not have been dreamed of.

Let us turn to Grabar's research into the work of Andrei Rublev.

Rublev was born in the third quarter of the XIV century (most likely between 1360 and 1370). He died between 1427 and 1430.

His name was known from the chronicles. A number of icons from the end of the XIV and the beginning of the XV century were tentatively attributed to him. But these icons could not give an idea of his mastery because the original painting was covered with a layer — sometimes several layers — of frequently common iconography.

Only after the Rublev icons (and those attributed to him) were cleaned did they shine in their original colors.

Only then was Rublev's mastery, as well as that of other iconographers of the era, truly discovered and evaluated.

## A.N. GRABAR (b. 1896)

Andrei Nikolaevich Grabar was born in Kiev.[127]
He enrolled in the historico-philological department of the University of Petersburg in 1914. His interest in the history of art was defined at that time. He graduated from the university in 1918.

He left for Bulgaria in 1920. He was appointed curator of the Archeological Museum in Sofiia. He studied Bulgarian antiquities. In 1922 he received a position as lecturer on the history of Byzantine art at the University of Strasbourg in France. It was there that he received his doctoral degree in 1928.

In 1937 he was made director of the department of Byzantine archeology at the *École des Hautes Études* in Paris. He worked there for nine years. In 1966 he was appointed professor at the *Collège de France*.

A survey of Grabar's scholarly works follows.[128]

Grabar's principle, though not sole, theme is Byzantine art in its various aspects and manifestations. I begin with Grabar's study, "The Christ 'Not-Made-By-Human-Hands' of the Lan Cathedral" ["Nerukotvornyi Spas Lanskogo Soboro"] (Zographica, 3 *Seminarium Kondakovianum*, Prague, 1930). This is an artistic edition with many illustrations.

The image of Christ 'not made by human hands' is, according to tradition, linked to the name of the devout woman Veronica. According to legend, she gave Christ, who was exhausted by the weight of the cross that he was carrying for his crucifixion, her kerchief ("ubrus") to wipe away the sweat and blood. Christ took the kerchief, wiped himself with it, and his image was imprinted upon it. There is another tradition as well.

Grabar finds that the history of the image of Christ 'not made by human hands' and the traditions associated with it have been inadequately studied.

Be that as it may, the Lan icon, according to Grabar, is a fine artistic work.

The circumstance that there is an ancient Slavonic inscription, "the Lord's image on the ubrus," lends the Lan icon a special interest. The icon was moved to Lan from a neighboring village in 1249.

Grabar wrote several valuable articles in the *Seminarium Kondakovianum*. His study, "The Iconographic Scheme of Pentecost" ["Ikonograficheskaia Skhema Piatidesiatnitsy"] appeared in volume II, (1928). Pentecost (the descent of the Holy Spirit upon the apostles) is described in the second chapter of the Acts of the Apostles. In Byzantine iconography the twelve apostles sit on a high arc within which the representations of all the nations are shown. The dove of the Holy Spirit soars above the apostles.

This is one of the abstract constructions characteristic of Byzantine art.

However, Grabar thinks that aesthetic motifs could also have influenced this scheme's historical development.

In volumes IV and V of the *Seminarium Kondakovianum* two articles by Grabar appeared on "Monuments of Greco-Eastern Miniatures" ["Pamiatniki Greko-Vostochnoi Miniatiury"] (1931 and 1932).

In the introduction to the first article Grabar discusses the little known miniatures of Greek manuscripts at the beginning of our era. Miniatures of this type are radically different from the great majority of Byzantine miniatures and carry the imprint of the Near East — Syria, Mesopotamia, Asia Minor, and Persia.

In his article Grabar printed a number of miniatures from the Vatican New Testament of 949.

In the second article Grabar analyzes the miniatures in the anthology of the sermons of John Chrysostom (also of the X century).

In his article on the frescos of the staircase of the Kievan Cathedral of St. Sophia and imperial Byzantine iconography (in French, the Kondakov Institute, VII, Prague, 1935), Grabar follows in Kondakov's footsteps.

He feels that the study of these frescos based precisely on Byzantine imperial art is necessary. The depiction of triumphal games and celebrations in the presence of the Emperor in the hippodrome of Constantinople were in the program of the imperial cycle of celebrations.

The frescos of the Kiev Cathedral may be seen as the expression of the favor shown by the Byzantine Emperors to the Kievan Prince whom they considered to be their vassal.

One of Grabar's fundamental works came out in 1936: *L'Empereur dans l'Art Byzantin* (Paris, 1936). The book is divided into three sections: 1) A survey of the most important artistic monuments and their themes; 2) A survey of the development of Byzantine imperial art commencing with the IV century; 3) The interrelation of imperial and Christian art. The book contains many illustrations.

In the introduction Grabar states that Byzantine art was permeated by the Church's influence but that the idea of a monarchy based on divine right played an essential role in Byzantine civilization. The Emperor was God's representative on earth.

Though Grabar analyzes the iconography of a number of Byzantine emperors in his book, he asserts that this was not his chief goal.

For him, the physical characteristics of the emperors are not essential (even though he describes them). Rather, what is basic for him is the Emperor (capitalized) and the symbolism of his power. This was his principle task — and he fulfilled it superbly.

### V. V. STASOV (1824-1906)

Vladimir Vasil'evich Stasov was born in Petersburg.[129] His father was a talented architect (who died in 1848). His mother, Mariia Abramovna Suchkova, died in 1831 from the then raging cholera.

In 1836 Stasov's father placed him in the just-opened School of Jurisprudence of which he retained the fondest memories. He graduated from it in 1843.

Upon graduating from the School of Jurisprudence, Stasov entered government service in the Senate, then at the Ministry of Justice. He resigned in 1851 and went abroad. It so happened that Anatolii Nikolaevich Demidov, the son of Russia's former ambassador to Florence, came to Petersburg at this time. Having inherited an enormous fortune from his father as well as a love for art and collecting, Demidov acquired a splendid estate near Florence and the palace of San Donato along with the princely title.

After this he was called the Prince of San Donato, but only abroad. This title was not recognized in Russia.

He came to Petersburg in order to find a Russian private secretary who knew languages and was well versed in art. Stasov was pointed out to him. Demidov tested him in a fashion and offered him to spend several years with him in San Donato. Stasov joyfully agreed.

Most of the time Stasov lived in Demidov's palace but frequently took trips all over Italy. He studied monuments of art and antiquities everywhere and surveyed museums and libraries.

Stasov returned to Russia in May, 1854. For a time he was employed by Baron (Count from 1872) M.A. Korf, director of the Public Library.

In the fall of 1872 Stasov was appointed librarian of the art division and from this time on the Public Library became the focus of his life and scholarly-library work. During the last years of his life Stasov's herculean health was strained and death came as deliverance.

Stasov's work was broad and varied. Music occupied a very significant place in his life. Stasov was the inspirer of the new current in Russian music — the so-called 'mighty bunch' (Balakirev, Musorgskii, Borodin, Rimskii-Korsakov, Kiui). I do not touch on this aspect of his activity.

Stasov's scholarly work encompassed a number of fields — archeology, art history, ethnography, popular literature, Russian art, sculpture, and architecture. Stasov treated all of this with a passion. He lived that which he was working on.

His basic approach to all his works — his scholarly world outlook it may be said — was that the answers to all questions in the history of culture could not be sought in Western Europe. One had to look to the East. Stasov was greatly pleased that his point of view was accepted by N.P. Kondakov in a letter dated March 30, 1887.

"Having formerly been an advocate of Westernism in archeology, I lay down my arms and come over to the Easternizers. Of them I esteem you as one who always stands for the Eastern origin of barbarian medieval culture."

In 1873, commissioned by the Archeological Society, Stasov went to Kerch to investigate and describe the catacomb then just found in the mountain of Mithridates. Stasov investigated and described the marvelous frescos which were outstanding in terms of their historical and archeological importance. He published his study with detailed drawings and plans.

Because the ground in which the catacomb was built was very unstable, Stasov addressed Count Stroganov, the chairman of the Archeological Society, with a report in which he indicated the necessity of moving the frescos to Petersburg after strengthening them with a special compound. But, with an incomprehensible indifference and inertia, Stroganov did nothing. The catacomb was flooded and the frescos destroyed.

In 1886 Stasov published an extensive collection of drawings titled *Slavic and Eastern Ornament in Manuscripts of the IV to XIX Centuries* [*Slavianskii i Vostochnyi Ornament po Rukopisiam ot IV do XIX Veka*]. This was the result of thirty years study in the major European libraries and museums. Funds for this were allocated by royal will, through the State treasury.

Stasov's work on the origin of the Russian *bylinas* (1886) played a particularly significant role in the history of Russian literature.

Prevalent at that time in the study of the Russian epic were popular sentimentality or mystical and allegorical

interpretations. It was considered that the *bylinas* represented a distinctive national work, a depository of ancient
folk legends.

Stasov rebelled against the prevailing views and stepped
forth with a new theory. He strove to prove that the Russian
*bylinas* were a retelling of Eastern (primarily Mongolian and
Turkic) epic works. He felt that the time of adoption was
considerably later, most likely during the era of Tatar domi-
nance over Rus'.

Stasov's declaration made a great disturbance in the
scholarly world. All sorts of objections and attacks fell on
him from all sides.

When passions had subsided, the positive elements of
Stasov's work began to be clarified. His views helped to
obviate the mythological, sentimental, and allegorical theories and views and led to a re-examination of all previous
interpretations of the Russian epic.

Some of Stasov's assertions were confirmed by future
researchers.

The notion of the Eastern origin of some of the Russian
*bylinas* was stated anew by G.N. Potapin (1835-1920) and
developed by V.F. Miller (1848-1913).

## A. A. SPITSYN (1858-1931)

Aleksandr Andreevich Spitsyn graduated from the University of Petersburg.[130]

Spitsyn revealed an interest in archeology while still at
the university. This was partly due to Bestuzhev-Riumin's influence.

Spitsyn was from Viatka by birth. He returned for
family reasons upon graduating from the university. There he
published his candidate's work, *Catalogue of the Antiquities
of the Viatka Region* [*Katalog Drevnostei Viatskogo Kraia*].
The book was sympathetically noted by Count A.S. Uvarov.

Due to material circumstances, trips and excavations
were not possible for Spitsyn. He delved into local history
and teaching.

Nevertheless, he was able to prepare for the VII Archeological Congress and published a work in 1886 titled *Program for Gathering Information on the Antiquities of the Viatka Province* [*Programma dlia Sobiraniia Svedenii po Drevnostiam Viatskoi Gubernii*]. Countess P.S. Uvarova (widow of Count A.S. Uvarov) noticed Spitsyn and quickly assigned him a sum of money to travel over the Viatka region. In this way, the VII Archeological Congress (which met in Iaroslavl in 1887) put Spitsyn on the scholarly road.

He was elected a member of the Archeological Commission in 1892.

Spitsyn was distinguished by an extraordinary capacity for work. His school may be called the empirical. "He did not write substantial monographs which solved the fundamental problems of Russian archeology," says the student, V.V. Sakhanev. "But he did more. By elaborating on, systematizing, and publishing materials, dating and linking them to specific peoples, he prepared the possibility of a scholarly construction of Russian archeology."

Spitsyn's development of the methods of archeological investigation is of great merit. He attributed major significance to technical execution in excavation and attempted to instill in all the view that during excavation the monument was destroyed forever. Thus, erroneous conclusions made on the basis of excavations cannot be verified by a new excavation. Hence, he demanded that a minute diary be kept containing constant measurements, sketches, drawings, and photographs.

From 1909 Spitsyn began to lecture at the University of Petersburg. This was the first university course in Russia on Russian archeology. During the first year, at Spitsyn's initiative, an archeological cabinet was established at the University of Petersburg. It had a good library and a small museum.

In 1917 Spitsyn published *Russian Historical Geography* [*Russkaia Istoricheskaia Geografiia*] to serve as a text.

In conclusion, I deem it necessary to make special mention of Spitsyn's work, "The Tmutarakan Stone" ["Tmutarakanskii Kamen' "] (*Transactions of the Russian Division of the Russian Archeological Society*, vol. XI, 1915).

The Tmutarakan stone was discovered on the Taman peninsula at the end of the XVIII century. The inscription on it states that Prince Gleb Sviatoslavovich (nephew of Iaroslav the Wise) measured the breadth of the Kerchen sound. The stone was later transferred to the Hermitage in Petersburg.

The discovery of the Tmutarakan stone was a sensation. The inscription was published by Count Musin-Pushkin in 1794.

Opinions subsequently changed. Many suspected the authenticity of the inscription. Musin-Pushkin was accused of forgery.[131]

Spitsyn was also sceptical of the Tmutarakan inscription. Like many of his predecessors, he did not agree with the placement of Tmutarakan on the Taman peninsula.

Finally, however, sorting out all possible doubts, he came to the conclusion that there are no visible signs of forgery and that one could be wholly reconciled to the inscription.

## V. A. GORODTSOV (1860-1945)

Vasilii Alekseevich Gorodtsov was an infantry officer as a youth and became interested in archeology during service. He resigned and devoted the rest of his life to archeology.

He started excavations at the beginning of the 1890's and continued to work at excavations for almost forty years.[132]

At the beginning of the 1900's he was appointed director of the Moscow Historical Museum. He was also the director and one of the founders of the Moscow Archeological Institute. He taught field archeology there. In 1914 he published a *Guide for Carrying Out Archeological Excavations* [*Rukovodstvo dlia Proizvodstva Arkheologicheskikh Raskopok*].

Spitsyn was the head of the Petersburg archeological

school, Gorodtsov that of Moscow.

Gorodtsov wrote an enormous quantity of archeological notes and studies, among them a number of long scholarly works. He worked almost exclusively in the field of primitive archeology.

His students — A. Artsikhovskii, B. Grekov, S.V. Kiselev, A. Briusov — were all outstanding archeologists.

Gorodtsov was the first, on the basis of his famous excavations in the Donets, to prove the existence of the bronze age on Russian territory. He established the basic stages of its development.

He then proceeded to write a long monograph on the bronze age. The scheme of this work, *The Bronze Period in the USSR* [*Bronzovoi Period v SSSR*] was published in volume VII of the *Large Soviet Encyclopedia* (1927). The complete monograph was not published.

The scheme of the periodization and chronology of the bronze culture in Russia as elaborated by Gorodtsov was dominant in Russian archeology for a long time.

In the 1920's Gorodtsov headed the archeological section of the then formed Russian Association of Scholarly-Research Institutes of the Social Sciences [RANION]. He also chaired the archeological department of Moscow University.

The Stalin era of the "great change" in the first half of the 1930's was catastrophic for Russian archeology. The majority of Russia's foremost archeologists was subjected to repression.

Gorodtsov was removed from all of his posts and suspended from work. He died in 1945, forgotten and neglected by almost everyone.

## B. V. FARMAKOVSKII (1870-1928)

Boris Vladimirovich Farmakovskii was born in Viatka. He studied at the Richelieu gymnasium in Odessa and at the University of Odessa.[133]

Upon graduating from the university, he spent several

years in Greece where at the time excavations were being conducted at Delphi by the French and in Athens by the German archeologist, Dernfeld. He learned a lot from the later. For three years (1899-1902) he was the learned secretary of the Russian Archeological Institute in Constantinople. During this time, among other things, he studied the Byzantine scroll with miniatures which was in the Institute's library (it was published in volume VI of the Institute's *Proceedings*). This work elicited the attention of Kondakov.

Farmakovskii wrote his master's thesis on the topic of "Attic Vase Painting and Its Relationship to Monumental Art in the Period Immediately Following the Persian Wars" ["Atticheskaia Vazovaia Zhivopis' i ee Otnoshenie k Iskusstvu Monumental'nomu v Epokhu Neposredstvenno Posle Persidskikh Voin"] (Petersburg, 1902).

This is an enormous volume which contains an essay on the history of Attic vase painting from the ancient style to the end of the production of painted vases.

Farmakovskii's principle achievement as an archeologist was his excavations at Ol'viia. Ol'viia was an ancient Greek colony on the Black Sea near the mouth of the Bug.

He conducted these excavations yearly from 1901 to 1915. He renewed them in 1924 and continued through 1926.

As a result of these excavations, Farmakovskii gathered much new data for comprehending the relationship of Greek art to that of the East and the so-called "severe style." His marvelous study, *The Archaic Period in Russia* [*Arkhaicheskii Period v Rossii*] (1914) is seen in this connection.

## D. V. AINALOV (1862-1939)

Dmitrii Vlas'evich Ainalov was a prominent researcher of Byzantine art — chiefly painting and mosaics. For his master's thesis he presented his book, *Mosaics of the IV and V Centuries* [*Mozaiki IV i V Vekov*] (Moscow, 1895), for the doctoral, *Hellenic Foundations of Byzantine Art* [*Ellinisticheskie Osnovy Vizantiiskogo Iskusstva*] (Petersburg, 1900).

His capital work, *Byzantine Painting in the XIV Century*
[*Vizantiiskaia Zhivopis' XIV Veka*] came out in 1917. There
are three chapters in this book:
CHAPTER ONE. Constantinople and Venetian Schools
1. The Mosaics of the Kariye Djami.
2. Mosaics of the St. Mark's Cathedral in Venice.
3. Venetian and Constantinopolitan Manner.
CHAPTER TWO. Some Monuments of the Constantinopolitan School at the end of the XIII and in the
XIV Century.
CHAPTER THREE. Characteristics of the New Byzantine Manner In Russian Church Paintings of the XIV
Century.

The mosaics of the Kariye Djami were studied and
published by N.P. Kondakov in 1880. At that time, it was
felt that these mosaics were the work of XIII century Italian
masters. Kondakov came to the conclusion that these mosaics belonged to Byzantine art of the period of the second
flowering of Byzantine painting during the XI-XIII centuries.

Ainalov realized the significance of Kondakov's ideas
but he broadened the scope of the investigation by giving an
analysis and survey of the "Constantinopolitan" and the
"Venetian" schools and their interaction.

Ainalov wrote a noteworthy article titled "The Art of
Palestine in the Middle Ages" ["Iskusstvo Palestiny v Srednie
Veka"] for volume XXV of the *Vizantiiskii Vremennik* in
1927.

Beginning with the IV century A.D., with the conversion to Christianity of the Roman-Byzantine Empire, pilgrim-
ages to Palestine from Europe began. Pilgrims strove to see
with their own eyes the places mentioned in the Bible and
the New Testament.

In this regard, there is a new turn in human thought, a
new symbolism of medieval civilization.

"It was here, precisely in Palestine," says Ainalov, "that
the proud ancient idea of the earth's focus being in Greece,
in Athens or Delphi fell. Medieval man transferred the focus
of the earth to the places where Christ was crucified.

"A new art was created in Palestine. It glorified the acts of the Bible and the New Testament in the very places where they had occurred. . .

"A new mixed art was formed in Palestine. Its sources are in the popular styles of the Christian countries of the East and the West."

In 1928 Ainalov wrote two articles in volume II of *Seminarium Kondakovianum*: "A New Iconographic Image of Christ" ["Novyi Ikonograficheskii Obraz Khrista"] and "Academician N.P. Kondakov as Art Historian and Methodologist" ["Akademik N.P. Kondakov kak Istorik Iskusstva i Metodolog"]. The unusual image of Christ of which Ainalov speaks in this article is found in the Christ Church in Nereditsa near Novgorod in the paintings of the altar apse. Christ is represented in full height as a youth with shortly cropped hair. Ainalov explains this depiction as an apocryphal one, according to which Christ was a priest-preacher of the Jerusalem temple.

According to the New Testament, Christ taught in synagogues on Saturdays (Luke 4: 16-18). In an epilogue, the editors of the *Seminarium Kondakovianum* characterized this work by Ainalov as "extremely important and interesting."

### V. N. LAZAREV (b. 1897)

Viktor Nikolaevich Lazarev was born in Moscow. He studied at Moscow University.[134]

From 1924 to 1936, Lazarev worked in the Pushkin State Museum of the fine arts. In 1935 he was made a professor at Moscow University. From 1945 to 1966 he was research associate at the Institute of Art History. In 1943 he was elected associate member of the Academy of Sciences.

Lazarev's learned work may be divided into two phases.

In the 1930's he worked primarily on the history of Western European art, but from the end of the 1940's almost exclusively on the history of Byzantine and ancient Russian painting.

One earlier work also belongs to the second period — Lazarev's "N.P. Kondakov" (published by the author, Moscow, 1925).

Lazarev's book on the XVII century Dutch painter, Johannes Vermeer of Delft, was published in 1933. Vermeer belonged to a group of Dutch painters who depicted the life of the middle class.

From the Dutch Lazarev switched to the French. His book on the Le Nain brothers came out in 1936. The Le Nain brothers worked in the middle of the XVII century. In the main they painted scenes of common life, evidently aiding each other.

Chronologically, his book on Jean Baptiste Chardin (1699-1799) belongs to the second period (it was published in 1947).

Chardin began by painting still life — fruits, vegetables, flowers, killed animals — with such mastery that many art lovers took his canvases to be the works of famous Flemish and Dutch masters. Later Chardin switched to the depiction of the domestic life of poor people. The paintings of this second category are distinguished by the harmony of color, softeners, and richness of the hush.

Lazarev's "The Portrait in Eighteenth Century European Art" ["Portret v Evropeiskom Iskusstve Vosemnadtsatogo Veka"] appeared in 1937.

Lazarev's monumental work, the two volume *History of Byzantine Painting* [*Istoriia Vizantiiskoi Zhivopisi*] was published in 1947. His *Art of Novgorod* [*Iskusstvo Novgoroda*] came out in that same year.

I will not cite Lazarev's later works on the history of Byzantine and Italian printing. I will only note his chief works on ancient Russian art.

In 1960 Lazarev published *The Mosaics of St. Sofiia of Kiev* [*Mozaiki Sviatoi Sofii Kievskoi*], *Andrei Rublev*, and *The Frescos of Old Laduga* [*Freski Staroi Ladogi*]. In the following year he published *Theophanes the Greek and his School* [*Feofan Grek i ego Shkola*].

Theophanes the Greek (born in the 1330's) came to

Russia about 1378 and remained there until the end of his life (he died between 1405-1415). Theophanes was an outstanding master and vivid personality who laid new paths for mural painting, iconography, and miniatures.

He had many Russian colleagues and pupils.

In 1963 and 1964 two anthologies of Lazarev's work were published: *Ancient Russian Art of the XV and the Beginning of the XVI Century* [*Drevnerusskoe Iskusstvo XV i Nachalo XVI Veka*] and *Ancient Russian Art of the XVII Century* [*Drevnerusskoe Iskusstvo XVII Veka*].

In the richness of his scholarly work, Lazarev occupies a prominent place among the art scholars and Byzantinists of our time in world literature.

## CHAPTER XXXII

## ORIENTAL STUDIES

### by ALEXIS SCHERBATOW[135]

Russian historians, linguists, ethnographers, and travelers did much for the study of Asian history, culture, and languages.

### N. Ia. BICHURIN (1777-1853)

Bichurin was an outstanding expert in the Chinese language who left many works on China, Mongolia, and adjoining countries.

Nikita Iakovlevich Bichurin was born near Kazan where he graduated from the seminary. His name as a monk was Iakinf.

He took the tonsure and was appointed archimandrite of the Voznesenskii Monastery in Irkutsk.

In 1807 he was made head of the religious mission to Peking where he remained until 1822. He was defrocked and exiled to the Valaam Monastery because of disorders in the mission.

In 1826 he moved to Petersburg where he received a position in the Ministry of Foreign Affairs as translator from the Chinese.

He wrote the following works: *Notes on Mongolia* [*Zapiski o Mongolii*] (1828), *Description of Dzhungariia and Eastern Turkestan* [*Opisanie Dzhungarii i Vostochnogo Turkestana*] (1828), *History of the First Four Khans of the House of Jenghiz Khan* [*Istoriia Pervykh Chetyrekh Khanov iz Doma Chingiskhana*] (1829), *Description of Peking* [*Opisanie Pekina*], *Historical Survey of the Oi-rots, or Kalmyks* [*Istoricheskoe Obozrenie Oi Rotov ili Kalmykov*] (1834), *China: Its Inhabitants, Mores, Customs, and Education* [*Kitai ego Zhiteli, Nravy, Obychai, Prosveshchenie*] (1840), *Statistical Description of the Chinese Empire* [*Statisticheskoe Opisanie Kitaiskoi Imperii*] (1842), *China in Its Civic and Moral State* [*Kitai v Grazhdanskom i Nravstvennom Sostoianii*] (1848), *Collection of Information on the Peoples Inhabiting Central Asia in Ancient Times* [*Sobranie Svedenii o Narodakh, Obitavshikh v Srednei Azii v Drevneishie Vremena*] (1851).

It is interesting that the latter work was re-issued by the Academy of Sciences of the USSR, 1950-1953. It contained commentaries by Soviet orientalists A. Bernshtam and N.V. Kiuner.

## V. V. GRIGOR'EV (1806-1881)

Vasilii Vasil'evich Grigor'ev graduated from the department of Eastern languages at the University of Petersburg. His first work *History of the Mongols* [*Istoriia Mongolov*] was published in 1834. From 1838 he was professor of Eastern languages at the Richelieu lycée in Odessa. He wrote several articles in the *Transactions of the Odessa Society of History and the Antiquities* on "Kufic Coins of the VII, VIII, IX, X, and XI Centuries" ["O Kuficheskikh Monetakh VII, VIII, IX, X, i XI Vekov"] found on Russian imperial territory.

This is a very important source for the study of Russia's

most ancient period of history. His articles on Eastern culture were also published in the *Odessa Almanac* and the *Novorossiisk Calendar*.

In 1842 he wrote his dissertation, "On the Authenticity of the Charters Granted to the Russian Clergy by the Khans of the Golden Horde" ["O Dostovernosti Iarlykov, Dannykh Khanami Zolotoi Ordy, Russkomu Dukhovenstvu"].

In 1844 he moved to Petersburg where he helped Nadezhdin to edit the *Journal of the Ministry of the Interior*. In 1851 he received a position in the Orenburg district — as head of the frontier expedition. This post provided him with the opportunity of writing several articles devoted to the Turkestan region.

His articles "On Certain Events in Bukhara, Kokand, and Katgar" ["O Nekotorykh Sobytiiakh v Bukhare, Kokande, i Katgare"] were based on the "Notes of the Murza Shems Bukhara" ["Zapiski Murzy Shems Bukhara"]. In other articles, Grigor'ev attempted to clarify Russian tasks in Central Asia. He returned to the University of Petersburg in 1862. His main works relate to this period: *Kabulistan and Kafiristan* (1867), *Eastern Turkestan* [*Vostochnyi Turkestan*] (1869-1873), and the monograph *On the Scythian People, the Saks* [*O Skifskom Narode Sakakh*] (1871).

For the Third International Congress of Orientalists in Petersburg in 1876, Grigor'ev published an anthology of his articles titled *Russia and Asia* [*Rossiia i Aziia*]. He left the university in 1878. In 1881 he published his interesting work *On the Campaigns of Alexander the Great into Western Turkestan* [*O Pokhodakh Aleksandra Velikogo v Zap. lnyi Turkestan*].

As a publicist, he was close to the Slavophiles. As a scholar, he was an outstanding specialist on Central Asian history.

## I. N. BEREZIN (1819-1895)

Il'ia Nikolaevich Berezin graduated from the Eastern studies department of the University of Kazan. He received the master's degree in Eastern literature and was sent on a three year assignment to Transcaucasia — to Dagestan, Asiatic Turkey, and Persia. A report on the trip was published in the *Transactions of the University of Kazan* (1845-1846). In 1846 he was appointed professor of Turkish language at the University of Kazan. His *Description of Turkish-Tatar Manuscripts* [*Opisanie Turetsko-Tatarskikh Rukopisei*] preserved in the Petersburg libraries appeared in the same year and was continued to 1849. He also wrote: *Studies on Muslim Dialects* [*Issledovanie o Musul'manskikh Narechiiakh*] (1849-1853); *Journey in Northern Persia* [*Puteshestvie po Severnoi Persii*], and *Library of Eastern Historians* [*Biblioteka Vostochnykh Istorikov*] (1850-1851). The first volume of the latter contains a manuscript found by Berezin titled *History of the Mongols and Turks in the Dzhagatai Dialect Called Sheibani Name* [*Istoriia Mongolov i Turok na Dzhagataiskom Narechii pod Nazvaniem Sheibani Name*] with Russian translation, notes and supplement. Volume two contains the manuscript found by Berezin titled *History of the Mongols and Turks in the Kazan Dialect Called Dzhami-et-Tevaril* [*Istoriia Mongolov i Turok na Kazanskom Narechii pod Nazvaniem Dzhami-et-Tevaril*] with Russian translation, notes, and supplement. In addition, there were the monographs *Bulgars on the Volga* [*Bulgar na Volge*] (1853); *The First Mongol Invasion of Russia* [*Pervoe Nashestvie Mongolov na Rossiiu*]; and *The Second Invasion of the Mongols* [*Vtoroe Nashestvie Mongolov*] (1852-1854 are the dates for these).

He received a chair at the University of Petersburg in the department of Eastern languages.

Many of his works date to the period 1857-1888. There is volume one of the *History of the Mongols* [*Istoriia Mongolov*] of Rashid-al-Din, which contained a Russian translation and notes; the *History of Jenghiz Khan* [*Istoriia Chingiz Khana*], Persian text, 1861-1865; and the *Essay on the Internal Structure of Dzhugui's Ulus* [*Ocherk Vnutrennego Ustroistva Ulusa Dzhugieva*] (1864). Many of his specialized articles appeared in the *Transactions of the Eastern Division of the*

*Imperial Russian Geographical Society.*

## P. I. KAFAROV (1817-1878)

Petr Ivanovich Kafarov was a famous Russian expert on China. He was born in Chistopol. Upon graduating from the theological academy, he was tonsured and given the name Palladii. From 1840, he was a member of the Russian religious mission in Peking where, with minor breaks, he spent 38 years.

He compiled a large Sino-Russian dictionary in two volumes (1888). He translated a very interesting manuscript from the Chinese, *Journey of the Daoss Monk Chan-Chun to the West* [*Puteshestvie Daosskogo Monakha Chan-Chunia na Zapad*]; also, *An Old Mongolian Legend About Jenghiz Khan* [*Starinnoe Mongol'skoe Skazanie o Chingiz Khane*] (1866), and *An Old Chinese Legend About Jenghiz Khan* [*Starinnoe Kitaiskoe Skazanie o Chingiz Khane*] (1877). Many of his works are devoted to the study of the history of religion in China: Christianity, Islam, and Buddhism. He wrote on the history of Chinese relations with Russia and other countries and a historical essay on the Ussurian region which appeared in volume eight of the *Transactions of the Imperial Russian Geographical Society*. This work was recently re-issued in the USSR and in China. He also wrote *Muslim Chinese Literature* [*Kitaiskaia Literatura Magometan*] (Petersburg, 1878).

## V. P. VASIL'EV (1818-1900)

Vasilii Pavlovich Vasil'ev was born in Nizhnii Novgorod. He enrolled at the University of Kazan in 1834 in the Eastern language division of the historico-philological department. He graduated from the university in 1837. From 1840 he was with the religious mission in Peking where he lived nine consecutive years without leaving. He learned the Chinese, Tibetan, Sanskrit, Mongolian, and Manchurian languages and literatures.

He returned from China in 1851 and received an appointment at the University of Kazan at the chair of Chinese and Manchurian literature. His scholarly and literary work commences from this point. He published a *Manchurian-Russian Dictionary* [*Man'chzhursko-Russkii Slovar'*] and an *Analysis of Chinese Hieroglyphics* [*Analiz Kitaiskikh Ieroglifov*] (1866).

His most important works are: *Buddhism: The Dogmas, History, and Literature* [*Buddizm, ego Dogmaty, Istoriia i Literatura*] (1851-1869). This book was a landmark in the study of Buddhism and was translated into German and French. Then, came the translation and interpretation of *Shchinzin* (1822); and *Essays on the History of Chinese Literature* [*Ocherki Istorii Kitaiskoi Literatury*]. His works on Eastern Asian geography are also very important. While yet in Peking, Vasil'ev published a large map of Chinese possessions (in Chinese). In addition, he compiled historical maps of China for twelve dynasties that ruled there. Next to the current place names, these maps contained their names during each period of a given rule. These maps were recently published by Mao Tse-tung's government.

Vasil'ev wrote many historical works: *History and Antiquities of the Eastern Part of Central Asia from the X to the XIII Centuries* [*Istoriia i Drevnosti Vostochnoi Chasti Srednei Azii s X po XIII Vek*] ; *About the Kidans, Chzhurgzhens, and the Mongol-Tatars* [*O Kidaniakh, Chzhurgzheniakh i Mongolo-Tatarakh*] with a translation from the Chinese appended (1861); *Information Regarding the Manchurians During the Period of the Yuan and Ming Dynasties* [*Svedeniia o Man'chzhurakh vo Vremena Dinastii Iuan' i Min*] (1861). His *Russo-Chinese Treaties* [*Russkoe-Kitaiskie Traktaty*] is also very important.

Besides these outstanding works, Vasil'ev also wrote interesting articles in various journals and newspapers. For example, "Russia and Central Asia" ["Rossiia i Srednaia Aziia"] (*Commodity News*, 1872 [*Birzhevye Vedomosti*]), and "The Present State of Asia: Chinese Progress" ["Sovremennoe Polozhenie Azii: Kitaiskii Progress"] .

Vasil'ev also collaborated on the *Northern Bee* [*Severnaia Pchela*], *Golos* [*Voice*], and *New Times* [*Novoe Vremia*].

## V. I. MEZHOV (1831-1894)

Vladimir Izmailovich Mezhov was born in Saratov. Upon graduating from the Gatchina Orphans Institute, he took a post at the Imperial Public Library.

He is known for his important bibliographical works on Russia, Siberia, and the Asiatic countries. See, for example, *Siberian Bibliography* [*Sibirskaia Bibliografiia*] volume III, 1891-1892. He also wrote many works on the ethnography, statistics, and bibliography of Turkestan. These played a significant role in the study of this region.

## V. V. RADLOV (1837-1918)

Vasilii Vasil'evich Radlov was born in Berlin and moved to Petersburg in 1858.

He was a famous orientalist, linguist, and ethnographer, a specialist in Tatar languages and literatures. Radlov traveled through the Altai, the eastern Kirghiz steppes, and Tashkent. In 1871 he settled in Kazan. From 1874 he held the post of regional inspector of Muslim schools. He learned the Turkic dialects (those of the pre-Volga and Bashkiriia) as well as the Cheremis languages. In 1884 he was appointed director of the Petersburg museum and elected academician. He left for the Crimea in 1886 to study the Crim Tatar tongue. In 1891 he headed an expedition sponsored by the Academy of Sciences to study ancient monuments on the Orkhon river in Mongolia.

Radlov's most important work is *Examples of the Folk Literature of the Turkic Tribes Living in Southern Siberia and the Dzhungarian Steppe* [*Obraztsy Narodnoi Literatury Tiurkskikh Plemen, Zhivushchikh v Iuzhnoi Sibiri i Dzhungarskoi Stepi*]. It contained the texts and a German translation. This collection is very important linguistically, ethnographically, and historically. He made possible the study of Turkic dialects which were not known to that time. They were preserved in a pure state without the admixture of Arabic and Persian words because these tribes lived a solitary life and were not under Islam's influence. The stories, legends, and beliefs collected by Radlov provide us with a picture of the life of these primitive Turkic tribes.

## N. M. PRZHEVAL'SKII (1839-1888)

Nikolai Mikhailovich Przheval'skii was born in the village of Kimborovo near Smolensk to a poor gentry family. At the age of sixteen he graduated from the Smolensk gymnasium with the privilege of grade one in the civil service. In 1855 he joined the Riazan infantry regiment. He was made officer from the junkers in the Polotsk infantry regiment in 1856. He was accepted into the Academy of the General Staff and graduated with honors in 1861. In 1867 he was assigned to Eastern Siberia where his task was to study the Ussurian district annexed to Russia a short time before. There he explored Lake Khanka and the regions bordering Korea. It was here that Przheval'skii gathered much material on north Asian ornithology. In 1871 Przheval'skii made his first trip to Central Asia. First he went to Peking where he received permission from the Chinese goverment for his trip. From Peking, Przheval'skii proceeded to Lake Dalai-Nor, then rested in Kolgan. He explored the mountain range of the Suma-Khodi in In-Shan and the Adashan mountains. He returned to Kolgan having covered 3,000 km. In 1872 he moved on to Kuku-Nor, then to Tibet, on to the upper reaches of the Golubaia river and then to the Ugra in 1873. From there he crossed the central Gobi desert to Kiakhta. The result of this journey was his book, *Mongolia and the Land of the Tunguts* [*Mongolia i Strana Tungutov*], volume I, SPB, 1875, volume II, SPB, 1876. During these three years he covered some 11,000 km. Przheval'skii made three other long trips through Tibet and Chinese Turkestan. Przheval'-

skii's major achievements are: the geographic and natural historical exploration of the Kuen'-Lun mountains, the peaks of Northern Tibet, the basins of the Lob-Nor and Kuku-Nor, and the sources of the Yellow river. Przheval'skii discovered a whole series of animal life such as the wild camel, a wild horse which was later named the Przheval'skii horse, the Tibetan bear, and a number of other mammals. Przheval'skii also gathered an enormous zoological and botanical collection.

In 1888 Przheval'skii was preparing for his fifth journey. He moved across Samarkand and into Sinkiang, caught a cold while hunting and died on October 26, in the town of Karakol. This town was named Przheval'sk after his death.

The services performed by Przheval'skii in the study of Central Asia were enormous. He spent more than nine years there and covered over 30,000 km. Until Przheval'skii, no place in Central Asia had been charted on a map. Similarly, the nature of this vast land was completely unknown.

Przheval'skii explained the enormous area from the Pamirs to the Great Khangan [Hangayn Nurvu] range in the East. This was a distance of 4,500 km. From north to south, from the Altai to central Tibet, the distance was 1,100 km.

His chief works aside from the book on the first travels are: *The Third Journey in Central Asia* [*Tret'e Puteshestvie v Tsentral'noi Azii*] (1883), *The Fourth Journey in Central Asia* [*Chetvertoe Puteshestvie v Tsentral'noi Azii*] (1888), and *Passages and Metereological Diaries* [*Marshruty i Meteorologicheskie Dnevniki*]. The most detailed biography of Przheval'skii was written by N. F. Dubrovin (SPB, 1890).

## N. I. VESELOVSKII (1848-1918)

Nikolai Ivanovich Veselovskii was born in Moscow in 1848 to a prosperous gentry family. Upon graduating from the gymnasium, Veselovskii enrolled in the department of Eastern languages at the University of Petersburg. In 1890 he was appointed professor at the University of Petersburg. He taught historical archeology in the university's archeological division. Veselovskii specialized in the archeology and history of Central Asia. He participated in several expeditions to that region. He took part in, then headed, the excavations of the ancient cities of Khozrep. Veselovskii studied the history of the Scythians and the Saks not only in Central Asia but also in the south and south-west of Russia. He excavated hundreds of burial mounds [kurgans], including the famous kurgans of Solokh and Maikop. These kurgans provided the Petersburg Hermitage with marvelous articles of gold and silver as well as vases and Scythian artifacts of daily use.

In 1975, in the Metropolitan Museum in New York, they were included in the Scythian treasury collection which those people in the United States who were interested in Scythian art could see.

Veselovskii's works are very broad in scope. They include: *Essay on the Historico-Geographical Data of the Khiva Kanate From Ancient Times to the Present* [*Ocherk Istoriko-Geograficheskikh Svedenii o Khivinskom Khanstve s Drevneishikh Vremen do Nastoiashchego Vremeni*] (1872); *Documents of Muscovite Rus's Diplomatic Relations with Persia* [*Pamiatniki Diplomaticheskikh Snoshenii Moskovskoi Rusi s Persiei*] (1890-1898); *Kurgans of the Kuban Region During the Period of Roman Rule* [*Kurgany Kubanskoi Oblasti v Period Rimskogo Vladychestva*] (1900); *Regarding the Location of cis-Saraisk Giulistan* [*O Mestopolozhenii Giulistana pri Saraiskogo*] (1907); *Tanais the Younger* [*Tanais Mladshii*] (1909); *Statuettes of pre-Mycenean Culture in the Kurgans of Southern Russia and in the Caucasus* [*Statuetki do Mikenskoi Kul'tury v Kurganakh Iuzhnoi Rossii i na Kavkaze*]. In the latter work Veselovskii proved the affinity with and influence of Thracian culture on the Scythians.

Also there is the *Tatar Influence on Ambassadorial Ceremony in the Muscovite Period of Russian History* [*Tatarskoe Vliianie na Russkii Posol'skii Tseremonial v Moskovskii Period Russkoi Istorii*]. Veselovskii feels that the Muscovite princes and tsars borrowed not only from Byzantium as it was commonly accepted before, but also took very much from the Tatars. Veselovskii wrote frequently for the *Trans-*

*actions of the Eastern Division of the Imperial Russian
Archeological Society.* He also engaged in the study of archeology in the Caucasus, Georgian territory, and in the excavations of the ancient Greek Tanais.

## V. R. BARON ROZEN (1849-1908)

Viktor Romanovich Rozen belonged to an old Swedish gentry family which migrated to Estland in the XIV century. His ancestors became Russian citizens after the Treaty of Nystadt. Rozen graduated from the classical gymnasium and enrolled in the Eastern studies department of the University of Petersburg. Upon graduating from the university, he left for Germany where he enrolled at the University of Leipzig. There he received his doctorate in Arabic philology. In 1893 he was appointed dean of the faculty of Eastern languages at the University of Petersburg and elected member of the Imperial Academy of Sciences.

Furthermore, after 1885 he was the chairman of the Eastern division of the Imperial Russian Archeological Society.

His most important works are: *Ancient Arabic Poetry and Its Criticism* [*Drevne Arabskaia Poeziia i ee Kritika*] (1872) and *The Information of al-Bakr and Other Writers About Rus' and the Slavs* [*Izvestiia al-Bakri i Drugikh Avtorov o Rusi i Slavianakh*] (1878). The latter was published as an appendix to volume XXXI of the *Transactions of the Imperial Academy of Sciences.* This very interesting work was widely used by Slavists not only in Russia but Western Europe as well. In 1883 he published *Emperor Basil of Bulgaria* [*Imperator Vasilii Bolgarskii*]. He also wrote several substantial works in German and French. In addition, he wrote many short articles, notes, reviews, and essays.

## A. M. POZDNEEV (1851-1920)

Aleksei Matveevich Pozdneev, the son of a priest, was born in the Orlov province. He graduated from the Orlov seminary and enrolled in the department of Eastern languages at the University of Petersburg. He took part in the expedition to Mongolia organized by the Imperial Geographic Society in 1874.

Upon returning from Mongolia, Pozdneev defended his dissertation (in 1883) on "The Mongolian Chronicle Erdeniin-Erikhe, with Explanations and Materials for the History of Khalkha from 1636-1736" ["Mongol'skaia Letopis' Erdeniin-Erikhe, s Poiasneniiami i Materialamy dlia Istorii Khalkhi s 1636-1736 gg."] and received his doctorate in Mongolian literature. From 1884, Pozdneev was professor of Mongolian literature at the University of Petersburg. He learned not only the Mongolian language and literature but the Manchurian language and literature as well. From 1889, he taught Manchurian. Professor Pozdneev was the first one in Europe to introduce a course of readings in the history of the literature of various Mongolian dialects. At the University of Petersburg he also introduced the mandatory reading of official papers written in the official Mongolian language.

The extent of his work was very broad. From 1881, he edited the publication of Great Britain's library society in the Mongolian, Chinese, and Manchurian languages. In 1887, on behalf of the Minister of State Properties, he compiled an educational project for the Kalmyks of the Astrakhan province. In 1892, the Ministry of Foreign Affairs sent Professor Pozdneev to Mongolia to investigate the internal state and administration of this extensive area which was officially part of the Chinese Empire. Pozdneev made two very lengthy trips. During these trips, he made an extensive collection of Chinese, Mongolian, and Manchurian works in manuscript and in print. He also gathered a rare collection of idols and other items of the Lamai cult.

After the second trip, he wrote a book called *Mongolia and the Mongols* [*Mongoliia i Mongoly*]. This book contains a bibliography of all his works.

## A. V. ELISEEV (1858-1895)

Aleksandr Vasil'evich Eliseev was the son of a well-known Petersburg doctor. He enrolled in the Medical Surgical Academy upon the completion of which he traveled widely. He spent 1881 and 1883-1884 in Syria, Palestine, and Egypt on behalf of the Palestinian society. He visited Asia Minor in 1886 and the Far East in 1889. Specifically, he studied Russian colonization of the Ussuri region and the possibility of an extensive migration there from European Russia.

He wrote several interesting reports for the Ministry of the Interior. After this trip, Eliseev spent some time in Japan and on the island of Ceylon.

Eliseev studied the countries he visited in terms of anthropology, ethnography, and medicine. Beginning in 1878, he describes his travels in both scholarly and other periodicals such as *Nature and People [Priroda i Liudi]*. He also published his book *Over the Wide World [Po Belu Svetu]* in three volumes. This book is of considerable historical interest and was recently re-issued.

## F. I. SHCHERBATSKOI (1866-1942)

Fedor Ippolitovich Shcherbatskoi was born in Moscow. Upon graduating from the classical gymnasium, he enrolled in the historico-philological department of the University of Petersburg. He studied under the direction of Professor Manaev. Upon graduating from the University of Petersburg in 1889, he went to Germany where he attended courses at the universities of Vienna and Bonn.

In 1900 he was assigned to Mongolia where, thanks to his brilliant knowledge of the Tibetan language, he had the opportunity for an extensive utilization of Buddhist monasteries for the study of Buddhist philosophy.

Shcherbatskoi decided to devote himself wholly to Hindu philosophy and Hindu studies. His book, *Theory of Poetry in India [Teoriia Poezii v Indii]* appeared in 1902. He considered Hindu philosophy to be "at the center of India's highest achievements in the spiritual sphere." Shcherbatskoi used the very abundant collections of the Academy of Sciences' Asiatic Museum for his philosophical works. Shcherbatskoi wrote many works on Hindu and Buddhist philosophy.

His most important works are: *Logic in Ancient India* [*Logika v Drevnei Indii*] (1902); *A Buddhist Philosopher on Monotheism* [*Buddiiskii Filosof o Edinobozhii*] (1904); and *Epistemology and Logic According to the Teachings of Contemporary Buddhists* [*Teoriia Poznaniia i Logika po Ucheniiu Pozdneishikh Buddistov*] which was published in the same year. Shcherbatskoi went to India in 1910 and spent three years there. He arrived at the conclusion that his approach to Hindu philosophy and logic was correct and that Hindu culture was not the product of abstract dreamers who were totally devoid of historical traditions. Shcherbatskoi proved in his works how logically the mind of Hindu scholars worked at all times.

In India his works are very famous and the majority of them have been translated into English and Hindu. He was a member of the Academy of Sciences from 1918.

It is interesting to note that Shcherbatskoi, like B.A. Turaev, had considerable influence on Iu.N. Roerich.

## B. A. TURAEV (1868-1920)

A prominent Russian scholar and historian of the ancient East, Boris Aleksandrovich Turaev, was born in Vil'nius where he was educated at Vil'nius's first classical gymnasium. When he graduated, he enrolled at the University of Petersburg in the historico-philological department. There he studied Egyptology. Upon graduating from the university, as an especially brilliant and very promising student, he was sent abroad in 1891. He studied under professors Erman and Mastero (in Egyptology) and Schroeder (in Assyriology and the Ethiopian tongues). For several years Turaev did scholarly research in the museums of Berlin, London, and Paris and Italian cities. In 1896 he was invited to lecture at the University of Petersburg. In 1898 he brilliantly defended his master's thesis in Egyptology. The topic was "The God Tot" ["Bog Tot"]. In 1902 he defended his doctoral dissertation on the topic "A Study in the Field of Egyptological Sources on the History of Ethiopia" ["Issledovanie v Oblasti Egiptologicheskikh Istochnikov Istorii Efiopii"]. This dissertation brought him wide renown in the scholarly world. Turaev always used primary sources in the ancient languages which he knew very well.

Turaev was not only a brilliant historian but also a philologist, archeologist, and art historian. He did much work in studying and publishing ancient Egyptian documents and manuscripts preserved in Russian museums and newspaper collections.

Turaev's most significant works are: *History of the Ancient East* [*Istoriia Drevnego Vostoka*] in two parts, 1911-1912, and the third part published posthumously in 1936, and *Description of Ethiopian Manuscripts* [*Opisanie Efiopskikh Rukopisei*] (Kiev, 1897).

Turaev published articles in the *Transactions of the Eastern Section of the Imperial Archives*, the *Journal of the Ministry of Public Education*, and the *Historical Survey of the Academy of Sciences*.

Turaev was the creator of the classical school of historians of the ancient East. He died from starvation in Petersburg in the winter of 1920.

## V. V. BARTOL'D (1869-1930)

A member of the Academy of Sciences and one of Russia's outstanding orientalists, Bartol'd graduated from the University of Petersburg. Upon graduating, he took courses at several Western European universities.

He was appointed professor at the University of Petersburg in 1901. Bartol'd knew Turkish, Arabic, and Persian well.

His many works are principally on the history of the

Near East and the culture of Muslim nations. Bartol'd was a top expert in primary sources and in sociology. He did much for Near Eastern archeology. His excavations in Samarkand in 1904 brought him wide fame and also helped to popularize the history of the East before and after Tamerlane. Incidentally, it is thanks to him that Tamerlane's mausoleum and mosque were restored and cleansed.

His works are: "Christianity in Turkestan in the Pre-Historic Period" ["Khristianstvo v Turkestane v Doistoricheskii Period"] in volume 8 of the *Transactions of the Eastern Section of the Imperial Russian Archeological Society*; "The Formation of Jenghiz Khan's Empire" ["Obrazovanie Imperii Chingiz Khana"], volume 10 of the same source; "Turkestan During the Era of the Mongol Invasions" ["Turkestan v Epokhu Mongol'skogo Nashestviia"] volume 2, *SPB*, 1898-1900; "Essay on the History of the *Semirech'ia*" ["Ocherk Istorii Semirech'ia"] (1898); *Knowledge of the Aral Sea in the Lower Reaches of the Amu-Darya from Ancient Times to the XVII Century [Svedenie ob Aral'skom More v Nizov'iakh Amu-Dar'i s Drevneishikh Vremen do XVII Veka]* (1902); *History of the Study of the East in Europe and Russia [Istoriia Izucheniia Vostoka v Evrope i Rossii]* (1925); *The Muslim World [Musul'manskii Mir]* (1922); *Islam* (1918); *Muslim Culture [Kul'tura Magometanstva]* (1918); *History of Turkestan [Istoriia Turkestana]* (1922); *Ulug Bey and His Time [Ulugbek i ego Vremia]* (1918); and many other works including many articles in scholarly journals.

## S. F. OL'DENBURG (1863-1934)

Sergei Fedorovich Ol'denburg was descended from an old gentry family. His ancestors moved to Russia under Peter the Great. Upon graduating from the gymnasium, Ol'denburg enrolled in the Eastern department at the University of Petersburg. He received his degree for the paper titled "Essay on the Phonetics and Morphology of the Irakritian Dialect of Magakha" ["Ocherk Fonetiki Morfologii

Irakritskogo Narechiia Magakhi"]. Ol'denburg was sent
abroad by the university for scholarly research. He worked
on Buddhist manuscripts in the Paris, London, and Cambridge libraries. Upon returning to Petersburg, he received
the master's degree for his thesis on "Buddhist Legends"
["Buddiiskie Legendy"] and received a professorship at the
University of Petersburg. Ol'denburg left for the university in
1899. He was elected academician in 1900 and was permanent secretary of the Academy of Sciences from 1904 to
1929.

In 1917 he was briefly the Minister of Public Education
in the Provisional Government. He was also the director of
the Institute of Oriental Studies at the Academy of Sciences
from 1930-1934.

Ol'denburg especially studied northern Buddhism which
moved into China and then into Japan.

In 1897 Ol'denburg and many European scholars began
to publish Buddhist literary monuments with his own notes.
This series was called *Library of Buddhism* [*Biblioteka
Buddika*]. The finding of ancient Indian manuscripts in
Kashgariia and other parts of Central Asia drew his attention
to Indian paleography. Ol'denburg sorted out and translated
these manuscripts successfully. From 1909-1910 he headed
the learned expedition to Chinese Turkestan. He also headed
the second expedition, 1914-1915.

Ol'denburg achieved great results thanks to the first of
such important manuscripts.

Ol'denburg's works were principally published in the
publications of the Academy of Sciences and the Russian
Archeological Society. The *Transactions of the Institute of
Oriental Studies of the Academy of Sciences of the USSR*
dedicated volume 4, 1935, to S.F. Ol'denburg.

Many of his works were translated into foreign languages.

## A. E. KRYMSKII (1871-1942)

Agafangel Efimovich Krymskii was born in Vladimir-

Volynsk. Upon graduating from the gymnasium, he enrolled in the Lazar Institute of Oriental languages (which later came to be known as the Institute of Oriental Languages). He was graduated in 1892. In that very year Krymskii enrolled in the historico-philological department of Moscow University wherefrom he was graduated in 1896. From 1898 to 1918 he was a professor at Moscow University. The Revolution forced him to move to Kiev where he was a professor at the university from 1918-1941. After Kiev was occupied by the Germans, he moved to his native Vladimir-Volynsk where he died. Krymskii was a member of the Ukrainian Academy of Sciences.

Krymskii was not only an orientalist but a famous Russo-Ukrainian writer. He published several books and novels in Ukrainian. Some of his works were disallowed by the Russian censorship so he published them in L'vov (in Austria) prior to World War I. Under the Soviet regime he was arrested several times for Ukrainian nationalism.

Krymskii was a specialist on the Near East and the Arab world. In 1896 Krymskii was sent by Moscow University to Syria which was then a province of the Ottoman Empire. He spent two years there. During this period he worked in depositories of Arabic manuscripts chiefly in Damascus but also in Bagdad. Krymskii learned the Arabic language and Arabic literature very well.

He was a contributor to many scholarly Arabic journals. He was a professor of Arabic literature and Near Eastern history. Until the Revolution he was also the secretary of the Eastern commission of the Imperial Moscow Archeological Society.

His principal works on the history of the Near East are: *History of Mohammedanism* [*Istoriia Musul'manstva*], parts I-III (1903-1904); *History of Turkey and Its Literature* [*Istoriia Turtsii i ee Literatury*] (1910-1914); *History of the Arabs and Arabic Literature Both Secular and Spiritual* [*Istoriia Arabov i Arabskoi Literatury Svetskoi i Dukhovnoi*] (1911-1913); *Sources for the History of Mohammed and the Literature About Him* [*Istochniki dlia Istorii Mokhkhameda i Literatura o Nem*] ; and *The Arsacids, Sassanids, and the Conquest of Iran by the Arabs* [*Arshakidy, Sasanidy i Zavoevanie Irana Arabami*] (1905).

## V. A. GORDLEVSKII (1876-1956)

Vladimir Aleksandrovich Gordlevskii, a specialist on the Near East (mainly Turkey), entered the Lazar Institute of Oriental Languages from which he was graduated in 1899. He enrolled in the historico-philological department at Moscow University. He was sent to Turkey in 1903 to do scholarly work. He learned both colloquial and literary Turkish excellently. Gordlevskii is the author of an extensive Turkish-Russian dictionary (1911).

His works on the history of Asia Minor and Turkey are generally of great interest. He gained considerable recognition in Turkey. His *Government of the Seljuks of Asia Minor* [*Gosudarstvo Sel'dzhukadov Maloi Azii*] (1941) gives a superb survey of life during the XI-XIII centuries. Also interesting is his *Internal State of Turkey in the Second Half of the XVI Century* [*Vnutrenee Sostoianie Turtsii vo Vtoroi Polovine XVI Veka*] — an era of Turkish might.

From 1918 to 1948 he was a professor at the Moscow Institute of Oriental Studies. Gordlevskii was a major specialist in Turkish language, folklore, and literature and also the medieval history of Asia Minor. From 1948, he was a fellow of the Academy of Sciences of the USSR.

## P. K. KOKOVTSEV (1861-1942)

Pavel Konstantinovich Kokovtsev was from an old gentry family from Novgorod. He was born in Polovsk and died from starvation during the siege of Leningrad.

In 1880 he enrolled in the department of Oriental languages at the University of Petersburg from which he was graduated in 1884. In 1893 he received the master's degree in Hebrew literature for his thesis "A Book of Comparisons of the Hebrew Language with the Arabic [of] Abu-Ibrahim"

["Kniga Sravneniia Evreiskogo Iazyka s Arabskim Abu-Ibragima"] (Isaac ibn-Barun, a Spanish Jew of the end of the XI and the beginning of the XII Century).

Kokovtsev was professor at the University of Petersburg and ordinary academician of the Academy of Sciences.

He wrote many works on Jewish and Judaeo-Arabic literature: *From the Book of Conversations and Records of Moses ibi Ezra* [*Iz Knigi Besed i Upominaniia Moiseia ibi Ezra*] (1885); *The Interpretation of Tankhum of Jerusalem of the Book of the Prophet Iona* [*Tolkovanie Tankhuma iz Ierusalima na Knigu Proroka Iony*] (1892); *Another Manuscript Fragment of the Jerusalem Talmud* [*Eshche Odin Rukopisnyi Fragment Ierusalimskogo Talmuda*] (1894); *A New Jewish Document on the Khazars and Khazar-Russian-Byzantine Relations* [*Novyi Evreiskii Dokument o Khazarakh i Khazaro-Russko-Vizantiiskikh Otnosheniiakh*] (1913). On Semitic epigraphy and Aramaic dialectology, Kokovtsev published *Ancient Aramaic Inscriptions from Nirab* [*Drevnearameiskie Nadpisi iz Niraba*] (1899) and *New Aramaic Inscriptions from Palmyra* [*Novye Arameiskie Nadpisi iz Pal'miry*] (1903). Kokovtsev also published, with commentaries, *A Byzantine Document of Semitic Epigraphy, A Palmyrian Trade Agreement* [*Vizantiiskii Pamiatnik Semitskoi Epigrafiki, Torgovyi Dogovor Pal'miry*]. All of these works have great significance for the study of the Semitic ancient Near East.

## I. Iu. KRACHKOVSKII (1883-1951)

Ignatii Iulianovich Krachkovskii was born in Vil'nius. He graduated from the Vil'nius classical gymnasium and enrolled in the department of Eastern languages at the University of Petersburg. Upon graduating from the university, he remained there and was professor of oriental studies from 1910 to 1918. He was a member of many foreign academies and oriental societies. He was one of the creators of the school of Arabic studies in the USSR after World War II. Krachkovskii studied Arabic-Christian literature as well as

Ethiopian literature and culture. His *Introduction to Ethiopian Philology* [*Vvedenie v Efiopskuiu Filologiiu*] was highly evaluated by European scholars. Krachkovskii especially studied the historico-cultural documents of ancient southern Africa. He was an outstanding expert of modern Arabic and its various dialects. His most important works are: *Over Arabic Manuscripts* [*Nad Arabskimi Rukopisiami*] (1949; this was re-issued four times to 1965); *Abu-l Faradzh-al-Boba-Damasskii*) (1914); and *Twentieth Century Arabic Literature* [*Arabskaia Literatura XX Veka*]. He was a member of the Academy of Sciences and the chairman of the Arabic Association of the USSR.

## B. Ia. VLADIMIRTSOV (1884 – 1931)

Boris Iakovlevich Vladimirtsov was born in Kamenets-Podol'sk on June 20, 1884. He enrolled in the department of Eastern Languages at the University of Petersburg in 1904. Professors there at the time were such famous experts on Mongolia as V. Kotvich and A. Rudnev and the leading scholar of the day, V.V. Bartol'd. While still a student, Vladimirtsov was already interested in the Mongolian peoples. In 1907 he left for Astrakhan province in order to study Kalmyk dialects, but especially to study the Derbets who lived there. In 1908 Vladimirtsov was sent by the Russian Committee for the Study of Central and Eastern Asia to Western Mongolia to study the Derbet tongue of the Kobdosk region. This trip and his observations laid the foundation for the linguistic and ethnographic study of the Western Mongolian peoples. His first scholarly work, *Legend Regarding the Origin of the Derbet Princes* [*Legenda o Proiskhozhdenii Derbetskikh Kniazei*] was well received in the scholarly world. Upon graduating from the university, Vladimirtsov was left at the chair of Mongolian studies. In 1911 he was again sent by the committee to Western Mongolia to study the language of the Baits. These journeys left a deep imprint on his soul. He devoted the rest of his work to the study of Mongolian life.

He was sent to London and Paris in 1912 on educational assignment. In Paris he worked at the National Library and also attended the lectures of Pelliot, a famous orientalist. In London he studied the Mongolian archives in the British Museum — the largest collection of Mongolian books and manuscripts in Europe.

His most important works are: "Turkish Elements in the Mongolian Language" ["Turetskie Elementy v Mongol'skom Iazyke"] (*Transactions of the Oriental Division of the Russian Archeological Society*, 1911); *Turkish Khaton People* [*Turetskii Narodets Khatony*] (1916); *The Mongolian-Oiratian Heroic Epic* [*Mongolo-Oiratskii Geroicheskii Epos*] ; *Buddhism in Tibet and Mongolia* [*Buddizm v Tibete i Mongolii*] (1922). His comparative grammar of the Mongolian literary language and the Khalkha dialect, with introduction and phonetics, appeared in 1929. *Mongolian Nomadic Feudalism* [*Mongol'skii Kochevoi Feodalizm*] was published posthumously in 1934.

Vladimirtsov kept detailed diaries. One of his necrologies stated that his diaries never saw the light of day. After his death they were lost during the war years of 1941-1945 and were not found. It is possible that his friendship with Baron Ungern prior to the Revolution made the publication of his diaries impossible in the 1930's and perhaps does so today as well.

For Mongolian specialists the loss of Vladimirtsov's diaries is grievous because these diaries contained valuable observations and notes on interesting facts of the life of Mongol princes and the Mongolian people. Vladimirtsov belonged to the Russian classical school of oriental studies. He was one of those few scholars who, in his learned work, united studies in history, ethnography, language, and literature of the people being studied.

Vladimirtsov deepened and developed Mongol studies by his works. He did just as much in the study of the literature and folklore of the Mongolian peoples.

## V.D. SMIRNOV (1846 – 1922)

Vasilii Dmitrievich Smirnov was a specialist in Turkish language, literature, and history. He graduated from the oriental studies department of the University of Petersburg. In 1873 he defended his thesis for the master's degree. It was titled "Kochubey of Gomiudzain and other Turkish XVIII Century Writers on the Reasons for Turkey's Fall" ["Kochubei Gomiudzhinskii i Drugie Turetskie Pisateli XVIII Veka o Prichinakh Upadka Turtsii"]. Smirnov was appointed professor to the chair of Turkish-Tatar Literature at the University of Petersburg.

Smirnov made several scholarly trips to Turkey where he became familiar with Turkish libraries and the State archives of Istanbul. In 1887 he defended his dissertation, for which he received the doctorate, on "The Crimean Khanate Under the Direction of the Ottoman Porte Until the Beginning of the XVII Century" ["Krymskoe Khanstvo pod Verkhovenstvom Otomanskoi Porty do Nachala XVII Veka"].

Smirnov did much research in the area of Eastern elements in the word content of the Russian language. All of his works on Turkish literature and history were based on detailed study of the Turkish sources and all of them have retained their significance to our day.

His main works are: "Turkish Civilization" ["Turetskaia Tsivilizatsiia"] (in *European Herald* [*Vestnik Evropy*] 1878); *An Episode from Prussia's Eastern Policy* [*Epizod iz Vostochnoi Politiki Prussii*]; *Official Turkey* [*Offitsial'naia Turtsiia*]; *Archeological Excursion to Crimea* [*Arkheologicheskaia Ekskursiia v Krym*] (1886); *Masterpieces of Ottoman Literature* [*Obraztsovye Proizvedeniia Osmanskoi Literatury*] (1891); *Essay on the History of Ottoman Literature* [*Ocherk Istorii Osmanskoi Literatury*] (1892).

Smirnov also published a very important description of Turkish manuscripts — the collection of the scholarly. division of Eastern languages at the Ministry of Foreign Affairs.

## V.M. ALEKSEEV (1881 - 1951)

Vasilii Mikhailovich Alekseev graduated from the department of Oriental languages at the University of Petersburg. He was a member of the Academy of Sciences of the USSR. He studied Chinese and Chinese dialects as well as Chinese literature.

His works are: *The Chinese Poem and Poets* [*Kitaiskaia Poema i Poety*] (1916) and *Chinese Hieroglyphic Written Language and Its Latinization* [*Kitaiskaia Ieroglificheskaia Pis'mennost' i ee Latinizatsiia*].

## G.N. ROERICH (1902 - 1960)

Georgii Nikolaevich Roerich was born in the province of Novgorod on the estate of his father, the famous artist N.K. Roerich.

While still in the gymnasium, Roerich began to display interest in the history of the ancient centers of culture, particularly India and Egypt. Roerich initially spent his student years in England when he graduated from the Indian-Iranian division of the department of oriental languages at the University of London, then in America at Harvard University. He received his bachelor's degree in Indian Philology in 1922. Roerich completed his preparation in Paris at the department of oriental languages at the Sorbonne. There he received the master's degree in Indian Philology. Roerich knew many European languages and also knew Greek, Latin, Persian, Sanskrit, Tibetan, Chinese, and Mongolian.

In 1923 the young Roerich took active part in an expedition to Central Asia organized by his father.

His works are: *Five Years of Research in N. Roerich's Central Asian Expedition* [*Piat' let Issledovanii v Tsentral'noi Asiatskoi Ekspeditsii N. Rerikha*]; *Tibetan Pictures* [*Tibetskie Kartiny*] (1925); *Biography of Dkharmavamin — A Tibetan Pilgrim Monk* [*Biografiia Dkharmavamina — Tibetskogo Monakha Palomnika*]; *Blue Annals 1392 - 1481*

[*Golubye Annaly 1392 - 1481*] (Translated by Roerich);
*The Savage Style of Northern Tibetan Nomadic Tribes*
[*Zhivotnyi Stil' Kochuiushchikh Plemen Severnogo Tibeta*]
(1920). Roerich returned to the USSR not long before his death.
He was appointed head of the division of the history, philosophy, and religion of India at the Institute of Asian Peoples
at the Academy of Sciences of the USSR. Furthermore, he
coordinated all research in the field of the history of cultural
and political ties of Mongolia, Tibet, and China in the past
as well as their links to Russia.

In 1961 the Academy of Sciences of the USSR published a *Festschrift* in honor of G. N. Roerich. It was edited
by A.M. Piatigorskii.

## V.F. MINORSKII (1877 - 1966)

Vladimir Fedorovich Minorskii was born in 1887 in
Karchava on the Volga (this city has now been submerged
by the Moscow Sea). He graduated from the gymnasium
with a gold medallion in 1896. In 1900 he graduated from
the juridical department of Moscow University and enrolled in the Lazar Institute of Eastern Languages. Upon
graduating from the latter, he entered the foreign service.
He served in Persia from 1904 to 1908. In 1912 he was
assigned to the Russian embassy in Istanbul. He was assigned
to the Russian embassy in Persia in 1916 and moved to Paris
from Persia in 1919. In 1923 he lectured on Persian literature at the national school of oriental languages and also
taught Persian literature and the history of the Muslim world.

In 1930 he was appointed professor of Persian literature at the University of London.

Minorskii was a member of the "Societé Asiatique"
(1920), the "Royal Asiatic Society"(1938), and the
*"Deutsche Morgenländische Gesellschaft."* (1937).

Minorskii was present and read papers at the congress
of orientalists in London (1923), Rome (1935), and Brussels

(1938). He was also present in Teheran at the celebrations in honor of the 1,000th anniversary of Firuz.

Minorskii left many works, over 150 articles, reviews, and notes in Russian, French, and English. He began to publish in 1901.

His principal works are: *With Russian Citizens of the Sultan* [*U Russkikh Poddannykh Sultana*] (1902) and *A Persian Geographer of 982 A.D. on Central Asia* [*Persidskii Geograf 982 A.D. o Tsentral'noi Azii*] (1937). With G. V. Vernadsky he wrote "The Composition of the Great Yasa of Genghiz Khan" ["*O Sostave Velikoi Iasy Chingiz-Khana*"]. His Catalogue of Turkish Manuscripts in the A. Chester Beatty collection was also published.

Minorskii contributed to many scholarly journals.

## S.I. RUDENKO (1885 – 1970)

Sergei Ivanovich Rudenko received his degree in anthropology from the University of Petersburg. In 1912 he was sent on assignment to Orenburg province and the eastern Altai. We have no information on his activity from 1916 - 1925 and again from 1929 - 1947. His name is not to be found in Soviet encyclopedias.

His chief interest at the university was archeology. The works of the famous V. V. Radlov strongly influenced Rudenko.

In 1891, in the Altai mountains, Radlov discovered two large burial mounds, the Katandil and the Berel, with stone covers on top. These mounds turned out to be frozen. Thus, articles of wood, leather, and fabric, and clothing and other items were well preserved. This circumstance led to the attention of the Russian Museum (presently this is called the Ethnographic Museum of the Peoples of the USSR). In 1926 a special expedition was equipped. It was to check a group of ancient burial mounds in the Ulan river basin in the eastern Altai. In 1929 the museum was able to equip an expedition to excavate the first burial mound in the Pazyryk valley. In all likelihood Rudenko took part in this expedition. Despite spectacular results, the excavations were interrupted during the years of collectivization, the Ezhevschina, and World War II.

The excavations were resumed by the Academy of Sciences in 1948 with the participation of the Hermitage. Rudenko headed this expedition. In succeeding years the whole group of burial mounds was uncovered. This is to Rudenko's great credit.

His main works are: *Bashkirians, An Experiment in the Ethnological Monograph* [*Bashkiry, Opyt Etnologicheskoi Monografii*] (1916 - 1925). *The Second Pazyryk Burial Mound. Results of the work of the Expedition of the Academy of Sciences* [*Vtoroi Pazyrykskii Kurgan. Rezul'taty Rabot Ekspeditsii Akademii Nauk*] (1954); *Art of the Scythians of the Altai* [*Iskusstvo Skifov Altaia*] (1949); *Culture of the Inhabitants of the Altai Mountains During Scythian Times* [*Kul'tura Naseleniia Gornogo Altaia v Skifskoe Vremia*] (1953); *The Siberian Collection of Peter I* [*Sibirskaia Kollektsiia Petra I* ] (1962); *Culture of the Huns and the Noinulian Burial Mounds* [*Kul'tura Khunnov i Noinulinskie Kurgany*] (Academy of Sciences, 1962); *The World's Most Ancient Artistic Rugs and Weaves from the Frozen Burial Mounds of the Altai Mountains* [*Drevneishie v Mire Khudozhestvennye Kovry i Tkani iz Oledenelykh Kurganov Gornogo Altaia*] (1968).

Professor M. W. Thompson of University of California at Berkeley translated Rudenko's *Second Pazyryk Burial Mound* and provided commentaries.

## V.A. RIASANOVSKII (1884 – 1968)

Valentin Aleksandrovich Riasanovskii was born near Kostroma on his parents' estate. He graduated from the classical gymnasium in Kostroma in 1903 and from the juridical department of Moscow University in 1908. He also studied in Germany in 1911 and at the Don University in 1917.

Riasanovskii was ordinary professor of law from 1918 - 1922 at the universities of Tomsk, Irkutsk, and Vladivostok.

He was also a law professor in Kharbin (Manchuria) from
1922 - 1934. His principle specialty was jurisprudence. A
great merit of Riasanovskii is the study of Mongolian law.
Riasanovskii not only studied Mongolian law, but also the
law of the large Mongolian tribes, the Buriats and the Kalmyks. Riasanovskii wrote more than 140 scholarly works,
articles, and reviews.

All of Riasanovskii's works can be divided into two
groups. His works on Russian law and procedure belong to
the first group; his scholarly works on the jurisprudence of
eastern Asian peoples belongs to the second.

His most important works are: *Common Law of the
Buriats* [*Obychnoe Pravo Buriat*] (1921); *Mongolian Law
(Principally Common)* [*Mongol'skoe Pravo (Preimushchest-
venno Obychnoe)*] (1931); *Is Mongolian Law Common Law*
[*Iavliaetsia li Mongol'skoe Pravo Obychnym*] (1932); *Con-
temporary Chinese Law* [*Sovremennoe Pravo Kitaia*] (1927);
*Fundamental Sources of Chinese Land, Mining, and Forest
Law* [*Osnovnye Nachala Zemel'nogo, Gornogo i Lesnogo
Prava Kitaia*] (1928); *On the Scholarly Elaboration and Codi-
fication of Buriat Common Law* [*O Nauchnoi Razrabotke i
Kodifikatsii Buriatskogo Obychnogo Prava*] (1921); *On the
Question of the Influence of Mongol Culture and Mongol
Law on Russian Culture and Law* [*K Voprosu Vliianiia Mon-
gol'skoi Kul'tury i Mongol'skogo Prava na Russkuiu Kul'-
turu i Pravo*] (1921); *Survey of Documents in Mongolian
Law* [*Obzor Pamiatnikov Mongol'skogo Prava*] (1932);
*The Great Yasa of Jenghiz-Khan* [*Velikaia Iasa Chingiz-
Khana*] (1933); *Fundamental Institutions of Chinese Civil
Law* [*Osnovnye Instituty Kitaiskogo Grazhdanskogo Prava*];
and *The Civil Code of the Chinese Republic* [*Grazhdanskoe
Ulozhenie Kitaiskoi Respubliki*] (1935, in five volumes).

Riasanovskii also wrote many works in English and
French. His book *Mongolian Law* was translated into Japanese in 1935.

# APPENDIX I
## On Vernadsky's Works

**by Nikolay Andreyev**

In the lobbies at the Byzantine Congress (at which many scholars of contiguous disciplines were present) at Oxford in 1966, S. B. Shishman (Paris) reminded those present that George Vernadsky would be 80 years old in 1967. In private discussions he raised the question of whether it might not be a good idea to publish an international anthology of works in honor of this outstanding historian. This idea was fervently welcomed by all those who heard of it at the Oxford session, particularly by scholars from Eastern Europe. They immediately promised to submit their studies for the Vernadsky *Festschrift*.

Naturally, the publication of this collection was to take place in the West, preferably in France or Belgium. Unfortunately, because of financial reasons, the plan could not be realized though A.N. Grabar (Paris) and other scholars worked on this for more than two years.

In the meantime, N. E. Andreyev (Cambridge) began to verify and supplement Vernadsky's bibliography and prepare an anniversary biographical essay which was translated into French by S.B. Shishman. The bibliography was inclusive to 1973. G. Vernadsky checked it a month before his death and reported that all had been included. N.E. Andreyev wrote him of the idea to publish the complete bibliography of his works.

The foundation of the bibliography published below is the bibliography published in a *Festschrift* for Professor Vernadsky prepared by his American disciples and col-

leagues: *Essays in Russian History: A Collection Dedicated to George Vernadsky*, edited by Allan D. Ferguson
and Alfred Levin. Archon Books, Hamden, Connecticut,
1964, pp. XIII – XXV.

This bibliography was verified. translated from the
Latin type, the only one used in the American edition, into
the original print, i.e. sometimes into the Cyrillic. Furthermore, consideration was taken of the new and old orthography in the works written in Russian. Works that were
missed were included in the appropriate sections of the list.
S.B. Shishman took upon himself the task of typing the
whole list in accordance with the rules accepted for publishing the bibliography in the Slavic publishing houses of
France where these materials were to be originally published.
They show the direction, sweep, and character of G.V.
Vernadsky's scholarly works. [See the appropriate appendix
for the bibliography.]

### G.V. VERNADSKY (August 20, 1887 – June 12, 1973)

George Vernadsky as a historian possessed those characteristics of a scholar which, in fairness, created a lofty
reputation for many representatives of Russian scholarship,
namely: factuality in construction, the striving to be
guided by primary sources, courage in the statement of a
problem, tolerance for other opinions, objectivity and
fearlessness in conclusions. It was precisely in these traits
that the tradition of his highly intelligent family told: his
grandfather, Ivan Vasil'evich Vernadsky, was professor of
political economy at Kiev and Moscow universities, then a
professor at the Pedagogical Institute and at the Alexandrian
Lycee in St. Petersburg. His father, Vladimir Ivanovich
Vernadsky, was one of the most prominent scholars in the
field of minerology and biochemistry. In 1906 he was
elected an adjunct of the Imperial Academy of Sciences
extraordinary academician in 1909, and ordinary acade-
demician in 1912. This was the tradition mastered by him,
first in the fifth classical gymnasium in Moscow, which gave

him the "taste" of history and a basic foundation in both modern and ancient languages, then at Moscow University. There he had such brilliant scholars as D.M. Petrushevskii, A. N. Savin, M. M. Bogoslovskii, M. K. Liubavskii, R. Iu. Vipper, A. A. Kizevetter, Iu. V. Got'e, A. I. Iakovlev, and even Kliuchevskii "himself" who was still lecturing but who no longer conducted seminars. In this way the "Moscow historical school" was Vernadsky's foundation. To this we must add the positive impressions gained from several months in Germany at the University of Freiburg. There he attended lectures on history by Georg von Below, Friedrich Meinecke and Heinrich Rickert. The latter taught the philosophy of history, "especially giving a push to thought," as Vernadsky later noted.

However, our historian linked his research more with the University of St. Petersburg where he was drawn by the possibility of studying under S.F. Platonov whose publications he knew well and admired. True, Vernadsky commenced his academic studies in Moscow. He studied documents on "Siberian affairs" at the archives of the Ministry of Justice. The results were three articles on Siberian history (see the entries in the bibliography for 1914 and 1915). But, because of a number of various reasons and considerations, of which Vernadsky speaks in his interesting memoirs (see entry no. 187 in the Vernadsky bibliography), he contacted Platonov in 1912 requesting him to be his adviser in preparing for a master's degree at the University of St. Petersburg. Platonov agreed. Thus, Vernadsky also found himself involved in the "Petersburg historical school." He passed a series of master's examinations: ancient history under M.I. Rostovtsev, medieval history under A.A. Grevs, modern history under N.I. Kareev, Russian history under S.F. Platonov. All of them were scholarly stars of the first magnitude. The master's theme was chosen finally in the XVIII century. The candidate was interested in the "broad international links of Russian Freemasonry under Catherine II and the possibility of studying it within the background of European intellectual history." The presence of many yet unpublished, or wholly unused, documents on this topic decided the question. "Siberian affairs," which also much attracted the attention of the young scholar, were in Moscow and Vernadsky felt himself to be linked to the University of St.Petersburg. His former history teacher at the gymnasium, an expert on Old Belief and an Old Believer himself, Ia. L. Barskov, had, at this time, become one of the senior scholarly officials in the State archives in Petersburg. He was well acquainted with the unpublished documents preserved there, as well as with those in the manuscript division of the Imperial Public Library and the rich collection of XVIII century books in the latter. Barskov fervently suggested that Vernadsky use some of the masonic materials for the dissertation (he published a bit "on the masons" himself in 1915). A.S. Lappo-Danilevskii and other experts on the period also approved this topic. Platonov, incidentally, had initially intended to offer Vernadsky a topic on Muscovite Russia. Later, he was inclined to accept a biography of Count P.I. Shuvalov, a statesman of the Elizabethan era. This theme had also been discussed by Vernadsky as a possible one for the master's degree. But Platonov also agreed on the topic of Freemasonry under Catherine II. He understood the interests of the candidate who desired to analyze a phenomenon of XVIII century Russia linked to European ideas in this period.

The master's thesis (see no. 8 in the Vernadsky bibliography) was successfully defended by Vernadsky at a public session on October 22, 1917. Official opponents assigned by the department were, in addition to S. F. Platonov, S. V. Rozhdestvenskii and I. A. Shliapkin. Remarks from the public were also made. The department unanimously granted Vernadsky the master's degree in Russian history.

This ended a very important period in Vernadsky's life. It gave him high professional qualifications and introduced him into the academic world. It acquainted him with a number of brilliant representatives of Russian historical scholarship. Many of them became his friends. Furthermore, it was during this period that he gained his first experience in university teaching. Vernadsky, as a *privat-docent*, held seminars on Siberian history and on the history of Russian freemasonry. He who understands the specifics of the process of the formation of a young scholar will easily imagine the extraordinary significance that entry into the field of research held for Vernadsky. Of course, the complement of his teachers and advisers, examiners and colleagues, and, not in the least, their very personalities, were the source of a spiritual richness and the object of a conscious and sub-conscious evaluation and re-evaluation of them. In essence, it was precisely they, with whom Vernadsky became personally acquainted, who formed what was referred to as Russian historical scholarship in the pre-revolutionary period. This acquaintanceship, even a half-century later, proved extremely valuable when, not long before his death, he commenced to unite his essays on the history of Russian historical scholarship. These were published in the *Transactions of the Association of Russian-American Scholars in the U.S.A.*

It should be noted, by the way, that the young historian, at the request of V.A. Pypina-Liatskaia, edited and supplied extensive notes for her father's book, A.N. Pypin's, *Russian Freemasonry, the XVIII and the First Quarter of the XIX c.*, which came out in 1916. (But Vernadsky did not deem it necessary to include this book, or others during his life in the U.S.A. which he edited, in his bibliography. He included in his bibliography only his original publications (see at end of the bibliography). His master's thesis was published in the spring of 1917. Some of his works of that period were published in 1918 and 1924 (see the Vernadsky bibliography, nos. 9, 27) in Soviet publications though the old orthography was still used.

On October 25, 1917,Vernadsky left the capital without suspecting the Bolshevik take over of power.

Vernadsky spent the 1917 — 1918 academic year at the University of Perm. He taught a course on the history of Russia in the XVIII and XIX centuries. Vernadsky got there by accident. He was on his way to Omsk in September, where he had been chosen for the chair of Russian history at the Omsk

Polytechnic Institute. But the train became stuck at Perm and the local university immediately offered him a position. The "deepening of the Revolution" (see no. 184 in the Vernadsky bibliography) forced Vernadsky to leave, first to Moscow then, from there, to the south of Russia. It is remarkable that Vernadsky tried to continue his academic work everywhere. In a letter to this author (dated March 13, 1967), Vernadsky reported that, in September of 1918, he gave a lecture at the Historical Society of Nestor the Chronicler in Kiev. The theme treated the Russian gentry under Peter III and Catherine II and "as far as I can remember, this lecture was published in this society's *Readings.*" Unfortunately, this author has not been able to locate the corresponding volume of the *Readings*. Three queries on this topic (to the History Institute of the Ukrainian Academy of Sciences of the USSR, and to one of the Soviet historians working on this period) provided no results.

Vernadsky moved to the Crimea in the fall of 1918. He was appointed professor of Russian history by the Simferopol branch of the historico-philological department of the University of Kiev. Soon thereafter this branch was transformed into an independent university, called Taura. As in other Russian cities, Vernadsky met friendly and highly qualified colleagues and a responsive and talented student body (see no. 185 in the Vernadsky bibliography).In addition to teaching, he continued the study of the Tatar language which he had begun in Perm. In both places his teachers were local mullahs. The valuable archive of V.S. Popov was transferred to the university from a private collection. Popov was chancellery head of Prince G.A. Potemkin of Taura (Taurida). Vernadsky studied these archival materials enthusiastically and gave several lectures based on them. These were published in the *Proceedings* of the Tauridian archival commission (see the bibliographical listing for 1919).

From the Crimea, where, for a short time (from mid-September to the evacuation on October 30, 1920), Vernadsky was drawn into the activity of General Wrangel's government (he took the part of press secretary which, at the suggestion of P.B. Struve, was offered to him by the commander-in-chief), he left for exile.

Vernadsky spent five months in Constantinople where, despite the difficulties of daily life, he was able to commence the study of "literary Turkish" under the guidance of a learned Arab who spoke Russian. He moved to Athens where he spent one year, until March of 1922. At that time he received an invitation to move to Prague to the just-organized Russian Educational Collegium. Soon after his arrival, he was appointed professor at the just-created Russian juridical faculty there. It is not uninteresting to observe that, while in Athens, he worked as a librarian at the Greek Archeological Society and, simultaneously, tried to learn modern Greek (he had already known classical Greek well from his gymnasium days).

Prague turned out to be an important stage in our historian's scholarly activity. It was here that the basic themes of his research interests were charted. In the latest period of his life he continued to develop and, of course, supplement them. In Prague, Vernadsky lectured on the history of Russian Law and on the history of institutions in Russia's imperial period. In addition, he gave a course on the sources of ecclesiastical law. The result of these studies in legal problems was the valuable book *Essay on the History of Law in the Russian State in the XVIII and XIXcc.* [*Ocherk Istorii Prava Russkogo Gosudarstva XVIII − XIX v.v.*] and a number of articles which touched on various problems of Russian and Byzantine law (see the Vernadsky bibliography for the years 1923 − 1928).

In Prague, Vernadsky entered the circle of interests of academician N. P. Kondakov, the great Russian Byzantinist, archeologist, and historian of medieval art. The result of this fruitful scholarly contact, one noted in Vernadsky's works, was an intense attention paid to Byzantine and specially Russo-Byzantine problematics. It is not accidental that it was precisely Professor Vernadsky who gave a speech concerning the significance of N.P. Kondakov's scholarly work when, in 1924, academic Prague was celebrating the latter's

80th birthday. He also wrote of him later (see the Vernadsky bibliography, nos. 28, 37, 42).

After Kondakov's death on February 17, 1925, Vernadsky and A.P. Kalitinskii, a former professor of the Moscow Archeological Institute, headed the newly-formed learned concord, the seminar in Kondakov's name (*Seminarium Kondakovianum*). Later it was re-organized into an institute in Kondakov's name (*Kondakov Institute*).

As before, Vernadsky again formed many new academic friends, both Russian and Czech. Among the latter,the name of Liubor Niderle should be singled out. He was the true creator of critical Slavistics and an outstanding student of Slavic antiquity (see item 48 in the Vernadsky bibliography).

Also in Prague, Vernadsky, along with the geographer and economist P. N. Savitskii, the philologist Prince N. S. Trubetskoi, historian of political ideas N. A. Alekseev, and a series of other scholars and social figures, joined in the elaboration of the Eurasian doctrine. The doctrine strove to depict Russia as a certain Euro-Asian unity, as a special, whole geographical world which possessed its own original historical ways. Russia's link with Asia and the East was more organic than it commonly thought. The dissimilarity with the West seemed natural. The peculiar traits of Russian history were dictated by its geographical development and the fate of the Eurasian "ocean-continent." In the ideological plane this applied to Orthodoxy which was the deciding factor in the nation's cultural development (and not only in ancient Russia). Vernadsky's book, *Outline of Russian History* [*Nachertanie Russkoi Istorii*] was, in a sense, one of the pillars of the Eurasians. This book and Vernadsky's articles which dealt with Eurasian problematics were basically taken negatively by the majority of the Russian emigration. This held true for other Eurasian works. They were not viewed as a new approach to Russian historiography and Russian thought. What was perceived in them above all was the "Eurasian temptation" of the post-revolutionary stream which rejected the "privacy of European beginnings" in Russian history. Many other points of criticism were appended, including the purely political. The official Soviet view of Eurasianism was even more laconically abrupt: "geographical materialism plus priestism."

However, in the perspective of decades, the Eurasian "reappraisal of values" in the field of Russian history, which was inseparably linked to Vernadsky's work and ideas, is not only of interest as a "particular viewpoint" but is useful for Russian historical scholarship. The Eurasian viewpoint served to sharpen Russian historical thought (the new statement of the East-West theme supported by geography and philology), stimulated the broadening of the historical range (the view of Russia from another "center," the steppe, and the Asian, so to speak), aided in better understanding some aspects of the Russian historical process (the relationship of Rus' to the nomad cultures), and, finally, underscored the significance the Orthodox Church which was gradually being forgotten or undervalued by historians of the Westernizing trend. Works on Eurasianism which appeared in Russian (see, e.g., V.A. Riasanovskii, *Survey of Russian Culture* [*Obzor Russkoi Kul'tury*], New York, 1947, chapter IV: "The Problem of Mongol Influence on Russian Culture", pp. 381-411; archpriest V. Zenkovskii, *Russian Thinkers and Europe* [*Russkie Mysliteli i Evropa*] Wiesbaden, 1961; Nicholas V. Riasanovskii, "The Emergence of Eurasianism," *California Slavic Studies*, V, 1966, pp. 39-72) show that, despite a number of disputable assertions, the "Eurasian interpretation" of Russia's past must be considered in the structuring of historical schemes. It is not accidental that P. N. Miliukov, a pertinacious opponent of Eurasianism, immediately felt the force and the weaknesses of the Eurasian ideas. In the anniversary edition in Paris in the 1930's and in the 1964 edition of his *Outlines of Russian Culture* (by Mouton in The Hague), Miliukov frequently argues with the Eurasians within the text and between the lines. Simultaneously, he borrowed their significantly important idea of "geographical development." It may also be confirmed that Vernadsky's historical views drew the attention of Soviet historians more than once. This was not just in terms of the "official vilification"of his books (appropos of these absurd attacks on Vernadsky's works, one prominent Soviet scholar said in private conversation at a historians' congress in Vienna: "Vernadsky should not be offended. He is too noticeable a scholar not to be chosen as a *persona non grata* in the war against objective historical research"). The deceased academician M.N. Tikhomirov stated privately that Vernadsky's works were "full of ideas" and called him a "major scholar." All of these facts (and much else) are, undoubtedly, indicative signs that "Vernadsky's theses" do not go unnoticed in the development of concepts regarding Russia's past.

Vernadsky's works gained especial significance after his arrival in the United States in 1927. He was invited by Yale University at the recommendation of M.I. Rostovtsev who was already working there. Vernadsky's academic work flowered here. It established a reputation for him as one of the leading specialists in the study of Russian history.

Of the 194 Vernadsky "works" known to us, 142 relate to the American period of work. Frequently these works are strictly factual, capacious in content, laconic in style. They are volumes of several hundred pages written with a remarkable combination of scholarly meaning and broad accesibility of form. Such, for example, is the so-called "Short Vernadsky," his one-volume *History of Russia* which, since 1929, has gone through six editions in English and been translated into Dutch, Hebrew, Spanish, and Japanese. It has become a very widely spread source for the study of Russia in Anglo-Saxon nations. Such also is his very intelligibly conceived book of 1936, the *Political and Diplomatic History of Russia* which was re-issued in 1966.

From 1943 to 1969, five monumental volumes appeared (the latter divided into two books) in the series *A History of Russia* published by Yale Univeristy Press and conceived for publication in conjunction with M.M. Karpovich. The latter was to have written on Russian History from the XVIII century. That is why the series bears both their names though Karpovich was not able to write anything for this publication. The significance of this "detailed Vernadsky" is absolutely exceptional. All of these volumes are more than introductions to the corresponding period of Russian history. Essentially, they provide an encyclopedic orientation to a vast amount of material, supply readers with a comprehension of the fundamental problems of studying Russia's past, and furnish them with a superb bibliography (see nos. 103, 125, 135, 155, 178 in the Vernadsky bibliography). Obviously, not all shades of Vernadsky's theses backed by the materials in these books were accepted by specialists. A number of points were criticized. It should be stressed that Vernadsky valued "vital criticism," though he rarely entered into academic polemics. He recognized the right of other historians to comprehend the material in a way different from him. However, he did defend his points of view. It was precisely for this reason that he wrote the very interesting book *Origin of Russia*. In it he strove to show a more organic link of slavic tribes with the East, its ancient civilizations, and with the nomadic peoples than it was commonly held. This volume also appeared in French and Italian.

In Russian, Vernadsky published *An Experiment in the History of Eurasia from the Middle of the VI Century to the Present Time* [*Opyt Istorii Evrazii s Poloviny VI Veka do Nastoiashchego Vremeni*] in 1934. In 1938 he wrote *Aspects of Russian Culture* [*Zven'ia Russkoi Kul'tury*], volume one. Evidently, this was a preliminary work for his major volumes in English. The World War and research deflected Vernadsky's attention away from major Russian publications.

In the many shorter works the attention of our historian is occupied by a variety of themes: the steppe world of the nomads, historico-legal topics in Kievan and Muscovite Rus', the origin and development of serfdom (specifically, a very useful item is the concise summation of the data of this most important of Russian topics, see bibliography no. 145), Mongol "legal norms," problems of the Russian Church, individual aspects of the most ancient periods of the history of the Slavs, topics on Pushkin, and many others. These include much detailed analyses as, for example, "The Lay of Prince Igor" (bibliography, no. 166), the analysis of the circumstances in the death of Tsarevich [Dmitrii] in Uglich (see items nos. 142 and 146), and the evaluation of the historical role of the Tatar Prince Simeon Bekbulatovich (see item no. 173).

The crown of Vernadsky's scholarly works was his *Essays on the History of Scholarship in Russia* published in the *Transactions of the Association of Russian-American Scholars in the USA* (see items 186,188,190,191, and 192 in the bibliography). This theme had long interested Vernadsky who found that the information on the development of various fields of knowledge in Russia was poorly known even to historians of Russian culture. Fortunately, he was able to execute his plan, though not fully. It is enough now to observe their complete objectivity, the evident thoroughness of the summaries and the thoughtfulness of the individual characteristics. Particularly successful were the essays on the historians of the end of the XIX and the beginning of the XX centuries ( here the author was evidently aided by his personal recollections from the period of his academic youth) (see the opening pages of this article). In any case, all of these "Essays" are truly a valuable contribution to the history of Russian cultural development. They are particularly valuable in that they were written by a master's pen and a specialist in the subject.

We should underline the fact that Vernadsky proceeded throughout his long life as a scholar to move along his own path without fearing to go "against the tide." He always strove to work from primary sources. This was what enabled him to be so individualistic in the solution of various problems. From here stems the completeness of exposition, the absence of generalities in the text and the lack of fear as a reputable historian in rejecting generally accepted clichés even if they were "professed" by the majority. These were precisely the traits that drew respect even from the opponents of "Vernadsky's theses."

In the presence of the enormous variety of his scholarly themes, did Vernadsky have a *principal idea*, one that was characteristic in terms of interpreting material and central to schematic construction? The author of these lines sees this idea in the *idea of empire* which subsequently showed and which, in essence, was dominant in Vernadsky's works. In actuality, Vernadsky, in analyzing the activity of Sviatoslav, Grand Prince of Kiev and son of Igor and St. Ol'ga, shows how a plan was to create an "empire" with the capital on the Danube. But the Byzantines destroyed the idea. Vernadsky convincingly shows in many works and on a multitude of pages how Rus' was taught the "imperial consciousness"— by the co-existence of the Slavs with the Finns and the nomads of the steppe, by Byzantium (both lay and ecclesiastical), and the State of Genghiz Khan's successors, the "militarized empire of the Mongols." He convincingly depicts how, commencing with Ivan III and flowering under Ivan IV, this "imperial ideology," which included a number of ethnic non-Slavic political forms within the Russian State, which was propped up after Byzantium's fall by the doctrine of Moscow the Third Rome, endured the tribulations of the Time of Troubles, strengthened during the XVII century, and was crowned under Peter the Great by the creation of a grandiose Russian Empire. He shows marvelously how the imperial idea diminished and was elevated, faded and was reborn until, reaching the Russian revolutions of 1917 and the civil war, it was liquidated in the Soviet State.

For Vernadsky, Russia was not the "people's prison" or the "gendarme of Europe." For Vernadsky the historian, Russia signified not the ascendancy of Russians over "aliens" or the "heterodox" but the peaceful creative co-existence of free and equal peoples, both eastern and western, in the boundless spaces of Eurasia. These peoples were united into a single government and empire. This was accomplished by geography ("Russia is a special geographical world" — the thesis of P.N. Savitskii accepted by Vernadsky), the community of a many-centuried historical fate, the lengthy time of "the crown of Monomakh" as the symbol of political continuity, and the synthesis of cultural and economic goals. Vernadsky (who politically was an adherent of the ideas of the Party of People's Freedom, the Constitutional Demo-

crats, the "cadets") knew exceptionally well the regional
interests of the population and the ethnic complexities in
Russia (see, in particular, item 99 in the bibliography in
regard to Bogdan Khmel'nitskii; also see no. 172 on the historical foundation of Russian-Kalmyk relations. This is not to
mention the relevant chapters in his general courses on Russian history). Vernadsky was himself of "Ukrainian blood."
It is not accidental that his father, Vladimir Ivanovich Vernadskii, became the first president of the Ukrainian Academy
of Sciences. However, Vernadsky, not without reason, felt
Pushkin's affirmative genius to be dear to him (see the bibliography, nos. 12, 19, 79, 80). The latter, in the final analysis, glorified not only the freedom of romanticism but also
the severe might of empire. As Vernadsky repeatedly shared
in his works (on Byzantium, the Mongols, and Russia)
great powers of creation frequently manifested themselves
in empires. Also, there was a certain constructive development of existing possibilities and the fashioning of the
strengths of separate nationalities for the achievement of
goals which were of State significance. It is exactly in this
sense that Vernadsky the historian's principle idea in his historical composition is the demonstration of the fate of the
*imperial idea* within the spaces of Russia-Eurasia.

To avoid misunderstanding, it should be stressed that,
in old concept, the term "imperial" signifies "political,"
more specifically "State." This derives from "empire" as
one of the historical forms of political unification, precisely
in the sense in which the word "imperial" is used by V.O.
Kliuchevskii in his works. The term "imperial" should not
be equated with the term "imperialistic" introduced by
Marxists for political aims and applied to certain phenomena
at the end of the XIX and the beginning of the XX centuries.
This levels, simplifies, and vulgarizes the essence of historical
phenomena.

Vernadsky was a member of many learned societies in
various countries. His 70th birthday was noted by the journal, the *Oxford Slavic Papers* which were then edited by
S.A. Konovalov. A bibliography of Vernadsky's works ap-

peared there and D.D. Obolenskii wrote an article on Vernadsky as a medievalist. In 1964 this bibliography (supplemented, of course) and the article were included in a special *Festschrift — Essays in Russian History. A Collection Dedicated to George Vernadsky.* Edited by Alan D. Ferguson and Alfred Levin. Archon Books, Hamden, Connecticut. Included therein were studies by eight of Vernadsky's students who had become professors in various American universities. In the dedication they characterized Vernadsky's scholarly work as that of a "scholar's scholar" and felt his contribution to historical knowledge and to the task of furthering Russian studies in the U.S.A. to be absolutely exceptional.

Vernadsky, in truth, as we can see even from his bibliography, devoted his whole life to indefatigable and inspired work on Russian history which he devotedly loved. It is necessary to say that, in this learned, true exploit, he was unswervingly supported by his wife, Nina Vladimirovna Il'-inskaia whom Vernadsky married in 1907 and who died in 1971. His sincere love was also expressed in letters to his sister, N.V. Toll, and he possessed an unusual loyalty of friendship (in letters to the author of this article, we can single out two names: Petr Nikolaevich Savitskii and Sergei Germanovich Pushkarev — both were privy to Vernadsky's ideological paths and historical works).

# APPENDIX II
## Bibliography of Vernadsky's Works

by Nikolay Andreyev

### 1914

1. "O Dvizhenii russkikh na vostok," *Nauchnyi istoricheskii zhurnal*, III, 52-61.

2. "Protiv solntsa, rasprostranenie russkago gosudarstva k vostoku," *Russkaia mysl'* (Mowcow); XXV, 56-79.

### 1915

3. "Vengerskii pokhod 1849 goda," *Russkaia mysl'*, No. 2, 78-88.

4. "Gosudarevy sluzhilye i promyshlennye liudi v vostochnoi Siberi XVII veka," *Zhurnal Ministerstva narodnago prosveshcheniia*, New Series, LV, 332-354.

5. "Iz istorii prusskoi reaktsii tridtsatykh i sorokovykh godov: dnevnik Farngagen fon Enze," *Russkaia mysl'*, No. 7, 39-49.

6. "Ugorskaia Rus' i eia vozrozhdenie v sredine XIX veka," *Golos minuvshago* (Moscow).

7. "Manifest Petra III o vol'nosti dvorianskoi i zakonodatel'naia komissiia 1754-1766 gg.," *Istoricheskoe obozrenie*, XX (Petrograd).

### 1917

8. "Russkoe masonstvo v tsarstvovanie Ekateriny II," *Zapiski Istoriko-filogicheskago universiteta*, CXXXVII, XXIV, 286 pp.

### 1918

9. *Nikolai Ivanovich Novikov* (Petrograd), V + 163 pp.

10. "Imperatritsa Ekaterina II i zakonodatel'naia komissiia 1767-1768 godov," *Sbornik Obshchestva istoricheskikh, filosofskikh i sotsial'nykh nauk pri Permskom universitete*, I, p. 23.

11. "Pis'mo N. I. Turgeneva po krest'ianskomy voprosy 1859 g.," *ibid.*, p. 11.

### 1919

12. "K istorii kolonizatsii Azovskago poberezh'ia 1698-1701," *Izvestiia Tavricheskoi uchenoi arkhivnoi komissii* (Simferopol').

13. "Skrytyi istochnik konstitutsii Nikity Murav'eva i Gosudarstvennaia ustavnaia gramota Novosil'tseva," *Izvestiia Tavricheskago universiteta*, I (Simferopol').

14. "Pis'ma Garnovskago Potemkinu," *ibid.*

15. "Stikhotvorenie kn. Potemkina na osnovanie Ekaterinoslava," *ibid.*

16. "Tavel'skii arkhiv V. S. Popova," *ibid.*

17. "Zapiska o neobkhogimosti priobreteniia Kryma," *ibid.*

18. "A. S. Lappo-Danilevskii kak istorik Rossii XVIII v." *Izvestiia Tavricheskoi Uchenoi Arkhivnoi Komissii*," No. 56, 156-160.

## 1923

19. "Bizantské popisy pudy," *Cesky casopis historicky*, XXIX, 443-457.

20. "Le césarévitch Paul et les francs-maçons de Moscou," *Revue des études slaves*, III, 268-285.

21. "Mednyi vsadnik v tvorchestve Pushkina," *Slavica*, II, 645-654.

22. "Soedinenie Tsarkvei v istoricheskoi deistvitel'nosti," *Rossiia i Latinstvo, sbornik statei* (Berlin), pp. 80-120.

## 1924

23. *Ocherk istorii prava russkago gosudarstva XVIII–XIX vv.* (*period imperii*), (Prague), 166 pp.

24. "Dikaja Vira" a "Ljudskaja vira" v staroruskim pravu, *Sbornik ved pravnich a statnich*, XXIV (Prague), 80-85.

25. "Zametki o krest'ianskoi obshchine v Vizantii," *Uchenye zapiski, osnovannyia Russkoi uchebnoi kollegiei v Prage*, 1, 2, 81-97.

26. "Ob odnom vozmozhnom istochnike *Russkoi Pravdy*," *ibid.*, 99-101.

27. "Zametki o literaturno-izdatel'skoi deiatel'nosti N. I. Novikova," *Istoriko-literaturnyi sbornik. Posviashchaetsia V. I. Sreznevskomu* (Leningrad), 85-91.

28. *O znachenii nauchnoi deiatel'nosti N. P. Kondakova. K vos'midesiatileiiu so gnia rozhdeniia, 1844* – I, XI, 1924 (Speech given at the III Conference of Russian Scholars in Prague on September 25, 1924).

29. "Pushkin kak istorik," *Uchenye zapiski osnovannyia Russkoi uchebnoi kollegiei v Prage*, 1, 2, pp. 61-79 (translated into Italian by Ettore Lo Getto in *Russia*, III [Naples]), 180-199.

## 1925

30. *Gosudarstvennaia ustavnaia gramota Rossiiskoi Imperii 1820 goda, istoriko-iuridicheskii ocherk* (Prague), III, pp. 263 + VIII + IV.

31. "Dva podviga sv. Aleksandra Nevskogo," *Evraziiskii vremennik*, IV, 318-337.

32. "Zametki o vizantiiskikh gramotakh XIII v.," *Sbornik v chest' na Vasil I. Zlatarski po sluchai na 30-godishnatamu nauchna i profesorska deinost'. Prigotoven ot negovite uchenitsi i pochitateli* (Sofiia), 35-43.

33. "Zamechaniia o iuridicheskoi prirode krepostnogo prava," *Sbornik statei, posviashchennykh P. B. Struve* (Prague), 253-265.

34. "M. Weingart Byzantseé kroniky v literature cirkevne-slovanské Prehled a rozbor filologicky. Cast I." V. Bratislave (1922) (Spisy filosofické faculty University Komenského y Bratislave, cast II), Retsenziia v *Slavia*, III, 485-486.

35. "N. Banescu, membre correspondante de l'Académie Roumain. Changements politiques dans les balkans aprés la conquête de l'Empire Bulgare de Samuel (1018). Nouveaux duchés byzantins: Bulgarie et Paristrion. Académie Roumaine. Bulletin de la section historique. X, pp. 49-72 (Bucarest), 1923, c. 24, X. pp. 49-72. Retsenziia v *Slavia*, III, 1924-1925, 549-550.

36. Serbisch-byzantinische Urkunden des Meteron Klosters hrst. von Nikos

A. Bees. Wierdabdruck aus der Zeitschrift *Byzantis*, Bd. II (Berlin-Wilmersdorf), Verlag der Byzantinisch-Neugriechischen Jahrbücher. s.a. (1923-?), 100 pp.
Retsenziia v *Slavia*, III, 1924-1925, 550-551.

37. "I. P. Kondakov, k ego vos'midesiatiletiiu (1844-1924)," *Slavia*, III, 560-563.

38. "Risskà ustavni litsina Ruského cisarstvi," *Sbornik ved pravnich a stàtnich*, XXV, 394-425.

39. "Sur les origines de la loi agraire byzantine," *Byzantion*, II, 169-180.

40. "Un projet de déclaration de droits de l'homme et du citoyen en Russie en 1801," *Revue historique de droit français et étranger*, 4ᵉ série, IV, 436-445.

## 1926

41. "Vizantiiskiia ucheniia o vlasti tsapia i patriarkha," *Recueil d'études dédiées à la mémoire de N. P. Kondakov* (Prague), 264 pp.

44. "Akademik F. I. Uspenskii," *Seminarium Kondakovianum*, I, 307-308.

45. "Alexandre Ier et le probléme slave pendant la premiére moité de son régne," *Revue des études slaves*, VII, 93-111.

46. "Beträge zur Geschichte der freimauerei und des Mystizismus in Russland," *Zeitschrift für slavische Philologie*, IV, 162-178.

47. "Zolotaia Orda, Egipet i Vizantiia v ikh vzaimootnosheniiakh v tsarstvovanie Mikhaila Paleologa," *Seminarium Kondakovianum*, I, 73-84.

48. "L. G. Niderle," *ibid.*, 313-314.

49. "Mongol'skoe igo v russkoi istorii," *Evraziiskii vremenik*, V, 153-164.

50. "Obzor trudov po vizantinovedeniiu s 1914 g. I: Trudy, vyzhedshie vne predelov Rossii," *Slavia*, V, 395-408; 639-653.

51. "Pamiatniki iskusstva i stariny srednevekovogo Peloponnesa," *Izvestiia Krymskogo obshchestva istorii, arkheologii i etnografii*, I (Simferopol'), 29-33.

52. "Zur Geschichte des entwurfs einer Konstitution für Russland vom Jahre 1819," *Historische Zeitschrift*, CXXXV, 423-427.

## 1928

53. "Die Kirchliche-politische Lehre der Epanagoge und ihr Einfluss auf das russische Leben im XVII Jahrhundert," *Byzantinisch-neugriechische Jahubücher*, VI, 119-142.

## 1929

54. *A History of Russia* (New Haven), 397 pp.

55. "Al'do Al'bertoni," *Seminarium Kondakovianum*, III, 294.

56. "K voprosy o veroispovedanii mongol'skikh poslov 1223 g.," *ibid.*, 145-148.

57. "Relations byzantino-russes au XIIᵉ siécle," *Byzantion*, IV, 296-276.

58. "Materialy dlia biografii A. S. Lappo-Danilevskogo," (Akademiia Nauk SSSR), *Ocherki po istorii znanii*, VI (Leningrad), 55 pp.

## 1930

59. "Note sur les vètements sacerdoutaux du partiarche Nikon," *Orient et Byzance*, IV, 412-415.

60. "S. V. Iushkov, Issledovaniia po istorii russkogo prave," (Novouzensk, 1926); retsenziia v: *Zeitschrift für slavische Philologie*, VII, 263-269.

61. *A History of Russia*, 2nd revised edition (New Haven), XIX, 413 pp.

## 1931

62. *Lenin, Red Dictator* (New Haven), VII 351 pp.

63. "Dschingis Khan," *Menschen die Geschichte machten*, II, 90-95.

64. "Swjatoslaw," *ibid.*, I. 322-327.

65. "Timur," *ibid.*, 162-167.

66. "M. I. Rostovtsev (K shestidesiatiletiiu ego)," *Seminarium Kondakovianum*, IV, 239-244.

67. "The Tactics of Leo the Wise and the Epanagogue," *Byzantion*, VII, 333-335.

## 1932

68. *The Russian Revolution*, 1917-1932 (New York), VIII, 133 pp.

## 1933

69. *La Charte constitutionelle de l'Empire russe de l'an 1820* (Paris), 283 pp.

70. "The Expansion of Russia," *Transactions of the Connecticut Academy of Arts and Sciences*, XXXI, 391-425.

71. "The Heresy of the Judaizers and the Policies of Ivan III of Moscow," *Speculum*, VIII, 436-454.

## 1934

72. Opyt istorii Evrazii s poloviny VI veka do nastoiashchego vremeni (Berlin), 189.

73. "L'industrie russe sous Pierre le Grand," *Le Monde slave*, nouvelle série, IV, 283-299.

## 1935

74. "A propos des origines du servage de *Kabala* dans le droit russe," *Revue historique de droit français et étranger*, 4 ème série, XIV, 360-367.

## 1936

75. *Political and Diplomatic History of Russia* (Boston), X, 499 pp. (reproduced by the Micro Photo division, Bell & Howell Co., Wooster, Ohio, 1966).

76. "A Japanese Drawing of the Russian Settlement in Aniva Bay, Karafuto (1854)," *Seminarium Kondakovianum*, VIII, 79-86;

77. "Notes on the History of the Vigurs in the Late Middle Ages," *Journal of the American Oriental Society*, LVI, 453-461.

## 1937

78. "The Baltic Commerce of the West Russian and Lithuanian Cities During the Middle Ages," *Baltic and Scandinavian Countries*, III, 399-409.

79. "Pushkin and the Decembrists," *Centennial Essays for Pushkin* (Cambridge, MA.), 45-76.

80. "Pushkin and His Time," *Transactions of the Connecticut Academy of Arts and Sciences*, XXXIII, 18-36.

81. "Studies in the History of Moscovian Private Law of the XVIth and XVIIth Centuries: Inheritance in the Case of the Childless Wife," *Studi in memo-*

531           *Russian Historiography: A History*

*ria di Aldo Albertoni*, III (Padua), 435-454.

## 1938
82. *Zven'ia russkoi kul'tury*, I (Brussels), 229 pp.
83. "A.A. Vasil'ev (k semidesiatiletiiu ego)," *Annales de l'institut Kondakov (Seminarium Kondakovianum)*, X, 1-17.
84. "Feudalism in Russia," *VIIIᵉ Congrès international des sciences historiques, Communications présentées, II (Paris), 302-305.*
85. "Goten und Anten in Südrussland," *Südostdeutsche Forschungen*, III, 265-279.
86. "The Scope and Contents of Chingis Khan's Yasa," *Harvard Journal of Asiatic Studies*, III, 337-360.
87. "The Spali of Jordanis and the Spori of Procopius," *Byzantion*, XIII, 263-266.

## 1939
88. "O sostave Velikoi Iasy Chingiz Khana, " *Issledovaniia i materialy po istorii Rosii i Vostoka* (Brussels), 5-39.
89. "Feudalism in Russia," *Speculum*, XIV, 300-323.
90. "Russian Interests in Mongolia and Manchuria," *Proceedings of the Institute of International Relations*, Sixth (San Francisco Bay) Session (Berkeley, California), 168-173.
91. "Iron Mining and Iron Industries in Medieval Russia," *Études dédiées à la mémoire d'André Andréadis* (Athens), 361-366.
92. "Juwaini's Version of Chingis Khan's Yasa," *Annales de l'institut Kondakov (Seminarium Kondakovianum)*, XII, 33-45.
93. "Lebedia: Studies on the Magyar Background of Kievan Russia," *Byzantion*, XIV, 179-203. (A German translation: "Studien zur ungarischen Frühgeschichte in *Südosteuropäische Arbeiten*, XLVII, 9-31).
94. "On the Origins of the Antae," *Journal of the American Oriental Society*, LIX, 56-66.

## 1940
95. "Byzantium and Southern Russia: Two Notes – I. The Eparchy of Gothia; II. The Date of the Conversion of the Khazars to Judaism," *Byzantion*, XV, 67-86.
96. "European Trouble Zone," *Yale Review*, XXIX, 248-272.
97. "William Egbert Wheeler – d. 28th of February 1939," *Annales de l'Institut Kondakov (Seminarium Kondakovianum)*, XI, 254-255.
98. "J. S. Curtiss, Church and State in Russia: 1900-1917," (New York, 1940); reviewed in *Church History*, IX, 394-408.

## 1941
99. *Bohdan, Hetman of Ukraine* (New Haven), VII, 150 pp.
100. "Flavius Ardabur Aspar," *Südost-Forschungen*, VI, 38-73.
101. "The Status of the Russian Church During the First Half-Century Following Vladimir's Conversion," *Slavonic and East European Review*, XX, 294-314.

## 1942
102. "A Review of Russian Policy," *Yale Review*, XXXI, 514-533.

## 1943
103. *Ancient Russia* (*A History of Russia* by George Vernadsky, vol. I), (New Haven), XIV, 425 pp.
104. "Slovo o polku Igoreve v istoricheskom otnoshenii," *Novosel'e*, 3 (New York), 53-56.
105. "Sur l'origine des Alains," *Byzantion*, XVI, 81-86.

## 1944
106. "The Beginnings of the Czech State," *Byzantion*, XVII, 315-328.
107. "Paul Mil'ukov," *Annuaire de l'Institut de philologie et d'histoire orientales et slaves*, VII, (New York), 531.
108. "Svantovit, dieu des Slaves baltiques," *ibid.*, 339-356.
109. "Three Notes on the Social History of Kievan Russia," *Slavonic and East European Review*, XXII, 81-92.
110. "Trends in Russian Foreign Policy," *Yale Review*, XXXIII, 699-720.
111. "R.H. Fisher, The Russian Fur Trade, 1550-1700," (Berkeley, California, 1943); reviewed in *American Historical Review*, XLIX, 704-706.
112. *A History of Russia*, revised edition (New Haven), VI, 517 pp. Translations into: Dutch – *Geschiednis van Rusland*: I (up to 1917 only; Amsterdam, 1947); Hebrew (1945); Spanish (Buenos Aires, 1947).
113. *Ancient Russia*, 2nd edition (New Haven).
114. A translation of V.I. Vernadsky, "Problems of Biogeochemistry, II: The Fundamental Matter-Energy Differences between the Living and the Inert Natural Bodies of the Biosphere," *Transactions of the Connecticut Academy of Arts and Sciences*, XXXV, 483-517.

## 1945
115. "Great Moravia and White Chorvatia," *Journal of the American Oriental Society*, LXV, 257-259.
116. "La Geste d'Igor au point de vue historique," *Annuaire de l'Institut de philologie et d'histoire orientale et slaves*, VIII (New York), 217-234.
117. "Le patriarche russe," *Renaisance*, II/III (New York), 437-445.
118. "On Some Parallel Trends in Russian and Turkish History," *Transactions of the Connecticut Academy of Arts and Sciences*, XXXVI, 25-36.
119. "Russia's Place in the World, 1861-1945," *Pacific Historical Review*, XIV, 275-289.
120. A translation of V. I. Vernadsky, "The Biosphere and the Noösphere," edited by G.E. Hutchinson, *American Scientist*, XXXIII, 1-12.

## 1946
121. "The Rus' in the Crimea and the Russo-Byzantine Treaty of 945," *Byzantine Metabyzantina*, I, 249-260.

## 1947
122. *Medieval Russian Laws*. Translation, introduction and notes (Records of civilization: Sources and Studies, edited by A.P. Evans, 41), (New York), 106 pp.

123. 'Le plan français et le plan américain dans les réformes et les projets de réforme en russie à l'époque déAlexandre Ier," *Cahiers d'histoire de la révolution française*, I, 143-167.

124. An English translation: "Reforms under Czar Alexander I: French and American Influences," *Review of Politics*, IX, 47-64.

## 1948

125. *Kievan Russia* (*A History of Russia* by George Vernadsky, vol. II), (New Haven), XII, 412 pp. Pages 163-172 appeared as "On Feudalism in Kievan Russia," in the *American Slavic and East European Review* (1948), VII, 3-14.

126. "A. Eck, Le grand domaine dans la Russie du moyen âge," (Bucharest, 1945); V. B. El'iashevich, *Istoriia prava pozemel'noi sobstvennosti v Rossii* (Paris, 1948); "S.V. Veselovskii, Feodal'noe, Zemlevladenie v severo-vostochnoi Rusi, I, gl. 1-2," (Moscow-Leningrad, 1947); Retsenziia v *Speculum*, XXIII, 691-696.

127. "M.N. Tukhomirov, Drevnerusskie gorod," (Moscow, 1946); reviewed in *American Slavic and East European Review*, VII, 189-190.

## 1949

128. "The Problem of the Early Russian Campaigns in the Black Sea Area," *American Slavic and East European Review*, VIII, 1-10.

## 1950

129. "The Eurasian Nomads and Their Art in the History of Civilization," *Saeculum*, I, 74-86.

## 1951

130. "Der sarmatische Hintergrund der garmanischen Völkerwanderung," *Saeculum*, II, 340-392.

131. "The Royal Serfs (*servi regales*) of the Ruthenian Law and Their Origin," *Speculum*, XXVI, 255-264.

132. "K.I. Zaitsev, Kievskaia Rus'," (Shanghai, 1949); reviewed in *Speculum*, XXVI, 432-435.

133. *A History of Russia* (New Haven), 3rd edition, revised, X, 533 pp. Translated into Japanese in 1954. The book was revised and expanded in 1954, 1961, and 1969.

## 1952

134. "The Riddle of the Gothi Tetraxitae," *Südost-Forschungen*, XI, 281-283.

## 1953

135. *The Mongols and Russia* (*A History of Russia* by George Vernadsky, vol. III; New Haven), XI, 462 pp.

136. A' Chinese translation: *Mêng-ku yu O-lo-ssu*, 2 volumes in 1, published in 1955 without the author's permission.

137. "Anent the epic poetry of the Alans," *Annuaire de l'Institut de philologie et d'histoire orientales et slaves*, XII (Mélanges Henry Grêgoire, IV), 1952 (published in 1953), 517-538.

138. "A Note on the Name *Antes*," *Journal of the American Oriental Society*, LXXIII, 192.

139. B. Nolde, *La formation de l'Empire russe*, 2 vols., Paris, 1952-1953. Reviewed in *American Historical Review*, LVIII (1953), 377-378 and LIX (1954), 620-622.

140. "The Russo-Byzantine War of 1043," *Südöst Forschungen*, XII, 47-67.

## 1954
141. "A Note on the Russian Word *cisclo*," *Speculum*, XXIX, 335.

142. "The Death of the Tsarevich Dimitry, A Reconsideration of the Case," *Oxford Slavonic Papers*, V, 1-19.

## 1955
143. A. Iakovliv, *Dogovir get'mana Bogdana Khmel'nitskogo z Moskoviskim tsarem Oleksiem Mikhailovichem*, 164 pp., New York, 1954. Reviewed in *American Slavic and East European Review*, XIV, 128-130.

144. H. Paszkiewicz, *The Origin of Russia*, New York, 1954. Reviewed in *Speculum*, XXX, 293-301.

145. "Serfdom in Russia," *Relazioni del X Congresso Internationale di Scienze Sotriche Roma*, 4-11 Settembre 1955, volume III: *Storia del medioevo*, Firenze, 247-277. Reprinted in a slightly abridged version and without footnotes in *Readings in Russian History* by S. Harkave, vol. I, New York, 212-228.

146. "Die Tragödie von Uglic und ihre Folgen," *Jahrbücher für Geschichte Osteuropas*, III, 41-49.

## 1956
147. "Das Frühe Slawentum, das Ostslawentum bis zum Mongolensturm," *Historia Mundi*, V, 251-300.

148. "Note on the Origin of the Word *tamga*," *Journal of the American Oriental Society*, LXXVI, 188-189.

149. "The Origin of the Name Rus'," *Südost-Forschungen*, XV, 167-179.

150. "Toxar, t'ma, T'mutorokan," *For Roman Jakobson*, The Hague, 588-591.

## 1959
151. *The Origins of Russia* (Oxford: The Clarendon Press), 355 pp. French and Italian translations exist.

152. "M.M. Karpovich, pamiati druga," *Novyi zhurnal*, LVIII, 9-11.

153. "Problems of Ossetic and Russian Epos," *American Slavic and East European Review*, XVIII, 281-294.

154. *Russia at the Dawn of the Modern Age* (vol. IV in *A History of Russia*) (New Haven), 347 pp.

155. "Teaching and Writing Russian History in America," *The Russian Orthodox Journal*, XXXIII, 11-26.

## 1960
156. "Iz drevnei istorii Evrazii: Khunnu," *Novyi zhurnal*, LXII, 273-283.

157. "Povest' o Sukhane," *ibid.*, LIX, 196-202.

158. "Russia, Turkey and Circassia in the 1640's," *Südost-Forschungen*, XIX, 134-145.

159. "The Russo-Byzantine War of 1043," *Byzantinisch-neugriechische Jahrbucher*, XVIII (Athens), 123-143.

## 1961

160.  L.N. Gumilev, *Khunnu, Sredinnaia Aziia v drevnie vremena*, (Moscow, 1960). Reviewed in *American Historical Review*, LXVI, 711-712.

## 1962

161.  "Chelovek i zhivotnyi mir v istorii Rossii," *Novyi zhurnal*, LXVIII, 242-261.

162.  S. V. Kirikov, "Izmeneniia zhivotnogo mira v prirodnykh sonakh SSSR," 2 vols. (Moscow, 1959-1960). Reviewed in *Slavic Review*, XXI, 532-535.

163.  Introduction to I.J. Lederer (ed.), *Russian Foreign Policy: Essays in Historical Perspective* (New Haven), V-IX.

164.  "Ust' — Tsilemskie rukopisnye sborniki, cherty umstvennoi zhizni staroobriadtsev russkogo severa v XVIII-XX vekakh," *Novyi Zhurnal*, LXX, 201-222.

## 1963

165.  "Predislovie k: M. A. Taube, Iogann Taube, sovetnik Tsaria Ivana Groznogo," *Novyi zhurnal*, LXXI, 170-189.

166.  "The Eurasian Nomads and their Impact on Medieval Europe (A Reconsideration of the Problem)," *Studi medievali*, 3rd series, IV, 2, 1-34.

## 1964

167.  "P.N. Miliukov i mestorazvitie russkogo naroda," *Novyi zhurnal*, 77, 254-289.

168.  Marc Szeftel, *Documents de droit public relatifs à la Russie medievale* (Brussels). Reviewed in *Slavic Review*, No. 4, 740-741.

## 1965

169.  "Tserkov i gosudarstvo v sisteme Sbornogo Ulozheniia 1649 g.," *Na temy Russkie i obshchie*, sbornik v chest' I.S. Timasheva (New York), 79-94.

170.  "Jurij Arbatskij (1911-1963)," *Südost-Forschungen*, XXIV, 257-259.

## 1966

171.  "The Prijutino Brotherhood, Preliminary Communication," *Orbis sriptus, Festschrift für D. Tschizevskij*, pp. 857-863.

172.  "Istoricheskaia osnova russko-kalmytskikh otnoshenii," *Kalmyk-Oirat Symposium* (Philadelphia), 11-50.

## 1967

173.  "Ivan Groznyi i Simeon Bekbulatovich," *To Honor Roman Jakobson* (The Hague), 2133-2157.

## 1968

174.  "Pamiati A.V. Florovskogo," *Novoe Russkoe Slovo* (New York, April 18).

175.  "S. G. Pushkarev, K ego vosimidesiatiletiiu," *ibid.*, (July 30).

176.  "P.N. Savitskii," *Novyi zhurnal*, No. 92, 273-277.

## 1969

177.  "Bratstvo Priiutino," *Novyi zhurnal*, No. 93, 147-171.

178. *The Tsardom of Moscow 1547-1682* (*A History of Russia*, volumes 1 and 2) (New Haven), 481 pp; 482-873pp.

179. "The Rise of Science in Russia 1700-1917," *Russian Review*, 28, 37-52.

180. "Bratstvo Priiutno," *Novyi zhurnal*, No. 95, 202-215; No. 9, 153-171; No. 97, 218-237.

181. "Iz vospominanii" (Gody ucheniia S.F. Platonov), *Novyi zhurnal*, No. 100, 196-221.

182. Andrei Nikolaevich Krasnov (1862-1914), *Zapiski Russkoi Akademicheskoi Gruppy v SShA* (New York), III, 5-20.

183. "N.O. Losskii," *Zapiski Russkoi Akademicheskoi Gruppy v SShA* (New York), IV, 183-186.

## 1971
184. "Perm'-Moskva-Kiev" (Vospominaniia), *Novyi zhurnal*, No. 104, 177-188.

185. "Krym" (Vospominaniia), *Novyi zhurnal*, No. 105, 203-224.

186. "Ocherki po istorii nauki v Rossii 1725-1920, Chast' I. Vosemnadtsatyi vek," *Zapiski Russkoi Akademicheskoi Gruppy v SShA* (New York), V, 195-233.

## 1972
187. "Konstantinopol', 1920-1921," (Vospominaniia), *Novyi zhurnal*, No. 108, 202-217.

188. "Ocherki po istorii nauki v Rossi. Pervyi otdel. Istoricheskaia nauka," *Zapiski Russkoi Akademicheskoi Gruppy v SShA* (New York), VI, 160-225.

189. *Kievan Russia* (New Haven: Yale University Press), 412 pp. Reprint of the 1948 edition with a new introduction and additional bibliography.

190. "Ocherki po istorii Nauki v Rossii (Chast' III)," *Zapiski Russkoi Akademicheskoi Gruppy v SShA* (New York), VII, 17-112.

## 1974
191. "Ocherki po istorii nauki v Rossii (Chast' IV)," *Zapiski Russkoi Akademicheskoi Gruppy v SShA* (New York), VIII, 17-212.

## 1975
192. "Ocherki po istorii nauki v Rossii (Chast' V)," *Zapiski Russkoi Akademicheskoi Gruppy v SShA* (New York), IX, 133-164.

## FORTHCOMING
193. "Russlands Ungarn-Feldzug von 1849," *Ferdinandy Festschrift*.

194. *Patriarch Nikon on Church and State, Nikon's Refutation*. Edited with introduction and notes by George Vernadsky and Valerie A. Tumins (The Hague: Mouton).

## EDITORSHIPS OF G.V. VERNADSKY
A) A.N. Pypin *Russkoe Masonstvo* (XVIII i pervaia chetvert' XIX veka). Redaktsiia i primechaniia G. V. Vernadskago. Petrograd, 1916.

B) Editor (together with Ralph T. Fisher of *Dictionary of Russian Historical Terms from the Eleventh Century to 1917*). Compiled by Sergei Pushkarev. Yale University Press, 1970.

C) Senior Editor of *A Source Book for Russian History from Early Times to 1917*, compiled by Sergei G. Pushkarev. 3 vols. Yale University Press, 1972.

# APPENDIX III
## Bibliography of the Russian Church
### by NIKOLAY ANDREYEV
[Listed according to the sequence of the Russian alphabet]
— IN RUSSIAN —

Aristov, I. Ia. *Pervye vremena Khristianstva v Rossii po tserkovovno-istoriche-skomy soderzhaniiu russkikh letopisei.* St. Petersburg, 1888.

Arsen'ev, N.S. *Pravoslavie, katolichestvo, protestantizm. Paris, 1948.*

Arkhangel'skii, A.S. *Prepodobnyi Nil Sorskii.* St. Petersburg, 1882.

Barsov, T.V. *Konstantinopol'skii patriarkh i ego vlast' nad russkoi tserkov'iu.* St. Petersburg, 1878. Republished by Mouton in 1968.

　　　 *Sv. Sinod v ego proshlom.* St. Petersburg, 1896.

　　　 *Sinodal'nye uchrezhdeniia prezhnego.* St. Petersburg, 1897.

　　　 *Sinodal'nye uchrezhdeniia novogo vremeni.* St Petersburg, 1899.

Barsukov, N.P. *Istochniki russkoi agiografii.* St. Petersburg, 1882.

Bednov, E.D. *Pravoslavnaia Tserkov' v Pol'she i v Litve.* Ekaterinoslav, 1908.

Blagovidov, F. V. *Ober-prokurory sviateishego Sinoda v XVIII i v pervoi polovine XIX st. Kazan',* 1899; 1900.

Bukharev, I. *Zhitiia vsekh sviatykh, prazdnuemykh pravoslavnoiu greko-rossii-skoiu Tserkoviiu.* Moscow, 1896;1906.

Vasil'ev, V.P. *Ocherk Istorii kanonizatsii russkikh sviatykh.* Moscow, 1893.

Verkhovskoi, S.S. *Pravoslavie v zhizni. Sbornik statei.* New York, 1953.

Gibbenet, N. *Istoricheskoe issledovanie dela patriarkha Nikona,* I–II. 1882-1884.

Glubokovskii, N.N. *Russkaia bogoslovskaia nauka v ee istoricheskom razvitii i noveishem sostoianin.* Warsaw, 1928.

Golubev, S.T. *Kievskii mitropolit Petr Mogila i ego spodvizhniki,* I–II. Kiev, 1883-1898.

Golubinskii, E. E. *Istoriia kanonizatsii sviatykh v russkoi tserkvi.* Moscow, 1903.

　　　　　　　. *Prepodobnyi Sergii Radonezhskii i sozdannaia im Troitskaia lavra.* Moscow, 1893.

Gorskii, A. V. *Istoricheskoe opisanie Sviato-Troitskoi Sergievoi lavry,* I-II, Moscow, 1852.

　　　　　　　. *Maksim Grek, Sviatogorets.* Moscow, 1859.

Gorchakov, M.I. *Monastyrskii prikaz.* St. Petersburg, 1868.

　　　　　　　. *O zemel'nykh vladeniiakh vserossiiskikh mitropolitov, patriar-khov i sv. Sinoda.* St. Petersburg, 1871; Trans. by Michigan University in

1965.

Denisov, L. I. *Pravoslavnye monastyri Rossiiskoi Imperii. Polnyi spisok vsekh 1105 nyne sushchestvuiushchikh muzhskikh i zhenskikh monastyrei.* Moscow, 1908.

Dimitrii, Bishop. *Miasetseslov (tserkovnyi kalendar').* 1878-1883, 1893-1901.

Zhevakhov, N.D. *Vospominaniia tovarishcha oberprokurora sv. Sinoda.* Vol. I, Munich, 1923; Vol. II, *Novyi Sad*, 1928.

Zhmakin, V. *Mitropolit Daniil i ego sochineniia.* Moscow, 1881.

Zhukovskii, P.N. *Seimovaia bor'ba pravoslavnogo zapadno-russkogo dvorianstva s tserkovnoi uniei do 1609 goda.* St. Petersburg, 1901.

Zaitsev, B.K. *Prepodobnyi Sergii Radonezhskii.* Paris, 1925.

Zen'kovskii, V.V. *Istoriia russkoi filosofii.* I-II. Paris, 1948-50. Translated by Columbia University Press.

Ivantsov-Platonov, A.I. *O russkom tserkovnom upravlenii.* Moscow, 1898.

Ignatii, Arkhimandrit. *Kratkoe zhizneopisanie russkikh sviatykh*, I-II. St. Petersburg, 1875.

Ikonnikov, V.S. *Opyt issledovaniia o kul'turnom znachenii Vizantii v Russkoi istorii.* Kiev, 1896.

——————— *Maksim Grek e ego vremia.* Kiev, 1866; 1915.

Il'in, V.N. *Prepodobnyi Serafim Sarovskii.* Paris, 1925; New York, 1971.

Ioann, Arkiepiskop (Shakhovskoi). *Beloe inochestvo.* Berlin, 1932.

———————. *Filosofiia pravoslavnogo pastyrstva.* Berlin, 1938.

Kazanskii, P.S. *Istoriia pravoslavnogo russkogo monashestva (do serediny XIV v.).* Moscow, 1885.

Karsavin, L.P. *Ottsi i uchiteli Tserkvi.* Paris, 1926.

Kirillov, I. *Moskva – Tretii Rim.* Moscow 1914.

Kliuchevskii, V.O. *Drevnerusskie zhitiia sviatykh kak istoricheskii istochnik.* Moscow, 1871. Translated by Mouton in 1968.

——————— *Znachenie prepodobnogo Sergiia dlia Russkogo naroda i gosudarstva.* Moscow, 1913.

———————. *Tserkov' i Rossii.* Paris, 1969.

Kologrivov, I. *Ocherki po istorii russkoi sviatosti.* Brussels, 1961. Translated into French.

Konstantin, Arkhimandrit. *Sv. Serafim Sarovskii i puti Rossii.* Ladomirovo, 1939.

——————— *Materialy k izucheniiu sviatoi Rusi.* Ladomirovo, 1940.

——————— *K poznaniiu pravoslaviia.* Shanghai, 1948.

Kontsevich, I.M. *Optina pustyn' i ee vremia.* Jordanville, N.Y. 1964.

Kostomarov, N.I. *Deiateli russkoi tserkvi v starinu.* Munich, 1922.

———————. *Russkaia istoriia v zhizneopisaniiakh ee glavneishikh deiatelei.* St. Petersburg, 1876-1880.

Koialovich, M.O. *Litovskaia (Brest-Litovskaia) tserkovnaia uniia*, I-II. St. Petersburg, 1859-1862.

Kudriavtsev, M. *Istoriia pravoslavnogo monashestva v severo-vostochnoi Rossii so vremeni prepodobnogo Sergiia.* 1881.

Lavrov, A. *Ocherk istorii russkoi tserkvi*. Moscow, 1880.

Lebedev, A.P. *Sobranie sochinenii*. Vol I – *Tserkovnaia istoriografiia*. Moscow, 1898.

Leonid, Arkhimandrit. *Sviataia Rus' ili svedeniia o vsekh sviatykh i podvizhnikakh na Rusi (do XVIII v.)*. St. Petersburg, 1891.

Lopukhin, P.S. *Prepodobnyi Serafim Sarovskii i puti Russii*. Ladomirovo, 1939.

Liashevskii, Protoierei Stefan. *Istoriia khristianstva v zemle russkoi s* I-go *veka po* II-i. Baltimore, 1968.

Maevskii, V.A. *Na nive tserkovnoi. Istoricheskie spravki*. Madrid, 1968.

Malinin, V.N. *Starets Eleasorova monastyra Filopei i ego poslaniia*. Kiev, 1901.

Nafanail, Bishop. *Zhitiia sviatykh*, Munich, 1969-1972.

Nikitskii, A.I. *Ocherk vnutrennei istorii tserkvi i velikom Novgorode*. St. Petersburg, 1897.

Pavlov, A. S. *Istoricheskii ocherk sekuliarizatsii tserkovnykh zemel' v Rossii*. Odessa, 1871.

Papkov, A.A. Bratstva. *Ocherk istorii zapadnorusskikh pravoslavnykh bratstv*. Moscow, 1900.

Parkhomenko, V.A. *Nachalo khristianstva na Rusi*. Poltava, 1913.

Pushkarev, S.G. *Rol' pravoslavnoi tserkvi v istorii russkoi kul'tury i gosudarstvennosti*. Ladomirovo, 1938.

Ratshin, A. *Polnoe sobranie istoricheskikh svedenii o vsekh byvshikh v drevnosti i nyne sushchvuiushchikh monastyriakh i primechatel'nykh tserkvakh v Rossii*. Moscow, 1852.

Rostislavov, D.I. *O pravoslavnom belom i chernom dukhovenstve v Rossii*, I-II. Leipzig, 1866.

Runkevich, S.G. *Istoriia russkoi tserkvi pod upravleniem sv. Sinoda*, I-II. St. Petersburg, 1900-1901.

Riazanovskii, V. A. *Obzor russkoi kul'tury*. I-II. New York, 1947-1948.

Samarin, Iu. F. *Stefan Iavorskii i Feofan Prokopovich. Sochineniia*, Vol. V., Moscow, 1880.

Sergievskii, N. *Sviatitel' Tikhon, episkop Voronezhskii i Zadonskii*. Moscow, 1898. Translated by Jordanville in 1965.

Serebianskii, N. I. *Ocherki po istorii monastyrskoi zhizni v Pskovskoi zemle*. Moscow, 1908.

Smirnov, N. P. *Zlatai tsep' sviatosti na Russii*. Buenos Aires, 1958.

Solov'ev, A. V. *Sviataia Rus'. Ocherk razvitiia religiozno-obshchestvennoi idei*. Belgrade, 1927.

Stavrovskii, A.V. *Khristianskaia Rossiia*. Buenos Aires, 1954.

Stroev, P.M. *Spiski ierarkhov i nastoiatelei monastyrei Rossiiskoi Tserkvi*. St. Petersburg, 1877.

──────────. *Spiski ierarkhov Rossiiskoi Tserkvi*. St. Petersburg, 1882.

Subbotin, N.I. *Delo patriarkha Nikona*. Moscow, 1862.

Suvorov, N. S. *Uchebnik tserkovnogo prava*. Moscow, 1912.

# 541 Russian Historiography: A History

Tel'berg, G. G. *Zaria Khristianstva na Rusi.* Shanghai, 1939.

Titov, F.I. *Russkaia pravoslavnaia tserkov' v Pol'sko-litovskom gosudarstve v XVII-XVIII vv.* Kiev, 1905.

Timofievich, A. *Prepodobnyi Serafim Sarovskii.* Spring Valley, N.Y., 1953.

Tikhomirov, N. *Galitskaia mitropolitiia.* St. Petersburg, 1896.

Troitskii, Protoierei Dimitrii. *Zhitie prepodobnogo Serafima Sarovskogo i ego torzhestvennoe proslavlenie.* Tallin, 1939.

Kharlampovich, K. F. *Malorossiiskoe vliianie na veliko-russkuiu tserkovnuiu zhizn'.* Kazan', 1914.

Chetverikov, Protoierei Sergii. *Optina pustyn'.* Paris, 1926.
——————. *Starets Paisii Velichkovskii,* I-II. Pechery, 1938. Forthcoming English translation by Nordland Publishing Company.

Chizhevskii, I.L. *Ustroistvo pravoslavnoi Rossiiskoi Tserkvi, ee uchrezhdenii i deistvuiushchie uzakoneniia po ee upravleniiu.* Khar'kov, 1898.

Chistovich, I.A. *Ocherk istorii zapadnorusskoi tserkvi,* I-II. St. Petersburg, 1882-1884.
——————. *Feofan Prokopovich i ego vremia.* St. Petersburg, 1868.
——————. *Istoriia perevoda Biblii na russkii iazyk.* St. Petersburg, 1879; 1899.

Shliapkin, I.A. *Sv. Dimitrii Rostovskii i ego vremia.* St. Petersburg, 1891.

Shmeman, Protoierei Aleksandr. *Istoricheskii put' pravoslaviia.* New York, 1954.

Shpakov, A. Ia. *Gosudarstvo i tserkov' v ikh vzaimootnosheniiakh v Moskovskom gosudarstve ot Florentinskoi unii do uchrezhdeniia patriarshestva.* Vol. I, Kiev; Vol. II, Odessa, 1912.

Iushkov, S.V. *Ocherki iz istorii prikhodskoi zhizni na severe Rossii XVII-XVIII vv.* St. Petersburg, 1912.

## BOOKS IN ENGLISH, FRENCH, GERMAN

Amann, A.M., S.J. *Abriß der ostslavischen Kirchengeschichte.* Vienna, 1950.

Andreyev, Nikolay. *Studies in Muscovy: Western Influence and Byzantine Inheritance.* London, 1970 (partly in Russian).

Arseniew, N. S. *Die Kirche des Morgenlandes.* Berlin 1926.
—————— *Ostkirche und Mystik.* Munich, 1925; 1943.
—————— *Holy Moscow.* New York, 1940.
—————— *Von dem Geist und dem Glauben der Kirche des Ostens.* Leipzig, 1941.

Billington, James H. *The Icon and the Axe. An Interpretive History of Russian Culture.* New York, 1966.

Bogolepov, Alexander A. *Church Reforms in Russia 1905-1918.* Bridgeport, Connecticut, 1966.

Boulgakoff, S.N. *L'Orthodoxie.* Paris, 1932. English translation in 1935 entitled *The Orthodox Church.*

Bubnov, N. N. *Östliches Christentum,* I-II. Munich, 1925; III, 1956.

Cracraft, James. *The Church Reform of Peter the Great*. Stanford, 1971.
Curtiss, John. *Church and State in Russia. The Last Years of the Empire* 1900-1917. New York, 1940.

Eck, A. *Le Moyen Age Russe*. Paris, 1933.
Evdokimov, P.N. *L'Orthodoxie*. Paris, 1959.

Fedotov, George P. [*The Collected Works* by Nordland Publishing Co.]
  Vol. I – *St. Filipp. Metropolitan of Moscow – Encounter with Ivan the Terrible*. Belmont, Ma., 1978.
  Vol. II – *A Treasury of Russian Spirituality*, Belmont, MA., 1975.
  Vol. III – *The Russian Religious Mind (I): Kievan Christianity – The 10th-13th Centuries*. Belmont, MA., 1975.
  Vol. IV – *The Russian Religious Mind (II): The Middle Ages – The 13th-15th Centuries*. Belmont, MA., 1975.
Florovsky, Georges. [*The Collected Works* by Nordland Publishing Co.]
  Vol. I – *Bible, Church, Tradition: An Eastern Orthodox View*. Belmont, MA., 1972.
  Vol. II – *Christianity and Culture*. Belmont, MA., 1973.
  Vol. III – *Creation and Redemption*. Belmont, MA., 1976.
  Vol. IV – *Aspects of Church History*. Belmont, MA., 1974.
  Vol. V – *Ways of Russian Theology: Part One*
  Vol VI – *Ways of Russian Theology: Part Two*
Fortescue, Adrian. *Orthodox Eastern Church*. London, 1904; 1907; 1916; 1920.

Grunwald, Constantin. *Quand la Russie avait des Saints*. Paris, 1958. English translation, *Saints of Russian*. London, 1960.

Iswolsky, Héléne. *Soul of Russia*. Milwaukee, 1943.
————. *Christ in Russia: The History, Tradition and Life of the Russian Church*. New York, 1960; London, 1962.
Kologrivoff, Ivan. *Essai sur la sainteté en Russie*. Bruges, 1953.
Kulomzina, Sophia. *The Orthodox Christian Church Through the Ages*. New York, 1956.

Lagovskii, I.A. *Die russische Orthodoxe Kirche*. Riga, 1938.
Leroy-Beaulieu, Anatole. *L'empire des tsars et les Russes*. I-III. Paris, 1881-1889; English translation: *The Empire of the Tsars and the Russians*. London, 1896; 1903.
Lossky, N.O. *History of Russian Philosophy*. New York, 1951.
Lowrie, Donald A. *The Light of Russia. An Introduction to the Russian Church*. Prague, 1923.

Medlin, W.K. *Moscow and East Rome. A Political Study of the Relations of Church and State in Muscovite Russia*. Geneva, 1952.
Meyendorff, John. *The Orthodox Church*. London, 1964.
Miliukov, Paul. *Outlines of Russian Culture* (3 vols.). Part I. *Religion and Church*. Ed. by M. Karpovich. Philadelphia, 1943; New York, 1960.

Palmer, William. *The Patriarch* [*Nikon*] *and the Tsar* (6 vols.). London 1871-1876; 2nd ed. 1905.

Pierling, Paul, S.J. *La Russie et le Siége* (3 vols.). Paris, 1896-1901; 1907;

Schmemann, Alexander. *The Historical Road of Eastern Orthodoxy.* New York, 1963.

Seraphim, Metropolitan. *Die Ostkirche.* Stuttgart, 1950.

Smolich, Igor. *Geschichte der russischen Kirche*, 1700-1917. Vol. I (1700-1869). Leiden, 1964.

——————————. *Russisches Mönchtum:*   *Entstehung, Entwicklung und Wesen, 988-1917.* Würzburg, 1953.

——————————. *Leben und Lehre der Starzen.* Wien, 1936; Köln, 1952.

Solov'ev, A. V. *Holy Russia. The History of a Russian-Social Idea.* Mouton, 1959.

Teodorovich, Nicholas. *The Great Prince Vladimir. His Life and Work.* 1957.

Treadgold, Donald W. *The West in Russia and China.* Vol. I: Russia: 1472-1917. Cambridge University Press, 1973.

Tshizewskij, Dmitrij. *Das heilige Russland.* Hamburg, 1959.

Zenkovsky, V.V. *History of Russian Philosophy.* (2 vols.). New York, 1953.

Zernov, N.M. *Moscow the Third Rome.* New York-London, 1937.

——————————. *St. Sergius, Builder of Russia.* London, 1939.

—————————— *The Church of the Eastern Christians.* New York-London, 1942.

—————————— *The Christian East.* Delhi, 1956.

——————————. *Eastern Christendom. A Study of the Origin and Development of the Eastern Orthodox Church.* New York-London, 1961.

——————————. *The Russian Religious Renaissance of the XXth Century.* New York-London, 1963.

—————————— *Three London Prophets: Khomiakov, Dostoevsky, Soloviev.* London, 1944.

# APPENDIX IV
## Bibliography of the Schism of Old Believers
### by NIKOLAY ANDREYEV
### [IN RUSSIAN]

Anderson, V.M. *Staroobriadchestvo i sektantstvo*. St. Petersburg, 1909.

Borozdin, A.K. *Russkoe Religioznoe raznomyslie (sbornik statei)*. St. Petersburg, 1907.

Golubinskii, E.E. *K nashei polemike s staroobriadtsami*. Moscow, 1905

Druzhinin, V.G. *Raskol na Donu v kontse XVII v.* Spb. 1889. Translated by Mouton in 1970.

Ivanovskii, N.I. *Rukovodstvo po istorii i oblicheniiu staroobriadcheskogo raskola*. Kazan', 1889; 1897,

Karlovich, V. *Istoricheskie issledovannia, sluzhashchie k opravdaniiu staroobriadtsev*. I-III. Moscow, 1881-1886.

Kel'siev, V. I. *Sbornik pravitel'stvennykh svedenii o raskol'nikakh*. I-IV. London, 1860-1862.

Kirillov, I.A. *Pravda staroi very*. Moscow, 1916.

Plotnikov, K. *Istoriia russkogo raskola staroobriadchestva*. St. Petersburg, 1914.

Prugavin, A. S. *Staroobriadchestvo vo 2-oi polovine XIX v.* Moscow, 1904.

——————. *Raskol-sektantstvo. Materialy dlia izucheniia religiozno-bytovykh dvizhenii russkogo naroda*. Moscow, 1887.

Rybakov, A.S. *Staraia vera, Staroobriadcheskaia khrestomatiia*. Moscow 1914.

Sapozhnikov, D.I. *Samosozhzhenie v russkom raskole so* 2-i poloviny XVII v. do kontsa XVIII. Moscow, 1891.

Sakharov, F.K. *Literatura istorii i oblicheniia russkogo raskola*, I-III. Tambov, 1887; St. Petersburg, 1892-1900.

Senatov, V.G. *Filosofiia istorii staroobriadchestva*. I-II. Moscow 1908-1912.

Smirnov, P.S. *Istoriia russkogo raskola staroobriadstva*. Riazan', 1893; St. Petersburg, 1903.

——————. *Proiskhozhdenie samosozhzheniia v russkom raskole*. St. Petersburg, 1895.

——————. *Vnutrenine voprosy v raskole v XVII v. Issledovanie iz nachal'noi istorii raskola po vnov' otkrytym pamiatnikam, izdannym i rukopisnym*. St. Petersburg, 1898.

Sokolov, N.S. *Raskol v Saratovskom krae*. Saratov, 1888.

Strel'bitskii, I.Kh. *Istoriia raskola, izvestnogo pod imenem staroobriadchestva*. Odessa, 1898.

Subbotin, N.I. *Sovremennye dvizheniia v raskole*. Moscow, 1865.

**[In English]**

Avvakum, *The Life of Archpriest Avvakum.* Preface by D.S. Mirsky. London, 1924. Reprinted in 1963 by Archon Books.

Bolshakoff, S. *Russian Nonconformity: The Story of Unofficial Religion in Russia.* Philadelphia, 1950.

Conybeare, Frederic C. *Russian Dissenters.* 1921.

Crummey, R.O. *Old Believers and the World of Antichrist. The Vyg Community and the Russian State*, 1694-1855. Wisconsin Un. Press, 1970.

Pascal, Pierre. *Avvakum et les débuts du raskol.* Paris, 1938; 1963.

# NOTES

1.    D. Obolensky (ed.), *The Penguin Book of Russian Verse* (Baltimore, Md., 1962), pp. 52-54.

2.    The figures are those of A. V. Kartashev, *Ocherki po Istorii Russkoi Tserkvi*, II, p. 548. I am obliged to K.G. Belousow for this note.

3.    P. Miliukov, *Ocherki po Istorii Russkoi Kul'tury*, v. II, part 2, p. 743.

4.    A.A. Kornilov, *Kurs Istorii Rossii XIX Veka* (reprint of the 2nd edition, Moscow, 1918), v. I, p. 19.

5.    *Ibid.*, p.26.

6.    See the introductory remarks of R.O. Jakobson in "La Geste du Prince Igor," *Annuaire de l'Institut de Philologie et d'Histoire Orientales et Slaves*, VI (New York, 1948), pp. 5-11.

7.    Prince D.S. Mirskii, *A History of Russian Literature from the Earliest Times to the Death of Dostoevsky* (New York,) pp. 79-80.

8.    See the recent study by S.A. Zenkovsky, *Russkoe Staroobriadchestvo* [*Russia's Old Believers*] (München, 1970).

9.    From 1867 to 1917, a total of 148 volumes of the *Sbornik Imperatorskogo Russkogo Istoricheskog Obshchestva* [*Collection of the Imperial Russian Historical Society*] were published. (–ed.)

10.   An originally stylized and thoughtful description of the Russian museum (formerly the Museum of Alexander III), and in particular of these sections, was given by V.A. Soloukhin in his book, *Letters from a Russian Museum* [*Pisma iz Russkogo muzeia*] (Moscow, 1967).

11.   Let us recall that the census listed only males (irrespective of age).

12.   See P.N. Miliukov, *Memoirs*, 2nd vol., (New York, 1955).

13.   See Mel'gunov, *Reminiscences and Diaries* I (Paris, 1964).

14.   See S. F. Platonov, "A. Ia. Efim," *Delo i Dni* (1920), I, pp. 617-619.

15. In 1966 the University of Kiev published this book: P.G. Markov, *A. Ia. Efimenko–Historian of the Ukraine* (Kiev, 1966).

16. There is an article by S. Sliusarenko in the *Dragomanov Anthology* [*Dragomanovskii Sbornik*] (Prague, 1933) on Dragomanov's works in Roman history.

17. See Yaroslav Bilynsky, "Drahomanov, Franko, and the Relations between the Dniepr Ukraine and Galicia," in *Annals of the Ukrainian Academy of Arts and Sciences in the U.S.*, vol. VII, pp. 1542-1566.

18. M. Pavlik, *Mikhailo Petrovich Dragomanov. Jubilee, Death, Autobiography, and Bibliography* [*Mikhailo Petrovich Dragomanov. Ego Iubilei, Smert', Avtobiografiia, i Spis Tvoriv*] (Lvov, 1896), pp. 331-397. I have no information on the fate of the Russian MS of Dragomanov's autobiography. Citations from the autobiography are in my own translation from Ukrainian into Russian.

19. In this chapter of his book Dragomanov discovers an insufficient knowledge of the views of mid-XIX century Russian society. Rich material on the real views of Russian scholars and literary circles toward Western Russia is gathered in the book by V. A. Frantsev, *Pushkin and the Polish Revolt of 1830-1831* [*Pushkin i Pol'skoe Vosstanie 1830-1831*] (Prague, 1921). Frantsev also touches on the later period in this book.

20. This autobiography was published in the *Materials for the Biographic Dictionary of Active Members of the Academy of Sciences* [*Materialy dlia Biograficheskogo Slovaria Deistvitel'nykh Chlenov Akademii Nauk*], vol. I (Petrograd, 1915), pp. 405-413.

21. The College of Economics was established in 1726 to administer the landed properties of ecclesiastics and religious institutions and for the collection of State duties. The College of Economics was closed in 1786. The supervision of Church properties, which had been the State's, now passed to the provincial financial boards.

22. This lecture was immediately published in Oxford in English. It was later published in Russian in *Voice of the Past* [*Golos Minuvshego*] (1914), no. 12.

23. See. I.I. Petrunkevich, *From the Notes of a Social Activist* [*Iz Zapisok Obshchestvennogo Deiatelia*] (Prague, 1934), pp. 104-105.

24. *Leo Tolstoy's Historical Scepticism* (Oxford Slavonic Papers, II, 1951), pp. 17-54.

25. D.I. Mendelev, *Problems of Russia's Economic Development* [*Problemy Ekonomicheskogo Razvitiia Rossii*] (Moscow, 1960). An Anthology of articles.

26. On the Russian school of world history, see V. Buzeskul, *World History and Its Representatives in Russia in the XIX and the Beginning of the XX Centuries* [*Vseobshchaia Istoriia i Ee Predstaviteli v Russii v XIX i Nachale XX Veka*] (2 parts, Leningrad, 1929-1931).

27. See. S.A. Satin, *The Education of Women in Pre-Revolutionary Russia* [*Obrazovanie Zhenshchin v Dorevoliutsionnoi Rossii*] (New York, 1966), pp. 76-77.

28. A short biography of Vasil'evskii is available in *Materials for the Biographic Dictionary of Active Members of the Academy of Sciences*, part I.

29. There is a brief biography of F.I. Uspenskii in part II of *Materials for the Biographic Dictionary of Active Members of the Academy of Sciences* (Petrograd, 1917). See also the anthology *In Commemoration of Academician F.I. Uspenskii* [*Pamiati Akademika F.I. Uspenskii*] (Leningrad, 1929). It contains Uspenskii's bibliography and articles regarding his scholarly work by Buzeskul and Zhebelev. A short and penetrating obituary was written by N.P. Toll' (Seminarium Kondakovianum, Prague, 1928), p. 328.

30. M.M. Kovalevskii's autobiography appeared in the *Materials for the Biographic Dictionary of Active Members of the Academy of Sciences*, vol. II, 1917. See also Buzeskul, *World History*, part I (Leningrad, 1929), pp. 201-218.

31. Vinogradov's autobiography appears in vol. II of *Materials for the Biographic Dictionary of Active Members of the Academy of Sciences* (1917).

32. See V. Buzeskul, *World History and Its Representatives in Russia*, part II (Leningrad, 1931), pp. 202-204.

33. See E. Ch. Skrzhinskaia, "I. M. Grevs. A Bibliographic Essay" ["I.M. Grevs. Bibliograficheskii Ocherk"] (appendix to Grevs' *Tacitus* [*Tatsit*], posthumously published (Moscow-Leningrad, 1946).

34. Grevs, "In Years of Youth" ["V Gody Iunosti"] *Byloe* [*The Past*], no. 12 (1918) and no. 16 (1921). Also see G. V. Vernadskii, "The Priutino Brotherhood," *Novyi Zhurnal* [*The New Review*] no. 83 (1968).

35. See G.V. Vernadsky, "A.A. Vasil'ev," *Annals of the N.P. Kondakov Institute*, X. pp. 1-17 (with an appendix containing the bibliography of Vasil'ev's works through 1937.

36. See Otto Böss, *Die Lehre der Eurasier* (Wiesbaden, 1961).

37. Karsavin's last years are described in *Orientalia Christiana* (Rome, 1952): "On the Life and Death of the Russian Metaphysician, Lev Karsavin" (in German).

38.  On Kareev, see chapter XXIII, *Philosophy of History.*

39.  See A.G. Mazour, *The Writing of History in the Soviet Union* (Stanford, California, 1971), pp. 65-66.

40.  See A.G. Mazour, *Outline of Modern Russian Historiography* (Berkeley, California, 1939), pp. 96-97.

41.  Platonov gives a vivid description of Bestuzhev-Riumin in his memoirs (see chapter XIII on Bestuzhev-Riumin).

42.  Vasilii Ivanovich Sergeevich (1832-1910) was an outstanding historian of Russian law, ordinary professor at and rector of the University of Petersburg. He was the author of a major three-volume work, *Russian Juridical Antiquities [Russkie Iuridicheskie Drevnosti]* (of which volume I was published in St. Petersburg in 1890). The whole work was re-issued at the beginning of the XX c. with the title of *Antiquities of Russian Law. Vol. I, Territory and Population* (3rd ed., St. Petersburg, 1909) *[Drevnosti Russkogo Prava. To. I, Territoriia i Naselenie]* This volume documents and describes in detail the juridical and social state of every group of the population in pre-Petrine Russia. Volume II, *Veche and the Prince; Advisers to the Prince* (3rd ed. 1908) *[Veche i Kniaz; Sovetniki Kniazia]* was based on many citations from the texts of chronicles. It describes the political structure of ancient Russian principalities in which monarchical rule in the person of the prince was combined with democratic rule in the person of the people's assemblies of the *veche.* Volume III was titled *Landownership, Obligations, and the Tax System* (1st ed., St. Petersburg, 1903) *[Zemlevladenie, Tiaglo, Poriadok Oblozheniia].* Another important work by Sergeevich is the anthology of historico-juridical studies titled *Lectures and Studies in the Ancient History of Russian Law [Lektsii i Issledovanie po Drevnie Istorii Russkogo Prava]* (St. Petersburg, 1883; 4th ed., St. Petersburg, 1910) —ed.

43.  The *Pomestnyi Prikaz* was the government department in charge of registering the lands given on condition of service. —N.L.

44.  See G.Vernadsky, "The Priutino Brotherhood," *The New Review [Novyi Zhurnal]*, no. 93 (1968), p. 150.

45.  In Russian historiography there were many attempts to explain the name *Rus'.* Kunik and Thomsen believed its derivation to be from the Swedish *Roslagen*, the name of the shoreline of the Swedish province of Upland (or from the Finnish *"Ruotsi"* which means "rowers" and applied to the Swedish Vikings). Budilovich derived *Rus'* from the Gothic tongue. At one time Kostomarov insisted on a derivation from Lithuanian. Shakhmatov believed that in antiquity *Rus'* was the name of Varangian retinues in general, not the name of an individual Varangian tribe. G.V. Vernadsky believed that the initial *Rus'* was an Alan tribe and that the name *Rus'* was Alan (*Rukhs-as* - light skinned Alans).

46. They were re-issued as a separate book: S.B. Veselovskii, *Studies on the History of the Oprichnina* [*Issledovaniia po Istorii Oprichniny*] (Moscow, 1963).

47. It was initially published in the journal *Russian Thought* [*Russkaia Mysl'*] (1890-1892).

48. See A.V. Florovsky, *The Czechs and the Eastern Slavs* [*Chekhi i Vostochnye Slaviane*] I (Prague, 1935), pp. 376-384. Valerie Tumins, *Tsar Ivan IV's Reply to Jan Rokyt* (The Hague: Mouton, 1971).

49. See V. Grigor'ev, "Bibliography of M.A. D'iakonov's Works" ["Spisok Trudov M.A. D'iakonova"] in *Russian Historical Journal*, 7 (Petrogrod, 1921), pp. 26-30. A. E. Presniakov, "M. A. D'iakonov's Works on Russian History" ["Trudy M.A. D'iakonova po Russkoi Istorii"], *ibid.*, pp. 8-25. A work by D'iakonov that should be mentioned is *The Power of the Moscow Sovereign: Essays on the History of the Political Ideas of Ancient Russia to the End of the XVI Century* [*Vlast' Moskovskikh Gosudarei. Ocherki iz Istorii Politicheskikh Idei Drevnei Rusi do Kontsa XVI Veka*] (St. Petersburg, 1889).

50. Ikonnikov's autobiography is published in *Materials for the Biographic Dictionary of the Academy of Sciences*, part II (1917), pp. 304-311. See also *Encyclopedic Dictionary*, half volume, 24 (1894), p. 889.

51. See A.A. Kizevetter's memoirs, *At the Crossroads of Two Centuries* [*Na Rubezhe Dvukh Stoletii*] (Prague, 1929).

52. On Miliukov, see ch. XIX. Liubavskii was mentioned in a different connection in chapter XX.

53. This is generally phrased in terms of the nobility's emancipation from compulsory service to the State. −N.L.

54. The anthology, *The XVIII Century* [*XVIII Vek*] (Leningrad, no. 940), pp. 54-76.

55. The second oldest was I.I. Lappo (b. 1869). He has been mentioned in Chapter XX on the historians of the south-west region.

56. For Leontovich's views see chapter XX (on the historians of the south-west region).

57. See P.M. Dmitrieva, *Legend of the Vladimir Princes* [*Skazanie o Kn'iaz'iakh Vladimirskikh*] (Moscow-Leningrad, 1955), pp. 130-135.

58. The *Gramota Polnaia* was a document by which a man became fully a slave. In this case the action is undertaken by the person himself. −N.L.

59. *"Istpart"* is the acronym for *Istoriia Partii [History of the Party]*. Here, of course, it also refers to commissions. —N.L.

60. A detailed biography of P. B. Struve was written by Harvard University professor Richard Pipes (Volume I, Harvard University Press, 1970). Volume II is in preparation.

61. A.D. Kalmykow, *Memoirs of a Russian Diplomat* (Yale University Press, 1971), p. 9.

62. A valuable source for the following was the publication of Gleb Petrovich Struve's "Correspondence of I.A. Bunin and P.B. Struve" ["Perepiska I.A. Bunina i P.B. Struve"] (*Transactions of the Association of Russian-American Scholars in the USA*, II, 1968), 61-111.

63. Boris Ischboldin, *History of Russian Non-Marxian Social-Economic Thought* (New Delhi, India), p. 242.

64. See G.V. Vernadsky, "The First Year of the Ukrainian Academy of Science 1918-1919," *Annals of the Ukrainian Academy of Arts and Sciences in the U.S.*, Vol. XI (1964-1968), pp. 18-22.

65. A.A. Shakhmatov's autobiography and the bibliography of his scholarly works appears in the book *A.A. Shakhmatov–1864-1920* (Leningrad, 1930). Also see A. E. Presniakov, "A. A. Shakhmatov" (an obituary). *Dela i Dni* (1920), book I, pp. 611-614.

66. In order to become acquainted with the contemporary level of the concepts of feudalism in historical scholarship in general and of feudalism in Europe, see I.M. Grevs, "Feudalism," *Encyclopedic Dictionary of Brockhaus-Effron*, half-volume 70 (1902), pp. 491-535. On feudalism in Russia– Miliukov, Liubavskii, Kareev, *Ibid.*, pp. 548-558. See also G. Vernadsky, "Feudalism in Russia," *Speculum*, XIV (1939), pp. 300-323.

67. Compare M. Liubavskii, *Ancient Russian History [Drevniaia Russkaia Istoriia]* (1918), pp. 179-180.

68. Biographical information on Veselovskii and a list of his main works are contained in the editor's introduction to Veselovskii's book *Studies on the History of the Oprichnina [Issledovaniia po Istorii Oprichniny]* (Moscow, 1963) which was published posthumously.

69. A.G. Mazour, *The Writing of History in the Soviet Union* (Stanford, California, 1971), p. 70.

70. Grekov's biography appears in volume one of his *Selected Works [Isbrannye Trudy]* (1957). See also V.I. Shunkov, "Boris Dmitrievich Grekov (His Creative Path)" ["Boris Dmitrievich Grekov (Tvorcheskii Put' ")] in the anthology dedicated to Grekov on the occasion of his 70th birthday

(1952), pp. 5-12. A bibliography of his works also appears there, pp. 20-36. In addition, I utilize my own personal recollections. Grekov's *Selected Works* appeared in four volumes, 1957-1960.

71.   The *Stoglav* is generally referred to as the Council of a Hundred Chapters. —N.L.

72.   G.V. Vernadsky, "In Memory of A.V. Florovskii" ["Pamiati A.V. Florovskogo"] in *Novoe Russkoe Slovo* (New York, April 18, 1968).

73.   A.V. Florovsky, *Cesti Jesuité na Rusi* (Prague, 1941).

74.   This chapter was added at the insistent request of K. G. Belousow. —Ed.

75.   G. Vernadsky, "Russlands Ugarn, Feldzug von 1849," *Ferdinandy Festschrift* (West Berlin, 1972).

76.   The book was published in the series *Transactions of the Historico-Philological Department of the University of Petersburg* (Petrogrod, 1917).

77.   A.N. Pypin, *Russian Freemasonry. The XVIII and the First Quarter of the XIX c.* [*Russkoe Massonstvo. XVIII i Pervaia Chetvert' XIX v.*]. Edited with notes by G.V. Vernadsky (Petrograd, 1916).

78.   See *Contemporary Authors*, vol. 7-8, 1965 (Detroit, Michigan: Gale Research Company).

79.   See *Materials for the Bibliography of Russian Scholarly Works Abroad. 1920-1930* [*Materialy dlia Bibliografii Russkikh Nauchnykh Trudov za Rubezhom. 1920-1930*] issue I (Belgrade, 1931), pp. 253-254; issue II (1941), pp. 270-271.

80.   *Transactions of the Association of Russian-American Scholars in the USA*, vol. II (1968).

81.   *Ibid.*

82.   It was on Pushkarev's initiative that Mel'gunov's work appeared in English translation: S.P. Mel'gunov, *The Bolshevik Seizure of Power*. Edited and abridged by S.G. Pushkarev in collaboration with Boris S. Pushkarev. Translated by James S. Beaver (Clio Press, Santa Barbara California, 1972). [Note slight title change in abridged version. —N.L.].

83.   Sergei Pushkarev, *The Emergence of Modern Russia. 1801-1917.* Translated by Robert H. McNeal and Tiva Yedlin (New York, 1963).

84.   *Dictionary of Russian Historical Terms from the Eleventh Century to 1917* (Yale University Press, 1970).

85.  See Philip E. Mosely, "Professor Michael Karpovich," *Harvard Slavic Studies*, IV (Harvard University Press, 1957), 1-13.

86.  "Klyuchevsky and Recent Trends in Russian Historiography," *Slavonic and East European Review* (American Series, II, part one); 31-39.

87.  On Rozhkov see chapter XXVI (Kliuchevskii's Students).

88.  See N.N. Alekseev, *The Ways and Fates of Marxism* [*Puti i Sud'y Marksizma* (Berlin, 1936).

89.  On Plekhanov see V.A. Riazanovskii [Riasanovsky], *Survey of Russian Culture*, part II, issue two (New York, 1948), pp. 90-97. Information of Plekhanov and his relations with Lenin may also be found in the book by George Vernadsky, *Lenin* (Yale University Press, 1931) and Richard Pipes, *Struve* (Harvard University Press, 1970).

90.  It is published in Plekhanov's collected works, vol. XX-XXII (Moscow, 1925-1927).

91.  I.I. Smirnov, *Essays on the Political History of the Russian State in the '30's to the '50's of the XVI Century* (Moscow-Leningrad, 1958), p. 144, footnote 12.

92.  Professor Vernadsky wrote only the two outlines on Metropolitan Makarii and Professor Golubinskii. Professor Pushkarev completed the chapter because Professor Vernadsky died suddenly in 1973. —Ed.

93.  On Khomiakov and Iurii Samarin see chapter IX (Slavophiles and Westernizers).

94.  See M.D. Priselkov, "Metropolitan Makarii Bulgakov", *Russian Historical Journal* [*Russkii Istoricheskii Zhurnal*], no. 5 (1918), pp. 177-196. Contains a bibliography of Makarii's works.

95.  E.E. Golubinskii's biography is published in *Materials for a Biographical Dictionary of Active Members of the Academy of Sciences*, part I (Petrograd, 1915). See also N.N. Glubokovskii, *Russian Theological Scholarship in Its Historical Development* [*Russkaia Bogoslovskaia Nauka v ee Istoricheskom Razvitii* (Warsaw, 1928).

96.  This is the complete title in Russian. The standard citation is ChOIDR.

97.  In the article on Metropolitan Platon in volume XIV of the *Russian Biographical Dictionary*, biographical literature on this memorable hierarch is specified. It begins with the book by I.M. Snegirev, *The Life of Metropolitan Platon of Moscow* [*Zhizn' Moskovskogo Mitropolita Platona*], 4th ed. (Moscow, 1891).

98. Archbishop Filaret (Gumilevskii), a severe critic, points to the absence in Metropolitan Evgenii's works of general ideas and of a "systematic view of historical phenomena." In his *Dictionary* he finds many omissions and inaccuracies with an abundance of unimportant biographical detail. But he recognizes that the wealth of factual information gathered in Metropolitan Evgenii's works "was very useful to lovers of our nation's history. This is his merit." (*Survey of Russian Spiritual Literature*, pp. 443-444). The bibliography of Metropolitan Evgenii's works is to be found in the *Orthodox Theological Encyclopedia* [*Pravoslavnaia Bogoslovskaia Entsiklopediia*] vol. V, pp. 189-190. Literature about him commences on page 191 with the book by Professor E.F. Shmurlo, "Metropolitan Evgenii as a Scholar" ["Mitropolit Evgenii kak Uchennyi"] (*SPB*, 1888).

99. Information on the life and works of Archbishop Filaret is available in the book by I. S. Listovskii, *Filaret, Archbishop of Chernigov* [*Filaret, Arkhiepiskop Chernigovskii*] (Moscow, 1887; Chernigov, 1894), and in the article by Professor I.N. Korsunskii in the *Russian Biographical Dictionary*, vol. XXI, pp. 80-83.

100. In my essay I included the survey of Metropolitan Filaret for such was (judging by his draft notes) the intention of Professor Vernadsky, even though this famous hierarch was not a major *historian* of the Russian Church.

101. Formally Professor Verkhovskoi is right: there was no juridically formulated dominion of the Moscow Tsars over the Church. But in actuality the dependence of the Church hierarchy on the sovereign (beginning with the appointment of candidates to hierarchical posts) was very considerable; see the above-cited quotations from N.F. Kapterev's book, *Patriarch Nikon and Tsar Aleksei Mikhailovich*. The Russian Church was never really independent of secular rule.

102. An evaluation of the Petrine Church reform and the synodal period in the Russian Church that is far from being so pessimistic is to be found in Professor A.V. Kartashev's book, *Essays on the History of the Russian Church* (Paris, 1959). See below.

103a. We will not enter into polemics with Miliukov here. But it is interesting to compare his opinion with the completely contrasting opinion of Professor Kartashev (*Essays*, vol. II, p. 319). He notes that "The rise in the strength of the Russian Church in terms of enlightened theology" in the XIX c., witnessed the participation of both lay and clerical philosophers (Khomiakov, the Aksakov brothers, Vladimir Solov'ev, the Trubetskoi brothers) and continues: "The religio-Orthodox phenomenon in Russian literature, which became universal, must be viewed at a parallel level. This Christian breath of our literature on the whole world is a direct offspring of the thousand year educational influence of the Russian Church." We should recall also that in the emergence of the cultural activity of the Russian intelligentsia (in the name of which Miliukov expands with such self-confidence) an enormous role was played by "seminarians", i.e. pupils of ecclesiastical schools. These ranged from the Vladimir seminarian M. M. Speranskii to the Penza seminarian, V. O. Kliuchevskii.

103. The full title is: *Russian Émigré Writers: Biographical information and Bibliography of Books on Theology, Religious Philosophy, Church History, and Orthodox Culture 1921-1972* [*Russkie Pisateli Emigratsii: Biograficheskie Svedeniia i Bibliografiia Knig pa Bogosloviiu, Religioznoi Filosofii, Tserkovnoi Istorii, i Pravoslavnoi Kul'ture 1921-1972*].

104. It is true that in pre-Petrine Rus' the Church also was not independent from the State and that the appointment of new hierarchs depended on the Tsar's will. Nevertheless, the Church constituted a special organization that was autonomous in its internal life. The secular government, in relationship to the Church and religion, was limited by certain age-old traditions and customs. Peter transformed Church organization into one of the units of government-wide administration (under the vigilant supervision of a secular official, *Ober-Procurator*). The clergy became a sort of government-service class.

105. Many books about Fr. Ioann of Kronstadt were written during his life and posthumously (for a listing of these see the book by Fr. A. Semenov-Tian-Shanskii cited below). During his lifetime, a book titled *Father Ioann of Kronstadt. A Complete Biography* [*Otets Ioann Kronshtadtskii. Polnaia Biografiia*] was published by the Hieromonk Mikhail, a *docent* of the St. Petersburg Theological Academy (SPB: 1903). A whole series of books about him was published in exiled Russia: I.K. Surskii (Ia.V. Il'iashevich), *Father Ioann of Kronstadt* [*Otets Ioann Kronshtadtskii*] (Belgrade, 1938); Mefodii, Hieromonk, *Father Ioann of Kronstadt*, (Sliven, 1938); Archpriest Sergii Chetverikov, *The Spiritual Image of Father Ioann of Kronstadt and his Pastoral Precepts* [*Dukhovnyi Oblik Otsa Ioanna Kronshtadtskogo i Ego Pastyrskie Zavety*] (Berlin, 1939); A. Nikolaevskii, *The Great Pastor of the Russian Land, Father Ioann of Kronstadt* [*Velikii Pastyr' Zemli Russkoi, Otets Ioann Khronshtadtskii*] (München, 1948); A. A. Sologub, *Father Ioann of Kronstadt – Life, Work, and Miracles* [*Otets Ioann Chronshtadtskii – Zhizn', Deiatel'nost' i Chudesa*] (Jordanville, 1951); A. Semenov-Tian-Shanskii, *Father Ioann of Khronstadt* (Chekhov Publishing House; New York, 1955); P.M. Chizhov, *Father Ioann of Kronstadt. The Activity and the End of the Good Pastor, Great Supplicant, and Spiritual Luminary of the Russian Land* [*Otets Ioann Kronshtadtskii. Deiatel'nost' i Konchina Dobrogo Pastyria, Velikogo Molitvennika i Dukhovnogo Svetil'nika Zemli Russkoi*] (Jordanville, 1958); Archimandrite Konstantin (Professor K.I. Zaitsev), *The Spiritual Make-up of Father Ioann of Kronstadt* [*Dukhovnyi Oblik Otsa Ioanna Kronshtadtskogo*] (Jordanville, 1964).

106. I fear that the reader, having read my list of five, will ask in surprise; but where is the world-famous religio-philosophical thinker and writer, N.A. Berdiaev? My "omission" is not accidental. The many religio-philosophical and socio-political writings of Berdiaev present a picture of constant and

changing guests (and wanderings) in the attempt to find some sort of truth and new religion. But in actuality, Berdiaev did not study the history of the Russian Orthodox Church *per se* (at least such works do not appear in the bibliography of his books).

107. Actually V.O. Kliuchevskii used deeply-felt words in the description and defense of "belief in ritual": "The religious-world view and attitude of each society are inextricably linked to the texts and rituals which educated it." "A ritual or a text is a phonograph of a sort in which the moral moment, which once elicited kind deeds and feelings in people, is frozen." (*Course of Russian History*, part III, Lecture 54).

108. At the beginning of his *Life* Avvakum warns the reader of his common-folk style ". . . for I love my native Russian tongue and am not used to coloring my language with philosophic doggerel" (A.K. Borozdin, *Archpriest Avvakum* [*Protopop Avvakum*], appendix no. 25, p. 71).

109. Several biographies were written about archpriest Avvakum (aside from the "hagiographical" literature of old-believer authors who venerated Avvakum as a holy martyr and spiritual father of the old belief). A.K. Borozdin, *Archpriest Avvakum. An Essay from the History of the Intellectual Life of Russian Society in the XVII c.* [*Protopop Avvakum. Ocherk iz Istorii Umstvennoi Zhizni Russkogo Obshchestva v XVII v.*], 2nd ed., SPB, 1900; V.A. Miakotin, *Archpriest Avvakum, His Life and Work* [*Protopop Avvakum, Ego Zhizn' i Deiatel'nost'*], SPB, 1894; S. P. Mel'gunov, *The Great Zealot Archpriest Avvakum* [*Velikii Podvizhnik Protopop Avvakum*], Moscow, 1907.

110. For a listing of these see Robert O. Crummey, *The Old Believers and the World of Antichrist* (Madison, Wisconsin; 1970), pp. 230-234.

111. Shchapov's book on the Schism (1859) and his brochure, *Zemstvo and the Schism* (1862) were re-issued in his collected works, vol. I, *SPB* (1906), pp. 173-450 and 451-504.

112. Let us note in passing that the Schism was especially successful among the peasants of the northern provinces where there were no landed gentry or serfdom at all.

113. The Tsar's decree of April 17, 1905, on religious toleration ordered the removal from official terminology of the appellation "schismatics" and to replace it with the term "old believers."

114. Count A.S. Uvarov was discussed in chapter XVII (on sources of historical scholarship) in connection with archeological congresses.

115. See G.V. Vernadsky, "M.I. Rostovtsev. On His Sixtieth Birthday" ["M.I. Rostovtsev. K Shestidesiatiletiiu Ego"], *Seminarium Kondakovianum*, v. IV (1931), pp. 239-252. See also *Encyclopedic Dictionary*, half vol. 53

(1899), p. 132.

116. I thank N.P. Toll and Frank Gilliam for help in compiling this list.

117. A bibliography of Rostovtsev's works prior to 1931 is appended to my article about him in *Seminarium Kondakovianum*, vol. IV, pp. 245-252. See also *Materials for the Bibliography of Russian Scholarly Work Abroad [Materialy dlia Bibliografii Russkikh Nauchnykh Trudov za Rubezhom]*, issue I (Belgrade, 1931), pp. 264-265 and *Who Was Who in America*, vol. 3 (1951-1960), page 744.

118. *Iranians and Greeks in South Russia* (Oxford, 1922), pp. VI and VIII.

119. Kondakov's autobiography was published in *Materials for the Bibliographic Dictionary of Active Members of the Academy of Sciences*, I (1915), pp. 338-340. I have provided a biographical sketch of Kondakov in a *Festschrift* for him (*Recueil Kondakov*, Prague, 1926), pp. XX-XXX (in French) See also *Encyclopedic Dictionary*, half-volume 30, p. 927.

120. On the sagave style see M. I. Rostovtsev, "Central Asia, Russia, China, and the Savage Style," *Seminarium Kondakovianum* (Prague, 1929).

121. S.A. Zhebelev, "Ia.I. Smirnov," *Seminarium Kondakovianum* (Prague, 1928), pp. 1-18.

122. For a list see the appendix to Zhebelev's article, pp. 16-18.

123. See the article by E.A. Lapkovskaia, "A Water Carrier Found in the Crimea and a Series of Items Related to It" ["Vodolei Naidennyi v Krymu, i Krug Rodstvennykh emu proizvedenii'] in the anthology *History and Archeology of Medieval Crimea [Istoriia i Arkheologiia Srednevekovogo Kryma]*, pp. 176-189.

124. See N. Beliaev, "Sergei Aleksandrovich Zhebelev," *Seminarium Kondakovianum*, I (Prague, 1927), pp. 308-312.

125. On Zhebelev's works through 1922, see V. Buzeskul, *World History and Its Representatives in Russia in the XIX and the Beginning of the XX Centuries*, II (1931), pp. 143-147 and p. 192.

126. *Problems of Restoration: An Anthology from the Central State Restoration Workshops [Voprosy Restavratsii, Sbornik Tsentral'nykh Gosudarstvennykh Restavratsionnykh Masterskikh]*, vol. I-II, ed. by Igor Grabar (Moscow, 1926-1928). Grabar was the director of these workshops.

127. See N. Zernov, *The Russian Religious Renaissance of the Twentieth Century* (London, 1963), pp. 370-371; in addition, see *International Who's Who*, 1970-1971, p. 602.

128. *Répertoire International des médiévistes* (1965), pp. 246-147. I concentrate more on Grabar's earlier works which are not cited in the *Répertoire*.

129. Vladimir Karenin, *Vladimir Stasov* (two parts, Leningrad, no date). "Vladimir Karenin" is the pseudonym of Varvara Dmitrievna Stasova, Komarova by marriage (1862-1942). See also S. Bulich, "Stasov, Vladimir Vasil'-evich," in *Encyclopedic Dictionary*, half volume 61 (1900), pp. 466-468.

130. See A.A. Spitsyn, "My Scholarly Works" ["Moi Nauchnye Raboty"] in *Seminarium Kondakovianum*, II (1928), pp. 331-332; V. Sakmanev, "A.A. Spitsyn – For A.A. Spitsyn's 70th Birthday " ["A.A. Spitsyn. K 70ti-letiiu so Dnia Rozhdeniia A.A. Spitsyna"], *ibid.*, pp. 343-346; M.A. Miller, "Archeology in the USSR" (München, 1954), pp. 29, 43.

131. See A.G. Kuz'min, "Does the Problem of the Tmutarakan Stone Exist" ["Sushchestvuet li Problema Tmutarakanskogo Kamina?"] in *Soviet Archeology* (1969), issue 3, pp. 278-283.

132. M.A. Miller, *Archeology in the USSR* (München, 1954), pp. 28, 33, 40,,41, 52, 59, 81, 82, 96. On Miller see P. E. Kovalevskii, *Foreign Russia [Zarubezhnaia Russiia]* (Paris, 1971), p. 170.

133. V. Buzeskul, *World History and Its Representatives in Russia in the XIX and the Beginning of the XX Centuries*, part II (Leningrad, 1931), pp. 166-170; M.A. Miller, *Archeology in the USSR* (München, 1954), p. 30; Rostovtsev, *Iranians and Greeks in South Russia* (Oxford, 1922), index of names, pp. 3, 20, 28, 65, 95; E.H. Minns, *Scythians and Greeks* (Cambridge, 1913), chapter XV. See also in index under Pharmacovskij, B.V.

134. For a brief bio-bibliography of Lazarev see the *International Who's Who 1907-1971*, p. 919.

135. This section was written by Professor Alexis P. Scherbatow, a member of the History Faculty of Fairleigh Dickinson University. Professor Vernadsky had compiled a partial list and was in the process of completing the list at the time of his sudden death. He had not begun the work of writing.

136. Dr. Nickolay Andreyev is Reader in Russian Studies at Cambridge University, England.

# INDEX

Petersburg Theological Academy 376, 388, 408, 416, 417, 419, 437.
Petersburg, University of 48, 67, 68, 99-101, 108, 110, 112, 118, 119, 127, 148, 168, 180, 181, 186, 191, 205-208, 210, 212, 218-220, 225, 226, 230, 234, 237, 240, 241, 245, 246, 261, 284, 287, 288, 291, 298, 302, 304, 307, 309, 312-314, 316, 328, 329, 337, 339, 343, 450, 455, 462-465, 471, 476, 477, 485-487, 492, 494-500, 502-504, 506, 509, 514, 515.
Petr, Metropolitan of Moscow 424.
*Petrashevtsy* 78, 79, 120.
Petrunkevich, A. I. 222, 229, 269, 322, 335.
Petrunkevich, I. I. 190, 191.
Petrushevskii, D. M. 223, 224, 236, 237, 264, 345, 352, 365, 514.
Philosophy 38, 48, 64, 69-71, 74, 76, 81, 82, 88, 114, 115, 117, 138, 180, 182, 185, 186, 188, 192, 193, 199, 202, 213, 230, 242, 497.
*Philosophy of History* (Hegel) 69, 70, 75, 76, 94.
Photius, Patriarch of Constantinople 409.
Piatigorskii, A. M. 508.
Pil'niak, B. 259.
Pirogov, N. I. 161.
Pisarev 106.
*Pistsovye knigi* 274, 276, 278.
Plato 466.
Platon, Metropolitan 380-382.
Platonov, S. F. ii, 110, 130, 147, 166, 168, 239-252, 254-256, 258-260, 282-284, 287, 288, 291, 292, 295, 296, 298, 299, 302-304, 307, 312, 325, 339, 342, 343, 353, 374, 514, 515.
Plekhanov, G. 152, 328, 369-371.
Pleve, V. K. 153, 281, 282.
Pobedonostsev, K. 267.
Pogodin, M. P. 60-62, 71, 85, 89, 92, 93, 384.
Pokrovskii, M. N. 167, 221, 238, 328, 372-374.
Pokryshkin 151.

Poland 101, 102, 170, 171, 176, 177, 184, 201, 256-258, 317, 347, 350, 360, 409.
Polevoi, N. A. 60, 62-66.
Polievktov, M. A. 291, 292, 294, 295.
Polish Revolution of 1863 176, 177, 201.
Politics 76, 77, 86, 115, 140, 152, 155, 158, 167, 176, 179, 188, 191, 214, 217, 224, 231, 234, 249, 263-265, 270-272, 293, 294, 297, 301, 311, 316, 318, 321, 322, 324, 327, 333, 357, 363, 365, 366, 370, 371, 373, 398, 417, 422, 439, 441, 443-446, 500, 525.
Pomponius Atticus 221.
Popov, A. N. 87.
Popov, N. 436.
Popov, V. S. 354, 517.
Popovskii 15.
Populism 160, 276, 320, 368, 369, 439.
Pordedge 71.
Positivism 185, 231, 232, 401.
Potapin, G. N. 476.
Potemkin, G. 41, 354, 517.
Potresov 371.
Pozdneev, A. M. 494, 495.
Praetorius 348.
Prakhov, A. V. 463.
Presniakov, A. E. 246, 262, 287-290, 304, 307, 312, 313, 338, 365.
*Primary Chronicle* 390.
Princeton University 428.
Priselkov, M. D. 328, 343-345, 390-392, 409.
Priutino Brotherhood 219, 316, 317.
Procopius of Caesarea 243, 348.
Prokich, B. 344.
Protasov, S. I. 450.
Protestantism 74, 82, 88, 400, 411, 414, 429.
Prugavin. A. S. 444, 446.
Prussia 44, 88, 203, 293.
Przheval'skii, N. M. 491, 492.
Psychology 114, 132, 138, 142.
Pufendorf, Samuel 38.
Pugachev, Emilian 53, 54.